Discover who we are...

and you will think the world of us.

The fact that we are the fourth-largest chemical company in the world, manufacture over 15,000 products in 40 countries and sell them in over 150 may have been unknown to you. With global sales of $21 billion ($4 billion in the U.S.), it is ironic that you may never have heard of us.

We make the world a little safer.

In the immediate future driving cars will be safer, because airbags actuated and inflated by components from ICI will inflate in 4/100ths of a second to protect the front-seat occupants.

Today, criminals can more accurately be tied to their crimes through high-tech DNA FINGERPRINTING[SM] which our Cellmark Diagnostics business is pioneering in the United States.

Innovative waterborne coatings introduced by Glidden reduce dependence on atmosphere-polluting alternatives. The magnitude of that is enormous. Happily, eight out of ten beverage and soft-drink cans are protected with our coating technology.

We make the world a little healthier.

1.5 million people suffering from hypertension in the U.S. control it with the first one-tablet-a-day beta blocker, which we manufacture.

We discovered the leading oral medication for advanced and post-surgical treatment of breast cancer.

Mylanta® and Mylanta-II,® the only antacids that are homogenized and pasteurized for smoother, better taste, are used by more than 12.7 million adults each year in the United States.

Discover who we are...

and you will think the world of us.

The fact that we are the fourth-largest chemical company in the world, manufacture over 15,000 products in 40 countries and sell them in over 150 may have been unknown to you. With global sales of $21 billion ($4 billion in the U.S.), it is ironic that you may never have heard of us.

We make the world a little safer.
In the immediate future driving cars will be safer, because airbags actuated and inflated by components from ICI will inflate in 4/100ths of a second to protect the front-seat occupants.

Today, criminals can more accurately be tied to their crimes through high-tech DNA FINGERPRINTING[SM] which our Cellmark Diagnostics business is pioneering in the United States.

Innovative waterborne coatings intro-duced by Glidden reduce dependence on atmosphere-polluting alternatives. The magnitude of that is enormous. Happily, eight out of ten beverage and soft-drink cans are protected with our coating technology.

We make the world a little healthier.
1.5 million people suffering from hypertension in the U.S. control it with the first one-tablet-a-day beta blocker, which we manufacture.

We discovered the leading oral medication for advanced and post-surgical treatment of breast cancer.

Mylanta® and Mylanta-II,® the only antacids that are homogenized and pasteurized for smoother, better taste, are used by more than 12.7 million adults each year in the United States.

We make the world more durable.

Thoro products have waterproofed and protected the Olympic Speed Skating Oval at Calgary, the Tower of London and the observatory at Mt. Washington, New Hampshire.

One out of every two cars manufactured in the United States is built using Molub-Alloy® or Tribol® lubricants supplied by ICI's Tribol.

We make the world more beautiful.

We are the world's largest manufacturer of paint, and we make enough of it to cover 10 million homes each year.

America's fashion designers choose our Tactel® textile fiber for apparel ranging from fine hosiery to weather-tough skiwear.

We hold the leading position in North America in supplying ink for snack food and confectionery packaging.

We make the world more efficient.

We have the fastest-growing agrochemical business in the United States.

Worldwide, we are the third-largest producer of crop-protection chemicals and the fourth-largest agricultural products company in the U.S.

We help to store and retrieve the world's information more effectively by providing Melinex® film base for a variety of information storage devices.

We are at the leading edge of polyurethanes technology, contributing significantly to the U.S. automotive parts, recreational footwear and construction markets.

At ICI we bring a lot to the world. And we are about to bring much more.

World Problems World Solutions **ICI** *World Class*

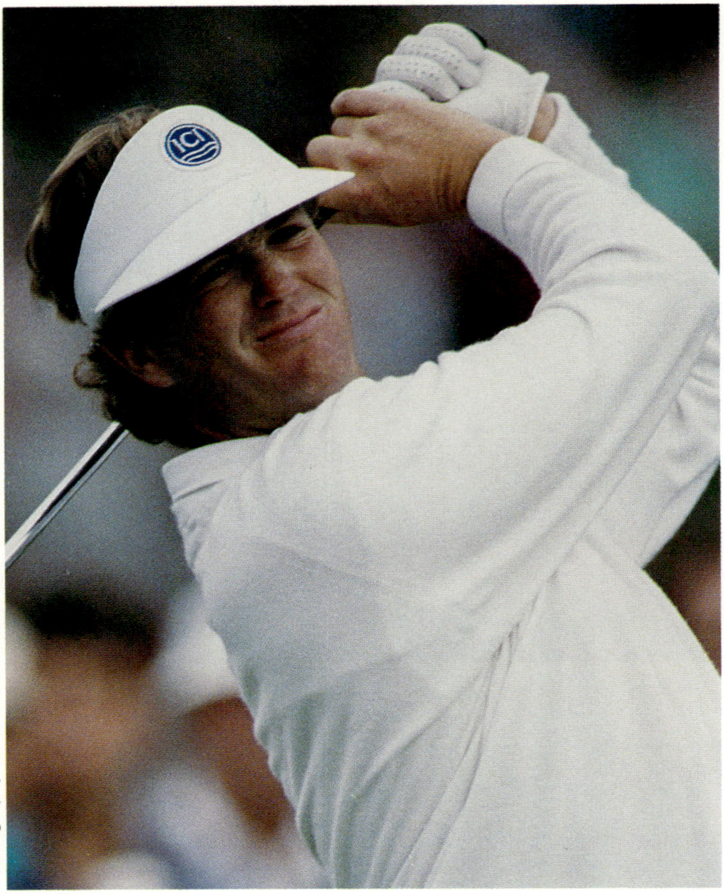

Photography:Tom Treick

ICI salutes Peter Jacobsen, a world class golfer

Presents

Mark H. McCormack's World of Professional Golf 1989

Photographs by Lawrence Levy

An IMG PUBLISHING Book
Distributed By
Contemporary Books, Inc.
180 North Michigan Avenue
Chicago, IL 60601
1989

An IMG PUBLISHING Book
Distributed By
Contemporary Books, Inc.
180 North Michigan Ave.
Chicago, IL 60601

First published 1989
© International Merchandising Corp. 1989

ISBN 0-9615344-5-1

Printed and bound in the United States of America.

Contents

1   The Sony Ranking   1
2   The Year In Retrospect   9
3   The Masters Tournament   24
4   The U.S. Open   40
5   The British Open   61
6   The PGA Championship   81
7   The World Match Play Championship   96
8   The Dunhill Cup   110
9   The U.S. Tour   125
10   The U.S. Senior Tour   172
11   The European Tour   202
12   The African Tours   234
13   The Australasian Tour   254
14   The Asia/Japan Tour   269
15   The LPGA Tour   295

APPENDIXES
World Money List   318
The Sony Ranking   322
World's Winners of 1988   326
Multiple Winners of 1988   330
Career World Money List   331
LPGA Money List   332
The U.S. Tour   334
The U.S. Senior Tour   392
The European Tour   426
The African Tours   464
The Australasian Tour   477
The Asia/Japan Tour   493
The LPGA Tour   531

1. The Sony Ranking

Throughout the history of professional golf, there has been the question: Who is the best?

Allan Robertson or Tom Morris?

Ben Hogan, Sam Snead or Byron Nelson?

Arnold Palmer, Jack Nicklaus or Gary Player?

When this annual publication was begun 23 years ago, one of the features was a ratings system to address that question, but our method was not based upon the computer technology now widely available; neither did it have an official endorsement nor significant exposure beyond the readership of this book.

Then, in 1986, the Sony Ranking was introduced, administered by our company, International Management Group, utilizing Sony equipment and having the sanction of the Championship Committee of the Royal and Ancient Golf Club of St. Andrews. In the short time since, this system of evaluating golfers has earned nearly global acceptance. Newspapers and golf periodicals throughout the world regularly publish these rankings which are updated weekly.

Some of the most respected people in golf worldwide bring their opinions to bear on the workings of the Sony Ranking. The Sony Advisory Committee, which meets at St. Andrews each October, consists of:

Brenda Blumberg, advisor to the South African PGA

Peter Dobereiner, golf correspondent for The Observer (London)

Taizo Kawata, member of the International Committee of the Japan Golf Association

Graham Marsh, executive of the Australian PGA

Colin Phillips, secretary of the Australian Golf Union

Richard Rahusen, chairman of the European Golf Association Technical Committee

Pat Reilly, president of the PGA of America

Ken Schofield, executive director of the PGA European Tour

Frank Tatum, past president of the United States Golf Association

Peter Townsend, former British Walker and Ryder Cup player and a member of the PGA European Tour Tournament Policy Board

The recommendations of the Sony Advisory Committee, of which I also am a member, are passed on to the R&A for approval, and the rankings are compiled and released to the news media and to the governing bodies of professional golf each Monday from London.

The premise of the Sony Ranking is simply that golfers need to be rated over periods of more than one year. This reflects the nature of the game, a sport in which an all-time great player in peak form might win only 20 percent of the time, and might have lapses of six months, a year or more without victory. A prime example: Gary Player, who despite one of the finest careers imaginable, never had two successive outstanding years.

Consider what happened to the professional tennis ranking when Bjorn Borg retired. Even though Borg was still playing a lot of exhibitions, 11 months after retiring, he was out of the top 400 in the world, yet everyone knew Borg was still somewhere high in the top 50 in terms of ability.

Think also of perhaps the greatest golfer ever, Jack Nicklaus, now on the downside of his career. If any reader of this book were to rank in order of preference, the golfers whom they would want to play for their lives tomorrow morning, Nicklaus would certainly be somewhere on the list. Yet, based only on the current year's ranking, Nicklaus would not even be in the top 200.

What is a proper period of time for the ranking to include? Surely, no one believes the first-round tournament leaders in their morning's newspapers are necessarily the best in the world, although their scores were the lowest for the previous day. If the measure were a week, the winner of every tournament would top the list.

Taken to the other extreme, ranking could include play over 10 years or more. The Sony Advisory Committee decided that three years was appropriate.

The Sony Ranking awards points according to the stature of the tournaments and the strength of the golfers competing, then multiplies those points by *four* for the current year, by *two* for the preceding year, and by *one* for the year before that, reflecting three years' performance, but weighted in favor of the current year.

There are six grades of tournaments, from the major championships to regional events. Grade One consists of the traditional four majors, followed by The Players Championship in a special category, Grade One-A.

The next tier, Grade Two, includes such highly-regarded events as The Nestle Invitational (formerly Bay Hill Classic), Memorial Tournament and NEC World Series of Golf in the United States; Volvo PGA Championship, Panasonic European Open and Lancome Trophy in Europe; Japan Open and Dunlop Phoenix in Japan, and the Panasonic Australian Open.

Grade Three consists of most of the rest of the U.S. tournaments and leading events in Europe, Japan and Australia. Other tournaments are listed on a descending scale in Grades Four, Five and Six.

Points are awarded to the 50 high finishers (with 50 points to the winner) in Grade One and to the 40 high finishers (with 40 points to the winner) in Grade One-A.

In Grades Two to Six there is a lower points framework but this is supplemented by bonus points which are awarded depending on the number of top-50 ranked players participating in the event, thus reflecting the quality of the field.

In Grade Two, a minimum of 32 points are awarded to the winner (with points to the top 32 finishers), which can escalate to a maximum of 40 points to the winner for an exceptionally good participating field. Similarly, the winners of Grade Three events may receive between 16 and 35 points, and so forth down to Grade Six, where the winner may receive between two and 10 points. The points for those in second place and below are also increased accordingly.

The complete points system is as follows:

GRADE ONE			**GRADE ONE-A**	
First	50 points		First	40 points
Second	30		Second	24
Third	20		Third	16
Fourth	15		Fourth	12
Fifth	12		Fifth	10
Sixth	10		Sixth	8
Seventh	9		Seventh	7
Eighth	8		Eighth	6
Ninth	7		Ninth	6
10th	7		10th/12th	5
11th/12th	6		13th/16th	4
13th/15th	5		17th/22nd	3
16th/20th	4		23rd/34th	2
21st/27th	3		35th/40th	1
28th/42nd	2			
43rd/50th	1			

(Note: No bonus points for Grade One or One-A)

GRADE TWO

	Minimum			Maximum
First	32 points		First	40 points
Second	19		Second	24
Third	13		Third	16
Fourth	10		Fourth	12
Fifth	8		Fifth	10
Sixth	6		Sixth	8
Seventh	6		Seventh	7
Eighth	5		Eighth	6
Ninth	5		Ninth	6
10th/12th	4		10th/12th	5
13th/18th	3		13th/16th	4
19th/28th	2		17th/22nd	3
29th/32nd	1		23rd/34th	2
			35th/40th	1

GRADE THREE

	Minimum			Maximum
First	16 points		First	35 points
Second	10		Second	21
Third	6		Third	14
Fourth	5		Fourth	11
Fifth	4		Fifth	9
Sixth/Eighth	3		Sixth	7
Ninth/15th	2		Seventh	6
16th	1		Eighth	6
			Ninth/10th	5
			11th/13th	4

14th/20th	3
21st/30th	2
31st/35th	1

GRADE FOUR

	Minimum		Maximum
First	8 points	First	25 points
Second	5	Second	15
Third	3	Third	10
Fourth	2	Fourth	8
Fifth	2	Fifth	6
Sixth	2	Sixth	5
Seventh	2	Seventh	5
Eighth	1	Eighth	4
		Ninth	4
		10th/13th	3
		14th/22nd	2
		23rd/25th	1

GRADE FIVE

	Minimum		Maximum
First	4 points	First	15 points
Second/Third	2	Second	9
Fourth	1	Third	6
		Fourth	5
		Fifth	4
		Sixth/Seventh	3
		Eighth/14th	2
		15th	1

GRADE SIX

	Minimum		Maximum
First	2 points	First	10 points
Second	1	Second	6
		Third	4
		Fourth	3
		Fifth/Ninth	2
		10th	1

In the first three years, the Sony Ranking was based upon a rolling three-year total, but during 1989 the system will be revised so that instead of a *total* number of points, players will be ranked according to their *average* number of points per event over a three-year period. As approved by the R&A, the minimum will be 20 tournaments per year and the divisor will thus be a minimum of 60 (three times 20). The intent is to set the minimum at a unthreatening and low level, yet a reasonable one. The intended effect will be to not unfairly penalize or reward golfers who play either fewer or more events than the norm. A first-year player might get himself into the top 40 by accumulating perhaps 300 points, which divided by 60 would give him an average of five points per event.

The Sony Ranking

(As of December 31, 1988)

POS.	PLAYER, TOUR	POINTS	POS.	PLAYER, TOUR	POINTS
1	Seve Ballesteros, Eur 1	1458	46	Corey Pavin, USA 28	373
2	Greg Norman, ANZ 1	1365	47	Masahiro Kuramoto, Jpn 4	364
3	Sandy Lyle, Eur 2	1297	48	Bruce Lietzke, USA 29	360
4	Nick Faldo, Eur 3	1103	49	Des Smyth, Eur 9	343
5	Curtis Strange, USA 1	1092	50	Mark James, Eur 10	336
6	Ben Crenshaw, USA 2	898	51	Jodie Mudd, USA 30	334
7	Ian Woosnam, Eur 4	854	52	Naomichi Ozaki, Jpn 5	323
8	David Frost, Afr 1	843	53	Tateo Ozaki, Jpn 6	313
9	Paul Azinger, USA 3	825	54	Graham Marsh, ANZ 5	312
10	Mark Calcavecchia, USA 4	819	55T	Hal Sutton, USA 31	311
11	Masashi Ozaki, Jpn 1	781	55T	Howard Clark, Eur 11	311
12	Chip Beck, USA 5	770	57	D.A. Weibring, USA 32	310
13	Tom Kite, USA 6	726	58	Fuzzy Zoeller, USA 33	309
14	Lanny Wadkins, USA 7	721	59	Mark Wiebe, USA 34	305
15	Bernhard Langer, Eur 5	696	60	John Mahaffey, USA 35	303
16	Payne Stewart USA 8	672	61T	Jose Rivero, Eur 12	302
17	Ken Green, USA 9	661	61T	Brian Jones, ANZ 6	302
18	Mark McNulty, Afr 2	645	63	Ray Floyd, USA 36	294
19	Fred Couples, USA 10	638	64	Peter Jacobsen, USA 37	290
20	Jose-Maria Olazabal, Eur 6	629	65	Dave Barr, Can 1	289
21	Joey Sindelar, USA 11	599	66	Gary Koch, USA 38	287
22	Rodger Davis, ANZ 2	589	67	Fulton Allem, Afr 4	276
23	Larry Nelson, USA 12	576	68	Bobby Wadkins, USA 39	275
24	David Ishii, USA 13	532	69	Doug Tewell, USA 40	263
25	Mark O'Meara, USA 14	518	70T	Gil Morgan, USA 41	251
26T	Mark McCumber, USA 15T	516	70T	David Graham, ANZ 7	251
26T	Steve Pate, USA 15T	516	72	Craig Parry, ANZ 8	250
28	Larry Mize, USA 17	511	73	Gene Sauers, USA 42	243
29	Tom Watson, USA 18	505	74	Andy Bean, USA 43	240
30T	Jeff Sluman, USA 19	503	75	Donnie Hammond, USA 44	233
30T	Isao Aoki, Jpn 2	503	76	Wayne Grady, ANZ 9	231
32	Tsuneyuki Nakajima, Jpn 3	494	77	Tze-Chung Chen, Asa 1	230
33	Scott Simpson, USA 20	493	78	Mac O'Grady, USA 45	229
34	Bob Tway, USA 21	486	79	Anders Forsbrand, Eur 13	228
35	Mike Reid, USA 22	485	80	Clarence Rose, USA 46	227
36	Dan Pohl, USA 23	473	81T	Steve Jones, USA 47T	222
37	Craig Stadler, USA 24	461	81T	Bob Lohr, USA 47T	222
38	Ian Baker-Finch, ANZ 3	454	83	John Cook, USA 49	219
39	Scott Hoch, USA 25	452	84	Tony Johnstone, Afr 5	218
40	Don Pooley, USA 26	445	85T	Eamonn Darcy, Eur 14	217
41	Nick Price, Afr 3	438	85T	Hajime Meshiai, Jpn 7	217
42	Peter Senior, ANZ 4	429	87	Scott Verplank, USA 50	214
43	Jay Haas, USA 27	405	88	Bill Glasson, USA 51	212
44	Ronan Rafferty, Eur 7	395	89	Toru Nakamura, Jpn 8	209
45	Gordon Brand, Jr., Eur 8	387	90	Davis Love, USA 52	206

POS.	PLAYER, TOUR	POINTS	POS.	PLAYER, TOUR	POINTS
91	Wayne Levi, USA 53	205	146	Tom Byrum, USA 82	113
92	Dave Rummells, USA 54	202	147T	Yoshikazu Yokoshima, Jpn 17	112
93	Curt Byrum, USA 55	201	147T	Chris Moody, Eur 27	112
94T	Tom Purtzer, USA 56	197	149T	Mike Harwood, ANZ 12	108
94T	Gordon J. Brand, Eur 15	197	149T	Philip Walton, Eur 28	108
96	Andrew Magee, USA 57	194	151	Brett Ogle, ANZ 13	107
97	Dan Forsman, USA 58	191	152T	Richard Zokol, Can 2	106
98	Calvin Peete, USA 59	190	152T	Bob Shearer, ANZ 14	106
99	Sam Torrance, Eur 16	187	152T	Tommy Armour, USA 83	106
100	John Bland, Afr 6	186	155	Tsukasa Watanabe, Jpn 18	104
101	Ken Brown, Eur 17	184	156T	Russ Cochran, USA 84	103
102T	Mike Hulbert, USA 60	182	156T	Manuel Pinero, Eur 29	103
102T	Katsunari Takahashi, Jpn 9	182	156T	Wayne Riley, ANZ 15	103
104	Morris Hatalsky, USA 61	181	159	Mats Lanner, Eur 30	102
105	Peter Fowler, ANZ 10	180	160	Ove Sellberg, Eur 31	99
106	Tim Simpson, USA 62	172	161T	Saburo Fujiki, Jpn 19	96
107	Bob Gilder, USA 63	171	161T	Steve Elkington, ANZ 16	96
108T	Hale Irwin, USA 64T	170	163T	Mike Clayton, ANZ 17T	95
108T	Kenny Knox, USA 64T	170	163T	Terry Gale, ANZ 17T	95
108T	Peter Baker, Eur 18	170	165T	Mike Donald, USA 85	94
111	Roger Chapman, Eur 19	169	165T	Frank Nobilo, ANZ 19	94
112	Mark Brooks, USA 66	168	165T	Miguel Martin, Eur 32	94
113T	Roger Mackay, ANZ 11	166	168	Ian Mosey, Eur 33	91
113T	Barry Lane, Eur 20	166	169	Rick Fehr, USA 86	90
115	Mark Mouland, Eur 21	165	170T	Johnny Miller, USA 87T	89
116	J.C. Snead, USA 67	163	170T	Howard Twitty, USA 87T	89
117	Yoshimi Niizeki, Jpn 10	159	170T	Nobumitsu Yuhara, Jpn 20	89
118T	Robert Wrenn, USA 68	154	173	John Huston, USA 89	88
118T	Hugh Baiocchi, Afr 7	154	174	Bill Sander, USA 90	86
120	Christy O'Connor, Jr., Eur 22	153	175	Denis Watson, Afr 9	85
121	Jim Benepe, USA 69	152	176	Lyndsay Stephen, ANZ 20	83
122	Denis Durnian, Eur 23	150	177T	Bobby Clampett, USA 91T	82
123	Brad Faxon, USA 70	149	177T	Sam Randolph, USA 91T	82
124	Tom Sieckmann, USA 71	148	179T	Ronnie Black, USA 93	81
125	David Feherty, Eur 24	146	179T	Ossie Moore, ANZ 21	81
126T	Roger Maltbie, USA 72	144	179T	Yoshiyuki Isomura, Jpn 21	81
126T	Nobuo Serizawa, Jpn 11	144	182T	Bob Eastwood, USA 94T	80
128	Seiichi Kanai, Jpn 12	140	182T	Loren Roberts, USA 94T	80
129	Ed Fiori, USA 73	139	182T	Yasuhiro Funatogawa, Jpn 22	80
130T	David Edwards, USA 74	137	182T	Wayne Westner, Afr 10	80
130T	Jose-Maria Canizares, Eur 25	137	186	Tadami Ueno, Jpn 23	79
132	Jim Carter, USA 75	136	187T	Pat McGowan, USA 96T	78
133	Blaine McCallister, USA 76	133	187T	David Ogrin, USA 96T	78
134T	Jack Nicklaus, USA 77	130	187T	David Llewellyn, Eur 34	78
134T	Koichi Suzuki, Jpn 13	130	187T	Gerry Taylor, ANZ 22	78
136	Keith Clearwater, USA 78	128	187T	Dick Mast, USA 96T	78
137T	Buddy Gardner, USA 79T	126	187T	Brian Tennyson, USA 96T	78
137T	Jim Hallet, USA 79T	126	193T	Richard Boxall, Eur 35	76
139	George Burns, USA 81	122	193T	Kenny Perry, USA 100	76
140	Hiroshi Makino, Jpn 14	119	195	Lennie Clements, USA 101	73
141T	Yoshitaka Yamamoto, Jpn 15	116	196	Jay Don Blake, USA 102	72
141T	Jeff Hawkes, Afr 8	116	197	Masanobu Kimura, Jpn 24	71
141T	Tze-Ming Chen, Asa 2	116	198T	Dave Eichelberger, USA 103T	70
144T	Carl Mason, Eur 26	114	198T	Hubert Green, USA 103T	70
144T	Ikuo Shirahama, Jpn 16	114	198T	Gary Hallberg, USA 103T	70

Seve Ballesteros' extraordinary play enabled him near year's end to replace Greg Norman as No. 1 in the world, but it took seven victories (including the British Open) and then a runner-up finish in the Volvo Masters for the Spaniard to do so. Such were the worldwide performances by the top five players that Curtis Strange could do no more than hold his No. 5 position after winning the U.S. Open and four other events, three in the United States and one in Australia.

Supporters of Ballesteros and Strange in particular — many, I suspect, unwilling to accept or to take the time to understand the system — were critical of the Sony Ranking during the year. "(Name of your choice) is the best golfer in the world." We read that a lot in 1988, especially in the stirring newspaper and magazine accounts of the victories by Sandy Lyle in the Masters, by Strange in the U.S. Open and by Ballesteros in the British Open.

All the while, the Sony Ranking, the system that would be recognized as the final authority on such matters, was telling us that Norman was the best golf player on earth. It was reasonable that many people wondered aloud and in print, What's going on here? Who is the No. 1 golfer after all? This led to the criticism of the Sony Ranking. One American golfer called it a contrived list, but I can assure you there's no way we could contrive a list to make that particular critic No. 1. The fact is, the Sony Ranking is an impartial measure that is far better than any golfer's tunnel-visioned perspective or any journalist's view, prejudiced by the spirit of the moment.

Although Norman lost his No. 1 position, Greg still won four times in Australia, once in the United States and once in Europe, and was a stroke away from four additional victories before a wrist injury at the U.S. Open sidelined him for seven weeks. Lyle had three victories in the United States, all in the first four months of the year, and two more triumphs in Europe. Nick Faldo was the most consistent golfer of the year, with two victories, eight seconds, and 15 top-four finishes worldwide.

More than 62 percent of the Sony Ranking points available in 1988 were awarded in U.S. events; the remaining 38 percent of the points were divided among the European, Japanese, Asian, Australian and African tours. The American and European tours each placed four golfers in the top 10, the same as at the end of 1987. For Europe, Ballesteros, Lyle and Ian Woosnam held their places, and Faldo took over from Bernhard Langer, who fell from third to 15th. For the United States, Strange and Ben Crenshaw remained in the top 10, while Paul Azinger and Mark Calcavecchia replaced Lanny Wadkins and Payne Stewart. South Africa's David Frost took over from Zimbabwe's Mark McNulty, and the remaining position was held by the Australian, Norman.

There were 11 newcomers in the top 50, with Ken Green the highest entry in 17th place, followed by Joey Sindelar in 21st place. Jeff Sluman, the U.S. PGA Championship winner, climbed from 75th to 30th place, and the last three in the top 50 — Bruce Lietzke, Des Smyth and Mark James — all rose from outside the top 100.

A number of young players made an impact in 1988, led by 22-year-old Jose-Maria Olazabal of Spain, who reached 20th place. Craig Parry (age 22) of Australia and Andrew Magee of the United States (26) reached the top 100, while significant progress was also made by Peter Baker (21) of

England, Mark Brooks (27) of the United States, Barry Lane (28) of England, Jim Benepe (24) of the United States, Jim Carter (27) of the United States and Brett Ogle (24) of Australia.

Some older golfers fell in the ranking, as one would expect, an exception being Jumbo Ozaki, age 41, who won six times in Japan and climbed from 18th to 11th place. Those declining included former major champions Jack Nicklaus, Raymond Floyd and Johnny Miller, all three among the dozen oldest players in the top 200.

The changing of the guard is an on-going process in professional golf, but it was never so evident before the creation of the Sony Ranking.

2. The Year In Retrospect

When asked to summarize his year, Ben Crenshaw responded, "Well, first of all, I wish I had been smart enough to buy a lot of Nabisco stock."

That could be a general assessment, as well, for all the uncertainty of the future, the news in professional golf in 1988 was mostly on the courses of the world.

RJR Nabisco, major sponsor of the U.S. PGA Tour, was subject to a $24.7 billion takeover by Kohlberg Kravis Roberts & Co.

The LPGA Tour hired another commissioner, William A. Blue, 48, former director of international marketing for the Kahlua Group, after John D. Laupheimer resigned.

Frank Hannigan quit as Senior Executive Director of the United States Golf Association to work for ABC Television and to write a magazine column.

The so-called "Grooves Controversy" continued.

The "World Tour" remained a topic of discussion.

We could be thankful, in a year when drug abuse tarnished the image of many sports including the Olympic Games, that golf was untouched. Drug problems probably do exist in golf, as throughout society, but no drug has been shown to enhance a golfer's performance.

Now, for what *did* happen in professional golf: The top five golfers on the Sony Ranking's three-year scale were also the top five of 1988 and won three of the four major championships, led by Severiano Ballesteros and his seven worldwide victories, including the British Open. Sandy Lyle won the Masters, Curtis Strange won the U.S. Open (defeating Nick Faldo in a playoff) and the one "outsider" to win a major was Jeff Sluman, whose PGA Championship victory raised him from 75th to 30th in the ranking. Following were the Sony Ranking leaders *for 1988 only*:

1.	Seve Ballesteros, Spain	964
2.	Sandy Lyle, Scotland	920
3.	Nick Faldo, England	804
4.	Greg Norman, Australia	792
5.	Curtis Strange, U.S.	724
6.	Mark Calcavecchia, U.S.	592
7.	David Frost, South Africa	580
8.	Chip Beck, U.S.	572
9.	Ben Crenshaw, U.S.	564
10.	Ken Green, U.S.	544

Our annual World Money List revealed that seven players won more than $1 million — not including the Nabisco Grand Prix and other such bonus, appearance and endorsement awards. Only two had previously reached this plateau, Greg Norman with $1,146,584 in 1986 and Ian Woosnam with $1,793,268 in 1987. The leading money winners of 1988:

1.	Severiano Ballesteros, Spain	$1,261,275
2.	Fulton Allem, South Africa	1,191,231

3.	Curtis Strange, U.S.	1,184,775
4.	Sandy Lyle, Scotland	1,182,438
5.	Ken Green, U.S.	1,085,994
6.	Jumbo Ozaki, Japan	1,082,985
7.	Chip Beck, U.S.	1,017,418
8.	Ben Crenshaw, U.S.	992,128
9.	Greg Norman, Australia	957,497
10.	Nick Faldo, England	922,732
11.	Joey Sindelar, U.S.	922,315
12.	Fred Couples, U.S.	889,684

Behind Ballesteros' seven triumphs on the list of worldwide multiple winners were Norman and Jumbo Ozaki with six victories each, Ozaki's coming exclusively in Japan. Lyle, Strange and Japan's Masahiro Kuramoto each won five times. Further down the list, Ken Green achieved his lofty standing in the World Money list with three late-year victories, Chip Beck won twice early, and Faldo, Ben Crenshaw, Joey Sindelar and Fulton Allem were also among those with two worldwide wins, Allem taking first prize in the Million Dollar Challenge at Sun City, Bophuthatswana, for the great majority of his money total.

All things considered, no matter how you stack them, these five golfers were the most outstanding worldwide in 1988: Ballesteros, Norman, Lyle, Faldo and Strange.

Let's consider them and their years in detail.

Ballesteros, in reaching No. 1 on the Sony Ranking, achieved his victories in seven different countries: Mallorca Open in Spain, Manufacturers Hanover Westchester Classic in the United States, British Open, Scandinavian Enterprise Open in Sweden, German Open, Lancome Trophy in France, and VISA Taiheiyo Masters in Japan.

He was fourth or better in 15 of his 25 tournaments, and in 16 starts on the European tour he set an earnings record of £451,559 and had a record scoring average of 68.85, playing the circuit at 130 under par for the year.

His brilliance — after a 1987 campaign in which he won only the Cannes Open, and after a three-year hiatus between major championships — was warmly received, even by the Americans, who are limited to watching Seve eight times per year because of his on-going conflict with the PGA Tour, which insists on a 15-tournament minimum while Ballesteros says he will agree to only perhaps 12 events. He now can play only the three major championships, plus five more tournaments (on an invitation basis) in America.

In an understandable overstatement, *Golf Digest* editor Jerry Tarde wrote "In case you didn't hear, a 31-year-old Spaniard just may have saved golf." I do not agree with those who say no one can create excitement as Ballesteros can, but I *do* agree with Jack Nicklaus' sentiment. "I mean," Jack says, "have you ever heard of Seve *hurting* a tournament?"

"He's got the greatest imagination for playing golf of anyone in history," says Crenshaw.

His role as the player to break the American stranglehold on major championships cannot be denied. "Seeing Sandy (Lyle) and Nick (Faldo) win the British Open and watching Bernhard (Langer) win the Masters, I gave a little credit to myself," Ballesteros told Tarde for his article. "I think

I was the one who proved we had the ability to win majors. I think I helped give confidence to the European players."

Even though Ballesteros won 16 tournaments around the world between the 1984 and 1988 British Opens, he suffered two major setbacks, both at the Masters. In 1986, he hit a four iron into the pond fronting the 15th green while Nicklaus was winning his sixth Masters, and in 1987 he three-putted the first playoff hole against Norman and eventual winner Larry Mize. Both instances were tremendous blows to his confidence.

Off the course, Ballesteros had to deal with the trauma of his father's death and, not publicly known until recently, of breaking from his former manager, Ed Barner. In an amazing revelation after the British Open, Ballesteros said that cost "big money."

Ballesteros is now represented by Joe Collett, a former Barner lieutenant now living in Spain. Observers also credit his better attitude and success to the hiring of an English caddy, Ian Wright, rather than employing one of his brothers, with whom he frequently argued on the course.

Another settling influence over 1988 — although it was not publicized until after the fact — was Seve's forthcoming marriage in November to his long-time girl friend, Carmen Botin. She is also from Santander, Spain, and is a graduate of Brown University. Her familiarity with America will be a plus, should Seve ever again play regularly in the U.S.

Ballesteros may never surpass the artistry of his finish at the British Open. Noting the plaque at Lytham to commemorate a shot by Bobby Jones in 1926, Dan Jenkins wrote, "It might not be possible to commemorate Seve's final-round 65 with plaques, for it would render the course unplayable."

There actually were three key shots that enabled Ballesteros to clinch the victory over courageous Nick Price. At the par-five seventh hole, with Price leading by one stroke, first Price hit a two iron within five feet of the cup, then Ballesteros struck a five iron to six feet for a matching eagle. They dueled on to the 16th, and there Seve hit a nine iron that missed by three inches of going into the hole. One stroke in front while playing the 18th, Ballesteros hit his approach shot too far left and five yards off the green. Just when it looked as if Price might tie him, Seve nearly holed a wedge shot from 60 feet.

"I think I played about as well as this game can be played," Ballesteros said, and he found no disagreement.

There's something about Greg Norman that makes you want to pull for him. Even though he has become a famous sports figure, Norman remains an ordinary guy. The Australians have a healthy attitude about fame; they don't believe in it. There's hardly any question that Norman is the most popular of the present-day golfers, with close ties to three of the four major circuits: He was born in Australia, developed his game in Europe and now lives in the United States.

What a year 1988 might have been for Norman, if not for a wrist injury at the U.S. Open which kept him out of action for seven weeks. Without question, it cost Norman the No. 1 position he had held since the inception of the Sony Ranking, and possibly a couple of wins. He still had six victories — second in the world only to Ballesteros' seven — five before the injury and one afterwards. He had 13 top-four finishes, two less than Ballesteros.

Through May, Norman was averaging a victory a month, and winning about half the time he was in contention. He won the Palm Meadows Cup in Australia, was one stroke out of playoffs at the AT&T Pebble Beach National Pro-Am and Australian Masters, won the ESP Open in Australia (by seven shots), won the Australian Tournament Players Championship (by eight shots), won the MCI Heritage Classic, lost a playoff in the Independent Insurance Agent (Houston) Open, won the Lancia Italian Open, and lost a playoff in the Westchester Classic, the week before the U.S. Open.

Aside from a tie for 23rd in a Las Vegas windstorm, Norman's worst performances in that span were ties for 11th place in the Hertz Bay Hill Classic and the Players Championship, sixth in the Memorial Tournament and fifth in the Masters Tournament.

His first tournament back after the injury, Norman tied for ninth in the PGA Championship. He continued to play well until the last couple of events, and even won the Panasonic New South Wales Open in Australia (and lost a playoff for the Australian PGA title), but I suspect Norman was looking mostly in the latter portion of the year to being prepared for 1989.

Norman's year will, and should, be remembered for his friendship with a teenage leukemia victim, Jamie Hutton, who was granted a wish by a charitable foundation to meet Norman and watch him play in the Heritage tournament. They formed an immediate bond, as close as brothers, even though they had known each other only for days, and in storybook fashion Norman went on to win the tournament, then presented his trophy to the boy.

That emotional sequence captured public attention as no other occurrence in golf — or sports — for the year, and Greg remained in close contact with Jamie as he battled for his life.

Before this year, Sandy Lyle was probably best known in the United States — aside from winning the British Open — for his remark when asked the difference between that revered event and the Players Championship. Not known for especially clever responses, Sandy replied perfectly, "About 120 years."

From now on, Lyle will be remembered for what golf historian Herbert Warren Wind described as "the greatest bunker shot in the history of the game" — his seven iron on the 18th hole to win the Masters. The most comparable shot, according to Wind, was that by Masters founder Bobby Jones in the 1926 British Open.

Lyle needed a par to tie Mark Calcavecchia when he took a one iron on the 18th tee, intending to sacrifice distance but keep the ball in the fairway. He pulled the shot and the ball went into the lower of two bunkers. Then 143 yards from the flag, Lyle said, "The thing I needed was a decent lie." He had one, and knew when he hit the ball that it was the right distance. It pitched on the green, bounced about 20 feet past the flag, then slowly rolled back, finishing 10 feet above the hole. Now he had that birdie putt to win. The ball was dead on line all the way and fell into the middle of the cup.

He became the first player since Arnold Palmer in 1960 to win the Masters with a birdie on the last hole, knowing he needed a birdie to do it. That year, Palmer passed Ken Venturi by hitting a six iron five feet left of the flag and holing the putt.

The 32-year-old Scot was also the first Briton to win the Masters, and in the process took his third (and final) victory in America for the year. Earlier, he won the Phoenix Open in a playoff and the week before the Masters, the K-Mart Greater Greensboro Open. Lyle by then had won $591,821 and led the U.S. money list by $213,783. His American tour was virtually over in April, but he continued to lead the money list for most of the year before placing seventh with $726,934.

On the European circuit, Lyle had two more victories for his total of five for the year, winning the Dunhill British Masters and, most coveted, the Suntory World Match Play Championship. He had been runner-up in the autumn classic at Wentworth four times, but finally won the championship by a 2-and-1 margin over Nick Faldo in an all-British final. Lyle was fifth on the European money list with £186,017 (plus an unofficial £75,000 from the World Match Play).

The Wentworth triumph provided a convincing finale to Lyle's year, in which he was a top-four finisher 10 times and won half of those. He beat some impressive competition en route to the title. In order, he went 34 holes against Nick Price, 30 against Seve Ballesteros and 35 against Faldo. In 99 holes, he had 34 birdies, three eagles, 13 bogeys and one double bogey — a cumulative 25 under par.

"I never gave up hope of winning this event," Lyle said, "After all those years of near-misses, it feels great to have finally won this title. I knew that if I continued playing as I had for the last couple of years, then my time would come."

It certainly had. He had been a powerhouse on both sides of the Atlantic. And significantly, I think, Lyle had done it on his own. In the British press, his wife (a former golf professional) was given credit in motivating him to success through the 1985 British Open and the 1987 Players Championship. Their marriage ended shortly after the latter event and, after about six months to regroup, Lyle served notice by winning the German Masters in the autumn of 1987. In the next seven months, through the Augusta victory, he won over $1 million.

Faldo, who also had to sort out his family life before taking a place on the world stage (he and second wife Gill have one daughter, two-year-old Natalie), began 1988 with the award of an MBE (Member of the British Empire) but after that, prizes were hard to come by. Whereas the other top performers of the year won about half the time when they were in contention, Nick had 15 finishes in the top four — exactly half of his 30 starts — but just two victories, in the Peugeot French Open and the Volvo Masters, the final event of the European circuit.

Only Ballesteros and Lyle accumulated more Sony Ranking points than did Faldo, who started the year ranked 14th and advanced to fourth place, ahead even of Curtis Strange, to whom he lost in the U.S. Open playoff. That was one of eight runner-up placings for Faldo, seven of which were on the European tour, where he was second to Ballesteros on the money list with £347,971. He was victimized twice each by Lyle (including the World Match Play) and Woosnam.

Faldo had the lowest aggregate score of any golfer in the major championships; he was tied for 30th in the Masters, second in the U.S. Open, third in the British Open and tied for fourth in the PGA Championship.

These were Faldo's second-place showings, three of which were playoffs: Torras Hostench Barcelona Open (playoff to David Whelan), Peugeot Spanish Open (to Mark James), Dunhill British Masters (to Lyle), U.S. Open (playoff to Strange), Benson & Hedges International Open (playoff to Peter Baker), Carrolls Irish Open (to Woosnam), Panasonic European Open (to Woosnam) and World Match Play (to Lyle).

Faldo won the 1987 British Open with 18 consecutive pars and, as much as Nick won it, Paul Azinger lost it by bogeying the last two holes. The Europeans already knew how good a player Faldo was, with his 15 career victories, and he demonstrated it to the Americans in the U.S. Open. Still, Faldo was frustrated by the tag of a par-maker. "You don't try *not* to make birdies," Faldo said many times.

He got those birdies in a come-from-behind victory over Ballesteros and Lyle in the Volvo Masters, shooting 68 in the last round. "I knew something had to happen," Faldo said. "Seve told me to stick with it. He said I was doing everything right and would soon win. Those kind words gave me a big boost."

Supporters of Curtis Strange may find it hard to understand why Strange, after winning the U.S. Open and four other tournaments, did no more than maintain his No. 5 position on the Sony Ranking. There were two reasons: the performances of the four golfers ahead of Strange in the ranking and Curtis' inconsistency. He was a top-four finisher only six times, a top-10 finisher only eight times.

True, Norman and Faldo might have traded their years for the U.S. Open title but statistically, at least, they had better records than Strange.

In the United States, Strange was the best. For the third time, he was chosen Player of the Year by one or more national magazines, and this year he also received PGA honors. Including the Nabisco bonus of $175,000 for leading the money list, Strange became the first to win over $1 million in a year on the PGA Tour, with $1,147,644. His four American victories gave him 15 for the decade, one less than the leader, Tom Watson. But those are just numbers; winning the U.S. Open went far beyond that.

Curtis told the press at Brookline, "This is my *first* major. But we're not going to stop here; we're really not going to stop here." Before then, some wondered whether Strange would win a major title, or even whether he cared. Then, after receiving the trophy, he silenced the huge gathering of reporters by tearfully recalling his father, Tom, a golf professional who died 19 years earlier, when Curtis was 14. His voice nearly breaking, he began by saying:

"This was for my dad."

Then he paused, took a breath, and went on.

"I've been waiting a long time to do this, to thank the people who gave me the advice I needed, the enthusiasm, and the knowledge to continue on. I have to thank my dad. This was for him."

By the time Strange won the U.S. Open, he was a favorite of the media. It wasn't always that way. He came out of Wake Forest in 1976, after his junior year, a former NCAA champion who was expected to become a star. That didn't happen, not right away. Strange missed qualifying on his first try, had some concerns about his health (which proved to be not serious), and at the same time was adjusting to a shorter swing under the tutelage of home state pro Chandler Harper, the former PGA champion, and Jimmy Ballard.

It wasn't until 1979 that Strange won, at Pensacola, then he won four more tournaments in the next five years, but he was far short of his ambitions as a player and had an undesirable reputation. He was not projecting his personality to the crowds and also carried the burden of an incident in 1982 at Arnold Palmer's Bay Hill tournament, when he blew his temper in front of a volunteer, and was publicly chastised by Palmer.

The turn-around came at the 1985 Masters. Strange began the tournament with an 80 then clawed his way back to take a four-stroke lead into the last nine holes. On the verge of a historic comeback, Curtis then put shots into the water on the 13th and 15th holes and Bernhard Langer won the tournament. The press was half-expecting Curtis to stalk away in anger, but he went to the interview and conducted himself marvelously.

"I think the press decided I handled that pretty well," Curtis has said, "but I did have problems with guys who would say it was a learning process. I didn't learn a doggone thing out of that back nine. I missed two shots...at the wrong time."

Strange went on in 1985 to win three tournaments and to lead the money list, accomplishments which he repeated in 1987. By then, his public relations problems were over. Curtis hadn't changed that much, although he was more comfortable with the crowds and the press, and the press was making an effort to understand him. They came to recognize that Strange was no different than, for example, Raymond Floyd. Says Curtis, "All the personality guys on tour become stonefaces as soon as they get into contention. And all the great players I have watched have been tough."

You couldn't be any tougher than Strange was in beating Greg Norman in the Independent Insurance Agent (Houston) Open, the first of his 1988 wins. Strange's shot to get into the playoff was second only to Sandy Lyle's bunker shot to win the Masters as the shot of the year.

After Noman birdied No. 17 to take the lead, then was safely on the 18th green with his second shot, Strange stood in the middle of the fairway and faced a 192-yard approach over water to a tightly-guarded pin. In an era when too many golfers would have been thinking of securing second-place money, Curtis took dead aim with his three iron. To say it was a bold shot would be an understatement. "I thought it was going into the water," Norman said. The ball scarcely cleared the lake, then came within four feet of the hole. A birdie and the playoff followed, with Strange winning at the same (and third extra) hole on a 25-foot birdie.

His third victory of the year (also including the season-opening Sanctuary Cove Classic in Australia) came at the Memorial, when he won by two strokes, equalling the course record at Muirfield Village with 64 in the third round and firing a 67 in the final round.

After some misadventures in the fourth round of the U.S. Open, including a bogey on the 17th hole, Strange took Nick Faldo to the 18-hole playoff with his second most-memorable shot of the year, a delicate bunker shot from in front of the 18th green to within a foot of the hole. The playoff was both thrilling and suspenseful, although the scores were Strange, 71, and Faldo, 75. Curtis won it on a brutal stretch of par-four holes, the 11th through the 13th, where he improved his lead from one to three strokes, a margin which he was not about to squander from there onwards.

Strange concluded the year by winning the Nabisco Championship, and the riches that went with that title, with another sensational stroke, a four iron over the front bunker to within 18 inches of the cup at Pebble Beach's No. 17 on the second hole of a playoff against Tom Kite, after Strange had bogeyed the same hole in regulation play.

A statistical comparison of the top five golfers on the Sony Ranking:

Player	Events	Wins	Top-Four Finishes	Masters	U.S. Open	British Open	PGA	U.S.	Eur.	Jpn.	Aust.
Seve Ballesteros	25	7	15	T-11	T-32	1	MC	7	16	2	0
Greg Norman	27	6	13	T-5	WD	DNP	T-9	14	3	2	8
Sandy Lyle	32	5	10	1	T-25	T-7	DNP	17	14	1	0
Nick Faldo	30	2	15	T-30	2	3	T-4	9	17	0	4
Curtis Strange	31	5	6	T-21	1	T-13	T-31	24	4	2	1

The year ended with the unsettling development of RJR Nabisco being taken over by Kohlberg Kravis Roberts & Co. RJR Nabisco was completing its second year as major sponsor, carrying the Nabisco banner on the PGA Tour and Vantage (cigarettes) on the Senior PGA Tour. Early speculation was that KKR would retain the tobacco business (also including Winston, Salem and Camel cigarettes) and sell off most of the rest. Then-chairman F. Ross Johnson, who led an unsuccessful takeover bid, was expected to be ousted and no one knew how the new management would view sponsorship of professional golf.

In the days following the takeover, RJR Nabisco spokesman Ed Redding said, "As far as I can anticipate we should be fulfilling all our commitments." As of this writing, the 1989 sponsorship was in full force, the only change being the previously-announced transfer of PGA Senior Tour sponsorship to the new Premier brand of cigarettes.

There were no announcements from the PGA Tour offices, but the message being circulated was that Deane Beman's crew felt they had a secure 10-year commitment. In other words, RJR Nabisco (or the spin-off corporations) would continue the sponsorship or pay to terminate the deal; either way, the PGA Tour felt it was fully protected.

The news midway of the year was that the tour was planning to ban all square-grooved clubs, starting with the 1989 circuit. Earlier, the United States Golf Association had banned only one model, the Ping Eye 2, beginning with its 1990 competitions. The tour later backed off and committed to a cooperative testing program with the USGA, the results expected to be announced in March, 1989. As anticipated, the older players were unhappy with the reversal. "Square grooves ruin the game," Jack Nicklaus said. "The good players aren't separating themselves from the field with shotmaking anymore." Comforting is the thought that in 1989, at last, we will get the final word on this tiresome subject.

Refinements in golf balls and the so-called "metal woods" have altered the game in recent years as much as the square-grooved irons. This year, a couple of fellows whom you would not expect — Nicklaus, then Lanny Wadkins — were among those switching to metal woods. "The young players blow it by me far too much, and I've got to get some of that back," Wadkins said. "When Jack found more distance, that convinced me. I never thought

I would see him put away the persimmon. I never thought I would be doing the same, come to think of it.

"I do have one advantage left, however, but for how long I don't know. It's called intimidation. I have discovered I can give a young player a 'look' and he'll wonder what this mean old veteran is thinking. At this stage, I'll take any advantage I can get."

Wadkins won the Hawaiian Open and Colonial National Invitation events and was 10th on the money list with $616,596. The rest of the top 10 were a fairly even blend of veterans and young players, traditionalists and high-tech pros.

Following Curtis Strange, in the No. 2 position was Chip Beck, who took until his ninth year on the tour to win a tournament then won twice in 1988, gaining titles at the Nissan Los Angeles Open by four strokes and USF&G (New Orleans) Classic, where he was 26 under par. Beck also was second three times, including a 25-under-par playoff loss to Bob Lohr in the Walt Disney World/Oldsmobile Classic. His U.S. earnings were $916,818, including a Nabisco bonus of $106,000 for being second on the money list. He won the Vardon Trophy with a 69.46 scoring average.

Victories at the Honda Classic and The International propelled Joey Sindelar to No. 3 on the money list with $813,732 (including $68,000 in Nabisco bonus money), while Ken Green took fourth place with $779,181 ($47,000 from Nabisco) after a spectacular autumn run. Green won back-to-back tournaments (a feat duplicated this year in the U.S. only by Sandy Lyle) at the Canadian Open and Greater Milwaukee Open, then was tied for sixth at the B.C. Open, tied for second at the Pensacola Open, tied for 12th at the Walt Disney World/Oldsmobile Classic, tied for fourth at the Northern Telecom Tucson Open, tied for third at the Nabisco Championship and won for the third time in Japan's prestigious Dunlop Phoenix event.

The next two on the money list, Tom Kite ($760,405) and Mark Calcavecchia ($751,912), had years in the "what if" category. Kite had his string broken after winning tournaments for seven consecutive years, and it took Strange's brilliant four-iron shot in the playoff for the Nabisco Championship to do it. Kite was second two other times and a top-four finisher six times. Calcavecchia was standing by, waiting for a playoff at the Masters, when Sandy Lyle struck the shot of the year from a fairway bunker with his seven iron to snatch away that championship. He later won the Bank of Boston Classic, was second in three other tournaments, and tied for third in the Nabisco Championship.

Lyle was No. 7 in the U.S., then came Ben Crenshaw ($696,895). The last time I looked, the Doral Ryder Open was not a major championship, but Crenshaw was chosen Player of the Year by an American monthly after having won just that tournament. (He won the World Cup individual title after publication.) He did have a good year: fourth in the Masters, tied for second in the Colonial National Invitation and tied for third in the GTE Byron Nelson Classic. He also placed in the top 20 of all four majors.

Like Chip Beck, when South Africa's David Frost finally won on the U.S. circuit, he followed soon with another victory. Frost's titles came in the late-year Southern Open and Northern Telecom Tucson Open, and he was ninth on the money list with $691,500. He also placed second or third six times, and finished in the top 10 in both the Masters and British Open.

Other multiple winners in the U.S. (for a total of eight) were Steve Pate (No. 12 on the money list with $582,473), who won early in the MONY Tournament of Champions and Shearson Lehman Hutton Andy Williams Open, and Bill Glasson (No. 30 on the money list with $380,651), who won late in the B.C. Open and Centel Classic.

Scarcely mentioned previously is someone who could well have been in the first paragraph, Paul Azinger. This is one fine player, as evidenced by his No. 9 spot in the Sony Ranking. He could have won the 1987 British Open, and the fates were against him in this year's PGA Championship, where he was second to Jeff Sluman. Paul was a wire-to-wire winner of the Hertz Bay Hill Classic at Arnold Palmer's Orlando club where he once worked as a summer camp counselor. A three-time winner in 1987, Azinger earned $594,850 for 11th place on the money list, and was top-10 finisher nine times.

A few words about Sluman: One of the year's most outstanding rounds was his last-day 65 at Oak Tree to win the PGA Championship by three strokes. He's the smallest player on the U.S. tour (5-feet-7), but hits the ball surprisingly long distances and has a sound short game. He was the first player since Jerry Pate in 1976 to make his first victory a major championship, and certainly should win more.

Other mentions must be made of 1988 highlights. Mark McCumber's delight at winning the Players Championship before the home folks in Jacksonville, Florida, was certainly one. Another was Jim Benepe's win in his first PGA Tour start, in the Beatrice Western Open, although it was at the unfortunate expense of Peter Jacobsen. And what about Scott Verplank's first victory as a professional in the Buick Open? The winner of the Western Open as an amateur in 1985, Verplank certainly was over-due.

Who would have thought that Payne Stewart would not win during the year? (He was second twice and placed 11 times in the top 10). Others of whom you would have expected victories included Fred Couples, Mark O'Meara, Bob Tway, Craig Stadler, Tom Watson, Fuzzy Zoeller, Larry Mize and Raymond Floyd.

Mention of Floyd brings to mind the forthcoming year and the Ryder Cup Matches scheduled for The Belfry in England this autumn. Floyd was selected to be captain of the U.S. team which has lost to Europe in the last two outings. "I welcome the opportunity and the challenge," Raymond said at the time of the announcement. "Some may not like the pressure and the responsibility, but I think it's an ideal situation. I was flattered and honored to be asked to be captain.

"We will travel together, stay together, eat together, and if we have any problems we will iron them out together. And when any of our players are not competing in a given round, I will expect to see them out there in the gallery rooting for their teammates. In most cases, golf is an individual game. In this case, we will be a unit."

In response to criticism of past team selections, Floyd will be given one wild-card choice, two if the PGA champion is already eligible. Says Floyd, "If that happens, I'm going to have two friends and a bunch of enemies. But our prime concern is, and will be, to bring the Ryder Cup back to the U.S."

The European holders of the Ryder Cup had an eventful year, their first under the title sponsorship of Volvo. The sponsorship was structured along similar lines to that between RJR Nabisco and the American circuit. The tour was officially known as the Volvo Tour, and the Swedish car manufacturer paid about £5 million in prize money alone, sponsoring the PGA Championship, Belgian Open and Volvo Masters, as well as the Seniors British Open. The contract is for five years.

Total prize money reached £10 million and there were 34 tournaments, an increase of eight events, starting with the Mallorca Open in March — when Seve Ballesteros gave indication of the year to come by winning the first of his seven titles, five of which were on the European circuit as he earned that record £451,559 in prize money.

Ballesteros provided the highlight of the year, winning the British Open, backing up Ryder Cup captain Tony Jacklin's prediction that an American would not win. "I can't see beyond a European win, and I can't see an American winning," Jacklin had said, in the year's most controversial statement. "But I'm biased. I don't think they're as good as we are now."

The Americans were steamed, and Lanny Wadkins got right to the point, as expected. "It's absurd," he said.

Fortunately for Jacklin, Ballesteros played that extraordinary final round to keep the title in European hands, when it seemed that Nick Price, a Zimbabwean who has applied for American citizenship, was about to snatch it away.

Other memorable events included Sandy Lyle's adding the Dunhill British Masters and Suntory World Match Play titles to the outstanding record he built in America, and Nick Faldo coming directly off his playoff loss to Curtis Strange in the U.S. Open to win the Peugeot French Open, then wrapping up the year with a triumph in the Volvo Masters. Also not to be forgotten was Ireland (with a team consisting of Eammon Darcy, Des Smyth and Ronan Rafferty) winning the Dunhill Cup over heavily-favored Australia at St. Andrews.

Still unproven in America, Spain's young star, Jose-Maria Olazabal charged back to take the Volvo Belgian Open and the German Masters after going winless in 1987. Olazabal was third on the money list with £285,964, following Ballesteros and Faldo, as previously mentioned.

Placing fourth with £234,990 was quite an accomplishment for Ian Woosnam, following a disastrous start to his year, when he left America with a string of missed cuts. The winner of eight tournaments and almost $1.8 million the previous year, Woosnam had his problems compounded by the considerable attention he received in the American press.

It took Lyle five years to win in the United States, and so Woosnam should not be too discouraged, and I don't think he was. He wanted to get back on his game, which he did in winning the Volvo PGA Championship, Carrolls Irish Open and Panasonic European Open — three of Europe's most important titles. He finished with World Money List earnings of $633,144, for 25th place.

Other European champions of note included veterans Mark McNulty, Rodger Davis, Mark James and Howard Clark, plus eight first-time winners, the most ever: David Whelan, David Llewellyn, Derrick Cooper, Mike Harwood, Barry Lane, Peter Baker, Frank Nobilo and Chris Moody.

Bernhard Langer had a recurrence of his putting difficulties and fell to No. 78 on the World Money List with $330,161. I still have a hard time believing he *five-putted from three feet* in the British Open. "It's the worst case I've ever seen," said his caddy, Peter Coleman. "Anything from two to eight feet is a disaster area." It brought to mind Henry Longhurst's fatalistic line about the putting yips, "Once you've had 'em, you've got 'em."

But don't bet against Bernhard. He did win the Epson Grand Prix tournament.

The African tours provided, as usual, a warm-up to the European circuit, then the bonanza of the Million Dollar Challenge in Sun City, Bophuthatswana, at year's end. The five-event Safari tour featured someone by the name of Vijay Singh, from Fiji, then living in Malaysia. Never heard of him? Consider his record in Africa: He won the tour-opening Nigerian Open, tied for fifth in the Ivory Coast Open, placed third in the 555 Kenya Open, was second in the Zimbabwe Open and 10th in the Zambian Open. It was quite a run, even if we did not hear from Singh again. Other Safari winners were Gordon J. Brand, Chris Platts, Roger Chapman and David Llewellyn.

The South African-based Sunshine circuit was again fertile territory for Fulton Allem. The South African native won the first tournament, the Palaboro Classic, and the last, the Million Dollar Challenge. Winners of other events included Mark James, Tony Johnstone, Wayne Westner and John Bland.

It was a big year in Australian golf, with the introduction of several new tournaments and the playing of the Bicentennial Classic and the World Cup, although the latter event — as has become typical of the World Cup — was not what it might have been, because of the bureaucracy which left Australia's best pair of golfers, Greg Norman and Rodger Davis, without invitations, along with U.S. Open champion Curtis Strange.

Davis, who earlier won a tournament in Europe, was a popular winner of the Bicentennial Classic at Royal Melbourne, and the United States, with Ben Crenshaw and Mark McCumber, won the World Cup, Crenshaw also taking the individual title.

There was a great send-off to the year, with Strange winning the new Sanctuary Cove Classic and Norman following with a victory in the Palm Meadows Cup, the first of Greg's four Australian triumphs.

In other early-season tournaments, Ian Baker-Finch won the Australian Masters and a then-unknown American, Jim Benepe, won the Victorian Open. Benepe would later win in his first start on the U.S. PGA Tour at the Beatrice Western Open.

Aside from the Bicentennial and World Cup events, the latter half of the season featured victories by Mark Calcavecchia in the Panasonic Australian Open, Wayne Grady in a playoff over Norman in the Australian PGA Championship, and Britain over the host country in the first Test Match.

If you were to describe the 1988 Japanese circuit in a word, it would be Ozaki. The three Ozaki brothers — Masashi (Jumbo), Naomichi (Joe) and Tateo (Jet) — together won $2,292,246 and 12 tournaments. They won four consecutive tournaments; then a while later, five out of seven. Jumbo, the eldest Ozaki brother at age 41, climbed to No. 11 on the Sony Ranking with six victories and earnings of $1,082,985. Joe won four events and $672,803, and Jet won two tournaments and $536,458, placing all three among the top 33 finishers on the World Money List.

Even though he couldn't take on the whole Ozaki family, Masahiro Kuramoto also had a great year with five victories and earnings of $559,852.

In the Asian events which preceded the Japanese tour, there were three two-time winners: Hsieh Chin Sheng, Wayne Smith and Ian Baker-Finch. When the Japanese circuit began, Jumbo Ozaki won the Dunlop Open. Following wins by Jet in the Japan PGA and Joe in the Niigata Open, Jumbo won two more — for four in a row by the Ozakis — taking the Nikkei Cup and Maruman Open. Jet's next victory was the Suntory Open, followed by Joe's win in the ANA Sapporo event, then three weeks later, Jumbo went on another streak to win the Japan Open, Golf Digest and Bridgestone tournaments.

American David Ishii, who led the 1987 Japanese circuit, had only one victory, in the Japan Match Play. Other overseas winners included Scott Simpson in the Chunichi Crowns, Seve Ballesteros in the VISA Taiheiyo Masters, Ken Green in the Dunlop Phoenix and Larry Mize in the Casio World Open.

The crowning moment of the 1988 Senior PGA Tour came, appropriately, at the USGA Senior Open when Gary Player took advantage of Bob Charles' mistakes — three bogeys over the last four holes — to gain a playoff, then won the title the following day, 68-70. There was not much to separate the two old rivals, Charles winning seven times and Player, six, in the United States and overseas.

Three of Player's victories were major titles, also including the General Foods PGA Seniors Championship and the Volvo Seniors British Open. Five of Charles' triumphs were on the American circuit, one was in Japan and one, South Africa. Other standouts were Orville Moody with four victories, Bruce Crampton and Dave Hill with three each, and Miller Barber, Don Bies, Billy Casper, Chi Chi Rodriguez and Walter Zembriski with two each. Also among the 16 different winners was Arnold Palmer, with his first victory in two years.

The loss in the USGA Senior Open was one of the biggest disappointments in Charles' career. "I had it in my pocket; it was my tournament. Then it was one bad shot, one unlucky shot and one wrong club, and it cost me (the title)," Charles said.

Five American wins — at tour stops in New York, Albuquerque, Sacramento, Lexington and Atlanta — along with 19 other top-10 finishes (including two playoff losses) propelled Charles to earnings of $533,929, a record for the Senior PGA Tour. Conducting a more limited schedule as he commuted from South Africa, Player won $435,914 with his U.S. victories in the Open, PGA and tour stops in Naples, Oklahoma City and Indianapolis.

Moody and Hill each had three individual victories and one each in team events. Moody shot a scorching 263 total in the Vintage Chrysler Invitational at Indian Wells, the lowest score in the history of the senior circuit, and also won tournaments in Dallas and Grand Rapids. Hill won the Senior Tournament of Champions plus the events in Charlotte and Syracuse.

The younger seniors have usually done better than the older seniors, and there were few exceptions in 1988. Time seemed to be passing for Don January and Gene Littler, who for the first year did not post senior victories. Rodriguez had a good record, but nothing to compare with his 1987 results of seven victories and then-record earnings of $509,145. Though both were double winners, Barber and Casper were no longer dominant, as they were a few years earlier.

At the same time, no new stars emerged. Bies was the only first-year winner, and the tour's spotlight event, the Vantage Championship, was won by former ironworker Walter Zembriski.

It will be another year before the greatly-anticipated arrival on the Senior PGA Tour of Jack Nicklaus and Lee Trevino, at which time, Player says, "I truly believe this tour will be more popular than the regular tour."

Every success of the Senior PGA Tour had been viewed in some quarters as a threat to the LPGA Tour. While the senior circuit grew to over 40 events in this decade, the LPGA managed to increase its purses from $5.1 million to over $12 million, quite an accomplishment, I would think, since they were operating in the same marketplace. There have been struggles to keep television and sponsorship contracts, however, and new commissioner William A. Blue will have his hands full in trying to satisfy the LPGA members, some of whom, for reasons I cannot fathom, were not satisfied with the job done by John Laupheimer (who was hired by our company, IMG, shortly after he resigned from the LPGA).

Competitively, at least, the LPGA was very healthy. Five players won three tournaments each, and the four designated major championships were won by four more players. Player of the Year? Officially, it was Nancy Lopez, winner of the LPGA's Rolex award, but you could justifiably have chosen any one of a half-dozen or more golfers.

Lopez was among the three-tournament winners; the others were Juli Inkster, Ayako Okamoto, Betsy King and Rosie Jones, whose victories included the prestigious Nestle World Championship. Major championships were won by Amy Alcott (Nabisco Dinah Shore), Sherri Turner (Mazda LPGA Championship), Sally Little (duMaurier Classic) and Liselotte Neumann (U.S. Women's Open). Turner, Patty Sheehan and Laura Davies each won two tournaments.

Six players won more than $300,000, led by Turner with $350,851, then Sheehan ($326,171), Jones ($323,392), Lopez ($322,154), Colleen Walker ($318,116 including one victory) and Okamoto ($300,206). Jan Stephenson did not win a tournament but was in the top 10, holding ninth place on the money list with $236,739.

There were nine first-time winners — Davies (who won the 1987 U.S. Women's Open when she was not an LPGA member), Turner, Neumann, Ok-Hee Ku, Mei-Chi Cheng, Shirley Furlong, Terry Jo Myers, Martha Nause and Patty Jordon.

"It's not going to be easy anymore to win four or five times a year, not with all these good, young players out here," said Lopez, who won the Rolex Player of the Year honors for the fourth time. "They're not afraid of anything. They don't blink when they get in contention. And that can only be good for the tour."

Turner and Newmann produced the year's biggest surprises. Turner, another of the Furman University products, blossomed in her fifth LPGA season and won the Mazda LPGA Championship and Corning Classic on consecutive weeks. From among the first-year players, Sweden's Neumann followed

England's Davies to the U.S. Women's Open crown. Known as Lotte, Neumann won several European titles before gaining her LPGA player's card. She was the fifth foreign winner of the U.S. Women's Open and, at age 22 years, two months, the youngest professional winner. (France's Catherine Lacoste, an amateur, was five days past her 22nd birthday when she won in 1967.)

Before turning to the 1988 season in detail, we recall the passing of...Gerald Micklem, 76, past captain of the Royal and Ancient Golf Club of St. Andrews, and one of the world's most noted golf administrators...Vivien Jacklin, 44, wife of European Ryder Cup captain Tony Jacklin...Well-respected golf instructors Davis Love, Jr., John Popa and Jim Hodges in an airplane crash...Dan Sikes, 58, winner of six PGA Tour and two Senior PGA Tour titles.

3. The Masters Tournament

Of golf's four major championships, only the Masters Tournament is played annually on the same course, Augusta National Golf Club, so that followers of the game have come to know the holes, especially those that make up the back nine, as intimately as they do characters in a favorite play. Each has a rich history of glorious moments: No. 10 is where Ben Crenshaw sank a 60-foot putt on his way to victory in 1984, No. 11 is Larry Mize and his chip-in in 1987 (although technically, it was the second hole of a playoff), No. 15, Gene Sarazen in 1934, No. 16, Jack Nicklaus' putt in 1975 and his near hole-in-one in 1986. There are dozens more.

There are also memories of disaster: Tom Weiskopf's 13 at No. 12, Seve Ballesteros hitting into the water at No. 15 to let Nicklaus win in 1986; Billy Joe Patton and Curtis Strange know how he felt. The finishing hole, No. 18, finished Arnold Palmer in 1961; par to win, bogey to tie, Palmer took six, thus losing to Gary Player by a stroke.

For those who saw the 1988 edition of the Masters, No. 18 had its most glorious moment in the 52-year history of the tournament. Debate is welcomed. Doug Ford holed out from a bunker in 1957, but even two putts would have brought him home a winner. Better was Player's birdie putt in 1978, capping a brilliant 64, but there were still three men on the course who were in position to win.

No, what happened at the 18th in the late afternoon sunshine of Sunday, April 10, 1988 deserves a position at the top of the list, at the same time negating what would have been one of the more memorable disasters at No. 12. Ah, but we are getting ahead of ourselves. As usual there were assorted points of interest earlier in the week — the concerns of the tournament chairman, suggestions and complaints by former champions and a watery grave for a souvenir. Let us check them out.

Among the many Masters traditions is the tournament's version of the fireside chat, in which the chairman, currently Hord Hardin, meets with the media the day before play begins and discusses the state of the world, the world in question stretching from Washington Road in front of the club to Berckman Road behind it. The primary topic this year was money, Hardin's concern being that every tournament on the PGA Tour calendar from the Los Angeles Open Presented by Nissan to Hardee's in Coal Valley, Illinois, to the Canon Sammy Davis Greater Hartford Open now offers purses that resemble the national debt. Hardin indicated that in the future the Masters might have to pull in its financial oars, offer a paltry $1 million, and let the Federal Express St. Jude Classic, the Texas Open Presented by Nabisco and the Walt Disney World/Oldsmobile Classic go by.

"Maybe I'm in dreamland," said Hardin, "and I will never say never, but I just don't believe the members of this club would want to continue if the only alternative was to get as much out of television as we could, or to sandbag our patrons for every nickel, or to have hospitality houses all over the place. I'd hate to see us charge for parking or ask $150 for a series badge. (Note: that day is coming, Hord. Series badges have risen from $20 to $80 over the last 15 years.) I'd hate to see us give up the 56 minutes (per hour) of golf on television we provide fans from around the world."

Hardin said the members of Augusta National would never yield to corporate sponsorship. "I don't visualize us having the Pizza Hut Masters." He worried that if the Masters didn't keep up in prize money younger players would start skipping it, especially if it were flanked by a couple of $5 million events.

But hours later, when Tom Watson heard what Hardin had said, he argued to the contrary. "This is for prestige, for tradition," said the two-time champion. "Winning this is a career-making opportunity. It's not 'where did you finish in the U.S. Open or the PGA?' but 'did you make the top 16 or eight and qualify for the Masters?' Everyone wants to play here."

Hardin also addressed himself to the possibility of a Senior Masters, a reflection of the growing popularity of the Senior Tour. Both Arnold Palmer and Jack Nicklaus had endorsed such a notion, but Hardin had reservations. "Anything those two fellows suggest deserves serious consideration," Hardin began. "But it's not a new subject. We've been asked in the past to have a separate tournament on a separate week and we've rejected that. Now it's been suggested we have a tournament within a tournament, but I think it would be confusing to the public to have two champions."

One of Hardin's concerns was the size of the field, 90 this year, which perforce would expand if top seniors such as Chi Chi Rodriguez, Bruce Crampton and perhaps a dozen more were added. "We're looking for ways to reduce the size of the field," said Hardin. "I think 80 is ideal."

On Wednesday morning, as the field took its final practice swings, everyone was a potential winner. That's the nice thing about Wednesdays. The local papers, in their usual thorough coverage, saw the bright side of virtually every player's chances. A *Golfweek Magazine* poll had Greg Norman beating out Seve Ballesteros as the favorite. Tom Watson was third. Nothing so terrible about those three choices, but the remainder of the poll — down to 38 places — may stand as a classic of fuzzy forecasting. There were Marks (Calcavecchia, O'Meara and McCumber), Steves (Beck and Jones) and Scotts (Hoch and Simpson), but nowhere on the list was a Sandy, meaning Lyle. The Scotsman came to Augusta as the tour's leading money winner, with wins at Phoenix and at Greensboro the week before. He was also a former British Open and TPC winner. You'd think that might get him...oh say, the 35th spot, just ahead of Keith Clearwater. But no.

Of the many sporting wagers made on the eve of play, a recent entry has been Americans vs. foreigners. Years ago the prospect of a foreigner winning ranked just above an amateur. Gary Player stood alone. But then came Ballesteros and Bernhard Langer and the successive Ryder Cup victories by the European team and now it is a close call. A betting man could take foreigners in all four majors and feel most comfortable. Lyle, Langer, Ballesteros, Norman and Nick Faldo have all won majors. The top U.S. fivesome on the 1987 money list would give you Curtis Strange, Paul Azinger, Crenshaw, Simpson and Watson. One vote for the foreigners.

What's more, we haven't even mentioned the man who may be just as good as any of the big boys, Ian Woosnam, the five feet, four and half-inch package of dynamite from Wales. Woosnam was making his first appearance at Augusta, and he revealed just a trace of bitterness that he had not been invited sooner. "I would have liked to have been here last year," he said. "I was playing well at the time and in fact won the Jersey Open the same week." Despite his size, Woosnam can hit with the big boys, even further than most of them. The practice range at Augusta is 270 yards long, with a screen at the end to keep the longest shots on the property. On Tuesday Woosnam hit one over the top of the screen and onto Washington Road.

The weather during the early practice rounds was ideal, but dark clouds gathered toward noon Wednesday and around 2:00 in the afternoon, heavy rain interrupted the traditional par-three event. When the skies cleared, many of the players had long since decided to call it a day, which was okay with Tommy Nakajima. Tommy went out early, posted a 24, usually a stroke or two off the pace, and found himself the winner.

Fans who stayed to the end gathered in some treats. On the final hole, Norman hit his tee shot across Ike's Pond to the green, then trotted downhill to a lower tee and hit another. What club he used I do not know, but he intentionally sculled the ball so that it skipped four times like a flat rock, the final skip taking it to the front edge of the green. It was a demonstration of the man's joie de vivre, but it also showed just how talented he and his fellow pros are.

The second tidbit involved the last twosome, Scott Verplank and — wait a minute — who is that gentleman? Old. Very old, certainly not a contestant. A club member, perhaps, keeping Verplank from having to play alone. As he played the eighth hole it was determined the man was Paul Runyan, 80, winner of the 1934 and 1938 PGA. That's a half century and more. On No. 9, Verplank hit his shot over the green into a bunker and now here came Runyan. The hole is about 155 yards long and for Runyan, it must have been a three iron or so because the ball crossed the pond like a low-flying honker. But it made it, hit the embankment and trickled up toward the pin, 10 feet away. Okay, he missed his birdie, but he beat Verplank, 55 years his junior.

By Wednesday at 5 p.m., you couldn't have asked for a more pleasant late-afternoon, although patrons were denied the pleasure of sitting on the veranda, sipping a drink and anticipating the upcoming tournament. Club stewards had folded the umbrellas above the tables, and the chairs were wet. At least the clearing brought with it the prospect of similar weather the next day.

Well, not quite. Thursday was, in the words of Jack Nicklaus, who has been attending the Masters more than 25 years, "one of the most difficult I've ever seen." Tom Watson took a military view. "A day like today is survival," he said. "You're in retreat. There are not many who advanced against the enemy today." Seve Ballesteros, a visitor 13 times, said he had never seen the course as difficult. Ben Crenshaw, the ultimate player/historian, felt the wind took everyone's game "into another dimension," one in which yardages meant nothing. "You had to feel your way around out there," he said. He added that he was "very proud" of his 72.

And well he might have been. There are years when even-par gets you polite applause, little more, because it is five or even six strokes off the pace. But on this day of winds and cool temperatures, especially late in the day, 72 was three strokes from the lead, with only six players better. The mean score was 77 and 21 players shot 80 or worse.

The day was not so belligerent at 8:30 in the morning when those two old warriors, Gene Sarazen and Sam Snead, performed the annual ritual of driving off the first tee. The pines were swaying to a southwest breeze, but the sun was out and such days often become gorgeous when the winds die. Both gentlemen hit their drives well, Snead not much shorter than a number of contestants would, and off they went in their cart, which was waiting for them a discreet 100 yards off the tee. A quarter of an hour later Mark O'Meara and Bobby Wadkins launched the official tournament and three hours later, O'Meara's name had made its way onto the leaderboard, alongside such traditional names as last year's champion (Mize), the winners of the three other majors, Scott Simpson, Faldo and Larry Nelson, and the two amateur champions, Billy Mayfair and Paul Mayo. O'Meara was at red 2, two under par, after 14 holes, but just as those of us wandering about the front nine were anticipating another birdie at the par-five 15th, we saw that O'Meara had bogeyed the hole.

Next came the harbinger of just how tough the course would be this day. O'Meara's tee shot at the par-three 16th, hit with a five iron, left him just short. His chip put him on the fringe, 10 feet above the hole, from where he putted, "just barely" touching the ball. It caught the downhill and rolled 60 feet away, from where it took him three more putts. Triple bogey-six and a 74.

The two low scores, 69s, came from an old pro and a comparative youngster, players born a day and 12 years apart. Larry Nelson, 40, winner of the 1983 U.S. Open and two PGAs, 1981 and 1987, posted his score first. If there was a key to his five-birdie, two-bogey round, it was laissez-faire attitude toward the wind. "I figured my distance, looked up to see which way the wind was blowing and just hit the shot," said Nelson, "I wasn't doing anything funny, not trying to do anything better than I can. If the wind stopped, or if it gusted, I couldn't do anything about it."

Nelson had more or less dropped off the tour during 1985-86, feeling that he had better prepare for a career outside of golf, unwilling to continue playing if he could not excel. When he decided to return, he worked vigorously, running several times a week and building up his upper body strength. He came to Augusta still seething over an article in a golf magazine that implied his achievements were flukes. "It was a stab in the back," he said. "When you win three major championships, the third is no fluke. Winning the PGA last year meant more to me than any other tournament. It was as if I said 'Well, I'm back, whether anybody likes it or not.' Then I finished second at the Western, fourth in the World Series and won the Disney."

If there's anything that breaks the heart of a working stiff golf writer for a daily publication, it's a low round late in the day, long after the first day's lead story has been filed. Hello, Robert Wrenn. Playing in a late pairing, as befits someone who has not yet emerged as a gallery attraction, Wrenn made the leaderboard quickly when he birdied the first two holes and turned in 33. Bogeys at Nos. 11 and 14 brought him back to earth, but at No. 15 he displayed an attitude the tour needs more of. Faced with a decision whether or not to try and carry the pond with his second shot, he thought "Heck, I don't get to Augusta very often. I'll give it a lash."

Wrenn birdied the hole and came to No. 18 with a red 2 beside his name. One more par would give him a nifty 70 and a paragraph in everyone's story. But Wrenn stuck his approach eight feet from the flagstick and when he sunk the putt in the gathering darkness and uncomfortable chill, the Masters had a co-leader.

"Don't wake me up" said the 28-year-old Wrenn, who had qualified for the Masters by winning the Buick Open in late July. "I'm tickled to death. If someone had given me a 69 before I went out there, I wouldn't have even thought about playing. With the wind like it was, it was a completely different golf course. Where the pins were made the greens difficult to read and you only have a few minutes to figure it out. You'd better be right or you'll be out there all day. You have to pack a sandwich on some of these greens."

Toward the very end of the day, a day in which play lasted until after 7:00, Gary Koch came up No. 18 about to join Wrenn and Nelson at 69, but his approach wandered into the righthand bunker. The pin was set back, so Gary had plenty of room and it seemed likely he would get down in two. But when he swung and the ball stayed in and his second try barely made it, he was in trouble. Sure enough, his first putt left him a tricky three-footer and when he missed that, he had a triple-bogey seven and a 72.

If Koch felt badly about 72 — and he did, skipping the press interview — Crenshaw and Watson were delighted. Watson pulled off the best shot of the day when, after driving into the pines on the right of No. 14, he hit a calculated ground ball six inches from the pin. Ben credited Carl Jackson, an Augusta National caddy who has carried his bag since 1976. "He's so helpful on a day like this," said Crenshaw. "There are some putts out there I defy anyone to read unless you've been here many times. Like No. 17 today, that's impossible. No. 7 is the other."

Sandwiched between the leaders and the threesome at par were four players at 71: Calcavecchia, Langer, Lyle and Don Pooley. When Calcavecchia teed off at No. 8 he had the look of a man destined for a not-so-pleasant weekend of fishing, resting or whatever. He was three over, but his spirits were high. "I told myself that everyone was having a tough time," he said. "Then I made that putt and it changed my round." That putt was an eight-footer for a birdie and he followed it with four more against only one bogey on the back.

Calcavecchia began to feel pain in his left shoulder earlier in the year and at the TPC, where he finished 64th, it became too much. He sought the advice of a surgeon, Dr. Frank Job, who put him on an exercise program which helped. Even so, he said his shoulder hurt during the round whenever he drove.

Langer also had physical problems, a bothersome back that had been troubling him for months. His round was a quiet, but efficient one, three birdies, two bogeys. As for Pooley, many people didn't realize he had shot 71 until they picked up their morning papers. He was in the final pairing of the day, one that finished at 7:11 p.m., just barely beating the darkness. It was the latest finish in memory, due to the wind that caused such indecision and club-changing on the part of the players.

Of the four 71s, Lyle's commanded the most attention. He had won the week before and while you could argue this was bad — no one had won both Greensboro and the Masters since Sam Snead in 1949 — it was proof the man was playing well. The one-under round was Lyle's best start at Augusta; the last three years he had averaged 77. In 1986 he had rebounded well enough that he was paired with Nicklaus on Sunday, thus having the best seat in the house as Jack shot 65 to win his sixth Masters.

On Thursday Lyle had enough birdies, five, for a truly fine round, but he kept tossing in bogeys. He was even-par with only one par after five holes. He is a very long hitter and was able to birdie three of the par-fives. A sour note was a bogey at No. 18, never a nice way to end a round. It was caused, he said, when his three-foot putt hit a spike mark. "The ball was knocked clean off line," he said. After discussing the wind, a common post-round topic this day, Lyle revealed he had not practiced as hard as he usually does. "On the first tee I felt more rested, more relaxed than usual," he said.

And what of last year's playoff trio? Mize made no birdies and on a day as rugged as this, you had to make bogeys. The result? A 78. Norman was only one stroke better, putting miserably, especially on the back nine where he double-bogeyed No. 10, then bogeyed the 14th through the 16th. Of the 1987 playoff trio, only Seve looked good and, in fact, was two-under and a possible leader when he teed off at No. 15.

Ah, the 15th, Seve. You remember it well. Par-five, water in front of the green, right? This time Seve, trying to reach the green in one, hooked his drive violently. One of the pleasant things about Augusta National from a wild hitter's point of view is that, unlike a U.S. Open course, you can drive it almost anywhere and not be in too much trouble. But there are limits. Seve managed to find some thorny bushes in the wide expanse between the 14th and 15th fairways. He spent fully 10 minutes circling the long row — there was no cutting between them — seeing if he couldn't scrape the ball out somehow, so that he could stick his third shot on the green. No go. He took a drop, laid up, hit it on and two-putted for a bogey.

Alas, that was just the prelude to disaster. At No. 16 he hit a six iron 35 feet from the pin. Later he was to say: "I putted past the hole. I miss, miss again and make it. Four putts can happen to anybody. Unfortunately it happened to me today."

There is reason to believe the pin placement on No. 16 was too difficult, which is to say unfair. Ian Woosnam also four-putted on his way to an 81, as had O'Meara hours earlier. Occasionally the folks who set the pins err, and this appears to be one of those times.

The leaders after the first round:

Larry Nelson	69	Ken Brown	73
Robert Wrenn	69	Davis Love III	73
Bernhard Langer	71	Andy Bean	73
Mark Calcavecchia	71	Tom Kite	73
Sandy Lyle	71	David Frost	73
Don Pooley	71	Gary Hallberg	73
Ben Crenshaw	72	Chip Beck	73
Tom Watson	72	Seve Ballesteros	73
Gary Koch	72		

Friday was the kind of Georgia day you have in mind when you contemplate another trip to the Masters. Gentle wind, mild temperatures. Good spectator weather. Good golfing weather too except that, according to many players, the greens were as hard as Interstate 95. Or, as Gary Hallberg said, it was like putting on a pool table with potato chips on it. The winds of the preceding day had dried out the surfaces; the ball rolled on forever.

The loudest — and most startling — objection came from Fuzzy Zoeller, startling because he had just posted a 66 that come nightfall would place him near the lead despite a first-round 76. Zoeller traced the problem to a round 15 years earlier in another tournament, another course — Johnny Miller's 63 at Oakmont on the final round of the U.S. Open. "If the players today are that good," said Zoeller, "why not let us play and if we shoot 63, pat us on the back? Why do we have to go back the next year and play crap like this? Putting on tricked-up greens is no fun at all. Now you must tap the ball and hope it stops 10 feet away. If that's golf, I'm in the wrong league."

Arnold Palmer joined in. "I'm tired of seeing 10-foot putts roll 40 feet away," said Arnold. "They need to redesign some of the bent grass or go back to Bermuda."

Nicklaus felt the greens were the fastest he'd seen at Augusta in 30 years, but said it was their inconsistancy, not their speed, that annoyed him. Watson agreed the greens were fast but felt they were fair. "This man (course superintendent Paul Latshaw) knows what he's doing," said Watson. "He's not going to let the greens get away from him." But some players felt a few of the greens were already gone. Earlier in the week Crenshaw had said that he had taken a close look at the 11th green and found "nothing living out there." Curtis Strange, who four-putted the ninth, said there wasn't "a blade of grass on the surface. I have to question whether Mr. Roberts and Mr. Jones wanted it this way."

In spite of everything, the game went on and 17 players brought home sub-par rounds, although one, Jay Haas' 71, was not quite good enough to let him make the cut of 151. Raymond Floyd proved what champions are made of when he cut 11 shots off his opening round with a 69. Over the next two days he would add a 68 and 71 to tie for 11th, a splendid recovery.

Zoeller teed off at 11:40, with Strange right behind him. Fuzzy made a lot of putts for a man who hated the greens. He rolled in 10-footers at the first two holes and a pair of tricky downhillers at Nos. 7 and 9. He made a routine two-putt birdie at No. 13, nearly holed out at No. 16 and made one last 10-footer at No. 17. He had seven birdies, one bogey (at the fifth). "I just hit the ball on the green in certain areas that left me with makable putts," he said. "It's been about two years since I put my game together like this — putting, driver, irons."

Halfway through his round, Strange was every bit as upset with Augusta National as was Zoeller. He had just four-putted the ninth green, a disaster that placed him in jeopardy of missing the cut. Two pars took him to the 12th tee, still seething. His playing partner, Roger Maltbie, had used a six iron on the dangerous par-three hole and had rolled past the flagstick, so Curtis chose a seven iron. "The green was so brown I couldn't see the flagstick," Strange said. What he did see seconds after he had hit his shot was Zoeller and T.C. Chen on the 13th tee both raise their arms. Strange's ball had bounced twice and rolled in for a hole-in-one, the first in the Masters since 1972 (Charles Coody at No. 6) and only the third at No. 12.

What happened next was, well, unexpected. Curtis retrieved his ball from the cup and flipped it into Rae's Creek, the water in front of the green. Why? "I don't know why," Strange said, "I just did it.

"The shot sure turned my game around. Funny how that happens."

Birdies at the par-fives and an additional one at No. 17, gave Strange 31 for the back side, 70 for the round. By Friday evening instead of packing his bags he was only eight strokes behind the leader.

Ah yes, the leader. Larry Nelson, perhaps. No, Nelson had fallen from first to 19th. He birdied the first hole to go four-under, but that was his high-water mark. "Yesterday my bad shots turned out good," he said when he had staggered home with his 78. "Today my good shots turned out bad." Nor did things improve, Nelson adding two 75s to wind up 33rd.

Then maybe Wrenn was leading. No, again. "Obviously I was nervous," he said after his 75. "When you see yourself on TV and read about it in the papers, it's obviously on your mind a lot more than the guy who shot 76." Which is what Wrenn shot Saturday, followed by a 74 to finish 25th, missing the top 24 by a stroke.

The 36-hole leader was the man who had been playing the best golf all year, Sandy Lyle. His 71 Thursday had put him in splendid position and Friday he posted the day's second best score, 67, to go six under par for the tournament. After a bogey at the first, the toughest hole on the course through the first two rounds, Lyle birdied four times on the front nine — Nos. 2, 5, 7 and 9 — and twice on the back, the conventional Nos. 13 and 15.

After which the press all learned about foot rubs and other assorted Lyle trivia. He calls himself a Scotsman although he was born in England and lives there. But both his parents were Scots, so the claim is not invalid. He was taught the game at age three by his father, Alex, has resided in England most of his life, was married and has two sons, but is now divorced. He was in Augusta with his girlfriend, a tall young woman named Jolanda Huurman who was seen reading a paperback during those sometimes-lengthy waiting periods between her friend's shots. Huurman was a sports masseuse on the European Tour when Lyle met her. Lyle was suffering from a slight head cold at Augusta and was having trouble breathing at night. Huurman had a cure. "She's been tickling my toes at night," Lyle revealed. "It clears my head." One has to wonder what Bobby Jones would make of it.

Calcavecchia, for one, thought it was great and threatened to have his wife give him a massage that night. Calcavecchia had been in the press room because his 69 had put him in second, two shots back. You'll remember he had been three-over after seven holes on Thursday. Friday's early holes were no better except that he managed some Harry Houdini escapes. At No. 3 he was 15 yards over the green, but got down in two. At No. 4 he sank a 20-footer for par, at No. 6 a 15-footer and at No. 7 one half that distance.

So instead of three over (or worse), he was even-par and in a great mood. He birdied Nos. 8, 15 and 17, again leaning on the putting skills for which he is rapidly becoming known on the tour. "If I could concentrate like this every week I'd be a lot better player," he said. "After those first seven holes I felt like I was stealing from the course."

Calcavecchia is regarded as one of the better young U.S. players. In the early 1980s he was one of those players who appears and then drops off the tour; his five-year earnings were less than $90,000. At the 1986 Honda Classic he caddied for Ken Green. A year later, he won it. His earnings in 1987 were $522,423, good for 10th on the money list.

Tied with Zoeller, four strokes behind Lyle, was The Hat, Gary Hallberg, who had a 69. "The key was to stay in slow motion," he said mysteriously. "I drove over here slow and ate slow. It's taken me 10 years to discover that staying in slow motion pays off."

One stroke further behind at 143 was Watson, along with Pooley, Langer, Chip Beck and Fred Couples. Standing on the sixth tee, Watson was two under for his round and had the look of someone who might shoot his own 66. Instead he finished with 12 pars and a bogey. "I'm not making any putts," he said.

Langer's round was the exact opposite; it was an even-par 72 with only six pars in it. There were five birdies, five bogeys, an eagle and a double bogey, an emotional roller-coaster for anyone following him. As for Langer's back, "it's still stiff," he said.

Ballesteros, Crenshaw and Stadler were among those at 145, Stadler shooting 69 to return from the dead. Nicklaus made his 27th cut in 30 Masters with 75-73. Norman's 73 was a four-stroke improvement, but he needed considerably more than that. Tom Kite was heading south for the second straight year after a decade of close calls. Last year he tied for 24th. This year, after an opening 73, he shot 76-77-76 to finish 44th. But at least that was better than the defending champion, Mize. His 78-71 made the cut, but 76-79 put him in a tie for last place. What an elevator ride.

Here is the scoreboard spectators saw as they left the course Friday evening:

Sandy Lyle	71-67—138	Hubert Green	74-70—144
Mark Calcavecchia	71-69—140	Robert Wrenn	69-75—144
Fuzzy Zoeller	76-66—142	Seve Ballesteros	73-72—145
Gary Hallberg	73-69—142	Mark McNulty	74-71—145
Fred Couples	75-68—143	Craig Stadler	76-69—145
Chip Beck	63-70—143	Gary Koch	72-73—145
Tom Watson	72-71—143	Ben Crenshaw	72-73—145
Don Pooley	71-72—143	Tommy Nakajima	74-72—146
Bernhard Langer	71-72—143	Curtis Strange	76-70—146

On Saturday, Lyle and Calcavecchia were the final pairing. When they teed off at 1:45, the day was balmy, the breezes normal. Nothing seemed to be happening on the course. Third rounds are known as "moving day" on the tour. A year ago Greg Norman shot 66 to pick up six shots on eventual winner Larry Mize. The year before Norman was moved on himself; he had a six-stroke lead on Nick Price, shot 68 and found his lead over Price reduced to one, as Price set a course record with a 63. (That same year Jack Nicklaus made "moving day" Sunday, shooting 65 to win his sixth Masters.)

Nothing like that was happening on this Saturday afternoon. The first pairing was already in; Ken Brown had shot a creditable 69, Payne Stewart 71, an indication the course might be vulnerable, but no one playing an hour or so ahead and starting about 10 shots behind was, say, four or five under after six holes. Both leaders had to wait a bit at No. 1 as Hallberg, just ahead, double-bogeyed the hole on his way to three sixes, seven fives and a round of 80. So much for slow motion.

One group ahead of Hallberg, Chip Beck was also disappearing from the leaderboard, going four over from No. 3 to No. 5. Watson, in theory an ideal choice to make a move, did so, but backwards. Opening with a pair of bogeys, he shot 73 and was never a factor.

Lyle looked for a time like a man in a hurry to wrap things up. He birdied the second hole, as indeed he did all four rounds. Lyle is so long off the tee the par-fives at Augusta are all reachable, even though at least two of them — Nos. 2 and 8 — are considerably longer than they were 10 years ago. For the tournament he was eight under on the par-fives, even on the par-threes, one-over on the par-fours.

Calcavecchia matched Lyle's birdie at the second, but when he three-putted from 25 feet at the third — a rare occurrence for him — as Lyle birdied the hole after knocking his approach stiff, he was four strokes back.

At this moment, and for the next half hour or so, a most popular person with journalists on the golf course was one Raymond Jacobs of the *Glasgow Herald*. Raymond, a veteran Masters observer, put in many years tracking Great Britain's hopes: Tony Jacklin, possible; Peter Butler, most unlikely; whoever was British amateur champ at the time, no chance. But now here was a real live Scotsman with a four-stroke lead. As the gallery took the long hike out No. 5, Jacobs' brain was picked for all he knew about his countryman, although Raymond was quick to point out that Lyle had forsaken Scotland for England many years ago and had just recently referred to Scotland as home.

Lyle gave a stroke back at the fifth hole when he three-putted but the par-five eighth provided him with the birdie that allowed him to turn in 34, eight under for the tournament. Calcavecchia had played No. 4 through No. 9 in straight pars, so he was exactly where he started, four under, but now four shots back. Of the 46 golfers on the course, no one played the front nine better than Lyle, and only two players matched him.

One of those, Doug Tewell, can be dispatched quickly. He shot 68 to theoretically put himself into the picture, but a 73 Sunday earned only a 14th place finish and a return trip next year. The other, Ben Crenshaw, was a more serious threat, as might have been expected.

Crenshaw, with his 72-73, was seven groups and about an hour ahead of Lyle. He had one of the more remarkable rounds in memory. He followed his 34 with a 33, but what made the round memorable was that he failed to birdie a single par-five. Over the last seven holes he posted five threes, plus the two par-fives. He had nary a bogey. It did not become a super round until the very end when he closed with a pair of birdies, sinking a 30-foot putt for a birdie at No. 17 and a 12-footer at No. 18.

Like Zoeller had the day before, Ben expressed concern about the greens. "I can't say it was fun out there," he said. "If you're above the hole, you just have to breathe on it. Fortunately I hit a lot of good irons where I could really take a swing at the putt."

Ben's 67 placed him at four under, but as Lyle and Calcavecchia started down the 10th fairway, Crenshaw had not yet made his finishing rush and was simply one of a cluster of folks six or so shots behind. The last pair sailed through the rugged 10th, 11th and 12th in even par, which is always what any golfer wants.

As Lyle stood on the 13th tee, he saw where Hallberg had hit his tee shot. "He was way around the corner, with only a four iron left to the green," Lyle said. (Little did he know that Hallberg would make six on the hole on his way to the 80.) "Maybe I was too casual. I'd gotten through No. 12 and felt good. I took too much of a gamble trying to get around the corner and I paid the penalty."

The 13th, as most people know, is the classic par-five, dogleg left. Drive perfectly along the leftside and the birdie is probable, eagle possible. Drive right and you have to lay up, trying for the birdie with a pitch and putt. Lyle hooked his drive and caught the woods on the left. Unplayable, one stroke penalty. It was routine after that, a four-iron lay up, pitch to 30 feet, two putts, bogey.

Calcavecchia, meanwhile, parred the hole to gain a stroke but immediately gave it back by bogeying No. 14, missing a short putt, so that coming to No. 15 Lyle was still ahead of him by four, although by this time Crenshaw, passing close by at No. 17, was also four back.

The 15th, easily reachable this day, proved more than that for Lyle. His second shot carried not only the pond but the green and the best he could do was chip and two-putt for a par. Calcavecchia did far better, putting a four iron 12 feet away, the ball barely clearing the embankment. In the clubhouse, one person was heard to say: "Gutsy but foolish. Today he makes it, tomorrow it goes in the water." But Calcavecchia capitalized on today's shot, sinking the putt for an eagle three. Lyle's lead was cut in half, to two strokes.

And then cut in half again. At No. 16 Lyle's tee shot was just off the green. He elected to putt and the ball caught some thick grass. It took him two more to get down. "I thought my first putt was perfect," he said. "An inch more and it would have reached the green. I never hit a bad shot on the hole and wound up with four. That's the way it goes."

Only one shot behind, Calcavecchia immediately made it two when he hit his approach at No. 17 into the front bunker. Both players parred No. 18, so that now both had shot even-par 72s and Lyle's lead at 6:15 p.m. was the same as it had been four and a half hours earlier. But now Calcavecchia had been joined by Crenshaw at two strokes back.

And, of course, there were others. Hallberg, Beck and Watson may have disappeared, but Zoeller, Langer and Couples had not, all of them four behind. None of them had done anything spectacular, just steady. All three were 35 going out, Couples and Langer 36 coming in. Fuzzy stood on the 15th tee at three under for the tournament, but he bogeyed that birdie hole and No. 16 as well for a 37 and 72.

As usual, Zoeller had much to say. He thought the greens were slightly improved. "It's amazing what you can get done if you bitch a little," he said. "But they should take a picture of No. 11 and frame it. It's as hard as this wall.

"A lot of players came up to me and told me it was about time someone spoke up. Except Tom Watson. He said, 'What's wrong with them? They're just challenging.'" When told Watson had four-putted the 16th, Zoeller couldn't resist the needle. "I hope he enjoyed every stroke," he said. "It's a darn shame it wasn't a six. I didn't say that, did I?"

Another view was presented by an elderly gentleman I know. "Zoeller says they've taken the fun out of golf," he said. "He makes half a million a year from golf. It's his job and he gets well paid. Why should it be fun?"

Couples had a ragged back nine, three bogeys and only pars at Nos. 13 and 15, but birdies at Nos. 16 and 17 gave him his 71. Still, he didn't think much of his chances. "I don't think 68 will do it and 68 is tough," he said. Langer predicted the tournament would not be decided until the last putt dropped, qualifying him for job as a gypsy fortune teller or at least a TV golf analyst. He also complained that officials had watered the fairways too much, the greens not enough. "I had mud on my ball several times," he said. "It's hard enough hitting into these greens without having mud on your ball."

There were three other players under par, one-under to be exact, and two of them were not ready to concede to Lyle, even though he was five strokes ahead. "He can play great golf," Ballesteros admitted. "When he plays good, he's hard to beat. But...he can be inconsistent. The tournament is not over. I remember one year I led by 10 strokes on the back nine and lost seven at Amen Corner."

Stadler was pleased with his position, considering his first-round 76. "The putts are starting to drop," he said. "Five shots is very easy to make up." However the taciturn Don Pooley was not optimistic, perhaps with reason. His lowest score at Augusta was 71, and a 71 on Sunday obviously would not do it. "There are too many people ahead of me," he said. "I'd have to shoot 65."

Press headquarters, as is its custom in this modern age, issued a blizzard of computer printouts, one of which graphically showed how fragile a five-shot lead can be. It was a hole-by-hole comparison of the leaders for the third round and Lyle's and Crenshaw's happened to follow one another. Their back nines looked like this:

Lyle	4 4 3	6 4 5	4 4 4	38
Crenshaw	4 4 3	5 3 5	3 3 3	33

To repeat what Craig Stadler had said, five shots is very easy to make up. Sunday would show how right he was.

The leaders after the third round:

Sandy Lyle	71-67-72—210
Mark Calcavecchia	71-69-72—212
Ben Crenshaw	72-73-67—212
Fred Couples	75-68-71—214
Bernhard Langer	71-72-71—214
Fuzzy Zoeller	76-66-72—214
Seve Ballesteros	73-72-70—215
Craig Stadler	76-69-70—215
Don Pooley	71-72-72—215
Doug Tewell	75-73-68—216

Tom Watson	72-71-73—216
Raymond Floyd	80-69-68—217
Dan Pohl	78-70-69—217

Well before Lyle teed off Sunday, there was, as television commentators are wont to say, action out on the course. Greg Norman, at a disspiriting five-over, 11 strokes back, was clearly out of it unless he did something ridiculous, like shoot 60. Teeing off at 1:19, a little more than one and a half hours ahead of Lyle, Norman reduced the front nine to rubble. Put it this way; he parred the first, fourth and fifth. The rest were birdies. That added up to 30, tying Johnny Miller's third-round effort in 1975.

Now all Norman had to do— although he couldn't know it at the time— was shoot another 30. Not impossible. That's what 46-year-old Jack Nicklaus did when he won two years ago. But suddenly the putts that dropped earlier stayed inches from the cup and the best Norman could do was 34, picking up birdies on the par-fives. His 64 placed him at three under for the tournament. He needed Lyle to shoot 75, Calcavecchia and Crenshaw 73s and so on down the line. Those things did not happen. Even so, when his round was over, the Shark disdained a beer until he had been mathematically eliminated.

Even with a 64, Norman was unhappy. "I'm more disappointed this year than last," he said. "Last year it was someone else's great shot that beat me. This time it's my own fault I wasn't around at the end."

As Lyle prepared to start his final round, there was another round in progress of much more concern to him than Norman's. The quiet man, Don Pooley, playing a half hour ahead, had birdied the first two holes. Five shots back at the start of the round, he was now three. And as Lyle was approaching the first green, Pooley birdied the third. Two back. What's going on? It's one thing for a player 11 strokes back to shoot 64, but a man only five back who shoots, say, 67, is even more dangerous. But minutes later Pooley bogeyed the fourth and was never again a serious threat. He did post a creditable 70 to tie Norman for fifth place, so he will be invited to the party next year.

The final four pairings were Ballesteros/Stadler, Couples/Zoeller, Calcavecchia/Langer and Lyle/Crenshaw. Of those eight players, four — Seve, Fred, Fuzzy and Ben — were never, or at best only momentarily, factors. Crenshaw, for instance, birdied Nos. 2 and 3, but he had bogeyed the first and when he did likewise at the sixth and seventh, he was done for. Couples never drew closer than three back and more often it was farther. Seve shot 73, Fuzzy 76.

Langer held on longer. Late in the day he was as close as two shots behind, with the 15th and its eagle possibility coming up. But Bernhard knocked it in the water instead, then finished with two more bogeys for a 73. The record books will say he finished in a tie for ninth, but in truth he was a serious contender until late in the day, whereas others, such as David Frost, who was eighth, were never a factor.

So really the battle Sunday afternoon involved three men. Stadler, starting at one under, five back, made the obligatory birdie at No. 2, but was just one of the aforementioned crowd of lurkers until he birdied the seventh. Pumped up, he hit two monster shots to reach the eighth green and holed a 30-footer for an eagle, the only eagle made at the par-five hole all week.

A par at No. 9 and the Walrus had gone out in 32, moving to five under.

But let's get back to Lyle, and to Calcavecchia. All week long Mark had struggled on the front nine and Sunday was no exception. He began with six straight fours, meaning that after a birdie at the second, he bogeyed both the par-threes. And when he added another bogey at No. 7 — making it three out of the last four holes — he was on his way to a 38. As he teed off on No. 8, hit a big drive and began the uphill walk to his ball, a look at the leaderboard near the seventh green told him he was now five strokes behind Lyle.

The leader had survived one major scare and had not only survived but improved. He was one under for the round when he came to the fourth hole, but he hit his five iron over the green on the left side, a certain bogey half the time. Choosing a sand wedge, he chipped the ball onto the putting surface, up to the cup and in. He bogeyed the sixth when his eight-iron tee shot missed the green and he needed a 12-foot putt to save par, but as he drove at the eighth, he was in good shape with a four-stroke lead over Stadler, who had just eagled the hole and a five-stroke lead on Calcavecchia.

Up ahead, Calcavecchia had taken his driver a second time and had nearly reached the eighth green. He chipped close, tapped in and was only four back, a distance that held when Lyle couldn't sink a 10-footer for his birdie, cutting the lead to three. But only for five minutes. Lyle's seven-iron approach stopped a foot from the flagstick and he too had a birdie. After nine holes, he had doubled his lead over Calcavecchia and was three ahead of Stadler.

But as veteran observers point out, the tournament doesn't begin until the back nine on Sunday. An oversimplification, perhaps, but true more times than not. All three leading players parred the 10th, but all three posted different scores on No. 11. Stadler parred it. Calcavecchia rolled in an 18-footer for a birdie to tie Stadler at five under. Lyle's seven-iron approach sailed slightly over the green and when he failed to get down in two, his bogey dropped him to seven under.

On to the 12th, the historic 12th, the treacherous 12th. Stadler and Calcavecchia got their pars, the latter holing a seven-footer and both said a silent prayer and moved on. Not Lyle. There are so many reasons why the 155-yard par-three is a killer; its green is narrow, with Rae's Creek in front, as well as a bunker, and a steep bank of wild growth behind it. The Sunday pin placement is always to the right, behind the bunker. Prudent shots are to the left, leaving a long putt or chip, but eliminating disaster. This is especially good advice for the leader. But even so, there are often tricky winds. The breeze at the tee is not necessarily going in the same direction as that by the green, which is at one end of a natural funnel formed by the 13th fairway. The tee is set back around a forest of pines, protected from that funnel.

Lyle chose an eight iron and hit directly at the flagstick, but the ball began to drift slightly right. It hit on the top of the bank to the right of the bunker, then rolled back into the creek. He stood on the tee as if stunned, then slowly walked to the drop area and hit another, this one to the back fringe, from where he was able to chip close and sink the putt. But that was a five, a double-bogey, and now his lead was gone. He was five under, tied with Calcavecchia.

And tied with Stadler too, you say? In theory, the Walrus might have been the leader, since he had just finished No. 13, a birdie hole. But instead, Stadler came away with a bogey-six when his approach at No. 13 fell short into the watery ditch that is part of Rae's Creek. Now he was only four under, one back. Minutes later Calcavecchia, having reached the 13th green in two, two-putted from 35 feet for the birdie that gave him the lead for the first time. And when Lyle failed to match him, putting his second shot into a bunker behind the green and taking three to get down, the one-stroke lead took on added stature.

Stadler wasn't giving up. He hit a good approach to No. 14 and dropped the putt, then reached the 15th in two and two-putted for another birdie. In the course of the 25 minutes that took, he was back in a tie for the lead with Calcavecchia, who had parred No. 14 but needed a 10-footer to get his five at the 15th.

At this point Lyle's prospects did not seem bright. He seemed still shaken by his disaster at No. 12, sandwiched by his bogey at No. 11 and his non-birdie at No. 13. He desperately needed the routine birdie at No. 15 that would tie him with the other two. His drive was long enough to allow an easy approach over the pond in front of the green and as he walked down the fairway, he could see from the leaderboard by the 17th that he needed to catch only one player — Calcavecchia. Stadler, riding an elevator, had three-putted No. 16 to drop back to five under.

If this news buoyed him, it didn't show. He hit a five iron over the green, chipped back to six feet but missed from there. Calcavecchia, threatened with a bogey at No. 16, had holed a 10-footer for par and was walking aggressively to the 17th tee. If he could par in, Lyle would need a birdie on one of the last three holes to tie, holes that are as easy to bogey as to birdie.

But at No. 16 Lyle hit a seven iron — a club he would use to good effect a half hour later — and landed the ball 15 feet from the pin. He was faced with a slick, downhill putt but he was up to the task, the ball rolling slowly in. The noise around the 16th green was audible up by No. 17 and Calcavecchia must have heard it. He had a reasonable birdie putt coming up, but he missed and remained at six under.

Playing No. 18, Stadler needed a birdie to match that figure, and he gave himself a chance with a splendid approach to 12 feet. He stroked his putt well, but alas, like so many putts at No. 18 on Sundays past, it just missed. Now he would need bogeys by the other two.

Stranger things have happened. Lyle made a routine par at No. 17, but up ahead, Calcavecchia was just short of the green with his approach. Not a difficult shot except that he was battling for a Masters title. "I was just hoping to get my chip five or six feet from the pin," he said later. He did better, the ball stopping two feet short. Calcavecchia drew an exaggerated sigh of relief, tapping his heart and, seconds later, tapping in.

As he did so, Lyle had already driven and, walking up the hill that is the 18th fairway, he was feeling as if he might have just given away the title. He had decided to go with a one iron, had pulled it slightly and wound up in the first of two fairway bunkers, the very area he hoped to avoid by hitting with an iron. Fortunately, his ball was sitting up nicely in the sand and back far enough from the steep front face that he had a shot.

The distance was 140 yards from the pin, which was in its usual Sunday place, on the lower level of the two-tiered green and over to the left, just behind the front bunker.

At this moment, as Lyle pondered his club selection, Calcavecchia had every reason to think he had won the Masters. At the worst, he would be driving off the 10th tee in a playoff. So you can imagine how shaken he was when Lyle pulled his seven iron from his bag, climbed down into the sand, dug in his shoes, swung, picked the ball clean and sent it dead on a line for the pin. The ball landed and bounced 22 feet beyond the flagstick and then as CBS golf analyst Ken Venturi began to shout "Watch this, watch this," the ball began to trickle back down the incline, finally coming to rest 10 feet above the pin.

Lyle's putt was merely an extenuation of that backward roll. He tapped the ball and it never moved left or right of the center of the cup. It had enough speed to reach it and not too much to roll too far by, had it slipped left or right at the last second. It was dead in and Calcavecchia was simply dead. Lyle did a variation on the Highland Fling, then stopped abruptly as if he remembered where he was.

Lyle would be well-advised to take good care of that seven iron of his. It had bailed him out of that bunker at No. 18, and off the tee at No. 16 it had set up the tying birdie. But hours earlier, at No. 2, he had hit it a huge distance on his second shot to give himself an eagle try from 12 feet. He missed the putt but made a birdie. And at No. 9, he put his seven-iron approach a foot from the pin for still another birdie. He made five birdies for the day and the seven iron set up all but one, that most fortunate one at the fourth where he overhit the green (with a five iron) and chipped in (sand wedge).

Hord Hardin had worried after Jack Nicklaus had won so dramatically in 1986 that whatever followed would be anticlimatic. So he got Larry Mize beating Greg Norman and Seve Ballesteros in a playoff, winning on an improbable chip-in. Now Hardin knew the next tournament had to be a let-down. And he was delighted to be wrong, the winner sinking a birdie putt on No. 18 for the victory, the first time that had been done since Arnold Palmer did it in 1960 to beat Ken Venturi.

Whatever you do, don't bet Augusta National won't cook something up next year that's just as exciting. It's become one of those Masters traditions.

4. The U.S. Open

Curtis Strange had always been an enigma. Blessed with enormous talent, and certainly expert teaching from his father, Tom Strange, who had been the professional at the Bow Creek Country Club, in Virginia Beach, Virginia, Curtis grew up to be the best amateur of his time. He won the Southeastern, Eastern, Western, and the North and South Amateurs, and the NCAA championship as a freshman at Wake Forest, and yet he didn't win the National Amateur.

He was the best player in the 1976 PGA Tour qualifying tournament, and yet he didn't qualify. He played the European tour instead, then made it to the American tour in the spring of 1977. Two years later he won more than $100,000 in a single year, and never won less than $200,000 since. He had been the tour's leading money winner in 1985, and nearly became the first to win $1 million in 1987, ranking first again. He succeeded in 1988, topping $1 million and ranking as the leading money-winner for the third time.

Old pros like Bob Rosburg considered him a virtuoso, a consummate shotmaker who could make the golf ball do whatever he wanted it to do. From 1980 through 1987 he averaged 70.94 strokes per round, the fifth best through that period. His 1987 figures were especially impressive — averaged 70.56 strokes per round, hit 75 percent of the fairways on driving holes, 70 percent of the greens, ranked 15th among all golfers in putting, and birdied slightly more than 21 percent of the holes he played.

He won his first tournament, the Pensacola Open of 1979, two years after joining the tour, and added 11 more through the end of 1987. In a game that had been dominated in recent years by Greg Norman, Sandy Lyle and Seve Ballesteros, more than one of the players who competed against him week after week believed Curtis Strange was the best player in the game. He had everything.

And yet, in his entire career, Strange hadn't won a tournament anyone could remember the next month. He was the best American golfer since Tom Watson, and he was certainly among the five best players in the game, but the world wondered if he had a national championship in him. Perhaps even more important, they wondered if he cared.

In five days at The Country Club, though, in the affluent Boston suburb of Brookline, we learned that Strange did indeed have a national championship in him, and that he cared very much. After struggling to shoot even-par 71 and defeat Nick Faldo in a playoff for the United States Open Championship, he spoke of how he had won for his father, who had died 19 years earlier, when Curtis was 14, of how long he had waited for this moment, and of how he wasn't going to stop there, that the Open was his *first* major, implying there would be more.

Good luck to him, but even if he doesn't win another, this one will be remembered a long time, not only because he won after nearly throwing the championship away with some shoddy play over the last few holes of the fourth round, but also because of the setting. Strange won his Open over one of the most sacred shrines in American golf. It was there at The Country Club that Francis Ouimet, the 20-year-old Massachusetts Amateur champion, defeated Harry Vardon, one of the five or six greatest players ever, and Ted Ray in another playoff.

This had been the most significant Open ever played, because for the first time a serious challenge from the British homeland had been turned back, and Americans had taken the first step toward dominating the game. British-born golfers had won every United States Open played in those early years. Vardon himself had been one of them. He came over in 1900 with J.H. Taylor, who was probably just as good a golfer, although not as stylish. They ran away with the Open, Vardon taking first place and Taylor second. The third man finished seven strokes behind Taylor.

Johnny McDermott had broken the British grip and become the first American-born Open champion in 1911, then repeated in 1912, but he had only beaten other Americans or British golfers living in the United States, and they were not the best of the British golfers. Vardon and Ray were, and by outscoring them on a dreary, rainy Saturday morning in September of 1913, Ouimet had proved Americans could beat the best of British golfers.

The significance of that moment notwithstanding, the Open had returned to The Country Club only twice, first in 1963, and again in 1988, observing the 50th and the 75th anniversaries of Ouimet's landmark victory.

Although those who qualified in 1988 played over much of the same ground as Ouimet, Vardon, and Ray, the golf course had changed over the years. Many of those old holes were still around — indeed, the finish, the 14th through the 18th, are pretty much the same as they had been in 1913 — but through a succession of revisions not only by earlier golf course architects but also by greenkeepers, and through natural evolutions brought about by years of play, The Country Club had changed.

Preparing for the 1988 Open, the club brought in Rees Jones, the younger son of Robert Trent Jones, the world's best-known golf course architect, to revise it once again.

Rees approached the job cautiously. He said that by changing those holes, he felt he would be tinkering with history, and that he had to aim for two objectives. First, he believed he had to maintain the integrity of the original design, which actually dates back to 1909, keeping alive what was left of the contours those pioneers played over, and restoring what had been altered, and second, he felt the course had to be strengthened for the modern golfer.

Restoring the original design was more difficult than it seemed. The Panama Canal hadn't opened when Ouimet won, the continent had been linked by the railroads only 45 years, the last of the Indian wars had petered out just 13 years earlier, and vast stretches of prairie still hadn't been settled. No one alive in the late 1980s remembered what The Country Club had been like. Before Jones turned a spadeful of earth, he searched the club's archives, resurrecting the work plans of those who had made significant changes, and talked to the oldest members and club staff, asking what they could recall. Weighing what he had learned, he determined his assignment was not to remodel the course but to restore it.

Jones's studies convinced him, for example, that some greens had shrunk, and bunkers that had been close enough to fortify particular sectors in the old days weren't close enough any longer to have an effect. Furthermore, aprons abutting those lost areas of green were either unnaturally wide or unusually narrow, and many of them had evolved in strange configurations. Jones restored 10 of those greens to what his survey indicated had been their original size, added area to one of them, and completely redesigned and rebuilt three others.

Restored very carefully, using rakes and spades, the greens were relatively small, which is typical of vintage golf courses. What they seemed to lack in dramatic contours was offset by the heaving ground, caused by the freezes and thaws of nearly a century of harsh New England winters. Putting on those greens in June, the time of the Open, figured to be difficult, not only because of these little breaks, but also because of the normally quick pace of Open greens.

The restoration work went beyond the greens. Jones rebuilt a tee, a blind fairway beyond a saddle on the ninth, a par five, added and rebuilt some bunkers, and relocated some others to better positions. Wherever he could, he restored their original dimensions, and then gave them and their grassy perimeters a ragged, unkempt, vintage look, complementing the Early American image of brown fescue grass hemming in fairways generally narrowed to between 30 and 35 yards.

Along with those changes, Jones increased the course length to 7,010 yards. It had measured 6,345 yards in 1913, which was plenty long enough for the equipment and techniques of the day, and 6,870 yards in 1963.

Of all the holes at The Country Club, the 17th most nearly qualified as hallowed ground. It was here that Ouimet made the last birdie he needed to catch Vardon and Ray, and it was here he birdied again the next day, and where Vardon risked cutting the corner of a dogleg and lost the gamble; his ball carried into a bunker. Studying his charts Jones discovered the green he looked at wasn't the original at all; Geoffrey Cornish, another architect, had built a new one in 1958 because the municipal government had taken away some land to widen a road.

Knowing this, Jones didn't feel badly at all about building a new green, with bunkers flanking the entrance, and with a strongly contoured surface rising to a terraced deck at the rear.

Looking over what he had done with the 17th, Jones felt the Open could be won or lost on that green. He was very nearly right.

Although he was generally satisfied with what he had done, he was disappointed he couldn't do what he wanted with the finishing hole. When he began his restoration work, he had hoped he could rebuild the 18th green to its original shape and recreate what he called the rear deck, which he found so evident in the old pictures of Ouimet and the Englishmen, but he had to bow to pressures and allow more space for Open spectators. It couldn't be done.

Nevertheless, when he had finished, Jones had brought to life a classic golf course that somehow had been hidden all those years. It was as if within three years extraordinary segments of our golf heritage had turned up unexpectedly. Shinnecock Hills was the first to re-emerge, as the site of the 1986 Open, which Raymond Floyd had won so decisively by playing superb, attacking golf through the later stages of the fourth round. The Country Club was the second, and the more surprising of the two, for those who knew Shinnecock well knew also it was among the finest anywhere; The

Country Club had no such reputation, but through imagination and ingenuity, it turned into one of the country's best examinations in golf.

Many of those in the Open field had played The Country Club in the past — Ben Crenshaw and Gary Koch in the 1968 Junior Amateur; Koch and Danny Edwards in the 1973 Walker Cup; Jim Hallet, Bill Andrade, Brad Faxon, and Mark Brooks in the 1982 Amateur; and both Jack Nicklaus and Gary Player in the 1963 Open. Even so most of them were as surprised as those who had never seen it before.

The transformation had begun 25 or 26 years earlier. The members knew the Open had been awarded to The Country Club mainly to observe the Ouimet Open. They knew as well that while they had some very fine holes — the third is one of the best par fours in all of golf — taken as a whole, the golf course was not as strong as they would like. They set about turning it into a more fitting test for the national championship. First, some members stumbled upon an ingenious scheme that would turn a mild little par four from a 350-yard drive and pitch into an immensely stronger hole of 450 yards by playing the second shot over the regular green, across a pond, and onto the green of the par three that normally follows. With that move, the hole would become a terror. But there was one slight problem; it was part of The Country Club's third nine, not part of the members' normal round. The solution seems fairly simple today: play this as the 11th hole, turn then to a par five of that same third nine, shorten the tee and make it a par four, then follow with a marvelous par four down a hill and past a pond, and then pick up with the 14th of the regular course.

They made one other move. The hole that would become the 10th under this routing was another mild par four with a blind tee shot over a hill. Surveying the area, Ted Emerson noticed the 13th tee of the regular course behind and to the right. The 13th hole runs in the opposite direction, but when Emerson climbed the grade and looked back, he saw it could become a much better hole if it were played from this tee. Again there was a problem: to see up the 10th fairway, he had to look past a giant oak tree that blocked the route up the fairway.

Turning to John Kealty, the course superintendent, Emerson said, "John, this would be a terrific hole from here if it weren't for that bloody oak."

"You know, Mr. Emerson," Kealty said, "I think that oak's diseased."

It was gone within a week, and after it had been felled, Kealty was able to report with some satisfaction, that it had indeed begun to rot. From that tee, the 10th became the first brick in what Ben Crenshaw called "the wall," a tough stretch of long par-four holes running through the 13th that became the heart of what turned out to be a superb golf course.

The 12th was the only one of those holes that didn't work. Set up as a 450-yard par four, it was strong enough and gave up birdies grudgingly, but its blind approach over a scraggly bluff that rose 30 feet or more above fairway level seemed out of character with the rest of the course.

Nevertheless, the players thought The Country Club was wonderful, winding through wooded hills and shallow valleys, its deep green fairways and greens framed by shaggy, brownish rough, its rolling ground seldom presenting a level lie, and its greens so small they were often difficult to hit.

Returning to the game's roots had always excited Ben Crenshaw. After his first practice round he said, "This course is a throwback. It's very honest in so many ways, because it challenges your whole game. You pretty well go through the bag here; you hit every club and play different shots. It's a very special place."

They liked it more than the newer creations they play through the year. Greg Norman said, "I think it's fabulous. I'd rather play this than a TPC course." Even the occasional blind shot didn't disturb him. "You know where you're going; that's why we play practice rounds."

Tom Watson said the course had character, and Hale Irwin, always a man with an opinion, said he was impressed, and that The Country Club was the kind of course where the Open ought to be played.

Curtis Strange said, "The course seems to flow in a very natural way, probably just like it was when it was first built. This is how I enjoy playing. It's all natural. I love the small greens."

Strange had come to The Country Club at the peak of his game. After winning in Australia, he had begun the year slowly in the United States, placing higher than 21st only once in his first 10 tournaments, and falling as low as 78th in one, missing the cut at Pebble Beach, and being disqualified from The Players Championship. Strange began to hit his stride in May, winning the Independent Insurance Agents Classic, in Houston, early in the month, and then the Memorial Tournament, in Columbus, Ohio, toward the end. He was so impressive during that period, Irwin called him the best player in the game.

Perhaps national pride swayed Irwin's judgement, because through the decade of the 1980s, Europe had developed a series of first-class players capable of winning consistently at the highest levels of the game — Seve Ballesteros, Sandy Lyle, Nick Faldo, Bernhard Langer, Norman (an Australian, he played in Europe before settling in the United States) and before long Jose-Maria Olazabal should be among them — and the United States hadn't kept up.

Granted it is easier for a first class golfer to win on the European tour than on the American tour because it is undeniable the United States has greater depth, but not since Tom Watson was at his peak had an American golfer stood at the head of the game.

Many thought that by the middle of 1988, Sandy Lyle stood ahead of everybody, and furthermore, if he wasn't the game's best player, then Norman was, or maybe it was Ballesteros, or perhaps even Faldo, all of them foreigners. Lyle had already won three tournaments on the 1988 American tour, most notably the Masters, along with the British Masters on the European tour. At the time of the Open he stood at the top of the PGA Tour's money list, with $608,478. At the end of the season, he still ranked third, even though he had played in the States only once after the Open.

On the other hand, even though Faldo had placed second in three of his five European starts, he had not been impressive in the United States since his first start of the year, when he placed third in the Tournament of Champions. He had played in only six American events since then, missed two cuts, and placed no higher than 29th in the others. Not a majestic record, to be sure, and there was a tendency to dismiss his British Open victory of 1987, since it was as much a case of Paul Azinger's having lost, but we were about to find out just how good Faldo was.

There was no secret about Ballesteros. A fierce, unyielding competitor, he had been the game's most dynamic figure ever since he had won the 1984 British Open, nosing out Tom Watson in a tight battle through the last few holes. While he had played sensational golf in Europe, winning 13 tournaments between that 1984 British Open and the time he left Europe to come to the United States, in June, he had won nothing in the States over that period. Then he won the Westchester Classic, in suburban New York, the week before the Open.

He gives the impression he loves to compete, and more than anything else, loves to beat American golfers. He had been the spiritual force behind Europe's Ryder Cup victory in September of 1987, driving his teammates to play above themselves, and guiding his young countryman Olazabal through the four-ball and foursomes segments of the match.

As the years pass, that 1984 British Open becomes more significant; unless the pattern changes, it could be known in some future time as James Burke's television show states, the day the universe changed. Until then Americans had ruled golf. They had won all but one British Open from 1970 through 1983, but they had not won another since then, and they'd been pressed hard in every other tournament of international stature.

While European golfers hadn't taken command in other major tournaments, they'd threatened. Beginning in 1980, they had won four Masters Tournaments, Lyle had won the 1987 Players' Championship, and Denis Watson the 1984 World Series, hardly matching what they had done with the British Open, but progress nonetheless, and while they'd won neither a U.S. Open nor a PGA Championship — the only foreign winners in those had been American tour regulars, like Gary Player and David Graham — they had been close. Faldo certainly had opportunities at Brookline, and Norman had the 1986 Open in his hands but threw it away in the last round. Don't forget either that Nicklaus had won the 1986 Masters as much because Ballesteros hit that dreadful iron into the water at the 15th as through his own magnificent 30 on the last nine holes.

At the same time, from 1986 through 1988, no one had played the four major international competitions so consistently well as Crenshaw. In those 12 tournaments he had finished fourth in four, sixth and seventh in two others, and 11th or worse in four more. He had played especially well in 1987, placing fourth in the U.S. and British Opens and the Masters, and seventh in the PGA, and was never more than five strokes out of first. He had missed tying Larry Mize, Norman, and Ballesteros by only one stroke in the Masters, and had finished only two strokes behind Faldo in the British Open. Earlier in 1988 he had placed fourth in the Masters once again, only three shots behind Lyle. Still, yearn for an Open championship though he might, Ben had won only the 1984 Masters among the major events.

Strange, of course, hadn't done that much. Never in position to win the U.S. Open, he had his best finish in 1984, the year Fuzzy Zoeller defeated Greg Norman in a playoff. Curtis placed fourth, but he had never once looked as if he could win after he shot 74 in the third round; he finished five strokes behind. He placed fourth again in 1987, but once more he was only a fringe player, shooting 283, six strokes behind Scott Simpson. He had never placed high in the British Open, indeed, he didn't play in it very often, nor have an impact when he did, which is fairly close to his effect in the PGA. Among the significant tournaments, Strange had been close to winning only the 1985 Masters, struggling back from an opening 80 and climbing into first place by following up with 65 and 68, but then he lost the tournament in the fourth round by hitting shots into the water on both the 13th and 15th holes. Langer won, and Strange placed second, tied with Ballesteros and Raymond Floyd.

He was disappointed in his Masters finish, to be sure. In the days that followed, Nicklaus told him the experience could either make him or break him, but Curtis projected the attitude he didn't much care what tournaments he won so long as they paid a lot of money. He did, of course, win a lot of it, and he won a number of tournaments, not so many he became the obvious successor to Watson — Strange had never won more than three tournaments in a single year, while Watson had won 16 from 1978 through 1980 — but enough to establish himself as one of America's best, perhaps its very best.

Nicklaus evidently had had great faith in him. Needing to have his team win nine of the 12 singles matches on the last day to save the 1987 Ryder Cup Match, Nicklaus sent Strange out against Ballesteros. Down by three holes after the fifth, Strange fought back to within one hole, but he lost the 14th and fell by 2 and 1. The Europeans won.

That was, of course, a low point, but he had won three times in 1987, beginning with the Canadian Open, in July, and in the last week of May of 1988 shot 64-67 in the last two rounds and won the Memorial, his third of the year; a man who wins six tournaments within a year must be taken seriously. Then, he evidently had changed his attitude as well, and said he had never felt better coming into the Open.

"Since that 1985 Masters," he said, "I've been more interested in the majors. I picked up a lot of confidence after playing so well down the stretch against a very strong field at the Memorial. I've been thinking about the Open every day for the last couple of weeks; I've worked very hard preparing for it, particularly with my mental approach. You know going in you must be more patient; you know you're going to work for pars and work like hell for birdies. The guys who've won in the past have been patient, steady players.

"It's going to be an interesting week; the top players in the world are playing well right now."

The Open had continued to grow, setting a record for the number of entrants for the fourth consecutive year. All told, 5,775 professionals and amateurs entered; the total was whittled down to 156 for the Open proper through a series of two qualifying rounds. Of course several categories of golfers — for example Open champions of the previous 10 years — were exempt from qualifying at all.

Complementing them, five foreign golfers were given special exemptions based on their playing records. Rodger Davis, an Australian; Mark McNulty, a South African; Jumbo Ozaki, a Japanese; and David Ishii, an American who plays the Japanese tour, accepted their invitations and played at Brookline, but Ian Woosnam had injured his wrist in a fall and passed it up. It was a pity, because Woosnam, a short, stocky, but powerful man who stands only 5-foot-4½ but hits the ball amazing distances, is an appealing golfer. While he hadn't won one of the major tournaments, he had played particularly well in 1987, and played a significant role in the Europeans' Ryder Cup victory.

An unusual mix assembled at Brookline. Of the 156 who teed off the first day, 42 were in their first Opens, and two others were returning to familiar ground. Both Nicklaus and Player had been in the starting field at this same course 25 years earlier, Nicklaus as the defending champion (he didn't make the cut). Nicklaus was 48 at the time of the Open, and Player was 52. Neither remotely approached the ages of the oldest men who had played in the Open. Sam Snead had played in 1977, at 65.

Early in the week it had become certain the Open would draw well. The 23,000 season tickets had been sold out for nearly a year, and the crowds for the practice rounds had been huge; an additional 10,000 daily tickets had been sold, and Tuesday's crowd was estimated at 30,000. Traffic had been a mess at first, but club officials brought it under control within a few days.

Fans had turned out early on Thursday morning. A man from Rhode Island was waiting in his car at 4:30 when a club official opened the gate to the parking lot. An hour later about 100 cars were already parked at another of the three big lots close to the club, and spectators streamed in throughout the day. The place had a carnival atmosphere. A group of hospitality tents stood on the club's normal practice area, between the first and 18th fairways (the club sold 33 of them at $100,000 each), and extensions of the golf shop were scattered about. Joe Lynch, the chief concessionaire, said, "I've done 15 or so U.S. Opens, but I've never seen anything like this. We're doubling everything we've ever done."

Like the rest of the country, New England had been locked in an intense heat wave. The temperature had risen above 90 for the fourth consecutive day on Wednesday, and 14 people had died in Boston from causes linked to the heat. Lynch had arrived with 10,000 beer cups to last the week. They sold 65,000 beers during the first two practice days, 43,000 of them on Wednesday.

In spite of the heat and even though New England, like the rest of the country, had had little rainfall through the spring, the golf course looked in prime condition, lush and green, with only a few spots ringed with white paint indicating ground under repair. Dry conditions helped in one way; because the grounds crew could control irrigation, the greens were firm and fast, just as the USGA believes they should be for the national championship.

Because 156 men were playing, and because Open rounds always take a long time for no reason other than it is the Open, the first group of three men started at 6:45 with about 100 fans grouped around the tee. The heat wave seemed to have broken; the weather was cool, and a light haze hung over The Country Club, not so thick you couldn't follow the flight of the ball, but dense enough to cloud your view of the green, 452 yards away. Still low, the sun would burn away the haze before long, and warm the air.

Golfers who play at this level use code words. When they say a course is fair, they mean it's easy, and they had agreed almost universally that The Country Club was fair. We could look, then, for some blistering scores. Early returns indicated they might be right. Off at 7:12, in the fourth group of the day, Dick Mast birdied five holes, bogeyed three others, and shot 69. Surely someone would play a bit steadier later in the day. Someone did; nearly an hour later Bob Gilder came in with 68 on four birdies and one bogey, bunkering his approach to the fourth, a dangerous short par four of 338 yards a daring and desperate man might drive.

It was only a little after noon by then, and the round would go on for another eight hours. It seemed certain scores would come tumbling down. They didn't. No one bettered Gilder's 68, but two others matched it. Only one of them who figured to last longer than this one day.

Mike Nicolette, a 31-year-old Pennsylvanian so far down the exempt list he plays in tour tournaments only when about 100 others don't show up, put together two nines of 34 in the middle of the day, and Sandy Lyle, one of the late starters, birdied two of the last three holes as he raced home in 33 after an even par 35 going out.

Nicolette's finish was nerve wracking. Three under with only the 17th and 18th to play, he gambled on both the 17th and 18th, trying to pick up more strokes, and bunkered both his approaches, but he escaped from both and saved his pars.

"I got a little greedy at the end," he said. "I wanted the lead outright, and tried to get close to the pins. Another three feet and I'd have been on instead of in the bunkers."

Nor was Lyle's round pretty. Even though he seldom used his driver, preferring to tee off with either his one iron or a fairway wood, he hit only five of the 15 fairways on driving holes (The Country Club had three par-three holes, two par fives, and 13 par fours), and one-putted four greens to save pars.

His was a puzzling round that could mean either that like all great players he had made his figures even though he had been off his game, or that he was so far off stride he would go steadily downhill. No one could tell just yet.

Meantime, he certainly couldn't relax, because Paul Azinger, Larry Mize, Scott Simpson, and above all Seve Ballesteros lurked only a stroke behind him, tied with Mast at 69. Mast, of course, like Nicolette, wasn't expected to hang on, but the others certainly might. Simpson had come into the Open as the defending champion, Mize had won the 1987 Masters, and Azinger had nearly won the 1987 British Open, missing two makeable birdie putts on the last six holes and dropping two more strokes on the last two at Muirfield, giving Faldo the opening he needed. Ballesteros was by then the most dangerous late-round player in the game.

An absolute magician around the greens, Ballesteros saved what otherwise would have been a disappointing beginning by using only 11 putts on the second nine. He had birdied five holes and bogeyed three through the first 13, and then closed out by one-putting the 15th, 16th, 17th, and 18th for pars, holing putts that ranged from three through 10 feet. Twice he escaped from bunkers, on the 16th and the 18th.

He was one of the few who had used his driver consistently, but he had driven into the rough on seven holes, and had struggled to work the ball close to the greens. He claimed, though, he wasn't afraid to miss the fairways at The Country Club, saying, "I can make pars from this rough; it's not as bad as other Opens. It's still difficult to hit the greens from the rough, but at least I can get around the greens where I can chip and putt."

Strange, meanwhile, had begun in mid-morning, and had lost two strokes to par at the end of the seventh, a strong par three of 201 yards, which was particularly difficult to hold, but then he birdied the eighth and ninth, turned in 35, and then saved his round with an eagle-three on the 14th, a par five of 527 yards that could be reached with the second shot after a powerful though chancy drive. Curtis came back with another 35 and tied for ninth place with Lanny Wadkins, another Virginian, and Craig Stadler.

The leaders after the first round:

Sandy Lyle	68
Bob Gilder	68
Mike Nicolette	68
Seve Ballesteros	69
Scott Simpson	69
Larry Mize	69
Paul Azinger	69
Curtis Strange	70
Lanny Wadkins	70
Craig Stadler	70

At the end of the first round, then, seven men had shot 69 or better, and three others had broken par 71. By now the players realized The Country Club would give up good scores, and they began to pour it on. With Simpson leading the way with his marvelous 66, and Strange, Mize, Faldo, Fred Couples, Jay Haas, and Larry Nelson adding 67s, 17 men broke 70 the next day, and four more matched it — 21 men under par.

When the day ended, Simpson had shot ahead, with 135, and led Mize, who had 136, by one stroke. Strange and Gilder followed, at 137, and Faldo and Lyle were another two strokes behind, at 139.

Simpson felt especially gratified by his position. No one had expected much of him, even though he was the defender. His victory over Watson a year earlier had been looked on as a sort of fluke; he wasn't thought to be that good.

Perhaps, but he played the last six holes at Olympic in three under par, the best finish in 20 years, and his 206 for the last 64 holes was only two strokes off the Open record. Now, a year later, he was playing better than anyone believed he could. His driving had been superb in the first round — he missed only one fairway — and had the nerves to make up for a few not-so-good irons with saving putts.

Tall and lean at 6-foot-2 and 180 pounds, Simpson was 32 in 1988. His swing was hardly a smooth, fluid, natural movement; rather it was more mechanical and contrived, and yet it was working like no other. He rushed to the turn in 30 strokes, five under par, and then birdied the 10th, all on putts of 10 feet or less. Six under now, but here he ran into trouble, pulling his approach to the 11th. His ball hit a tree, rebounded into the pond in front of the green, and he made a double-bogey six. Birdies on the 14th and 16th made up for those lost strokes, but he dropped another at the 18th, where he overshot the green with his approach.

A day earlier, Simpson had dismissed his chances of winning, saying we would have a new champion. Now he had second thoughts.

"My thinking has changed. I always thought I had a chance, but now it's a little more likely."

While no one had taken Simpson seriously until now, even fewer were aware Gilder was in the field, and now he stood only two strokes behind the leader, ahead of Faldo, Lyle, and Azinger, and tied with Strange. Once among the tour's more consistent money-winners, Gilder hadn't won a tournament since the 1983 Phoenix Open. He had become involved in tour politics as a member of the Policy Board, and then became disenchanted because of restrictions placed on him in that position.

Gilder had objected to the way certain players had been seeded for the first Tucson match play tournament, in 1984. He told a reporter for the *Arizona Republic* how he felt, especially criticizing Deane Beman, the tour commissioner. He was fined $1,000.

"I tried to make some changes, and didn't get any support. Nobody cares. I was very upset at the time. I learned if they want you to keep your mouth shut, you keep your mouth shut. I couldn't say what I wanted without being fined, so I said the hell with it."

Gilder had spent the two weeks leading up to the Open preparing in a strange way — by racing sports cars in the Pacific Northwest, where he lives.

He had led off by shooting 68, then followed up with 69, but even though he was firmly set among the leaders, he had played erratic golf. He had made 11 birdies in 36 holes, five in the first round, six in the second, but he had also made six bogeys, three of them over the last seven holes of the second round. It didn't seem likely he could continue to play like that and remain among the leaders.

Strange, meanwhile, seemed to be making his move. Playing some especially good iron shots that consistently settled close to the pins, he went out in 32, holing three birdie putts of 15 feet or less, then picked up another on the 12th, a truly difficult hole (the field averaged 4.35 strokes in the first round, made only 12 birdies but 39 bogeys). His blind approach missed the green, but he chipped in.

He made his only bogey on the 15th, a straightaway par four of 434 yards played from an elevated tee, hooking his drive into the left rough, then playing an eight iron that nearly carried to the club's lawn bowling greens, well beyond the far side of the fairway.

"I tried to duck hook it, which was stupid," he said. "I hit everything back there — the tree behind my ball, grass, rocks, and dirt under it, and I think I grazed the tree in front of me."

No matter; he escaped with a bogey-five then closed with some shaky golf, missing the 16th green but saving par with a good chip, missing a birdie opportunity from 12 feet on the 17th, then bunkering his five iron to the 18th but again saving par by holing an eight-footer. After signing his scorecard, he strode to the practice tee to work out his problems.

While the day ended with some surprising leaders, most of those one would expect were near the top, with one exception. Greg Norman had had to withdraw. He had shot 74 in the first round, and had lost two more strokes through the first eight holes of the second. Playing his third shot to the ninth, a 510-yard par five, from behind a creek 150 yards short of the green, Norman lashed into a seven iron. His clubhead struck a rock just below the soil under his ball. Norman cringed; he had hurt his left wrist.

Larry Mize said it sounded like he hit a boulder. Mize walked over to Greg and asked if he was all right.

"We'll see," Norman said.

His seven iron had missed the ninth green, but he saved his par by holing a 25-footer, drove into the rough from the 10th tee, then played a six iron for his approach. It hurt. He turned to Mize and Craig Stadler, his playing partners, and said, "Fellas, I can't play."

"There's no sense ruining yourself," Mize said.

Norman wrapped his wrist in a towel, exchanged scorecards with Mize, the walked away. The injury kept him out of the British Open, played a month later.

The 36-hole cut fell at 146, matching the lowest ever, and among others it caught Jack Nicklaus, who had been playing in his 32nd consecutive Open, more than anyone ever. Jack shot 147. This was the second Open cut he had missed within the last four years, and only the third since he had become a professional, 27 years earlier. Ironically, he had also missed the cut in 1963, the last Open played at The Country Club (he had missed twice as an amateur).

The cut also caught Mac O'Grady, like Nicklaus by one stroke. Earlier in the week, O'Grady had walked across the street to the house where Francis Ouimet had lived in 1913, rubbed his hands across the clapboard siding, and snipped off a branch of a spruce tree growing on the grounds, tucking it into his golf bag for good luck. Midway through the first round, when things weren't going so well, and he was on his way to shooting 75, he zipped open his bag and tossed the twig aside. So much for sentiment.

The leaders after the second round:

Scott Simpson	69-66	135
Larry Mize	69-67	136
Bob Gilder	68-69	137
Curtis Strange	70-67	137
Fred Couples	72-67	139
Sandy Lyle	68-71	139
Paul Azinger	69-70	139
Nick Faldo	72-67	139
D.A. Weibring	71-69	140
Lanny Wadkins	70-71	140

The weather had been hot and sultry early in the week, but the mornings and evenings had turned cool as the days passed, and clouds had moved in, obscuring the sun, and bringing with them the threat of rain. Darkness had fallen so early on Friday, the day of the second round, six golfers couldn't finish; they had to return early Saturday morning.

A light overnight rain had softened the greens and apparently slowed their pace; they had been reading over 11 feet on the Stimpmeter, the device that measures how far a ball will roll, but by the time Lee Trevino, the first man off, left the first tee, at 9:02, they had slowed down perhaps a foot, taking away some of their sting.

The softer, more receptive, and slower putting greens were not much help to Lyle; he was about to learn he couldn't go on as he had and remain a contender. He had played some loose golf through the first two rounds, although managing to hang within four strokes of the lead, but his game continued to slip away from him on Saturday, the day of the third round. Missing greens, chipping and pitching poorly, and not putting well enough to make up for his mistakes, he shot 75, and was never a factor again.

Ballesteros continued his slide, shooting 72 and falling into 23rd place, Crenshaw once again broke everyone's heart by dropping even further back, into a tie for 34th place, and Mike Nicolette and Dick Mast, who had begun the Open with such great hopes, dropped out of the race.

The Open defined itself on this day. Curtis Strange shot to the top, Nick Faldo moved into contention, and Scott Simpson, Bob Gilder, and Larry Mize continued to lurk within a stroke or two of the lead.

Simpson played his worst round so far, shooting 72, a stroke over par, and slipping to 207 for the 54 holes. Swinging poorly early in the round, he lost two strokes on the fifth, where he drove into the rough, needed three more strokes to reach the green, and never fully recovered.

For a time the Open looked as if it had turned into a three-man race among Strange, Faldo, and Gilder, with Gilder at one time holding the lead. He was paired with Strange in the next-to-last grouping, just ahead of Simpson and Mize, and Faldo played two pairs ahead of them.

Four strokes behind Simpson as the day began, Faldo opened by dropping a five iron within 10 feet of the cup on the second, a testy, uphill 185-yard par three, then holing the putt for a birdie-two. He stood four under par for 38 holes then, still three strokes behind Simpson, who hadn't been summoned to the tee. A lost stroke at the deceptive fourth pulled him back to where he had started, but then two more birdies brought him to the turn in 33, five under, and now solidly in the race. By the time Faldo had played through the ninth, Simpson had double-bogeyed the fifth, stood at five under par himself, and not only had fallen into a tie with Nick, but had dropped behind Gilder and Strange.

Gilder had continued to confound everyone by playing such tough, aggressive golf, and refusing to yield to the pressures of the Open. Two strokes behind Simpson at the end of the day, Gilder birdied both the third and fourth, drilling an iron within six feet of the cup on the third, and running in a 20-footer on the fourth, dropping to seven under par, and taking over first place when Simpson played the fifth so badly.

For a time it was impossible to keep up with the changing situation. Strange was playing at the top of his game. Lofting a blind seven iron over the shoulder of a hill to within two feet of the cup, he birdied the third, then holed a 10-footer on the eighth, and an 18-footer at the ninth. Racing to the turn in 32, he caught Gilder at the eighth and passed him at the ninth. After his birdie on the fourth, Gilder made five routine pars, reaching the ninth in 33; Mize was playing indifferent golf, making a bogey here, a par there, and balancing them out through the first nine, shooting 35, and after birdieing the ninth, Faldo had turned in 33.

As each man passed the ninth hole, then, Strange had moved ahead at eight under par, Gilder was seven under, Simpson and Mize six under, and Faldo five under.

Thunder had rumbled in the distance and the sky had become increasingly darker as the leaders moved into the home nine. Rain seemed imminent. Strange had just saved his par on the 11th by holing a 15-footer after missing the green, and had walked to the 12th tee when lightning flashed in the distance. He refused to go on; minutes later a siren wailed, suspending play. Rain poured down, driven by swirling winds, soaking the course, and sending players and spectators alike to whatever shelter they could find — under trees, around refreshment stands, back to the clubhouse, or for some, back to their cars and an early drive home.

It was a minute or two after four o'clock then, and more than an hour would pass before the siren sounded again, signaling the field to resume play. The rain had stopped by then, but periodic showers fell throughout the rest of the afternoon.

Gilder complained he was told to play too quickly, saying, "They kind of said, 'Okay, now hit,' and we weren't ready, I think."

The delay and the quick start seemed to have no effect on Gilder, though, until a few holes later. He birdied the 14th, the par five, but then drew his drive into the rough alongside the 15th fairway. Soaked by rain, the grass was especially heavy and slippery, and Gilder couldn't control his second shot; his right foot slipped on the slick grass, and he pulled his ball into the rough again. He tried once more, and still didn't get out. On in four, he two-putted for six. He had been eight under after the 14th, but now he dropped to six under, where he finished.

Up ahead, Faldo had gone into one of those strange periods when he can make nothing but pars. He ran off eight of them beginning with the ninth, but then holed an 18-footer on the home hole, finished the day with 68, and stood at 207 for 54 holes, six under par.

With four holes to play, Strange was turning the Open into a rout. He had gone nine under par with a birdie on the 14th, his fourth of the day, after an unlikely start. He drove into a fairway bunker, advanced his ball only to within five-iron range, then rolled in a 20-footer.

One hole later he was three strokes clear of the field; even though he had fallen back to six under par, Gilder was closest to him, tied with Simpson, who had just birdied the 14th, Faldo hadn't yet birdied the 18th, so he was five under, and Mize stood at four under. Three more pars and Strange would have an impressive cushion going into the last round on Sunday.

Here Strange revived speculation he might never win a tournament that matters. His tee shot to the 16th drifted into the right bunker, possibly carried by the wind, and he missed an eight-footer, dropping one stroke of his lead, and then, after reaching the 17th green with his approach, rolled his 20-footer about three feet past the cup. His second putt glided toward the hole, caught the right lip, then made a 180-degree turn, and came back toward him. Another stroke gone, and now he had Gilder, Simpson, and Faldo by only one stroke.

He almost lost all of his lead on the 18th, an excellent finishing hole of 438 yards with an elevated green guarded by a deep bunker reaching from one side to the other. He had played this hole twice before, and had caught the bunker both times, bogeying the first day, saving par the next. Now he was in it again.

Still, the shot he faced was not particularly difficult as bunker shots go. His ball was lying on an uphill slope, and the hole was set in the left front of the green, about 15 feet back and perhaps 20 feet in from the left edge. With an unusually restive gallery strangely hushed, Strange dug in, made nice contact with the sand just behind the ball, and flew it out to within eight feet of the cup. This was no gimme, though, and he still had work to do. Stepping up to the putt, he set himself, tapped the ball firmly, and rolled it right into the center of the hole. He had made his par, shot 69, and had held onto a shaky lead of one stroke. Faldo had come in with 68, making up lots of ground, and jumping from a tie for fifth place into a tie for second, Gilder had shot 70, and Simpson and Mize 72s.

The leaders after the third round:

Curtis Strange	70-67-69—206
Nick Faldo	72-67-68—207
Bob Gilder	68-69-70—207
Scott Simpson	69-66-72—207
Larry Mize	69-67-72—208
D.A. Weibring	71-69-68—208
Mark O'Meara	71-72-66—209
Fred Couples	72-67-71—210
Lanny Wadkins	70-71-70—211

D.A Weibring, a solid golfer but one who usually plays a supporting role on the tour, had moved in among the contenders by shooting 68, and now stood within two shots of the lead. Still he felt the Open had already been settled. He saw Strange in front and said, "He's a competitor. You can see it in his eyes, just like you can see it in Raymond Floyd's eyes, just like you can see it in Jack Nicklaus's eyes. You can see it in Larry Bird's eyes (basketball star Larry Bird had been in the gallery), you can see a very deep sense of concentration, of intent. Curtis has a fire."

Mark O'Meara had stormed around The Country Club in 66, playing wonderful irons that consistently placed him within 20 feet or less of the cup, and rolling in four good birdie putts on the last nine. A man capable of bursts of low scoring, O'Meara lurked three strokes off the lead, certainly within range, but like Weibring, he felt Strange would win.

"You look at Curtis and the way he's played," O'Meara said, "and you look at his tournament record. When he's been in contention, you know he's going to win. Before the last round at the Memorial I told my caddy, 'Curtis is going to win.'"

Of course he did win the Memorial, but both Weibring and O'Meara were looking at Strange's record in weekly tour tournaments, not at how he had performed on the big occasions. His record was just the opposite in those; he had been a contender only a few times, and had failed. Still, he was playing better than he had ever played before.

The hot and sultry weather of the first few days had given way to rain and overcast, but Sunday morning promised to be a pleasant day. Crowds began drifting in hours before the first group was to begin, at 9:37, while the ground still lay under a morning mist, and the sun hadn't burned through the light haze. A wispy fog rose from the pond by the 11th green, pushed along by a lazy breeze, and two fans walked in the rough separating the 10th and 11th fairways, looking for the tree stump where Arnold Palmer had driven his ball in the playoff a quarter of a century earlier, made seven, and lost to Julius Boros.

As the leader, Strange would go off last, at 2:25, and since Faldo had posted his 207 before either Simpson or Gilder, he would go with him.

Curtis opened with tentative golf. He bogeyed both the second and third holes, allowing Faldo, who was making his par figures, to move ahead. Strange was falling back, Faldo seemed capable of making nothing but pars, and the Open was there to be won if only somebody could make some birdies. None of those close enough to the leaders could do it.

Playing directly in front of them, Simpson was driving badly and was falling apart. His hopes collapsed at the fourth, where he dropped his approach into a greenside bunker, then bladed his recovery over the green and into some deep and tangled rough. He double-bogeyed, shot 39 out, and that was the end of him.

Mize, too, was playing loose golf, went out in 36, then stumbled home in 40. Putting badly, Gilder could make no headway. He had climbed within two strokes of the leader by birdieing the ninth, but then he drove into the rough on the 10th and bogeyed, and couldn't make it up. Peter Jacobsen had ripped the old course apart, shooting 64 early in the day, but he had begun 16 strokes behind Strange. Steve Pate made a move, shooting 32 going out, but like Jacobsen he had begun the day too far back, and neither O'Meara nor Weibring could put together a sustained string of low scoring.

Only Paul Azinger seemed to have a chance, and that was a very slender one. Playing inspired irons that constantly left him with 15 feet, Azinger birdied six holes on the first nine, shot 30 (he bogeyed the fifth), and dropped to three under par for 63 holes. By the time Strange and Faldo had finished the fourth, Azinger had played through the 14th still three under. He was closing in, only two strokes behind Strange, three behind Faldo, and they both had many holes to play.

Azinger made a routine four at the 15th, then played a classic faded seven iron to the 16th that rose high, drifted a touch to the right, and seemed to come straight down, stopping close to the pin. He holed the putt, took one long stride and scooped the ball from the cup, then headed for the 17th tee. He had fallen six under par for the day, four under for 70 holes, but he still needed another birdie to put more pressure on the leaders.

A two iron to center-fairway on the 17th, then a long wait while the pair ahead stumbled around, and finally a seven iron aimed at the green's treacherous rear shelf. Azinger's ball reached the upper tier but ran off the back, and his chip had too much speed; it ran away down the slope to the lower level, and he was finished. Back to Strange and Faldo.

Curtis struggled through the first nine in 36, holing a long birdie putt on the 201-yard seventh; Faldo, with nine pars, shot 35. They were dead level, and the Open would be determined between them. No one else mattered.

The duel was becoming intense, with neither man able to take command by putting together a string of sub-par holes, although they both had opportunities. Strange moved ahead by holing a 15-footer at the 10th, but then missed from 20 feet at the 11th, from 15 feet at the 13th, and from six feet at the 14th.

Faldo, meanwhile, had missed two greens through the 12th hole, saved his pars on those, and two putted the others. Then he bunkered his approach to the 13th, and once again saved his par. He was locked in his groove, but now he came to the 14th, the easier of the two par fives, a birdie hole.

A driver and a two iron left him at the base of the hill leading upward to the green, and then a sand wedge within holing distance, his best opportunity of the day.

First his ball slid past the cup, then Strange missed.

Looking on from the hillside rising from the green, Gill Faldo, Nick's wife, shook her head.

"Neither of those two guys made a birdie on this hole. Shameful," she muttered.

Each man had lost the opportunity to move ahead and perhaps win the championship on a hole that should be birdied. It looked as if each man's chance depended on the other's making a mistake, for Strange obviously was not sharp, and Faldo seemed capable of making nothing but pars.

Nick broke the string on the 15th, drilling a three wood into the center of the fairway short of the main entrance road, which slices directly across to the clubhouse, then laying a seven iron within five feet of the cup and holing the putt. When Strange parred, Faldo had caught up. Three more hard holes to play.

We were then to see two of the key holes of the Open. Up first on the 16th tee, Faldo cut his six iron a little too much, and his ball splashed into the right bunker. Strange next. With the green open, he put too much into his shot; his ball hit the back of the green, then bounded into the heavy rough beyond. With the hole cut only about 15 feet from the green's edge, Faldo blasted 20 feet or so past, leaving himself a difficult putt for his par. Strange, though, was even worse off; chopping through the wiry growth with his sand wedge, he barely reached the green, his ball stopping at least 25 feet short of the hole. Now it looked as if both men would bogey, and they would go on to the 17th still tied.

Strange had not putted well throughout the day, even though he had rolled in a 30-footer on the seventh and a 15-footer on the 10th, but here he pulled himself together and ran the putt home. Seven under now. When Faldo missed, Curtis had gone a stroke ahead. Two more steady holes and the Open would be his.

The day was warm, and the sun burned down as they moved to the 17th tee. The crowd had become increasingly unruly throughout the day, and the marshaling had broken down early. Boston must be the yuppie capital of the world. Go to a Red Sox game, and anybody over the age of 40 stands out in the crowd. It was nearly the same at The Country Club; most of the crowd was young and out for a good time. Up ahead, the two big grandstands on either side of the 18th green were crammed with spectators. As Strange and Faldo walked toward their drives, they could hear chanting (from a beer commercial) in the distance. The group in one grandstand called out "Tastes great," and across the way the others objected, "Less filling."

The hole had been cut on the upper level of the 17th once again, a difficult spot to reach because it was so shallow. Using his three wood, Strange outdrove Faldo, who had played a one iron, and then Nick left his eight-iron approach on the lower level, about 40 feet short of the flag. Curtis realized Faldo faced a difficult putt; his ball would have to climb the slope to the upper tier, and he would have to gauge the speed just right to stop it close to the hole. Strange wanted his approach on that upper tier, and debated between using a pitching wedge and a nine iron. Going with the nine iron, he hit a daring attacking shot that carried to the rear shelf and braked about 15 feet beyond the hole. He held the Open in his hand.

After Faldo lagged his ball close, assuring himself of his par, Strange stepped up to his ball. This would not be an easy shot. He faced a downhill putt on a slippery green; miss and this ball could roll down the slope and onto the lower level, as Azinger's had done earlier in the day. While the crowd held its breath, Curtis tapped the ball as softly as he dared. It crept toward the hole, and then Curtis couldn't believe what he saw. The ball had picked up speed as it reached the hole, and glided six or seven feet past. He was in shock; now he would have to struggle to save his lead. He studied his second putt a long time, and then missed. He three-putted, and now he and Faldo were tied once again.

Shaken by the putt, Strange pulled his three wood into the left rough after Faldo, also driving with a three wood, had placed his ball in the fairway.

By now the galleries had gone out of control. Ignoring instructions from the marshals, they broke through the ropes lining the perimeter of the hole, romped along in the fairway, and clustered around the players. It was frightening, because the crowd was so huge, but the fans settled down long enough for Faldo and Strange to finish the hole.

The crowd was still restive when Nick ripped into a four iron that pulled up about 15 to 18 feet right of the cup, cut toward the right front of the green. The putt was holeable; now it was up to Strange.

Expecting his ball to fly from the rough, Curtis chose a seven iron, but his shot came up short, and for the third straight day he had to play from the front bunker.

He came out beautifully, leaving his ball only about a foot from the cup, but by now the Open was out of his hands. You can't play defense in golf, and with one good putt, Faldo could walk off with the championship.

His line was relatively straight and only slightly downhill. Once again the fans settled down as Nick stepped up to his ball. He tapped it, and the crowd noise swelled as the ball ran true toward the cup. Strange stared at him, trying to read his eyes, which he figured would tell him how the ball was running. Nick's eyes widened as the ball approached the cup, but then the crowd groaned as it slipped past the right edge, missing by about an inch. Strange let out his breath, and tapped in his one-footer. Strange had shot 72, Faldo 71, and they had tied at 278, six under par for 72 holes. Once again an Open at The Country Club would end in a playoff. Twice before it had involved three men; this time only two would play. It had taken 75 years, from 1913 to 1988, to eliminate one man.

Curtis was angry with himself for playing what he considered such a bad round. Standing on the practice tee at about 7:30 that night, he said, "I played horrible and I putted just as bad. On the back nine I had an opportunity to put everybody away, and I just didn't do it. The only consolation is that I didn't lose the tournament."

Looking back to the 17th green, where he had lost his best chance, he said, "Even now I wish I could drop another ball and see if I could stop it close to the hole. I really didn't hit it hard at all. I hit the damn putt as easy as I thought I should have. The green was simply much faster than I expected. I honestly can't get upset with myself."

Then, looking a little pensive, "I just don't feel like I ought to be here," and with a tight smile added, "I'm sure Nick's saying the same thing."

Monday playoffs hadn't usually drawn very big crowds, since this is, after all, a working day, but because of the consistently large turnouts throughout the week, no one knew what to expect. By the time the gates opened, at 11 o'clock, three hours before play was to begin, fans were already lined up. By 1:30 the first and second holes had been encircled from tee to green, and other galleries had grouped about greens up ahead. Marshals, who had expected to be through by then, turned out once more, and kept order by forming a cordon along the restraining ropes. About 25,000 spectators had turned out; no one had seen anything like it.

It is unfortunate in a way they couldn't have seen better golf, for neither Strange nor Faldo was at his peak. Swirling, gusting, unpredictable winds caused The Country Club to play even harder than it had earlier in the championship, preventing either man from attacking, until Faldo had to take chances late in the day.

Realizing he was facing the opportunity of his life, and that he had possibly thrown the Open away with his loose play through the final holes of the fourth round, Strange had slept very little Sunday night, but he showed none of the effects once play began; his nerves seemed stronger than ever. Through the first nine holes, with a vagrant, swirling wind impossible to predict, Curtis hit only three of seven fairways on driving holes, was bunkered twice, and hit just three greens. Yet he holed those nerve-wracking five and six footers he had to hole, and stood at one under par, a stroke ahead of Faldo.

Both men had squeezed the most from their games. While Faldo had driven much better than Strange, hitting six of the seven fairways, he too had reached only three greens, although he was on the collars of most of those he missed. Yet Strange was out in 34, with birdies on two holes where he hit greens — the fifth, where his eight iron had left him 10 feet from the cup, and the seventh, where for the second straight day he holed a long putt. Faldo had shot 35, with a bogey at the third, where unluckily his four-iron approach had drifted into a bunker no more than 20 feet left of the hole, and a birdie at the seventh, where he had holed an eight-footer on top of Strange's birdie. The two men were locked in a tense, tight battle that looked as if it would go down to the final stroke.

Suddenly though Strange opened a two-stroke gap when Nick's five-iron second skipped off the 11th green onto the apron, snuggling against high-standing grass, where he had trouble chipping. He bogeyed, Strange parred, and with seven hard holes to play, Curtis looked to be in command.

Just as quickly he lost one of those strokes, leaving his four iron short and right of the 12th green, his eighth missed green of the round, and taking five.

Curtis won the Open on the 13th, the last hole of Crenshaw's wall. The fairway runs downhill to a green set in a wooded dell. Coming off the ball, Faldo drove into the right rough, only his second missed fairway of the day, then overshot the hole with his six iron, leaving himself a nasty 35-foot downhill putt. Strange, meanwhile, had driven perfectly, finding a level lie at left center fairway, then nailed his six iron perhaps 18 or 20 feet left of the hole.

Nearly impossible to control, Faldo's putt skimmed past the cup and rolled well beyond. Strange then stepped up to his ball, and gave it a firm rap. It broke first right, then left, then tumbled into the hole. A birdie-three, and when Faldo missed coming back, Curtis stood three strokes ahead. Nothing could stop him now.

Desperate now, Faldo went with his driver on the the 14th, hit his ball perfectly, then ripped a four iron to the back of the green. Two putts and a birdie-four cut Strange's margin to two strokes. Closer, but he needed more birdies. Then, from the right rough of the 15th, Nick pulled his eight iron, missing the green's collar, but by only a foot or so. Playing an eight iron as well, Strange caught the right greenside bunker.

Farther from the hole than Faldo, Strange played first and pitched out 10 or 12 feet from the hole. Now Nick had a chance. He had such a decent lie he could chip, and with a stroke of good luck, perhaps roll it in, picking up at least one stroke and maybe two if Curtis bogeyed. Instead, Faldo's ball exploded from his clubface and rolled across the green and into the rough on the other side. Both men bogeyed. Only a miracle or a collapse by Strange could change the outcome.

Faldo lost whatever improbable hope he had left when he overshot the 17th, leaving himself no chance at all of stopping his ball near the hole. He bogeyed, Strange saved another par from a bunker, his sixth one-putt par of the round, and walked through the cheering crowd to the 18th green holding a three-stroke lead.

After struggling through those last few holes, fighting off the tension, and saving pars where a player with less steel might have lost his composure and his will, Curtis finally felt he had won the Open. He played a safe two iron that left him about 220 yards from the green, and now the gallery buzzed, wondering how he would play his next shot. Surely he wouldn't go for the green from that distance; he might hit that bunker a fourth straight day, some said, and who knows what might happen. Sure he will, others answered. He'll take the chance and go for it.

He went for it. Lashing into a two iron once again, he played a wonderful shot that cleared the bunker and somehow stopped on the green. Faldo's ball plopped into the sand, but it really didn't matter. Strange coaxed his ball into the cup with his second putt, and the great crowd thundered. He did have a national championship in him after all.

Curtis had shot 71 in the playoff round, and Faldo had struggled home in 40, for 75. Off to the side, Sarah Strange, Curtis' wife, hugged Allan Strange, his twin brother, while the crowd stood and cheered.

Formalities of the prize ceremony over with, both men appeared before the press, where Curtis surprised nearly everyone who had known him only casually by showing a part of himself he had kept hidden, and depths of emotion and purpose not many had dreamed he had.

Seated in the huge press facility, he silenced the noisy gathering of reporters with his first sentence. His voice nearly breaking, he began by saying:

"This was for my dad."

Then he paused, took a breath, and went on.

"I've been waiting a long time to do this, to thank the people who gave me the advice I needed, the enthusiasm, and the knowledge to continue on. I have to thank my dad. This was for him.

"He started me out years ago, when I was nine. I would arrive at work with him in the morning, and go home with him late at night. I did it for four or five years. I learned the basics of my golf swing from him, and it's still with me. I learned a lot from him, many things I probably can't remember but that I do subconsciously, and a couple of things I do remember and still think about damn near every day. I just wish he could have been here."

He sat quietly for a second in the hushed room, then went on again. "This is the greatest thing I have ever done; this is the greatest feeling I have ever had. It means a lot to me. It means that all the work and time and effort I've put into it has paid off. It got me to the next level.

"It means what every little boy dreams about when he plays by himself late in the afternoon. He has three or four balls; one's Hogan, one's Palmer, one's Nicklaus, the other is Strange. Ninety-nine percent of the time those dreams don't come true.

"It gives me confidence to go on to the British Open this year, and the PGA, and if I fall on my face there, then I'll come back next year and do my best."

Then, his face brightening and the smile becoming more natural and engaging, he slapped his palm against a table and said, "This is my *first* major. But we're not going to stop here; we're really not going to stop here."

5. The British Open

Tony Jacklin — British golf idol of a generation ago and now a national hero as non-playing captain of two successive winning European Ryder Cup teams — came out of semi-retirement to play in the 1988 British Open at Royal Lytham and St. Annes. Because of his stature, Jacklin was asked, routinely enough, whether he had a prediction for this Open. As they say in the old American horse operas, he shot from the hip.

"Looking at the favorites this week," Jacklin said evenly, "I can't see beyond a European win, and I can't see an American winning. But I'm biased. I don't think they're as good as we are now."

The Europeans took it as a tribute, the Americans as something quite different. "It wasn't a smart statement to make at all," said Paul Azinger, the 1987 Open co-runnerup. "Jacklin's comments will certainly change the way I feel if I am in contention on Sunday. I'll be less nervous and out to prove something to him. And the other Americans will feel the same way after this." Said Craig Stadler: "I'm really surprised Tony would say something like that." Lanny Wadkins, as quick-firing with his observations as with his clubs, was more to the point. "It's absurd," he said. "Tony seems to be trying to turn this into a patriotic thing. I don't give a damn whether Ben Crenshaw is American or Sandy Lyle Scottish, I just want to beat the hell out of both of them. Those two Ryder Cup wins must have gone to Tony's head." Crenshaw was mild-mannered, as always. "I always respect what Tony has to say," he said, "but I have to disagree with him. Any of us is capable of winning, otherwise we wouldn't be here." And said reigning U.S. Open champion Curtis Strange, tabbed by Jacklin as one of the best three players in the world (with Greg Norman and Seve Ballesteros), "I'll let my score do the talking. That's the way it should be." Jacklin got one strong endorsement from the Americans. "Tony's right," said five-time Open champion Tom Watson. "Just look at the record."

That was early in the week. At the end, Jacklin was more than just right. The best the Americans could do was a distant fourth place, a tie between Fred Couples and Gary Koch at three-under-par 281. Third place went to England's Nick Faldo, the 1987 champion, at five-under-par 279. Nick Price, the Zimbabwean who led most of the way, finished second at nine-under-par 275. And the champion again was that flamboyant Spaniard, Severiano Ballesteros, who came smashing through with a 65 in the final round to win by two from Price at 11-under-par 273. History had come full circle. Ballesteros won the first of his three Opens at Lytham in 1979. And he was surprised that someone would think anything had changed since then.

"My putter is the same, my three-wood is the same, my sand wedge, my clothes — all the same," he said, grinning. "The only difference is, I'm nine years older." He was 22 when he won in 1979, and he was 31 now. He was dressed again, that final day, in white shirt, blue slacks, and blue sweater. There was something else that was the same. The Ballesteros who overran the unfortunate Nick Price was just as electrifying as the one who won in 1979. Except now he was a more mature man with a more mature game.

He was like an expert horseman that finally had broken an unbreakable stallion. He had brought his game pretty much under control. For the time being, at least.

Ballesteros' victory in July, 1988, may have had greater significance for those with a broader view. History indeed may have come full circle, in just nine short years. The thought might have struck some that the upheaval in world golf began with Ballesteros' victory at Lytham in 1979. It probably didn't seem to have all that much impact at the time. Just a brash 22-year-old becoming the first Spaniard to win the British Open, or any of the majors, for that matter. It was a high moment, but it was after all, just another in a long line of British Opens. But look back at it from 1988: Golf hasn't been the same since.

Michael Bonallack, secretary of the Royal and Ancient Golf Club of St. Andrews, was not to be outdone when it came to predictions. He was looking for a record attendance for the Open, or second-largest, at least. The target was the record of 193,000 set at St. Andrews in 1984. Subject, of course, to the weather. A timely point, as the R&A would discover in the third round.

"It is a fine balancing act to get a course right in this country," Bonallack said. It rained only one day in the six weeks preceding the Open. The greens had to be watered just to keep them alive. And of course, it rained hard on Monday and Tuesday of Open week. "Now they're in danger of getting soft," Bonallack said. But the fairways were fine and the rough, though not as severe as at Muirfield the year before, was tournament-tough. "I think that makes it a driver's course," Bonallack said. "The fairways are 12 yards or more, on the average, wider than Muirfield's."

The course also had been changed somewhat from the one Ballesteros won on in 1979. Among the changes: The sloping sixth fairway was extended to the right, and the green altered and extended to the left, with a new bunker on the right. A new back tee at No. 18 lengthened the hole by some 40 yards, to 412 yards, making it the testing par-four it was designed to be back when the ball didn't carry so far. The golfer now faced a carry of 235 yards. Another point about the elements. "In the wind," Bonallack said, "Lytham, along with Troon, has the hardest last nine holes on the championship rota." (Ian Woosnam, on playing the 463-yard, par-four 15th into the wind in practice: "With two drivers, you can't reach the green, and if you miss the fairway, you're dead. You could end up with eight at that hole very easily.")

So all that was left was the playing of the 1988 Open. It promised to be another classic. Everybody who was anybody was in the field, with one big exception. Greg Norman, the 1986 Open champion, was still sidelined by the sprained left wrist he suffered in the U.S. Open a month earlier. Otherwise, the cast was complete:

— Nick Faldo, the defending champion, ground out 18 consecutive pars in the final round to beat the faltering Paul Azinger at Muirfield in 1987. "I'm not thinking of it as a defense, just another Open," he said. "I need more practice to sort things out. I'm just trying to get my transition between the backswing and the downswing right. Probably secretly, I was more confident last year. I just felt I was going to do it. I'm not saying whether I've got that feeling yet."

— Sandy Lyle, the 1985 champion, was on hand with a terrific mixed bag of credentials. He won once in four appearances on the European tour, the Dunhill British Masters; and three times in 10 tournaments on the American tour, where he was the leading money-winner. He won the Phoenix Open, the Greater Greensboro Open, and, with a spectacular birdie on the final hole, the Masters. "My short game is pretty decent," Lyle said. "The main objective is to keep the ball in play for the second shot to the green. The bookies are making me the favorite. I am well prepared. I have had lots of practice."

— Curtis Strange won the U.S. Open a month earlier, beating Faldo in an 18-hole playoff. "I've been looking forward to this week," he said. "Realistically, I think I have a chance, and by Sunday I hope to have an opportunity to win. The U.S. Open — that was my first win in a major — has given me an added incentive to win."

— Bernhard Langer, with the 1985 Masters his only major, had been troubled by back problems. He overcame his aches long enough to win the Epson Grand Prix. That was in early May. "But I'm in good enough shape to play," he said. "When I swing well I can control the ball in most circumstances, even when it is windy. But right now I feel I am not always hitting it where I would like."

— Paul Azinger bogeyed the last two holes at Muirfield in 1987 to open the door to Faldo. "You learn from experience," he said. "It took a lot out of me last year, but I overcame it pretty well."

— Ian Woosnam owned 1987. He won eight times around the world and earned over $1.8 million. But 1988 was a different story. He had one victory, the Volvo PGA Championship, but he was way off form otherwise. One reason was the wrist injury he suffered falling off his son's mini-bike. It put him out of action for a month. "There is no problem with my wrist," Woosnam said at Lytham. "I feel a lot better, and more relaxed. Maybe where I went wrong earlier this year — I should have had more rest in the winter."

— Seve Ballesteros, who was in what for him was a slump, showed signs of stirring. He began the year by winning the Majorca Open, and he added the Westchester Classic in the United States. "I feel confident about this week," he said. "I am happy with my game, which is good. But to win any major today is very difficult because the quality of the players today is very good." Ballesteros was reminded that he hadn't won a major since the 1984 Open at St. Andrews. "I am not in a hurry to win another major," he said, smiling. "I have 10 years more to win another."

If Ballesteros was being patient, he certainly didn't show it in the next five days.

Brad Faxon had a good start, shooting 69, just two strokes off the pace set by Seve Ballesteros, who had finished earlier. Faxon birdied the sixth, narrowly missing his eagle putt of five feet, then the seventh, where he chipped to two feet. A bogey at No. 8 sent him around the turn in 34. His incoming nine was anything but routine. He birdied the 10th from 30 feet, bogeyed No. 14 and No. 15, then got both strokes back on the next two holes. An eight-iron into No. 16 and a seven-iron to No. 17 left him 12 feet both times, and he finished both off. Two putts from 40 feet gave him a par at the 18th and a one-under-par 35 on the punishing inward nine. He and Fred Couples (34) were the only two of the 153 starters to break its par in the first round.

There were 17 golfers within four strokes of Ballesteros' leading 67.

Australian Wayne Grady, playing in his fifth Open, joined Faxon in second place with a 69. He also two-putted for birdies at No. 6, from 30 feet, and No. 7, where his 12-foot eagle putt lipped out. A sand wedge out of the rough to eight feet set up his birdie-three at No. 13, but the 15th snatched the stroke right back from him when his four-iron approach came down short. "This is my first time in this position in a major," Grady said. "I might be pretty nervous tomorrow, but I felt very comfortable today." (The feeling didn't last. A 76 in the second round would take him out of the running.)

Nick Price, Peter Senior, Noel Ratcliffe, and Don Pooley shared fourth place at one-under-par 70. Ratcliffe, a two-time winner on the European tour, had to win a playoff in the qualifier to get into the Open. Then he wasted no time. He made his bid with an eagle-birdie-birdie dash, starting at the sixth. Senior turned in a four-birdie, three-bogey effort. Pooley, age 36, a tall, lanky, pleasant man, who joined the American tour in 1976, was in his first Open. "I wasn't thrilled to see the weather this morning," he said, "but I'm very happy to be here." He made his debut with a birdie at No. 1, after a six-iron to about 30 inches. Two holes later, he was two over par, with a bogey at the second and a double bogey at the third. Back he came, with three consecutive birdies starting at No. 6. He capped the inward half with one of only seven birdies at No. 18 in the first round for a par 36.

Price no sooner appeared on the leaderboard than talk began of his collapse down the stretch at Royal Troon in 1982. "I'm more mature now," he said. "I've learned a lot more." Fighting a wind he termed "relentless," Price played a rock-steady but unspectacular round. He was one of few challengers not to get at least one birdie at the vulnerable sixth and seventh. He made seven pars and one birdie — a 12-foot putt at No. 8 — and made the turn in 34. He played the inward nine even, with two birdies and two bogeys. "It was so difficult to get the ball close to the hole, whether with the wind or against it," he said. "Still, I played better than I have in the last six weeks." Then he turned prophet. "I had two chances to win major championships since Troon — the U.S. PGA in 1985 and the Masters in 1986," he said. "If I am in the hunt this time, I will be no stranger to it."

Nick Faldo came in at par 71, and wouldn't he have liked another crack at the 17th. He came to the tee of that treacherous hole at three under par. He left the green at only one under. "I hit a slightly bad tee shot in that howling left-to-right gale," he said. "It finished in a left bunker. I came out, and then I hit what I thought was a perfect nine iron." That ended up in another bunker. He blasted out weakly, 25 feet short of the cup, and two-putted for a double-bogey six. His troubles had started at No. 14, second only to No. 15 in difficulty the first day. It's 445 yards long, but in that wind it took him a driver, a three-wood second, and a pitch-and-run to get home. Then he two-putted from seven feet for a bogey. He survived the 15th and 16th, then tripped over the 17th. A three-putt bogey from 15 feet at the last hole completed the damage down that fearsome home stretch in the wind. He had played the last five holes in four over par. Fortunately, he already had some money in the bank. He had played the first 13 holes in four under par, with five birdies and a bogey. Frustrated, yes; but worried, no. "This is going to be a long championship," he said. "The weather forecast is not good for this week. There are going to be some screw-ups out there, and I have made mine already." Unfortunately, for Faldo, golf doesn't have a credit system for errors.

Faldo was one of 17 in that crush at 71. Another was a familiar but unexpected face — Bob Charles, the lanky New Zealand lefthander who won the 1963 Open at Lytham. Charles, now 52, had been reborn as a golfer. He was the leading money-winner on the U.S. Senior tour, had won South African and Japanese senior titles, and had come to Britain for a shot at the British Seniors title at Turnberry the week after the Open. Might as well win the Open first, he decided. The fourth hole almost changed his mind — a fairway bunker, then three putts from 30 feet for a double-bogey six. This from one of the finest putters the game has ever known. But that was merely a glitch in his computerized stroke. He needed only 16 putts going out, 10 coming in. On the inward half, where so many others staggered, he was solid par except for a bogey at No. 17. "I could win this week," Charles said. "The spark is still there." It sputtered briefly, but he managed to tie for 20th at 71-74-69-73—287.

Also at 71 was David Frost. But he got it the hard way. Frost was sitting pretty after three consecutive birdies through the eighth and a 32 at the turn. Then crash! At No. 10, he drove into rough so deep and snarled that his only thought was to get back to the fairway. But he moved the ball only about 18 inches — and then spent four minutes hunting for it. When he finally found the ball, it was unplayable. He ended up with a double-bogey six, on his way to an inward 39.

Almost lost in a crowd at 72 — amid well-known names such as Craig Stadler, Gary Player, Isao Aoki, Paul Azinger, and Gordon Brand Jr. — was a complete mystery man. All that was known about him at first was that he was an American named Greg Buckner. It wasn't his 72 that caught everyone's attention, but his outward nine. He streaked through the turn in 31 with an outburst of back-to-back eagles at the sixth (from six feet) and seventh (from 15) and a birdie at the eighth (from 15). He had gone five under par in only three holes. The incoming nine got him hard, a 41. Then he cleared up the mystery. Bruckner, 28, is from Manhattan Beach, California. He failed in three tries to win his American tour card, and so went to the Asian tour, and was fourth on the 1988 Order of Merit with $68,000. His big victory, the Singapore Open, was more of a thrill than he bargained for. He received his $33,000 prize in cash — 330 $100 bills. He stuffed the money into a paper bag, rushed back to his room, and hid it under the mattress. The next day, he converted it into a check and mailed it home. "I didn't want the police to find me carrying that kind of money," he said. "They might think I had just done a drug deal. They kill you for that." Bruckner's big moment began and ended in the first round. He would make the 36-hole cut, but then sink to a tie for 67th on 302.

Peter Akakasiaka, a lean six-footer, also had a big moment — he was the first Nigerian ever to play in the Open. Akakasiaka, who came through the qualifier, was doing well for a while. He was level par until he came to the closing stretch of par fours. He went six over par on the last five holes. (He went on to miss the cut at 77-79—156.)

Curtis Strange was as much a surprise as Faxon in the first round, but for the opposite reason. Strange was destroyed by the inward nine, making two double bogeys and three bogeys for a 43 and a stunning eight-over-par 79. "I'm somewhat embarrassed — but that's a harsh word," Strange said. "That's an extremely difficult eight, nine holes into the wind. I knew it would be tough coming in. When you don't hit solid in the wind, it magnifies your mistakes, and when it happens on a course like this, you get double bogeys." He got one at the par-four 13th, where he drove into a bunker and then put his third shot over the green; and the other at the par-four 15th, after catching a cross bunker with his approach. He got little comfort from the outward nine to begin with. Where others were almost frolicking, he was making a one-over-par 36. He bogeyed both the third and the fourth with two putts from about eight feet. He got his only birdie of the day at the par-five sixth, two-putting from 30 feet. "This won't be the last poor round I ever have," the spirited Strange said. He was down, but no one was silly enough to count him out.

Jack Nicklaus was another surprise. He was 20 strokes better than he expected to be — with a 75. "The way I felt, I thought I'd shoot 95," Nicklaus said. Two misfortunes hit the 48-year-old three-time champion. First, a severe upset stomach that kept him awake much of the night. And second, a 7:48 a.m. starting time. In recent years, Nicklaus had complained that he was forever getting the worst of the draw — out early into the bad weather the first day, then out late in the second, again when the weather perversely switched to bad. But 7:48 was even earlier than usual for him. (R&A Secretary Michael Bonallack was asked about the thinking behind Nicklaus's early start. "There was no thinking behind it at all," he said. "This was a draw, and his name came out of the hat for that time — and anyway, we were being filmed, so we couldn't put it back in.") Nicklaus was up early anyway, but not just to play golf. At 6:30, he was so ill he was thinking of withdrawing. But on he went. His spirits, if not his stomach, improved when he birdied the par-three first, holing a 10-foot putt after a downwind five-iron to the 203-yard hole. It was downhill from there, beginning with three putts at the second and two bunker shots at the third. Gary Player, another three-time champion, playing in his 34th consecutive Open and now a senior (over 50), returned a one-over-par 72. Fate was not as kind to two other former champions. Lee Trevino (75) did not hole a single birdie putt, and Tony Jacklin (80) dropped four strokes over the first four holes.

It was a day of disappointment, too, for some big names. Paul Azinger was at 36-36—72; Bernhard Langer, 36-37—73; Sandy Lyle, 34-39—73; Ben Crenshaw, 34-39—73; Tom Watson, 34-40—74; Raymond Floyd, 37-39—76, and the bloodiest back-nine victim of this group, Ian Woosnam, 33-43—76. Their outlook was not good. A sleeping giant had stirred, and gave them a "number" to shoot at.

Seve Ballesteros, an 8:54 starter, did not start his day in the best frame of mind. He woke about 6 o'clock on Thursday morning, took one look out the window at the bleak, gray skies and the treetops whipping in the wind, and muttered something in Spanish that is unprintable. But he would brighten soon. First, there was some light banter with his new caddy, a Briton named Ian Wright. Ballesteros bet Wright on the Tour de France cycling competition then going on. Ballesteros took Pedro Delgado and Jean-Francois

Bernard. Wright, humoring his man, took the only cycling name he knew
— Sean Kelly. "Your man can't ride," Ballesteros said, chuckling in triumph.
But Wright's other man could sure play. His opening salvo would rock the
field. Ballesteros hit a six-iron to two feet at the 206-yard first hole. One
birdie in the hopper. At No. 2, Ballesteros teed off with a three iron, then
put an eight iron two feet from the hole. Another birdie. At No. 3, it was
three iron, eight iron, and a 15-foot putt. Three consecutive birdies. "I did
not mind the weather then," Ballesteros said later. Then he poked a little
more fun at himself. "I was very confident," he said, "especially on the first
two holes — where I holed from two feet." (The explosive start recalled
memories of his devastating start in the fourth round of the 1983 Masters
— birdie-eagle-par-birdie that sent him on his way to his second green jacket.)

After two pars, he got two more birdies. At No. 6, he two-putted from
25 feet after his approach hit the stick; and at No. 7, showing awesome
power and accuracy, he covered the 549 yards with a one iron, four iron
combination, and two putted from 45 feet. He somehow missed a birdie
from four feet at No. 8, and a par at the ninth got him through the turn
in five-under-par 30. Next, the formidable inward nine, fighting the wind
all the way. He was steady with pars through the 13th. Then came the hole
that stung so many and almost cost him the championship, the 445-yard,
par-4 14th. It's a faint dogleg right, and the preferred landing area calls for
a precise shot in the wind that must avoid two bunkers to the right. That
sets up a second shot over cross bunkers. But Ballesteros was having none
of that. It was the old Ballesteros who stepped to the tee. He found a new
way to play the hole. He was at his heroic and almost-suicidal best. He
hooked his drive into tramped-down grass and, bold as ever, decided he
could reach the green with a two iron. He couldn't. He ended up in such
a tangled mess of bushes that only a huge crowd of searching spectators
saved him. At least it wasn't a lost ball. But he had to surrender to it, anyway.
It was an unplayable lie. "I don't think Daniel Boone could play from there,"
he said. (The press corps was amazed that a Spaniard would know of a
legendary frontiersman from early American history. No mystery, Ballesteros
said. When he was a boy, Spanish television carried reruns of the American
series on the woodsman.)

Ballesteros had to summon his playing partner, Fuzzy Zoeller, to decide
on the drop. They deliberated for some time. "What's he waiting for —
the Forestry Commission?" a spectator cracked. Ballesteros eventually backed
up some 50 yards, to the ladies' tee at No. 6, and of course hit a seven
iron 125 yards to 15 feet, and of course sank the putt to salvage a sensational
bogey-five.

He also played No. 15 without touching the fairway — and made his
par-four. His tee shot ended up near the ladies' restroom to the right, his
second shot in the rough to the left, followed by a pitch and a six-foot
putt. The wild ride wasn't over yet. After a routine par at No. 16, he made
a spectacular birdie at No. 17. He slashed a blind, six-iron approach out
of the rough that hit the green and curled away from an eagle at the last
instant and left him only three feet away. He settled for the birdie. At the
18th, well..."Three feet more left," he said, with a shrug, "and it would
have been all right, and I would make four there." But it wasn't three feet
more left. It was in the bushes. He suffered his second unplayable lie in

five holes. He took the penalty drop, hit a six iron short, pitched on to three feet, and holed the putt for his bogey-five and the 67. He was among the early finishers, coming in shortly after 1 p.m. He had left the number up there for everyone else to shoot at. But no one else would touch it. This was vintage Ballesteros. He faced almost every conceivable shot, and he used every club in his bag except the three wood and the nine iron. He had taken on Lytham at its nastiest and he beat it. He had brought his ship in with some hairy navigation. How about one last dig at the captain?

"It is very difficult to shoot four under," Ballesteros said, with one eyebrow raised, "but not the way I play."

The leaders after the first round:

Seve Ballesteros	67	Jay Haas	71
Brad Faxon	69	Bob Tway	71
Wayne Grady	69	Bob Charles	71
Peter Senior	70	Andy Bean	71
Noel Ratcliffe	70	Nick Faldo	71
Nick Price	70	Howard Clark	71
Don Pooley	70	Gary Koch	71
David J. Russell	71	Mark James	71
David Frost	71	Andrew Sherborne	71

Tony Jacklin, who triggered that little flap when he said the Americans were no longer good enough to win the British Open, was not merely a ceremonial visitor to Lytham. Jacklin, 44, now living on Spain's Costa del Sol, had come to play at the site of his 1969 Open victory. But his was a bittersweet return. He didn't come just to re-live old glories. He was a sad man, and he needed to forget for a little while. Just 10 weeks earlier, his wife, Vivienne, suffered a brain hemorhage near their home, and died. "I can never forget my sadness," Jacklin said. "It's just that some days you feel better than others. I had to make a choice, and I don't really think it was difficult for me to come back. I mean, this is a golf course and golf is what I do. So here I am, plowing on. Lytham is a sentimental journey for me, and will always be my course. Probably by the end of it, I'll be sorry I entered. But I hope not. I only play socially now. And now that I'm here again, I'd just like to put four good rounds together. That would mean a lot to me — especially here." And so he retraced the steps that had thrust him into international stardom. But only for two rounds. Golf doesn't pay attention to people or their problems. He returned 80-70—159 and was just one of the 81 who missed the 36-hole cut. It came in at seven-over-par 149 and took some unexpected victims.

Among them: Zimbabwe's Tony Johnstone, Ireland's Eamonn Darcy, Spain's Jose-Maria Canizares, America-based Australian David Graham, and Americans Lee Trevino, a two-time champion, 1987 Masters champion Larry Mize, young Scott Verplank, veteran Raymond Floyd, and Mark Calcavecchia, who challenged for a while in the 1987 Open and was runner-up victim of Sandy Lyle's stunning final-hole birdie in the 1988 Masters. Possibly the most surprised victim was Barry Lane, the young Englishman who the week before won the Bell's Scottish Open. Lane crashed with 78-85—163.

The round, played before a one-day record crowd of 43,111, belonged to Nick Price, the easy-smiling man of such scattered geography. He had come within six holes of winning the 1982 Open at Troon. Now he was within 36 holes of winning at Lytham. Price, playing in the breezes early on Friday, broke through on the outward nine with an eagle-birdie-birdie burst from the sixth and returned a four-under-par 67. That gave him a 36-hole total of five-under-par 137 and a one-stroke lead on first-round leader Seve Ballesteros, who got caught in the heavier winds of the sunny, cool afternoon and had to settle for a 71—138.

"The real secret to this course," Price said, "is to make a good score going out, then hold on coming in." He took his own advice with a vengeance. He eagled the par-five sixth with a drive, a 182-yard seven-iron, and a 35-foot putt. Then he birdied the par-five seventh with two putts from 30 feet, and the par-four eighth from 15, and made the turn in 31. He more than held on coming in, posting a strong par 36. He took his only bogey at No. 12, where he left his two-iron tee shot short, pitched to six feet, and two-putted for a four. He got the stroke back at No. 15, on a birdie-three from 12 feet, then made a superb save at No. 18, where a weak chip shot from behind the green left him a par putt that must have seemed a mile long. It was 20 feet. He made it.

Anyone who expected Ballesteros to fret over slipping out of the lead was disappointed. "I am playing well," he said, after his 71. "I feel I have more confidence now. I feel my putting is getting better. I had good breaks out there. Nothing really went wrong for me. Everything so far is on my side." This was the original Ballesteros speaking, the one who used to take a golf round in his hands and shape it to his liking. He bogeyed No. 3 after hitting his tee shot into a bunker. He shook that off. He even shrugged at two eagles that got away. He missed the first from 10 feet at No. 6. "The wind took the ball to the right a little," he said. At No. 7, a 35-footer just missed. The two birdies he did get surely had a certain calming effect. The 14th hurt him for the second consecutive day. He drove into the left rough and was short with his six-iron second. His chip shot wasn't much better, and he two-putted for a bogey-five. Even so, the second round left him in a fine frame of mind. "The course is playing fair and conditions cannot be any better," he said. "So far, I am beating the pressure, but as you all know, the pressure is very difficult to beat." Someone asked what it would take now to win. Ballesteros just shrugged and grinned. "If I can have two 71s," he said, "I will sign right now."

The Americans were stirring. They were starting to crowd the leaderboard. Nine of them were within seven strokes of Price's lead. The closest was Craig Stadler, tied for third with defending champion Nick Faldo at 140, three behind Price. Stadler, after an opening 72, returned a 68 and had a simple explanation for both rounds: Putting. "I missed everything yesterday," he said, "and I made everything today." He went from 34 putts in the first round — when he missed four from two feet or less — to 25 in the second. And the wind was kinder, he said. "You can stand up and hit a shot and hit a short putt without being blown over," he said. Stadler was using a gift putter. It was a left-over from the 100 given as prizes to the amateurs at a pro-am for junior golf at San Diego earlier in the season. Some gift

— two-putt birdies at the sixth (from 20 feet) and the seventh (from 40), a 20-foot par save at No. 11, a 40-foot birdie at No. 12, and a 20-foot birdie at No. 13. The putter let him down only once, a two-putt from six feet at No. 16 for his only bogey of the round. (The glow wouldn't last. He was headed for trouble.)

Next, at 141, came Andy Bean, the big, amiable Floridian, after a weird day. You might say Bean backed his way onto the leaderboard. On the easier outgoing nine, where everyone else was picking up strokes, he was dropping them. He staggered to a three-bogey 38. Then he did the unthinkable. He took the brutal incoming nine apart for a five-birdie, one-bogey 32, the lowest back-nine of the Open so far. "I was two different people on the golf course today," the redhead said. Here's some perspective for that accomplishment: There were 139 scores of 40 or more on the inward nine through the first two rounds. These included 46s by Barry Lane, Mark Mouland, and Britain's Alan McCloskey; 45s by Mark Calcavecchia and Davis Love III; and 43s by Curtis Strange, Ian Woosnam, and Eamonn Darcy. Only two of 153 starters broke the par of 36 in the first round — Brad Faxon (35) and Fred Couples (34). And in the second, only seven. So Bean's 32 was two strokes better than anyone else's. That's not exactly what Price was talking about when he said you had to "hold on" coming in.

Sandy Lyle certainly hung on. After an outward 33, he ground out nine consecutive pars coming home for a 69—142. He saved par at No. 12 with a spectacular bunker shot. He popped the ball over the lip of the bunker with just six inches to spare, and got it to one foot and holed for his par three. Lyle called it the "greatest bunker shot of his career." Someone mentioned his shot from the fairway bunker that set up his winning birdie in the Masters just three months earlier. "Oh," Lyle said, "that was a seven iron." The two surprise players of the first round gave ground but held on probably better than expected. Faxon had 74—143, and Greg Bruckner, 74—146. England's Paul Broadhurst, on 73-73—146, was the only one of eight amateurs to make the cut and thus assured himself of the amateur's medal. (He went on to finish 74-76 for 296, 12 over par.)

Nick Faldo came in at 69—140, tied for second with Stadler, three strokes off the 36-hole lead. "You have to birdie the so-called easy holes and par the tough holes," Faldo said. "I have been birdieing the right ones and bogeying the others." He missed five fairways coming in, thus missing three birdie chances and taking two bogeys. That ruined a very promising round that had begun with an outward 31, where he birdied the second, then three in succession from No. 4. He bogeyed No. 14 after driving into the rough, then had a real adventure at No. 17 — a drive into a fairway bunker, a 65-yard blast out, his third into a bunker near the green, then a blast out and a three-foot putt for his bogey-five. He had made six there in the first round.

U.S. Open champion Curtis Strange was in real danger of missing the cut after his opening 79. But he bore down, improved by 10 strokes to a 69, and made it with no room to spare on 148. No one was surprised by Strange's dramatic turnaround. It recalled his U-turn in the 1985 Masters, when he went 80-65. "When I birdied No. 10 into the wind," he said, "that got me to two under for the day, and I knew if I held on I would make the cut." Jack Nicklaus was another survivor. He had recovered from the stomach ailment that almost forced him to withdraw from the first round, and both his game and his spirits improved. He twitted the press corps. "I don't know why you're bothering with me — at 145," he said. He returned a bumpy one-under-par 70 that started with a bogey at No. 1, where he two-putted from five feet after coming out of a bunker, and an eagle-three at No. 6, where he holed a 45-foot putt.

So the pressure was on Nick Price now to hold his lead. This stirred up the painful memory of the 1982 Open at Royal Troon. Back then, Price was dogging the footsteps of Bobby Clampett, who was hot through the first two rounds. When Clampett finally faded in the final round, Price found himself leading by three strokes with just six holes to play. And then he also faded. Tom Watson, who had finished, had his fifth Open championship. The general opinion up to now was that Price had choked badly. Price just gave that big smile. No way, he said. Actually, it was quite the reverse.

"I got ahead of myself," Price said. "I had birdied 10, 11, and 12. Watson at that stage bogeyed a hole, and I was three ahead, and I was so confident I couldn't lose the championship. Remember — I was 25 then, and how many guys at 25 have the opportunity to win a major championship?" So with the Open victory at his fingertips, Price proceeded to drop three strokes over the last six holes and lost. He was determined not to repeat that error. "I learned a golden lesson: never get ahead of yourself, never get too confident," he said. "If I ever forgot about what happened to me that day, I'd be a fool."

The leaders after the second round:

Nick Price	70-67—137	Isao Aoki	72-71—143
Seve Ballesteros	67-71—138	Brad Faxon	69-74—143
Nick Faldo	71-69—140	Howard Clark	71-72—143
Craig Stadler	72-68—140	Gary Koch	71-72—143
Andy Bean	71-70—141	Andrew Sherborne	71-72—143
Sandy Lyle	73-69—142	Peter Senior	70-73—143
Fred Couples	73-69—142	Eduardo Romero	72-71—143
Bob Tway	71-71—142	Wayne Riley	72-71—143
Don Pooley	70-73—143	Chip Beck	72-71—143

On Saturday, it rained. And rained and rained and rained. Play was suspended at 12:20 p.m., and at 1:45 p.m., R&A officials declared play abandoned. It was the first Open wash-out since 1961 at Royal Birkdale. And for the first time in Open history, the final round would be played on Monday.

There was one happy golfer, and one not-so-happy golfer on Saturday. Only 30 of the 71 qualifiers had started their third round before play was suspended, and no one had finished. The wash-out was great news to Brian Marchbank, who had already had his share of narrow escapes. First, he got into the Open through the qualifier, and at that had to pick up five strokes to par over the last six holes to do it. In the Open, he stood 73-74—147 through the first two rounds, making the cut by only one stroke, and he had to hole a bunker shot on the final hole to do it. Then on Saturday, he dropped five strokes in the first seven holes. The wash-out spared him.

But sometimes one man's blessing is another man's curse. Enter the case of Hubert Green, Marchbank's playing partner. At 74-73—147, he began the day tied with Marchbank, but at the end of the same seven holes, he was 10 strokes ahead. For where Marchbank dropped five strokes, Green had made one of the greatest starts in Open history. He went five under par over those first seven holes. He birdied the second through the fourth, then the sixth and seventh. Green turned stoic when play was suspended, though one had the impression he was biting his tongue, and who could blame him? "If play is cancelled," he said, "it can't be helped. No use worrying. What they have to do, they have to do. If they have to cancel it, it's not the end of the world. It's a game called golf. I'm not complaining. Life's been good to me."

"Obviously, we are very disappointed with what has happened," said Alistair Low, Championship Committee chairman. He explained that the R&A was following the practice of the European tour, to cancel a round if less than half the field had not finished. In this case, nobody had finished. The R&A planned feverishly, and this might well be the pattern for future wash-outs: For a Sunday double round, and a three-ball format instead of a two-ball since fewer tee times would be required. And in case of a playoff, the sudden-death in place of the five-hole aggregate. But all that planning turned out to be futile. The course was so swamped that there was no chance for a double round on Sunday. In fact, there were serious doubts that even one round could be played on Sunday. By midnight Saturday, the fairways at the fourth, seventh, 11th, and 14th holes were completely under water. Course workers were out at 4:30 a.m. Sunday, manning pumps and a "waterhog," a kind of water vacuum sweeper. Tons of straw were brought in and spread on the most heavily damaged walkways.

At 7 a.m. Sunday, the forecast was for clouds and occasional drizzle, temperatures in the mid-60s, and a freshening wind in the afternoon. Then there was a welcome sight by noon Sunday — the sun breaking through big white clouds. The course had drained well, and the golfers said it was in remarkably fine condition after all that rain.

Green picked up where he left off on Saturday, but only for a short while. He was three under par through the seventh. Then a double-bogey five at the ninth set him back. An inward 39 left him at 73—220. Ironically, Marchbank matched him. The fireworks this time came from David J. Russell of England, who had one victory in his 14 years on the European tour. Russell hit the flagstick with his tee shot at No. 1, tapped in a two-inch putt for his birdie, and he was off and winging. He chopped two more strokes off par with a 15-foot eagle putt at No. 6, and he made the turn in a stunning six-under-par 29. "That's my best-ever nine holes," Russell said. He kept getting encouragement from his playing partner, one Jack Nicklaus, who was struggling to a 75. "Now come back in 29," Nicklaus said. Not at Lytham. An out-of-bounds tee shot at the 12th cost Russell a double-bogey five, and he came home in 40 for a 69—214, one over par. Perhaps Nicklaus was an inspiration. But the marvel is that Russell could even swing a club. Russell said he considers Nicklaus the greatest golfer who ever lived, and when he discovered he was paired with the man, his mind went blank. At the putting green before the round, his wife asked him whether she could get him anything. "No," Russell said. "Just take me home." The first hole was a blur, he said.

He didn't realize that he had hit the stick. His head didn't start to clear until he saw where his tee shot had finished — at two inches. Another hole or two, and he settled down. Then it was Nicklaus' turn to admire him.

Craig Stadler, playing with Nick Price and Seve Ballesteros, started the third round just three strokes off the lead. But he got lost coming home. He made two triple bogeys and three bogeys for a 44, and an 81—221. He was out of it. Lanny Wadkins seemed ready to take off on one of his famous hot streaks. Seven strokes off the lead at the start, he made up two of them with one swing. He holed his five-iron tee shot at No. 1. (David Graham is believed the only other player known to have started a major with an ace, that in the 1979 Open at Lytham, which is the only Open course with a par-three first hole). But Wadkins cooled down and settled for 71—215, nine off the lead.

The jockeying began in earnest. Larry Nelson, the American PGA champion, was running on automatic pilot. He returned a remarkable bogey-free 68. (It would be one of only two spotless rounds among the top 15 finishers. Curtis Strange was to post the other, also a 68, in the fourth round.) Nelson got his three birdies on putts of three, six, and 25 feet and joined Don Pooley (69), Andy Bean (71), and Argentina's Eduardo Romero (69) at one-under-par 212. Brad Faxon, the young American so thrilled to be in the Open, rebounded from a second-round 74 with a 70 and was a stroke further back at par 213. "I couldn't have dreamed of anything better," Faxon said. "First having to qualify, and now I'm in good position for the last round. I've had everything I wanted by this performance." Strange turned in his second consecutive 69, but he wasn't deluding himself. "That 79 in the first round means I'm out of the running," he said. "But I didn't come all this way to play badly."

Now the final battle began shaping up. First came Sandy Lyle. An opening 73 had left him on the distant fringes, a second-round 69 brought him closer, and now a third-round 67 put him smack in the middle of things, just three off the lead by the end of the day. He took just one bogey, a three-putt from 15 feet at No. 4. "I got a little bit overconfident," he said. "I pushed the first one four feet past and missed coming back." Lyle was on the scent. He got up and down from bunkers three times, including at the two closing holes. He was hitting his deadly one iron beautifully, his approaches were good, and he didn't have to work miracles for his five birdies — an eight-foot putt at No. 3, two putts from long range at Nos. 6 and 7, a 15-footer at No. 11, and a three-footer at No. 14.

Faldo hurt himself both early and late and still managed a 68—208. A quick bogey had him shaking his head. "To practice all morning," Faldo said, "and then walk out and miss from two feet on the first hole." (That, by the way, dropped him five strokes off the lead when Price, playing in the last group just behind, birdied No. 1.) He two-putted from six feet for a bogey at No. 15, and at No. 17 bogeyed again after driving into a fairway bunker. Otherwise, he burned up the greeens for six birdies — two putts from 18 feet at No. 6, and one-putts from 12, 15, 18, 18, 20, and 25 feet. Now, how confident was he of retaining his championship? "Top secret!" he said. "There are four good players there, and nobody is likely to go backward, so it's going to be a long struggle. But if I were to be the first Briton to win two in seccession, it would be everything."

Ballesteros started off getting nowhere fast. "It was a tough day, especially going out," he said. "I saw everybody picking up shots and I was only even par at the turn." It could have been much worse. Ballesteros worked his magic again. He turned certain disaster into a mere bogey at the sixth. He hooked his tee shot into the bushes. When he saw the fix he was in, he considered declaring an unplayable lie, then thought the better of it. "If I drop two club-lengths to the right. I still would not have a backswing," he said. So he had to invent a shot. He turned his sand wedge upside-down and hit left-handed. The ball moved a foot. "Then I could not declare it unplayable because I was in the same situation again," he said. So he swung the upside-down sand wedge left-handed again, this time harder, and the ball came out. Now he could get a crack at it. He put an eight-iron on the green and two-putted from 25 feet for a remarkable six, his only bogey of the round. Someone asked whether he practices left-handed shots. "You know me," Ballesteros said. "I'm all over the place, so I practice left-hand, right-hand more than anybody." He got the stroke back immediately with a routine birdie at No. 7 on a six-foot putt.

Coming in, he carded one birdie, holing from three feet at No. 13, and he finally beat his old enemy, No. 14, getting a par on a six-foot putt — his only par there for the entire Open. He wrapped up a one-under-par 70 and tied Faldo for second at 208, five under. He had played the third round with Nick Price, and he didn't see any signs of fatal shakes in the man. He knew his work was cut out for him. "It is going to be tough tomorrow," he said. "There are many with a chance to win. I think it will be good for me to go out and shoot a couple under par on the first nine and play solid on the back side." If he only knew what was coming.

You'd be hard-pressed to say that Price was shaking. True, his tee shots were straying, but his short game kept rescuing him. He led most of the way through the third round, sometimes by only one stroke, sometimes by three. His worst position was a tie for the lead with Faldo, and that was brief. Price broke the tie when he birdied No. 15 shortly after Faldo had bogeyed it just in front of him. Price was playing in a tough spot. He was paired with the dangerous Ballesteros, Faldo was just up ahead, and Lyle another group ahead. His chief threats had him more or less in sight all the way. He didn't seem to notice. He returned his third consecutive sub-par round, a 69, and at seven-under-par 206 stayed in the lead by two strokes over Faldo and Ballesteros.

Price wasted no time setting the pace for the third round, getting a birdie from eight feet at No. 1 to Ballesteros' par and Faldo's bogey up ahead. He suffered two bogeys going out, two-putting No. 4 from 35 feet after driving into a bunker, and two-putting No. 8 from six feet. He offset them with two birdies, a 10-foot putt at No. 6 and a 12-footer at No. 9, and made the turn in one-under-par 34. He tamed the fierce back nine with a one-under-par 35. He saved par at No. 11 by holing from 12 feet after a weak chip, birdied No. 13 from eight feet, and birdied No. 15 from three feet after a wonderful two-iron approach. "That was probably the best two iron of my life," he said. His only bogey coming in was at No. 17. He bunkered his tee shot, escaped, and hit a seven iron to 35 feet and two-putted. Then he saved his four at the 18th with two putts from 60 feet. "Whether I was two or three behind or ahead," Price said, "it is very comforting to know my game has held up as well as it has, and has given me the chance to win tomorrow. I feel I am in total control of my game and myself, and when I feel like that, I know I will play really well. And I don't worry about what the other people do because I have the confidence in my own ability." Then he headed for the practice tee. "There are four or five things I've been working on for the last six months," he said, "and I'm going out to find out what is missing."

They say if you don't bring it with you, you won't find it here. Whatever was missing, only Price knew. He certainly seemed to be in command of himself. He had had plenty of opportunities to crack, but he didn't. The final round figured to be a different matter, though. For one thing, it was the final round. That's when the pressure is greatest on the leader, especially over the last nine holes. Price was not unaccustomed to winning. He had won the World Series of Golf in 1983 and The Lancome Trophy in 1985, and a handful of South African and European events. But this was the Open. And worse, Price would start the final day with three hardened winners on his heels. This raised the question of Troon again. Could he handle the pressure? The jury was divided.

"There was pressure today," said Ballesteros. "But the pressure's not really in the third round. It comes tomorrow, on the back nine."

Said Faldo: "Price has played in this situation before, and he's been around a long time. The third day is the test day. If you have survived the pressure on the third day, it eases the pressure for the last day."

Lyle didn't agree. "I think Nick will feel the pressure a lot. He has nothing to lose, but he still has to win."

Just as surely as the Ghost of Troon was raised, so was the question of Price's national background. Not that it was an issue, but because it was so confusing, and it would have to be cleared up in case this man of many maps were to win the Open. Once again he tried to straighten it out: His father was English and was in the army in India; his mother was Welsh. Following his father's discharge after World War II, they were headed for Kenya, but stopped off in Durban, South Africa, and liked it. Nick was born there. When he was about 18 months old, the family moved to what was then Rhodesia. He grew up there, served in the Rhodesian Air Force in the 1970s. Rhodesia then became Zimbabwe, and is now Price's home country. Some of the confusion stems from his early golfing years, when he listed himself out of South Africa because of political sanctions against Rhodesia at the time.

"So," he told the press corps, chuckling, "I was born in South Africa, raised in Rhodesia, I have a British passport, and I live in the U.S. — you pick one." Then he addressed the British writers. "Actually," he said, "I was raised with the same manners and customs as you, so I'm as British as you are."

"You'll be even *more* British," came a British voice, "if you win."

Later, outside the press tent, Price smiled patiently and went through it all again for yet another gathering of writers, most of them Americans. Then he revealed that he had begun the process of getting American citizenship. An American accent came from the back of pack.

"Can you get it in time," the man said, "for an American to win the British Open?"

The leaders after the third round:

Nick Price	70-67-69—206
Seve Ballesteros	67-71-70—208
Nick Faldo	71-69-68—208
Sandy Lyle	73-69-67—209
Larry Nelson	73-71-68—212
Eduardo Romero	72-71-69—212
Don Pooley	70-73-69—212
Andy Bean	71-70-71—212

Monday was back-to-work day. But somehow, not for 15,080 people. They found a way to turn out for the Open's first-ever Monday finish. It was a fitting finale. The crowds all week had been staggering. Not only did this Open break the single-day record with the 43,111 on Friday, it broke all previous records. The total for the nine days (Sunday through Monday) was 205,285 — 12,000 over the previous record at St. Andrews in 1984 and 70,000 over the last time the Open was at Lytham, in 1979. The Monday crowd got its money's worth.

Long-hitting Fred Couples triggered some shock waves early in the final round — an outward 30 highlighted by thunderous back-to-back eagles. His drive at the 490-yard sixth left him only a nine iron to the green. He put it to 15 feet. At the 549-yard seventh, a driver and a four-iron left him only 25 feet from the flag. He holed both putts. (In four passes at those two holes, he had a bogey, two pars, three birdies, and two eagles. All told, six under par.) He was five under par through the 16th, but any chance he had at picking up more ground on the leaders behind him evaporated with bogeys on the last two holes. His 68 tied him at 281 with fellow American Gary Koch for fourth. That was the best the Americans could do. Tony Jacklin was right. And Lytham had struck again. Seven Opens at Lytham, and no American pro had won. "I'll be back next year," Couples vowed.

So will Argentina's Eduardo Romero, one would think. Romero was playing in his second Open — he missed the cut at Royal St. George's in 1985 — and he was giving everybody a thrill, including the leaders. After rounds of 72-71-69, he was three under par for the round and four under for the championship through the 12th. His bid to become the second Argentinian to win the Open — after Roberto de Vicenzo in 1967 — died down Lytham's punishing stretch. Romero bogeyed five of the last six holes. But for a relatively obscure golfer in only his second Open, it was a strong showing. His closing 73—285 left him tied for 13th with Curtis Strange (68) and Larry Nelson (73). Romero was not impressed with himself. "I was expecting a top-three finish," he said through an intepreter. When it came to disappointments, however, it was Bernhard Langer who wrote the saddest tale of all. Langer, not quite yet 31, had been a force in world golf for years. He was a challenger in several Opens. But he was doomed in this one. He was still troubled by the back problems that he feared, even earlier in the year, might require surgery. And possibly worse, his putting yips had returned like a recurrent nightmare. He carded 73-75-75 through the first three rounds. In the fourth, he went out in 34, then suffered an awesome crash coming in, a 46. He played the last five holes in nine over par. He took five putts at No. 17

for an eight, and three more putts at No. 18. With a 19-over-par 303, Langer was 69th out of the 71 finishers.

The early fireworks were over. The crowd turned its attention to the end of the field, the final battle. Couples, who teed off at 12:15 p.m., a half-hour before the leaders, flirted with the lead for a while. His brace of eagles got him down to five under par, which put him a stroke or two off the lead as the duel was shaping up behind him. A bogey at the 10th wiped out his final hopes. Only one other man intruded. That was Sandy Lyle, in the next-to-last threesome. Back-to-back birdies put him at six under par through No. 7. Now here was a measure of the intensity of that last round: Lyle bogeyed No. 9, he was still five under par, but he was no longer in the picture. He had been lost in the smoke. Lyle kept sliding and finished 74—283, tied for seventh.

It came down to the final threesome: Price, leading at seven under; and Faldo and Ballesteros tied for second at five under. They teed off at 12:45 p.m. By the time they reached the turn about two hours later, it was a two-man chase, but only for a while. Faldo was playing excellent golf and Price was brilliant. But it wasn't enough. Ballesteros was incandescent.

Here's the way it went:

Nothing changed at the first hole. All three parred it. The first bump came at No. 2. Price bogeyed, missing a five-foot par putt. "That put me in a negative frame of mind," he said. Faldo also bogeyed, three-putting. Ballesteros two-putted from 15 feet for his par. Price's lead was down to one, over Ballesteros. Faldo caught up with Ballesteros at the third with a birdie from eight feet. Price and Ballesteros both parred, and Price led them by one. All three parred the fourth and fifth. Then began one of the great duels in Open history. It was a three-man battle for only one more hole, the sixth. All three birdied. Now here is where the action reached a fever pitch. When a man does no worse than make a par, and it knocks him out of the chase, golf has got to some other level. That's what happened to Faldo. The pace was brutal.

"The seventh hole killed me," Faldo said. "I hit a good four iron to the green, then found that where I was, I could not even putt. I had to putt it uphill and three-putted, while the other guys were close." Faldo also parred the eighth and ninth. Exit the defending champion. Faldo completed a round of par 71 and finished third with five-under-par 279. In retrospect, No. 7 killed him all through the Open. He could do no better than make his par-five each day while practically everyone else was making hay. Of the top 15 finishers, only Faldo, Gary Koch, and Eduardo Romero made all pars there. Isao Aoki was the next least opportunistic, playing it in a birdie and three pars. The hole took a fearful beating.

With Faldo falling behind by merely standing still, now began a piece of art that will forever hang in the halls of golf: the Price-Ballesteros shootout.

At No. 7, Price put his second shot to about four feet, Ballesteros to six. Both holed for eagle-threes. Price was nine under, Ballesteros eight.

At No. 8, Ballesteros birdied from 18 feet. Price two-putted for par. They were tied at nine under.

At No. 9, Ballesteros missed his first green of the day, but chipped close. Price two putted from 20 feet. They came away with par-threes.

At No. 10, Price put his second to about four feet, a certain birdie. He was about to re-take the lead. But Ballesteros got down first from 20 feet. Two birdies, and they were still tied.

At No. 11, Price faced a 12-foot birdie putt. He needed it to keep pace. But it lipped out. He made his par. Ballesteros had already drilled in a 20-footer for a birdie. Now Ballesteros led by one.

The tension had stretched too thin to bear. The crowd was howling. Price had played the six-hole stretch, from the sixth through the 11th, in four under par with an eagle and two birdies. But Ballesteros had destroyed them. He played them in six under, with an eagle and four birdies, and went from one stroke behind to one ahead. But not for long.

At the 203-yard, par-three 12th, Ballesteros, trying a low four iron, missed the green by 30 yards. He was in the high, thin rough to the right. He pitched to about five feet, then two-putted for a four. It was his first bogey of the round; his first in 24 holes. Price was not about to let this opportunity slip away. His tee shot was on the front edge below the shelf, about 20 feet from the hole. He two-putted for his par and caught Ballesteros at 10 under par. Then came an exchange that would have utterly demoralized a lesser man. But which one?

Price nearly holed his second shot at the 342-yard 13th. The ball rolled dangerously toward the hole, then stopped a mere two inches away. It had to be an unsettling sight to Ballesteros when he came to the green and saw his man poised to take the lead. He himself was still a long 18 feet from the hole. But if the view bothered him, he didn't show it. In fact, he didn't even seem to notice. He studied his line briefly, got over the ball, and in absolutely cold blood rammed the birdie in. Price's heart had to sink. But he showed no emotion. He tapped in his birdie and joined Ballesteros at 11 under par. Not that it would help Faldo, who could do nothing but tag along four strokes behind, but both Price and Ballesteros both bogeyed the 14th — Ballesteros for the third time in the Open, Price for the second. This was one Price let get away. Both missed the green. Ballesteros, master of the short game, failed this time. He chipped five feet past. Price's chip was only three feet away. Ballesteros missed his par putt. Then somehow, Price missed the three-footer. They were still tied at 10 under par. They remained deadlocked with pars at the 15th, Price holing from six feet after a weak chip, and Ballesteros two-putting from the edge. This couldn't last. And it didn't.

Two more holes will take their place in golf history, as tributes both to Ballesteros' fire and genius and Price's spirit.

At No. 16, Ballesteros hit a one-iron into the middle of the fairway. Price also hit the fairway. He put his second to 12 feet, and Ballesteros hit a stunning nine iron, 135 yards to within three inches of the hole. It was the reverse of what happened back at No. 13. Now it was Price's turn to give Ballesteros a jolt and birdie first. But his putt tailed off, and he tapped in for his par-four. Ballesteros nudged in his "gimme" for a birdie, and he led by one. It was 4:34 p.m., just shy of four hours from their start. It seemed the Open was over. But it wasn't.

Ballesteros had played the 17th in a birdie and two pars, Price in two pars and a bogey. Ballesteros drove into the fairway and put his second on the green, about 25 feet from the hole. Price's tee shot ended up in some muddy tire tracks. He got a free drop, and put his second on the front edge, 30 feet short. Both missed the birdie putts and tapped in for pars.

They went to No. 18 with Ballesteros a stroke ahead. It should have been routine now, but Ballesteros had one last piece of theater to produce, a no-fairway finish. He hit his driver into the light rough to the left, then missed the green to the left. It was the "safe" side, but he was in thick rough, some 50 dangerous feet from the flag. Price hit the green with his second, some 35 feet from the hole. There was his chance. It was a slim one, but a chance nonetheless. Ballesteros was in excellent position to bogey. But then he stepped up to his ball in the high grass, and Price was dead. The Spaniard, summoning that pressure-proof magic, executed a dazzling chip shot that burned the hole and stopped about six inches away. Price just looked and shook his head. Sometimes, Ballesteros is simply beyond belief. So Price needed a birdie, just to tie. No reason to be coy now. Second place was his. He was five huge strokes ahead of the third-place Faldo. He charged the putt hard. It missed and went eight feet past, and he two-putted from there for a bogey-five and a 69. Ordinarily, a leader who scores 69 in the final round almost certainly will win. In fact, before the round Price had told his caddie, Dave McNeilly, "Let's just go out and shoot a 69 and not worry about anyone else." There was nothing ordinary about this time. Ballesteros had just shot a six-under-par 65. It was a masterpiece.

"I don't know what to say," said Ballesteros, who finished at 11-under-par 273 to win by two strokes. "You can only hope for a round like that once every 25, maybe 50 years. So far, it is the best round of my life. I played as good as you can hope to play this game.

"Nick Price showed he was a champion, too. I was just a little bit luckier. It's a pity there can be only one champion. I want to tell you, Nick, if you keep playing the way you did today, you will be the champion soon."

Nick Price did not lose this Open. He simply was beaten. There is a huge distinction, and it put the Ghost of Troon to rest. "I'm not feeling down," Price said. "If I had played badly, I might be. But when you're beaten by somebody, especially the way he played, you just bow out gracefully. It was such a thrill to play to this standard of golf. Seve was very gracious, but he definitely played better than I did."

Another ghost also was put to rest — the Ghost of Augusta that had been haunting Ballesteros. With this amazing victory, Ballesteros burned the accumulation of two years of dark thoughts and doubt off his back. He had carried that gloomy load since the final round of the 1986 Masters, where he was leading by two strokes with four holes to play and then somehow dumped a simple medium-iron approach shot into the water in front of No. 15 green. That opened the door to the Jack Nicklaus Miracle.

"That second in the water — that very much hurt my confidence," Ballesteros said. That was a strange, new feeling for him. A lack of confidence was never his problem. In any golf event you care to think of, he could soar like an eagle or crash in flames, but he never lost his equilibrium, never doubted himself. The 1986 Masters changed that. And if he wasn't low enough after that one, he was the next year. Two images remain from the 1987 Masters: Larry Mize sinking that miracle chip shot to beat Greg Norman on the second extra hole, and Ballesteros stalking off the course, silent and in tears, after bowing out at the first extra hole by missing a five-foot par putt. Had the magic gone? Ballesteros faced that grim thought privately and in silence. It simmered in him, giving off dark fumes. He never revealed his fears, not until he proved to himself that they were groundless. This he did by winning the 1988 British Open. Then he felt free to speak. He astonished the press corps. No one suspected he had sunk so low. Actually, it all came out in only two fragments of sentences, but they said it all.

"I was wondering if my time..." Ballesteros said. "You know..."

He never completed either sentence. He didn't have to.

"Now I can put that way back," he said, brightening with the old claret jug safely in hand, "and remember this."

So the old Ballesteros was back — the wild shots (but fewer of them), the spectacular recoveries, the routine genius. But he was different, too. He was now more mature and less wild, but he was still impatient, still brilliantly inventive, and fiery as ever. He had rid himself of one burden, but now he had a new one. Maybe other golfers can win and go their way, but not Ballesteros. The 1988 British Open — the way he won it, and what it meant — seemed a great catharsis. It vented the built-up pressures of frustration and doubt, and it exorcised the evil spirits of failures, but it presented him with a new devil. Since Ballesteros is more talented, more is expected of him, and this explains the interesting question that came next from someone in the press corps: Now that he was free of those old devils, was there any reason why he shouldn't win, oh, five or six more majors?

Ballesteros grinned at the man. He might have had the Spanish word "loco" in mind for an answer, but instead he slipped comfortably into current American vernacular.

"What you think?" Ballesteros said. "This game is a piece of cake or what?"

6. The PGA Championship

Say this for the PGA Championship. While it may be the last of the four major championships and comes at a time of the year when it's hot, the players are tired, often off their games and it goes to places that the USGA might not go for the U.S. Open, it's never dull.

Such was the 1988 event.

From three shots off the pace, Jeff Sluman turned in a nifty six-under-par 65 to tie David Graham's 65 in 1979 for the lowest winning final round in a PGA Championship. The only thing it broke was the heart of Paul Azinger, who shot even par and made every putt he had to make on the back nine. Every one. And still lost by three shots.

For almost all of his PGA Tour career, Sluman was remembered for one thing, being in the wrong place at a time when a young man decided to jump into the lake at the island 17th green at the Tournament Players Club. It came just as Sluman prepared to knock in a three-foot birdie putt that would have meant victory in the 1987 Players Championship. Distracted, Sluman backed off, reloaded, missed and three sudden-death playoff holes later lost the title to Sandy Lyle.

Now, however, Sluman could finally put the one that got away behind him. Winning the PGA Championship can do that for a guy.

First, the controversy. The PGA was played at 7,015-yard Oak Tree Golf Club in Edmond, Oklahoma. The course was designed by Pete Dye, not one of the players' favorite architects, and holds the highest course rating of any in the country, 76.9 for its par of 71. Horror stories abounded from members of the Oak Tree Gang of Willie Wood, Scott Verplank, Bob Tway, Gil Morgan, Doug Tewell, Andrew Magee and David Edwards.

And for the umpteenth time, the PGA of America was brought to task by the media for continuing its policy of playing the championship at the hottest time of the year in some of the hot spots of America, also including Tulsa, Birmingham, and West Palm Beach. Why not February or March when everybody is keyed up to play? Or May. Anytime but August.

Several of the leading players, however, came to the defense of the PGA and its championship. Raymond Floyd was one. "I see no problem with having the tournament this time of year," he said. "I know some people are golfed out by now, but, fellows, this is a major championship. If you can't get yourself ready to play in a major, no matter where it is or when it is, you shouldn't be here. Besides, the earlier months are taken up with other tournaments."

Unfamiliarity often breeds contempt. But a few practice rounds had most in the field praising Oak Tree. For one, the fairways were generous, the rough manageable and the greens measured only 9.9 on the Stimpmeter. That was a far cry from the 1987 championship at PGA National where the fairways were narrow, the rough impossible and the greens more dirt than grass.

With such generosity provided by the PGA this time, the players stopped grumbling and decided Oak Tree was playable after all.

"Nothing wrong here," said Azinger. "There are no let-up holes out there. It's all golf course. And if the wind blows, it may be more than any of us want. But the course is set up so we can drive the ball off the tee with a driver. That hasn't always been the case."

And from defending champion Larry Nelson: "Oak Tree is a great golf course. This will be the Merion or the Baltusrol of the 2000's. I wish people would get off this stuff about what happened on some course 30 years ago. We're making history today.

"The USGA has a habit of finding courses that are the least accessible. At Merion, they had to bus us three miles to the practice area. Here, you've got it all right outside the clubhouse. Oak Tree is as good a championship course as I've played since I've been playing the PGA Championship."

Adding to the pre-tournament drama was the presence of Greg Norman, and the absence of Sandy Lyle. Norman had injured a wrist during the second round of the U.S. Open in June and hadn't played since. This was to be his coming-out party.

"It's been a long and frustrating 7½ weeks for me," Norman said. "First not being able to complete the U.S. Open, then having to miss the British Open, basically two major championships that you revolve your whole career around. The worst time was when the starting times were published in the paper on Tuesday and my name wasn't in there. It hit me pretty hard.

"I guess I've played six rounds in those seven weeks, most of that recently. I started just hitting 90-yard sand wedge shots, then gradually worked my way before resuming my normal practice routine. The wrist is fine. If it wasn't I wouldn't be playing here. I would have taken more time off and waited it out. I think the time off will make me more competitive; maybe it's been a blessing in disguise. I'm ready to play and think my game is pretty strong coming in here."

Lyle, the Masters champion and leading money winner, chose to sit it out, taking the week off before the Irish Open. Nobody could believe he would skip a major, especially with the opportunity to become the first player since Tom Watson in 1982 to win two majors in the same year.

And some of his competitors questioned his motives. One of them was Curtis Strange, who in the past has been on the receiving end of such criticism for bypassing the British Open. "It's hard for me to comment about Sandy not coming here to play," Strange said. "If he thinks he's doing what is right for him, so be it, but this is a major championship and it would be great for someone to win two in a year, much less one. He's a good player, and yes, he should be here."

Because the 1984 U.S. Amateur had been the only tournament held at Oak Tree, predicting a winning score for the week was like choosing the correct numbers in a lottery. Where do you start?

"It all depends on the wind," said Nelson. "They will be low if it doesn't blow, and by low, I mean well under par. And par might be good enough if it blows 15 miles an hour every day, and 300 could win if it gets up to 30 miles an hour."

The early betting line was that one of the Oak Tree Gang would win it. Guys like Tway and Verplank and Morgan and Tewell had played it hundreds of times, knew all the angles and every slope on every green. But Jack Nicklaus, who never picks a winner unless he knows it probably won't be him, liked the chances of Severiano Ballesteros.

"This is a course that demands great imagination around the greens and nobody has more imagination than Seve does," Nicklaus said. "This course also is made for him. He can use his driver off the tee because the fairways are generous and the rough isn't that severe. And he's an excellent putter."

Nicklaus didn't much like Norman's chances, however. "He's going to have a difficult time on this course because the short game is going to come into play and that's one thing you will have trouble coming back from if you've been off for a while."

What everyone did agree on was that come Sunday night a quality champion would be crowned.

"To win here, you've got to play all the shots," Nicklaus said, "and I like that in a major championship. You usually get a truer champion that way. Whoever that is come Sunday will have earned it. And, I think it's going to be a close finish. I don't see anyone running away with it. The course is too demanding."

Demanding, however, was hardly the order of the day for the first round as Oak Tree's tough-guy reputation was dismantled from the early morn to late evening. Only a slight breeze greeted the field and the course rating was held up to ridicule.

The course record of 68 stood only half the day as John Cook and Chip Beck came in with four-under 67s. And that was only the beginning. Before the day was over, Bob Gilder turned in a first-round leading and course record 66, while Azinger and Nick Faldo matched Beck and Cook with 67s and seven others shot 68s.

In the latter group was Norman, Floyd, Craig Stadler, Rocco Mediate, Peter Senior, Mike Reid and Jay Overton, the director of golf at Innisbrook Golf Resort in Tarpon Springs, Florida. The 69 shooters were led by former PGA champion Hal Sutton and included another club pro, Bob Makoski, Sluman, Steve Jones, Tommy Nakajima and Dan Pohl. Hardly a Hall-of-Famer in the group.

There were 13 players at one-under 70, including defending champion Nelson, Ben Crenshaw, Payne Stewart and low Oak Tree Gang member Doug Tewell. In all, 31 players broke par of 71 and another 12 matched it.

"When you play a golf course with no wind, you have a yardage book and the greens are receptive, I don't care how hard it is, it's playable," Azinger said of so many low first round scores. "A lot has been made of the course rating, but that's for amateurs. And today, I don't think a good amateur would have had trouble getting around here in under 77."

It was so playable that Gilder hit 16 greens, 12 fairways and had no bogeys. He went out in 33 with birdies at Nos. 4, 7 and 8, and came in in 33 with birdies at Nos. 14 and 16. He missed the second green, but chipped to 18 inches, and missed No. 9, then saved his par from a foot.

"I didn't make any mistakes. I never drove it out of the fairway and I had a shot at the pin on every hole," said Gilder of his five-birdie, no-bogey round. "I gave myself a lot of opportunities; I just didn't take advantage of all of them.

"I look forward to any golf course that is tough. It's not as difficult to concentrate on a course like this. It makes you play hard. Frankly, I don't like easy courses, and this one isn't easy despite all the low scores today."

If Gilder had confined his comments to birdies, bogeys and saves, he would have been better served. But he wasn't content to be the first round leader. He livened up the story by blasting all four major championships for weakening their fields for various reasons. His salvo scored a direct hit on the PGA of America and on the 37-year-old Overton, who qualified for the PGA with a tie for 23rd in the Club Pro Championship.

The PGA of America allows the top 40 players in the Club Pro Championship, held each October, to play in the PGA Championship, and that, according to Gilder, weakened the field.

"They (PGA) have a right to do that," Gilder said, "and I have nothing against the club pros personally. Some of them are my friends. But they are not as good golfers as the next 40 pros on the tour list, who can't play in the PGA Championship because of the 40 club pros.

"The club pros have other things to occupy their minds. They're not making their livings out here playing golf. So, it just stands to reason they won't be as good at it as those who earn their living that way."

When told of Gilder's comment, Overton put on his best club pro smile and public relations demeanor. "If Bob was grading our skill level on scoring ability, then he makes a point," he said. "We're not going to beat Greg Norman for four rounds. But, there are some very good golf club professionals. It is the PGA Championship. That encompasses all professionals in the country."

Overton wasn't about to take himself too seriously, but it isn't often a club pro makes his way into the interview room after any round of a major championship. This was his fifth PGA — he'd missed the cut in four previous ones — and he came to Oak Tree with one thing in mind: to have a good time.

"We club pros usually put too much pressure on ourselves in tournaments like this," he said. "Next week we're back at our club jobs, running a mixed four-ball or something. This is a reward. I certainly didn't expect to shoot 68, but I'm going to enjoy it while I can."

Overton's attitude was shared by Azinger, who on Monday didn't give himself a chance of ever competing. He'd suffered muscle spasms the week before while playing the second round at Memphis and had to withdraw. He came to Oak Tree looking for a miracle cure and found it.

"I've never had any back problems, never even given it a thought," Azinger said. "All of a sudden, out of nowhere, it happened. I was half paralyzed with muscle spasms. Frankly, I thought there was no way I was going to play here. But, I came on out and got some treatment from the same doctor who treated Gil Morgan and now I feel much better. Within 36 hours I went from no way I could play to I knew I could play."

After three days of heat treatment and massages, he played as well as ever. Six birdies, two bogeys and only twice did he drive it out of the fairway. He birdied No. 3 from four feet, chipped in from 45 feet on No. 4, ran afoul of No. 5 — his bugaboo all week — and made bogey, but came back to birdie seven and eight to turn in 33.

On the back, he birdied No. 11 from 25 feet, bogeyed the 15th and birdied No. 16 from four feet.

"I'm pleasantly surprised," Azinger said. "When you have a dramatic change in your body, you're never sure what's going to happen. I didn't give my back a single thought today. It could go out tomorrow, but I'm not going to worry about it. I'm just going to play as long as it will let me."

One of Azinger's incentives to play well was his pairing with Arnold Palmer, who though not eligible through regular qualifications was given an exemption by the PGA.

"I was inspired," Azinger said. "I'm in his Army, definitely. I hate to see him make a bogey. If he has a four-footer, I want him to make it, and I don't feel that way about anybody else."

Cook, who had struggled most of the year with a sour putter, played a strong front side with birdies at one, three, five and nine to turn in 32, but leveled off on the back, sandwiching birdies at Nos. 13 and 16 with bogeys at Nos. 14 and 15. But he wasn't complaining.

"My record this year is nothing to brag about, but I've played better than I've scored," he said. "I'm proud of the round I shot today. I finally made a few putts."

Beck had five birdies — Nos. 5, 6, 8, 12 and 16 — on putts ranging from 18 inches to three feet. His lone bogey came as a result of a poor drive at No. 7, one of the most penal holes from the tee on the course.

At first glance, Overton was viewed as one of those first-round wonders who has his career round on Thursday then fades into the field. But he had played with gusto, making five birdies and two bogeys. "Every once in a while, we can play a round like this," said the 37-year-old Overton. "Notice I said every once in a while."

Stadler looked all the world like a first round co-leader after 17 holes, standing five under par. He birdied the first from three feet, the third from four feet, the fourth from six feet, then missed from inside 10 feet at six, seven and eight to turn in 33.

On the incoming nine, he wasn't as pure, but he wasn't bad. The former Masters champion birdied the 10th from 20 feet, then fought off a bogey at No. 12 with birdies at Nos. 14 from 12 feet and 16 from three feet to move into a tie with Gilder. But he forgot to finish.

On the 429-yard devilish 18th, where a good tee shot is more important than a good putt, Stadler hit a bad one, which led to a double-bogey six. After driving into the right rough, he hacked a five iron left of the green into a deep swale, left his next shot short of the green, pitched poorly and two-putted from 20 feet. It was a downer from which he never recovered the remainder of the week.

"I hit the ball so well for the first four or five holes, I was in my own little world," said Stadler, who hasn't won on the PGA Tour since the 1984 Byron Nelson Classic. "I could have shot nothing on the front side. At six, seven and eight, I missed from four feet, four feet and 10 feet."

And of his finish? "I played through 17 holes, then I quit. At 18, I hit a lousy tee shot, a lousy chip and a miserable putt. But, that's done and over with. It will be brought up only one more time — tonight when I talk with my wife."

The presence of Norman among the leaders raised quite a few eyebrows, including his own, considering his lengthy absence from competition. He had four birdies and a lone bogey.

"I'm very, very happy about coming back and performing the way I did. My concentration was good on the practice tee and it carried onto the course. I'm very excited about the way I played today," Norman said.

It didn't hurt his confidence that in his first competitive round in almost two months he started with birdies on two of the first three holes and after making his only bogey at No. 11 finished with birdies at Nos. 15 and 16.

"I told myself before the round not to expect too much, to just get out there and play like you know how to play," Norman said. "I concentrated on every shot. I never set a score to shoot. But now I'm excited about the next three days."

Old warhorse Floyd used all the experience of his many years to carve out his 69. He was all over the place and played an adventuresome round — six up-and-down saves for pars, an eagle on No. 16 from 15 inches, a chip in from 30 feet for birdie at No. 9, a couple of bogeys and a pair of birdies.

"When you've played as long as I have, you probably have rounds like this, but I don't remember one," said Floyd, who has won a Masters, a U.S. Open and two PGA titles. "It certainly wasn't boring. I did the things necessary to shoot 68."

On the other end of that spectrum was Sluman. He missed the cut in the U.S. Open and admitted to being uptight before the round began as evidenced by a bogey on the second hole.

"I really want to play well this week," said the 30-year-old New Yorker, in what proved to be the understatement of the week.

The leaders after the first round:

Bob Gilder	66	Ray Floyd	68
Paul Azinger	67	Greg Norman	68
John Cook	67	Mike Reid	68
Nick Faldo	67	Bob Makoski	69
Chip Beck	67	Jeff Sluman	69
Jay Overton	68	Steve Jones	69
Peter Senior	68	Tommy Nakajima	69
Craig Stadler	68	Dan Pohl	69
Rocco Mediate	68	Hal Sutton	69

Ever notice how some people have a knack for putting their foot in their mouth? Gilder filled that role in this PGA. No sooner had he criticized the presence of club pros in the field than he found himself trailing one (Overton) and tied with another (Makoski) as the championship hit the midway point.

Overton followed his surprising 68 with a 66, which matched Gilder's course record in the first round. He moved up to second place, one stroke behind Azinger who also shot 66.

Gilder tumbled into a tie for 28th with a second-round 75, eight shots behind Azinger.

Overton was one of Friday's early starters and as he walked between the 14th green and 15th tee leading the tournament, he spied a scoreboard and smiled. He was six under par on his round, nine under for the championship and playing one for all his fellow club pros.

Overton grew up in North Carolina, near Pinehurst, and graduated from Campbell College, where he won the NAIA national championship. He turned pro in 1973, got the head job at Pinehurst Country Club in 1977, and left in 1978 to become director of golf at Innisbrook Resort. His playing credentials include winning the North Florida PGA Section championship twice, the Izod International, and in 1979 he was a member of the PGA Cup team.

When Jay was 23 months old, his father, Jimmy, had Sam Snead put a club in his son's hands. What else could he become but a golf professional?

And this was his zenith. One stroke out of the lead in the PGA Championship the day after a professional golfer said the club pros weakened the field.

"I spent most of the day defending him (Gilder) when people asked about his comments," Overton said. "I didn't think they were that bad; there was a lot of truth in them. But when I saw the leaderboard out at 14, I thought about him teeing off and how he'd sure be surprised to see a club pro on top."

Overton wasn't leading when the round was over, but he was close enough that his observation was meaningful. Behind Azinger and Overton came Floyd (68) and Cook (69) at 136; David Graham (67), Dave Rummells (64), Steve Jones (68), Tommy Nakajima (68) and Gary Koch (65) at 137.

While Overton surely was the surprise of the day, he was only a small part of Friday's overall big story:

— There was the continued assault on Oak Tree, which was knocked silly by 35 rounds under 70, including Rummell's course-record 64, and the 65 of Koch. Adding insult was the cut figure. It came at a PGA Championship record low of 144, two over par. There were 10 eagles, nine of them on No. 16, and one hole-in-one, by David Edwards on No. 13.

"I think PGA officials set up the course easier than they could have because they were afraid of high scores," said Doug Tewell, a member of the Oak Tree Gang. "The members here have played it under much tougher conditions. The scores should be low."

"I feel bad for the golf course," said Verplank, who missed the cut. "It's not as easy as it's playing. It's too soft. I could use a little more speed and a little more firmness."

— There was British Open champion Severiano Ballesteros missing the cut. He finally found a shot he couldn't execute, a cut shot over a four-foot high wall while he stood only a couple of feet away from it. That's where Ballesteros found himself after hitting his tee shot over the green at the 149-yard 13th, called the Postage Stamp, for obvious reasons.

After surveying the shot carefully, Ballesterous swung a sharp decending blow. He caught it thin. The ball banged off the rock wall and barely missed hitting him in the head as it sailed past him into the heavy brush.

From there, he played a miraculous shot, like so many he's executed the world over. But it hit a hard spot on the green, bounced over a slight ridge and rolled 25 feet into the heavy fringe. Obviously perturbed by a good pitch gone bad, Ballesteros then chilly-dipped his fourth shot, barely reaching the putting surface.

Still facing the ridge between him and the pin, Ballesteros again chipped, this time within 10 feet and made the putt for six. He went on to shoot 75 and miss the cut by two strokes.

"My pitch landed in the middle of the green, on the left side where you're supposed to hit. I kicked out like a rock," he said. "Things like that are unfair. If I'd known it, I would have played a different shot. I was real surprised."

Ballesteros had opened with a respectable 71 and the last thing he expected was an early exit. "I played very well. Very good putts, they just didn't fall in. I feel my game is very good; it just didn't show up in the score. The 13th, that one killed me."

— There was Jack Nicklaus losing two balls on one hole, the 16th, where he made nine on the way to a 79 and a two-day total of 151. He missed the cut for only the third time in PGA Championships, once in each decade, 1968, 1979 and 1988.

It was the first time as an amateur or professional he had lost two balls in the same round. And he looked like an everyday hacker as he played the innocent-looking 479-yard par-five hole.

"I tried to hit my drive over some trees and blocked it," Nicklaus said. "It went into the hazard and I couldn't find it, so I had to go back and drop another ball. Then I hit a three wood up into the valley and nobody could find that one, either.

"The fans said it hit a tree and dropped out. I said, 'Fine, let's find it,' but we couldn't and I had to go back and play again. By the time I finally got to the green I three-putted for a nine."

— There was the Oak Tree Gang. Only three of their number made the cut and among the missing was Verplank, who in 1984 won the U.S. Amateur at Oak Tree.

For his part, Overton continued to amaze. Few players knew who he was and even fewer spectators and television cameramen.

"As I was walking the last six or seven holes, I could hear people in the gallery saying, 'Which one is he?' And on the 16th hole, there was a cameraman right over the creek in a tower trying to pick up my second shot. Right before I took my swing, I could hear him say to somebody, 'C'mon, give me the color of his shirt. Which one is he? C'mon somebody help me.' He had no idea which one I was."

After shooting three under par Thursday, Overton was more sensational Friday. He made six birdies, on Nos. 1, 2, 6, 8, 10 and 11. His only bogey came at No. 17 where he drove into the greenside bunker and couldn't get up and down for his par.

"To tell you I was trying to score that well would not be the truth. I was just trying to keep the ball in play and good things happened. Now I've finally made the cut in the PGA," he said. "Even if I hit the ball in the water six times on No. 1 Saturday I'm going to be happy."

More puzzling than the showing of Overton was the tameness of Oak Tree. It was like a baited hunting field to this gang of birdie hunters. As Rummells said of his 64, which included two bogeys, "I thought I could shoot in the 50s today. I know we're not seeing Oak Tree at its toughest, but maybe its easiest. If the wind comes up, you'll see the scores get way up there."

Floyd defended the course, saying, "I don't think the scores are that low considering the conditions we have. I think the golf course has stood on its own for two days. If we had these conditions at other places you'd see a lot of 65s and 66s, not the few we've seen here."

Meanwhile, Azinger just kept rolling along. Six birdies, two bogeys Thursday; six birdies, one bogey Friday. He started Friday with an eight-footer at No. 1, made one from 18 feet at No. 3, from two inches at the sixth and from 20 feet at No. 7 to turn in 32. He birdied No. 10 after hitting a pitching wedge to eight feet, bogeyed No. 15 from the front bunker and birdied No. 16 from a foot away.

"The last two days I've been as consistent as I've ever been," Azinger said. "The difference today might have been I was more comfortable with the putter. But the greens are the slowest of any major I've ever played in. My back? I haven't had any trouble swinging, but I really haven't slept that well and that has caused some fatigue late in the round. I did get a little tired today."

Floyd started his round with a bogey and ended it with another. In between, he had birdies at Nos. 2, 6, 7, 12 and 13. "I missed four shots all day, that's all," Floyd said. "With the conditions the way they are, perfect, you have to take advantage of them."

Rummells got off to a flying start. After bogeying his final two holes in a first round 73, the 30-year-old Floridian went on a birdie binge Friday. He had nine of them, including five straight from Nos. 4 through 8. His first of two bogeys was a three-putt from 35 feet at No. 9. After turning in 31, he birdied Nos. 13, 16 and 18 on the back and bogeyed No. 15 after missing the green, only one of two all day.

"I wasn't in a good mood yesterday because I let a pretty good round get away on the last two holes," Rummells said. "Today, I got off to a good start and stayed with it. I tried to stay on an even keel and not get too excited. Used to be if I made four or five in a row, I'd almost run down the fairway."

Koch also made his birdies in bunches. Back-to-back at two and three, 10 and 11 and 15 and 16. Others came at seven and 13. He had bogeys at four and 14.

The cut went deep. Among those who missed it, other than Ballesteros and Nicklaus, were Palmer, 1987 Masters champion Larry Mize, 1987 U.S. Open champion Scott Simpson, Lee Trevino, Gil Morgan, Bernhard Langer and Mac O'Grady, who left with these words, "I have nothing to say about this place. I wish it didn't exist."

The leaders after the second round:

Paul Azinger	67-66—133	Nick Faldo	67-71—138
Jay Overton	68-66—134	Doug Tewell	70-68—138
Ray Floyd	68-68—136	Chip Beck	67-72—139
John Cook	67-69—136	Greg Norman	68-71—139
David Graham	70-67—137	Mike Reid	68-71—139
Dave Rummells	73-64—137	Jeff Sluman	69-70—139
Steve Jones	69-68—137	Payne Stewart	70-69—139
Tommy Nakajima	69-68—137	Dave Stockton	70-69—139
Gary Koch	72-65—137		

As sure as God made little green apples, you had to know two things would occur before the PGA Championship ended. One, that club pro Jay Overton wouldn't shoot under par every day, and two, that the Oklahoma wind would blow and scores would soar.

They both occurred on the same day, Saturday's third round.

Paired with Azinger in the final group, Overton finally reached his comfort zone. After making just three bogeys and standing at eight under par after 36 holes, he had six bogeys Saturday, shot 76 and fell into a tie for eighth at 210, six strokes behind Azinger, who had 71 and continued to lead.

Rummells moved to within a stroke of Azinger with a 68, while Sluman made his first notable presence in this championship with a 68 to stand third, just three back. Nick Faldo (70) was fourth and tied for fifth were Kenny Knox (68), Steve Jones (72) and Payne Stewart (70). Still within sight of the leaders were a group of six at 210, six behind, Dan Pohl (70), Crenshaw (69), Mark McNulty (67), David Graham (73), Floyd (74) and Overton.

There also were non-survivors. After hanging close for two days, Cook shot 76 and fell eight back. And the one who fell the farthest was Hubert Green. He started the day at 143, shot an 83 and withdrew. He double-bogeyed the first three holes, birdied the fifth, bogeyed six and seven and turned in 43. He then bogeyed Nos. 12 and 14, double-bogeyed No. 15, birdied No. 16 and double-bogeyed No. 17 for a back-nine 40.

Blame it on the wind. Non-existant the first two rounds when 74 sub-par scores were reported, it blew a steady 12-14 miles per hour and gusted as high as 25. As a result, only seven players broke 70 and just 10 others matched it.

"It was like we were on a different golf course today," Azinger said. "What's tough about this wind is that it's a crosswind on a lot of tee shots. I felt uneasy most of the time on the tee today."

"You had to be more conscious of it today," said Knox, who was six under on his round through 10 holes, had a double-bogey, bogey finish for 68. "The course is definitely harder than it was the first two days and now we're getting the scores we anticipated. I really let a good one get away there at the end."

After solid starts the first two rounds, Azinger got off a little shaky Saturday, scrambling for pars on the first two holes with putts of six and 20 feet. He settled down with a routine par at the third. Then came the shot heard all over the golf course.

Azinger pulled out a six iron on the downwind 200-yard par-three fourth. His shot hit the green, took two bounces and went into the cup. Azinger threw his right fist in the air, tossed his visor toward the heavens and slammed the club back into the bag.

At that point he led by four shots.

"That was the single most exhilarating experience of my life, except when my daughter was born," Azinger said. "I'd never gotten a roar like that. It was a Jack Nicklaus or Arnold Palmer-type cheer."

It was the second ace of the day. About 30 minutes earlier, Floyd holed out on the 171-yard eighth. But it didn't help him much. He shot 74 and fell six behind the leader.

What Azinger had taken from the course at No. 4, he gave back on No. 5, making double-bogey seven. A layup two-iron shot intended for the front bunker got away from him, hit the cart path and bounced into the lake. "I had 270 yards to the hole and I was just trying to hit it up there in the bunker. I guess I came off the shot. It was stupid," Azinger said. "There was no excuse for that. But I didn't hit a lot of shots good today. I was lucky to shoot 71."

Azinger bogeyed the ninth, missing a four-foot par putt, scrambled to save pars at Nos. 11 and 12, then made his first birdie of the day at No. 13 with a seven-foot putt. He missed great chances at Nos. 15 and 16 to put some distance between himself and the field.

"I really hit two good shots on those holes," Azinger said. "At 15, I had a five-foot putt for birdie and missed it, and at 16, I hit a five iron and had it seven feet for eagle and missed that. I was quite surprised at the speed of the greens; they were much quicker today and it took a lot of adjusting on my part. I felt I had to be more defensive and that sometimes hurts other parts of my game. Like at 18. I hit a terrible drive — I hit a lot of suspect tee shots today — into the right woods, hit a four-iron shot and made a poor pitch. Bogey. Not a good way to end your round."

Overton was over par and out of contention early, making bogeys on three of the first five holes. Still, he had a blast.

"Playing in the last twosome in a major championship isn't something that happens all the time," he said. "This is a one-in-a-million thing for a club pro or amateur, and I thoroughly enjoyed myself. I was surprised at how relaxed I was. I wasn't thinking, 'Golly gee, I hope I don't mess up.' Today the course played a little tougher with the wind. I got caught two or three times by gusts, and I didn't make any putts."

Though he had previously witnessed a hole-in-one in competition, Overton said the ace by Azinger was incredible, considering everything.

"Everyone went so crazy it was deafening in that little corridor of the course," he said. "It took such a long time for things to settle down. I told Paul it was a great shot, and I think I made the statement that he'd go on and win the tournament. That shot just opened the door for him."

For the second straight day, Rummells had the hot hand. After shooting his course-record 64 on Friday, the 30-year old non-winner described his game this way. "I can usually tell on the driving range if I'm going to play well. And if I don't make a putt the first five holes I'm usually done for the day. A lot of guys out here are mechanical. I'm just the opposite. I play on feel and confidence. If I get off to a good start, I feel like I'll get it close on every hole."

He had that feel again in round No. 3. He birdied the first hole from two feet, chipped in for another birdie at No. 8 and made a 50-foot birdie putt at No. 9.

"It was a totally different golf course today. It was a monster. I felt like I was working 12 hours out there. I didn't look at the leaderboard much," Rummells said. "It wasn't a day to let your mind wander. I didn't make that many birdies, but nobody else did either. But I still feel like I'm hitting the ball solid. Now, I hope the wind blows 80 miles an hour Sunday because the harder it blows, the better my chances. If I get out early tomorrow and make a few birdies, it should put some pressure on Paul. Even though I'm two shots back, I feel good about my chances because I know I can make a lot of birdies."

Azinger has been in this position before in a major. He led the 1987 British Open after 54 holes but let it get away in the final round with bogeys on the final two holes and Faldo won with 18 straight pars. "If I don't win tomorrow it more than likely will not be because I succumbed to the pressure," he said. "I felt I handled it pretty good in the British Open, but yes, I gave it away."

Sluman, also a non-winner on the PGA Tour, had been solid and consistent for three days with rounds of 69-70-68. Saturday, however, he had to scramble for what he got. He missed eight greens, but saved par six times, at No. 1 from 10 feet, at six and seven from a foot, at Nos. 11 and 12 from two feet and at No. 18 from three feet.

He had five birdies, at Nos. 2, 3, 10, 14 and 16. His bogeys came at nine and 17.

Despite his steady climb up the leaderboard, the 5-7, 135-pound Sluman was getting little attention. But, then, he doesn't expect it or let it bother him.

"I'm not going to be a Greg Norman or Jack Nicklaus," he said. "All I can do is play my own game and if I do that, I have a chance. Today I tried not to worry too much about what was going on around me. It took a lot of concentration because of the wind. About Sunday? Paul will be tough to catch, he's a great player. He's proven he can win and he's been through the pressure of major championships. That should help him."

Sluman said his home-away-from-home this week had been a factor in his play. He stayed with Willie Wood and his wife Holly, who live across the street at Oak Tree Country Club.

"Sure beats looking at four walls in a hotel room," Sluman said. "Holly's a great cook and Willie's one of the nicest guys I've ever met."

Prior to Saturday's round, Wood stepped outside, judged the wind and offered Sluman some advice on how to play the course. Wood wasn't playing in the tournament, having failed to qualify. But he knows it as well as anyone and better than most.

"Willie told me certain holes would play downwind a little more than I thought they would, and he was right," Sluman said. "I'd have to give him an assist today."

The leaders after the third round:

Paul Azinger	67-66-71—204
Dave Rummells	73-64-68—205
Jeff Sluman	69-70-68—207
Nick Faldo	67-71-70—208
Kenny Knox	72-69-68—209
Steve Jones	69-68-72—209
Payne Stewart	70-69-70—209
Jay Overton	68-66-76—210
David Graham	70-67-73—210
Ben Crenshaw	70-71-69—210
Ray Floyd	68-68-74—210
Mark McNulty	73-70-67—210
Dan Pohl	69-71-70—210

With his final-round 65, Sluman completed 72 holes around Oak Tree in 272 strokes, 12 under par and picked up the $160,000 winner's share of the $1 million purse.

"I think Jeff Sluman probably played one of the best final rounds in a major championship," said a dejected Azinger. "There are a lot of nervous moments on this golf course. There are a lot of places to make double bogeys. But he never made a bad shot. When you give a tournament away, it nags at you. But when somebody snatches it away, there's nothing you can do."

Azinger teed off one stroke in front of Rummells and had Sluman by three. All looked in order for this lanky Floridian when he birdied the first hole, especially after Rummells made bogey there, another one at No. 2. He wasn't to be heard from again, finishing with 75. Azinger was hardly charging, waiting for others to make the mistakes. It was good strategy for four holes. It was to be No. 5 that proved to be Azinger's undoing. It is a 590-yard, par-five, not easy, but hardly one of those to toss and turn over. Good drive, layup, wedge and a birdie possibility. Azinger played this hole four over, Sluman two under.

Pivotable? You bet. Six shots usually are.

Sunday, down by three, Sluman holed out a 115-yard wedge shot for eagle-three. Azinger later bogeyed it. The momentum and the moment were no longer his. He bogeyed the sixth and never sniffed the lead again.

"That hole was my nemesis," Azinger said. "I never could figure out how to play it and as it turned out it cost me the championship."

It wasn't until the seventh hole, however, that Azinger knew he was behind. He looked at the leaderboard thinking he was one in front and discovered he was two behind, which seems strange considering Sluman was playing just in front of him.

Azinger now was chasing the man, who, with every hole became more in control, while he became more tentative. He followed his bogey at No. 5 with a three-putt bogey at six, where just in front of him Sluman had made par. At the seventh, Sluman made a 10-footer to go up by two. Azinger hit his approach inside 10 feet, but tried to coax it into the hole and missed.

"I hit a very tentative putt, thinking I still had a one-shot lead," Azinger said. "I remember going over to my bag and wondering if I ought to take a look at the scoreboard. When I looked up, it was kind of a shock. He's 10 under, I'm eight under, two behind when I thought I was one ahead.

"It's amazing how much different I felt at that moment. It's hard to help it, but you hit tentative shots when ahead. As soon as I found out I was behind, I felt like I could swing again. It really changed my frame of mind."

But it was too late. Sluman was gone. He birdied No. 10 to go up three, birdied No. 12 to lead by four, lost a shot with a bogey at No. 13, then in all likelihood buried Azinger and raised himself on the 14th. A probable three-putt bogey stared him square in the face. Instead he made a 15-foot par putt and followed that with a birdie on No. 15. That sealed it.

"After No. 5, I didn't look at the scoreboard until No. 15," Sluman said. "When I saw I had a four-shot lead, I felt in control of the tournament. The mind does funny things to you, but I felt comfortable."

Behind him, Azinger was doing all he could do. But he had too far to go and not enough holes to get there. The back nine at Oak Tree isn't the place to make up strokes if the fellow you're chasing has his game on cruise control. He birdied No. 16, then hit the pin at the par-three 17th, his ball stopping three inches away. Ever so close to a hole-in-one, but he had to settle for a two. It was dramatic, but is wasn't enough. He needed a three at No. 18 to tie and made five.

"I thought as nervous as he must be, he could make a mistake," Azinger said. "I felt if I could just stay close enough, as hard as those finishing holes are, something might happen to him. To be honest with you, I didn't expect Jeff to shoot 65. Even when he was five under, I didn't think he could keep going. But in all honesty, I didn't hit enough good shots to win. When I'm playing my best, I hit the ball pin high. I didn't do that today.

"This is the hardest course I've ever played under pressure. There are a lot of nervous holes out there; every tee shot, wedge shot. But Jeff just never, never hit a bad shot. He never made a mistake."

Rummells couldn't make anything but mistakes. His game plan was to get off to a fast start. Instead he went into reverse. He bogeyed the first two holes, missing short par putts, and his confidence was shot.

"Sometimes I get discouraged and start getting down on myself," Rummells said. "That's what happened today. My caddy tried to help get me back up, but nothing worked. I told you guys that for me to play well I had to hit a lot of greens, like 15 or 16. Today, I hit 11."

Rummells denied the pressure of being in contention was partly responsible. "I didn't feel nervous at all. I had no reason to be nervous. Honestly, except for the front nine Friday I really haven't played that well this week."

Then Rummells paid tribute to the champion. "Jeff just played too well. Nobody lost it. He won it. Anybody who plays that well on the last day deserves to win. I knew when he started playing well he was going to be tough to beat. Jeff doesn't get much publicity, but he's one of the best players out here and when he gets his swing in a groove, watch out."

With the victory, Sluman became the first player making a major his first PGA Tour victory since Jerry Pate at the 1976 U.S. Open, and Pate was ABC's roving reporter for Sluman's last-round pairing with Faldo.

Speaking of Faldo, he made a momentary dash at the championship when a birdie at No. 11 moved him to within four strokes. But he bogeyed the next and the last two, missed four short putts, and finally settled into a tie for fourth with Tom Kite. "This putter won't be flying first class on the way home," Faldo said.

Tommy Nakajima charged with a final round of 67 to end at six under par and claim third, but he never was closer than six strokes from the lead.

And what of the Oak Tree Gang? So much for the home advantage. David Edwards finished as the top Oak Tree Boy with a 72-hole total of 285, tying five others for 25th place. Tway began the day at one under but shot 77 and tied for 48th. Magee placed 69th and Tewell was 70th.

The other order of business was that of Overton and Gilder. After playing so well the first two rounds then fading in the third, Overton closed out with a 74 to finish at even-par 284. Gilder rallied from that disastrous second round 75 to shoot 71-68 and tie for sixth with Rummells.

When Sluman went to bed Saturday night, he thought he had a chance because nobody gave him a chance. The pressure was on Azinger to hold what he had. Sluman could go for the gold.

"I just wanted to get off to a good solid start and get it under par and try to put some pressure on Paul," Sluman said. "He can be tough if you let him sail along with a three or four-shot lead. I wanted to let him know I was out there, and the sooner the better.

"As soon as I hit the wedge shot at five, I knew it was going to be close. When it went in, it was the first time in 95-degree heat that I've had chills all up and down my body. All day long, I thought if I could get it to nine or 10 under I might have a chance."

And Sluman was in some pretty good company, being penciled in alongside this year's major championship winners, Lyle, Strange, and Ballesteros.

"It makes me feel pretty good to be in with that group," Sluman said. "Anytime you win a major it's a great tournament to win. I can't imagine how Jack Nicklaus feels with 20 of them. If he felt like this 20 times, he's very up in life. I guess I proved I can play on the weekend, huh?

That last remark was in reference to the critics who wondered if Sluman had what it takes to get it to the house. Earlier in the year, he had led in Greensboro after two rounds with a blistering 15-under par 129, but shot 144 on the weekend. Seven weeks later, he started the final round leading the Byron Nelson Classic, then went up in smoke with a 76 and finished tied for 13th.

The PGA Tour statistics told it all. Before that cut, Sluman's scoring average of 70.23 ranked fourth; his third round average of 71.5 was 112th and fourth round 71.90 was 106th best. Few doubted his ability to play, but many questioned his staying power.

No more. His final two rounds of 68-65, nine under par, was five shots better than the next best of Kite, who finished 71-67.

"You can look at it a lot of different ways," Sluman said, "but now the pressure is off. It's a pretty good feeling. Maybe this is the one folks will remember."

Then Sluman was off for his victory celebration and also to say a thank-you to his hosts for the week, the Woods.

So what kind of celebration did the new PGA championship have in mind?

"Oh, I guess we'll have a couple of beers with Willie and Holly and maybe I'll even get a chance to change one of their kids' diapers."

7. The World Match Play Championship

One of the charms of anniversaries is that they compel us to look back and reflect. And so it was with the 1988 Suntory World Match Play Championship. The event was celebrating its 25th birthday. Who could resist recalling the inaugural in 1964? Fittingly, it was won by the most dynamic figure of the day, perhaps the most dynamic of all time, Arnold Palmer. What an electrifying introduction. Palmer met Gary Player in the semifinal, and started like dynamite — eagle, par, birdie, birdie, birdie, birdie — and was five up after six holes. Palmer won, 8 and 6. The championship match was not so simple. Palmer's opponent was the redoubtable Neil Coles. Before a swarming crowd, Palmer had a bulldog by the tail. Palmer was two up after the first nine, and if a repeat of the Player defeat seemed imminent, Coles was having none of it. Coles got those two back, and two others for good measure, and was two up at lunch, and three up through 21 holes. But Palmer hauled himself together, chipped in twice from off the green, and holed a clutch birdie putt to win on the 35th hole. It was the first of his two titles.

It seemed odd that through the first 23 years, the British, noted for their devotion to match play, couldn't crack this tournament. They finally did it in 1987, when Ian Woosnam broke through. And 1988 would guarantee another Briton on the winner's stand. It was an all-British final, Sandy Lyle against Nick Faldo. Over the years, Lyle had carried the battle like no Briton had. After Coles in 1964, no Briton even reached the final for 16 years until Lyle, in 1980. He was runner-up that year, and runner-up three other times — 1982, and 1986 and 1987. That's called knocking on the door. This time Lyle, the Masters champion, kicked it in for his fifth victory of the year, and he beat an all-star cast doing it. His victims: Nick Price, British Open runner-up; Seve Ballesteros, British Open champion, and Faldo, U.S. Open runner-up. Few victories were so richly deserved and so authoritatively taken.

The World Match Play week began under a storm very different from the one that ripped Wentworth and much of England during the 1987 tournament. This one came from the press. The principal target was the American contingent, described by one newspaper as "(Jeff) Sluman and his equally anonymous colleagues, Mark McCumber and Joey Sindelar." Curtis Strange, the U.S. Open champion and the sharpest American golfer of the moment, turned down his Match Play invitation because of other commitments. The papers brooded about this. One offered that the absence of a magnetic American character on the order of Ballesteros "is threatening the whole future of the World Match Play event." Lyle's performance soon enough lifted those clouds.

For the first time in the World Match Play's 25 years, all four seeds were Europeans — Lyle, Ballesteros, Woosnam, and Faldo. But one thing drew flak from Lyle. Sluman, in August, had won the American PGA, his first professional victory. Lyle figured it was "degrading" for the PGA champion not to be seeded. Sluman shrugged off the issue. "I'm here," he said. "I guess I should be happy just to be invited. It just means I'll have to play four rounds instead of three to win. But it's nice that Sandy has had so many nice things to say about me." Faldo, it developed, was seeded off his higher position on the Sony Ranking, No. 4 to Sluman's No. 36. In addition, Faldo also had played well in all four major championships, especially the U.S. Open, where he was runner-up to Strange in a playoff.

Like the press, Woosnam also was not impressed with the American field. In addition to PGA champion Sluman, there were Sindelar, a two-time winner, and McCumber, who had won the American tour's flagship event, The Players Championship. "Forget the Americans," Woosnam said. "I rate Sandy Lyle, Seve Ballesteros, Nick Faldo, and myself as the hot favorites. It's no secret that I love to see the Americans get beaten. They dominated the game for so long, but that's all over now." The record book was on his side. In the World Match Play, the last American to win was Bill Rogers, in 1979.

Woosnam, who won eight times and amassed more than $1.8 million in 1987, was the comeback player of 1988. "Everybody was writing me off as a one-season wonder when things went wrong early on," he said. "But I bounced back to win the Volvo PGA Championship here in May and Carroll's Irish Open in August."

Ballesteros arrived as a bit of damaged goods, thanks to a bicycle accident. He could chuckle about it now, this thing that might have been a career-threatening incident. It happened the previous Friday, when he was riding for exercise at his home, at Pedrena, Spain. "I was going uphill and I changed gears," he said. "Two seconds later, something went wrong at the back and the bike wobbled and I fell sideways. I landed on my left hip and arm, and I thought at first that I had broken my arm." Fortunately, he came away with nothing more than pain and stiffness, and a hip he described as all "black, blue, and yellow." The matter ended right then and there at his pre-tournament interview. "I played 18 holes on Sunday and on Monday, and with no ill effects," he said.

He turned his attention to the World Match Play, and his chances for a fifth title. "It will be very difficult, but I will try my best," Ballesteros said. "Whether I will get the chance to meet Ian Woosnam again and get my revenge for last year's defeat, we will have to wait and see. I will take it one step at a time. But it would be nice to equal Gary Player's record." He didn't meet Woosnam again, and he didn't match Player with a fifth championship. And he did not blame the cycling accident. He did produce, however, a remarkable round in his first outing, against Mark McCumber. It was a bewildering display, alternating between weekend hacker and absolute genius.

The other four members of the 12-man field were Zimbabwe's Mark McNulty, who played in 1987, and Australia's Rodger Davis (1986), and two newcomers. These were Barry Lane, the promising young Englishman who won his first tournament in July, Bell's Scottish Open, and Japan's Nobuo Serizawa. Serizawa, approaching his 29th birthday, opted for a World Match Play berth rather than play in the Japan Open the same week. He was a two-time winner in Japan in 1987, taking the Nikkei Cup and the ACOM Doubles, and was runner-up in the Bridgestone tournament.

Lane, a heavy hitter, had discovered what so many before him had learned. He had geared back on the power, the better to keep the ball in play. But he'd been having his troubles. "I haven't been playing well lately," he said. "It was a lack of form, mainly because I was playing too much. But it's better now. I took last week off, and started playing again on Friday, I'm hitting the ball better." Well enough to beat Lyle in a practice round. "We weren't playing all that seriously," Lane said. "But I beat him 4 and 3, and I took the money anyhow."

With that, the pre-tournament chatter and speculation was over. It was time to tee it up.

Oddly enough, the same press that was bemoaning the fate of the World Match Play because of the weakness of the American contingent suddenly was proclaiming the dawn of a new age for the Americans. "Woosnam has to match his word with a big deed," one headline shouted, recalling his grim prediction. "Sindelar leads America out of the shadows," said another. And so it went. What caused this sudden warming trend was an American sweep in the first round. All three came through — Sluman, Sindelar and McCumber, along with Zimbabwean Nick Price. It seemed that the press, which had shown contempt for American golf, actually was happy to see it alive and well. But no one could have been happier than the Americans themselves.

The first round was greeted by typical British weather. It was chilly, with a buffeting wind all day. And the course was heavy from a brisk rain that had forced a delay of about an hour. Sluman was first out, against Serizawa.

Sluman had played a college event at St. Andrews in 1977, but he counted the World Match Play as his first real outing in Britain. It was a smashing debut, a 6 and 5 victory over Serizawa. Neither could get more than a one-hole lead through the first 10 holes, and Serizawa squared the match at the 11th with a birdie-three from eight feet. Then they parted company for good. Serizawa drove into the trees at No. 12, and Sluman went one up with par five. Serizawa, beginning to look nervous, drove into the trees again at No. 15, took a penalty drop and three more strokes to reach the green, where Sluman lay two. He conceded the hole. Sluman then birdied No. 17 with two putts from a huge 80 feet, and added another birdie at No. 18 on two putts from 15 feet after Serizawa caught the trees again for the third time in the morning round. Sluman had a four-hole cushion for the afternoon.

Golf is such a maddening game. Barry Lane figured he was playing much better. Suddenly, he wasn't. He fell hard to Sindelar, 5 and 4. But he may have logged a dubious distinction shared by no one else in World Match Play history — his comeback was stopped short by a raincoat.

It happened in the afternoon. Lane was rallying. In a span of seven holes, he had whacked his deficit from a huge seven down to just three with seven to play. Then at No. 12, his one-iron second got slightly away from him and ended up in the flap of a spectator's raincoat. "I asked him," Lane joked later, "if he would mind walking onto the green and dropping the ball, but he declined." Lane got a free drop, of course, but his ball came to rest in a heel print. "I just couldn't make good contact because of the way the ball was lying," he said. "Such a pity, because I felt I was coming back into the game. I started to play well in the afternoon, but it was all too late."

His wedge shot out of the heel print went zipping nearly 30 feet past the flag, and he two-putted for his par five. Sindelar jumped on the opportunity. He pulled the surging Lane up short as through he were reining in a frisky horse, holing an eight-footer for a birdie. He was now four up. The disappointed

Lane then bogeyed No. 13 with two putts from 15 feet, and Sindelar closed him out with a half in par threes at No. 14.

McCumber was on a runaway against McNulty, then came a little undone in the afternoon and had to birdie the last three holes to escape with a one-hole victory. McNulty, who made the 1988 Cannes Open the seventh European tour victory of his career, took the early lead with two strong birdies. A wedge to three feet at the fourth and a 25-foot putt at the sixth staked him to a two-hole lead through the turn in the morning. He dropped the 10th, missing the green with his tee shot. Then before he knew what hit him, he was three down.

McCumber, a bold player capable of exciting streaks, burst into the lead with a thrilling save and four consecutive winners. First, he shocked McNulty at the par-four 11th, where he had to wedge his errant tee shot out of the trees, was short with his next, then holed a pitch from 75 feet for his halving par. At No. 13, McNulty, after a penalty drop, reached the green in four. McCumber won it with a par and the match was square. McCumber turned deadly on the greens, holing birdie putts of 45 and 35 feet to win the 14th and 15th, then went three up at No. 16 with a wedge to 18 inches for a par to McNulty's three-putt bogey. They halved the last two holes in birdies, and McCumber enjoyed a three-up lead at lunch. But he knew McNulty too well to believe it was anywhere near over, and he was right.

McCumber couldn't maintain the pace in the afternoon, but he was fairly steady for a while. He lost the third on a bogey, regained a three-up lead with a birdie at the fourth, and went through the turn two up after losing the ninth on a two-putt bogey — his third bogey on the outward nine. Five holes later, he was trailing. McNulty birdied the 12th from nine feet, squared the match at the 13th on McCumber's bogey, and went ahead by one at the par-three 14th with a three-foot birdie putt after a splendid five-iron tee shot. But he couldn't hold on. He drove into the trees at the 15th, put his second into a ditch and needed a penalty drop to get out. McCumber squared the match with a routine par-four. Now came the decisive holes.

The streaky McCumber ran off three consecutive birdies. The first of them proved to be the winner against McNulty's par-birdie-birdie finish. "My happiest hole," McCumber said, "was No. 16. I hit a wedge to four feet for a birdie, and he two-putted." The birdie put him one up with two to play. They had to play both. "At No. 17, I had a 66-foot putt and lagged it to one foot," McCumber said. "He tried for an eagle and ran three feet by. But he made it." They halved in birdies. McNulty made one final stab at the 18th, pitching softly to eight feet and getting his birdie. But McCumber, after driving into the right rough, ended up pitching to about four feet, and followed him in for a birdie and the win.

Just ahead of them, Nick Price and Rodger Davis had hooked up in the oddest match of the day. Except for Davis's bogey at the sixth, they halved relentlessly in pars through the 11th in the morning. "One of us needed to take the bull by the horns and get something going," Price said. He took his own advice. He came smashing to the front, playing the last seven holes in four under par on an eagle, three birdies, and a bogey while Davis continued to run off pars the rest of the way. Price struck hard at the par-five 12th, sticking a one-iron approach to three feet and holing for an eagle. He followed that up with a six-iron to six feet and a birdie at No. 13 to go three up.

He gave back a hole with a three-putt bogey at No. 15, then birdied both closing par-fives — a sand wedge to two feet at No. 17, and two putts from 40 feet at No. 18. His four-up morning lead was comforting, but hardly safe.

Price dropped the first hole in the afternoon, then fortunately for him, Davis turned sour at the same time he did. They halved the third and fourth awkwardly, in bogeys. At No. 3, Davis topped his three-wood second, and had to make a 25-foot putt for his five while Price two-putted from nine feet. At No. 4, both took penalty drops, Davis from the trees on his drive, Price out of water after his second. They exchanged winning birdies at the sixth and seventh, then Price's lead was down to two through the turn on a bogey at No. 9. The struggle, it turned out, was just getting started.

Davis gave the hole back with a bogey at the 11th, and they halved the 12th in birdies, both men pitching to one foot. Now Davis finally came to life. He cut Price's lead to two holes with a birdie at No. 15 on a nine-foot birdie putt, and Price gave him another when he three-putted the 16th for a bogey. Price's lead was down to one. He couldn't wait much longer. The difference was what Price called "my best shot of the day" — a three-wood second at No. 17 that covered 270 yards and just missed the green to the left. He pitched to five feet. Davis missed his birdie try. Price didn't. It was Price, 2 and 1. On to the second round, and the coming-out party of the four seeds.

Woosnam knew what he was talking about — no American would win the 1988 World Match Play. The four seeded Europeans moved into action in the second round, and the Americans moved out: Woosnam crushed Jeff Sluman, 7 and 6; Nick Faldo did likewise to Joey Sindelar, 5 and 4; Sandy Lyle made an inspired comeback and ousted Nick Price, 3 and 2, and in a weird match, Seve Ballesteros came back from the dead and beat Mark McCumber on the 37th hole in a real battle. It wasn't pretty, but it was breathtaking. It was Ballesteros at his bull-fighting best.

The day was cool, mostly sunny under big rolling clouds, and battered by winds that sent trees whipping and made each golf shot an adventure. Americans rarely see winds of such power and duration. Or, as Sluman put it out on the course, "I'll be glad to get out of the wind." Said Woosnam, "That's what it's like here." Discomfort aside, Sluman didn't blame the wind. "He didn't putt too well, morning or afternoon," Woosnam said. "This afternoon, he lost Nos. 10 and 11 by three-putting, and that was pretty well the end of it."

Woosnam closed Sluman out with a birdie from 11 feet at the 12th in the afternoon. Sluman led only once, and that was at the very first hole. Despite his lack of power, he conquered the 471-yard brute dead into the heavy wind with a driver, three wood, and a 12-foot birdie putt. Woosnam squared the match with a birdie-two at the second, and the march was on. While Sluman was putting his way into an early trip home, Woosnam was building himself a comfortable cushion. He lost only four holes on over-par scores — three bogeys and his worst hole of the day, a double-bogey six at No. 15 in the morning, where he two-putted from three feet. He was three up at lunch time.

"I am playing pretty well," Woosnam said. "I hit a couple of bad shots, but I hit some balls in between and discovered why I was hitting them to the right. I was aiming to the right with my feet and aiming straight with the clubface." Once he got his sights adjusted, he was on his way. Woosnam had four birdies in the outward nine in the morning, and returned a three-under-par 69 to Sluman's 71. All told, Woosnam had 10 birdies for the day, three of them in the afternoon when Sluman self-destructed with five bogeys and a double bogey in the 12 holes. Woosnam was riding high. He was set for a new challenge, the man he beat one-up in the second round in 1987. "If I meet Faldo tomorrow," Woosnam said, "he will be trying to get his revenge. But I will have something to say about that."

Faldo it would be. In the match behind Woosnam's, Faldo was dismissing Sindelar with cool efficiency. He never trailed. He was never worse off than all-square, and then only for an eye-blink. Sindelar caught him with a 36-foot birdie putt at No. 8 in the morning, then slipped immediately. At the ninth, he drove into the trees and bogeyed. Faldo bumped his lead to two holes with a birdie from 25 feet at No. 12, then to three when Sindelar bogeyed No. 15 after catching a bunker. Faldo was his consistent self, with a three-birdie, one-bogey 70 to Sindelar's 73, and led by three holes at lunch.

It was hardly a promising picture for Sindelar. He was struggling just to bring his game under control in the stiff winds. He got a straw to cling to at the third, but he failed to take advantage of it. Faldo hit his second into a greenside bunker. Now the green was open. But Sindelar was short with his approach, and they halved in two-putt bogey-fives. Faldo went five up at No. 4 on an eagle against Sindelar's birdie. Heading into the final turn, Sindelar got two holes back on a 25-foot birdie at No. 8 and Faldo's bogey out of a bunker at No. 9. Then the bottom fell out of his comeback on three-putt bogeys at No. 13 and No. 14. He had three-putted four times in the day. The 5-and-4 victory sent Faldo into the semifinals against Woosnam the next day. It would be a duel of two men who had hugged each other as Ryder Cup champions a year earlier. But the Ryder Cup was long time ago.

So was Woosnam's one-up victory over Faldo in the 1987 World Match Play. "It didn't leave any scars," Faldo said. "I'll take 10 under again, like I shot last year against him to his eight under — and lost."

The attention turned to Sandy Lyle. "Today," he said, "I was in reverse for a while." The man can really shift gears, though. Who can forget the 1982 World Match Play, when he was six down to Faldo at lunch and came back to win. This time, he was a mere three down to Nick Price with 12 holes to play.

Lyle birdied the first and Price squared the match with a tap-in birdie at the fourth after a great bunker shot. Price then exploded for three straight birdies from the seventh. The first two put him two ahead — a 12-foot at No. 7 and a 27-footer at No. 8. He chipped in from 35 feet at No. 9, and Lyle matched him with a 30-foot putt. Price was two up at the turn.

Then just as abruptly, they were all-square again. Price missed the 10th green and bogeyed, and Lyle squared the match at No. 11 with a birdie from nine feet. They were riding a seesaw now. Lyle went one ahead with a birdie at No. 13, then staggered to three consecutive losing bogeys from the 14th. Price, making three pars, found himself two ahead, and that's how they stood at lunch.

Lyle was thinking it couldn't get any worse, but it did. He crashed at the first three holes in the afternoon. "I couldn't believe such a bad start," he said. Who could? Trees at the first, bogey; three putts from 15 feet at the second, double bogey; a bunker at the third, bogey. Price said thank you, parred steadily along, and was five up through No. 3. Then another of golf's mysteries unfolded: They switched roles.

Over the next 13 holes, Lyle made five birdies and no bogeys while Price suffered three bogeys and a double bogey. Lyle had stopped the bleeding of that disastrous start with a two-putt birdie at No. 4. He was four down. Price gave a hole back at No. 6, three-putting from 28 feet. "That's when things started to change," Lyle said. At the seventh, he birdied from 35 feet. Two down. And at the ninth, Price bunkered his second shot and double-bogeyed. One down. Lyle didn't waste the opportunity. He squared the match at No. 10, with a birdie-two from four feet. "Nick started to hit a few scattered shots, and he was losing his rhythm," Lyle said. Two holes later, at the 12th, Lyle was in the lead for the first time in 17 holes when Price had to take a penalty drop after driving into the trees. It cost him a bogey-six. Lyle upped his lead to two holes at No. 13, firing an effortless combination of one iron and a great six iron — "a banana hook, my best shot of the day" — to 10 feet. He dropped the birdie putt. Both men faced discouraging putts in the 70-foot range at the 15th. Lyle got down in two for a winning par and a three-up lead. It ended at the 16th, with a half in birdies. Lyle did it in style, holing from 20 feet to end one of the great comebacks in World Match Play history.

"I just whittled away at his lead, and he lost a bit of his composure," Lyle said. "Just one of those things."

The final match of the day was the most thrilling — Seve Ballesteros beating Mark McCumber on the 37th hole. It seems a contradiction in terms to say that Ballesteros was both awful and brilliant. But this was Ballesteros. He was four down through the first round, three down with eight to play. But it wasn't his comeback. There have been greater. No, in this case it was because Ballesteros was cast in the role of Indiana Jones, the American movie hero who escapes one frightful peril after another. McCumber was playing well enough to win. But Ballesteros was playing some other game. The morning round was merely an appetizer.

"I did not play very well the whole day," Ballesteros said. "The match was in McCumber's hands." Ballesteros led just twice — at the first, on McCumber's bogey, and at the 37th, where he won. McCumber's putter was working well. Overworking might be the better word. He was giving it too much to do with his approaches. Two examples: At No. 12, he went to three-up with a birdie, but he had to two-putt from 90 feet to do it. At No. 17, he had to cover 75 feet in two putts to save a half in birdies. He was four up at lunch. But he soon would pay dearly for those weak approaches.

It seemed inconsequential at the time, but McCumber made the first mistake of the afternoon when he tried to reach the first green with a driver out of the rough, hitting dead into a heavy wind. The ball came down in the hollow about 100 yards short of the green. He punched a low approach under the wind, but 45 feet short of the hole. Ballesteros, meanwhile, had hit a colossal drive off the fairway and finished 70 feet from the hole. Both men two-putted. Ballesteros won the hole with the par.

Now Indiana Jones made his first appearance of the afternoon. At No. 3, Ballesteros hooked his tee shot beyond the left gallery ropes. His only chance to reach the green was with a wood shot from the heavy grass that had to skirt the trees on the left by inches. He did it. Two putts from 90 feet matched McCumber's par for a half. McCumber's lead fell to two when he bunkered his approach at No. 4. But Ballesteros was nothing if not generous. He four-putted the sixth from 60 feet, and McCumber was back to three up. Then came No. 7, and it was here that Ballesteros authored a shot that belongs in a hall of fame. The pity was that so few could get close enough to see it.

Wentworth's seventh is a downhill-uphill par four of 399 yards, with a little creek bisecting the fairway at the shelf at the bottom of the hill. McCumber played the hole beautifully — a tee shot down to the shelf, a seven iron up to the green, to nine feet. Ballesteros hooked his drive horribly into a dense little stand of trees just short of the creek. His situation was hopeless. His ball lay on some dry twigs just inches from a fallen tree in front of him. Behind him stood two slender trees that he could clear by just inches with his swing. And 15 feet in front of him, where the trees opened onto the fairway, a leafy branch hung head-high, right in his line of flight. The only sane shot was a chip back to the fairway about 30 yards away. But Ballesteros took his seven-iron, and stood up to the ball. The spectators were stunned. When Ballesteros addressed the ball, the green was well over his left shoulder. He slashed mightily, and hit a phenominal hook.

Some fans drifted in and silently reconstructed the shot. "He hit *that* from *there*?" one man said. "That was the greatest shot I've ever seen!" Ballesteros was unimpressed. "Too much hook," he said later, shaking his head, "I missed the green." The bogey dropped him four behind.

It wasn't even his best shot of the day, Ballesteros insisted. "The one at No. 9 was even more difficult," he said. At No. 9 — after winning the eighth with a birdie — Ballesteros hooked his second to the uphill green into dense trees and high grass, about 40 yards short. After long study, he hit a low wedge that cleared the greenside bunker, rolled, and stopped eight feet from the hole. He made his par. Poor McCumber. Another win snatched away. He played out of the fairway, but got no better than a half.

Golf is played between the ears, they say. Ballesteros's escapes had to be wearing on McCumber. That thing at No. 10 surely didn't help. At the 186-yarder, Ballesteros missed the green badly to the right, his ball landing at the bottom of a steep slope. He would have to hit up onto a green he couldn't see. Worse, two slender silver birches stood directly in his path, side-by-side. But up came his ball, as though it had eyes, missing the left birch by only inches and rolling to within three feet of the hole. He dropped the putt for his par. McCumber had hit the green, but was 60 feet short. He two-putted for a half. Another sure win had evaporated. McCumber's lead fell to two at No. 11, where he three-putted from about 50 feet, then to one with three putts from 24 feet at No. 14. One had the odd sensation that both a triumph and a funeral were in progress at the same time. Something was needed to break the tension.

It came at the 15th. Ballesteros was just about to putt when he noticed a young boy, seated only an arm's length away, camera ready. "You shouldn't do that," Ballesteros said, backing away from the ball. Then he turned and faced the kid and grinned. "Go ahead," he said. The kid shot his picture, the gallery cheered, and Ballesteros returned to work. He two-putted for his par. McCumber, meanwhile, just missed a half from eight feet. He stamped his foot in frustration. He had led for 29 holes. Now the match was all-square.

But Ballesteros still was not out of the woods — literally speaking. At the par-four 16th, he had to chip backwards from near a shrub, hoping to reach the fairway. All he got was a little pop-up. His nine-iron shot caught the leaves of an overhanging branch and dropped 10 yards short of the green. But he chipped to a foot and salvaged his bogey. McCumber hit a good drive, but his approach was about 55 feet short of the hole. He three-putted for a half. It was his third and final three-putt of the afternoon — a half and two losers.

And still the adventures of Ballesteros rolled on. At No. 17, he sliced his ball (shades of the 1979 British Open) into a car park. He got a free drop, hit a three iron across the fairway into the left rough, pitched on, and two-putted from 16 feet for his par five. McCumber recovered nicely from the left rough, pitched to 12 feet, but couldn't get the winning birdie to drop. The 18th, at least, was routine. They halved in birdie-fours, and it was back to No. 1. A poor approach again killed McCumber. Both hit the fairway and the green. But McCumber was 75 feet from the hole, Ballesteros 10. McCumber missed his desperate birdie try. Ballesteros gave him no second chance. It was, by the way, only the third birdie of the day at No. 1, and only the second from on the green.

Ballesteros wasn't exactly proud of his game. "I shouldn't have won," he told McCumber. But he did win, and he would face Sandy Lyle the next day.

How does one escape from 32-32—64? That's the challenge Lyle put to Ballesteros when they met in the morning of the third round. Ballesteros could only shake his head — and Lyle's hand.

Ballesteros caught trees only twice in the morning. It cost him the eighth hole, but he escaped for a half at No. 12. He found no trees in the afternoon. So unlike his adventurous victory against McCumber, his match against Lyle was almost entirely trouble-free, except for Lyle. The amiable Scot was nothing but trouble.

The weather had moderated a little this Saturday. It was still cool and overcast, but the wind had slackened to brisk breezes. After an early exchange of birdies, Ballesteros got his only lead of the day at No. 3 on a routine par, where Lyle missed the green and two-putted from 10 feet. Amazingly, it was one of only two bogeys for the day for Lyle. He got the hole back at No. 4, two-putting from 75 feet for a birdie, and they were tied. At No. 8, Ballesteros's visit into the trees was academic. Lyle got home with a one-iron, nine-iron combination and holed from 10 feet for his birdie. Ballesteros couldn't resist one little tug at Lyle's leg. At the ninth, Ballesteros waited patiently while Lyle gravely studied the short par putt he needed for a half to retain his one-hole lead. Then Lyle bent over the ball. Just as he drew the putter back, a quiet voice came over his shoulder: "That's OK Sandy. I'll give you that one." Lyle straightened up and laughed. And the fact was, Lyle was in the lead to stay.

Ballesteros did make a strong rally late in the inward nine. He had fallen three behind to Lyle's birdies at the 10th, from six feet, and the 11th, from 25. Then Ballesteros made his move. He won the 13th with a birdie from 14 feet, halved the 15th in birdies, a 36-footer against Lyle's six-footer, and won the 17th with a birdie from 10 feet. He was breathing easier, only one down. Then came a tough one to swallow. At No. 18, Ballesteros got his fourth birdie in six holes with two putts from 40 feet. And lost the hole. Lyle had put his four-iron approach to nine feet and holed for an eagle-three. That put Lyle two up at lunch. Then it got worse in a hurry for Ballesteros.

In the afternoon, Lyle won No. 1 on a birdie from 10 feet, and No. 3 on Ballesteros's two-putt bogey. Then came a stunning development at the 344-yard sixth. Lyle was in the fairway, 86 yards from the hole. He flicked his sand wedge, and the ball hit about six inches from the flag, bounced four feet past, and spun back and dropped into the cup. Lyle's caddy, Dave Musgrove, just grinned. "I talked him into using the right club for once," he said. It was Lyle's second eagle of the day, and only the second on a par-four hole in the World Match Play's 25-year history. Peter Oosterhuis got the first against Hale Irwin in 1977. Lyle was now five up with 12 to play.

Ballesteros fell six behind with a bogey at No. 10. He matched Lyle's birdie at No. 11 to stay barely alive, and the end came at the 12th. Fittingly, Lyle did it on his own. He reached the green with a three iron and two-putted from 40 feet. The birdie-four rang up a 7 and 6 victory, snuffing out Ballesteros's hopes this year of tying Gary Player's record of five World Match Play victories. It was only Ballesteros's 10th loss against 25 victories, but it matched his worst defeat ever, the 7 and 6 whipping by Rodger Davis in 1986, when he was ill. It was a measure of Ballesteros's play that aside from these, his worst previous losses were by 3 and 2, first to Simon Owen in 1978, then to Peter Jacobsen in 1980. He fell to a very hot hand this time. "The way Sandy played today, he would beat anybody," Ballesteros said. "I have no excuses. He played superbly, and when he did make a slight mistake, I made one, too." For the 30 holes, Lyle had made two bogeys and was 13 under par. Next, the final. He was the first player to reach the final three successive times. The World Match Play title had been elusive as smoke. Four tries, four misses. He lost to Greg Norman in 1980, Ballesteros in 1982, Norman in 1986, and Ian Woosnam in 1987.

"Now I may get this one right," Lyle said, with a wry smile. "The odds are in my favor. But tomorrow is another day."

He was similarly resigned on the question of his opponent. It would be either Nick Faldo or Woosnam, the defending champion. They had teed off a half hour earlier than Lyle and Ballesteros, and were still grinding away out on the course as Lyle was speaking. "Whoever I play, it's going to be a tough game," Lyle said. "I think Faldo is more on his game than Woosnam at the moment."

And whichever man he played, it would be a rematch from a year ago. In 1987, he lost to Woosnam, one-up, in the World Match Play final, and he lost to Faldo, 67-69, in the Scotland-England match of the Dunhill Cup at St. Andrews. Before long, he knew who his man was going to be.

"When I three-putted the eighth to go three-down," Faldo was saying a short while later, "I was wondering where he was going to clean me up." The answer was — never.

That nagging question had popped into Faldo's mind at No. 8 in the afternoon round of the slugfest with Woosnam. In fact, he had been three down earlier in the day, at No. 14 in the morning. Woosnam just couldn't put him away. "I kept clawing away," Faldo said, "and I don't know what the key was, really." The key was probably what's known as guts.

It was a donnybrook from the start. They halved the first four holes in three pars and a birdie before anyone could inch ahead. That was Woosnam, on a par at No. 5, when Faldo let a six-foot par putt get away from him. Then they were square at No. 7, when Woosnam bogeyed, two-putting from eight feet. Woosnam went one-up at the ninth when Faldo missed a par from only four feet. Then it was all square at the 11th when Faldo did get down from four feet for a birdie. Woosnam's rush started innocently enough. At No. 12, he came out of a bunker to 10 feet and holed the putt for a birdie-four while the troubled Faldo missed from five feet. At No. 13, Woosnam hit a nine iron to seven feet and holed for a second birdie, and he got his third in succession at the par-three 14th from five feet. Just that fast, Faldo was three down.

Faldo rallied for two quick birdies set up by a good wedge and a brilliant one — to seven feet at No. 16, and to 18 inches at No. 17. The two winners left him only one down at lunch. Now, that was more like it.

But things quickly turned sour again. In the afternoon, Faldo bogeyed the third, and Woosnam holed a nine-foot birdie putt at No. 6 to go three up. At the seventh, Woosnam took three to reach the green and two putts to get down, and his lead was two. Back it went to three at No. 8 on a par four when Faldo needed three putts from 25 feet. That's when the troubling question began to creep into Faldo's mind. Things brightened a little for him when Woosnam's game began to shake. He two-putted from three feet and bogeyed No. 9, and Faldo was quick to jump through the opening. After a half in pars at the 10th, Faldo squared the match with bang-bang birdies — a wedge to four feet at No. 11, and a 20-foot putt at No. 12. What had looked like a runaway for Woosnam had suddenly turned into a heavyweight bout.

After 30 long and unsettling holes, Faldo finally took his first lead at No. 13 on a routine par. Woosnam's poor eight-iron approach left him in his worst position of the day, fully 60 feet from the flag. He three-putted, and the bogey put him one down. He would not lead again. He birdied No. 16 from three feet to square the match, but Faldo pushed into the lead again at the 17th, covering 50 feet in two putts for a birdie. Woosnam's last chance came at the final hole, but he couldn't pull it in. He drove onto a path, hit the driver again, then a sand wedge to 45 feet. Remarkably, he drained the long putt for a birdie-four. But Faldo was home with a driver and three-wood combination to 55 feet. He two-putted for his own birdie and the half that gave him the one-hole victory. Faldo was in the final for the second time. He was hungry to reverse the 1983 result, when he lost to Greg Norman, 4 and 2. He was also hungry for some revenge for that shocker in the first round of the 1982 World Match Play, when Lyle was six down after 18 holes and came back to beat him, 2 and 1.

It would be an interesting final. Both men were residents and members at Wentworth. What a club championship this would be.

"Tomorrow it's the Wentworth Members' Championship!" Faldo cracked. "Will they make me an honorary member if I win?"

Both men knew what to expect, of course. Lyle would have to ignore Faldo's slow play. Faldo, on the other hand, would have to contend with something else. "I know that Sandy will always be 30, 40 yards ahead of me from the tee," he said, "but if I can reach the par fours in two, I'll be happy."

Actually, "tomorrow" never came. Overnight Saturday, a steady rain began to fall. And it fell and fell. By Sunday morning, Wentworth's Burma Road course was more suited to water skiing than golf. Eight fairways were unplayable. The 11th, for example, was a small lagoon. Play was abandoned and rescheduled for Monday.

The weather on Monday had improved immensely. It was cool, mostly clear, and the breezes were comparatively light. The rains of the day before made for heavy going in mud for a surprisingly large workday gallery, but the course was playable. Given the conditions, tournament officials scratched the playoff for third and fourth places between Ballesteros and Woosnam, and declared a tie.

Lyle, entering his third consecutive World Match Play final, began the day with some encouragement still fresh in his ear from his good friend and his most recent conquest. Ballesteros had stopped by Lyle's home after Sunday's rain-out. "You are good enough to win," Ballesteros told him. "Go out there and do it."

The Lyle-backers were in heaven. Lyle put on two phenomenal bursts. In the morning, he played the last five holes in five under par, and the last three in four under. In the afternoon, he birdied the last four in succession. He made few mistakes — just two bogeys in the morning, three in the afternoon. But compared to Faldo, he was shaky. Faldo was his wonderfully consistent self. He made just three bogeys all day, two in the morning and just one in the afternoon. The fatal trouble was, he didn't make enough birdies. He had nine, but six of them were merely for halves. Lyle had 12, and an eagle for good measure.

First blood came on a bogey. Faldo missed the green at the par-three second in the morning, wedged to six feet, and two-putted. He was one down. Lyle's tee shot to the par-three fifth cost him that hole. It was a poor five iron that ended up 70 feet and three putts from the hole. The match was square. Lyle inched back in front at No. 8 with a birdie-three from four feet. But Faldo hauled him right back, rolling in a 35-footer for a birdie-three at the ninth. They were all square again. They halved the 12th and 14th in birdies, and in between Faldo missed a ripe opportunity. At the par-four 13th, Lyle left his approach in bogey range, 60 feet from the hole. Faldo missed the green with his second, but pitched close enough to get his par. Lyle proceeded to three-putt and bogey, but Faldo missed his nine-footer. One of those Lyle outbursts was in the offing, and what an outburst it was.

At the 16th, he holed from 21 feet for a birdie and was one up. At the 17th, a two-iron got to within 35 feet, and the putt went down — his third eagle of the tournament. He was two up. And at the 18th, a miracle birdie saved him and the lead. That one had to hurt Faldo. He had had a lot to look forward to when Lyle, hitting first, drove into some trees. Faldo had his opening. He was in great shape with a drive into the fairway, a three wood to 40 feet. Lyle was in deep trouble. He was a long way from the green on the 502-yard hole. Reaching the green was out of the question. He needed his nine iron just to get out of the trees. Then he missed the green with his eight-iron approach. Who could blame Faldo if he was set to chalk up a win? Now Lyle was lying three, still 25 yards from the hole, and the most he could hope for was to chip close and get down with one putt for his five. Faldo ought to be able to two-putt and get that winning birdie. Lyle spoiled the script. He holed his chip for a birdie. "That was a real morale-booster," Lyle said. But not for Faldo. Now the disappointed Faldo needed an eagle to win the hole. He tried gamely from 40 feet, just missed, and tapped in for a half. Lunch could not have been much fun. Lyle had just gone birdie-par-birdie-eagle-birdie. He had played the inward nine in 32 — his fourth 32 in two consecutive matches. He had a medal score of 66 to Faldo's 68, and he was two up.

Now it got strange. Lyle's lead evaporated almost instantly after lunch through a generosity he never intended. At the par-three second, he missed the green, then blew a two-foot par putt. And at the third, after a weak wedge, he two-putted from 28 feet. Faldo put up two pars and the match was all square. It stayed that way through the turn. The 1988 World Match Play had come down to the last nine holes.

And it really was a whole new ball game. After 27 holes of playing catch-up, Faldo took the lead for the first time. Actually, Lyle handed it to him. Both were in the 30-foot range at the par-three 10th. Faldo two-putted for a par, and Lyle committed a strange error. He somehow failed to notice that his putt was downhill. He sent it eight feet past the hole, and missed coming back. His three-putt bogey put Faldo one up. Faldo's lead lasted for one hole. At No. 11, Lyle hit a wedge to six feet and squared the match with the birdie. Faldo pushed ahead again at No. 12, with a one-iron second and two putts from 20 feet for a winning birdie. It was his second lead in three holes, his second all day. Lyle was jittery. He had just seen an old enemy — failure. "I thought I was staring at another defeat when Nick went one up," he said. But Faldo's lead this time lasted for only two holes.

They came to the 179-yard 14th. "I thought I was in right trouble," Lyle said later. "Especially when my ball was obviously miles away." He was almost that bad off. He had put his six-iron tee shot some 32 feet from the hole, while Faldo's five iron was just 10 feet away. But Lyle holed his for the birdie, and Faldo parred. "That," said Faldo, "was a typical match-play turnaround." They were all-square. The match had come down to the last four holes. It would not go the distance.

"The closing holes give you few breathers," Lyle was to say later. That's true enough. But you couldn't prove it by him. He has the deed to them. For the second time in the day, he exploded down the stretch — this time, four consecutive birdies. First, a 32-footer at No. 14 squared the match. Then the crucial point. At the 466-yard, par-four 15th, Lyle opted to go with his deadly one iron off the tee. It wasn't so deadly this time. He hit it fat. Faldo, on the other hand, was rock-steady. A hefty three wood off the tee, and a three-iron approach put him 25 feet from the hole. Now came the difference. Lyle recovered from his mis-hit tee shot with a dazzling 215-yard four-iron to within three feet. Faldo proceeded to suffer his only three-putt of the day, and only his second of the tournament. Lyle was not going to three-putt from three feet. Faldo conceded the birdie, and Lyle was one up. He was in the lead for good.

Lyle had his teeth in it now. At No. 16, he holed a six-footer for the third birdie, following Faldo in from a similar distance for a half. Then Lyle wrapped it up at No. 17, if unartistically. Faldo's three-wood second was short, but his sand wedge pitch got him to within birdie range, 15 feet. Lyle's two-iron approach reached the green, but was 75 feet from the hole. Unaccountably, he ran his first putt 20 feet past the hole. Lyle was still putting, and Faldo was still breathing. Lyle lined up that 20-footer, then almost casually rapped it in — his fourth consecutive birdie. Now Faldo needed his 15-footer to stay alive. He didn't get it. After four visits to the final, the third in succession, Sandy Lyle had got it right this time. He had the World Match Play title, 2 and 1.

There was little for Faldo to say. He had made only three bogeys in 35 holes, only one of them in the afternoon. The match was squared no fewer than five times, and twice in the final eight holes. He even had led twice in that stretch. But for the eighth time this season, he had finished second. "I am very disappointed," he said. "Especially after playing well all day." And he had played relentlessly well. But he had caught a hot opponent. He had enough good humor left for a wry quip at the presentation ceremony. "I hope you've been hiding your faces from the TV," he said to the Monday gallery. "These four-day work-weeks..."

Lyle's results were convincing. He had beaten some impressive competition. In order, he went 34 holes against British Open runner-up Nick Price, 30 against British Open champion Seve Ballesteros, and 35 against Faldo, another of Europe's best. In 99 holes, he had 34 birdies, three eagles, 13 bogeys, and one double bogey — a cumulative 25 under par.

"I never gave up hope of winning this event," Lyle said. "After all those years of near-misses, it feels great to have finally won this title. I knew that if I continued playing as I had for the last couple of years, then my time would come."

It certainly had. He had been a powerhouse on both sides of the Atlantic. In America, he won the Phoenix Open, the Greater Greensboro Open, and then the Masters. In Europe, he added the Dunhill British Masters, and now the World Match Play. It was a pretty fair year's work.

8. The Dunhill Cup

There were no big surprises in the first three years of the Dunhill Cup, unless you count the Americans — for *not* winning. The Australians had won the first two, the English the third in 1987.

U.S. Open champion Curtis Strange, the hottest golfer in the United States, was back at St. Andrews leading another assault. Masters champion Sandy Lyle, a five-time winner this year, was on hand to head the 1987 runner-up Scots. Nick Faldo, U.S. Open runner-up, led the defending champion English. British Open champion Seve Ballesteros headed a strong Spanish team, and Greg Norman, now recovered from his wrist injury, led the Australians. And the Welsh were stirring. Ian Woosnam had shaken off an early-season slump. You could make book on it — the champion would come from this awesome group.

Someone should have kept an eye on the Irish.

"The Irish didn't win a medal in the Olympic Games," said the heroic Des Smyth. "So maybe this will make up for it." You could argue that this Irish victory was a fluke. After all, there was not so much as one major championship in the three of them, and they were in a Dunhill Cup field that read like anyone's Hall of Fame. But the facts prove otherwise. Eamonn Darcy, 36, master of the funny swing, captain Smyth, 35, and Ronan Rafferty, 24, not only marched over the Canadians, the Americans, the English, and the Australians, in order, but did it with unprecedented authority. For the first time in the Dunhill Cup's four years, all three team members were under par in all four matches.

"My boys are no mugs," Darcy was to say soon. "They will have to be beaten." They weren't.

Some things you can always count on. That's the way it is with the Road Hole. It's the center of the Old Course, even though it's the 17th hole. The golfer is either whipped from suffering there, or relieved at having escaped, and if he hasn't played it yet, he's worrying about it. And so it was at the 1988 Dunhill Cup.

Darcy kept the eighth-seeded Irish alive in their first outing by tiptoeing around the old beast. He was leading Canada's Dan Halldorson by two strokes coming to No. 17, and his goal was modest. "On the tee," Darcy said, "I decided to play for five." He got it — the hard way. He had put his tee shot into the left rough, then horrors — couldn't get out cleanly. His eight-iron shot was 100 yards short of the green. He played short with his third and finally got down from 10 feet for his five. But it was enough. Halldorson found a crushing way to make six. His three-iron approach went over the green, the road, and the stone wall. The double bogey left him at level par, and Darcy was three under. Darcy squared the match with a 69-72 victory.

Canada had taken a 1—0 lead in the first game when Dave Barr caught fire at No. 5, played a 10-hole stretch in seven under par, and sank Rafferty, 67-69. The decisive third game had Smyth against Canada's Richard Zokol, and it was a struggle until a weird three-hole disaster utterly destroyed Zokol.

They came to the par-four 12th deadlocked at three under par. Zokol then hit his tee shot into a pot bunker, needed two to get out, wedged on, and three-putted. Triple-bogey seven. He drove into a bunker again at No. 13, and yet again at No. 14. He had to come out the back door both times. Bogey-five, double bogey-seven. He had gone six over par on three holes. "None of my tee shots was that bad, just a little off line," the groggy Zokol said. "But they derailed me." Smyth parred in from the turn for a 69 to Zokol's 76. It was Ireland's match, 2-1. "We knew it was probably the toughest match of the day," Darcy said. "When we saw the draw, we were a little disappointed not to get an easy ride in the first round. But my boys are not going to give it away. I think we have a great chance tomorrow."

Darcy was the only one who thought so. Tomorrow would bring the Irish up against the No. 1-seeded Americans, who had made short work of the Phillipines, 3-0, in the first outing of the day. Unlike the howling Wednesday, Thursday was an excellent day for golf — cool, calm, overcast, and dry. The last time Strange played the Old Course was in the playoff for third place against Australia in 1987. That was the day he posted the course-record 62. The weather was similar this time, and he led off with a 70-75 win over Eddie Bagtas. Chip Beck, the leading American money-winner, who had been robbed of a practice round by bad weather on Wednesday, posted an easy 68-81 day over Rudy Lavares. Mark McCumber had only a slightly tougher time against Frankie Minoza. They were tied at one over par coming to the ninth. Then McCumber got one of his two birdies and Minoza plunged to a double-bogey six and suddenly was three behind. They ended that way, McCumber winning, 72-75, for the American sweep.

Only one thing was in doubt — could Strange, or anybody, oblige with another record performance this year? "The course is in fabulous shape," he said. "The greens are soft, and if conditions hold, someone's going to shoot some low scores. But," he said, laughing, "not a 61, I hope."

The Americans and the Irish were safely in, and were quickly joined by Spain, 3-0, over Zimbabwe. It was almost a moral victory for the Zimbabweans. They were simply delighted just to be in the field. Tim Price, their captain, older brother of British Open runner-up Nick Price, pretty much said it all when he confessed his awe at stepping out onto the mist-shrouded old links, with the hiss of the nearby sea in his ears, and then meeting his opponent. "I tried hard not to let it get to me," Price said. "But the first time I saw Seve, my heart nearly jumped out of my chest because of the admiration I have for the guy." The meeting had its light moment, when Ballesteros first saw Price's "Long Tom" putter, a putter about five feet long, which he swung, pendulum-style, from his lower throat. "I've stopped worrying about how stupid some people seem to think I look," he said. "I'll try anything, because my putting is the reason I've never felt able to give international golf a go." Ballesteros returned an unspectacular 72 to win by two strokes. The Spaniards locked up the win on Jose Rivero's 68-72 victory over Anthony Edwards in the next match. Then Morgan Shumba saw his dream end when he went four over par on the last three holes and bowed to Jose-Maria Olazabal, 74-78. He was not a completely unhappy man. "Aw, well, it's only a game," he said, smiling to a passerby who stopped for his autograph.

Two things occupied Norman's mind in the Australian's first outing — his injured wrist and David Graham's play. Both were solid in the 3-0 defeat of Brazil. "My wrist is not going to be completely fine, but not any worse," he said, after a 71-73 victory over Priscillo Diniz. "I'll put up with it because I don't want to consider surgery and I'm not keen to sit out for six to nine months." It was at the U.S. Open in June that Norman badly aggravated a boyhood injury and had to spend seven weeks recuperating. The injury required an adjustment in both his game and his thinking. He had become somewhat defensive. "I don't like taking big divots anymore, especially not with the long irons," he said. "I'm trying to protect it as much as I can."

The Australians, champions in 1985 and 1986, were in trouble only briefly against the Brazilians. Rodger Davis, leading off, was two strokes behind Rafael Navarro's 34 at the turn. Then he spurted to three consecutive birdies from the 10th and was on his way to a 69-73 victory. He hadn't missed a green. Graham, who remains an Australian although living in the United States for many years, joined the team when Peter Senior had to be hospitalized for a pinched disc. Graham barrelled past Carlos Dluosh, 68-79. Dluosh double-bogeyed the first and the fourth, and triple-bogeyed the 17th, where Graham got a birdie — the only birdie of the day out of 48 players.

Mark James got England off and running against France, erasing Frederic Regard, 66-75. Barry Lane, the promising young Englishman making his Dunhill Cup debut, returned a one-bogey 70 to outrun Michel Tapia, 75. Then came two elegant performances. Faldo returned a seven-birdie 65, lowest score of the day, against Emmanuel Dussart's two-birdie 70. Remarkably, neither man made a bogey. Poor Dussart. His 70 would have been enough to beat seven winners in this first round, including Ballesteros, Olazabal and Norman. Fate had put him in against the wrong man. Everything went right for Faldo as he equalled his all-time low on the Old Course, set in the 1979 British PGA Championship. What his approach shots didn't do, his putter made up for. His birdies: One each from four, six, and eight feet; two from 10 feet, one from 12 feet, and two putts on an overland monster of 90 feet at No. 5. It was his eighth Dunhill Cup victory against no defeats. "I changed my grip to an ordinary natural grip, and I changed putters," Faldo said. "I'm just getting the right feel."

Feel seemed to be something the fourth-seeded Scots lacked, even though they swept Thailand. They were off form, despite — or maybe because of — Captain Sandy's attempt to inspire them with a bit of homecooking the night before. "I sent the chef out in his deerstalker to shoot us a haggis," Lyle said.

This match, by the way, underlined golf's role as an international bond of good will. How else would one become friends with, or even hear of, Boonchu Ruanghit, Suthep Meesawad, and Somsakdi Srinsangar? The point was emphasized on the final hole of the final twosome of the match. Srinsangar had put up a good fight against the powerful Lyle. He was trying to salvage something. The Scots were leading, 2-0, but not with impressive play. Gordon Brand Jr. had beaten Ruangkit, 74-76, and Colin Montgomerie, another newcomer, triple-bogeyed No. 17 in his 72-80 win over Meesawad. Srinsangar wanted Thailand at least to make a showing. But what a disadvantage. He was hitting medium irons where Lyle was hitting a wedge. But he was stubborn. He was one under par and only a stroke behind through the 15th. Then two consecutive bogeys left him a 70-73 loser, and his team had been routed. Yet he was all smiles at No. 18. When the last putt dropped, he went to

Lyle and asked him to autograph a visor. He had just battled the Masters champion on the Old Course. What golfer could ask for more? The crowd at No. 18 understood. He got a rousing round of applause.

Seventh-seeded Japan, featuring two of the golfing Ozaki brothers, was in trouble only once against less-experienced Denmark, and that was in the captains' duel in the second pairing. No. 17 made the difference. Coming to that reef, Steen Tinning was four under par and one stroke ahead of Tateo "Jet" Ozaki. Tinning bogeyed, Ozaki parred, and they were all square. Then Jet birdied No. 18 for a 68-69 victory and a clinching 2-0 lead for Japan. Things might have been different except for Jacob Rasmussen's awful smashup on the incoming nine in the first match. He and Naomichi "Joe" Ozaki, the youngest brother, were tied at even par through the 10th. Rasmussen proceeded to come apart. He bogeyed five of the next seven holes, three of them in succession from the 15th, and fell heavily, 69-77. Hajime Meshiai made it a Japanese sweep in the finale, leading from the seventh hole on for a 72-75 victory over Anders Sorensen.

Sixth-seeded Wales, led by Woosnam, faced the toughest assignment after Ireland-Canada in meeting a team of experienced Swedes, all three of them European tour members. And the Swedes threw a real scare into the Welsh. The Road Hole made the difference. In the first pairing, Magnus Pearsson was only a stroke behind after David Llewellyn double-bogeyed the 12th. He dogged Llewellyn for four more holes, then got wiped out by a double bogey-six at the Road Hole, and lost 72-75. Mark Mouland clinched for Wales, but had to birdie No. 18 for a 70-71 win over Ove Sellberg. Sellberg was two behind through the 13th, then inched up with a birdie at No. 14. The match was squared at the 17th when Mouland double-bogeyed to Sellberg's bogey. Anders Forsbrand was on the verge of preventing a Welsh sweep until he came crashing down with an inward 40. He led Woosnam by two through the sixth and by one at the turn. Now the fighter in Woosnam surfaced. He went one ahead at No. 10 on a birdie-bogey exchange, the first of three birdies in a no-bogey inward 33. Forsbrand completed his crash with a six at No. 17, and Woosnam cruised in with a 69-75 victory and a sweep for Wales.

In the 16-match day, the Road Hole had decided one and was a dark influence in seven others. To a total of 48 players, it gave up one birdie, 18 pars, 18 bogeys, nine double bogeys, and two triple bogeys.

The seeded teams had come through untouched, except for Ireland's one loss to Canada, and the pairings for Friday set up a real international summit battle of golf: United States (No. 1 seed) vs. Ireland (8), Spain (2) vs. Japan (7), Australia (3) vs. Wales (6), and Scotland (4) vs. England (5) in a rematch.

Lyle, as captain of the higher-seeded team, had the option of choosing his opponent. He claimed Faldo. There were two reasons. The first was chess-like strategy. "The thought of putting Colin Montgomerie in against Nick did enter my mind," Lyle said, the idea being to sacrifice the newcomer and take the other two matches. But Lyle rejected the notion. "I thought if I took Nick, it would make it easier for the other two," he said. The reason was pure pride and confidence. "I think I can beat him," Lyle said, grinning. "He got me here last year, and I want my own back. Anyway, Nick had his good score today."

Faldo just shrugged. "That doesn't bother me in the slightest," he said. "I'm happy to take him on." He brushed off Lyle's strategy as well, and it was his turn to be the prophet. "That," he said, "could be their downfall."

So some spice had been tossed into the fire. In a little while, one of them would be wishing he could get it back.

Friday came in as a sunny, mild autumn day with little or no wind. And also with a throaty crowd of more then 10,000 home fans primed to cheer their beloved Scots against the "Auld Enemy" in the last of the day's four matches. They had plenty to cheer about — at first. Lyle's strategy sent the seasoned Gordon Brand Jr. out against the newcomer, Barry Lane. Brand took the lead with a birdie at No. 2 and stayed there. "The 10th hole was crucial," the big-hitting Lane said. "I was going for the green, and I put my drive into a bush. It was a lack of concentration." His position was marginal, and he was tempted to play the ball. But he thought the better of it and took a penalty drop. He bogeyed the hole, and Brand birdied to go up by three strokes. That was the first of two errors that would cost Lane the game. He got a stroke back with a birdie at No. 12. "Then at the 15th, I hit a six-iron fat and then three-putted from 10 feet," Lane said. A par would have squared the match, since Brand had bogeyed at No. 14. Instead, Lane was still a stroke behind, and it ended that way, Brand giving Scotland a 1-0 lead with a 71-73 win.

The home crowd was really warming up in the second game. Colin Montgomerie, 25, who turned professional in 1987, had a leg up on English veteran Mark James, 10 years and 13 pro seasons his senior. Montgomerie led by a stroke through the turn, 34-35. "He was knocking the pin out," James said. They matched birdies at the 10th, but in a way that James thought stung Montgomerie. "He was just two feet away in two," James said. But James got in ahead of him from much farther out to stay a stroke behind. "Then," said James, "I made two more birdies on the next two holes, and I think that knocked the stuffing out of him." James birdied No. 11 to Montgomerie's bogey and was one ahead, leading for the first time, and he upped his edge to two strokes at No. 12 with his third consecutive birdie. James went on to win, 69-71, and square the match. So it came down to the two protagonists, Lyle and Faldo. To the final hole, in fact.

They were brilliant.

Lyle opened with a withering burst of three consecutive birdies, and Faldo could match him only on the first two. It is hard to imagine a grittier duel. Twice Faldo was two behind, but he narrowed it finally to one with a birdie at the ninth. Lyle led through the turn, 31-32. They cooled off slightly, running pars from the 10th, Lyle holding that one-stroke lead, until the turning point came into view on the horizon — the Road Hole. Neither man would flirt with the out-of-bounds on the right, and both hit their drives into the left rough. Now came a crucial bit of strategy, dictated as only the Road Hole can. Faldo was once asked what his weakness was. "Some of the in-between wedge shots," he replied. This in mind, he didn't try for the green, but instead opted to set up a full wedge shot, much as Jack Nicklaus does. He could hit the full shot hard and get spin on the ball. He put his nine-iron second about 90 yards short of the green. Lyle, on the other hand, tried to get as close as he could. He hit a six-iron. Now he had an "in-between" wedge shot left. Faldo slashed his third perfectly. He could tell it was close, he said, "by the muffled Scottish applause." In fact, it was three feet from the flag. Lyle, unable to get the same spin on the ball, left his pitch 11 feet away. He two-putted for his only bogey in two days, and the only bogey between them in the round. And Faldo holed his to square the game at four under par. It would be settled at No. 18.

Both reached the green in two, and now the matter of deceptive perception came into play. Faldo was first to hit his second, and Lyle later said it seemed to be only five feet from the hole. In fact, it was about 12. "I might have been a bit more aggressive with my pitch if I had known he was so far away," Lyle said. He put his own about 15 feet from the hole. He putted first, and missed. Faldo read his downhill 12-footer perfectly, allowed for about four inches of borrow, and stroked. Suddenly, he was leaping and slamming his fist into the air. It was the only time he led the game. It was the only time it mattered. He had beaten Lyle, 67-68, and England won the match, 2-1. (It dawned on people later that Faldo had just completed two successive rounds on the Old Course without a bogey.)

"I will remember my last two holes for a long time," Faldo said. "It was great to beat Sandy, but it proves nothing. Not to me, anyway, though maybe it proves something to others."

As for Lyle, he had to face the question of his strategy. "I think it worked out pretty well," he said. "If I'd won I'd have been proved right. But coming home, I couldn't buy a putt. He got the breaks and I missed the putts, so it was just a bit unfortunate."

The day that ended with a bang had begun with one. The Road Hole was to claim another victim — spectacularly.

Mark Mouland got Wales off and winging against Australia, holing his approach at the second for an eagle-two and dropping a 40-foot birdie putt at No. 8. He carried a one-stroke lead over David Graham through the turn, 33-34. Graham, former U.S. Open and PGA champion, wouldn't stay put. While Mouland was parring from the 10th through the 16th, Graham crept into the lead with birdies at the 12th and 15th. Graham was four under par and a stroke ahead through No. 16. Time was running out. Mouland would have to make his move at No. 17. "I had to hit a good second shot, drawing it in," Mouland said. When he got to the green, his face fell. His ball was on the floor of the Road Bunker. Maybe he still had a chance. "I was in the bunker yesterday and knocked it out and took six," Mouland said. "I opened the face of my sand wedge as wide as I could. I'm normally a good bunker player." But this was no normal bunker. Before long, all Mouland could do was look up helplessly at Graham and laugh. It took him seven to get out of the hellish pit. He had to hole a 20-foot putt to save a 10. Graham won, 67-76, and gave Australia a 1-0 lead.

"Mark played very well," Graham said, "then paid the supreme price, as we all have at some time in our careers at No. 17 — shooting for the pin. After about the fifth attempt to get out, he motioned to me and laughed, and we both saw the funny side." Mouland's disaster raised memories of the 1987 Dunhill Cup, when Malaysia's Zainal Abidin Yusof made 10 without even getting near the bunker. The hapless Yusof merely put his second on the road. Then he tried to cover the few feet to the green, first with a wedge, then a putter. The ball kept coming back to him. Mouland apparently hadn't heard about Yusof. He was thinking about Japan's Tommy Nakajima, who made nine out of the bunker in the 1978 British Open. "I saw it on TV and I wondered why he couldn't get out of it," Mouland said. "Now I know."

Rodger Davis came from behind and edged David Llewellyn, 69-70, to clinch the match for Australia, 2-0. Davis saved the game at No. 17 when he got away with a three-putt bogey from 90 feet. Llewellyn was next in the bunker after Mouland, but he solved it by nearly holing his blast. He got down from about five feet for his par. Davis, though not happy about the bogey, was pleased about one thing — he had played the hole the way he wanted to. "I took a double bogey there last year," Davis said. "I remember Peter Thomson telling me that at No. 17, it doesn't really matter what you have in your hand for the second shot. Aim to the front right or let it run up the middle of the green, but never go anywhere near the pot bunker. I played it that way." Those words would have a grim humor to them two days later. In any event, Davis had come through in the nick of time.

"If you have had a bad day yourself," Greg Norman was saying, "with this format you have two guys who can get you through." And that's exactly what happened. Norman had a bad day and lost the third game to Ian Woosnam, 73-71. Norman led by a stroke through the fourth, and Woosnam caught him with a birdie at the fifth. Then the turning point: Norman four-putted No. 6 from 50 feet. The double bogey-six dropped him two behind Woosnam, who had parred. The margin grew quickly. Norman got one stroke back at No. 7, then his putting went sour. He bogeyed the next two with three-putts, from 12 feet at No. 8 and 18 feet at No. 9. Woosnam tacked on a birdie from four feet at No. 9, and was three under par and four strokes ahead, 33-37. Woosnam almost undid himself coming home, with bogeys at the 11th and 17th, but Norman could manage only one birdie and gave that stroke back with a bogey. "I'm happy with my game, tee-to-green, but not with my putting," Norman said. "I don't care who I play tomorrow, whether it's Seve or not."

It would be Australia against Spain in the semifinals. Ballesteros led off for the Spaniards against Japan and seemed to have clear sailing when Naomichi "Joe" Ozaki double-bogeyed the first two holes. "Joe really opened the door for Spain," Ballesteros said. "He was very nervous over the first four holes." Oddly enough, Ballesteros couldn't get anything going. Maybe he missed the heat of a real challenge. "It's difficult to play hard when you're four ahead after only two holes," he said. Although he had a four-stroke edge coming out of the gate, he turned in a so-so-72 to win by two and give Spain a 1-0 lead.

Spain won it in the next game, Jose Rivero erupted on the outward nine and giving Spain the match, 2-0, with a 65-68 victory over Hajime Meshiai. Rivero went one ahead with a birdie at the second, but made up no ground when Meshiai matched his eagle at No. 5. Rivero then sprinted to three consecutive birdies from the seventh and led at the turn, 30-34. Curtis Strange's course-record 62 was in reach. "But all I thought about was the match," Rivero said. That streak on the outward nine was a different world. "You feel very happy," he said, "and all the shots are very easy." Rivero added a birdie at the 14th and made no bogeys for an inward 35. Meshiai was game, but erratic play chilled his rally. He birdied the first two coming in, then bogeyed No. 12, and he birdied the 16th and 18th but bogeyed the 17th. In the third game, Tateo "Jet" Ozaki made a spirited close, a four-birdie 32, but it was too late. Jose-Maria Olazabal was four ahead at the turn, 33-37, and one more birdie, at the 10th, proved to be the winner. His bogey-free 68 edged Ozaki by a stroke for the Spanish sweep.

Only the tension of the England-Scotland battle in the final match could take the edge off what happened in the second match of the day, the American-Ireland collision. You half-suspected something was up when Ronan Rafferty shook off a one-stroke deficit at the turn and came on to beat Mark McCumber, 71-72. Eighth-seeded Ireland had 1-0 lead against first-seeded America, and as it ended, with Rafferty winning with a birdie at the 18th, the scoreboard showed Des Smyth tied with Chip Beck through the 17th, and Eamonn Darcy three ahead of Curtis Strange through the 16th. The biggest upset in the Dunhill Cup's young history was in progress.

Darcy had braced his men for the test. He told them what an incredible thing it would be for Ireland to beat the Americans. "Normally, it takes the whole of Europe," he said, thinking of the 1987 Ryder Cup, when he helped Europe to its second consecutive victory. It must have been an inspiring talk.

Rafferty stumbled to three consecutive bogeys from the fourth and trailed at the turn, 35-36. He leveled the match with a birdie at No. 12, then fell behind again with a bogey at No. 14. McCumber obliged him with a bogey at No. 17, and they went to the 18th tee all square. Rafferty's drive ended up on Grannie Clark's Wynd, the road that cuts across the first and last fairways. Hitting off asphalt is always a marginal proposition. "I played it a little like a fairway bunker shot," Rafferty said. He hit his eight iron to 10 feet and holed the putt for a 71-72 victory. Ireland led, 1-0. McCumber just shrugged. "I hit 16 greens, made two birdies and two bogeys," he said.

Ireland would have won outright in the next match, except for the Road Hole. Smyth led by a stroke at the turn, 35-36, erased Beck's tying birdie at the 11th and built his lead to two with birdies at No. 12 and No. 13. It was down to one when Beck birdied No. 15. At the 17th, Beck took three to reach the green and bogeyed. But Smyth was having troubles of his own and couldn't capitalize on the slip. He drove into the rough, caught the bunker with his third, and double-bogeyed. They parred No. 18 and halved the game, 71-71. Ireland held a precarious 1½-½ lead. It was up to Darcy.

And Darcy was in great shape. He and Strange were level in 33s at the turn. The big break came at the par-three 11th. Darcy faced an uphill birdie putt he judged to be about 15 feet long. An Irish golf writer insisted it was at least twice that long. "Okay," Darcy said later, grinning, "what's five feet between friends?" Whatever the length, he holed it to go one stroke up on Strange. He padded his lead to three with birdies at No. 13 and No. 14. Neither man had made a bogey yet. Strange's last real hope lay at No. 17 — if only Darcy would come to grief there. But Darcy, with a three-stroke cushion, wasn't about to. As he did in the first round, he played the Road Hole for a five. But he made four. The way Strange saw it, it was simply Darcy's time. "How do you figure it?" Strange said. "Eamonn hits his tee shot to the right, almost out of bounds. Then he hits his second near the bunker. He pitches away from the bunker, then holes a 30-footer for his par!" Strange also parred, and he birdied No. 18, but neither mattered. Darcy beat him, 66-68. The Irish had won, 2½-½.

The world of golf may have been shocked, but Strange wasn't. "Look, this Irish team is a good team," he said. "They scare you. You think you're supposed to win, but they're good, and they've been playing awfully well. Don't be surprised by anything they do."

The Irish secret, Smyth said later, was to keep the 24-year-old Rafferty, the baby of the team, happy. He recalled the chat he had with Darcy.

"Will we put Ronan first?" Darcy wondered.

"Don't do anything until you've spoken to him," Smyth said. "Maybe he could have said he would like to play Strange, but he said he'd like to play McCumber. And to have him playing the match he wanted was good."

"I decided to play Strange myself," Darcy said. "Anything to keep Ronan happy."

Rafferty wasn't the only one happy with that decision.

Saturday, the day of the third round of the Dunhill Cup — the semifinals — didn't dawn. It merely got lighter. Fog off the North Sea lay over St. Andrews like an immense blanket. The golfers waited. So did the spectators, and so did the nervous officials. And waited and waited. The Australians and Spaniards were scheduled first off, then the upstart Irish against the defending champion English. But no one was going anywhere. The fog lay so dense across the Old Course that if you stood beside the first tee, you couldn't see across the 18th fairway right alongside it. The Royal and Ancient clubhouse was just a spooky presence off to your left. Golf was out of the question. Even a duffer's wedge shot would be out of sight.

A late start would just be the front end of the problem. Would there be enough daylight left to finish that afternoon? Tournament officials fretted. They calculated that if play didn't begin by about 1:30 p.m., the day would have to be scratched. And they were just about to scratch it when the tide shifted and the fog went with it. After a wait of nearly three hours, Greg Norman and Seve Ballesteros — a battle of captains — led off at 1:20. But the problems weren't over yet. The fog would dictate an odd finish to this day. Perhaps an unprecedented one.

Ballesteros was in for a day of erratic iron play and capricious putting, and this wouldn't do against a guy like Norman. The first flaw — and there weren't many — appeared at the par-four fourth. Both men were on in two, Norman 40 feet from the hole, Ballesteros 45. Norman got down in two putts, but Ballesteros needed three. As turning points go, it was modest and early, but it was the turning point. Norman then bracketed Ballesteros's birdie at No. 8 with two of his own, first at the seventh, from three feet, then the ninth. "That's where it really started," Norman said. "I holed a 30-footer, and he missed from 18." Norman led at the turn, 33-35.

Norman birdied the 10th as well, from 10 feet, and the 14th from four, while Ballesteros two-putted his way to pay. Norman led by four strokes through No. 15. Ballesteros finally caught fire, but too late. He picked up two quick strokes on his six-foot birdie putt at No. 16 and Norman's only bogey of the day, at No. 17, where he three-putted from 80 feet. Then came the beginning of the end of an odd day. The fog returned.

"At No. 18, we stopped," Norman said. "We could just see the bridge, about 80 yards, maximum. Then it started to lift and everybody was backing up behind us. I was ready to go. I didn't want to come back in the morning to play one hole. But Seve had the honors and wasn't going to play." Ballesteros had to birdie No. 18, and Norman bogey it, to force a playoff. Finally, they played on. Ballesteros dropped a sand wedge four feet from the hole. Norman sent his approach 30 feet past the hole. "I knew I was going to make four," he said. "So I lagged the putt, and darn if it didn't go in for a birdie." Ballesteros followed him in, and Norman had the game, 67-69. "Greg was much better on the greens," Ballesteros said. "He holed a lot of putts, and I hit many good ones myself but I just didn't hole them." In fact, Ballesteros had four one-putts, ranging from three to six feet. Norman had five, including one from 10 feet, one from 20 and one from about 30. Australia led, 1-0.

Hard behind them came a game that could be decisive. Rodger Davis saw a three-stroke lead over Jose Rivero melt away to one by the time they came to the 18th tee. Both had started off weakly. Rivero's approach to No. 1 came down well short of the green, took a little bounce, and trickled up to the edge of Swilcan Burn — and dropped in. Davis also was short with his second, but it rolled dead just at the edge of the fatal drop. Both pitched close and holed out, but the penalty put Rivero into a hole. He spent the day trying to climb out. Davis led by three at the turn, 34-37, then by four with a birdie at No. 10. Then Rivero crept back in — a birdie from 10 feet at the 12th, and another from 35 at the 16th. By this time, the afternoon fog was thickening. "Really, we should not have hit our second shots at No. 16," Davis said. Then Davis made it even closer when he bogeyed No. 17 for the second consecutive day, missing the green with his second shot. Rivero's last chance was to win No. 18, and Davis almost gave it to him. "I was undecided whether to hit the driver or the three wood," Davis said. "I hit the driver, and where I was too close to the green, Jose had a full shot and got the spin." That put Rivero 10 feet from the flag. Davis's main concern was to avoid the Valley of Sin, that deep swale running along the left front of the green. His ball ended up 16 feet from the hole. His first putt missed, and now the door was open. Rivero needed the 10-foot birdie to at least tie. He didn't get it. Davis took the game, 71-72, and Australia had the match, 2-0.

The final game was academic, but it made for good viewing. Olazabal was one over par through the sixth, then set off on a birdie binge — four in succession from No. 7, holing putts of 10, one, eight, and eight feet, and he added another at No. 13 from 12 feet en route to a 69-73 win over David Graham. The Australians had advanced, 2-1, into the final for the third time in the Dunhill's four years, then stood back to see whether they would play the English or the Irish. Maddeningly enough, it would take yet another day to find out. One thing was certain though — the unheralded Irish couldn't keep this up much longer.

For the skeptics, the proof came in the first game. England's Barry Lane shrugged off a one-stroke deficit at the turn and went on a rampage for an inward 31 and a 65-68 victory over Ronan Rafferty. It was one of the finest rounds of Lane's life. The Irish still hadn't gone over par, and here they were, one match down. Lane fell one behind at No. 2 with his only bogey of the day, a two-putt from 18 feet. He registered three birdies over the next five holes and trailed at the turn, 33-34. Then it was a dogfight. Lane caught Rafferty with a birdie at the par-three 11th. He almost passed him, in fact. Lane nearly holed out his eight-iron tee shot. All he had left was a six-inch tap-in. Rafferty then ripped off three consecutive birdies from the 12th on putts of 15, four, and 15 feet, and Lane matched the last two, from four feet at No. 13 and from seven at No. 14. The spurt put Rafferty six under par, and Lane still trailed by a stroke. Then Rafferty made two fatal errors.

His six-iron approach at No. 15 was far off target, stopping 70 feet from the hole. He three-putted for his first bogey and was level with Lane, who parred. Rafferty played No. 17 cautiously, leaving himself a wedge third. Then he two-putted from eight feet for his second and last bogey. Lane, meanwhile, put a six iron to eight feet at the treacherous old monster, and holed it — only the second birdie at No. 17 in the entire tournament. It gave Lane the lead for the first time. He was six under and two ahead of Rafferty with a hole to play. Lane had all but a lock on this game, but he wasn't taking any chances. At the final hole, he lobbed a sand wedge shot to 18 feet and dropped the birdie putt for the 65-68 win. England was one up. It was all but over.

You couldn't blame the fans for thinking this way. In the match right behind them, Nick Faldo was having a devil of a time with Des Smyth but finally drew even at the 12th. But first, a funny thing happened in this game — Faldo finally bogeyed. At the par-four fourth, his four-iron approach missed the green and his wedge left him 45 feet from the flag. He two-putted for his five, breaking his streak of 39 consecutive holes without a bogey. He was a stroke behind. They charged into the turn. Faldo scored three consecutive birdies from the fifth on putts of seven, five, and 15 feet. Smyth matched him at the fifth, from 30 inches, and the seventh from two feet. They were tied going to No. 9. Smyth broke free, holing from 12 for a birdie-two against Faldo's two putts from eight feet, and Smyth led at the turn, 33-34, and kept the one-stroke edge until Faldo caught him with six-foot birdie at No. 12. Next came the turning point at — where else? — the Road Hole.

At No. 17, Faldo missed the green with his four iron, left a wedge shot 30 feet from the hole, and two-putted for only his second bogey in this Dunhill Cup. The normally cautious Smyth, however, had turned bold. When Faldo missed the green, Smyth went after it with a four-wood second, put it 20 feet from the hole, and got down in two for his par and a one-stroke lead. Now an odd thing happened at No. 18: Faldo refused to finish the hole.

The sun was a huge, orange disk hanging up in an almost clear sky, bathing the old gray town in a Van Gogh hue. But a thick fog was clutching the Old Course here and there, and particularly at the 18th green. The golfers were apparitions in the mist. Now it was 5:30 p.m. Both men had hit their tee shots, and Smyth — against his better judgment, it turned out — had also hit his wedge approach. The crowd's polite applause informed him he had reached the green up there somewhere in the mist. He couldn't see it.

"I probably acted impetuously," Smyth admitted later. "If I had it to do over again, I probably wouldn't play."

Faldo left no room for self-doubt. He simply refused to hit. He fretted, walked about, held discussions with an official. The fog lifted a bit, then fell again. The crowd in the stands behind the green set up a slow clap. "Get on with it!" someone called. But Faldo held firm. This shot would be crucial because suddenly England's hopes were hanging by a thread. England was leading, 1-0, but Faldo was a stroke down and in danger of losing the second game to Smyth, and behind them, Ireland's Eamonn Darcy was thrashing Mark James. This was the pivotal match.

"I could see the flag, but not the black-and-white stick," Faldo explained. "I couldn't see the hole, the edge of the green, or anything of the slope. If I had been playing on my own, I might have hit. But I am playing for the two other guys, and it is down to this match." Faldo was in his rights to hold fire. By 6 p.m., the fog had not lifted, and now darkness was falling. Play was called for the day.

This left Darcy and James with two holes to complete — and shouldered James with an awesome task. A collapse early in the inward half left him three strokes behind. Darcy had opened hot. Two short putts bracketing a 34-footer gave him birdies on the first three holes. James matched him only at the first, and so trailed by two with the game only three holes old. James also birdied the ninth. In between, Darcy wiped out his big advantage with two bogeys, then added a birdie at the seventh from four feet, and they were tied at the turn, 34-34.

Then a plague hit James. At the 10th, he missed with his approach, pitched to three feet, and two-putted. He bunkered his tee shot at No. 11, blasted out to 10 feet, and again two-putted. And at the 12th, it took him three to get on and two putts to get down from nine feet. Three consecutive bogeys. Darcy dropped a three-foot birdie at No. 12 to go to three under par and four ahead. James's position wasn't merely critical. It was all but hopeless. He lightened his load a little at No. 16, rolling in a 25-footer for a birdie to pick up a stroke. He was three behind. Then with Faldo and Smyth stalled at the 18th, and with darkness and fog draping the course, play was abandoned. All four would return early Sunday morning to settle things.

When the golfers come marching up the 18th fairway at the Old Course, they see one of the most famous scenes in golf: first the famed, sloping green, then the grandstand, and then beyond, a ponderous, dark stone building, Hamilton Hall, of the University of St. Andrews. When Nick Faldo arrived early on the gray, cool, calm Sunday morning to pick up where he left off the evening before, to complete the third round, he might have been able to shut out the jibes of the partisan Scottish crowd but he couldn't miss the big sign draped from a fifth-floor balcony of Hamilton Hall. It looked like a blanket. It was blue, with the message in white. To the right was a golf flag, to the left a sour-looking face with the corners of the mouth turned down. In between was a taunt shouting in block capital letter: SEE THIS ONE NICK?

There was no fog now, at 8:30 a.m. And if Faldo saw that sign, he gave no indication. He had work to do. He was trailing Des Smyth by a stroke. The England-Ireland match was hanging in the balance. If Faldo lost this game, Ireland would tie the match 1-1, and behind them, back at No. 17, Eamonn Darcy was comfortably ahead of Mark James. Faldo had 78 yards to a flag sitting just beyond the Valley of Sin. He had to get this one close. He — and England — needed a birdie. He took one last look, then hit a fine shot to just seven feet below the hole. Now the burden was on Smyth. That near-blind pitch he had hit through the fog the evening before had left him an uncomfortable thought to sleep on. Worse, it also left him uphill and to the right of the flag, about 60 long feet away.

Smyth stepped over the ball, then backed off. "I began to shake," he explained later. But he forced himself to go back. He did well to leave his first putt about three feet short, by no means a "gimme" on the treacherous green. Now Faldo stepped up. A birdie would clinch a tie, and if Smyth should miss that three-footer, it meant a win for him and England. But Faldo missed. The partisan fans broke into a wild cheer. Then they hushed. Smyth, the hero of the moment, needed some peace and quiet. He faced about the same putt that cost Doug Sanders the 1970 British Open Championship. Smyth gave one last glance, tapped the ball, and Faldo had suffered his only defeat in 11 Dunhill Cup games.

Smyth's 69-70 victory tied the match at 1-1. But actually, it was over. Darcy, going against James just behind, was not about to squander a three-stroke lead over two holes. In fact, he went one better. Again playing No. 17 for a safe bogey, he holed a 30-foot putt from off the green for his par, halving the hole with James. Then Darcy birdied the 18th, from eight feet, for a 68-72 win and a 2-1 Irish victory. The Irish were in the Dunhill Cup final for the first time. And against a formidable opponent. The Australians, led by Greg Norman, were in the final for the third time in four years. In the inaugural Dunhill Cup in 1985, they crushed the Americans by 12 strokes in a 3-0 sweep. In 1986, their victims were the Japanese, 3-0, by nine strokes.

The playoff for third and fourth place went off first, later Sunday morning. Faldo, unshaken by his loss to Smyth, remained his gritty self against Jose-Maria Olazabal. He birdied the first three holes, then held on against Olazabal's strong finish for a 66-67 victory. (Faldo bogeyed No. 13 — only his third bogey in 72 holes.) The Spanish tied the match in the second game when Barry Lane bogeyed three of the final five holes and lost to Seve Ballesteros, 71-72. Jose Rivero charged through the turn with three birdies to give Spain third place with a 69-70 win over Mark James in the final game.

Des Smyth was in a dark frame of mind when the championship match went off. He couldn't have drawn a worse opponent — Rodger Davis. "I thought of Rodger having beaten me twice," Smyth was to confess. "He beat me in this year's Epson Match Play, and he beat me in the PGA Championship two years ago at Wentworth in a playoff. I was beginning to think he had a sign on me." But this was the Old Course. That dragon Road Hole hadn't been fed for a while. It was soon to devour another victim.

They got under way at 12:45 p.m. It was a lurching start. Davis wasn't short with his approach to No. 1 this time. He hit a nine iron to 32 feet and birdied while Smyth wasted an excellent approach, needing two putts from six feet. Davis led by a stroke. But he was soon one down after bogeys at the fourth, where he three-putted from 34 feet, and the fifth, where he bunkered his drive. The par-three eighth was an early turning point. Davis birdied from 12 feet and Smyth bogeyed with three putts from 28. Davis led by one at the turn, 36-37. The margin was small, but the sign wasn't good. Until now, not one of the Irish had gone over par for any nine holes, out or in. Davis's putter failed him again at the par-three 11th. He took three putts from 32 feet, and they were tied at one over par. But he took the lead back at No. 12, a birdie from 14 feet, then went two ahead when

Smyth bunkered his tee shot at the 13th and bogeyed. They halved the 14th in short birdies, and Smyth got down to level par with a birdie at No. 16, hitting an excellent seven iron to 12 feet and holing the birdie putt. Davis was leading by a stroke with only two holes to play. The trouble was, one of those holes was No. 17.

Smyth teed off first and was safely to the left. Davis couldn't resist the opportunity. "I knew Des had not shot to the green from there," he said. So he stepped up to protect his one-stroke lead, but he wasn't about to tip-toe around this hole. He wanted to fly the ball over the jutting edge of the Old Course Golf and Country Club Hotel. He gave a mighty swing, then watched in horror as the ball drifted. He had gone too far right. The ball arced into the hotel gardens. He was out of bounds. Davis leaned on his driver, head bowed. Wearily, he reloaded. His second drive was into the fairway, and he put a six iron on the front of the green, some 75 feet from the hole. He three-putted from there — a fatal triple-bogey seven. Smyth wasn't about to challenge the hole now. He didn't have to. He played away from the bunker, hitting his three iron approach to the left of the green, some 40 feet from the flag. He was two strokes ahead. The 18th was an anticlimax. Davis pulled himself together and birdied from eight feet, but he was only following the leader. Smyth had already dropped an 18-footer for his birdie. Smyth not only kept the Irish under-par going with a 71-73 win, he gave the Irish a 1-0 lead.

Later, Davis could only shake his head. "I always hit it that way at No. 17," he said. "I just try to hit it on the right side so I could put my second in the middle of the green. And with the greens soft, you can pitch it on top and aim at the flag. But I cut it."

"I know how he felt," Smyth said. "I've done it myself." But Smyth had to shut Davis's disaster out of his mind. He himself still had to negotiate that menacing hole, especially the bunker. A man could make 10 with no trouble at all, as Mark Mouland had shown. It wasn't until Smyth did get past the thing that he could breathe a little freer. "I knew if I hit down the fairway, the pressure was on him," Smyth said. "He seemed to be cruising, and when I hit it down the fairway and then, with him out of bounds, when I hit my second shot left of the bunker, I thought I was home."

All the Irish needed now was a victory from Ronan Rafferty, and he was doing nicely against David Graham in the match behind. Graham went out in par 36, with a bogey at the second and a birdie-three at the seventh from 12 feet. Rafferty, on the other hand, was flawless. He birdied three holes in the middle, the fourth from 35 feet, the fifth from four, and the seventh from three, and led through the turn, 33-36. Graham would get no closer than two strokes coming home. Rafferty bogeyed the 13th after missing the green, but Graham couldn't get anything going. He three-putted the 14th from 25 feet for a bogey, and was three behind again. One last test.

"Standing on the 17th tee, we'd already heard the cheer," Rafferty said. He knew what the roar meant: It was the boisterous Scots, announcing Faldo's defeat when he missed his birdie putt up at No. 18. "It dawned on me," Rafferty said, face flushed. "It's me! I've got to do it up the last two holes!" He played the 17th gingerly, but not without breaking a sweat. His three-iron approach stopped rolling just in time. Another yard, and he'd have been in the Road Bunker. With great caution, he hit an exquisitely delicate pitch over the left shoulder of the bunker. "I had no other option," he said. The shot left him 30 feet from the hole. He was delighted just to be there. He tried to lag the putt close, to get a safe bogey. But the ball rolled right in. "I jumped so high, I nearly jumped over the Dunhill sign," Rafferty said. "I knew it was all over then." Graham, meanwhile, was three-putting from 60 feet for his five. He was four behind. The end was ceremonial, but Rafferty closed out in style — a birdie from 25 feet for a 69-74 victory. His putt dropped at 4:27 p.m. Ireland had won the Dunhill Cup.

There was still some drama to be played out, however. It was an ironic replay of the third place match of a year ago. Back then, Greg Norman was tagging along while Curtis Strange was burning up the Old Course with his record 62. Norman, it will be recalled, shot a very creditable 70 at the time. The cast was different this time, and the roles reversed. While Eamonn Darcy was working on a fine 71, Norman was working on a record. Norman had Strange's course-record 62 squarely in his sights. Norman was out in 30, including four consecutive birdies from the fifth. His shortest putts were a six-inch tap-in at No. 3 and a four-footer at No. 7. The other four ranged from 15 to 20 feet. He got three more birdies coming home — from 12 feet at No. 13, from three at No. 14, and from 25 at No. 16. But two short birdie putts got away, an eight-footer at No. 12 and a six-footer at No. 17, and he had to settle for a bogey-free, nine-under-par 63.

"And I wanted that record," Norman said. "I said, 'I am going to break it today or never.' But the team all played well. I didn't know what had happened to Rodger, but when I heard about his out-of-bounds — well, it's just one of those things. We had a shot today, but the fates looked the other way. The course was there to be played, and we didn't make it."

And the winners laughed.

"It has been a fantastic week for us," said Darcy, the Irish captain. "We've had a tough match every day, starting against Canada, the toughest match of the non-seeded teams, then America, and against England, nailbiting, and to have to come back this morning." Darcy had his uneasy moments in this final match. He knew early that he had no chance against Norman. He had made the turn in one-under-par 35, and was trailing by five whopping strokes. "I hit Greg on a hot day," he said. "And I was watching the two boys carefully in front of us, and I thought we were in big trouble. I knew Ronan was two shots ahead, but that Des was struggling. Then I heard that Davis had put it out of bounds, and when I saw the scoreboard, I couldn't believe it! Christmas had come early for us."

9. The U.S. Tour

The laments that the U.S. PGA Tour was suffering because it lacked a dominant figure were answered by Curtis Strange in 1988. Strange, who won three tournaments and more than $925,000 in 1987, outdid himself. He became the first to win over $1 million in the United States in a season, although that record could be downplayed because a major chunk of it ($535,000) came for his victory in the Nabisco Championship, including the $360,000 first prize and $175,000 in bonuses.

Strange also won the Memorial Tournament and Independent Insurance Agent (Houston) Open as well as, of course, scoring his first victory in a major event, beating Nick Faldo in a playoff by four strokes in the U.S. Open at The Country Club in Brookline, Massachusetts.

Strange was the major story in 1988, but he wasn't the entire story. Going into the Nabisco tournament, any of 14 players could have topped $1 million with a victory. Including non-member Seve Ballesteros, who won $165,202 in seven tournaments, a total of 112 players earned more than $100,000. Chip Beck, who placed second with $916,818, won more money in one year than anyone ever except Strange. Jack Nicklaus, a milestone-setter for money winnings, became the first to pass $5 million in a career although he won only $28,845 in nine tournaments. If the old system of the top 60 qualifying for tour cards was still in effect, it would have taken $191,489 to make it.

It was possible to earn nearly a fortune without winning a tournament. Tom Kite set a record for winnings in a season without a victory of $760,405. Kite had his seven-year winning streak ended, but he didn't give up without a fight. He lost playoffs to Morris Hatalsky in the Kemper Open and to Strange in the Nabisco Championship, and placed second in the Hertz Bay Hill Classic to Paul Azinger.

Beck, who had been knocking for his first victory, finally had the door opened in the Los Angeles Open. He stepped in again with a triumph in the USF&G Classic in New Orleans. He was one of 11 first-time winners and one of nine players who won more than once during the year. Strange led the multiple winners. The others were Sandy Lyle (Phoenix, Greensboro, Masters), Ken Green (Canadian, Milwaukee), Steve Pate (Tournament of Champions, Andy Williams), Lanny Wadkins (Hawaii, Colonial), Joey Sindelar (Honda, International), David Frost (Southern, Tucson) and Bill Glasson (B.C., Centel).

There were 13 first-time winners if you count Scott Verplank's first victory as a pro in the Buick Open (he won the Western Open as an amateur in 1985) and Frank Conner's triumph in the Deposit Guaranty, an unofficial tournament. The other first-timers were: Steve Jones (AT&T Pebble Beach), Jim Benepe (Western), Tom Sieckmann (Anheuser-Busch), Blaine McCallister (Hardee's), Mark Brooks (Hartford), Jeff Sluman (PGA Championship), Jodie Mudd (Memphis), Andrew Magee (Pensacola) and Bob Lohr (Disney).

Benepe was the most unlikely tournament winner. He got into his first PGA Tour tournament on a sponsor's exemption, then withstood mounting pressure to win the Western Open, a tournament that has had a history of bizarre happenings. Some other highlights were:

• Fred Couples needed only a par at the 72nd hole to beat out Lyle, who had finished with a bogey, for victory at Phoenix. Couples' tee shot hit a spectator and went into a lake. He bogeyed. At the same hole, the third in bunker. Then he hit a high recovery shot 10 feet above the hole and dropped the putt for victory.

• Greg Norman scored his only U.S. victory of the year amid high emotions in the Heritage Classic. Jamie Hutton, a 17-year-old from Wisconsin, had been diagnosed as having leukemia. Thursday's Child, a non-profit organization that tries to grant wishes, fulfilled Hutton's desire to meet Norman. Hutton spent the weekend with Norman, who won dramatically with a 66 in the final round at Harbour Town.

• Norman also was involved in what could have been the most interesting playoff of the year. Norman, Ken Green, Ballesteros and Frost tied after 72 holes at Westchester. But Ballesteros, who hates playoffs, ended it quickly, blasting out of a bunker and sinking a five-foot birdie putt at the first hole.

• Mike Reid, who scored his first triumph in 11 years in 1987, confounded the experts in the television booth in the World Series. At the first hole of a playoff with Tom Watson at rain-soaked Firestone Country Club, Reid's approach left him so far from the hole the announcers voiced their opinion he would three-putt. Watson was closer; he had a certain par. But Reid two-putted and Watson missed a tying putt from about three feet.

• Ken Green developed chest pains that were so severe he almost passed out early in the final round at Milwaukee, but he recovered to win by six strokes.

• Corey Pavin, who had been a non-contender through most of the year, suddenly put his game together in the Texas Open, winning by eight strokes with 259, the second lowest score in tour history.

For some better-known players, it was an empty season. Couples, Bob Tway, who last won in the 1986 PGA Championship; Craig Stadler, Tom Watson, Fuzzy Zoeller, Larry Mize and Raymond Floyd failed to score a victory. They earned nice livings, to be sure. But a pro golfer's career is measured more by the tournaments he has won than by the money he has amassed, no matter how big that dollar sign has become on the PGA Tour.

Spalding Invitational—$250,000
Winner: Lennie Clements

Lennie Clements picked up the $50,000 first prize in the Spalding Invitational with a 35-foot birdie putt at the first playoff hole against Ken Green, Tim Norris and Dan Pohl. One of six LPGA players in the field, Jan Stephenson, had a chance to make it a five-way playoff but missed a six-foot birdie putt at the 18th hole.

The non-tour event was played over two California courses, with three rounds at Carmel Valley Ranch and one at Pebble Beach. Clements started with a nine-under 62 at Carmel Valley that broke the course and tournament records. Norris and Mark Lye tied the record in the third round. Clements broke the shaft of his seven iron at the fifth hole at Pebble Beach in the second round and slipped three strokes behind Stephenson, who added a 69 to her opening 67, and five behind Bob Gilder, who stitched together

67s. Stephenson's 65 in the third round gave her the lead, but Clements regrouped for a 63 that left him one stroke back.

Stephenson bogeyed the first hole and Clements started birdie-birdie in the final round and the chase was on. Pohl, aided by eagles at the second and 10th holes, came flying in with 64 for 271. Green got off to a bad start, then righted himself for 65 and his 271. Norris got his 271 with a steady 68. Clements had a seven-foot birdie putt to win the tournment outright and missed, and seconds later Stephenson failed on a six-foot birdie putt that would have made the playoff.

The playoff ended quickly, Norris and Pohl reached the green, about 25 feet from the cup, with their approaches and Green hit his approach into a bunker. Clements' shot went past the cup to the fringe behind it, 35 feet away. His birdie putt was on line and the others were unable to match his three.

MONY Tournament of Champions—$500,000
Winner: Steve Pate

Steve Pate, whose first PGA Tour victory came in the 1987 Southwest Classic, picked up his second triumph in the MONY Tournament of Champions at La Costa Country Club in Carlsbad, California, winning by one stroke over Larry Nelson when the fourth round was washed out by unusually bad weather.

The first official tournament of the year brought together the 37 PGA Tour winners of 1987, plus British Open champion Nick Faldo. It appeared the only one upset by the abrupt ending was Nelson. The PGA champion had tied Pate for the lead with a birdie at the third hole when the final round was called off after four suspensions of play and a total delay of four hours.

The first round gave no indication of what was in store. The weather was favorable and the players jumped on it, with only nine failing to shoot par or below. Pate, a native Californian, turned in a bogey-free six-under 66 to take the lead. On Friday, he missed his first green, but again finished with a bogey-free 66 that left him one stroke ahead of Dave Barr, who opened with 67-66. Nelson trailed by three with 68-67, and Faldo, who had seven birdies in a row in a second-round 65, was three behind.

It rained Friday night, making the course play longer than in the first two rounds. Pate finally had his first over-par hole, a double bogey when his drive buried in a bunker, but also made five birdies on the front nine. He bogeyed three of the last five holes for 70 that left him at 202, and Nelson breathing down his neck at 203 after 68. Barr, with 73, and Faldo, with 71, were tied for third place at 206 and that's the way they finished.

Bob Hope Chrysler Classic—$1,000,000
Winner: Jay Haas

When Jay Haas called his family back home in South Carolina the morning of the final round of the Bob Hope Chrysler Classic, it was difficult to get his four children to come to the telephone. Reluctantly, they left the television set for a moment and Jay, Jr., came up with the question that might have set up Haas' seventh PGA Tour victory.

"Why are you nervous, Daddy?" Jay, Jr. said.

Haas had a one-stroke lead over Bob Tway, the 1986 PGA Player of the Year, and a two-stroke edge on Paul Azinger, the 1987 PGA Player of the Year. What's to worry about? Try to tell a six-year-old child.

The remark might have been just the tonic Haas needed. It relaxed him for a two-stroke victory over fast-closing David Edwards. "I felt if I shot a 70 I'd probably finish in second or third place," Haas said. But that was enough as Tway slipped to 72 and Azinger, 75. Edwards' 67 gave him second place, a stroke ahead of Tway.

The Hope Classic is a 90-hole tournament played over four courses in the Palm Springs, California, area. This year the final round was over the new PGA West Palmer Course. In contrast to the poor weather conditions that shortened the Tournament of Champions a week earlier, it was played in ideal weather. That was why Haas thought a two-under 70 would not enable him to win.

Low scores had been in abundance through the first four rounds. Haas opened with a nine-under 63 at Indian Wells for a one-stroke lead over Andy Bean and Sandy Lyle.

Dan Forsman, who had asked Haas how to shoot a 63 during a timeout on the practice range, must have learned something. Forsman shot a 10-under 62 in the second round for a 36-hole 130 that gave him a one-stroke lead. But Forsman followed with a 75 and never recovered.

Haas, nearly flawless through the first two rounds, made his first bogey of the tournament in the third round at the Palmer Course but managed 69 that gave him a share of the lead with Azinger at 200. Azinger turned in a brilliant 65 at Indian Wells. Tway, with a 67 at Indian Wells, was at 202.

Haas sank a 50-yard wedge shot for an eagle at Bermuda Dunes' eighth hole in the fourth round on the way to 68. He was one stroke ahead of Tway, who had 67, and Azinger, who slipped to 70.

Azinger's putting, not strong at the beginning of the tournament, virtually disintegrated in the final round. He five-putted from the apron at the par-three fourth hole, then left Haas and Tway to battle it out after he four-putted the 11th green. Haas and Tway had started erratically, and when Tway birdied the fifth and sixth holes, they were tied for the lead. Then came what proved to be the decisive hole at the 338-yard No. 7, Haas hit a sand wedge to within five feet of the hole, setting up a birdie. Tway's wedge play had been weak, and this time his approach was long. He bogeyed and the two-stroke swing gave Haas a lead he was able to keep just by stringing together pars.

Mark O'Meara got to within two strokes of Haas at the 14th hole, where his charge ran out. Edwards, who admitted he had no thoughts of winning, birdied the 17th with a 20-foot putt and sank a three-foot birdie at the final hole that got him to within a stroke of the lead until Haas finished off his victory with a 12-foot birdie.

Phoenix Open—$650,000
Winner: Sandy Lyle

There are no short hitters on the PGA Tour; some can hit the ball further than others. Sometimes length can be a detriment, as it was to Fred Couples in the final round of the Phoenix Open at the Tournament Players Club of Scottsdale.

At 6,990 yards, the Arizona course is not tailored for long hitters, although there are a few holes that give them an advantage. One is the 17th, a 332-yard par-four that a long hitter can drive. Another is the 438-yard No. 18, a par-four with a lake to the left of the fairway. Couples played those two holes in par-bogey in the final round, then double-bogeyed the 18th on the third playoff hole, handing the victory to Sandy Lyle, who bogeyed.

Except for the second round, which Chip Beck led with a 66-63, the tournament was a battle of long hitters — Lyle, Couples and Davis Love III. Love had six birdies and an eagle in an opening-round 63 for a three-stroke lead, then slipped two behind Beck with 68 the second day. Couples, with 67-65, and Lyle, with 68-68, were just part of a crowd of par-breakers.

Love overcame three bogeys for a five-under 66 in the third round for a 54-hole total of 197. Couples played just as erratically with almost as good results: four bogeys, four birdies, two eagles for 67 and 199. David Frost, who eventually placed third, was four back and Lyle, with three straight 68s, was tied with Beck, seven behind Love. Lyle later admitted he thought he had no chance to win, his outlook dampened by a shot in the the water at No. 18.

For a while the final round was a Couples-Love struggle. Love three-putted the eighth hole, Couples sank a 15-foot birdie at the ninth, and Love missed there from three feet. Suddenly Couples led Love by two strokes and Lyle by four. Love lasted two more holes, then dropped out of contention, finishing with 76 in fourth place.

Meanwhile, Lyle inched up on Couples. They were tied for the lead after a bogey by Couples at No. 12 and Lyle's birdies at Nos. 11, 13 and 15. Couples birdied the par-three 16th, then Lyle drove the inviting No. 17 and birdied. Couples also drove No. 17, but three-putted for par. He got another chance to win when Lyle bogeyed No. 18 after hitting his approach into a bunker. Couples' drive at the 18th was far left, so far that it hit on the other side of the lake, where the spectators were. His ball hit an unsuspecting woman and ricocheted into the lake. He did well to make bogey for 70 and 269, the same as Lyle, who finished with 65.

The playoff began at No. 10, then went to Nos. 17 and 18. Lyle made a great chip to within less than a yard of the hole to halve No. 10 after Couples missed a 12-foot birdie. Lyle missed a four-foot putt that would have won at No. 17, so once again they went to the fateful 18th. Couples again hit his drive into the lake and this time he didn't recover as well as he had earlier. His approach went into a bunker, and he wound up with double bogey, as Lyle came out of a bunker to win with a bogey.

AT&T Pebble Beach National Pro-Am—$700,000
Winner: Steve Jones

No matter what they call it, the AT&T Pebble Beach National Pro-Am may always be regarded as the Bing Crosby Pro-Am. It's still played on three Monterey Peninsula courses in California — Pebble Beach, Cypress Point and Spyglass Hill — as it was before Bing died and his widow moved the tournament name to North Carolina, and celebrities, most from stage and screen, dot the amateur portion.

The pros have gradually changed. When Steve Jones won, there must have been many in the crowd who knew little about him. But after Jones beat Bob Tway in a playoff for his first victory as a pro, many probably marked him down as a player to watch.

Jones is a native of Phoenix, and attended the University of Colorado. He won more than $150,000 in 1987. Each tournament chooses a team in the Nabisco Grand Prix, with the top teams at the end of the year earning money for the charities of the tournaments they represent. So it was that Jones' victory was greeted warmly by the AT&T Pebble Beach Pro-Am sponsors, who had chosen him as one of their players.

The medalist in the 1986 qualifying tournament, Jones popped into prominence in the 1987 Heritage Classic, leading by one stroke with one hole to play. As he took his club back, a gust of wind arose, and he drove out of bounds. The double bogey left him one stroke behind Davis Love.

Jones admitted he was thinking of that hole as he teed off in the final round at Pebble Beach. He had just bogeyed the 17th hole and needed a par to send the tournament into a playoff, or a birdie to win. The Pacific Ocean laps along the left side of the par-five 18th, and out of bounds is to the right.

Instead of playing safe with a iron, Jones hit a driver. "God teaches us to learn from our mistakes," he said.

He parred for a wobbly 74 that left him tied with Tway, who shot 68, at 280. Greg Norman attempted to make the playoff a threesome, but his 65 was one stroke short. Jones and Tway halved the first playoff hole with pars. The second was No. 17, which had nearly led to Jones' demise less than an hour earlier. Both hit the green, Tway a little closer to the hole. After Jones holed his 15-foot birdie putt, Tway was unable to match him.

Jones' putt was no surprise to anyone who had watched him in the final round. His putter saved his 74 from being an 80. He one-putted Nos. 10, 11, 12, 13 and 14. He was even more outstanding in the second round when he shot 64 for a 136 total that tied Mark Calcavecchia for the lead. Calcavecchia had opened with 67, tied for the lead with Jim Booros and Jim Gallagher. Jones came back with 70 in the third round, for a three-stroke lead over Craig Stadler and Bernhard Langer. Tway, with 67, trailed by six strokes and Norman was three behind him.

Hawaiian Open—$600,000
Winner: Lanny Wadkins

A few years ago, it was easy to identify Richard Zokol. He was the one wearing the portable tape player as he hovered over a shot. "The music helped me relax," he said. After a poor 1986 season, Zokol had to requalify and he came back in 1987 without the tape player. In the fifth tournament of 1988, he almost heard the music of a victory march.

Lanny Wadkins changed the tune in the final nine holes of the Hawaiian Open at the Waialae Country Club, but Zokol wasn't displeased by his second-place finish, one stroke behind Wadkins' 17-under 271. "If I had choked my brains out it would have been a failure. This was my best finish on tour." The $64,800 he earned was more than half what he made in 1987, his best year.

Zokol was in the chase from start to finish. He opened with a six-under 66, tying him for the lead with Jodie Mudd, whose round was marked by birdie putts of 40 and 60 feet. The wind, as usual, kept the players guessing, but most of them guessed right. Wadkins and Loren Roberts were among those with 68s. Roberts, who, like Zokol, had to requalify in 1987, took over the lead with a second-day 66 for 134. Zokol and Wadkins came in with 71s.

A cross-handed putter, Zokol needed only 26 putts for 65 that gave him a two-stoke lead over Roberts and Mark Brooks after 54 holes. Wadkins, with 66, was tied with Tom Watson, three strokes behind the leader. Wadkins and Watson were the ones who concerned Zokol the most. "If they play well, fine, I just want to play the best I can," he said.

Zokol played the front nine in 37 in the final round, and Wadkins moved a stroke ahead of him with 33 and Watson caught him with 34. Suddenly Watson was out of the chase when he four-putted the 10th hole for a triple-bogey seven. Wadkins matched his front-nine figures for 66. After Zokol hit his drive at the par-five 18th, he learned that he needed an eagle to make a playoff. He gave it a shot. His second with a two-iron reached the fringe of the green. He gamely tried to hole his chip shot, and it came up a foot short.

Shearson Lehman Hutton Andy Williams Open—$650,000
Winner: Steve Pate

A native Californian, Steve Pate said that before 1988, "I never seemed to play well out here." He won't be able to say that anymore. His victory in the Shearson Lehman Hutton Andy Williams (San Diego) Open was his second of the year, and both came in California.

Pate was not very proud of his first triumph, the MONY Tournament of Champions, which was ended after 54 holes by miserable weather. This victory was something to boast about. The Torrey Pines North and South courses had been hardened by winds, and it was obvious that the winning score would be well under par. It was 19 under par, Pate winning by one stroke over Jay Haas with 68-66-67-68—269.

The 7,000-yard long South course and the 6,660-yard North course are used in the first two rounds, with those making the cut playing the last two rounds on the South course. The North course, as expected, yielded the lowest scores, and the cut came at 142, two under. How much easier the North course played was illustrated by Gil Morgan, who was in danger of missing the cut after a 74 on the South, then bounced into contention with a 62 on the North.

Fred Couples opened with 63 on the North course, which technically gave him the lead, but most people including Couples thought Tom Watson's 65 on the South course was better. After a prediction of strong winds proved false, the birdies flew again in the second round, Morgan shooting 29 on the back nine as he tied the North course record with his 62.

Don Pooley shot 65 on the North for 132 and the second-round lead over Tom Kite and Bob Tway, who matched Pooley's 65. Brad Faxon, who also had 65 in the second round, sank a 30-foot eagle putt at the final hole for 66 in the third round and took the 54-hole lead with 200, 16 under par. Pate also made an eagle at the 18th hole — from six feet — for 67 that left him one stroke behind. Kite hit what he called "a West Texas rat hook" at the 14th hole into an unplayable lie as he managed 69 that left him tied at 202 with Willie Wood, Hal Sutton and Couples.

Last-round pressure seemed to affect many of the contenders, but Pate was able to offset it with his putter. Time and time again, he sank critical putts of four to 10 feet for birdies or pars after the eighth hole. His best, and most important, came at the final hole. Haas had made an 18-foot eagle putt at the final hole to cap a 66 and was in the clubhouse with 270 when Pate teed off at No. 18. Pate needed a birdie to win — not a very difficult task. He got the necessary four, sinking a putt of less than six feet for the $117,000 prize that gave him nearly $230,000 after less than two months of the season and left him a little more than $30,000 behind Haas, the leader.

Los Angeles Open—$750,000
Winner: Chip Beck

As time ran out on the 1987 PGA Tour season, a triumvirate of golfers stood alone in what was not good company. Mike Reid, Chip Beck and Bobby Wadkins had each spent more than 10 years on the tour without winning a tournament. Then Reid made it a duo by winning the Tucson Open near the end of the season.

Beck's turn finally came in the Los Angeles Open at Riviera Country Club, leaving only Wadkins to answer the tiresome question: "When are you going to win?"

Mac O'Grady, who tied Bill Sander for second place at Los Angeles, said he had told Beck a year and a half earlier that when he won his first tournament "over the next 10 years he would win about 20 times." And after the way Beck won at Riviera, O'Grady could prove to be correct. Despite a bogey at the final hole, Beck won by four strokes with 65-69-65-68—274, showing considerable poise and determination after Jay Haas closed in on him in the middle of the front nine in the final round.

The weather had left Riviera with its defenses down. The fairways were spotted and fast, and the greens soft and true, made softer in the last two rounds by rain. Beck's opening 65 tied him for the lead with Jumbo Ozaki, Dan Pohl and Haas. Haas, with 68, and Ben Crenshaw, with 64, took a one-stroke lead over five players, including Beck, after 36 holes.

Then Beck took over. His second 65 of the week gave him 199 for 54 holes, a tournament record, and a three-stroke lead on Haas, Ed Fiori and Steve Elkington. Beck made six birdies in eight holes, starting at the fifth, a feat he was to repeat in the final round.

Rain twice delayed play Sunday, the second time for about an hour and a half, after Beck had played one hole. He bogeyed the third hole but said, "I just figured, 'There are bogeys to be made out here' and I wasn't concerned." He proved his talk was not just so much bravado, when Haas pulled to within a stroke after six holes. Beck birdied the seventh by hitting a seven iron to within 18 inches of the hole, sank a 10-footer for birdie at No. 8 after Haas, playing in the group ahead of him, bogeyed the hole, then birdied the ninth and 11th holes with putts of 10 and three feet. He had a four-stroke lead on Reid and a smooth ride to his first victory.

Doral Ryder Open—$1,000,000
Winner: Ben Crenshaw

Was this the week for Bobby Wadkins to end his victory drought, as the tour swung east for the Doral Ryder Open? That was on the minds of many with one round to play on Doral Country Club's Blue Monster course. That and whether Jack Nicklaus, at age 48, could mount a charge to win a tournament he had captured 16 years earlier.

It was not to be for either. Wadkins, who has won the most money on tour without a victory, did a belly-flop in the last round, and Nicklaus' putting stroke failed him. Ben Crenshaw, almost unnoticed for three days, came out of the pack with a six-under 66 for 274 that gave him a one-stroke victory over Mark McCumber and Chip Beck.

Until Crenshaw fought his way to the top, Wadkins and Nicklaus were the center of attention. Nicklaus used a metal driver for the first time as he won the nine-hole shootout two days before the tournament, and he awed the spectators with the length and accuracy of his drives as he shot 68-69-71 through the first three rounds. But Nicklaus bogeyed three of the par-fives in the third round, and that was a tipoff there would be no charge the next day. Nicklaus finished with 75 as a gang of players roared past him.

Wadkins, with the help of teacher Peter Kostis, has a vastly improved putting stroke that quickly produced results. Wadkins led the first round with 67, one stroke ahead of four players, including Nicklaus and Beck. A second 67 on Friday gave Wadkins a two-stroke lead on Beck, who opened 68-68, and three on Nicklaus.

Wadkins, who has won overseas but whose U.S. career has been littered with ill-timed mistakes, committed one in the third round. Attempting to hit a 200-yard layup with a four iron at the 528-yard No. 8 hole, he overlooked how much his adrenaline was pumping and hit it into the water. He said he calmed down after that, but missed birdie putts of six to 15 feet on the first three holes of the back nine. Nevertheless, Wadkins parred in for 70 and maintained his two-stroke margin over Beck. McCumber, after an opening 71, shot his second straight 68 and was three strokes behind. Crenshaw, who had lost ground despite shooting 70-69-69, thought he had a chance to win if he shot 66 in the final round.

On a damp, windy and overcast day, Crenshaw shot his 66 Sunday, then sat by to see if anyone could match or beat his 274 total. Wadkins found the water at the fourth hole and took a double bogey that seemed to take all the life out of him. He shot 76 and skidded to a tie for 15th, six strokes behind Crenshaw. Only McCumber and Beck, who both had birdied No. 17, had a chance to catch Crenshaw. They had to birdie No. 18 to do it, no easy task. McCumber's putt from 20 feet stopped short. Beck's putt was wide. Crenshaw had his 14th victory in 15 years on the tour.

Honda Classic—$700,000
Winner: Joey Sindelar

In his first four years on the tour, Joey Sindelar had settled into a pattern. He spent the first three or four months sharpening his game, picked up the big checks when spring turned into summer, and won in the autumn before the home folks. Of his three victories, two came in the B.C. Open in Endicott, New York, not far from his home town of Horseheads. The other came in the Greater Greensboro Open, "and that's early for me."

Sindelar said his wife, Suzanne, told him to quit fiddling with his game and to go out and play. That's the advice he followed to victory in the Honda Classic at the TPC at Eagle Trace course in Coral Springs, Florida. After tying for third at San Diego and for fifth at Doral, Sindelar shook off his pursuers to win by two strokes with 68-70-68-70—276.

His opening 68 might have been the key to his triumph. The Thursday weather was abominable, nearly bad enough to have the round called off. A heavy rain and wind raked the course in the morning, and when the rain stopped the wind blew to about 35-40 miles an hour. Amid such conditions, Sindelar shot 68 that left him one stroke behind Ronnie Black, who had taken the brunt of the storm in his 67. The wind was like a policeman escorting the bad weather off the premises. The last three rounds were played in almost ideal weather.

As the weather improved, so did the scores. Ken Brown, Ed Fiori, Fred Wadsworth, Jodie Mudd, Tommy Nakajima and Dan Forsman tied for the second-round lead at 137 and six others, including Sandy Lyle, who shot 64, and Sindelar were tied at 138. A 68 on Saturday gave Sindelar a one-stroke edge on Brown, but the field was bunched behind them.

Brown indicated he expected to make a battle of it when he caught Sindelar with a birdie at the first hole in the final round, but he dropped back with a bogey at the third hole. Brown took himself out of the chase with a triple bogey at the eighth hole after hitting his second shot into the water. Shortly before that, Davis Love III, in sight of the lead after a birdie at the fourth hole and an eagle at the fifth, erased himself with an 11 at the par-three seventh hole.

Raymond Floyd, at age 45 making a bid to regain the excellence of years past, caught Sindelar and Brown with birdies at the first and fourth holes. Floyd bogeyed the fifth hole and took a triple bogey at the seventh. Even an eagle at the eighth hole was not enough to undo the damage. Mark McCumber, who played the first 15 holes in eight under par, ran out of gas. Lyle and Fiori had their bids crumpled by late bogeys. Fiori tied for second place with Payne Stewart, who came back from an unimpressive start to finish with two consecutive 67s.

Meanwhile, Sindelar and Brown raced to finish in daylight. They were asked whether they wanted to finish. Sindelar, who thought he had only a one-stroke lead on Lyle, and Brown completed their round with no time to spare for a playoff. It wasn't until he got to the 18th green that Sindelar learned Lyle had bogeyed the final hole, giving him a two-stroke lead, which he figured he could have held in darkness.

Hertz Bay Hill Classic—$750,000
Winner: Paul Azinger

The Bay Hill Club in Orlando, Florida, already held a number of memories for Paul Azinger before the Hertz Bay Hill Classic. Which is why his five-stroke victory might have been more cherished than the three wins he had scored in 1987, when he was named PGA Player of the Year.

While attending junior college in Florida, Azinger worked as a counselor at the Arnold Palmer Golf Academy in the summer, and was able to play Bay Hill every day. "It was great," he said. After losing, then regaining, his PGA Tour card, Azinger tied for fifth in the Bay Hill Classic, his best finish up to that point in a blossoming career. In 1986, paired with Palmer, he was medalist in the qualifing for the U.S. Open at Bay Hill. And two years later he was with Palmer again, accepting the $135,000 check for winning the Hertz Bay Hill Classic.

His first victory of 1988 also answered a few questions, mostly raised by the new media, such as: Was his three-win, $822,481 performance in 1987 a fluke? Was the bogey-bogey finish that cost him the 1987 British Open an indication that his rocket had run out of fuel? To all this, Azinger said no; "I had been putting a lot of pressure on myself. I didn't get over the British Open until last week."

Once he got that memory out of the way, he settled down to beat Tom Kite in a head-to-head battle that left the rest of the field mere spectators in the final round at Bay Hill. Azinger either led or was tied for the lead from the first round on as he shot five-under-par 66s in the first, second and fourth rounds and interspersed a 73 on a windy third round.

Azinger and Andrew Magee, who ultimately tied David Frost for third place, tied for the first-round lead and Azinger pulled in front by four strokes with his second 66 on a windy and wet day. Azinger played the third round with an inner ear infection that made him dizzy and made it a chore just to fix ball marks. But Kite was one of only two players able to conquer the wind for an under-70 score, his 69 cutting Azinger's lead from five strokes to one.

Azinger and Kite settled into a duel of their own early in the final round, matching stroke for stroke. Azinger's birdie and Kite's bogey at the par-three No. 7 gave Azinger a three-stroke lead, and Paul made it four with a birdie at No. 8. But Kite wasn't finished...and neither was Azinger. Kite chipped in for a birdie and Azinger bogeyed at No. 9, and the margin was down to two strokes.

At No. 10, Azinger sank a 10-foot birdie putt after Kite had one from 20 feet. Azinger bogeyed No. 11, and that's the hole Kite said cost him the victory. Faced with a two-foot putt for par, he hit it carelessly and missed, as Azinger retained his lead. At Nos. 12 and 13, Azinger again sank birdie putts on top of good-sized birdie putts by Kite. "I kept telling myself, 'You're the Player of the Year, you're the Phoenix Open champion, you're the Las Vegas Invitational champion, you're the Greater Hartford Open champion.' That gave me confidence," Azinger said.

At the 218-yard No. 14, Kite bogeyed after hitting a bunker with his tee shot and Azinger chipped in from 30 feet for a birdie, giving Azinger a four-stroke lead. And the next time he got over a putt he could add "...and Hertz Bay Hill champion."

The Players Championship—$1,250,000
Winner: Mark McCumber

In a continuing effort to gain major status, the Tournament Players Championship was renamed The Players Championship. The implication was that this is *THE* tournament for the touring pros, the one that draws a stronger field than the Masters, U.S. or British Opens, or the PGA Championship.

Maybe so, but after two rounds at the TPC at Sawgrass in Ponte Vedra, Florida, the event resembled any other tournament. Gone were the four major winners of the year before — Larry Mize, Scott Simpson, Nick Faldo and Larry Nelson. Gone, too, were Seve Ballesteros, Jack Nicklaus, Tom Watson, Ian Woosnam and Curtis Strange, whose departure was not because he missed the cut. He was disqualified for using a putter after he had bent it, thus changing the characteristics of the club.

Out of all this seeming disaster emerged a champion who provided the tournament with a poignant touch. With his family — his wife, two children, grandmother, parents, nieces, nephews and brothers — among the thousands who applauded him as he walked to the 72nd green, Mark McCumber found it difficult to hold back the tears. "I had trouble keeping my eyes clear to make the last putt," he said.

The last putt was routine. He already had the championship clinched, his 15-under-par 273 making him a winner by four strokes over Mike Reid, who finished with 67 and gained possession of second place by himself when David Frost bogeyed the last hole. The departure of many of the name players at the cut did not mean the tournament had its talent depleted. It took a player with a well-managed game to win at Sawgrass, and McCumber had come within one ill-advised shot of winning the PGA Championship the year before. It's difficult to win before the home folks, but McCumber held up well, shooting 65, 72, 67 and 69 for 273, and when he had the title in his grasp, he didn't let go.

McCumber completed his first round by sinking a 123-yard wedge shot for an eagle at the ninth hole, capping a seven-under 65 that gave him a a one-stroke lead over Greg Norman and Curt Byrum. Payne Stewart, playing in the relatively calm weather of the morning, duplicated McCumber's opening round Friday, sinking a 15-foot putt for an eagle at the 582-yard No. 9 for a 65 and a 36-hole 136 that put him one stroke in front of McCumber and Mike Reid.

Saturday's weather turned ugly early in the afternoon. Play was suspended for an hour and a half because of lightning, and was stopped for the day because of rain and lightning. Of the 72 players who made the cut, only 28 completed their rounds before the halt. Of those who had finished, Fulton Allem had the best round, a 65 that lifted him into contention. The leader on the course was Dan Pohl, who birdied four of his first five holes before calling it a day. McCumber had just birdied the second hole and parred the third when the siren went off.

When the players resumed their third round the next morning, the storm had passed, and so had Pohl's game. A ball into the lake at No. 18 cost him a double bogey and left him four strokes off the lead. McCumber, meanwhile, began at the par-three fourth by sinking a 25-foot putt for birdie, an eye-opener that launched a 67 that put him two strokes ahead of Frost when the break came before the final round, which started on both nines. McCumber was at 204, Frost (68) at 206 and Stewart (71) at 207.

Frost came out charging in the final round with birdies at the first two holes. McCumber matched his birdie at the par-three second hole. That kept him one stroke ahead, and no one got closer as McCumber played the course the way it was designed to be played. McCumber birdied the ninth hole and Frost bogeyed, giving McCumber a three-stroke lead to take into the back nine. It quickly got larger as he birdied Nos. 11 and 12 and Frost bogeyed 13 and 14. With four holes to play, all McCumber had to do was avoid major trouble and he did that, even taking a bogey at the last hole on purpose to sidestep a possible disaster.

K-Mart Greater Greensboro Open—$1,000,000
Winner: Sandy Lyle

Jeff Sluman should have known something out of the ordinary would happen in the final round of the Greater Greensboro Open. All he had to do was look at his playing companion, Sandy Lyle. A year earlier, Lyle had beaten Sluman in a playoff for the Tournament Players Championship after Sluman missed a possible winning putt at the 71st hole when a spectator had taken an impromptu dive into the adjacent lake. And earlier in the 1988 season, Lyle had won the Phoenix Open by beating Fred Couples in a playoff after Couples bogeyed the 72nd hole.

This time it was Ken Green who made the mistake that helped give Lyle his fourth victory on the American tour. Green had come charging from five strokes behind with some sensational putting on the final round to take a one-stroke lead over Lyle with one hole remaining. After Lyle had chipped close to save par at the 18th, Green needed only two putts from 35 feet to win. Suddenly his putting stroke deserted him. He left the first putt three feet short, then pushed his next putt, leaving him and Lyle tied at 17-under-par 271. At the first playoff hole, No. 16, Lyle sank a 10-foot birdie putt, making him 3-0 in playoffs on the U.S. tour.

"I wasn't in the best frame of mind for the playoff," Green said. His frame of mind had reached a peak in the final round, as he abandoned his supporting role to take command of a tournament that up to that point seemed destined to go to Lyle or Sluman.

With the weather at Forest Oaks Country Club unusually pleasant, Sluman shot a 23-putt, eight-under 64 in the first round to tie the course record. His lead was only two strokes. Sluman came back with 65 in the second round for a 15-under 129 that only let him keep his lead at two. Lyle was 11 strokes behind Sluman when he teed off in the second round. He sank a bunker shot for a eagle-three at the third hole and added three birdies on the front nine. Four more birdies on the back nine, the last a four-footer at the 18th green, gave him a record-breaking 63 and a total of 131, two shy of Sluman. Green, with 68-67, trailed by six.

"It's a tough course to beat three days in a row," said Sluman, who saw his dominance end in the third round with a 73, which he said was the best he could have done. Lyle also said he got the best he could out of his round as he fired a 68 that moved him two strokes ahead of Sluman. Green, with a 69, was five back and facing the likelihood of playing an extremely low round on the final day to win. "I should be hard to catch. I'd say 71 is the worst I'm going to do," Lyle said.

Lyle shot 72 and that wouldn't have been good enough if Green hadn't stumbled and fallen at the end. Lyle three-putted the third hole, and when he three-putted the sixth, he was in a tie for the lead with Sluman, one stroke ahead of the charging Green. But Lyle birdied Nos. 8 and 9, and when Sluman bogeyed No. 10, his lead was up to three again. Green birdied No. 13 and when Lyle bogeyed the hole and Sluman birdied it, Lyle and Green were tied for the lead, and Sluman was a stroke behind. At the 16th hole, all three turned on the dramatics. Green birdied from two feet; Sluman sank a bunker shot for a birdie; Lyle sank a 60-foot putt for birdie. Green broke the deadlock with a 30-foot birdie putt at the 17th hole. Sluman, desperate to keep pace, tried to chip in from off the edge of the green, hit a poor shot and bogeyed, dropping two strokes off the pace. Now all Green had to do was par the final hole to win. "It's going to be awhile before I get over this," Green said after the playoff.

Deposit Guaranty Golf Classic—$200,000
Winner: Frank Conner

The Deposit Guaranty Golf Classic is the only survivor of a handful of second-tour tournaments, those played opposite major events. It is populated by youngsters, veterans trying to prolong careers and regular tour players who did not qualify for the Masters.

Befitting the nature of the Hattiesburg, Mississippi tournament, the winner was Frank Conner, a former professional tennis player. Conner, 42, joined the PGA Tour in 1974, but his lone victory in the intervening years came in Morocco in 1982. He had been second four times, and his best year on the tour came in 1981, when he finished 51st with $85,009.

It was only Conner's second tournament of the year, but a five-under 65 the first day indicated that this might be his week. A 70 in the second round dropped him into a tie with Brian Mogg, who had 68-67. Dave Eichelberger shot 64 in the third round for a 202 that tied Lance Ten Broeck. Eichelberger made triple bogey on the sixth hole and skidded to 74 in the final round, and Ten Broeck struggled to 73.

Conner had a share of the lead in the third round until he double-bogeyed the last hole. "I wasn't going to let one hole ruin the week for me," Conner said. He birdied the sixth, seventh and eighth holes and saved par at the ninth in the final round and rode that momentum to a 63-267 and a five-stroke victory over Mogg. Defending champion David Ogrin was the only player who broke par every round, but he placed third, one stroke behind Mogg.

MCI Heritage Classic—$700,000
Winner: Greg Norman

There were a lot of wet eyes as Greg Norman scored his first PGA Tour victory in nearly two years at the MCI Heritage Classic over the Harbour Town Links on Hilton Head Island, South Carolina. "As I stood over the putt, I told myself 'This is for Jamie,'" Norman said of the three-foot putt that completed a 271 total for a one-stroke victory over Gil Morgan and David Frost.

Jamie Hutton, a 17-year-old from Monona, Wisconsin, had been diagnosed a month earlier as having leukemia. Thursday's Child granted Hutton's wish to meet Norman by flying him to the tournament. Norman charmed Hutton, who looked younger than his years. In the eyes of Hutton, Norman was a hero, a status Greg refused to accept. Nevertheless, Hutton saw it that way, and Norman grew in stature with Hutton when they talked over strategy for the final round after a poor-putting round the third day. "We decided to be more aggressive with my putter," Norman said.

Norman went into the final round four strokes behind Fred Couples and looked as if the difference was about to grow wider when Norman hit his first drive on the final round into the trees to the right. He saved par after threading an iron between the trees, and at the fifth hole he got his putter working as he birdied Nos. 5, 8, 9 and 10 to go to 12 under par. "That was the first time I knew I had the lead," he said. A birdie at No. 15 got him 13-under and he saved pars at Nos. 17 and 18 for 66.

If Norman got inspiration from Hutton, he also got a little help from his competitors, especially Couples. In the third round, after missing a short putt for par at the 17th, Couples carelessly tapped the ball backhanded and missed by six inches. He made a double bogey, and instead of a two-stroke lead on David Frost, he had only one, and instead of five on Norman he had only four. "I don't think it's going to bother me," Couples said, but he shot an indifferent 73 in the final round and placed fourth, three strokes behind.

Norman arrived fresh off 64 in the final round of the Masters. That, plus good weather and greens not nearly as slippery as Augusta National's, made him eager for the Heritage to begin. He came out flying, tying Paul Azinger for the first-round lead with a five-under 65. Azinger caught him by birdieing his final three holes. Norman failed to retain the magic in the second round, but he did birdie two of the final three holes for 69. Couples tacked 65 onto his opening 68, and Frost followed 69 with 64 for 133 and a one-stroke lead on Gil Morgan, who also had 64. The second day belonged to Jim Hallet, who tied the course record with 63. Hallet failed to break par in his other three rounds.

The Heritage tournament record is 14 under par. Couples and Frost were nine under after 36 holes. Speculation was that the record would fall. That speculation grew as Couples birdied four of the first eight holes in the third round, then got to 14-under and a five-stroke lead with birdies at the 13th and 14th holes. But the careless double bogey at No. 17 reduced him to 12-under. Frost birdied the 16th and 18th holes for 69 that moved him to within a stroke of the lead and Morgan, with a 69, was two strokes behind him. Norman was four back. But he was on a mission to grant a young man's wish. Just as he had done in the Masters, Norman put together a brilliant final round, a 66 that gave him a memorable victory.

USF&G Classic—$750,000
Winner: Chip Beck

With nine holes left in the USF&G Classic, the question was not whether Chip Beck could win, but whether he would break the PGA Tour record of 27 under par. Beck came within a stroke — actually four inches — of matching the record as he ran away with the victory. It was the second triumph of his career — the first came in the Los Angeles Open two months earlier.

After warming up with a three-under 69, Beck was awesome. He followed with 64, 65, 64 for a 262 total and a seven-stroke margin on the runnerup, Lanny Wadkins. Beck missed only seven greens, made only two bogeys and converted 28 of his 65 birdie opportunities. And he just kept getting better.

Hal Sutton, sinking birdie putts of 10, 20, 30 and 40 feet, led the first round by a stroke over Tom Byrum with 65 and then made a correct prophecy: "You'll need a lot of birdies to win." Wadkins, who opened with 67, added 65 in the second round to take a one-stroke lead over Beck, who moved into position with 64.

It was the final PGA Tour event at Lakewood Country Club in New Orleans, Louisiana, and Beck and Wadkins proceeded to bid it a fond farewell, Beck bettering the course record of 267 set by Lee Trevino in 1967. Beck's 65 in the third round gave him a three-stroke lead on Wadkins. "If he shoots another 65, it's going to be tough," Wadkins said. Tournament leaders, with the pressure of running in front, seldom shoot 65s in the final round. This was no ordinary week for Beck.

"My strategy was just to shoot for the pins," Beck said, and that approach paid off with three consecutive birdies midway through the front nine. That put him 22 under par and six strokes in front of Wadkins. Beck was 22 under with nine holes left and had a shot at the 72-hole record of 27-under held by Ben Hogan and Mike Souchak. Never mind Trevino's tournament record; that was already assured.

At the par-five No. 11, Beck wedged to two feet for a tap-in birdie to go 23 under. A 30-foot birdie putt at No. 14 and a par at No. 15 left him 24-under and needing birdies at the final three holes to match the record. At No. 16, he sank a 10-footer for birdie and at No. 17 he rolled in a startling 25-footer. Now he needed one more. His approach with an eight iron at the 18th hole left him 10 feet from the record. The putt was four inches short. "It was a little disappointing to leave it short. But, really, how can I be disappointed?" he said.

Independent Insurance Agent Open—$700,000
Winner: Curtis Strange

When Curtis Strange and Greg Norman met in a playoff for the Independent Insurance Agent Open championship, it was a showdown between two of the best players in the world. Norman was regarded as No. 1, but Strange had won the PGA Tour money title two of the three previous years.

Strange caught Norman with a sensational birdie at the final hole, both having 270 totals and a two-stroke margin on Tom Kite. In this event, formerly the Houston Open, Strange had beaten Lee Trevino in a playoff in 1980 and Calvin Peete in a playoff in 1986. When Curtis defeated Norman, he became the first to win the tournament three times.

Strange's victory was an impressive one. Norman birdied the 17th hole to go 18 under par. Strange trailed by a stroke going to the final hole and No. 18, a 445-yard par-four guarded by a large pond, is not a birdie hole. Norman reached the green from the rough on his second shot. To have a realistic shot at tying him, Strange had to hit his second shot close from 192 yards. He hit a three iron — "I thought it was going into the water," Norman said — to within four feet of the hole. "I felt like I could pull it off and you don't win anything backing off," Strange said. That capped a 67, the same score turned in by Norman, and sent them back to the par-three No. 16. Strange hit his tee shot 30 feet from the hole, Norman 18 feet closer. After Strange missed, Norman failed to sink the clincher. Both parred the 17th. Once again they were at the 18th and this time both were left with sizeable putts for birdies, Norman 45 feet and Strange 25. Strange was on almost the same line he had when he beat Peete and he said, "I told myself, I've done this before and I can do it again." And he did.

Raymond Floyd and Norman shot 65-70 to share the lead after the first and second rounds. However, the second round was halted by rain and lightning and only 45 players were able to complete their rounds before play was called off. Floyd, age 45, said the long Saturday didn't tire him, but he shot 76 and dropped out of the chase. Strange finished off 66 and Norman 68 that left them tied for the lead, a stroke ahead of Kite. "I came out in the afternoon and was brain dead," Norman said. George Burns eagled the par-five sixth hole and was tied for the lead, then he went into a slide, hitting bottom with a double bogey at the par-three 16th as he completed his second round. Then he came back hours later and made a hole-in-one at No. 16.

Norman, who had a great round defused by an out-of-bounds shot at the 13th hole in the third round, hit a tee shot into the water at the par-three third hole in the final round and in retrospect that was the difference between winning and losing. Kite dropped out of the chase with a bogey at the 14th, leaving Norman and Strange to battle it out down the stretch. Strange's magnificent three iron sent the tournament into extra holes and then his putter ended it. "I feel like I beat the best golfer in the world," he said.

Panasonic Las Vegas Invitational—$1,388,889
Winner: Gary Koch

It was this kind of week at the Panasonic Las Vegas Invitational: A rocket fuel plant caught fire and blew up in nearby Henderson, raising fears of a nuclear fallout; winds up to 55 miles per hour raked the area on Thursday, reducing the scheduled 90-hole tournament to 72 holes for the second year in a row...and Gary Koch won.

Koch is only 35, but he hadn't won since 1984, when he scored two of his previous five victories and earned more than $260,000. In 1987 he fell to 175th on the money list and lost his playing card. He was reduced to trying to qualify, playing in those tournaments in which he was exempt (where he had won in the past) and accepting invitations. One of the invitations came from the Panasonic Las Vegas Invitational, primarily because he was a member of the tournament's Nabisco Grand Prix team.

"It's a great feeling to know I can once again play with the best in the world," Koch said after he won by one stroke over Peter Jacobsen and Mark O'Meara with a 68-73-66-67—274 total. He earned $250,000, more than seven times what he collected in all of 1987.

Koch was almost unnoticed the final round. First came the explosion during the opening round on Wednesday, which flattened a marshmallow factory and sent reverberations that could be felt 20 miles away, causing more than $1 million in damage. Then came the winds, followed by cold weather. The wind was so strong that Greg Norman drove the green on the 410-yard opening hole at Spanish Trail.

Before the weather turned nasty, Bobby Wadkins fired an eight-under-par 64 at Desert Inn for a one-stroke lead over O'Meara and Curt Byrum in the first round. The wind gusts were steadily stronger late in the second round, and 71 players were still on the course when play was suspended. Instead of completing the second round Friday morning, officials decided to erase the scores and start all over. Bob Lohr, who had opened with a 66, turned in a 70 in the numbing weather for a one-stroke lead over Jacobsen, who had a 66. Wadkins faded to a 79 and Koch, with a 73, trailed by five.

The weather finally settled down on Saturday and the scoring picked up. Bill Kratzert tied the course record at Spanish Trail with a 63. Byrum shot a 67 and took a one-stroke lead on Jacobsen, who had a 68, and Ben Crenshaw, who had a 67. Koch's 67 left him three behind.

Many felt Crenshaw was the man to watch in the final round, but Crenshaw's putter lost its usual verve. Byrum, who had yet to win in his sixth year on the tour, jumped out to a two-stroke lead with a birdie at the first hole at Las Vegas Country Club, but the field soon closed up behind him. Koch, a good putter before his slump, birdied the first, fourth, sixth and eighth holes, then grabbed a share of the lead at 14 under par with a birdie at the par-five 10th hole. Then he went ahead with an eight-foot birdie putt at No. 12. A poor tee shot at the par-three 14th cost him a bogey and he fell back to 14 under again.

Meanwhile, Rick Fehr and Jacobsen were on the march. Fehr was 14 under when he teed off at the 18th hole, a 524-yard dogleg right that many can reach in two. Fehr hooked his drive out of bounds and his title chances disappeared. Jacobsen birdied three of four holes, the third a four-footer at the 16th that got him to 14 under. But he used the wrong club off the tee at the par-three 17th and three-putted from 100 feet. Up ahead, Koch parred the 18th hole for a 67 that left him one stroke ahead of O'Meara, who had finished with a 66, and awaited his fate.

Byrum hit a poor drive and was forced to lay up on his second shot. His wedge approach hit a retaining wall and bounced 25 feet back to the fringe. He missed the birdie putt from there. Jacobsen, faced with needing a birdie to tie, went for the green from 230 yards on his second shot. His ball landed in a back bunker and he failed to sink an 18-foot birdie putt after he came out. Like Koch, Jacobsen hadn't won since 1984, but the $122,222 he won for sharing second place eased his feelings.

GTE Byron Nelson Classic—$750,000
Winner: Bruce Lietzke

Bruce Lietzke has talked about retiring from the tour almost from the time he won his first tournament in 1977. In fact, there was a time in 1973, shortly after he left the University of Houston, that he did take a timeout from golf before turning pro. So it was no surprise that when he scored the 11th victory of his career in the Byron Nelson Classic — his first since 1984 — that Lietzke once again talked about the future.

"This tournament is named for a guy who left the tour in the prime of his career," Lietzke said after beating Clarence Rose on the first hole of a sudden-death playoff. "I'd be more than willing to give it up to maintain a normal life."

Lietzke, 37, has a growing family, son Stephen, born in 1983, and daughter Christine, born in 1986, and in 14 years on the tour he has made a comfortable living, his $135,000 winner's check pushing his career earnings past $2.5 million. That is not bad considering Lietzke has cut back his tournament schedule to 20-22 events in recent years. His payday nearly matched what he had earned in each of the previous three years.

Lietzke was born in Kansas, but he did a lot of golfing in Texas, an education that helped him win at the Las Colinas TPC course in Irving. The drought that was to grip the nation already had hit Texas. Only two inches of rain had fallen in the first four months of the year and the course was dry, the greens hard. The course called for a Texas-style game — pitch and run. Lietzke and Rose played that game the best.

Ben Crenshaw, another Texan who helped design the course, came out with 66-65 and by the middle of the third round he had a four-stroke lead. He then bogeyed three holes on the back nine and let numerous birdie opportunities escape him in the final round as he finished with a 271 that tied him for third place with David Graham, one stroke behind Lietzke and Rose. Graham broke 70 every round, finishing with a 68. Jeff Sluman took over when Crenshaw began to slip, taking a one-stroke lead over Lietzke and Crenshaw after 54 holes. But Sluman came apart for a 76 in the final round.

Then, Lietzke and Rose became locked in what became a head-to-head battle. Lietzke shot 66-69-66 and Rose 66-69-67 through the first three rounds. Lietzke said a bogey at the eighth hole after he used the wrong club "ticked me off" and turned his final round into a winner. He birdied the next hole, then he and Rose began a succession of pars. However, Lietzke's string was more a succession of missed birdies. Nevertheless, he took a one-stroke lead to the last hole after Rose fell behind with a bogey at No. 14. All he had to do to win was par the 18th hole. Lietzke hit his drive into the left rough, leaving himself with a 147-yard shot to the green. Instead of playing for the green and risk trying to two-putt from a good distance, Lietzke went for the pin . . . and came up with a buried lie in the bunker next to the green.

The pin was close to the bunker. Lietzke said afterward he was afraid if he played for the pin he might go over the green and lose everything with a double bogey. He blasted to the fat part of the green and two-putted for a 70 that tied Rose at 271. The playoff began at the 554-yard No. 15 and ended quickly. Both laid up on their second shots, about 100 yards short of the fairway bunkers in front of the green. Rose hit a six iron to the right rear fringe; Lietzke's approach came up 20 feet from the hole, giving him a straight-in putt. After Rose's chip rolled past the hole, Lietzke's birdie putt raced into the hole. It was the fifth second-place finish for Rose in a little more than six years on tour. "As long as I finish second, I must be playing good," he said.

Colonial National Invitation—$750,000
Winner: Lanny Wadkins

Lanny Wadkins said he didn't realize his poor history in the Colonial National Invitation tournament until he read it in a newspaper: In 35 rounds prior to the 1988 tournament he had not broken par. He knew, of course, that he had missed the cut in 1984 and 1985 and that he had not entered the tournament in 1986 and 1987. "I told my wife I would take a couple years off and maybe come back with a better taste in my mouth." It had been very galling for a man who calls nearby Dallas home.

Apparently, that plan worked as Wadkins not only broke par at the Colonial Country Club in Fort Worth, but broke it three times as he finished with a 10-under-par 67-68-70-65 — 270 and a one-stroke victory over Ben Crenshaw, Mark Calcavecchia and Joey Sindelar. Wadkins' friends had urged him to enter, partly because they wanted him to play, but also because they thought the course was the kind on which he could win.

At 7,116 yards, Colonial is a long course with plenty of trees and dogleg holes. And it was made even more difficult on the final round by gusting winds. It was perfect for a person such as Wadkins, who rarely plays cautiously. But he had a fight on his hands all the way, and still had his glove handy and his spikes on after completing his final round, anticipating a possible playoff. Crenshaw finished with birdies on the last four holes, but that only pulled him to within a stroke of Wadkins, who birdied the final hole with a five-foot putt; a decisive putt, as it turned out.

Clarence Rose had gone into the final round with a three-stroke lead on Sindelar, four on Crenshaw and five on Wadkins and improved his lead to four strokes with a birdie at the first hole. Rose was in and out of the lead after that, finally dropping out with a bogey at the eighth hole. Calcavecchia also had started the final round five strokes to the rear, but when he sank a 45-foot putt at the 12th hole he pulled into a tie for the lead with Sindelar. When Wadkins birdied the 14th hole it was a three-man deadlock. Calcavecchia went in front by himself with a seven-foot birdie putt at the 15th hole, but bogeyed the par-three 16th after an errant tee shot and was unable to match Wadkins' birdie at No. 18. Sindelar also was sunk by a par-three hole, hitting his tee shot into the water at No. 13, the resulting bogey putting him a stroke behind Wadkins. Sindelar birdied No. 15, but, like Calcavecchia, he could not sink a necessary 35-foot birdie putt at the final green.

Rose, riding a high after losing a playoff to Bruce Lietzke in the Byron Nelson Classic the week before, opened with a 67 that tied him for the first-round lead with Rose and Hoch remained in the lead after 36 holes with 68s, then Rose stepped in front with his third-round 65. Weather conditions the final day — wind following on the heels of a storm that caused a suspension of play for two hours on Friday — made it almost certain that it would be anybody's tournament the final round. It almost was Crenshaw's, which would have been a popular one because Crenshaw is a native Texan. Crenshaw made seven birdies. "But I made four bogeys and that's too many to win," he said.

Memorial Tournament—$930,250
Winner: Curtis Strange

Until the Memorial Tournament, there was a suspicion that maybe Seve Ballesteros, Greg Norman and Sandy Lyle were not the only ones who fit the appellation best golfer in the world. And after Curtis Strange won at Muirfield Village Golf Club near Columbus, Ohio, the suspicion had given way to certainty. Strange won by two strokes and did it impressively, shooting a course-record-equalling 64 in the third round and a 67 in the final round for a 14-under-par 274 total.

Muirfield Village is not the type of course that ordinarily gives up such low numbers. "The golf course played six or seven shots tougher than it did a couple of years ago," said Jack Nicklaus, who designed the 7,104-yard layout. Yet only two previous winners had shot lower 72-hole scores than Strange.

Strange shrugs off the "best" title. "I just go out and play golf the best way I can. I've got more important things to worry about. It isn't who's number one, two or three that's important; it's who wins the golf tournament." And the more you win...well, a rating is certain to follow. Strange's fifth victory in less than 11 months was worth $160,000, pushing his career earnings to $3,478,454 and into sixth place among the PGA Tour's all-time money winners.

Muirfield Village is a difficult course, but it needs an assist from the weather to bring out all its magnificence. It didn't get it; the weather was perfect every day and the course was hard and fast, the greens yielding and true. Strange's 64 was not the only record-tying round. Scott Hoch, who always plays well here, shot a 64 in the third round. He didn't break par in any of his other rounds, but that one day was enough to earn him a tie for sixth place. Nevertheless, the tournament was virtually a three-man affair with Strange, David Frost and Hale Irwin the central players in the final round.

Strange had been bothered by a back problem, but that had been attended to, and with the knowledge he had gained of the course from the Ryder Cup Matches the previous September, he was armed and ready to fire. "I came here in the right frame of mind. I was ready to play," he said. But there was some question of whether that was good enough as he opened with a 73 that left him five strokes behind Peter Jacobsen and John Mahaffey. Irwin, a two-time winner of the tournament, jumped into a one-stroke lead with a second-round 68 for 138. Strange still trailed by five.

Irwin still led after a 68 in the third round, but Strange pulled into range with his 64 and Frost, after rounds of 69, 70, 68, was tied with Strange, one stroke behind. Irwin hadn't won since the 1985 Memorial, he was 42, and a stomach virus had left him weak. It was amazing he had played so well for 54 holes. His margin over Strange was wider until he three-putted the final green from 40 feet and Strange sank a 25-foot birdie putt.

Irwin opened the final round with a bogey at the first hole and Frost bogeyed the second and third holes. When he birdied the seventh hole, Strange suddenly had a three-stroke lead. But Frost birdied five of the last six holes on the front nine, taking the lead as Strange bogeyed the ninth hole with a tee shot into the woods.

Unperturbed, Strange birdied the 10th hole, tying Frost for the lead, then went ahead to stay with an 18-inch birdie putt at the par-5 No. 15. The luckless Frost could only par the last seven holes. A birdie from 10 feet at the 17th green doubled Strange's lead and gave him a comfortable ride to the 18th hole. Irwin caught Frost with a birdie at the 18th. "He's (Strange) better than Seve and he beat Greg Norman in a playoff at Houston. He's difficult to beat because he doesn't let up," Irwin said.

Kemper Open—$800,000
Winner: Morris Hatalsky

Morris Hatalsky might have played a big part in the PGA Tour's changing one of its playing statistics. Since the tour began keeping figures for average number of putts a hole, Hatalsky always rated high; in 1987 his average was 1.748 and that was good enough for fourth place. Now, it would seem that somebody who averages fewer than 29 1/2 putts a round would do better than Hatalsky did, when he placed 70th among the money winners with a little more than $150,000. What had to be taken into consideration was that Hatalsky is not rated one of the better drivers; he misses a lot of greens. He has a good short game and often saves pars with his chipping. So the tour decided the putting statistic would only count for those holes reached in regulation (tee shot on a par-three, two strokes on a par-four, three on a par-five).

This is not to deny that Hatalsky is a good putter, or that he lives off his short game. Anybody who can chip and putt well can make up for deficiencies in other parts of his game. Power hitting is not a requisite on the tour. When the Kemper Open was played at Congressional Country Club, power was a big advantage, but with the move to the shorter TPC at Avenel course in Potomac, Maryland, in 1987, the Kemper became a shot-maker's tournament. And for the third time in his 12-year career, Hatalsky made more shots than anybody. For 74 holes, that is. After 72 holes Hatalsky and Tom Kite were even, both at 10-under-par 274. Kite, by the way, also is not one of the longer hitters.

Hatalsky hung on just to make the playoff. The 15th, 16th and 18th holes played into the wind in the final round. Hatalsky bogeyed four of the final six, a birdie at the 14th giving him a respite from his travails. With a par at the 444-yard No. 18 a likely winner, Hatalsky and Kite both bogeyed, giving Hatalsky a 72 and Kite a 69. The playoff began at the par-three 17th and both parred. At the tough 18th, Hatalsky's drive left him with 235 yards to the green; Kite had 225 left. Hatalsky hooked his second shot near the scorers' tent; Kite pushed his far right. "I couldn't have put it in a worse place," said Hatalsky of his lie. "I just threw this wedge up there, hoping and praying it would give me some kind of putt." His prayers were answered — his ball stopped five feet from the hole. Kite's pitch stopped 12 feet from the hole. After Kite missed, Hatalsky hit his putt, his mind went blank and when it came back on the putt was dropping, "That's the most excited I've ever been."

Howard Twitty and Webb Heintzelman grabbed the attention in the first round with 66s, Heintzelman especially causing surprise. Heintzelman was an assistant pro at a district club whose name was pulled out of a hat as one of the sponsor's exemptions. Heintzelman didn't break par in the next three rounds, but the $3,280 was far above an ordinary paycheck for an assistant club pro. Jim Hallet, who won his tour card on his fourth try, moved into the lead with a 65—133 in the second round. But now Hatalsky and Kite, with 66 and 67, respectively, were in position to make a run. Hatalsky shot a 68 and Kite a 71 in the third round, giving Hatalsky a two-stroke lead. One of those tied for second was Craig Stadler, who fired a 64.

Hatalsky had broken a thumb early in the season. Prior to the Kemper, his best showing was a tie for 30th. But here he was on the verge of his biggest victory and his caddy was inexperienced. His caddy was former baseball player Tim Foli, who played for the Pittsburgh Pirates and New York Mets. If Foli was without experience as a caddy, he had considerable experience with tense situations and that had to be a plus. Hatalsky began the final round with a birdie at the first hole and an eagle at the sixth and that gave him a three-stroke lead on Hallet.

Then Hatalsky showed signs of feeling the pressure. He saved par with a 40-foot chip-in at the seventh hole, bogeyed the eighth and saved par at the ninth. At the 13th, Hatalsky hit his drive out of bounds and did well to bogey as Stadler birdied and tied him for the lead. But Stadler took a double bogey at No. 14 as Hatalsky birdied, knocking Stadler out of the chase. Meanwhile, Kite was creeping up and caught Hatalsky when Hatalsky bogeyed Nos. 15 and 16. Then they were to play 18 twice, and Kite bogeyed it twice, which was one too many.

Manufacturers Hanover Westchester Classic—$700,000
Winner: Seve Ballesteros

It had been three years since Seve Ballesteros had won a PGA Tour tournament — the 1985 USF&G Classic — and a year since he had lost to J.C. Snead in a playoff at the Westchester Classic, a tuneup for the U.S. Open the following week.

Ballesteros manhandled the 10th and 18th holes en route to an eight-under-par 276 that tied him with Greg Norman, Ken Green and David Frost. Faced with a second successive playoff in the tournament, Ballesteros called on all his skills to prevent it going more than one hole.

The 10th hole, which Ballesteros had played in four under par in the tournament, is a 304-yard par-four that can be reached with a good drive. Nobody reached it in the playoff, but Ballesteros best handled the problem his drive left him. Green hit his tee shot into the trees to the right and short of the green. Frost also found trouble. Ballesteros's caddy, brother Vicente, talked him into switching from a three wood to a driver, and Ballesteros hit his drive into a bunker in front of the green. Norman unloaded, and fired his drive into the gallery to the right.

It took Green two more shots, and Norman and Frost one each to reach the green, none of them getting close to the hole. Ballesteros had to stand with his left foot in the sand and his right out of the bunker to hit his downhill lie in the bunker. "I was a little upset because I didn't put my drive in the fairway," he said.

But Ballesteros can handle bunker shots as well as anybody. He cut the ball to within five feet of the cup. Then after the other three had missed their birdie putts — Frost's was the shortest, from 18 feet — Ballesteros sank his birdie putt for the victory.

Ballesteros, who also won the Westchester Classic in 1983, was still smarting from a poor showing in the Spanish Open on his home course when he arrived at Westchester. His opening 72 left him six strokes behind Loren Roberts and Howard Twitty. A 68 the second day left him three behind Roberts, who added a 71 to his opening 66. Green took over with a 67 the third day as Roberts slipped to a 73, but Ballesteros ended his day with an exclamation point as he hit a pitch-and-run for an eagle-three at the 18th, a hole he played in six under for the tournament. That capped a 69 and left him three strokes behind Green.

At this point, it was Norman and Green who were doing the talking. "I'll need a 63 to win," Norman said as he joined the television crew while waiting for others to finish. Green, who was raised in Connecticut, said he viewed the Westchester and the Hartford Open as more important to him than the U.S. Open. "That's the only thing I care about. If I don't win, I don't care if I finish second or fifth or 25th. If I shoot 65 and don't win, I won't be happy."

Norman came close with his prediction. A 63 would have won for him. He shot 64, then waited in the TV tower to see if anybody would do better.

Ballesteros was the first to tie, his wedge to the 18th green setting up an easy birdie that finished off a 67. Frost and Green also birdied and Steve Elkington just missed making the playoff a fivesome with a long eagle putt. Then Ballesteros quickly brought the tournament to a conclusion for his sixth PGA Tour triumph.

Georgia-Pacific Atlanta Golf Classic—$600,000
Winner: Larry Nelson

After 54 holes, Larry Nelson had the Georgia-Pacific Atlanta Classic tournament won. Then in the middle of the final round at Atlanta Country Club he had to win it all over again. Nelson's one-stroke victory over Chip Beck was a reiteration of the old saying there's no such thing as a safe lead in golf and also was a tribute to Nelson's ability to pull his game together just when the pieces were falling everywhere.

After rounds of 63-66-66, Nelson, who lives near Atlanta, had a four-stroke lead on Paul Azinger, six on Lanny Wadkins and eight on Beck. His lead could have been six strokes, but he hit the water at the par-five No. 18 and bogeyed. "After I birdied No. 11 I thought I could birdie every hole on the back side," he said. Despite the bogey, he was 21 under par for three rounds and had a shot at the PGA Tour record of 27 under for 72 holes. Nelson admitted before he watered his ball at the 18th hole he had a loftier goal: 30 under.

There was some talk that Nelson was playing too well to be caught, but the bogey at the 54th hole gave some hope to those behind him. He began the final round as shaky as he ended the third. He double-bogeyed the fourth hole and bogeyed the sixth as Azinger birdied. Suddenly they were tied for the lead. With nine holes to go, Wadkins had moved to within a stroke of the lead and Beck was a stoke behind him. "I figured if nobody blew by me and I held on, I'd be OK," Nelson said. And so it was.

Azinger missed a birdie putt at the seventh hole and three-putted the ninth. Beck birdied Nos. 12 and 14, putting him in a tie for the lead. Beck hung tough, saving par at the 16th and 17th holes, then making a necessary birdie at the 18th for a 66—269. Azinger grabbed the lead with a birdie at No. 13, then bogeyed No. 14 as Nelson birdied and took a double-bogey at No. 15 that virtually eliminated him. "After I missed a 10-foot birdie put at No. 13, I knew I was running out of birdie holes," Nelson said. "I went to No. 14 knowing I needed a birdie there, pars at Nos. 15, 16 and 17 and a birdie at 18 to win." He did what he had to do, getting the decisive birdie at the 18th with two putts after reaching the green with a four wood for a 73—268.

Until the final round, the tournament was all Nelson's. His opening 63 gave him a one-stroke lead over Bobby Wadkins. His 66 in the second round expanded his advantage to four strokes as Wadkins double bogeyed two of his last four holes. With one hole to go in the third round, Nelson needed a par to tie the record of 22 under par for 54 holes. Then Nelson made a poor swing and the tournament began.

Beatrice Western Open—$900,000
Winner: Jim Benepe

Peter Jacobsen stood in the middle of the fairway of the 18th hole at Butler National Golf Club. Up ahead, he saw Jim Benepe three-putt for a bogey. All he needed was a par for his first victory in more than four years.

A flashback...

Benepe, who graduated from Northwestern University in 1986, had played around the world for the previous two years. He had competed in tournaments in 14 countries, winning the British Columbia Open in 1987 and the Victorian Open in Australia earlier in 1988. A former Western Junior champion and Western Amateur medalist from Sheridan, Wyoming, he got into the Western Open with a sponsor's exemption. His goal: don't embarrass himself, make the cut. Then he birdied the first hole in the first PGA Tour tournament in which he competed.

Benepe's goal became reality when he opened with a one-under-par 71 and followed that with a 68. Mark Hayes, Brian Mogg and Morris Hatalsky led the first round with 66s and Jacobsen, recovered from the back problems that had plagued him, took over with a 65 in the second round for a 135 total, four ahead of Benepe. In the third round, Benepe shot a 69 and victory was a flickering possibility. Jacobsen was playing so well it looked as if he would take a nearly insurmountable lead into the final round. Jacobsen seemed headed toward a six-stroke lead after 54 holes. Then he bogeyed Nos. 17 and 18 and said, "I just had the wrong club in my hands." Instead of a six-stroke lead, his 69 left him four in front of Benepe, Dan Forsman, Dave Eichelberger and Bill Britton.

Forsman began the final round with three birdies to temporarily tie for the lead before fading to a 73 and a tie for fifth place. Benepe alternated between bogeys and birdies, his most telling mistake a bogey at the 478-yard 12th hole. But Benepe kept his nerves under control and when he birdied the 16th hole from five feet, he and Jacobsen were tied for the lead.

Now Benepe was in the scorer's tent, signing for a 70 and 278 total, and excited about his performance, even if the bogey at No. 18 probably cost him a victory. And on the 18th fairway Jacobsen tried to keep his adrenaline from bubbling over. He had 165 yards to the pin. At the 13th hole he used a nine iron from 175 yards, but that shot was with the wind. Now he swung a six iron. The ball flew the green into the lake behind. The resulting double bogey gave him a 279, and gave Benepe an unexpected victory.

Anheuser-Busch Golf Classic—$650,000
Winner: Tom Sieckmann

If the field for the Anheuser-Busch Classic had been given odds as they do in some countries, Tom Sieckmann probably would have been one of the longest of odds to win. Sieckmann had won before, but it was in such places as Brazil, the Philippines, Thailand and Switzerland. He was struggling on the PGA Tour. Twice he had to go back to the qualifying tournament. As the 1988 tour moved into its second half, it looked as if he would face another such test. Prior to the Anheuser-Busch Classic at the Kingsmill Golf

Club in Williamsburg, Virginia, Sieckmann had made the cut in only three of 16 tournaments. He had won about $42,000.

But Sieckmann beat the odds. His 14-under-par 69-66-66-69 — 270 total tied Mark Wiebe (68-70-64-68) and he won the playoff on the second hole when Wiebe bogeyed after missing the green. "I think I am happier than Jack Nicklaus was when he won any of his majors because I have been so much further down than he ever was," said Sieckmann, who could point to the 177-yard No. 17 as the pivotal hole in his first triumph.

Wiebe, whose first victory came here in 1985, had missed the green at the par-three hole three times in the four rounds but managed to save par the last two times. After Wiebe had made a putt of about 15 feet from the fringe to save par at the first playoff hole, his iron to the 17th sailed to the left of the green, into patchy rough. His chip hit the pin, but the ball was going so fast it stopped 10 feet from the hole. Sieckmann, who had made a 12-foot birdie putt at the 17th hole to catch Wiebe less than an hour earlier, hit the green with his tee shot, then rolled his first putt to within four feet of the hole. Wiebe missed his par putt; Sieckmann, telling himself "I got to make it, that's all there is to it," holed his decisive putt.

The tournament began as if half the field were contenders. Dick Mast opened with a 64, one off the course record, then vanished. Peter Jacobsen took over with a 65 in the second round, and stayed in contention until the late holes of the final round. Jerry Pate, the 1976 U.S. Open champion who has been troubled by shoulder problems in recent years, made one of his best showings after opening with a 66 — "My first sub-70 round since the 1986 Los Angeles Open." He ultimately tied for 14th place, six strokes behind.

Sieckmann's 66 and Kenny Knox's 65 put them in a deadlock with Jacobsen after 54 holes. Wiebe moved into position, one stroke back, with a 64. Gene Sauers, with a 66—272, and Jeff Sluman, with 64—273, made a run at the leaders and Knox failed to get a charge going in the final round, tying Sauers with a 71. That left it to Sieckmann and Wiebe. Wiebe outscored Sieckmann, 68-69, but No. 17 proved his downfall.

Hardee's Golf Classic—$600,000
Winner: Blaine McCallister

With many of the big-name players competing in the British Open, it is not surprising that the Hardee's (formerly Quad Cities) Golf Classic often crowns a little-known or first-time champion. This time it was Blaine McCallister.

McCallister, age 29, was a three-time All-America at the University of Houston, but his pro career had been marked with little success. He went through the qualifying tournament three times. He lost to Gene Sauers in a playoff for the Bank of Boston title in 1986, his closest brush with victory.

By coincidence, Sauers was a lead character again in the Hardee's Classic at Oakwood Country Club in Coal Valley, Illinois. Sauers opened with an eight-under-par 62 and McCallister trailed him by six strokes. But not for long. Oakwood is an ego-builder and McCallister got his boosted with a 62 in the second round and a 63 in the third. His middle rounds matched

the low score for 36 holes set by Ron Streck in the Texas Open in 1978.
Those rounds also gave him a four-stroke lead to take into the final day.

Nobody came close to overtaking McCallister in the final round, although
Dan Forsman made a try. With four holes to go, McCallister had a seven-
stroke lead en route to a 68 and a 19-under 261, the lowest score on the
tour at that point in the season. Forsman, who shot a commendable 64-
66-67-67 — 264, also beating the tournament record of 265 set by Kenny
Knox a year earlier, cut the difference to three strokes before running out
of holes.

Canon Sammy Davis Jr. Greater Hartford Open—$700,000
Winner: Mark Brooks

The way the tour was going, it should have been easy to predict the winner
of the Canon Sammy Davis Jr. Greater Hartford Open. Just look for somebody
who had struggled to stay on the tour and had yet to win a tournament.
Somebody such as Mark Brooks.

A former All-America at the University of Texas, Brooks, age 27, shot
a 67 in the final round of the qualifying tournament in December of 1987
to regain his card. The experience seemed to solidify his game; he had won
more than $80,000 before traveling to Hartford. Then he more than doubled
his earnings by beating Joey Sindelar and Dave Barr in a playoff in a wet
and wonderful tournament at the TPC of Connecticut course in what was
Sammy Davis's finale after 15 years of lending his name to the tournament
and helping obtain the show business stars for the pro-am.

It rained on Thursday and Friday, but fortunately the course is built on
a sand and gravel pit, and the only delays of play were 90 minutes before
the first round began, 21 minutes in the first round and 15 minutes in the
second round. The wet weather softened the course and made it virtually
defenseless. Roger Maltbie opened with a seven-under-par 64 and Brooks,
Barr and Sindelar tied the tournament record with 15-under 269 totals.

Sindelar birdied the 16th and 17th holes as he finished with a 65. Barr
missed tying the course record by one stroke with a 63 that he capped with
a 12-foot birdie putt at the final hole. Brooks, whose best previous finish
had been a tie for eighth in the 1986 Hardee's Classic, left a winning 20-
foot birdie putt short at the 18th hole for a 69 that included an eagle-two
at the No. 12 hole.

Sindelar dropped out of the playoff at the first hole (No. 16) when he
hit his tee shot into the lake at the par-three hole. At the second hole (No.
17), Barr used a three wood off the tee and hit his ball off the cart path
and into the rough. With a poor lie, he hit his approach on the edge of
railroad ties, leaving himself with an almost impossible lie. Meanwhile, Brooks
hit the fairway, then followed with a seven iron to within 10 feet of the
hole. To retain any hope, Barr had to get close for a par, so he turned
over a sand wedge and, hitting lefthanded, ran the ball through the rough
and to within a yard of the hole. "It was one in a thousand shot," said
TV announcer Ken Venturi. But Brooks made sure it wouldn't be the winning
one as he sank his birdie putt.

Brooks had been in contention from the start, opening with a 66, then adding a 65 that gave him the lead for the first time in any tournament. With more than 15 players baying at his heels, Brooks shot a 69 in the third round and shared the lead with Mark Calcavecchia, who had a 67, and Ronnie Black, who had a 65. Calcavecchia and Black shot creditable 70s in the final round, but that left them a stroke out of the playoff. Brett Upper also could have joined the playoff with a birdie at the 18th hole but bogeyed and tied with Maltbie at 271.

Buick Open—$700,000
Winner: Scott Verplank

His career had gone downhill after Scott Verplank won the Western Open as an amateur in 1985. The victory qualified him for the PGA Tour in 1986 and 1987, but after disappointing seasons he had to compete in the qualifying tournament to regain his card. Golf was no fun for him. That, he finally learned in the middle of the 1988 season, was the crux of the matter. He talked to Bob Tway, the 1986 PGA champion, and sports psychologist Dr. Bob Rotella and his problem surfaced: he should relax, and not take the game so seriously.

So with the new attitude, Verplank, at 24 the youngest player on the tour, went out and had fun in the Buick Open at the immaculate Warwick Hills Country Club in Grand Blanc, Michigan, and scored his first victory as a pro, winning by two strokes over Doug Tewell with a 66-66-70-66 — 268 total, 20 under par.

It was obvious to the spectators that Verplank was enjoying himself, as he played the final holes with a wide grin on his face. At the 17th hole of the final round, Verplank hit his ball into a greenside bunker and his playing companion, Steve Elkington, told him "Suck it up." Puzzled, Verplank glanced at the leaderboard and saw he held a two-stroke lead. Instead of getting serious, Verplank retained his have-fun attitude and got up and down for a par, the third time he had saved par from a bunker in the final round.

Verplank kept saying "I just want to have fun" every time people asked him about the tournament and showed that when he passed up the final practice round to play tennis and see a movie. "I've been playing golf all my life. One day off wasn't going to hurt me." Obviously, it didn't. His opening 66 gave him a share of the lead with George Archer, Tim Simpson, Greg Ladehoff, Fred Couples and Scott Hoch. His second 66 gave him the lead by two strokes over Howard Twitty, who had a 65. Verplank shot a 70 in the third round and Elkington and Twitty caught him with 67 and 68, respectively.

But Elkington and Twitty faded early in the final round as Tewell took over as Verplank's major threat. Tewell raced in with a 64, but it wasn't enough as Verplank turned in his third 66. "I keep being runner-up when guys are making comebacks," Tewell said.

Federal Express St. Jude Classic—$953,842
Winner: Jodie Mudd

Jodie Mudd, six times a runner-up since joining the tour in 1982, continued the succession of first-time winners as he held on to win the Federal Express St. Jude Classic in its final appearance at Colonial Country Club in Cordova, Tennessee. Mudd became the fifth first-timer in six weeks, the seventh of the season.

It was a physical and mental battle for Mudd in the final round as he carved out a 15-under-par 68-68-67-70 — 273 total worth $171,692. His opening 68 left him two strokes behind Doug Tewell and Ed Fiori, and he moved into a share of the lead with Peter Jacobsen as they matched 68s through the first two rounds. Simpson shot his third straight 68 in the third round, but Mudd beat him by a stroke as he took sole possession of first place at 203. But the field was bunched up behind him and the stage was set for the final-day dramatics.

Included in Mudd's second-place finishes had been some last-round disasters. With that background, could he hold up under pressure with a good shot at his first victory? Dave Rummells seemed to have an answer when he birdied the first, second and fifth holes to take the lead at 15 under par. But Rummells failed to sustain his momentum, finishing with a 71 that relegated him to a tie for fourth place.

Mudd birdied Nos. 10 and 11 to go to 16 under par and three strokes ahead of Rummells, Jacobsen and Nick Price. "After I made the putt on 11 I felt like all I could do was lose the tournament," he said. And there were those who thought he was about to do it with one hole to play. At the 17th hole, Mudd's seven-iron approach landed a few inches from the lip of a bunker, leaving him with a difficult problem of just getting the ball on the green. He got out, but the best he could do was two-putt for bogey, only his second of the tournament (the other came at the 12th hole in the first round). Now his lead was down to one stroke over Price and Jacobsen, who both finished with 66s for 274.

The 18th at Colonial is a 548-yard hole loaded with danger. There's water down the left side and a menacing bunker on the right side of the fairway. Mudd walloped his drive down the middle, leaving him 215 yards from the hole and four strokes from his first victory. He played it safe, hitting a pitching wedge on his second shot to get in position for a shot to the green, then hitting a sand wedge from 100 yards — "I just wanted to make sure I got it over the water; I wasn't trying to get close."

He put the ball 35 feet from the hole, then rolled his first putt to within four feet of the hole. "I never dreamed it would come down to the last putt on the last hole," he said. But it did, and Mudd pushed aside the negative thoughts as he hit the putt true into the hole. "I was having some thoughts about whether I could win out here," he said. "But now that I've done it, I'm going to savor it."

The International—$1,115,280
Winner: Joey Sindelar

Jack Nicklaus didn't win The International at Castle Pines Golf Club in Colorado, but he certainly brought attention to the sometimes-puzzling tournament before Joey Sindelar was crowned champion. The International is unlike any other, a five-day event that reduces the size of the field every day and whose winner accumulates the most points — not necessarily the lowest score — the final day. It uses a modified Stableford system: eight points for double-eagle, five for eagle, two for birdie, none for par, minus one for bogey and minus three for double-bogey or worse.

It's a format that Nicklaus and some others do not like. He admitted before the start that if he had not designed the course he would not have entered. Others, chief among them Mike Reid, were outspoken in their desire for a tournament that is a departure from the usual. The Stableford system encourages gambling on shots, rather than rewarding conservative play. Ken Green had won the first tournament with 12 points and John Cook took the second with 11.

Although he doesn't like the format, Nicklaus had some success with it. He got through the first round on Wednesday — when half the field played — with three points, the same number accumulated by Sindelar. Reid led the scoring with 11 points. On Friday, Nicklaus made eight points. That was three fewer than Sindelar, Fred Couples and D.W. Weibring, but it got him comfortably into the third round and made him the PGA Tour's first $5 million man.

Then came Nicklaus' ignominious exit on Saturday. He had recovered from a minus-four start to get to plus-seven with two holes remaining. He needed only two pars to make the final round, and one of the holes left was the par-five No. 17, rated the easiest hole on the course. Nicklaus had overcome an unplayable lie at the third hole, but he was unable to overcome his troubles at No. 17. He hit his tee shot right, it hit a spectator on the head and ricocheted into the bushes. He tried to punch it out lefthanded and failed. So he declared the ball unplayable and took a drop, and the ball fell between two rocks. He attempted to extricate it with a mighty swing, but it stopped in an unplayable lie "and at that point I decided I had enough." He had had six birdies, but he also had enough penalties to drop him to a plus-three finish and it took plus-six to get into a playoff for the final spots in the fourth round.

Meanwhile, Sindelar, ranked seventh in percentage of birdie holes, worked his way toward his fifth victory, although for a while on Saturday it looked as if he would not be around on Sunday to get the chance. Castle Rock was hit by a rainstorm and play was delayed with Sindelar on the course with two holes to go. During the break, he made plane reservations out of town, believing he had no chance to qualify for the final round. When play resumed Sindelar birdied the last two holes for a plus-seven that avoided a playoff by one stroke and moved him into the 18-man final. Ben Crenshaw did even better, playing the final five holes in eagle, birdie, birdie, birdie, par to tie Jodie Mudd at 13 points, one behind the day's leader, Bruce Lietzke. Reid was one of three who survived a six-man playoff at plus-six.

Sindelar began pursuit of the $180,000 first prize and the year's money lead in the final round. Dan Pohl and Seve Pate started fast and Sindelar got in step behind them. He birdied Nos. 2, 3, 4 and 8, then lost a point with his only bogey of the day at the ninth hole. With seven points, he trailed Pohl as they went into the back nine. Sindelar birdied Nos. 10, 11 and 12 on putts of 12 feet or less and when he birdied No. 14 he was within a stroke of Pohl.

Pohl, playing up ahead of Sindelar, met with disaster at the 18th hole, taking a double-bogey that dropped him from 16 points to 13 and a tie with Pate for second place. That gave Sindelar the lead with 15 points and he clinched his victory with a birdie at the 17th hole. He wasn't required to play No. 18 — he did — because the worst he could have done was minus three, which would have left him with 14 points. That's another thing that's unique about The International — theoretically, a man could play 16 or 17 holes each day and win. The $180,000 purse increased Sindelar's winnings for the year to $672,212, second only to the record $925,941 won by Curtis Strange.

NEC World Series of Golf—$800,000
Winner: Mike Reid

The feeling that Tom Watson would beat Mike Reid in the playoff for the World Series of Golf was almost palpable. The fans at Firestone Country Club in Akron, Ohio, the television announcers and probably the viewers at home all but conceded the victory to Watson. After all, wasn't this the man on the verge of becoming the all-time leading money winner, a several times Player of the Year, a 32-time PGA Tour winner, a man who had come from four strokes behind to beat Reid in the 1980 Dunlop Phoenix tournament in Japan, a defeat that was engraved on Reid's memory? And wasn't Reid the man who had won $1 million before he won his first tournament, the Tucson Open in 1987, and was rated as one of the shortest hitters?

When they both reached the green with their second shots at the 410-yard No. 10, wasn't Reid the one who was supposed to three-putt from 35 feet, and Watson the one who was going to roll his first putt to within three feet and easily sink his par putt, as Reid probably pushed his second putt past the cup?

Instead of three-putting the first playoff hole, Reid two-putted, sinking his second from a little more than three feet and Watson, once a superior putter, pushed his tying putt past the hole. "My heart goes out to him because I've done the same thing," Reid said.

The $162,000 check would have pushed Watson past Jack Nicklaus for all-time winnings and he seemed to be pushing toward that even after an inelegant 74 in the opening round. Seve Ballesteros and Ian Woosnam passed up the tournament to play in Europe; of the 45 players in the field, 18 were first-time winners. Watson's opposition did not look very formidable.

The weather forecast was unsettled, which some thought might have worked against the short-hitting Reid — the ball doesn't roll very far on wet fairways — but Reid likes to play in foul weather. He learned how to play golf in

Sandy Lyle, with three American victories, became the first Briton to win the Masters.

Sandy Lyle's sensational bunker shot resulted in a tremendous ovation as the Scot approached the 18th green, where he holed a 10-foot birdie putt.

The Masters

Until Sandy Lyle's dramatic finish, Mark Calcavecchia thought he had at least a first-place tie in the Masters. He took second place, one stroke behind.

Curtis Strange had a crucial bunker shot (below) and putt to gain a playoff in the U.S. Open, then Curtis posted an even-par 71 for the victory.

U.S. Open

Sarah and Curtis
Strange celebrate the
U.S. Open triumph.

An injured wrist put Greg Norman out of the U.S. Open, and out of competition for two months.

Briton Nick Faldo had eight seconds in 1988, including the U.S. Open playoff loss.

Severiano Ballesteros lifted the British Open trophy for the third time at Royal Lytham & St. Annes.

British Open

Severiano Ballesteros chipped close to the 18th hole to secure his British Open win over surprisingly tough Nick Price (right).

Jeff Sluman at the PGA Championship: A hugh trophy for the small man.

PGA Championship

Paul Azinger was runner-up by three strokes in the PGA Championship.

A "paychex" of $160,000 awaited Jeff Sluman after his final-round 65, six under par.

After four runner-up finishes, Sandy Lyle finally won the Suntory World Match Play Championship.

World Match Play

In the all-British final, Nick Faldo (above) fell by a 2-and-1 margin to rival Sandy Lyle.

Moments of Victory

A familiar scene after important victories, caddies hug the champions: (clockwise on previous page): Sandy Lyle at the Masters, Curtis Strange at the U.S. Open and Jeff Sluman at the PGA Championship. At left, the one beneath is Mark McCumber, who surfaced to accept the trophy at the Players Championship.

Dunhill Cup

An excited Des Smyth (left) on the 18th green at St. Andrews. Above, the champion Irish team in the Dunhill Cup: (from left) Ronan Rafferty, captain Eammon Darcy and Smyth.

it. His opening 70 left him three strokes behind another first-time winner, Blaine McCallister, and four in front of Watson. Reid leap-frogged past McCallister with a 65 in the second round and into a tie for the lead with Ian Baker-Finch, who had a 67. Masters champion Sandy Lyle shot a 67 that left him a stroke behind at 136. Watson came back with a 69 that moved him up in the standings but still eight strokes out of the lead.

Overnight rains made the course play long, but softened the greens for the third round and Reid and Baker-Finch took advantage of the soft greens early. Baker-Finch seemingly took control with birdies on three of the first eight holes. But Baker-Finch slipped into reverse on the back nine as he took a 71 and watched Reid and former PGA champion Larry Nelson take over the lead. Nelson played the back nine in 30, with birdies at the final three holes — a 50-foot chip-in at No. 17 — for a 66 and Reid shot a 71. Watson made eight birdies en route to a 64 and suddenly he was one stroke out of the lead at 207 and playing on a course tailored for his game.

Baker-Finch hung around for a while in the final round. So did Nelson. A rain that halted play for 75 minutes seemed to dampen their enthusiasm as they both shot 71 and tied for third place at 277. That left the final battle to Reid and Watson and many remembered how Reid had finished his third round, with a double-bogey at the long 16th after hitting an approach into the lake and a bogey at No. 17 after missing the green. Watson birdied the 11th and 14th but he couldn't shake Reid. Watson shot a 68 for 275, but he missed good opportunities for birdies at Nos. 16 and 18 and Reid birdied the 17th for a 69 and 275.

The walk up the 10th fairway in the playoff was supposed to be ceremonial for Watson, but he ended it with a flat note by three-putting and Reid finally had a victory of note. "I never stopped believing I could get in the winner's circle," Reid said. "I just kept trying to give myself pep talks and saying, 'Behind every adversity there's opportunity.'"

Provident Classic—$450,000
Winner: Phil Blackmar

Phil Blackmar, at 6-7, 240 pounds, the biggest man on the PGA Tour, resuscitated a wilting career with some explosive putting at the finish of the Provident Classic, which included most of the players not eligible for the World Series of Golf.

Blackmar stood in the fairway at the 18th hole in Hixson, Tennessee, as Payne Stewart hit his second shot at the 501-yard, par-five No. 17, a hole Blackmar had birdied moments earlier to pull into a tie for the lead. Blackmar said he knew the worst Stewart would do was birdie No. 17. He had to make birdie at the 18th to have a chance to tie. Blackmar swayed on a nine-iron approach and his ball stopped 40 feet from the hole.

As he looked over his putt, the roar at the 17th told him Stewart had birdied. "I hadn't made anything longer than four feet," Blackmar said. His putt rolled true for a birdie and 65 that gave him a 264 total. Stewart, who missed an eagle putt of about 20 feet at No. 17, had a birdie putt of about the same distance at the 18th and he missed that one, too, for a 65 that tied him with Blackmar.

The playoff began at the dogleg 358-yard No. 1 hole. Stewart hit his approach 30 feet short of the hole; Blackmar was 25 feet beyond. Blackmar's putter was still hot. After Stewart didn't come close on his first putt, Blackmar sank his birdie putt. The $81,000 he won was more than three times what he had collected through the rest of the season.

Blackmar's putting heroics at the finish should have come as no surprise. His putter had kept him in contention in the tightly packed field, especially in the second round, when he shot a 64 that gave him a one-stroke lead with a 130 total at the halfway point. His putting stroke abandoned him momentarily in the third round when he three-putted the 18th hole for a 69 that tied him with Stewart, Bill Britton and Jim Dent at 199. Britton and Dent retreated in the final round, leaving Blackmar and Stewart to try to hold off a pack of pursuers who finally gave up the chase on the final nine.

Blackmar's only previous victory had come in a playoff, in the 1985 Hartford Open. His defeat left Stewart 0-4 in playoffs and in a philosophical mood. "I birdied three of the last four holes to get into the playoff. Phil had to play great golf to beat me. I can't dwell on being 0-4 in playoffs."

Canadian Open—$750,000
Winner: Ken Green

A change of dates — two months later in the season than in past years — had some effect on the caliber of the field for the Canadian Open and probably led to the poor condition of some greens at Glen Abbey Golf Club, but it didn't reduce the crowds or detract from Ken Green's dramatic victory.

Because of a rain delay, the final round had to be completed on Monday, with 22 players aiming at the three-stroke lead Green held overnight. Scott Verplank and Bill Glasson came closest to overtaking Green, who played his final six holes on Monday in two over par for an even-par 72 and 13-under-par 275 total, a Glen Abbey record that gave him the victory by one stroke over Glasson and Verplank.

"I was scared. I'm not a cold wind player and it was cold and windy. I definitely felt the pressure," said Green, who slept for three hours Sunday night, then started completion of his final round with a bogey at the 13th hole. He birdied the 14th from three feet, then hung on.

Verplank birdied Nos. 13 and 15, then missed a big opportunity when he three-putted the 16th hole for a par after reaching it in two. Glasson finished birdie-birdie-birdie, but he missed an 18-foot putt for an eagle at the final hole. Verplank finished with a 70 and Glasson, with a 67. Glasson's problem was that he three-putted two of the valley greens, a forgivable sin.

Glen Abbey's four holes in the valley of 16-Mile Creek — Nos. 11, 12, 13 and 14 — had been all but destroyed by pythium blight, a product of the summer-long drought. Yet Nos. 11 and 13 played under par, and Dave Barr made a hole-in-one at the 187-yard No. 12 with a six iron in the second round. PGA champion Jeff Sluman played the damaged holes sensationally in the first round, birdieing all four, then adding birdies at the par-five 16th and 18th holes for a 64 that gave him the lead. He never approached that excellence in the final three rounds.

Green added a 65 to his opening 70 on Friday and tied Sluman for the lead with a 68 for 203 in the third round as Sluman faded with a 73. Behind him, the field made advances: John Huston shot a 64 that put him to within four strokes, Larry Rinker shot a second straight 65 that set a course record for low consecutive rounds and Jay Delsing turned in a 68 that put him in second place.

Green played steadily if unspectacularly through the first 12 holes on Sunday as nobody close to him made a charge. The hole that kept his tournament together was the ninth and it came just before the rain. His approach buried in the mud below the green, but he dug it out and sank a 30-foot putt for par. Barr was the leader with 277 when the halt came and was feeling good. "If you told me I'd be 11 under at the end I'd have said it would win the tournament because Glen Abbey is one of the toughest courses we play," he said. But after the rain softened the course, his hopes diminished.

Green lost one-third of his three-stroke lead when he bogeyed his first hole, No. 13, when play resumed Monday, blaming a soft lie and a bad break — literally — for his bogey. As he was about to putt for parr, a large tree limb fell to the ground. But nobody was able to shake the lead out of Green.

Greater Milwaukee Open—$700,000
Winner: Ken Green

Ken Green scored his second straight victory in the Greater Milwaukee Open, but he didn't plan to try for three in a row. Instead of heading for the Bank of Boston Classic, Green made an appointment to see a cardiologist.

Green has a history of chest pains, but after numerous examinations, doctors had been unable to ascertain whether they were caused by his heart, stress, or something else. Maybe it was excitement. Even before the pains, Green said he had no intention of playing at Boston because "I'm an emotional person. When I won at Glen Abbey I was on clouds. I'm all drained out from the excitement."

He didn't seem to be drained out at Tuckaway Country Club. He shot an 11-under 61 in the third round that set a course and tournament record and won by six strokes with 70-69-61-68 — 268, a 20-under-par total just two strokes above the tournament record.

The 61 was the key, of course. It took him from five strokes behind co-leaders Jim Gallagher and Dave Barr and put him two strokes ahead. His 61 began with a birdie out of a bunker at the second hole, was kept going with a 30-foot eagle putt at the sixth hole and was capped with putts of 50, 18 and 15 feet for eagle-birdie-birdie at the final three holes.

The only question in the final round was whether he would finish. The chest pains began early in the round. "For three holes I was really hurting," he said. "And when I have pain I get dizzy. I tried not to pass out because I don't think they would have waited for me." He didn't pass out and of the four who tied for second place at 274 — Mark Calcavecchia, Gallagher, Dan Pohl and Donnie Hammond — the one who might have been just as happy as Green was Gallagher. He had to survive a local qualifier to get in the tournament and the $46,200 he won enabled him to regain exempt status.

Bank of Boston Classic—$600,000
Winner: Mark Calcavecchia

Mark Calcavecchia seemed to have a new grip on his game when he tied for second place in the Greater Milwaukee Open. Then he thought he had lost it when he shot a 70 in the third round of the Bank of Boston Classic. Disgusted, he went straight from Pleasant Valley Country Club to his hotel room, passing up time on the range to mentally replay his round. The third round of the Masters came to mind.

"I realized I was standing too far away from the ball, the same as in the third round of the Masters," Calcavecchia said. He placed second, one stroke behind Sandy Lyle, in the Masters, but this time there would be no second-place finish. Calcavecchia chipped-in from 40 feet for a birdie on the first hole and sank a 30-foot birdie putt on the last hole, the key shots in a 66 and 274 total that gave him a one-stroke victory over fast-closing Don Pooley. Pooley, who missed four months because of pneumonia and a shoulder injury, tied the tournament record with 63 that leap-frogged him past Fuzzy Zoeller, Dave Rummells and John Mahaffey.

The Masters was one of five second-place finishes for Calcavecchia since he won the Honda Classic in 1987. He went into the Bank of Boston Classic on a high, a 66 in the final round of the Milwaukee Classic earning him a tie for second place.

David Frost and Donnie Hammond bore up best under the cold and windy conditions the first day to share the lead at 67, four better than Calcavecchia. As the weather warmed and the winds died, Steve Pate and D.A. Weibring, both with 68-68, took command. Calcavecchia moved to within a stroke of the lead with a 67.

Pate and Weibring both shot 69s in the third round and were joined at the top by Larry Rinker, who had a 65. Calcavecchia, with a 70, trailed by three strokes and left the course in a foul mood. The final round eventually belonged to him, but first it looked as if it would be Zoeller's day. As the three leaders stalled, Zoeller moved two strokes ahead after 13 holes, playing the first 10 holes in four under par. Zoeller hit poor tee shots at the 13th and 17th holes and both resulted in double bogeys. "Two bad swings and I was a goner," he said.

As Zoeller went, Calcavecchia and Pooley took over. Pooley's 63 gave him the lead with a nine-under 275 total, and he was forced to wait in the clubhouse to see what his fate would be.

B.C. Open—$500,000
Winner: Bill Glasson

Bill Glasson was the PGA Tour's driving champion as a rookie in 1984 and it looked as if his ability to hit a golf ball a long distance might be a key to a successful career when he won the Kemper Open at Congressional Country Club in Bethesda, Maryland, the next year. But it wasn't until late in the 1988 season that that ability finally paid off again.

Glasson won the B.C. Open at the En Joie Golf Club in Endicott, New York, by two strokes, building a comfortable lead with birdies at the first three par-five holes, then smoothing out a game that had become somewhat ruffled on the closing holes. Glasson shot a 66-68-65-69 — 268, but his final round was not without terror.

Wayne Levi got the most agressive and gave Glasson the most uncomfortable moments. When Levi missed an 18-inch par putt at the 11th hole he trailed by five strokes and seemed to be a non-contender. But Levi birdied the 14th and 16th holes, both par-threes, and when Glasson bogeyed No. 14 the difference between them was two strokes. Glasson was visibly upset. He missed the green at the 175-yard No. 16 and admitted he "hit a chip as bad as I possibly could." But the ball stopped four feet from the hole, and his relief was evident. Levi made Glasson's walk in more pleasant by missing a 12-foot birdie putt at the 18th hole that left him with a tie for second place with Bruce Lietzke, who closed with a 64.

For years the B.C. Open had been a tournament for neighborhood boys — Joey Sindelar of nearby Horseheads, New York, won it in 1985 and 1987 and Levi, of Little Falls, New York, won in 1984. It appeared Sindelar might make it three wins in four years when he got off to a 67-65 start that tied him with Ed Dougherty for the 36-hole lead. Sindelar, with a 70, slipped three strokes behind Glasson when Glasson shot a 65 in the third round and Dougherty disappeared with a 77. Sindelar finished in a tie for ninth place at 274, worth $12,500. That moved him into the money lead with $705,515 as previous leader Chip Beck missed the 36-hole cut.

Southern Open—$400,000
Winner: David Frost

The only regret David Frost had after he scored his first triumph on the PGA Tour was that it came so late in the year. "If I had won earlier, I would have made $108,000," he said. The Southern Open at the Green Island Country Club in Columbus, Georgia, is a $400,000 tournament, not $600,000, even though winning there can be as difficult as finishing first in one of the higher-priced tournaments. For Frost, a native of South Africa, it will be remembered as the place where his streak of almosts ended. Frost had placed second in five tournaments in his first three years, and in 1988 he had three seconds and three thirds.

It appeared he might be heading for another runner-up finish as he stood in the middle of the fairway of the par-five finishing hole at Green Island. Up ahead, Bob Tway had a 10-foot birdie putt. If Tway made it, Frost had to eagle to tie him. "I was nervous and excited," Tway said, running the consequences through his mind as he sized up the putt. He missed.

"I told myself if Tway makes the putt, I definitely was going to go (for the green)," said Frost of his 242-yard approach. "Then he missed and I said, 'What the heck.'" Frost didn't reach the green, falling 30 yards short, but he left himself with an easy chip that he hit to six feet and made the tying birdie putt. The first playoff hole was almost a rerun of the 18th. Tway, still looking for his first victory since the 1986 PGA Championship, missed a 10-foot birdie putt at the first hole and Frost sank a five-footer for the victory.

Jeff Sluman, who had won the PGA title less than two months earlier, looked as if he were going to escape the jinx that follows PGA champions when he opened with 63-67 that gave him a two-stroke lead at the halfway point. But Sluman was pushed aside by Dave Barr in the third round, as Barr jumped in front with a nine-under-par 61. Barr had nine birdies, four from between 20 and 35 feet. Frost and Tway trailed by two strokes after 54 holes.

The final round was a four-man affair before Tway and Frost went into their act. Frost led by two strokes after 12 holes, but frittered away his lead with bogeys at the 13th and 14th holes. "That left me wondering if I ever was going to win," he said. Barr and George Archer were tied with Tway, but fell back when Tway birdied No. 16. Barr and Archer (who had a 65) tied Dan Forsman for third place at 271. Then came the Tway-Frost dramatics and Frost's victory surprised nobody. "It was just a matter of time before David was going to win a tournament," Tway said.

Gatlin Brothers Southwest Classic—$400,000
Winner: Tom Purtzer

Considering his ability, it is surprising that Tom Purtzer's victory in the Gatlin Brothers Southwest Classic in Abilene, Texas, was only his third in more than 13 years on the tour.

Purtzer opened with an eight-under-par 64 that tied him for the lead with Mark Brooks and Bobby Clampett. Two undistinguished rounds — 72, 69 — dropped him to three behind Brooks and Brad Bryant entering the final round. Then Purtzer produced another scintillating round, making it a two-man show with Brooks as he carved out a 64 to Brooks' 67, tying them after 72 holes at 19-under 269, two strokes under the tournament record. The playoff was nearly anticlimactic as Brooks three-putted the first hole, missing his second putt from five feet.

Brooks, a two-time All-America at the University of Texas, took a two-stroke lead after 36 holes with a 68 Friday, then was joined by Bryant after 54 holes when he shot a 70 and Bryant closed up with a second straight 68. Buddy Gardner shot a 65 and Mark O'Meara a 64 in the final round, but they began the day too far behind to intrude on the Purtzer-Brooks duel. Purtzer began the final round with birdies at Nos. 1, 2, 3 and 5 and he was in a deadlock for the lead with Brooks. When Brooks bogeyed No. 6, Purtzer was on top by himself. Brooks caught Purtzer with a birdie at No. 13 and they both birdied the par-five No. 15.

They were still tied when they teed off at the 562-yard No. 18. Texas courses are known for the roll the fairways give and Fairway Oaks was no different. Purtzer reached the green with his second shot, using a seven iron to get within 25 feet of the hole. He dropped the eagle putt, forcing Brooks to also eagle the hole to send the tournament into a playoff, the 14th in 41 tournaments. Brooks used a little more club, a six iron, to reach the 18th green in two. He also used a little more putter to make his eagle, holing a sensational 50-footer. But in the playoff, he couldn't sink a five-footer.

It was the last Gatlin Brothers Southwest Classic. The tournament was scheduled to become a Senior PGA Tour stop in 1989.

Texas Open—$600,000
Winner: Corey Pavin

Corey Pavin had virtually disappeared after winning the Hawaii Open early in 1987. In 45 tournaments since his Hawaii victory, Pavin had missed the cut 17 times, a surprise for a player considered one of the rising young stars.

So then what happens? Pavin pulls a gem out of a clinker of a season, winning the Texas Open by eight strokes and nearly matching PGA Tour records for 36, 54 and 72 holes. After trailing Mike Sullivan by one stroke with an opening 64, Pavin turned it into no contest. He followed with 63, 66, 66 for 259, matching the second lowest winning score in PGA Tour history and missing the record of 257 set by Mike Souchak in the 1955 Texas Open at nearby Brackenridge Park.

The tournament began as if it might be one for the books. Sullivan chipped in twice en route to his 63. Pavin made a hole-in-one with a seven iron at a 172-yard hole and Bobby Wadkins made threes at half his holes, and missed four birdie putts of eight feet or less. But Pavin took over with a 63 in the second round, his 127 just one stroke shy of Tommy Bolt's 36-hole record set 34 years previously. Pavin came close to matching Bolt's record twice at the finish, nearly holing a sand wedge approach at the 17th hole and having a 15-foot birdie putt stop on the edge of the cup at No. 18.

A 66 on Saturday improved Pavin's lead to five strokes over Tom Pernice and seven strokes over Tom Kite, and left Pavin only two strokes short of Gay Brewer's 54-hole record of 191 set in the 1967 Pensacola Open. It also elicited talk of players who have come from far behind to win. But this was not to be one of those weeks. Robert Wrenn blazed to a 62 in the final round, but all that got him was second place with 267. Kite made a brief run at Pavin, getting to within four strokes, but Pavin put him and the rest of the field away with another 66.

Pavin's margin of victory was the widest since Andy Bean won the 1979 Atlanta Classic by eight strokes. His victory also left him and Curtis Strange as the only players who have won at least one tournament over the past five years.

Pensacola Open—$400,000
Winner: Andrew Magee

Andrew Magee calls himself "one of the best whistlers" on the tour. In the final round of the Pensacola Open, Magee came out with a succession of Elvis Presley songs as an accompaniment to his first victory in his fourth year on the tour. But after he failed to birdie the 18th hole in the final round he thought he might be whistling a different tune, something like a blues song, perhaps. "I was sure it was a playoff," he said.

Tom Byrum had a downhill 25-foot putt for birdie that would have tied Magee at 271. He missed. Bruce Lietzke faced a sidehill 10-footer for birdie. He also missed. Ken Green, who had shared the lead with Magee earlier in the day, three-putted from 20 feet. Byrum, Lietzke and Green wound up in a tie for second place, one stroke behind Magee.

Magee, 26, a three-time All-America at the University of Oklahoma, became the 11th first-time winner on the tour. Magee had played the European tour briefly in 1984 before joining the PGA Tour and showed slow progress in his first three years. He married in 1987 and said, "it's time to get down to business." And that's what he did at Pensacola.

The Pensacola Open is one of those friendly tournaments in which it seems all the townspeople try to make the players feel at home. The tournament moved to the Tiger Point Golf Club on Santa Rosa Island, a layout designed by former U.S. Open champ Jerry Pate. Pate figured it would take "about 16 or 18 under" to win and he was correct. Magee won with 70-68-67-66 — 271, 17 under par.

Dan Pohl, Kenny Perry, Mark Hayes and Lance Ten Broeck shared the first-round lead with 66s, but only Pohl, who placed fifth at 274, was among the leaders at the finish. Scott Hoch and Hayes shared the lead at 135 after 36 holes, three strokes ahead of Magee. Bryum, with 64-65 in his middle rounds, had 201 after 54 holes and led Magee, Green, Ray Stewart and Lietzke by four strokes entering the final round. But with his first victory in sight Byrum could do no better than one-under 71 in the final round.

Walt Disney World/Oldsmobile Classic—$600,000
Winner: Bob Lohr

Everybody wanted to crown Bob Lohr as champion after he shot a brilliant 10-under-par 62 at the Palm course, the most difficult of the three courses used in the Disney/Oldsmobile Classic, in the first round. But Lohr knew he still had a long way to go and only a two-stroke lead on Fuzzy Zoeller to start. But after shooting 67-66 in the middle rounds and playing well in the final round, Lohr figured that, yes, maybe he was going to win. Then, walking off the 15th tee, he got a shock. He trailed Chip Beck by two strokes.

"I was flaming," Lohr said. "I led by two starting the round, I was three under and had played steady. And here I am, two behind." He might have stayed that way, too, had not thoughts of Ben Hogan's record for most strokes under par not crept into Beck's mind at the 18th hole. Beck admitted "there were a few extra thoughts" running through his mind as he contemplated his 168-yard approach to the final green. Beck was 26 under par; Hogan had set the PGA Tour record with 27 under 43 years earlier.

Beck said he failed to follow through on a seven iron and left his ball 40 feet from the hole. He three-putted for bogey. Lohr, watching from the fairway as Beck putted, knew his chances now were much better. Now he needed a birdie to tie, not a near-impossible eagle. Lohr hit an eight iron three feet from the hole and dropped the birdie putt that tied them at 263. That set up a playoff between a man (Lohr) who had never won on tour and another who had a shot at becoming the first million-dollar winner in one year. If Lohr was nervous about the situation, he didn't show it.

Lohr birdied the first playoff hole (No. 16) and Beck matched him. Both birdied the next two holes and once again they both birdied No. 16, Lohr sinking a 12-foot putt after Beck birdied from 15 feet. Now darkness was a problem, but they decided they wanted to play at least one more hole rather than come back the next afternoon. Beck pulled his approach at No.

17 far from the hole, and Lohr hit his into the rough behind the green. Beck ran his downhill putt eight feet past the hole. Lohr chipped to within five feet. Beck missed his comebacker and Lohr smoothly sank his winning putt.

Lohr knew his opening 62 was only a piece of the pie, and his second round and his last-round pairing played a big part in his victory. He shot a 67 in the second round — "That got my concentration back" — and was paired with Paul Azinger, his partner in the Chrysler Team Classic, in the final round. But in the end it was a mistake by Beck and his own ability that earned him his first victory.

Northern Telecom Tucson Open—$600,000
Winner: David Frost

The first week in November was maybe the best week in the life of David Frost. He won $90,000 in the Merrill Lynch Shootout Championship, the culmination of a series of weekly shootouts, on the Tuesday before the Seiko Tucson Open, then won $108,000 more in the tournament, gaining his second victory of the year and the second in his four years on the tour.

Frost beat Chip Beck in a special chip-off in the Shootout, which began with a 10-man field. He won the Tucson Open at the TPC at StarPass simply by playing the steadiest golf. Tom Purtzer tied the course record with a 10-under-par 62 in the second round and Mark Wiebe lowered it with a 61 in the third round, but Frost kept putting together low numbers — 66, 66, 67, 67 for 266 — as the others followed their dandies with disasters.

Russ Cochran, one of two lefthanders on the tour, jumped into the lead with an opening 65 and stayed there with another 65 the next day. He slipped to one stroke behind Frost and Wiebe after three rounds, then fell apart for a 75 in the final round, the decisive blow a quadruple bogey at the 15th hole. Wiebe's 61 in the third round followed a 65 in the second and it looked as if he and Frost would shoot it out for the title in the final round. But Wiebe came down with a stomach virus and was no match for Frost after Frost began the final round with three straight birdies.

As Wiebe faltered for a 73 and 272, Mark O'Meara, with a 70, and Mark Calcavecchia, with a 69, eased past him to tie for second place at 271, five strokes behind Frost.

Nabisco Championship—$2,000,000
Winner: Curtis Strange

"May the best man win" is a phrase often used in sports . . . and often not answered accurately. The best man or best team often doesn't win. Curtis Strange in 1987 is a case in point. Strange, with three victories and a record $925,941 in winnings, was arguably the best player on the PGA Tour. But he placed 30th (and last) in the first Nabisco Championship and Paul Azinger, who placed fourth, earned enough points to be crowned PGA Player of the Year.

Now it was 1988 and time again for the Nabisco Championship at the Pebble Beach Golf Links in California. Strange had won three U.S. tournaments, including the U.S. Open and Memorial. He was not the leading money winner, but he was among 14 players who could become the first to win $1 million in one year by taking the $360,000 offered as the first prize in the Nabisco tournament. And this time the best man won.

Strange played like a man possessed at Pebble Beach and neither horrid weather, nor Tim Kite, nor the memory of his 1987 performance could shake him. Strange beat Kite on the second hole of a playoff on the Monday morning following the rain-delayed fourth round, thus becoming the first $1 million-in-a-year winner in the U.S. with earnings of $1,147,644. "I guess the first one to do it is the one everybody will talk about, but a couple years from now four or five guys will be doing it," said Strange. "It's like Arnold Palmer becoming the first to win $1 million in a career. Now there are 40 or 50 who have done it."

It took Palmer 13 years to become the first to win $1 million in a career; Jack Nicklaus, the all-time money leader, took eight years. In his past two years Strange has won almost $2 million. It took Nicklaus almost 12 years to reach that plateau. But in the heyday of Palmer and Nicklaus no one was shelling out $2 million for a tournament.

Chip Beck, who began the year without a victory and had won twice, led the money list and Sandy Lyle, who had won three U.S. tournaments, including the Masters, and nearly $600,000 in the first four months, was the Player of the Year front-runner. Beck had to settle for second place in money ($916,818) and the Vardon Trophy for his adjusted scoring average of 69.46. Lyle placed second to Strange in PGA Player of the Year points, 80 to 75. Beck was third with 58 points.

So those were some of the things at stake in the richest tournament on the tour. Another, more personal, streak also was on the line — Kite's streak of at least one victory for seven years in a row. He might have made it eight if not for Strange and the weather.

Pebble Beach in November can be different than it is in February, when the tour makes its annual stop there. And this November it looked as if "Crosby weather" is something that occurs only in the winter . . . at least at the outset. There was little wind and no rain for the pro-am and the first two rounds of the tournament, and Pebble Beach was helpless. Strange was disqualified in the pro-am for signing his scorecard for a 64 when he had shot a 65, a mistake that only made him more alert in the first round of the tournament. He opened with a 64 and "I must have checked my scorecard six or seven times." It was a day for low scores: 16 men broke par and seven others matched it.

One of the few who failed to break par in the first round was Greg Norman, whose 75 beat only Mark Weibe, who had a 76. But Wiebe bounced back with a 64, picking up seven strokes on Strange, who had a 71. Kite, with 72-65, Bruce Lietzke, with 69-69, and Ken Green, with 67-70, trailed Strange by two strokes. Kite played four under par from the 12th hole in and birdied all four par-threes, no easy accomplishment at Pebble Beach.

Strange shot a 70 in the third round for 205 and led Green, who had a 69, and Mark Calcavecchia, who had a 65, by one stroke. Kite, with a 70, was two strokes back. A light rain was falling as Strange finished, giving off portents of what was to come. The forecast was for wind and rain on Sunday, but the weather was still favorable when Norman and Mark O'Meara, the first twosome, teed off. Norman, who had to catch a plane for Australia, and O'Meara played their round in 84 minutes, leaving the rest of the field to struggle with the quickly approaching bad weather.

Strange, in the last twosome, was at the 10th hole when the rain went from light to a downpour, covering some greens and forcing a halt to play. Kite had bogeyed the ninth, 10th and 11th holes and was "18½ steps" from the hole at the 12th green. He was thankful for the stop. The rain was bad enough; the wind nearly blew him away from his ball a few times, he said. But Kite could take solace in the fact that the weather was costing everybody else strokes, too.

After a 90-minute delay, Kite sank his birdie putt and found out that, indeed, everybody had lost ground in the rain. He was in second place, one stroke behind Strange. At the 16th hole, Strange came up short on a birdie putt that would put him three ahead and almost surely cinch the victory. At the par-three 17th, Strange hit his tee shot into the back bunker and failed to get it up and down for a par. Up ahead, Kite hit a pitching wedge eight feet from the hole at No. 18 and birdied, tying Strange for the lead. Strange could win with a birdie at No. 18. But with darkness descending he hit a nine iron fat 35 feet from the hole and two-putted. It was too dark for a playoff, so they were told to come back the next morning and settle matters. Strange had shot a 74 for 279, Kite a 72 for 279.

A couple thousand people showed up to watch a playoff that might be over in minutes. It was a few long minutes. The playoff began at the par-four No. 16 and both parred it. Strange, first up at the 17th hole, the one that cost him so dearly the day before, hit his tee shot no more than a yard from the hole. Now the pressure was on Kite, and he did what Strange had done the day before — hit his ball into a bunker behind the hole. Kite's explosion was short of the hole, farther from the pin than Strange's ball and on the same line. Kite sank his putt for par. Strange, taking advantage of the read, made the winning birdie putt.

Centel Classic—$500,000
Winner: Bill Glasson

For a month before the Centel Classic at Killearn Country Club in Tallahassee, Florida, Bill Glasson had been troubled by bronchitis. But that was a minor problem easily overcome, considering that two months earlier he had erased an ailment of even greater concern for many golfers — self-doubt. Glasson won the Kemper Open in 1985, then didn't win again until the B.C. Open in September of 1988, a period in which he had begun harboring doubts of whether he would ever win again.

But with the 30 top money winners competing in the Nabisco Championship in California, Glasson found the winning formula for the second time in the season, winning the Centel Classic by two strokes with 67-69-68-68 — 272. Glasson ended the first round two strokes behind Lance Ten Broeck and was in a crowd tied for second, one stroke in back of Bob Lohr, after 36 holes. Lohr (68), Chris Perry (66) and Kenny Perry (66) were tied for the lead with Glasson after 65 holes, but Tommy Armour III had pulled to within two strokes of the leaders with a 65 and was to be heard from in the finale.

Armour leaped ahead of the pack in the final round with birdies on five of the first six holes. That seemed to take the starch out of everybody except Glasson. With two holes to go, they were tied for the lead. The break came at the 17th hole. Armour bogeyed and Glasson took the lead with a par. Glasson birdied the final hole for a 68 that matched Armour's round.

As the last official tournament on the PGA Tour, the Centel also helped determine the 125 players who would retain their playing cards for 1989. Several were in jeopardy — on the bubble, as they say — among them Chris Perry, who was in 143rd place before the tournament began. Perry figured he would have to finish at least third to place among the elite; and he was correct, his third-place tie with Lohr, worth $29,000, jumping him into 121st among the money winners. Leonard Thompson ($3,031) and Jim Gallagher Jr. ($2,309) also won enough to keep their cards.

Isuzu Kapalua International—$600,000
Winner: Bob Gilder

Since he won the Phoenix Open in 1983, Bob Gilder's career had gone into a steady slide. His enthusiasm had wilted after his peak years of 1982 and 1983, and when it returned in 1986 his touch did not return with it. Nearing his 38th birthday, Gilder had placed 82nd among the money winners in 1988 with $144,523, a large chunk of that coming from his eighth-place finish in the U.S. Open. So it was when a select field of 44 pros gathered in Hawaii for the Isuzu Kapalua International, Gilder was a hungry golfer — for a victory and the money that goes with it.

The Kapalua event, staged at the Bay course of the Kapalua Bay Hotel on Maui, is not part of the PGA Tour, but the $150,000 first prize makes it one a man can cherish. Gilder admitted that was on his mind as he dueled John Mahaffey in the final round. "The more I tried, the more I thought of it."

Gilder was in the chase from the beginning and won because he didn't three-putt a green in 72 holes. Bill Glasson took the first-round lead with a 64, but Gilder and Mahaffey were only a stroke behind him. Glasson slipped to a 69 in the second round and Gilder and Mahaffey kept in step in first place with 64s. Gilder's 71 in the third round gave him a one-stroke lead on Corey Pavin, who strung together three straight 67s, and two on Mahaffey and Glasson.

Gilder said he gets nervous when he is being crowded, but he shook off any nervousness at the start of the final round, when he opened with three consecutive birdies. That virtually disposed of Glasson and Pavin, but Mahaffey wouldn't disappear. Gilder bogeyed the 11th hole and when Mahaffey birdied No. 14 they were separated by only a stroke. Unshaken, Gilder sank a 25-foot putt for birdie at the 15th hole and all but settled matters when Mahaffey drove into a ditch at the 16th hole, then three-putted after a marvelous recovery shot. Mahaffey eagled the 18th hole, but Gilder birdied it, giving them both 66s, but Gilder a 266 to Mahaffey's 268.

J.C. Penney Classic—$800,000
Winner: Amy Benz and John Huston

The J.C. Penney Classic at the Bardmoor Country Club in Largo, Florida, pairs members of the PGA Tour with members of the LPGA Tour in a Chapman-format tournament that is a vast departure from the weekly events. Each hits a tee shot, then they hit each other's ball on their second shot, then alternate hitting one ball from the spot of their best second shot. It's a fun event that often brings together old friends or neighbors. For instance, Amy Benz and John Huston were teammates on the boys' team in high school in Dunedin, Florida, and Missie Berteotti and Rocco Mediate are Western Pennsylvanians who took lessons from then Westmoreland Country Club pro Jim Ferree.

The home connections seemed to help. Huston and Benz won by two strokes with a 19-under-par 269, and Berteotti and Mediate tied Scott Hoch and Beth Daniel for third place at 272. Larry Mize and Martha Nause placed second at 271.

An opening 69 left Benz-Huston four strokes behind Patty Sheehan and Jay Haas. A 68 in the second round left them even further behind as Donna White and Morris Hatalsky shot a tournament-low 64 for 132. But that was the last hurrah for White-Hatalsky. Nause-Mize, with a 67, and Lori Garbacz and Mike Hulbert, with a 65, tied for the lead after 54 holes with 201, but now Benz-Huston were in position, tied at 202 with Sally Little and Mike Sullivan after a 65.

Berteotti and Mediate, who trailed by six strokes entering the final round, made a run at the title with a 65, but Benz and Huston continued their steady play as their nearest rivals faltered. With one hole to go, Benz and Huston held a one-stroke lead on Nause and Mize, who were playing in the group behind them. Huston hit a drive out of play, so their only option was to play Benz's ball at the par-five hole. No problem. Huston hit the second shot just short of the green and Benz hit a marvelous pitch to within three feet of the hole. Huston sank the birdie putt. When Nause and Mize got to the green, they thought they needed a birdie to tie — the scoreboard did not show Benz-Huston had birdied the hole — and Mize reacted with anguish when he missed a 12-foot birdie putt. But it didn't mean a thing.

Benz and Huston did not win a tournament on their respective tours in 1988, but Benz, with $117,059 (her finest year as a pro) and Huston, with $150,301 in his rookie season, had satisfying seasons. The taste of victory made it even more rewarding.

Chrysler Team Championship—$600,000
Winner: George Burns and Wayne Levi

The Chrysler Team Championship was similar to the J.C. Penney tournament a week before — two winless players won and Mike Hulbert found his bid for victory once again nipped. That's where the similarity between those tournaments ended.

The Chrysler is a better-ball tournament and produces lower scores than an alternate-stroke event such as the J.C. Penney. How much lower can be noted by the final round of George Burns and Wayne Levi, who shot a 59 . . . and went into a playoff with Hulbert and Bob Tway with a 36-under-par 252. A week earlier, Hulbert and Lori Garbacz had gone into the final round of the J.C. Penney in a tie for the lead only to slump badly in the final round.

This time Hulbert and his partner did not fade — they shot a 63 in the final round — but there's no defense in golf, no way to stop some other team from shooting a 59, such as that turned in by Burns-Levi. Well, there is one way — match them stroke for stroke. And that's what Hulbert and Tway tried to do in the stretch. They birdied their final three holes to force a playoff, the capper a birdie putt of more than 80 feet by Hulbert at the final green.

Burns had five birdies and an eagle and Levi had six birdies, the last one from 25 feet at the 18th hole, in their 59. And they didn't cool off in the playoff. After Hulbert and Tway both failed to birdie the par-four 15th hole, Burns and Levi both had putts that could win, Levi from 38 feet, Burns from 15 feet. Just trying to get close for a certain par, giving Burns a free shot at a winning birdie, Levi sank his putt.

The year had been a bummer for Burns and Levi. Burns had pneumonia and chicken pox, then underwent arthroscopic surgery on his right shoulder nine weeks before the tournament. He had won a little more than $30,000. Levi won more than $190,000, but he had a persistent thumb injury, missed seven weeks when his wife was late giving birth and suffered heat exhaustion. But in the final round of the Chrysler Team tournament they appeared to be 100 percent healthy. They had to be.

Just about every team had a round between 60 and 62 in the three-course — Cypress and Dunes courses at the Palm Beach Polo Club and Wellington Club — tournament. Bobby Clampett and Bill Glasson opened with a 60, one better than Hulbert-Tway. A 63 by Clampett-Glasson gave them a one-stroke edge on Jim Rutledge and Mike Smith, who had a 60 after 36 holes. Rutledge and Smith became the favorites of the gallery when they shot a 62 at the Cypress course in the third round for a one-stroke lead over Clampett-Glasson, who had a 64. Rutledge and Smith had both failed to win playing cards in the PGA Tour qualifying school a week earlier. A victory would have got them on the tour in 1989.

While Rutledge and Smith were getting the attention, Burns and Levi were trying to stay in range, waiting for a hot round. They had 63-67-63 and trailed by seven strokes. Unaccustomed to their position, Rutledge and Smith managed only a 67 in the final round, and in better-ball play that's not much better than par. Yet only two teams raced past them.

Kirin Cup—$1,000,000
Winner: United States

The Kirin Cup at the Kapalua Resort course in Hawaii brings together six players from each of four tours in a round-robin stroke-play match tournament. In its short time — it began as the Nissan Cup in 1985 — the United States had won twice and Japan once. Europe had placed second every time.

The U.S. was favored, with six players from among the top 15 money winners, including the top three — Curtis Strange, Chip Beck and Joey Sindelar. The others were Ben Crenshaw (8), Steve Pate (12) and Mike Reid (15). The European team, on the other hand, had none from its top seven. It consisted of Mark James (8), Ronan Rafferty (9), Jose Rivero (10), Gordon Brand Jr. (11), Mark Mouland (18) and Anders Forsbrand (22)

Isao Aoki and Tommy Nakajima headed the Japanese team. Their teammates were Hiroshi Makino, Massy Kuramoto, Nobou Sarizawa and Yoshimi Nilzeski. The Australia-New Zealand team was Ian Baker-Finch, Graham Marsh, Brian Jones, Rodger Davis, Peter Senior and Craig Parry.

Each team played each other, then the two with the most points met for the championship. The results were as expected. The U.S. defeated Australia-New Zealand, 10-2, and Europe beat Japan, 9-3, the first day. Australia-New Zealand's points came on Davis' 67-68 defeat of Strange. In a pivotal match, the U.S. whipped Europe, 10-2, the second day, giving the U.S. a 20-11 lead on Europe going into the final day of the round robin. Japan beat Australia-New Zealand, 7-5, leaving Japan one stroke behind Europe.

The U.S. needed only two victories the third day to move into the finals. It got four and a tie, Crenshaw beating Nilzeski, 67-75; Reid beating Sarizawa, 71-72; Beck beating Kuramoto, 69-71; Sindelar beating Aoki, 68-70, and Strange drawing with Nakajima, 69-69. Makino defeated Pate, 70-73, for Japan's only victory. The 9-3 U.S. triumph gave it 29 points. Europe grabbed second place with 16 points despite a 7-5 loss to Australia-New Zealand, which finished with 14 points. Japan had 13.

Heavy rain had wiped out one day of play, forcing two rounds the last day. "I could sure feel those 36 holes at the end," said Crenshaw, the captain of the U.S. team. Crenshaw beat Brand, 70-71, as the U.S. scored an 8-4 decision over Europe. The long day assured there would not be any of the low scores and outstanding shots of the first three matches. Sindelar, with a 68 that beat Rafferty by two strokes, had the best score. Strange won over Mouland, 70-71, and Beck beat James, 69-73, for the other U.S. points. Europe's victories were by Rivero, 72-76 over Reid, and Forsbrand, 70-71 over Pate. Australia-New Zealand defeated Japan, 8-4. The U.S. team divided $360,000, with Sindelar receiving a $4,000 bonus for garnering the most points — eight — in the four days.

10. The U.S. Senior Tour

The 1988 Senior PGA Tour produced 16 different winners, few of them surprising and two of them a cut above the rest. Bob Charles and Gary Player, close personal friends through most of their playing careers gave international golf another boost at the expense of the long-dominant Americans by placing one-two on the $14 million circuit's 1988 official money list, earning almost $1 million and accumulating 13 of the 40 available titles in senior golf, in the U.S. and abroad.

Charles, the lefthander from New Zealand, had certainly the finest season of his splendid career, although he might beg to differ and cite 1963 and his hard-won victory in the British Open, the crown jewel on his fine record. Bob won seven times in 1988, five on the Senior PGA Tour to go with victories in important senior events in Japan (Fuji Electric Grand Slam) and South Africa (First National Bank Classic in Johannesburg.) The five wins in America — at regular tour stops in New York, Albuquerque, Sacramento, Lexington and Atlanta — along with 19 other top-10 finishes that included two losses in playoffs carried Charles to a single-season earnings record on the circuit with $533,929, just $5,189 less than his official winnings during his entire career on the regular PGA Tour. Bob also had the year's best scoring average — 70.05 — in 23 events.

Player, whose wife Vivienne and Verity Charles were good friends in South Africa before either was married, scored six victories, playing a much more limited schedule because of his many other commitments, and three of them are considered "major" titles. Gary won his second PGA and U.S. Senior Open Championships among his five Senior PGA Tour victories and captured the second Senior British Open at Turnberry, Scotland. His $435,914 earnings ran his three-year senior career total over $1 million and the title total to 13.

Orville Moody and Dave Hill each posted three individual victories and a win each in team events, following up fine 1987 seasons. Hill scored in the Senior Tournament of Champions, the PaineWebber Invitational at Charlotte and at Syracuse on his own, then teamed with Colleen Walker to pick up the biggest check of his career — $250,000, his share in the Mazda Champions at season's end in Puerto Rico. Moody's individual wins came in the exclusive Vintage Invitational, the Senior Reunion at Dallas and in Grand Rapids and he teamed with Bruce Crampton to repeat in the Legends of Golf. Although well off his sensational pace of 1986, Crampton also picked up titles in Philadelphia and Seattle during the summer.

By most standards, Chi Chi Rodriguez had another good season in 1988, winning twice and collecting more than $300,000, but that record did not stack up well to his 1987 season of seven victories and a record $509,145 in earnings. Billy Casper and Miller Barber, veteran senior tour players, also were double winners, along with the new victors of the year — colorful Walt Zembriski and solid Don Bies, the only first-year titlist on the circuit. Zembriski, the rough-hewn former high-rise ironworker, joined Larry Mowry as the only two players to win as seniors without PGA Tour titles on their records. Zembriski broke the ice at Newport in July, months before capturing the rich Vantage Championship against a top-flight field in Winston-Salem.

Mowry, a double winner in 1987, added a third victory with the 1988 Las Vegas Classic title. The year's other victors were Harold Henning, Dale Douglass, Al Geiberger, Lee Elder and Arnold Palmer, who scored his first circuit triumph in more than three years in the Crestar Classic at Richmond. Elder and Geiberger overcame adversities in achieving their victories, Lee coming back from a heart attack in late 1987 and Al shaking off the tragic accidental death of his young son. Henning actually won twice, taking the non-tour Mauna Lani Challenge in Hawaii following the GTE Kaanapali Classic to go with his early-season victory in the GTE Classic at Los Angeles.

Two streaks ended. Don January and Gene Littler, who had won at least once in every one of their senior seasons, missed out in 1988. January, the biggest winner in senior golf with 26 titles on his official record, cut back his schedule drastically, then was idled late in the year by injuries incurred in a traffic accident.

The Chrysler Cup, the classy team event that pits senior teams representing the U.S. and the rest of the golfing world against each other, bounced back into the hands of the Americans in the annual competition at the TPC at Prestancia at Sarasota, Florida, in April, giving the U.S. a 2-1 edge in the competition.

MONY Senior Tournament of Champions—$100,000
Winner: Dave Hill

Dave Hill won the MONY Senior Tournament of Champions even though he was not in the lead when play ended on a damp January Sunday at LaCosta Country Club in Southern California. Now wait a minute... What happened was that Hill, beginning his first full senior season, had lost the one-stroke lead he had carried into the final round in the course of three rain delays. But, when the persistent rains returned and forced a fourth halt in play, officials decided the round could not be finished. With Monday action ruled out, the scoring reverted to the 54-hole totals and Hill had his second Senior PGA Tour victory.

Al Geiberger was the big loser to the weather. Geiberger, another 50-year-old who had joined the circuit during the 1987 season and who had won three times in the last three months, had splashed in a birdie at LaCosta's ninth hole Sunday for an outgoing 35 and a one-stroke lead over Hill, who shot 37 on the front nine. That's where the final downpour ended it, since Senior Tour regulations bar Monday finishes. The often outspoken Hill gladly accepted the victory, his first in a rain-shortened event. "I'll take a win any way I can get it," he cracked. "You get enough bad breaks. Once in a while, they turn around."

The Michigan native, a 13-tournament winner on the regular circuit who had scored his first senior victory at Melbourne, Florida, in the Fairfield Barnett Classic the previous November, never trailed at swank LaCosta, the long-time site of the Tournament of Champions. He opened with 68 to share the first-round lead with Billy Casper, whose game subsequently tailed off. Nursing a sore right elbow, Hill moved a stroke in front of Miller Barber with a 72 for 140 Friday. Barber had 69-72, putting him a shot better than Geiberger and Orville Moody after 36 holes.

Tinkering with his game and switching putters, Hill mustered a one-under-par 71 over the 6,815-yard course to get in with his 21 and the one-stroke lead over Barber and Geiberger. In the adventurous early going, he had a bogey-double bogey sequence, switched from one to the other putter among the 14 clubs in his bag and changed to a cross-handed putting grip. But he salvaged it all — and eventually the $30,000 victory — with a late stretch of three birdies.

First National Bank Classic—$150,000
Winner: Bob Charles

Bob Charles posted an early-in-the-year victory in a tournament that made a bigger impression on his bank account than the world of golf. The event — the First National Bank Classic — was played at Houghton Golf Club in Johannesburg, South Africa, in early February and the accounts of its progress made little impact elsewhere.

Charles overcame a three-stroke deficit in the final round of the 54-hole event, firing a 65 for his 10-under-par 206 total. Bruce Devlin, the leader after each of the first two rounds, finished second at 209. Devlin "stroked the ball beautifully" the first day at Houghton, shooting a 68 to lead Orville Moody by a shot, Charles and Harold Henning by two. Devlin added a 70 Saturday for 138, opening a three-stroke lead over Charles, Henning and Butch Baird as hot, muggy weather prevailed. Henning slumped to 74 Sunday and dropped into a third-place tie at 213 with Bruce Crampton.

General Foods PGA Senior Championship—$350,000
Winner: Gary Player

Although he would be the last person to downgrade any of the 131 victories on his brilliant record, Gary Player has always taken particular pride in his triumphs in major and national championships. With nine major titles, Player is one of only four men in the game's history who have won all four of the majors at least once. He is off on the same tack on the Senior PGA Tour. During his first two seasons, he numbered the prestigious PGA Senior, USGA Senior Open and the Senior TPC among his eight victories. In February, he rolled to another victory in the PGA Senior Championship at PGA National in Palm Beach Gardens. He posted a four-under-par 284 total against the 287 score of runner-up Chi Chi Rodriguez, the defending champion.

The early headlines belonged to Bob Charles. With the PGA's Champion course playing short at 6,530 yards and officials drawing some heat from many of the contestants because of that, Charles came within a stroke of the tournament record with an opening 64, jumping off to a five-stroke lead over seven players. Seven of the left-hander's eight birdies came from within eight feet, the other on a 40-foot chip-in at the par-three 16th. With the big lead, Charles remained in front Friday despite a 73. Three back at 149 were Al Geiberger and Orville Moody with Arnold Palmer, a two-time PGA

Seniors winner and holder of the 18-hole record of 63. In strong, cold morning winds, Charles played cautiously, taking a single bogey and making no birdies.

Rodriguez and Geiberger seized shares of the lead at 213 Saturday on another windy day that saw Charles blown to his first of two 78s. Player, one of the first-round runners-up with 69, added 73-72 the next two days and was just a shot behind the co-leaders at 214 with Bruce Devlin and Moody after 54 holes. Player eventually broke in front of the bunched-up field Sunday when his four-iron approach stopped inches from the cup at the eighth hole and the final three behind him all had trouble with the eighth and ninth holes. Gary never trailed after that, holing eight-footers for birdies at the 14th and 16th, shrugging off a harmless three-putt at the 17th. The victory paid $63,000. Geiberger and Barber tied for third behind Rodriguez at 288 with Palmer and Moody next at 289.

GTE Suncoast Classic—$300,000
Winner: Dale Douglass

Dale Douglass got off winging when he joined the Senior PGA Tour in 1986, winning more tournaments — four — than the three he had won during all of his long career on the regular PGA Tour. In 1987, though, he fared more as he had in his earlier career — many good showings but no victories — as he drifted from third to seventh on the year-end money list. He regained his winning way early in the 1988 campaign when he led from opening day and scored a two-stroke victory in the inaugural GTE Suncoast Classic, which returned senior golf to the Tampa, FLorida, area after a six-year absence.

GTE brought it back to Tampa Palms Country Club, where the course had only been open for four months and had no practice putting green yet. Nonetheless, it proved a good test and evoked little criticism as Douglass posted a six-under-par 210 for the victory and just six other players broke par.

Dale broke in front Friday with a five-under-par 67, bagging a two-stroke lead over Orville Moody and Don Massengale, three over Gary Player, Arnold Palmer and Bruce Devlin. He had six birdies, four in one five-hole stretch and two on the closing holes. Douglass continued his solid play Saturday, shooting 69 for 136 and a four-stroke lead over Bob Brue on a cold, blustery day when only two other men broke 70. Brue, who played the PGA Tour with limited success in the 1960s and calls his return to the tournament wars on the Senior PGA Tour "the greatest mulligan ever," shot 68 for his 140. Palmer and Player remained close at 141 and were joined there by Bob Charles, who shot 69.

Sunday was a struggle for the winner. After an early birdie, Dale started hitting just about everything left. He scrambled some pars but bogeyed the seventh and 11th, his lead dropping to a single stroke over Player. A bid by Palmer ended when he found water and triple-bogeyed the 10th hole. Player, too, fell back with bogeys at the 13th and 15th, giving Douglass enough breathing room that a hard-earned bogey at No. 16 still left him with a two-stroke lead over Moody, who had already finished with 67 for 212. Dale parred the last two holes for 74 and the two-shot win. It paid $45,000.

Aetna Challenge—$300,000
Winner: Gary Player

Gary Player gave a graphic illustration of what might happen if he were to remain in the United States for a full season of senior golf play with his performances in the Florida kickoff of the 1988 Senior PGA Tour season. The Hall-of-Famer from South Africa merely went one-three-one in his three starts in February in the Sunshine State, following his victory in the PGA Senior Championship and third-place finish in the GTE Suncoast Classic with his 130th career victory in the Aetna Challenge, another new senior event, this one at Naples' Pelican Bay.

The patrons who watched Sunday's finish got their money's worth as Player, Dave Hill and Harold Henning battled each other down the stretch. It set up this way: Hill, seeking his second 1988 victory, led the first day with 68, then yielded first place to Bob Charles Saturday, shooting 73 for 141 as the left-hander added a 70 to his opening 69. At 139, he led Player (70-70) and Henning (71-69) by a stroke. Hill, Bruce Devlin and Bobby Nichols were at 141, Nichols after the week's low round of 66. Player bemoaned the 70, feeling it should have been no worse than 63 or 64.

Henning held the hot hand on the front nine of Pelican Bay's 6,719-yard course and moved two shots ahead of Player and three in front of Hill when he birdied No. 11 to go seven under par. That was to be his last hurrah as he lost a stroke coming in, finishing with 70 and 210. The fireworks came from Hill and Player. Dave birdied the 13th and 14th while Gary was starting a string of four birdies at the 14th. Then, at the 16th, Hill switched from an eight- to a seven-iron and holed his tee shot on the 157-yarder to jump into the lead. Momentarily. Player followed Hill to the 16th tee and came within six inches of matching Dave's ace. That birdie tied the two and Player moved ahead to stay with the fourth consecutive birdie off a three-iron and five-iron at No. 17 after Hill had dropped a 10-footer to save par at the hole. The rookie senior kept his hopes alive with a brilliant approach from the woods at the final hole, but missed a long birdie putt. Player also parred there as both shot 67s, Gary's nine-under-par 207 etching the one-stroke victory.

Vintage Chrysler Invitational—$320,000
Winner: Orville Moody

Some might argue that Orville Moody's victory in the Vintage Chrysler Invitational was a bit incongruous, considering that the elongated putter that blazed the way is hardly "vintage." Regardless, Moody put on an overwhelming performance in capturing the prestigious 72-hole tournament at the plush Vintage Club at Indian Wells in Southern California's wealthy desert oasis.

It was virtually no contest from the first day on and Ol' Sarge equalled or destroyed a battery of course, tournament and Senior PGA Tour records in the process. To wit:

— A 64 in the first round tied the record on the shorter Desert course (6,240 yards), used by all the pros for one of their four rounds. That staked Moody to a two-shot lead over Gene Littler, the only two-time

Vintage winner. Orville was never headed after that.
— His 66 in the second round at the Mountain course (6,907 yards) gave him a four-stroke lead over Larry Mowry and the 130 matched the tour's all-time 36-hole record.
— With 70 on Saturday, Moody established a three-stroke lead over Al Geiberger, 200 to 203. No incursions of the record books that day.
— His closing 63 shattered the Mountain course record and his 263 total not only was the lowest Vintage score ever by eight strokes, but also was the best 72-hole score in the history of the Senior PGA Tour, a shot better than Miller Barber's 264 in the 1982 Suntree Classic.

Geiberger mustered a touch of an early threat Sunday, but Moody was almost phenomenal from the seventh hole on. With his version of the extra-long putters that tuck under the chin and work in a pendulum fashion, Sarge ran in birdie putts on nine of the last 12 holes, twice admittedly holing long ones he was just trying to get close. Geiberger shot 71 Sunday and was overtaken for second place by Harold Henning, who had closing rounds of 65-64 for his 274. The 11-stroke victory margin matched another all-time Senior PGA Tour record, set by Arnold Palmer when he won the 1985 Senior TPC at Canterbury.

GTE Classic—$275,000
Winner: Harold Hennings

Harold Henning had fared very well in his three seasons-plus on the Senior PGA Tour, winning well over a half-million dollars, but when he eased his way to victory in the GTE Classic in a virtual wind tunnel north of Los Angeles, he landed his first stroke-play title in the United States in nearly 22 years. The South African, who campaigned extensively on the regular PGA Tour in the 1960s, won the Texas Open in 1966 and his only success in the interim came in his first full senior season when he captured the rich Tucson Match Play Championship in 1985.

Henning, the fourth Senior Tour winner of 1988 who led or shared first place from start to finish, fulfilled, in a way, a previous three-year pattern, in which the Vintage victor added the Los Angeles title the subsequent week. Like Orville Moody, the 1988 Vintage king, Henning employs one of those outlandish-looking long putters for his work on the greens. All play, but especially putting, was an adventure at Wood Ranch Country Club as winds gusting to 40 miles per hour continually raked the Simi Valley course north of the metropolis. It calibrated the severely-contoured greens at billiard-table speed and had all of the pros talking to themselves, the winner included.

Harold carried over the effects of the 65-64 finish that lifted him into second place in the Vintage as he opened with 68 and a one-stroke lead over Walter Zembriski at Wood Ranch. He made six birdies but three-putted the slick greens twice. The next day was worse for Henning from the greens standpoint as he missed "10 little putts." He shot 73 and slipped into a first-place tie with Larry Mowry, who had six birdies in shooting 69 for his 141 and called Wood Ranch "by far the toughest course we play all year." Rookie senior Don Bies also shot 69 for 142, and Butch Baird and Orville Moody came in at 143.

The winds became even more intense out of the north Sunday, and Henning's decision to steer a highly conservative route around the course paid off with the $41,250 victory. His closest pursuers took themselves out of the picture as Harold chalked up 17 pars and a single bogey for another 73 and the only sub-par total — 214, two under. Mowry disappeared as a challenger when he put three balls in the water at No. 8 and took a 10. Double-bogeys at the first and 10th holes ruined Bies. So, Henning picked his way home with a three-shot victory over Bruce Crampton and Dale Douglass.

The Pointe/Del E. Webb Arizona Classic—$225,000
Winner: Al Geiberger

Most of the contending cast was the same, but a different winner emerged at Arizona's Sun City West. Al Geiberger, who had launched his Senior PGA Tour career with a flourish with three late-season victories, etched his fourth title into the record in The Pointe/Del E. Webb Arizona Classic, posting the first sub-200 score with his 17-under-par 199. That score in itself illustrated the contrast in conditions the pros faced at Hillcrest Golf Club not far from Phoenix to those they fought at Simi Valley in the GTE Classic the previous week.

Geiberger, who already had two seconds, a third and a fourth on his 1988 record, grabbed the lead Friday with a nine-under-par 63 that set a tournament record and gave him a three-stroke lead over Agim Bardha and Quinton Gray, two little-known players without PGA Tour experience. He admitted to thoughts of his all-time-record 59 on the regular circuit in 1977 when it was still possible after he reached 63. Saturday was a bit of a struggle for Al, though. He lost the lead during the round, but fought back with a 69 for 132, taking a two-stroke lead over Dave Hill into the final round. Orville Moody was three back after a 68-67—135 start.

After nine holes Sunday, Geiberger seemed heading for a runaway. He birdied the first two holes, was four under par after nine holes and birdied the par-five 10th. That put him five strokes in front of Hill and six ahead of Moody and he parred in, which should have made things a breeze. Instead, Moody and Hill came alive. Orville went birdie-eagle-birdie-birdie on the next four holes and closed to within a stroke. Hill's 15-foot birdie putt at the 15th put him just two back. A crucial par save at the 16th and Moody's six-foot miss of a birdie putt there preserved Geiberger's lead and Orville had no real birdie chances on the last two holes. So, he shot 65 and 200, Hill a third straight 67 for 201 and Geiberger had the $33,750 first prize. He was the third straight wire-to-wire leader or co-leader on the circuit.

Fuji Electric Grand Slam Championship—$360,000
Winner: Bob Charles

Seventeen regulars on the Senior PGA Tour ventured to Japan in late March for the 1988 Fuji Electric Grand Slam Championship, joining with a like number of Japanese seniors and a few other international players in a select, 40-man field. Bob Charles returned to the United States with his first 1988 victory and the year's biggest individual check — $75,000 — keeping intact the monopoly of the regulars from the U.S. circuit.

Charles picked up the big money for just two days of work, as a Saturday rainout shortened the tournament to 36 holes. The New Zealander opened Friday with 67 and took a one-stroke lead over four players — Americans Billy Casper and Don Massengale, Japanese Kanehiko Uchida and Ichirou Togawa. However, the day's biggest excitement was generated when Arnold Palmer, enroute to a 70, aced the 182-yard 14th hole with his four-iron tee shot.

The three-under-par 69 he shot Sunday gave Charles a one-stroke victory over Casper, who also shot 69, and fast-closing Larry Mowry, who produced a sizzling 64 after opening with 73. Palmer shot 68 and finished fourth at 138.

Doug Sanders Kingwood Celebrity Classic—$250,000
Winner: Chi Chi Rodriguez

More so than any other tournament on the Senior PGA Tour, the Doug Sanders Kingwood Celebrity Classic abounds with actors and comedians and musicians, all friends of the man who established the event and nurtured it into an offical Senior PGA Tour tournament. Perhaps, then, it was appropriate that Chi Chi Rodriguez, who is on stage most of the time, made the Houston tournament the occasion of his first 1988 victory and 11th in less than three years on the circuit. It pushed his senior earnings over the $1 million mark.

The experience of Rodriguez paid off at the end, but for two days it appeared that John Brodie — quarterback-sports announcer turned pro golfer for a second time — was about to score his first victory since shedding shoulder pads. Brodie, who took a brief shot at the PGA Tour in the late 1950s before launching his great football career with the San Francisco 49ers, opened with a three-under-par 69 at the Deerwood Club and shared the first-round lead with Bobby Nichols, who was still seeking his first individual victory on the Senior PGA Tour. Rodriguez was among five players who started with 70s. Brodie offset five birdies with two three-putt bogeys on the swift, tricky Deerwood greens, while Nichols bounced back from a two-bogeys start with five birdies of his own.

Brodie moved in front Saturday with a solid five-birdie, one-bogey round of 68 for 137. The 52-year-old Californian led Rodriguez by two as Chi Chi added 69 for 139. Miller Barber was at 140, Walt Zembriski at 141. Rodriguez caught Brodie Sunday with birdies at the fifth and sixth holes and went in front with another at the ninth. Bogeys at the 10th and 12th set Chi Chi back and gave Barber an opening that a balky putter frustrated. The clincher for Rodriguez came at the par-five 16th, where he reached the green with driver-four wood and sank the 25-foot eagle putt. Par-par in gave him a 69—108 and a two-stroke victory over Barber, who shot 70, and Brodie, who finished with 73. It was John's second runner-up finish on the Senior PGA Tour, the other coming in late 1987 at the GTE Kaanapali Classic.

Chrysler Cup—$600,000
Winners: United States

The United States took a page out of the International book of 1987 in capturing the 1988 edition of the Chrysler Cup team competition and taking a 2-1 advantage in the annual series, staged for the second time at the Tournament Players Club at Prestancia in Sarasota, Florida, in late April.

A fast start by the Internationals the previous spring had put the Americans in too deep a hole when "the Rest of the World" evened the score for the pasting it took in the inaugural competition in 1986 at Avenel near Washington. In 1988, it was United States that grabbed the big advantage, winning all four of the four-ball matches on opening Thursday and five of the eight singles matches Friday. Although that 26-6 margin only accounted for a third of the 100 total points, the Internationals found themselves a little too far behind, particularly when they split the four stroke four-ball contests Saturday. With the score then 40-20, they needed to win seven of the eight five-point singles stroke duels Sunday. They gave it a good run, landing five of them and losing each of the others by a single stroke. The final score was 55-45.

Billy Casper, Gene Littler and Chi Chi Rodriguez blocked out the International rally Sunday. Casper nipped Christy O'Connor, 72-73, and Gene Littler birdied the last two holes to edge Peter Thomson, 70-71. Littler's finish was spectacular. He chipped in from 50 feet at the 17th and wedged to eight inches at the 18th. Rodriguez actually clinched the victory in the final match, overcoming a double-bogey at the 15th with a birdie at the 17th for a 69-70 win over the remarkable, 65-year-old Roberto de Vicenzo. Bob Charles, Harold Henning, Bruce Crampton, Bruce Devlin and Captain Gary Player put the title within reach with their singles victories Sunday, Charles winning most decisively, 67-70, against Orville Moody.

The Littler and Rodriguez wins capped outstanding weeks for the two Americans, They contributed 25 points themselves as they went undefeated, Littler teaming with Dale Douglass and Al Geiberger, the team newcomer, in the two-man events, Rodriguez with captain Arnold Palmer and Orville Moody. Player and Crampton lost only in the U.S. sweep the first day.

Liberty Mutual Legends of Golf—$660,000
Winners: Bruce Crampton and Orville Moody

The dramatic repeat victory of Bruce Crampton and Orville Moody in the 1988 Liberty Mutual Legends of Golf had flashback qualities to it. The tense six-hole playoff it took for the Crampton-Moody combo to make it two in a row was reminiscent of the 1979 Legends which almost single-handedly established senior golf as a valid and exciting spectator sport. That was the year of another six-hole playoff on television that saw Julius Boros and Roberto de Vicenzo defeat Art Wall and Tommy Bolt amid a flurry of birdies.

One difference this time was that an NBC network decision deprived its viewers of the final three holes of the playoff, the TV brass opting for its regular programming at 7 p.m. So, the national viewers were watching Wilford

Brimley on "Our House" instead of Moody when the Sarge holed a 15-foot birdie putt at the sixth extra hole for the victory.

The events of the first three rounds paled in the heroics of the closing Sunday. For the record, Bob Charles/Bruce Devlin and Bobby Nichols/Butch Baird led the first day with 63, then Charles/Devlin followed with 62 to nose a stroke ahead of Nichols/Baird. The final-day dramatics were virtually assured when Charles/Devlin were joined at the top at 191 by Arnold Palmer/Miller Barber, who shot the week's low 61 Saturday, and Peter Thomson/Harold Henning, who posted 62. Tommy Aaron/Lou Graham, Nichols/Baird and Crampton/Moody were just a shot behind.

All except Nichols/Baird remained in the fight to the end, although a birdie famine on the front nine virtually doomed Palmer/Barber chances. The lightly-regarded Aaron/Graham team vaulted in front when Tommy holed his nine-iron approach at No. 16 for an eagle deuce and a two-stroke lead. They finished with 62, but Crampton/Moody followed them in with birdies at the 16th and 18th for the matching 62—254, forcing the playoff. After nondescript pars at the first hole, Aaron nearly duplicated the eagle at the 16th, the second playoff hole, his ball hitting the flagstick and bouncing five feet away. He missed the birdie, though. Moody and Aaron made birdies at the 18th. Back to the 15th and four pars. Then, at the critical 16th, Moody ran in a 15-footer with his long-handled putter for the victory, worth $60,000 to each of them. Graham and Aaron, making their first Legends starts, picked up $32,500 apiece. Roberto de Vicenzo and Charley Sifford scored a three-shot victory in the Legendary Champions division (over 60) with 262.

Vantage at the Dominion—$250,000
Winner: Billy Casper

Two former winners challenged through the stretch but were unable to sidetrack Billy Casper's bid for his first 1988 victory on the Senior PGA Tour and his 10th triumph from his campaigning with the after-50 set. Defending champion Chi Chi Rodriguez and the first Dominion winner in 1985, Don January, pushed Casper over the closing holes only to finish two-three to Billy, who had his putter working in a deadly fashion reminiscent of the regular PGA Tour days when he was in the process of piling up 51 titles in America and a few others abroad.

The rotund shotmaker nailed sizeable birdie putts back to back on the incoming nine and fought off the bids of Rodriguez and January, posting a five-under-par 67 and 205 to edge Chi Chi by a stroke and January by two over the 6,814 yards of the Dominion Country Club course at San Antonio, Texas, the first week of May.

Those three players emerged from a cluster of contenders who began the final round within a stroke of each other. Casper and Rodriguez shared the second-round lead with Dale Douglass, who fired the week's best score — 65 — Saturday. They were at 138. January was one back in the company of Al Geiberger, Charles Coody and Bobby Nichols, who had opened the tournament with 68 when he eagled his final hole of the day to take a one-shot lead over Geiberger and Walt Zembriski. Rodriguez went out in 32 Sunday to go 10 under, but Casper and January remained at his heels as the others faded. Chi Chi added another stroke to his lead at No. 10, but Casper rolled in birdie putts of 15 and 20 feet at the next two holes, later describing his work on the Dominion greens as "absolutely fantastic." Two holes later, Billy had a two-stroke lead. It happened at No. 14 where Chi Chi missed the green and flubbed his wedge pitch for bogey while Casper was wedging to five feet and holing for the birdie.

Casper bogeyed the next hole, but held his one-shot margin over Rodriguez the rest of the way. January fell two strokes off the pace when he bogeyed the 17th, overshooting the green. Rodriguez made a game bid to catch Casper on the par-five finishing hole, going for the green in two, but he pulled his four-wood second shot into the water to the left of the green and could do no better than match Casper's routine par, one stroke shy.

United Hospitals Classic—$225,000
Winner: Bruce Crampton

Until the Senior PGA Tour reached Philadelphia in mid-May, only one tournament had been extended into a playoff — the dramatic, six-hole overtime in the Legends of Golf. Partners Bruce Crampton and Orville Moody won that one. When the United Hospitals Classic at Chester Valley in suburban Philadelphia required a playoff, Crampton was again a participant and was again a winner, picking up his first 1988 title with a birdie on the first extra hole. It was his 15th win on the Senior Tour, matching the excellent record it took him 14 years to compile on the regular circuit in earlier years.

Crampton's victory came at the expense of Billy Casper, who was on the verge of back-to-back wins after moving ahead of Bruce and Lou Graham in a hard-fought stretch run over the rolling 6,406 yards of Chester Valley. Billy holed a 14-foot birdie putt at the 13th to deadlock with Crampton, who missed a three-footer and three-putted, and an 18-foot birdie putt at the 16th to move a stroke in front. He carried that margin to the 18th hole, where, with Graham out of it, he needed only a par to win. He hadn't had a bogey in 40 holes. However, Casper missed the green with his four-iron approach, chipped to three feet for an apparent save and victory only to push the short putt and force the playoff, as he finished with 68 and Crampton with 69 for their 205s. Graham also shot 69 for 206.

The overtime was abbreviated. Bruce put his five-iron tee shot at the par-three 15th three feet from the pin and ran it in after Casper missed from 25 feet.

The big guns stood back for one round. Quinton Gray, a former minor-league baseball player who took a brief and unsuccessful shot at the PGA Tour when he was 42, opened the tournament with 67, taking a one-shot lead over Bobby Nichols, Bruce Devlin and Dick Rhyan, who, like Gray, was one of five alternates who got into the field at the last minute. None of them lasted, though, Gray plunging to a 78 Saturday as Crampton shot 65 to lead Casper and Graham by a stroke with his 136 and set the stage for the exciting finish. Crampton's first-place check of $33,750 pushed him over the $1 million mark on the Senior PGA Tour, a feat accomplished before him only by Don January, Miller Barber, Gene Littler and Chi Chi Rodriguez.

Nynex/Golf Digest Commemorative—$300,000
Winner: Bob Charles

Enough of this also-ran stuff, Bob Charles seemed to imply when the Senior PGA Tour made its Metropolitan New York stop at Sleepy Hollow Country Club in mid-May. The New Zealander had been in frequent contention through the earlier months of the season and piled up some $80,000 winnings, but his only victory, lucrative though it was, had come in early February in a select-field event in South Africa.

Charles asserted himself right off the bat in New York. He opened with a course-record 63 and, challenged just once over the weekend, rolled to a four-stroke victory over Don Massengale and Harold Henning. His 14-under-par 196 broke Lee Elder's 1986 tournament record by three shots and was the low score during those first months of the season.

The first-round 63 staked Bob to a two-stroke lead over Larry Mowry and a three-shot margin on Charles Coody and Chick Evans, another of the little-remembered pros who popped up briefly on the PGA Tour in the 1960s. Charles widened the gap to three Saturday, adding a 67 for 130. Massengale shot 65 for 133 and Henning braced 67s for 134 as Mowry shot 70 for 135.

One of the game's truly great putters, Charles had a rare sinking spell on the greens on the front nine Sunday, taking 39 putts. But, he squared away his putting on the back nine. He birdied the 437-yard 12th hole for a third day in a row, but encountered a challenge when Bruce Crampton birdied the 11th hole and followed with three more in a row. However, Charles nailed another of his own when he reached the green of that par-five 15th in two and two-putted from 40 feet. Then, he iced matters when, in characteristic fashion of yore, he ran in a 40-footer for a final birdie at the 17th and finished with 67 for the 196. Crampton lost a share of second-place money when he bogeyed the 18th hole to end a stroke behind Massengale (67) and Henning (66), who had 200s. Mowry came back with 67 Sunday to pick off fifth place at 202 and Coody finished at 203.

Sunwest Bank/Charley Pride Classic—$250,000
Winner: Bob Charles

An absolute necessity in the makeup of a tournament professional is the ability to adapt to conditions. Nobody has been doing it more often and with much more success than Bob Charles as he has played the international field for the better part of the last three decades. Charles has played on all kinds of courses on all kinds of grass and turf in all kinds of weather almost continuously, since he remained active right up to his entry into senior golf.

Bob showed that adaptability when the Senior PGA Tour moved from the northern climate and course conditions of New York to the quite-different circumstances of Albuquerque, New Mexico, for the Sunwest Bank/Charley Pride Classic at Four Hills Country Club. A winner for the first time in 1988 at the Commemorative in the Empire State, Charles made it two in a row at Four Hills, clinching the victory in sensational fashion when he holed a 35-foot chip shot on the 18th green for a 69 and a two-stroke victory over Orville Moody, His only serious challenger. "I don't remember ever holing a longer chip shot to win a tournament," Bob recalled afterward. It was the first instance of back-to-back victories of the 1988 season.

Charles, who was the leader after all three rounds in New York, continued that practice in Albuquerque when he opened with 69 to share first place with Moody, Ben Smith, Peter Thomson and Lou Graham. Don Massengale and Bob Erickson had 70s. Moody broke the Charles spell Saturday, although he frittered away a big margin and settled for a 67. Orville birdied six holes on the front nine and had a four-shot lead at one point but when the round ended he was just a stroke ahead of Charles, 136-137.

Moody maintained the lead through much of the final round and no other challengers besides Charles emerged. Ultimately, the great Charles putting stroke did in the man with the elongated weapon, who said he had some stance problems in the windy conditions. Bob holed from 35 feet for birdies at the 15th and 16th to take the lead and his final chip-in widened it to the final margin. The $41,250 check gave the New Zealander winnings of $86,250 in eight days, more than he had won on the circuit all year.

Senior Players Reunion Pro-Am—$250,000
Winner: Orville Moody

They call it the Senior Players Reunion Pro-Am and it looked like they were all there when the time came to decide the winner at Bent Tree Country Club in Dallas. Four players posted 206s to force a gang playoff that Sunday, but Orville Moody's outsized putter broke it up quickly when he sank a 15-footer for a birdie on the first extra hole just it had carried him into the deadlock in the first place.

The $37,500 victory, Moody's second individual title of the season and seventh on the Senior PGA Tour, boosted his 1988 earnings over $200,000 for the year and over $1 million on the over-50 circuit. Earlier in the year, he had picked up an additional $60,000 when he partnered Bruce Crampton to the Legends of Golf championship for the second year in a row.

Moody, who had lost in a tight finish to Bob Charles the previous week in Albuquerque, faced an uphill battle against the streaking New Zealander Sunday. He went into the final round four strokes off the pace of Charles, who had fired a pair of 68s to lead five players by two strokes after Miller Barber had opened the unique, pro-amateur-styled tournament with a seven-under-par 65 and a three-shot lead over Don Massengale and him. Barber was not a later factor as he slipped to 74 Saturday.

In a wildly-fluctuating final round, seven different players had at least pieces of the lead and five, Harold Henning and Larry Mowry besides Moody, Charles and Massengale, had first place to themselves at one time or another. But Moody's putting was the decisive factor as he shot 66 despite three consecutive bogeys on the back nine. The critical putts were those for birdies from 15 feet at No. 16 and 30 feet on the 18th green. Massengale, showing well in his second senior season, shot 67 Sunday and nearly won the tournament outright. A chip at No. 17 stopped an inch short of the cup and he lipped out a four-foot birdie putt at No. 18. Nichols closed with 68, while Charles, gunning for his third straight victory, managed just a two-under 70 for his 206.

Moody, hitting last in the playoff, boomed a 280-yard drive far ahead of the conservative tee shots of the other three men and put his sand wedge approach 15 feet from the cup on Bent Tree's 10th green. Nichols hit the sand and the other two left themselves outside Orville. Nichols muffed his sand shot and Charles and Massengale missed their putts before Moody rolled his in.

Mazda Senior Tournament Players Championship—$400,000
Winner: Billy Casper

Billy Casper stirred together something old and something new and the amalgamation worked him into the Mazda Senior Tournament Players Championship, one of the crown jewels on the Senior PGA Tour. One of golf's greatest putters in his younger days, Casper recovered that sometimes-elusive stroke of old and put it to excellent use in the final rounds at the Valley course of the TPC at Sawgrass at the PGA Tour's Ponte Vedra, Florida, headquarters where the Senior TPC has been played the last two years. The other ingredient was a big, old hook, an action foreign to the Casper game of the past, and it required some overnight harnessing to enable Billy to shoot his closing 67 for 10-under-par 278 and a two-stroke victory.

Anybody who watched Casper's third round Saturday wouldn't have given him a chance Sunday. After trailing Bob Goalby (66) after the first round and taking the lead the second day with 69-68—137, Casper gave first place away Saturday amid a flurry of wild hooks with which he missed all except five fairways. "My chipping and putting were just unbelievable," Billy said of his 74 that day. "That's when I won the tournament. I could very easily have shot 90." The 74 left him two strokes off the pace of Miller Barber, who added 68s to his opening 73. Gary Player and Al Geiberger were a stroke back.

With the hook under confident control, Casper mounted a front-nine charge Sunday. He birdied the third, fourth and seventh holes to jump into the thick of things and later birdies at the 13th and 14th holes put him in the driver's seat. He scrambled a good bit to finish with four pars for the 67. Barber and Player made strong runs before coming a cropper at the 15th hole. Barber's tee shot landed on a concrete cart path and bounced out of bounds, while Player knocked his seven-iron approach over the green into the water. Geiberger, who finished second with a closing 70 and 280, could only match Casper's four pars on the final holes. Player, Barber and Don January wound up at 281.

The $60,000 victory was Casper's seventh individual title on the Senior Tour and 11th overall, counting two team victories and two unofficial events. Gardner Dickinson won the Super Seniors sideshow with a birdie on the first hole of a sudden-death playoff against Charley Sifford. They had shot 215s.

Northville Invitational—$350,000
Winner: Don Bies

It took a half season before the "haves" yielded to a "have-not" on the Senior PGA Tour. Every winner had been there before in his senior career until the circuit reached the Northville Invitational, which became an official event just in time for Don Bies, who "had not" a title in his first six months on the over-50 tour. The Seattle pro, who campaigned off and on the PGA Tour for some two decades, had gone 15 years before winning his only official victory in the 1975 Greater Hartford Open. It only required 12 starts on the Senior PGA Tour.

The Northville Invitational, at Long Island's Meadow Brook Club, was established in 1987 in the week of the U.S. Open, which was an inactive week on the Senior PGA Tour schedule. This year, it became a scheduled, official tournament in the same slot, but had no defending champion since the 1987 winner, Gary Player, was competing in the U.S. Open that week at Boston. The big purse attracted most of the other senior stars, so Bies outplayed a strong field in capturing the $52,500 first prize.

The Washington pro returned to tournament golf after dropping off the regular PGA Tour in 1980 to operate a restaurant in Seattle. His game didn't suffer from the absence from competition as he finished 10th or better in seven of his first 11 starts prior to the victory. Bies and Harold Henning shared the second-round lead with 136s after Bruce Devlin, another Senior Tour newcomer, shot a seven-birdie 66 in the first round, using a driver he appropriated from Orville Moody. Henning and Bobby Nichols shot 67s Friday while Bies was opening with 69.

Bies staked himself to a big lead early in the final round. He birdied the first two holes, then dropped a 20-foot eagle putt at the par-five third. When he birdied the fifth hole, he had a four-stroke lead over Henning and Bob Charles, who was to match Bies' 66 and be the only serious challenger. Don turned in 30 and played a solid 36, with a bogey and birdie, on the back nine for his 202 total and a two-stroke victory over Charles, who had two wins and a second in his previous four finishes. "It means a lot to me to beat fellows like Charles and all these good players," Bies pronounced afterward.

Southwestern Bell Classic—$250,000
Winner: Gary Player

Harold Henning took his playoff defeat in the Southwestern Bell Classic philosophically. A clubbing mistake led him to the loss to Gary Player at Quail Creek Golf and Country Club in Oklahoma City, but Henning, who has more than 50 titles to his credit, shrugged: "Gary has beaten me a lot of times in the past. It's nothing to be ashamed of." True. Henning's fine record pales when one considers the remarkable 133-victory history of his fellow South African, who captured his third victory on the 1988 Senior PGA Tour and 10th since joining the circuit in late 1985.

Interestingly, Player seems to have turned around a plague that stuck with him through most of his earlier career — an incredibly-poor record in playoffs, which he came to abhor. In defeating Henning with an eight-foot birdie putt on the first extra hole at Quail Creek, Gary won his second playoff in nine months. He won the same way in the PaineWebber Invitational the previous September.

The field was bunched most of the distance. Gene Littler, Bobby Nichols and Chi Chi Rodriguez, the defending champion, led eight other men by a stroke with their first-round 68s before Henning nudged two strokes in front Saturday with his 69-66—135, a nine-under-par total. Player was second, trailing by two, going into the final round.

Bruce Crampton made an early bid Sunday. He birdied the third and fourth holes while Henning was taking bogeys on the same holes and they were tied. Crampton was just a stroke behind Player and Henning at the turn, but a double-bogey at No. 11 ended his chances. Littler was tied for the lead after 10 holes, but eight pars coming in left him three shots in arrears of the playoff pair. That left it to Player and Henning, who forged a tie at 12 under when Henning dropped a 20-foot birdie putt at No. 15. Harold went in front with a six-foot birdie putt at the 16th, but Gary countered immediately with a six-footer at the 17th and missed outright victory at the 18th when he misread a six-footer at the 18th. Henning failed to allow for a sudden rise in the wind when the playoff began at the par-three 16th and put his seven-iron tee shot in the back trap. Player went with his eight-iron, dropped his tee shot eight feet behind the hole and canned the putt for the win.

Rancho Murieta Gold Rush—$350,000
Winner: Bob Charles

Bob Charles continued his dominant play on the Senior PGA Tour when the over-50 stars returned to California for the Fourth of July holiday weekend. The brilliant left-hander caged his third official victory and his fifth senior win of 1988 when he captured the Rancho Murieta Gold Rush title at the club of the same name outside of Sacramento. It jumped him past Orville Moody into the money-winning lead on the Senior Tour at that point in the long season.

Always a brilliant putter, Charles put his finger on a big reason for his current success on the senior circuit, sounding a bit incongruous. "I'm so much longer off the tee than I was 25 years ago. I know how to swing the club," he said after posting a two-stroke victory over Gary Player, the previous week's winner. His score was 207, nine under par.

Charles didn't really establish his victory move until he was well into the final round. Peter Thomson opened the tournament with a six-under-par 66, taking a one-stroke lead over Miller Barber. Then, Lou Graham entered the picture. He shot his second straight 68 for 136 and a two-stroke lead over Charles. The margin went to three when the left-hander opened the final round with a trapped approach and a bogey at the first hole. It was a windy Sunday and, after that starting misstep, Charles played solidly. "The wind and the pin placement made the course play harder than I thought it would," he reflected. "I don't like playing in the wind, but I have a lot of experience in the wind."

By the 15th hole, Bob had bagged four birdies and held a two-stroke lead over Graham. However, it was Player who took the final shot at the leader as Graham bogeyed two of the last three holes. Gary had got away to a rocky start and was one over par for the round after 11 holes, but he birdied three of the final seven for 70 to slip past Graham and three others — Thomson, Orville Moody and Al Geiberger — into second place. He had 209, they had 210.

Another frequent 1988 winner — Roberto de Vicenzo — scored his fourth Super Seniors victory with 145 despite a nine on the 36th hole.

GTE Northwest Classic—$300,000
Winner: Bruce Crampton

Bruce Crampton is pleased that the Senior PGA Tour "discovered" the Northwest. The inaugural GTE Northwest Classic at Seattle coincided with Crampton's first full season on the circuit and he made it one of his seven offical victories (eight wins in all in 1986) as he dominated senior golf that season. After slipping to 10th in the 1987 event, he came back with a second title in Seattle in July, holding off a series of contenders in the final round.

Crampton's stiffest challenges this year at Inglewood Country Club in suburban Kenmore came from Larry Mowry, Bruce Devlin and Don Bies, the first-year senior trying to win in front of his hometown friends and fans. Mowry put together a six-under-par 66 on opening Friday. The week's best round, it put Larry a shot in front of Bob Brue, with Crampton, Devlin, John Brodie and Chi Chi Rodriguez, the defending champion, at 69. Bies opened with 71. Crampton moved in front the second day with 68 for 137, a stroke in front of Mowry (72) and Bies (67).

The three formed the final grouping Sunday and at one time or another each of them held or shared first place. Bies, although admitting to "a little added pressure trying to win at home," birdied the first hole, but Crampton promptly established a two-stoke lead with birdies at the next two holes. Mowry made back-to-back birdies to catch Bruce at the turn. Bies birdied the 10th, Crampton bogeyed the 11th, Mowry bogeyed the 13th and they were all even. Don jumped into the lead with a birdie from 18 inches at the 14th as Mowry lost his bid with a double-bogey.

Both Crampton and Bies bogeyed the 15th, then Bruce took the lead for good with an 18-foot birdie putt at the par-three 16th as Don missed the green and bogeyed. After pars at the 17th, the two protagonists went for the green in two at the par-five 18th, Crampton reaching it 25 feet from the pin and Bies missing it to the right. His pitch hit the cup but he had to settle for a matching birdie to Crampton's two-putt. Had Bruce faltered there, he would have fallen into a tie and a playoff with Bies and Devlin, who had hit his three-wood second shot five feet from the cup at No. 18 and made the five-foot eagle putt. Crampton and Bies had 70s and Devlin a 69 to deadlock Don for second place at 208.

Showdown Classic—$350,000
Winner: Miller Barber

Perhaps the most impressive statistic relating to Miller Barber's excellent record on the PGA Tour was his feat of winning at least one tournament a year for eight straight seasons. He matched that in senior golf when he came from behind to win the Showdown Classic at Jeremy Ranch Country Club outside of Salt Lake City in mid-July, getting his first victory of 1988. The determined Barber had joined the Senior PGA Tour in 1981 and promptly won three official events. In successive years, he won three in 1982, four in 1983, four in 1984, four in 1985, one in 1986 and three in 1987.

Miller needed some help Sunday in capturing the Showdown Classic for a second year in a row and third time in four seasons. Ben Smith, a former auto mechanic shop operator who turned pro when he was 48 to take his shot at the Senior PGA Tour, succumbed to the pressure he had never before experienced in the stretch. He bogeyed the last two holes and two of the previous five for 76, dropping into a second-place tie at 209 with Orville Moody and Dick Rhyan. Barber, who had started the day four strokes off the lead and thinking he needed 66 or 67 to win, did it with a two-under-par 70 for his 207 and the $52,500 first-place check.

Smith opened with 66-67 and the 133 gave him the four-shot lead on Barber and Jim Cochran. Miller, who made only one bogey over the final 36 holes, caught Smith at the 14th hole Sunday as Ben three-putted, missing a 14-inch tap-in. It was the obvious turning point because Smith missed from five feet for the birdie that would have given him a three-stroke lead. Instead, it was one and he found himself in a three-way tie for first with Barber and Rhyan, when they both birdied the par-five 16th. Miller then prevailed simply by parring the last two holes as both Smith and Rhyan bogeyed both of them. Moody joined them with a 70 for his 209.

"I didn't win it. Ben gave it to me," Barber stated. "That first win is always the hardest. Once you win, you learn how and it becomes easier. I've done the very same thing that Ben did. I've had tournaments won and let them get away the last day. That's just golf." Smith called it "a great week for me, but I hit all my good shots the first two days and all my bad shots today. I guess what I needed was a bigger lead."

Volvo Seniors British Open—$270,000
Winner: Gary Player

Gary Player has always taken particular pride in his victories in significant tournaments, especially when his achievements have been those rarely accomplished or, more so, when they have been unprecedented. Thus, he was especially delighted with his wire-to-wire victory in the second Seniors British Open at prestigious Turnberry in Ayrshire, Scotland. With it, he laid claim to a well-recognized "Senior Grand Slam," a first in the relatively-young world of over-50 tournament golf.

Among the 133 previous victories in his very special career were the PGA Seniors (1986 and 1988), the USGA Senior Open (1987) and the Senior Tournament Players Championship (1987), the other legs of the Senior Slam.

Furthermore, it seems that only one man — Jack Nicklaus — has a chance to match another more-impressive feat when he becomes a senior, since only he and Player among active golfers have won the "regular" Grand Slam of the U.S. and British Opens, the PGA and the Masters.

Billy Casper was Player's most persistent pursuer during the four rounds over the famed Turnberry links. Gary opened with a potent 65 Thursday, seven birdies and only two birdie putts of great length, taking a three-stroke lead on Casper and Canadian Lou Garrison, the Canadian senior champion. Player followed with 66 Friday for a 131 in atypically-mild Scotland weather that normally would open a sizeable lead, but Casper shot 65 to close the gap by a stroke and Neil Coles, the defending champion and Britain's best senior player, added a 65 of his own for 135. Playing together, Casper and Coles made 14 birdies and an eagle Friday.

The defender made his bid Saturday, when both Player and Casper settled for par 72s. Coles produced a 69 to move within a stroke of Player's 203, but that was to be Neil's last gasp. Never a strong wind player, Coles was blown to a 79 in the final round and wound up in a sixth-place tie with Arnold Palmer at 283. Although Gary birdied two of the first three holes, he three-putted three times on the front nine and after 10 holes was tied at seven under with Casper and Harold Henning. Casper fell back with a bogey at the 11th, Player birdied the 12th, then three-putted again at the 13th and was tied with Henning until he birdied the 16th and Henning bogeyed. He was then home free, shooting 69 for eight-under-par 272. Casper birdied the last two holes for 68 and 273, a shot better than Henning.

Newport Cup—$250,000
Winner: Walter Zembriski

If there ever was a rags-to-riches story in golf, try one that could well be entitled, "The Emergence of Walter Zembriski." Here was a man who, filled with the nerve and determination it must take to be an iron-worker on high-rise construction, carried his love for golf through half a lifetime of struggles in the world of mini-tours and a brief, unsuccessful shot at the PGA Tour, never doing well enough to put his money in a bank account.

Then, he found it all beginning to pay off when he worked his way onto the Senior PGA Tour in 1985 and in the next two seasons was a $100,000-plus performer. The climax came this July when the blue-collar Zembriski captured the Newport Cup amid the fancy and storied trappings of the Newport Country Club on the Rhode Island seacoast, getting a big assist from torrential downpours on Saturday night and Sunday that forced a cancellation of the scheduled final round and gave him the title as the 36-hole leader. At 132, he was two strokes ahead of Charles Coody, another Senior Tour non-winner but a man with solid PGA Tour credentials.

Actually, Zembriski may not have needed any help from the weather. He had played two excellent rounds in taking over first place Saturday. He opened with 67, sharing second place with Coody and Lee Elder, two strokes behind lefty George Lanning, another Senior Tour player without an early-career tournament reputation. Then, Walter wielded a deadly putter Saturday in assuming the lead. He shot 65, a seven-under-par total, on the strength of just 24 putts, making eight birdies on putts ranging from three to 18 feet and taking a single bogey, while Coody was shooting his second 67 and Elder a 68, setting up his third-place finish after the rain-out decision. (Senior Tour regulations prohibit Monday play.)

"I can't remember when I've ever putted the ball better," Zembriski commented after that round. "I don't think I missed a makable putt all day." On Sunday, after he had been declared the winner, Walter said he had always dreamed of winning a Senior Tour tournament with a birdie on the final hole. "But, hey, I'm not going to beef (about the 36-hole nature of the victory). A win is a win, no matter how you get it."

Digital Classic—$300,000
Winner: Chi Chi Rodriguez

Chi Chi Rodriguez, a seven-time winner on the Senior PGA Tour in 1987, had scored only one victory nearly four months earlier on the 1988 circuit when the senior stars visited Massachusetts for the Digital Classic at Nashawtuc Country Club outside of Boston. You might have known the title drought would end there — and did. After all, Rodriguez had won the Digital in 1986 and 1987 at Nashawtuc, so it figured that he could do it again. His third consecutive Digital victory established a new Senior Tour record, as nobody had won the same event three consecutive years before then.

Chi Chi, never at a loss for words, said of his suddenly-nervous victory at 14-under-par 202, "The hungry tiger got his prey." He had jumped into a three-stroke lead in Saturday's second round and seemed to have everything well in hand until he dumped his five-iron tee shot into a pond at the 17th hole Sunday, took a double-bogey and opened the door to Bob Charles, his playing partner. But, Charles failed on birdie putts on that hole and the 18th to finish a stroke back. He closed with a 67 to the 69 of Rodriguez for his 203. His $26,000 prize (Chi Chi received $45,000) pushed him past Orville Moody into the lead on the Senior Tour money list.

Bobby Nichols, still seeking his first individual victory on the Senior PGA Tour, seized the first-round lead with a 67 and a one-stroke lead over Rodriguez and Al Geiberger. Chi Chi took charge Saturday. He birdied four of the last five holes for 65. His 133 staked him to a three-shot lead over Charles, who also shot 65 after opening with 71. The New Zealander got more than a little help in his round from a hole-in-one and an eagle. Dale Douglass matched the course record Saturday with 64 but still trailed by six because of his opening 75.

Rodriguez had matters going his way Sunday until the slip at the 17th and had to watch at the 18th green after missing his 20-foot birdie putt at the par-five finishing hole as Charles tried and missed his birdie putt for the tie from 10 feet.

USGA Senior Open—$325,000
Winner: Gary Player

Never one to look a gift horse in the mouth, Gary Player jumped on the opportunity Bob Charles had presented to him and rolled to his second straight victory in the USGA Senior Open, scoring a relatively-easy, two-stroke triumph in an 18-hole playoff at Medinah Country Club in Suburban Chicago. Charles, in the midst of a brilliant season in which he had already won five times and was the Senior PGA Tour's leading money-winner, had faltered just as he verged on his first major senior title and dropped back into a 72-hole tie with Player at even-par 288 over the demanding acres of the famed course, which had undergone modernizing remodeling for the Senior and, in 1990, the U.S. Open Championships.

Others captured most of the attention in the early rounds. Billy Casper, the 1983 Senior Open winner, and Walter Zembriski, who had bagged his first senior title two weeks earlier, shared the first-round lead at 69 as Player opened with 74 and Charles with 75. An up-and-down round of 71 over Medinah's 6,881 yards of fairways and tenacious rough moved Casper three strokes ahead of Harold Henning and Lou Graham Friday as blistering, humid temperatures lingered in Chicago. Both Player and Charles shot 70s that day, making sizeable moves up the standings. Saturday, they went to the top as Bob had another 70 and Gary posted 71 for their one-under-par 215s. On the way up, they passed Casper, who started bogey, double-bogey enroute to a 76 and 216, tying Graham there. Bruce Crampton was within a stroke of the lead until he triple-bogeyed the par-three 13th, a water hole, and wound up at 217. Zembriski had the worst disaster. After leading the tournament for 13 holes, he put two balls in the water and took an eight at the par-three 17th.

Charles moved in front early in Sunday's final round with only Player and Crampton in serious contention with him. Bob holed a 12-foot birdie putt at the 14th just after Bruce double-bogeyed the 15th to open a three-stroke lead over Player. However, as Gary parred in, Charles bogeyed the next three holes before parring the 18th for the tie. Crampton missed by a shot. Player quickly seized a three-stroke lead in Monday's playoff as Charles took two early bogeys. With four birdies on the first 13 holes, Player built his lead to four strokes and birdies by the New Zealander at the 14th and 17th merely reduced the final margin as Gary finished with 68 to Bob's 70 and collected the $65,000 first-place check for his fifth victory of the season and 13th as a senior.

MONY Syracuse Classic—$250,000
Winner: Dave Hill

As far as Dave Hill is concerned, Mutual of New York could sponsor every tournament on the Senior PGA Tour. The 51-year-old Michigan shotmaker started the 1988 season with a rain-aborted victory in MONY's Senior Tournament of Champions at LaCosta in January, went nearly seven months without a victory, then took out another winning policy at the MONY-sponsored Syracuse Classic in mid-August.

The victory, at Lafayette Country Club in suburban Jamesville, came much more easily for Hill, who opted to play the tournament when his game rebounded from a summer-long slump the week before just as the torrid summer heat was about to drive him home for a rest. He seized the lead in the second round and rolled in a five-stroke triumph, finishing 16-under-par at 200. Bobby Nichols and Butch Baird were next at 205.

Doug Dalziel, a native Scot from Carnoustie who had never campaigned on the regular tour, opened with 65 Friday and took a one-stroke lead over Lou Graham and lesser-known Jim Hatfield as Hill shot 68. Dave then took charge Saturday with a tournament-record 64, the result of an eagle, seven birdies and a bogey. He jumped three shots in front of Dalziel and four ahead of Baird, Ben Smith and George Lanning.

Smith made the strongest run at Hill Sunday. He went five under on the first eight holes to tie Dave, but immediately followed with double-bogey, bogey, bogey and was out of contention, particularly when Hill made two clutch, seven-foot par putts at Nos. 10 and 11. Baird made a run, too, but Hill's birdies at the 12th and 16th opened the ultimate five-stroke lead, making Nichols' strong finish only valuable in that it drew him into a second-place tie with Baird at 205 and fattened the paycheck to $19,650. Hill's payoff was $37,500.

Greater Grand Rapids Open—$250,000
Winner: Orville Moody

Jim Ferree and Billy Casper, the winners of the first two Greater Grand Rapids Opens, loomed within easy striking distance going into the final round, but the tournament crowned another new winner as Orville Moody continued his outstanding season with a breath-taking one-stroke victory. His final-round 70 and 10-under-par 203 gave him a one-stroke win, his fourth of the season.

Moody, who had won individual titles in the Senior Reunion and Vintage tournaments and teamed with Bruce Crampton again to repeat in the Legends of Golf, inched in front in Saturday's second round at the 6,453-yard Elks Country Club course at Grand Rapids. He had opened with 68, trailing Chi Chi Rodriguez by two and nine others by one, then moved a shot in front of Rodriguez and Harold Henning when he followed with 65 for 133, Casper and Ferree were just two back at that point. Moody had seven birdies in a round in which he missed just one green.

A two-under-par round of 70 proved to be enough Sunday, although Orville had his nervous moments, some of his own making. He built a four-stroke lead over the first 12 holes, but encountered serious challenges later on as Gary Player closed with a 66 and Chick Evans with a 67 to close the gap along with Rodriguez, who matched Moody's 70. Actually, Orville contributed to the final tension as he bogeyed three of the last five holes. But Player, Evans and Rodriguez came up one shot short at 204. The $37,500 first prize increased Moody's 1988 earnings to $355,182.

Vantage Presents Bank One Classic—$250,000
Winner: Bob Charles

Bob Charles pushed away from threats to his No. 1 position on the 1988 Senior PGA Tour when the circuit made its sixth visit to Griffin Gate Country Club in Lexington, Kentucky at the end of August. Orville Moody had moved close the week before when he won at Grand Rapids, but passed up Lexington. With one less serious challenger to contend with, Charles mustered his fourth Senior Tour title (to go with others in Japan and South Africa) with a one-stroke victory.

As it turned out, Bob's strongest opposition at Griffin Gate came from an unexpected quarter in the person of Dick Hendrickson, who got into the tournament off the alternate list that Tuesday. Hendrickson finished second, two shots ahead of five more prominent players, including Chrysler Cuppers Gary Player, Miller Barber and Dale Douglass.

Charles began the tournament Friday as if there would be no challenges at all. He fired a tournament-record-tying 63 with eight birdies and a bogey on the 6,595-yard, par-70 course, yet found himself just a shot ahead of Hendrickson and two in front of Player and Bob Boldt. Charles shot 66, Hendrickson 65 and they shared the lead after 36 holes, the rangy American bemoaning a two-foot par putt he had missed at the 17th green. The back nine was classic Charles as the New Zealander took just eight putts in his incoming 30 after a one-over front nine.

Again, Charles shot the front nine in 36 Sunday, but made good saves at the 13th and 14th holes to preserve his one-shot lead over Hendrickson and matched him stroke for stroke on the last four holes. He scrambled for a par at the 560-yard 18th as Dick's crisply-struck wedge third shot sucked back 40 feet below the hole, virtually eliminating his chances for a tying birdie putt. Charles' one-over 71 for 200 gave him the $37,500 first prize, while Hendrickson, who quit a club job to try the senior circuit, picked up his biggest check ever — $21,500. Walt Zembriski, with 65, and Bob Erickson joined Player, Barber and Douglass at 203.

GTE North Classic—$350,000
Winner: Gary Player

The game of "Can You Top That?" continued on the Senior PGA Tour when a new event — the GTE North Classic — was launched in Indianapolis. After Orville Moody and Bob Charles had matched his four-win seasonal total on successive Sundays the preceding two weeks at Grand Rapids and Lexington, Gary Player stepped out and landed his fifth U.S. senior title in the GTE North inaugural at Broadmoor Country Club.

The victory sprung from a single brilliant shot by Player in his duel with Dave Hill on the final holes of the $350,000 event. Hill, playing ahead of Gary, had executed some excellent shots himself, scoring birdies on three of the last four holes for a 65 and 13-under-par 203. His last birdie was a tap-in at the 18th. At the par-five 17th, Player also was 13 under and 227 yards from the cup after his tee shot. He then rifled a one-iron shot within two feet of the hole. That gave him his winning, two-stroke margin off his final 66 and total of 201.

Player started modestly with 70, trailing first-round-leader Charles Coody by four strokes Thursday, then moved into a tie for the lead after 36 holes with Dale Douglass. Both had 135s, Player with his 70-65 and Douglass with 67-68, but it was still just about anybody's ballgame. Four men were just a shot behind, Coody and two others two back and 15 others within five shots of the lead going into Saturday's final round.

Player birdied the first hole from the rough and never trailed after that, though he gave the close pursuers some hope when, after a second birdie at No. 3, he missed a birdie putt at No. 6 from inside a foot. Undaunted, he birdied the seventh and ninth, dropped back into his first tie with Hill when he bogeyed the 11th, then birdied again at the 13th to set up the exciting finish provided by Hill's fireworks. Actually, it could have been even tighter because Dave bogeyed the 16th amid his three birdies at the end. The victory paid $52,500, Hill collected $30,000 and Moody, Douglass and Miller Barber received $20,333 for their 204s.

Crestar Classic—$325,000
Winner: Arnold Palmer

Arnold Palmer had helped the six-year-old Crestar Classic get off the ground in its founding seasons, so, when he received an indirect SOS from tournament officials this year, he made a last-minute decision to play again, particularly since he had noted that his overall game seemed to be sharpening. The move, within hours of the entry deadline, turned out to be one of his wisest.

His game was sharp at the Hermitage, he jumped off in front the first day and scored his first Senior PGA Tour victory in more than three years. The triumph, Palmer's 92nd in his 34-year professional career, was by four strokes on rounds of 65-68-70 for a 13-under-par 203. It came just eight days after his 59th birthday and he was the oldest winner to that point on the 1988 circuit.

Palmer launched his wire-to-wire victory performance Friday with a seven-under-par 65, his best score of the season by four strokes. With nine birdies and two bogeys, he started two shots in front of Don Massengale, Gene Littler and Bobby Nichols. The last two birdies at the par-five 16th and the 17th provided the margin. Arnie widened the lead to three strokes Saturday, but early on was on the verge of a runaway. He was five under for the day at the sixth tee after nearly driving out of bounds off the first tee, then following with a birdie and two eagles, one a pitch-in over a trap and the other off a blazing 234-yard two-iron shot and an eight-foot putt. However, he faltered with bogeys at the 12th and 13th, saved par with a three-footer at the 14th and sank a downhill 25-footer on the last green for 68, 133 and the three-shot lead over Bobby Nichols and Walt Zembriski.

Larry Mowry, the defending champion, mustered the only serious threat Sunday. Palmer birdied the second and third holes and had his only bogey at the ninth after a wild drive. Mowry, who began the day six shots back, had four birdies on the front nine and moved within two of Palmer with his fifth birdie at the 15th. However, he bogeyed the 16th and 17th, then chipped in for a birdie at the 18th for 68 to tie Jim Ferree and Lee Elder for second at 207. Palmer's check was for $48,750, his biggest since his last previous victory in the non-tour UnionMutual Classic in September of 1986.

PaineWebber Invitational—$350,000
Winner: Dave Hill

Crisp irons gave back what a balky putter had taken away as Dave Hill rallied in dramatic fashion and captured his third victory of the season in the PaineWebber Invitational. Always a fine shotmaker, though such a perfectionist about it that he once went directly to the practice tee after shooting a 64, Hill had been going through the throes of poor putting in the weeks since his victory at Syracuse in early August, even resorting to occasional cross-handed strokes.

At Quail Hollow in Charlotte, the problems on the greens cropped up again early in the final round after he had taken a one-stroke edge over Bobby Nichols and Bob Charles at the 36-hole mark with his opening pair of 68s. Nichols had 69-68 and Charles 71-66. First-round-leader Don Massengale (67) and Arnold Palmer, coming off his victory at Richmond the previous Sunday, were another stroke back. The race scrambled when Hill three-putted three times, the third time for a double-bogey at No. 12, and nobody else close to the top really asserted himself.

Palmer made three early birdies, but none after the fifth hole. Instead, it was Crampton, coming off a four-week layoff because of his wife's illness, who charged into the lead. Bruce, five shots behind at the start of the day, birdied the first three holes, turned in 30 and was in the clubhouse early with 66 and 207. Enter Hill and his heroics. Standing 160 yards from the pin at the par-four 16th hole, Dave grabbed his seven iron, which had produced holes-in-one twice earlier in the year, and holed out for an eagle. Now he was nine under, tied for the lead with the already-finished Crampton. Hill neatly parred the testy, par-three 17th, but leaked his tee shot at the 18th into the right-hand fairway bunker. However, he hit "maybe my best fairway bunker shot ever," the four-iron shot stopping eight feet above the cup. This time, going cross-handed, he rolled in the cautiously-struck putt with his Palmer Peerless 504 No. 5 for the $45,000 victory. Ironically, using the same model putter minutes earlier, Arnold had just missed from considerably-longer range in his bid for a tie with Crampton. So, Palmer finished third with 70 for 208.

Pepsi Challenge—$300,000
Winner: Bob Charles

If anything is to jeopardize the continued existence of the Pepsi Challenge on the Senior PGA Tour, the powers-that-be certainly can blame it on the weather. Twice in the tournament's three-year history, a weekend round has been rained out, forcing a shortening of the event to 36 holes because of a circuit rule precluding extensions of play to Mondays. Weekend rounds are the big revenue producers, so the Pepsi sponsors in Atlanta, who had suffered the loss of Saturday income in 1986, were jolted again when an all-night deluge swamped Horseshoe Bend Country Club and wiped out Sunday play in 1988.

Somebody always benefits from a rain-out. This time, it was Bob Charles, who had held the 36-hole lead Saturday night, as had Walt Zembriski when rain ended the Newport Cup with two rounds on the books and Dave Hill, when Sunday downpours reverted the Senior Tournament of Champions title to him as the leader after Saturday's third round. Charles had staked a precarious one-stroke lead at Horseshoe Bend, following his opening 70 with a 69 to stand that critical shot ahead of three others — Harold Henning, little-known Dick Hendrickson and Bert Yancey, a Senior Tour freshman whose once-outstanding talents on the regular PGA Tour had eroded with lengthy and serious health problems.

Hendrickson, Yancey and lefty George Lanning led the first day with 68s, Doug Sanders posting a 69 and Charles his 70 with Joe Jimenez and Walt Zembriski. Charles started well Saturday, but bogeyed the 11th and 12th holes to tighten things up. But he birdied the par-five 18th from two feet for the decisive 69. Sanders appeared to have a shot at his second seniors victory Saturday, but three straight bogeys on the back nine ruined his bid. Yancey, who had just joined the circuit in August, lost his chance for what would have been a co-championship when he three-putted the 17th green and missed a six-foot eagle putt at the final hole.

The win was the fifth on the 1988 Senior PGA Tour for Charles, enabling him to again catch up to Gary Player in the year's win column. Bob had two other non-tour seniors victories earlier in the season.

Vantage Championship—$900,000
Winner: Walter Zembriski

If his victory in the abbreviated Newport Cup earlier in the season proved that Walter Zembriski "belonged" as an important player on the Senior PGA Tour, his impressive triumph in the Vantage Championship, the circuit's richest event by far, certified it in spades. The rough-hewn little man, who had banged around golf's minor-league periphery for half of his adult years, emerged from among a fair number of more celebrated contenders in the pressure-charged final round with a rock-steady performance that carried him to a three-stroke victory. Zembriski shot an even-par 70 and his winning 278 was the only sub-par score recorded in the tournament at Winston-Salem's Tanglewood Park, site of the 1974 PGA Championship.

Consider that Sunday situation. Here's a man who, although doing much better in senior golf the last two years or so, had had trouble making ends meet financially most of his life, locked in a Sunday battle for a first prize of $135,000, probably more money than his total earnings in 13 years on the mini-tours. Yet, he was the solid player almost all afternoon.

Zembriski jumped in front to stay with two early birdies as third-round leader Lou Graham began a collapse toward a 79 and a 10th-place finish. Walt had begun the Sunday round a shot behind Graham and one ahead of Dick Rhyan, another non-winner in his time on the regular PGA Tour. As Graham faded, the battle settled into a duel between Zembriski and Rhyan. Walt moved three shots ahead when Rhyan double-bogeyed the 11th hole, lost two on a birdie-bogey swing at the 13th, but got back to a two-shot margin with a birdie at the 14th, went three ahead when Rhyan bogeyed the 16th. Both bogeyed the 18th, the lost stroke dropping Rhyan into a three-way tie for second place with Dave Hill and Al Geiberger, the defending champion. Both closed with 69s for their 281.

The miserable Sunday had to be particularly painful for Graham, the former U.S. Open champion who had just turned 50 in January. He shared the first-round lead with Hill at 68 — Zembriski opened with 73 — and with Rhyan at 137 at 36 holes. After a second-round 68, Zembriski moved into the runner-up position at 208, a shot behind Graham, with 67, and went from there Sunday.

General Tire Classic—$250,000
Winner: Larry Mowry

Through a quirk in the tournament's qualifying format, Larry Mowry was not invited to play in the 1987 Senior PGA Tour event at Las Vegas even though he had won twice in the preceding two months. The paperwork snub was particularly painful for Mowry because he had lived and worked in Las Vegas in earlier years. Perhaps that circumstance gave Mowry extra incentive when the circuit returned to the Nevada gambling mecca for the 1988 tournament, now called the General Tire Classic. Whatever, the 51-year-old pro with the widely-varied golf career made it the scene of his first 1988 victory and third on the senior tour.

With a final round of 71 that Larry said "wasn't that pretty," he broke from a tie with Bob Charles and scored a two-stroke victory with a 12-under-par 204 on the Desert Inn Country Club course, the best-known tournament site in Las Vegas, a testing, 6,810-yarder that hosted the famed Tournament of Champions in its early years.

Charles, who had been in the thick of contention in the two previous editions of the tournament, was at it again in the early going. Six birdies helped him post 67 in the Friday round for a one-stroke lead over Jim Ferree, Orville Moody, Bobby Nichols and Mowry. The southpaw swinger improved a stroke Saturday with 66, but Mowry did him one better and forged the leadership tie at 133, three shots better than anybody else in the field.

In 1987, Al Geiberger gave Charles and the rest of the field no chance when he finished with a brilliant 62 to score a four-stroke victory after Bob had taken a three-stroke lead at the 36-hole mark. Mowry had a harder time of it this year, in fact calling it "the toughest win I've ever had." Although he nailed six birdies, Larry absorbed three bogeys and a double-bogey when he put his tee shot in the water at the par-three seventh. The last two birdies came at the 15th and 16th holes, providing him with a three-stroke cushion. Charles managed only a 73, tying for second with Nichols at 206. However, the $20,625 runnerup money pushed his No. 1 earnings to $512,729, a new single-season record, set in 1987 by Chi Chi Rodriguez with $509,145. Mowry's prize was $37,500.

Fairfield Barnett Classic—$225,000
Winner: Miller Barber

Miller Barber seems to have a rather select group of tournaments upon which he squanders his victory efforts. When he scored his third win over the years at Suntree Country Club in Melbourne, Florida, in early November, Barber matched his efforts in the U.S. Senior Open and at Jeremy Ranch in Utah. Add those triples to his pairs of victories at Charlotte and Newport and you have accounted for nearly half of Miller's 24 wins during his eight years of senior tour golf.

The most recent win at Suntree, this year called the Fairfield Barnett Classic, was one of Barber's more impressive ones. He jumped on the field the first two days and breezed to a five-stroke victory with a 19-under-par score of 197, which tied the Senior PGA Tour record in 54-hole-event winning scores against par. Bruce Crampton shot the same score in 1987 at Syracuse and Don January posted 194 on a par-71 course in winning the 1984 du Maurier Champions.

The 57-year-old Barber, who is closing in on $2 million in senior tour earnings, had only one bogey all week at Suntree. He birdied eight of the first 12 holes in Friday's opening round en route to shoot 64 and take a two-stroke lead over Homero Blancas, who had an even faster start — six under after seven holes with an ace at the fifth — but could do no further damage to par the rest of the way. Miller was nearly as sharp Saturday. His 65 produced a new senior tour record with the 15-under-par total of 129 and widened his gap over Blancas to five as Homero shot 68. Dave Hill and Walt Zembriski were two shots further back.

Barber gave nobody a real chance to run at him Sunday. He birdied the third and fourth holes, effectively choking off any real hopes for Blancas, who had a number of birdie chances but couldn't convert as he sought his first senior tour victory in his first season on that circuit. Still, his second-place finish was by far his best. His only previous top-10 finish was eighth at Dallas. Barber finished with 68, leaving a 10-footer for the 54-hole record just short. Blancas also had 68 for his 202. Hill was another four shots back in third place. The $33,750 victory gave Barber his 22nd individual title on the tour proper and 24th overall, the most of any of the senior competitors.

Gus Machado Classic—$300,000
Winner: Lee Elder

It was an anniversary of sorts, probably a good one to celebrate. It had been one year since Lee Elder had suffered a heart attack within hours after the finish of the Gus Machado Classic, the final event on the 1987 schedule of the Senior PGA Tour at Key Biscayne, Florida. That he had survived, regained his health and golf game and returned to tournament action provided Elder with ample cause to celebrate that nearly-fatal day when he returned for the 1988 Gus Machado event.

But, he had another excellent reason to celebrate by week's end at Key Biscayne this year. He owned the tournament championship, paralleling Miller Barber's wire-to-wire, five-stroke victory of the previous Sunday in Melbourne. Lee closed with a sparkling 65 for an 11-under-par 202, scoring his first senior tour victory in more than two years and eighth of the career on that circuit. His last previous win had been in the Commemorative in New York in the summer of 1986.

Harold Henning provided the early challenges to Elder. He was a shot off the pace after Lee opened with 67 and still just a stroke behind after

36 holes. Both had second-round 70s over the 6,715-yard municipal course at Miami. Butch Baird and Lou Graham were only two shots off the pace at 139. But, Elder's biggest threat came from farther back as Al Geiberger produced a course-record 63 Sunday. Elder had birdied two of the first three holes to fashion a three-shot lead and not even when Geiberger birdied six of seven holes starting at the ninth did the margin get any smaller. Lee birdied the 10th and 12th around an excellent par save at the 11th, then put it away with his final two birdies at the 14th and 15th.

Geiberger's 63 and 207 gave him the runnerup slot, two shots in front of Graham, Henning and Bob Charles. The $45,000 first prize jumped Elder's earnings to more than $150,000 for a season that might not have happened at all. This time Lee wound up in the clutches of celebrating family and friends, not in the hands of paramedics on the floor of a condominium.

The tournament will continue, it was announced, but not until early 1990 when the sponsors hope to have two new seniors, Jack Nicklaus and Lee Trevino, in the field.

GTE Kaanapali Classic—$300,000
Winner: Don Bies

The Senior PGA Tour closed its official season with one of its most exciting finishes as yet another first-year player made a stronger impact than he ever made in his younger days on the regular PGA Tour. Don Bies, who had just one victory and little more than $500,000 to show for more than two decades on the regular circuit, scored the second victory of his rookie senior season in the year-ender at Hawaii's Royal Kaanapali Golf Club in the GTE Kaanapali Classic, jumping his official earnings to almost $300,000.

Bies, who concedes that his young family and its precedence kept him from reaching the full potential that he obviously harbored back in the 1960s, finds the senior circuit more comfortable and his game has responded. "On the other tour, it was more grinding for me," he noted. "I had three small children and being on the tour added to the pressure."

Pressure was abundant at Royal Kaanapali in the final round. Unlike the situation when he won the earlier 1988 victory in the Northville Invitational on Long Island where he grabbed a sizeable lead early in the final round and stood off the challengers, Don was a pursuer in the GTE Kaanapali. John Brodie led the first day with 65, then fell away, being replaced at the top after Saturday's round by Don January, who made a remarkable, if ultimately demoralizing showing in Hawaii little more than two months after suffering severe injuries in an auto accident. January, with 66-68 — 134, took a one-stroke lead over Bies (68-67) and Harold Henning (67-68), two over Dave Hill and Jimmy Powell and expanded a stroke on it through the first 14 holes Sunday.

Then, at the par-five 15th, a gamble failed him. Trying to get close to the green by fading a driver shot out of the trees, Don instead knocked the shot straight and out of bounds, eventually taking a double-bogey. Bies three-putted for a bogey there, but caught January with a 20-foot birdie putt at the 16th and nailed the victory with a 25-foot birdie putt on the final green after January had rolled his longer effort close from off the back edge of the green. Bies finished with 69 for 204, 12 under par; January with 71 for 205. Dave Hill was third at 206.

Many of the Kaanapali players remained in Hawaii for the Mauna Lani Challenge at Waikoloa the following week and Harold Henning picked off the $45,000 first prize with his 66-66-70 — 202, a four-stroke victory over Bob Erickson in the unofficial, non-tour event.

Mazda Champions—$850,000
Winner: Dave Hill and Colleen Walker

Dave Hill and Colleen Walker were the 1988 beneficiaries of American golf's annual "Christmas comes early" program in mid-December. The Mazda Champions tournament officials stock their Santa Claus with $850,000 in prize money, $500,000 ticketed for the winners of the event, which pairs 12 stars of the Senior PGA and LPGA Tours in a Caribbean finale of the season. This year, Hill and Walker, who finished third on their respective money lists, accepted the whopping gifts after a splendid wire-to-wire victory performance. Hill landed the bonanza in his first Mazda appearance, while Walker has finished first and second in her two showings.

The slender Hill and his sturdier female partner opened the tournament at its new Puerto Rican locale with a 12-under-par 60 Friday and never looked back. The new site at the Hyatt-Dorado Beach had been determined, fortuitously, prior to the fall hurricane that raked the Tryall course in Jamaica, scene of the first three Mazda Champions clashes, and the Hyatt's East course yielded a record score. Hill and Walker followed the opening 60 with a 62 for 122 and a three-stroke lead over Chi Chi Rodriguez and Jan Stephenson, then closed with 64 for 186, a new record by five strokes. Rodriguez and Stephenson finished with 65 for 190 and the four-stroke victory margin set another Mazda mark.

Hill and Walker made it a strong team effort. Colleen sparkled particularly the second day. She nearly holed her approach at the first hole and went on to score three other birdies and an eagle at the par-five 10th. Dave was the major contributor Sunday, running in six birdie putts en route to the 30-under-par final score. Rodriguez holed a 25-footer on the final green for his team's 65 as he and Jan edged Orville Moody and Tammie Green, who got into the tournament for the first time as substitute for Japan's Ayako Okamota.

With Hill and Walker breezing toward the title, much of Sunday's attention turned to Arnold Palmer and Kathy Postlewait, who had been languishing in last place after 36 holes with rounds of 67-69. Palmer came up with one of the hottest rounds of his long and fabled career. He made nine birdies as he and Kathy shot the week's best score — 59 — and jumped to sixth place in the standings.

11. The European Tour

The real tip-off came in December, 1987, in a simple news release from the PGA European Tour offices: A total of 240 golfers from 23 countries had entered the tour's qualifying tournament at La Manga in Spain in hopes of joining the tour in 1988. But it wasn't the size of the entry that made this one different. It was the feel. This wasn't an entry, it was a stampede. Any golfer on speaking terms with his one iron was rushing to join the circuit. For sheer vigor and excitement, 1988 was a year without precedent on the PGA European Tour — new tournaments, new names, and more prize money than ever before. A historic transformation was in progress. The European tour was coming of age in a hurry.

These were the raw figures, compared to 10 years ago: The total prize pool had hit £10 million for the first time, up from £1 million, and there were 34 tournaments, up from 26. This was the impact of Volvo, the giant Swedish car manufacturer. Volvo pumped in about £5 million in prize money alone. The European tour was becoming a transatlantic version of the huge American tour, and in more ways than just richer purses. European players were being elevated to the stature of their American counterparts through amenities that long have been commonplace in the United States. Among them: the European now had courtesy cars at tournaments (Volvos, of course), lounges at the clubs, and 5,000 new balls at the practice range for each tournament. European golf had come a long way since Henry Cotton, denied access to the clubhouse, used to set up a picnic table outside his Rolls Royce and have lunch near the first tee.

The Volvo Tour was simply the regular PGA European Tour, still sanctioned and administered by the PGA European Tour. This was the first year of a five-year contract between Volvo and the tour that would see both prize money and the number of events increase in the future. Volvo stamped its name on the tour in exchange for providing money and amenities. Oddly enough, the Volvo Tour also included events sponsored by other car makers, Peugeot and Lancia. Volvo also sponsored three tournaments — the PGA Championship, the Belgian Open, and the season-ending Volvo Masters. The exact amount of money Volvo was committing in the five-year contract was not revealed, but observers speculate that it is an eight-digit figure. If the question is why, the answer is simple: High-profile marketing. Volvo, long a name in tennis and skiing, had discovered golf.

"Suddenly, it was our No. 1-rated sport," said Volvo Executive Vice President Carleric Haggstrom. "In terms of upward or downward growth, in terms of attractivity, you can soon see why we have come to the conclusion that golf is the right sport for us to be in. Golf now has its future to look forward to and the same perhaps cannot be said of tennis. We believe there is more mass development ahead and we want to grow, too. So golf and Volvo fit together nicely. That's why we are here." He added that Volvo was not spending "new" money on golf, but channeling it from other areas. The impact was felt in tennis. Volvo reduced its tennis sponsorship to nine Grand Prix events in 1988.

The 1988 schedule included three new tournaments — the Majorca Open at Santa Ponca in Spain, kicking off the new year in March, the English Open at Royal Birkdale in September, and the season-closing Volvo Masters in Spain in October.

The golfers gave Volvo its money's worth right out of the starting blocks, kicking off possibly the most exciting season in history. Seve Ballesteros set the tone. Ballesteros had been languishing (for him) since a crushing disappointment in the 1987 Masters, but came smashing through to run away with the new Majorca Open, starting the season. Then came David Whelan to set a different kind of tone. Whelan, an Englishman, had gone through the tour qualifying school six consecutive years before gaining his playing card in 1987. Two tournaments into the 1988 season, he had his first victory, the Barcelona Open.

Whelan might have seemed a chance winner at the moment, but by the time the season had run its course, there were eight first-time winners — the most ever, aside from the tour's first year, 1974. In fact, it looked like the Year of the First-Timer almost from the start. Right after Whelan's win, David Llewellyn took the Biarritz Open. Two tournaments later, Derrick Cooper won the Cepsa Madrid Open, followed immediately by Mike Harwood in the Portuguese Open. Spectators were scratching their heads. Six tournaments, four first-time winners. And they weren't finished yet. Barry Lane broke through in Bell's Scottish Open in July, then Peter Baker in the Benson & Hedges International a month later, followed immediately by Frank Nobilo in the PLM Open. Chris Moody was No. 8 in the Ebel European Masters/Swiss Open in September.

Had the big names all gone fishing? Not so. Oh, Sandy Lyle was busy working the American tour early in the year. In fact, with the Phoenix Open, Greater Greensboro Open, and the Masters all in his pocket, he topped the American money list much of the season. Ian Woosnam, who ruled the world in 1987, was mysteriously sagging in 1988. Burn-out from 1987? The wrist injury from the motorbike spill? The new clubs he took up under an endorsement? Whatever it was, Woosnam got it straightened out in time to win the Volvo PGA Championship in May, Carroll's Irish Open in August, and the Panasonic European Open in September. So much for the slump.

Nick Faldo was in a different kind of slump, one that most golfers would settle for. He seemed destined to spend the season in second place. After three seconds, he broke out to win the Peugeot French Open, then had four more seconds, including the Suntory World Match Play. He wrote a ringing *finis* to that frustration by coming from behind to win the final event, the Volvo Masters.

Back to Ballesteros. He sputtered along after that season-opening victory at Majorca, still dragging the old woes of the 1987 Masters. The amazing news was that he missed the 36-hole cut at the Cannes Open in mid-April, his first miss since 1982. Some saw this as a sign of decline. Then came a brilliant victory in the British Open and he was his old self. He added the Scandinavian Enterprise Open, German Open, and Lancome Trophy. In the second half of the season, he won three in three consecutive starts, four out of five. His performance in Europe was awesome. Through the German Open, his third win in three starts and his fourth victory in nine completed European starts, he was 100 under par and was making a birdie or an eagle on the average of less than every fourth hole. And he was winning at the rate of £98 a stroke. So much for the woes.

Jose-Maria Olazabal, after a winless 1987, roused himself and scored twice — the Volvo Belgian Open and the German Masters. Greg Norman, after an emotional victory dedicated to a leukemia-stricken boy in the MCI Heritage Classic in America, made one of his few scheduled European appearances and took the Lancia Italian Open in May. It was a bright sign that was to dim a month later when he injured his wrist in the U.S. Open and had to sit out for about two months. Sandy Lyle interrupted his reign in the United States and won the Dunhill British Masters.

It was not a bright year for everyone, however. Ryder Cupper Sam Torrance fell from grace, and teammate Bernhard Langer fell even farther. When the year ended, golf fans had to wonder whether they had seen the last of the popular West German as they had known him. He was struggling with two of the most fierce enemies a golfer can face — a bad back and a recurrence of that virulent case of the putting yips that had nearly crippled his game early in his career. He held both at bay early in the year and won the Epson Grand Prix of Europe in May. "If my back never gets any worse," he had said, "then I will be a very happy man." Langer tried various treatments for his back, short of surgery. He looked for any kind of help for his yips. In the British Open, he five-putted one hole. He even resorted to sports psychology and the extra-long putter so popular on the yips-ridden American senior tour. The Epson would be his only victory. After that, 1988 was one long slide. Langer came to the German Open late in August having missed six cuts in his previous seven starts.

So this was the 1988 European tour, the debut of the bigger, richer Volvo Tour. The effect was felt immediately. Two bright British amateurs — Paul Broadhurst, 22, and Wayne Henry, 18 — turned professional in early August. This was just a few weeks after Broadhurst won low-amateur honors in the British Open. In fact, he was the only amateur to make the 36-hole cut. He said he had been on the verge of turning pro for some time, and Henry simply wanted a change of scenery. "I was beginning to get a bit bored," he said. Both had been expected to represent England in some important amateur competitions. But the tide in European golf is shifting rapidly, much as it had in America years ago. The rich pro tours are attracting sharp amateurs as soon as they feel they can find their way in that fast traffic. The knock of opportunity is a siren song.

It promises to continue. The 1989 Volvo Tour, including minor events, was scheduled for 40 weeks of golf and £11.6 million in purses.

Majorca Open—£200,000
Winner: Seve Ballesteros

This wasn't a teacher-student showdown, but it was almost as good — a confrontation between Spanish countrymen on their home soil, one of the best golfers in the world, the other a young lion, his presumed successor. It was Seve Ballesteros, a month from his 31st birthday, against Jose-Maria Olazabal, 22. It lacked just one thing — the showdown itself. They went into the final round of the Majorca Open tied for the lead. Then Ballesteros ran away with it.

The Majorca Open, at the 7,150-yard, par-72 Santa Ponsa course, launched the 1988 season, the European tour's first under Volvo sponsorship. Ballesteros was the promoter through his organization, the Amen Corner company. It would hardly do for him to embarrass himself. And Ballesteros, looking for his first European victory in almost a year, didn't. He returned 70-68-67-67—272, 16 under par, to win by six from Olazabal (68-73-64-73—278).

It took a little warming up, though. Ballesteros didn't come to the top until the third round, when he found himself tied with Olazabal. Ballesteros suffered one uneasy moment, when he surrendered the first-round lead with some weird putting at No. 18. Playing in rain and chilly temperatures, he ran off six birdies, and he was within reach of a par, 45 feet from the hole. His first putt was three feet short, he ran his second four feet past, and missed that as well: a four-putt double-bogey six. "It isn't a problem," he insisted. "Breaking your arm or cutting your wrist is a problem, but taking four putts, especially in the first round, is not serious." He was at 70, two strokes behind Olazabal, who shared the lead on 68.

Neil Hansen, age 26, a former caddy and assistant club professional in England, had his big moment in the second round. A 66, including an eagle-three off a 250-yard three-wood and a 15-foot putt at No. 2, carried him into the 36-hole lead at 137. Ballesteros had begun to stir. His 68 put him second by a stroke, and Olazabal slipped to a 73 and fell to fourth at 141.

It was Olazabal's turn in the third round. An electrifying course-record 64 lifted him to the top, and Ballesteros shot a 67, and now it was their show. At 11-under-par 211, they shared a three-stroke lead over Hansen (who would sink to a tie for 15th with a closing 79—287).

Olazabal crashed on Santa Ponsa's par-threes in the finale. He bogeyed three of them. He was bunkered at No. 3, and fell behind. Ballesteros stepped further ahead with a birdie at the ninth. Then came the clinchers. Olazabal bogeyed the par-three 12th, missing his par from three feet. He found a spark of hope with a birdie at No. 13, and then his chances died at the par-three 15th. He three-putted from 15 feet for a bogey, and Ballesteros holed from six feet for a birdie-two. Chalk it up: Ballesteros's 33rd European victory in 165 starts in 15 years.

But it was back to square one for Ian Woosnam, the world's leader in 1987, when he won eight events and more than $1.8 million. He opened on 71, three off the lead, but he didn't make his first birdie until the 14th. A slip of the mind cost him a stroke in the second round. It was high enough at 77, but he signed for a four instead of a birdie-three at No. 17 and had to accept a 78. Woosnam was miffed, but others rejoiced. His error let 21 extra players into the final 36 holes on the cut at 149. Woosnam finally took out his frustrations on his two iron in the final round. He was out in 32, but came home in 39 for 71—291, and tied for 38th. He broke his two iron across his knee.

Torras Hostench Barcelona Open—£200,000
Winner: David Whelan

David Whelan, 26, former amateur Junior International from England, came into the Torras Hostench Barcelona Open just another face in the crowd. What could anybody expect from a man who had to go through the European tour qualifying school six consecutive years? But Whelan, who finally won his playing card in 1987, was persistence personified, and it paid off in his first victory. He became the tour's first new winner of the year.

It was simple. All he had to do was birdie the final hole to join a four-way tie, then come through a playoff against Barry Lane, a six-year veteran seeking his first win; veteran Mark Mouland, who had won once in his six previous years, and none other than one of the world's finest, 1987 British Open champion Nick Faldo. This was Faldo's tournament, by the way, until he bogeyed the final hole.

Whelan wasn't a stranger for long at Real Club de Golf El Prat. He had introduced himself to everybody in the second round with a seven-under-par 65. Then he crashed the playoff party — with a birdie on the final hole. That wrapped up a 12-under-par 276, with rounds of 68-65-74-69. The shootout cast was cut in half abruptly, on the first extra hole, when Faldo and Mouland each made a par-three. Whelan and Lane birdied, and then proceeded to slug it out for three more holes. Whelan ended it with a four on the fourth extra hole.

Faldo and American Michael Allen took the first-round lead with 66s, a stroke ahead of American John De Forest and Spanish amateur Jose Arruti. (Their time in the spotlight was brief. De Forest shot a 76 in the second round, Arruti a 76 in the third, and they finished tied for 55th.) Whelan was two strokes off the first-round lead with 68. Now came his time.

In the second round, he went out in 32, and coming in he got an eagle-three at the 547-yard 15th. The 65 would hold up as the lowest round of the tournament. It also gave him a 36-hole total of 11-under-par 133, to say nothing of possibly the most intense pressure yet of his young career. For lurking just behind were two of the tour's top guns, Faldo (68—134) and Jose-Maria Olazabal (69—136). Perhaps the pressure took its toll. Whelan's 74 in the third round seemed to write an end to his charge. It dropped him two strokes behind Faldo's lead (71—205), into a tie with Barry Lane (67) and Swedish newcomer Johan Rystrom (68). It was here, by the way, that Faldo really lost the tournament by dropping three strokes over the last five holes. He missed a two-foot par putt at No. 14, three-putted No. 16, and bogeyed the par-three 17th after bunkering his tee shot.

Still laboring, Faldo shot another 71 in the final round. Mouland caught him with a 68, and Lane and Whelan joined the deadlock with 69s (Whelan with that birdie at the 72nd hole). It was playoff time. Whelan went out carrying the tag "Least Likely To Succeed," and came back with one that said "Champion."

AGF Biarritz Open—£142,146
Winner: David Llewellyn

Here's one for trivia fans: What champion started a round with an eagle-three? That cuts the field down in a hurry. After all, how many golf courses start with a par-five hole? Well, Biarritz Golf Club does. No. 1 is short by par-five standards — just 460 yards. But an eagle is an eagle. It was there, in the third round, that David Llewellyn posted a sign saying "This tournament is mine." Llewellyn rang up the eagle-three, then charged to a course-record eight-under-par 60, and didn't let up until he had the AGF Biarritz Open in his bag. The 60-65 finish gave him a seven-stroke victory, the first big-tournament win of a career that began in 1970.

It was an inspiring win for the 36-year-old Welshman. Seventeen years earlier, he was the tour's rookie of the year. But the promise misfired. His earlier successes were two widely spaced African victories, the 1972 Kenya Open and the 1985 Ivory Coast Open. In 1987, a victory in a satellite event, the Vernons Open, set the stage for rebirth. Late in 1987 he paired with Ian Woosnam to win the World Cup for Wales, and early in 1988 won the Zambian Open on the Safari circuit.

But his Biarritz win wasn't the pushover it seemed. The 5,878-yard, par-68 course was a sitting duck despite the absence of the big European tour names who were in the United States that week, warming up for the Masters. Fully 31 of the field finished below par, and seven others right on it at 272. Llewellyn came in at 14-under-par with rounds of 64-69-60-65, a European tour record 258. Christy O'Connor Jr. was second at 265, and Barry Lane and Jose Rivero shared third at 266.

Llewellyn was a tag-along from the start. In the first round, postponed to Friday because of rain (thus necessitating a 36-hole finish on Sunday), Eamonn Darcy led him by a stroke with 63. Darcy had come within a whisker of getting his own 60. At the par-three 17th, his tee shot ended up in casual water at the edge of the green. His only relief was off the green, and it took him four to get down, for a double-bogey five. Darcy then drifted out of contention in the second round with his only score out of the 60s, a 71. In the second round, Llewellyn fell to a tie for fourth with a 69, his only over-par round, and he trailed halfway leader Jose Rivero (130) by three strokes. Then came Llewellyn's Sunday two-round explosion. It began with the eagle at No. 1, followed by a birdie at No. 2. A bogey-five at No. 3 made it seem that a routine round was in progress. But then he streaked off for seven more birdies, and only a lurch at the 18th kept him from the first sub-60 round in tour history. His approach putt from 45 feet was five feet short, and he missed from there and settled for a three-putt bogey-five. His 60 set the course record and tied the tour low-round record established by Baldovino Dassu in the 1971 Swiss Open.

So Llewellyn had set two records and tied one. He wasn't all that impressed. "Records only get broken," Llewellyn said. "But a win is a win, and nobody can take that away from you."

Cannes Open—£189,555
Winner: Mark McNulty

It isn't often that someone missing the 36-hole cut made as much news as the man who won, but this was one of those times. The winner was Mark McNulty, almost fresh from a bout with pneumonia and making his first appearance of the year on the European tour, where he was No. 2 on the Order of Merit in 1987. It was the 30th victory of his career, his sixth in Europe.

The cut victim was none other than Seve Ballesteros, back from the Masters. Ballesteros shot a near-unbelievable (for him) 76-78—154 at the par-72 Cannes-Mougins Golf Club and missed the cut by four strokes. Everyone was stunned, especially Ballesteros. "Everything was bad," he said. "And I feel sorry for all the people who were expecting to come and see me play. I gave everything in the Masters and I gave everything I had left here. Nothing went right." Despite his victory in the season-opening Majorca Open about a month earlier, his Cannes performance raised a predictable question: Was he on the way down? Not so, said friend and fellow Spaniard Manuel Pinero. "He just gets more tired coming straight back from America," Pinero said. "He's now 31, not 21."

For the record: Aside from the now-defunct Silk Cut Masters, where he signed an incorrect scorecard in 1983, the last time Ballesteros missed the cut was in the 1982 Sanyo Open.

There was plenty of firepower in the field from the outset, with such as McNulty, Joey Sindelar, Howard Clark, and Jose-Maria Olazabal on hand. But it was a couple of comparative unknowns who staked the early claim. Australian Wayne Riley took the first-round lead with 68, and Barry Lane, promising young Englishman, joined Sindelar, the big-hitting American, in second place at 69. Of the three, Sindelar was the only one who would maintain the challenge. (Lane blew to an 80 in the second round, en route to a tie for 35th, and Riley shot 75-75 in the middle two rounds and tied for 12th.) McNulty (72) wasn't even on the radar scope yet.

The cast changed completely for the second round. Ron Commans, another American, charged to the front with a 68 for the 36-hole lead at six-under-par 138, three strokes ahead of Denis Durnian (69) and Italy's Emanuele Bolognesi (a 76-77 finish would take him away). Commans held firm in the third round, his par-72 leaving him in the lead at six-under 210, two ahead of another change of characters. Sindelar reappeared with a 69-212, joined there by the promising Irishman, Philip Walton (68). And finally McNulty came into view. A solid 70 lifted him to fourth place on three-under-par 213. And so he began the final round three strokes off the lead.

As he had done so often in Africa, McNulty came rushing through in the final round to pluck the plum. First, Commans faded a bit too much, bogeying the 12th and 14th for a par-72. Walton disappeared with a 76. And Sindelar, pinned down by a double-bogey start, could manage only a 70. It looked like anybody's tournament, especially when McNulty bogeyed No. 1 after driving nearly into the hazard well right of the fairway. But he settled down quickly. He saved par from a bunker at No. 2, then caught Commans with a run of four birdies over the next six holes. He birdied the 10th, and rapped in a 45-foot birdie putt at No. 13, and was on his way to the 66 that gave him a nine-under-par 279 and a three-stroke victory over Commans and Sindelar. It was Commans' best finish in three years on the European tour.

"I really am delighted to win in my first event back on the European tour," McNulty said. "I couldn't dream of a better return here."

Cepsa Madrid Open—£200,000
Winner: Derrick Cooper

There's that old line about the travel-weary, quick-stop tourist that goes, "If it's Tuesday, this must be Belgium." Something like that was happening on the European tour: "Another new winner? This must be America." The European tour, just six tournaments old, was taking on a decidedly American flavor. Add England's Derrick Cooper, in the Cepsa Madrid Open, to the list — the third first-timer in five events, joining David Whelan (Barcelona Open) and David Llewellyn (Biarritz Open).

Cooper, just nearing his 33rd birthday, was hardly a new player on the European Tour. He had labored for nine years, and a couple of fourths in the mid-1980s was all he had to show for it. In four 1988 appearances, he ranged from 32nd to 131st. That makes him the definition of the surprise winner. And it was not a field of weekend golfers he was up against. Practically all of European golf was there, including Seve Ballesteros, Howard Clark, Mark McNulty, Sam Torrance, Eamonn Darcy, and Jose-Maria Olazabal. So it was not a walk through the tulips when Cooper finally emerged in the last round. Cooper returned 70-68-69-68 for 13-under-par total of 275 and a one-stroke victory over Manuel Pinero and Miguel Martin, who shared second at 276.

The Madrid Open looked like a home event all the way. Jose Ignacio Gervas led the first round with a 65. Cooper was five behind. Gervas also led the second with 69—134. Cooper was four behind. After the third round, there were three Spaniards ahead of him — Pinero, at 205, and Martin and Ballesteros at 206. Cooper was at 207. He hardly seemed a threat.

But Cooper swept through the last round with six birdies and an eagle, then stepped aside to fret while his challengers finished. Ballesteros fell short. "I didn't play well, and I didn't take my chances on the back nine," he said. A 72 left him at 278, in fourth place. Pinero and Martin needed a birdie at the last hole to tie. They couldn't pull it in. Cooper was a winner. He credited a new approach to tournament golf.

"I've done everything differently this year," he said.

He stayed home with his wife and two-year-old son rather than go abroad and get stale in the winter. He tuned up his game with golf guru Bob Torrance, Sam's father. And he grabbed a putter "on impulse" out of his shop at the Birch Wood Club in Warrington on his way to Spain. He also arrived at Puerta de Hierro at the last minute, to avoid boredom. "The first I saw of the course," he said, "was on the first tee in round one." And finally, the mind. "I've been too negative in the brain," he said. "So I talked to myself and kept calm." And then, of course, there was the example of the other first-timers.

"I thought about the victories of Whelan and Llewellyn," Cooper said, "and told myself, if they can do it, so can I." And so he did.

Portuguese Open—£200,000
Winner: Mike Harwood

Mike Harwood, a 6-foot-4 Australian, used to be known as the man who ended Greg Norman's rampage of six consecutive victories when his final-round 64 beat the Shark in the 1986 Australian PGA Championship. Thanks to another pressure-proof finish, now he's known as the Portuguese Open champion — another first-time winner on the European tour. Harwood, 29, in his third year on the tour, had known success elsewhere, but his previous best in Europe was a tie for sixth in the 1986 Italian Open.

Harwood won by a stroke over Eamonn Darcy, whose bid to force a playoff died when his long putt on the final hole hung on the lip of the cup. Harwood, coming from behind at the start, shot 73-70-68-69—280, eight under par at the 7,091-yard, par-72 Quinta do Lago course. But until the final round, he looked like anything but a winner. He had dug himself a big hole to start — an opening 73 that left him five big strokes off the hot pace set by Derrick Cooper and American Bill Malley, who shared the lead on 68. Both were looking for that elusive first victory. They'd have to wait a bit longer. In the second round, a 75 wiped out Cooper's hopes (he settled for a tie for 15th). And Malley suffered a gruesome, 15-stroke crash. He went from co-leader to out-the-door. He shot an 83 in the second round and missed the 36-hole cut (147) by four strokes.

Harwood started to make up some ground with a 70 in the second round. His one-under-par 143 total got him a stroke closer to the lead, now 139, shared by Peter Fowler (68), Stephen Bennett (70), and Darcy (70). Next it was Fowler's turn to go. A 73 in the third round took him away, and the lead went to England's Peter Baker, a promising third-year player. Baker returned a 67, the low score of the tournament, for a seven-under-par 209 total and a two-stroke edge. And Harwood had finally surfaced. A 68, his best of the week, vaulted him to a tie for second with Darcy (72) and Bennett (72). Des Smyth made his bid with a 68 that included the ninth hole-in-one of his career, a two-iron shot at the 210-yard sixth. That put him at 212.

But at the end, with Baker struggling to a 73, it came down to a Harwood-Darcy battle. Harwood did it like a hardened veteran. He holed a 20-yard bunker shot at No. 10, then dropped birdie putts of 15 feet at the 14th and 15th, and saved par with a six-footer at No. 16. Darcy's last hope was for a birdie on the final hole, and from 35 feet, he made Harwood's heart stop. The putt hung on the lip. Darcy would settle for 70—281, and Harwood would resume breathing. He had won.

Winning was not completely alien to him. In 1984 he won the Fiji Open and the Pacific Harbor Open, and in 1986 the Swedish Naturgas Open and the Australian PGA. But this one was special. "Both Portugal and Quinta do Lago will remain forever in my heart," he said. "It was here, on this excellent course and in this marvelous climate that I got my first European victory."

Epson Grand Prix of Europe—£275,000
Winner: Bernhard Langer

In a week in which he was practically a laboratory specimen, Bernhard Langer overcame an old enemy — a bad back — and rejoiced with a new friend — a putter — to breeze to a 4-and-3 victory in the final of the Epson Grand Prix of Europe Match Play Championship at St. Pierre Golf and Country Club at Chepstow, Wales. It was his first outing of the year on the European tour. And ironically, his victim was Mark McNulty, another victim of various ills, the most recent being a pneumonia attack that had sidelined him for 10 weeks.

"If my back never gets any worse than it is now," Langer proclaimed later, "then I will be a very happy man." Langer, who had done little on the American tour so far this year, had spent the two previous weeks back home in West Germany for treatment of bulging discs and a stress fracture. He surrendered to an orthopedic specialist, a physiotherapist, a chiropractor, and a masseur. Taking turns at him, they twisted, poked, shoved, jabbed, prodded, and what-not. Like everyone else in the legion of golfers with bad backs, Langer did not enjoy the prospect of surgery. Hence his proclamation of reserved relief.

Langer barely made it into the final. His battle with Rodger Davis in the semifinal came down to the final hole. Davis pulled his drive close to a wall and could not go for the flag. Then he let Langer in by two-putting for a bogey-four. In an earlier skin-of-his-teeth escape, Langer was two down with three to play against Bill Longmuir in the second round, but won the 16th and the 17th to catch him, then birdied the first extra hole to advance to the round of 16. Four seeded players were knocked out in the second round — Nick Faldo, by Antonio Garrido; Gordon Brand Jr., by Gordon J. Brand; defending champion Mats Lanner, by England's Glenn Ralph, and Peter Senior, by Spain's Miguel Martin.

McNulty, winner of the Cannes Open three weeks earlier, charged past Howard Clark for a 3-and-2 victory in the semifinals. Clark was one up after 11 holes, but McNulty took four of the next five. In a playoff for third place, Davis beat Clark, 3 and 2.

Langer wasn't happy with his putting in the semifinals. "I putted like a blind man," he said. Then he switched to a heavier putter that had more loft for the title match. The results were devastating to McNulty. Langer carded seven birdies and had eight single putts, and was five under par when he erased McNulty on the 15th green. Langer came through two uneasy moments. At No. 1, he had to play safe with a six-iron second after his tee shot ended up on a twig, and McNulty was just off the green with a wood second. Then Langer nearly holed his pitch, and made an easy birdie while McNulty three-putted. At No. 8, McNulty chipped in from off the green. Langer waved that new putter and matched the birdie with a 10-footer.

The victory was Langer's 18th on the European tour. His first was on the same St. Pierre course, in the 1980 Dunlop Masters.

Peugeot Spanish Open—£166,230
Winner: Mark James

There was plenty of fire in the Peugeot Spanish Open — some on the course, the rest by Seve Ballesteros off it, almost obscuring Mark James's first European victory in two years. Ballesteros was provoked by the low-60s scoring, rolling across Royal Pedrena like thunder. This was where he learned to play, not far from his home in Santander. He felt insulted.

"They have watered the greens, not watered the fairways, and cut the rough," Ballesteros said, in a sweeping indictment of the European tour. "It is not the same golf course. You have players who can't break par shooting 62s and 63s."

Ballesteros himself set the pace in the Wednesday pro-am with a course-record 61, nine under par. He wouldn't approach it again, but others did. One even matched it — Australian Wayne Riley in the third round. Whether Ballesteros's complaint was justified — he finished tied for 17th with rounds of 72-67-67-68—274 — the scoring suggests that Royal Pedrena could be had. This was the breakdown through 59th place (63 finishers): 61s-1, 62s-1, 63s-5, 64s-8, 65s-6, 66s-19, 67s-22, 68s-41, 69s-40.

"Obviously, it's not that difficult a course," said James, whose 63-68-63-68—262, 18 under par, won by three strokes over Nick Faldo. "But how difficult can a par-70, 6,340-yard course be? But it's a good test of golf, and you can get into a lot of trouble if you're not thinking."

Said Ken Schofield, executive director of the European Tour, "I think Seve is just a little frustrated."

Perhaps Faldo was, too. James kept slipping away. James began the final round three strokes ahead and quickly dropped two of them with bogeys at the second and third holes. He hung on, getting a big boost with a 30-yard pitch for a birdie-two at No. 10. Faldo pulled to within a stroke with a birdie at No. 14, but James was equal to the pressure, matching him birdie-for-birdie at No. 16 and No. 17 (especially at the 17th, where he rescued himself from the rough with an eight iron to eight feet). Faldo's last stab failed. At No. 18, he hit into the trees and made double-bogey six for a 68—265.

James had to do some chasing of his own. After sharing the first-round lead with Richard Boxall at 63, he fell four behind with a 68 to Boxall's 64 through 36 holes. James jumped ahead in the third round with his second 63, and led by three over Boxall (70) and Faldo, who added to the scoring barrage with a 62 that included seven birdies and an eagle. No question the 1987 British Open champion was on his game and would be a big problem in the final round.

"Until Nick hit into the trees on No. 18, the tournament was still up for grabs," James said. "I had to struggle all day. It wasn't the pressure of being the leader, because I knew my swing wasn't right on the practice tee. I had to keep fighting and hope Faldo didn't shoot a 64." Faldo didn't, and James, age 34, had his first European victory since the 1986 Benson and Hedges International, his ninth since joining the tour in 1976.

Italian Open—£212,000
Winner: Greg Norman

The 1988 Italian Open called for an accountant, not a scorekeeper. It took some juggling to keep the books straight. Heavy rains not only forced the postponement of the first round, but when play did begin on Friday, the water-logged Monticello course was shortened to 6,157 yards and par was cut to 69. Then it was restored to its normal 6,966 yards and par 72 for the third round on Saturday and the two-round finish on Sunday. Thus par became an even more elusive figure than usual on a course that took a beating. It was more than fleeting for two players. Kyi Hla Han, of Burma, aced the third hole in the second round, but it didn't help. His 72-70—142 missed the 36-hole cut by two strokes. Ian Woosnam, the giant of 1987, was still slumping. But his 68-68-69-69—274 suggested he was stirring at last.

No matter how you figured par, however, Greg Norman was seven strokes off the lead after the first round. He had shot a 69 — par for the day — and Bill McColl shot a 62 for the lead, and a lot of golfers were in between. These included Vicente Fernandez, David Whelan, and Ove Sellberg, all at 63. Norman had decided to make just three starts on the European tour for 1988, and this was not a promising beginning. A 68 in the second round, with the course restored to its par 72, didn't help much. He was at 137, five strokes behind Ron Commans, whose course-record 63 set the pace at 132 through 36 holes. All of which made Norman's victory that much sweeter. He had a lot of catching up to do.

The irrepressible Shark got right to it on Sunday morning, in the third round. Starting at No. 10, he birdied from 20 feet. At the 529-yard, par-five 11th, he hit a one-iron second shot to the green and two-putted for another birdie. He got another at No. 13, a 244-yard par-three, then eagled the 14th from 30 feet. He was out in 31, and started back with four consecutive threes, two of them birdies. Commans' freshly-set course record was right in his sights. Norman needed to birdie at the par-five ninth, his final hole. He didn't get it, but he tied the record with a 63 and shared the third-round lead on 13-under-par 200 with fellow Australian Craig Parry (67). The tightly bunched leaderboard had Commans third at 70—202 and Ronan Rafferty fourth at 67—203.

They went back out Sunday afternoon in the final round on the same playing schedule. Commans faded fast, a 77 dropping him all the way to 19th. Rafferty's bid fell short with a 69, and he finished third. Norman cooled off to a closing 70—270, 15 under par, then had to wait 90 minutes to see whether it would hold up. Parry, who had won his tour card just the preceding December, could catch him. But the birdies escaped him, and his last chance to force a tie and a playoff was snuffed out when he bunkered his approach to the final hole. He finished second by a stroke, 71—271, and Norman, who played the final 36 holes the same day in 11 under par, had his fifth victory of 1988.

Volvo PGA Championship—£300,000
Winner: Ian Woosnam

"I'm still not quite striking it like I want to," Ian Woosnam was saying to the press at the Volvo PGA Championship.

To which his playing partner, Mark McNulty, replied with a grin, "You don't have to listen to this bull. He's hitting it perfect!"

Woosnam had done a 180-degree turn. Nothing had gone right since the beginning of the year, and by late May he was one troubled man. Golfers often go from soaring success to awful crashes. The question is, will they snap out of it? Some don't. Woosnam did. He ripped through Wentworth in 67-70-70-67—274, 14 under par, taking the PGA by two strokes over Seve Ballesteros and Mark James. What a relief.

"My lowest point came in America earlier this year," Woosnam said. "When you're on your own with no one to talk to and you can't get home, it's terrible. The worst week was the Masters." Woosnam had made it a personal *cause celebre* about not having been invited to the Masters in the past. He finally got the invitation he valued so highly, and shot 81-74—155, and missed the 36-hole cut by four strokes. This from the man who had won eight times and over $1.8 million around the world the year before. Try as he might, he couldn't get his game going. He practiced till his hands bled and lost their feeling, and still he not only went winless, he missed five cuts. The light finally started to glow in the first round of the PGA.

Woosnam was one of eight tied for fourth after an encouraging five-under-par 67. He birdied three of four holes, starting at No. 5, en route to his seventh consecutive sub-par round, and was two behind the 65s returned by first-round leaders Jose Rivero and Andrew Oldcorn. In the second round, Rivero ruined himself with a 78 and Oldcorn slipped to a 73, and were replaced atop the leaderboard by Bernhard Langer (66—133, 11 under par). Woosnam slipped a notch, to fifth place with 70—137, and between him and the top were two formidable obstacles, Jose-Maria Olazabal (66—134) and Ballesteros (68—135). Langer's putter went bad the third day (74) and Olazabal self-destructed with a 78. The fast-improving Ballesteros rose to the top on 71—206, 10 under par, taking the lead on a two-putt birdie after reaching the 572-yard 16th with a three wood and a six iron. Woosnam shot another 70 and joined Langer and three others in second place, a stroke behind.

It came down to the final round. Now Woosnam would see whether his renewed faith was justified. "When I start playing well," he said, "my confidence comes flooding back and I know I'm going to win." He was nothing but confident on the outgoing nine. Now using McNulty's putting style — both index fingers down the shaft — he holed birdies from 10, 12, and 25 feet and made the turn in 32. They proved to be the margin he needed. Ballesteros, playing behind him, still had a chance to catch him with birdies at Wentworth's two closing par-five holes. But he took three from the edge at No. 17 and then, needing an eagle at No. 18 to tie, he pulled his approach. He had to settle for 70—276, a joint second with Mark James, two strokes behind Woosnam's 67—274, 14 under par. Woosnam had his first victory of 1988. Then he could look back on the private hell he'd been through for months.

"You can learn from everything," Woosnam said. "I've come through bad spells before. It does everybody good to be knocked down a peg. You're not going to be the best golfer in the world just like that — it isn't that easy. But," he added, "that's still my ambition."

Dunhill British Masters—£250,000
Winner: Sandy Lyle

Maybe there's something about the word "Masters" that appeals to Sandy Lyle. He already had one Masters title in his pocket this year, the first Briton ever to conquer Augusta National. He'd had some lean times since that shining moment about two months ago, in early April, but he was off and running from the opening gun in the Dunhill British Masters at Woburn. This was his first win in Britain since the 1985 British Open, his first in Europe since the 1987 German Masters. He led wire-to-wire, but it didn't come easy. In the final round, Lyle got a thrill from hard-charging Mark McNulty, the defending champion, and a challenge from fellow Ryder Cupper Nick Faldo. Still, the margin of victory, two strokes, was Lyle's smallest lead since his one-stroke edge in the first round.

Lyle returned 66-68-68-71—273, 15 under par. He led by one stroke through the first round, three through the second, and four through the third. He began with a seven-birdie, one-bogey 66, six under par, for a one-stroke lead over Tony Charnley. "This was not one of my best rounds," Lyle insisted, but he was pleased with his putting. He needed just 29 putts, which included a three-putt from 40 feet for his only bogey.

His deadly one iron staked him to a 68—134 in the second round, a three-stroke lead over Jose-Maria Olazabal and Ossie Moore. Lyle kept pumping one iron shots of 250 yards and more on the rain-heavy, 6,883-yard course. "I'd love to use the driver more often," he said, "but there's no point in it around here. It only takes one bad shot, and you're in the trees." He risked the driver at No. 14, and it cost him his only slip, a double-bogey six. At No. 7, he holed a bunker shot from 25 yards; at No. 8, a 60-foot putt, and at No. 9, a 20-footer. The field, meantime, lost one of its big names. Bernhard Langer struggled to a 148 total, and missed the cut in a European tournament for the first time in five years. "It happens to all of us at some time or another," Langer said. His problems: "I am playing poorly, putting badly, and I have no confidence."

Lyle seemed on the verge of a runaway. His 68 in the third round, his fifth consecutive sub-70 round, carried him to a four-stroke lead over Faldo. Only the formality of the fourth round stood between him and the presentation speeches. But suddenly it wasn't quite that simple. He had a fight on his hands. Faldo started it with a birdie at No. 1. Lyle responded at the 134-yard second, almost holing his nine-iron tee shot.

Then came Lyle's narrowest escape. At No. 5, Faldo holed from 20 feet for a two. At No. 6, Lyle suffered a double-bogey six, and his lead was down to one. But he quickly regained control, and he did it with the same seven iron that smoothed the way to his U.S. Masters victory — the shot from the fairway bunker that set up his closing birdie. This time he put his tee shot six inches from the flag on the 177-yard, par-three eighth. He backed that up with a birdie from 25 feet at No. 9, and went three clear.

He birdied the 10th as well. Faldo matched him there, but then bogeyed the short 11th and three-putted No. 14. Lyle was all but home free. McNulty's thrill came in the form of a charge down the stretch — an incoming 31 to tie his own course record of 65 and join Faldo in second place at 275.

Wang Four-Stars Pro-Celebrity—£201,600
Winner: Rodger Davis

It went from disappointment to delight for Rodger Davis. He had planned to tune up for next week's U.S. Open by playing this week in the Westchester Classic on the American tour. "But the invitation came so late that I decided to play here instead," he said. "What a good decision that was."

Indeed. Davis turned the sow's ear into a silk purse, making the Four-Stars Pro-Celebrity at Moor Park, Rickmansworth, England, his first victory in 18 months. Davis, who bolted into the second-round lead with a course-record 63, nine under par, locked up the win with a five-foot par putt on the final hole. His 69-63-71-72—275, 13 under par, gave him a one-stroke victory over Eamonn Darcy (72) and Jose-Maria Canizares (71).

The Four-Stars was notable for another reason, too — the return of Tony Jacklin after a three-year absence. It was a bittersweet return. His wife Vivien died just six weeks earlier. "Home is the last place I want to be at the moment," said the European Ryder Cup captain and former British and U.S. Open champion. He had played just six times in the previous three months, and so although his play was not notable, the fact that he returned was. He shot 80-79 in the first two rounds. "I was apprehensive, and it showed," Jacklin said. "My concentration went from time to time, circumstances being what they are. I'm not making any predictions, though, and I'm certainly not returning on a full-time basis." Jacklin said he planned to play in five or six tournaments a season, including, in 1988, the Bell's Scottish Open and the British Open at Royal Lytham and St. Annes, where he won the British Open in 1969. It was a third-round 73 that encouraged him. His final-round 83 gave him a 315 total, 27 over par, and put him in 102nd place, next-to-last.

Davis's 63 in the second round staked him to a three-stroke lead, at 12-under-par 132, after 36 holes. He overhauled Darcy, whose 68 left him second at 135. Davis struggled in the third round, and saw his cushion shrink in an outward 38. But he settled down coming home, and his birdie at No. 17 to Darcy's bogey-six left him the lead by one.

Darcy's putter betrayed him in the fourth round. He drove the green at the 320-yard 15th, but three-putted, missing his birdie on the second putt from 18 inches. Davis birdied the hole and pulled two strokes ahead, but at No. 17, he bogeyed after missing from four feet. But he led a charmed life.

Ahead of him, Canizares' 20-footer for a tying birdie lipped out at No. 18. Davis seemed set to give up the stroke anyway, when he drove into a bunker on the final hole, and could not reach the green. But he came out short of the green and chipped on. Darcy's last chance to tie died when he missed a 10-foot putt. Davis then stepped up and dropped the five-footer for his par and the title.

Volvo Belgian Open—£200,000
Winner: Jose-Maria Olazabal

Jose-Maria Olazabal, 22, the European Rookie of the Year in 1986 but winless in 1987, was not pleased. He had wanted to play in the U.S. Open this week, but he wasn't invited. He was informed he would have to qualify, and he was having none of that. Helping to win the 1987 Ryder Cup ought to count for something, he felt. So he opted for the Volvo Belgian Open, at Bercuit. The fates, it turned out, had opened a different door.

This was a curious victory, though. Opportunity kept hammering and Olazabal wouldn't answer the door. In the first round, an out-of-bounds tee shot at No. 18 kept him in check, and missing two short par putts kept him from opening up a big gap in the second. He seemed bent on self-destruction, unless one noted the results: A luxurious four-stroke victory over American Mike Smith at 67-69-64-69—269, 15 under par.

The first round ended in a very mixed bag, with four sharing the lead on 67, including a profusion of American Smiths. Mike, age 37, from Alabama, who led the 1987 European Tour qualifier, came home in 31 to the tie. Then there was Bob Smith, age 45, California, former American tour player. Also Britain's Paul Kent, age 25, 171st on the Order of Merit, who got into the Belgian Open by the skin of his teeth, as 10th alternate. He raced to four birdies over the last six holes. And then Olazabal, who had seven one-putt birdies over the first 12 holes, thought the lead was in his pocket until he hooked his tee shot out of bounds on the par-five 18th.

From there, a tie was the closest anyone would get the rest of the way. Gordon Brand Jr., fresh from a visit with a psychologist "to unscramble my mind," holed a nine-iron shot from 143 yards for an eagle-two at the 15th en route to a course-record 66 in the second round. That put him at 137, tied for second one stroke behind Olazabal, who continued to flirt with trouble, then dodge it. Olazabal missed two putts inside two feet and bogeyed twice, then made up for them with an eagle-three from 12 feet at No. 18 for 69—136.

The big jam at second place melted fast in the third round. Mike Smith rebounded from a 73 in the second round to a 63 and was second alone after 54 holes at 203, three behind Olazabal (64). Then the rout was on. Olazabal got two quick birdies in the final round, and was seven strokes clear with eight holes to play. He pretty much coasted in, and won by four over Smith (Mike). But the victory didn't completely soothe him. "I said, 'No, thank you,'" Olazabal said. "We showed the Americans we play good golf in Europe by beating them twice in the Ryder Cup, and I feel all the members of the winning team should have had automatic Open places."

Peugeot French Open — £283,420
Winner: Nick Faldo

Whoever first said golf wasn't meant to be fair must have had Denis Durnian in mind. When you lead all the way, and come within two holes of your first victory, only to have it snatched out of your hands — that isn't fair. But it is golf. Durnian, age 38, former club professional champion who joined the European tour full-time in 1987, led the Peugeot French Open at Chantilly through the first, second, and third rounds, and through the last 16 holes. Then poof! It was gone.

Durnian's game buckled, and Nick Faldo, tagging along behind, smelled blood — and pounced. Faldo, playoff runner-up to Curtis Strange in the U.S. Open the previous week, drilled a 30-foot putt on the final hole for an eagle-three and a two-stroke victory, his first win of 1988. Durnian fell to a tie for second with Wayne Riley, and could only shake his head. "I played the 17th like a 24-handicapper," he said. He pulled a two-iron approach shot into a clump of bushes, chopped out short of the green, chipped 20 feet past the hole, and made double-bogey six.

Faldo, never closer to Durnian than four strokes through the first three rounds, shot 71-67-68-68—274, six under par. Durnian, who returned 65-68-69-74—276, was comfortably out of Faldo's reach for three rounds. So down the stretch, Faldo had no reason to expect more than a tie. He was barely hanging on. He scrambled to save par at No. 15, and holed an eight-foot putt to save again at No. 16. But at No. 18, he smashed a three-wood 260 yards to the back of the green, then dropped the putt. He had done his part. Then Durnian did his, unfortunately for him.

Durnian's putting was fiercely hot in the first round. He had 25 putts overall, and 11 one-putt greens, seven of them ranging from 20 to 60 feet. His 65 gave him the lead by one over Keith Waters and Richard Boxall, one of the tour's hottest scorers. Boxall had four birdies and an eagle-two, raising his totals to 155 birdies and five eagles in 43 rounds.

Three big names never made an impact. Masters champion Sandy Lyle started with a 77 and missed the 36-hole cut. Strange, the U.S. Open champion, finished 13th at three-over-par 283, and Ballesteros tied for 14th at 284.

By a compelling coincidence, the final two holes were the pivotal ones. Durnian jumped to a five-stroke lead in the second round when he shook off a bogey at No. 17 and eagled No. 18, after a four iron to six feet. Faldo's six-birdie charge was blunted by a double-bogey at No. 17. The situation reversed itself in the final round — Durnian crashing to a double-bogey at No. 17, and Faldo making eagle at No. 18.

Monte Carlo Open—£210,084
Winner: Jose Rivero

Jose Rivero taught his putter a lesson: He sent it packing. It had betrayed him in the Peugeot French Open a week earlier, where he was embarrassed as the defending champion. A pair of 76s sent him out at the 36-hole cut. So he did what any exasperated golfer would do. When he arrived at the Monte Carlo Club, he went straight to the pro shop and bought a new putter. It paid handsome dividends immediately — the Monte Carlo title, the third European tour victory of his 13-year career and his first since the 1987 French Open.

"Maybe this putter is magical," Rivero said in tribute after outrunning Mark McNulty and Seve Ballesteros in the final round. Rivero had withstood the threat of two of the game's best for four rounds across the 6,198-yard, par-69 course to win by two over McNulty and five over Ballesteros. He played almost as though they weren't there. He was in a four-way tie for the lead in the first round, a group that included Ballesteros; he was one stroke behind McNulty, the 36-hole leader, and he tied with him after 54 holes. And in the last, he broke free down the stretch. Rivero returned 65-64-67-65—261, 15 under par. McNulty was 66-62-68-67—263, and Ballesteros 65-66-67-68—266.

Ballesteros's final figure, five behind the winner, was deceptive. He actually drew even with Rivero through the 14th. Then he came to the par-4 15th, a mere 294 yards long, and he found it too tempting. He decided to go for the kill, right then and there. The green was well within his powerful reach. But this time he hooked his drive into heavy rough, pin-high, then came out short, pitched about six feet beyond the hole, and three-putted for a double-bogey six. If that didn't hurt enough, Rivero holed from 12 feet for a birdie. The three-stroke swing took Ballesteros out of the running. Rivero had six birdies in the round, including a 50-foot chip-in from sand at No. 4. He was grateful for that one. "You don't expect that every day," he offered.

But it was good golf, not good luck, that kept him in the thick of things from the start. Ballesteros was at his explosive best in the first round. An outburst of five birdies in six holes carried him into a share of the lead at 65 with Rivero, Britain's Andrew Sherborne, and Sweden's Jesper Parnevik. Ever unpredictable, Ballesteros bogeyed three of the first five holes in the second round, and though he recovered for a 66, he had to stand aside for the onrushing McNulty, who crashed into the lead with a 62. Rivero, returning after a two-hour suspension of play due to fog, lipped the cup with a 40-yard chip shot on his final hole and finished 36 holes a stroke behind McNulty, 128-129. Ballesteros stood third at 131.

The incoming nine in the third round was crucial. McNulty put on a burst with some brilliant iron play that set him up for three birdies from three feet or less. They pulled him level with Rivero, who matched him in birdies but who also hurt himself with two bogeys. So Rivero (67) and McNulty (68) went into the final round tied at 196, with Ballesteros (67-198) breathing down their necks. Now the final drama. Ballesteros and McNulty both had outstanding records. Rivero had only the two previous victories — the Lawrence Batley International in 1984 and the French Open in 1987. He was not in an enviable position. The question was, could he hold up under the combined pressure of those two?

Rivero had answered the question in the third round. "It could still be my week," he insisted. It turned out he was right.

Bell's Scottish Open—£250,000
Winner: Barry Lane

"People kept telling me I had the potential," an elated Barry Lane said, "but you never really know until you actually win a big tournament." Lane, a 28-year-old Englishman, who set a record with seven trips through the European tour qualifying school, was weary of hearing about potential. In 12 years as a professional, his work was modest or less — victories in the 36-hole Equity & Law Challenge in 1987, the 1983 Jamaica Open, and two assistant club pro tournaments. Came the Bell's Scottish Open at the Gleneagles Kings Course, and his persistence was rewarded. He came from nowhere, ignored his nearest pursuers, Jose Rivero and reigning Masters champion Sandy Lyle, and took his first big championship by three strokes — the fifth first-time winner in 1988.

At the outset, Lane was just another name in the field. His one-under-par 70 left him six strokes behind the blistering 64 start by Rivero and Fred Couples. A 67-137 had him five behind Couples (68) after 36 holes. He finally sniffed the heady air at the top with a 66 for a share of the third-round lead at 203 with Peter Fowler (69) and Roger Chapman (67). Then a closing 68 did it, a 13-under-par 271. Lyle (68) eagled the final hole to catch Rivero (68) for a share of second on 274.

Rain, winds, and five-hour rounds failed to dampen Couples and Rivero (64s) in the first round. Couples enjoyed a no-bogey, seven-birdie trip, the last of which was a narrow miss of a 15-foot eagle putt at No. 18 that cost him sole possession of the lead. Rivero, winner of the Monte Carlo Open the week before, started with a three-putt bogey on the first hole, then raced off for six birdies and an eagle-three.

Couples shook off a headache and the rain for a 68—132 and the solo lead through 36 holes. Slow play bothered him more than the headache. "It seemed like forever out there, and I just didn't feel like standing around in the rain," he said. "But I could have felt a lot better and probably shot 75." Mike Harwood (65—133) was second, and two others blazed their way into share of third with Rivero (70—134). Fowler, former Australian Open champion, returned a nine-birdie 63. Britain's Stephen Bennett burned up the last five holes with an eagle and four consecutive birdies for a 65.

Then came the first of two big moments for Lane. "I don't mind leading at all," he said. "You have to go through that experience if you aspire to be one of the top guys." It was the power hitter's first lead ever in a big event. His 66, best of the day, included three putts at the 18th. He shared the lead with Fowler (69) and Roger Chapman (67) at 203.

Then one by one, they fell away in the final round. Couples, who slipped with a third-round 72, disappeared with a 76. Chapman (72) finished fourth, and Fowler (73) fifth. The outgoing nine did most of them in. But not Lane. He bogeyed the third, but rebounded for three birdies in succession for an outward 33. When he birdied No. 12 on a 25-foot putt, he was six shots ahead. It was clear sailing from there to his second big moment: His first victory, plus a berth in the British Open the next week.

KLM Dutch Open—£250,000
Winner: Mark Mouland

Some 20 months earlier, in November, 1986, Mark Mouland was happy just to be alive. But the auto accident broke, among other things, his right ankle and his left foot. Hardly the kind of thing an aspiring young golfer needs. "I still get pain," the Welshman said. But his spirit and persistence paid off handsomely in the KLM Dutch Open at Hilversum. With an explosive finish, he came from seven strokes behind in the final round to snap up the victory. Mouland shot 72-68-69-65—274, 14 under par, edging Des Smyth by one.

Mouland's victory actually was narrower than that. It almost didn't happen at all. Only the alertness of Argentina's Vicente Fernandez saved him at the last instant. Mouland and Fernandez, his playing partner in the final round, had forgotten to exchange scorecards at the first tee. They were putting their scores on the wrong cards all through the round. Fernandez spotted the error at the finish — just in time.

The tournament opened on a strange note, too. This may have been the Dutch Open, but it was Murphy's Law that ruled for England's David A. Russell. Murphy's Law may be summed up: If anything can go wrong, it probably will. Forget the probably. It did. Russell found a new way to draw a penalty. He struck a pine cone with his practice swing, the cone hit his ball, the ball moved a foot. It cost Russell a penalty stroke and a share of the first-round lead. With four birdies, an eagle, and the penalty, he was at 66, one behind leader Andrew Murray, of England. Both later drifted back.

Tony Johnstone, three-time winner on the South African tour the previous winter, moved to the front in the second round. For the moment, he won the technique-vs.-concentration battle he had been having with himself and posted a 66 that included eight one-putts and birdies on two of the last three holes. He stood on 134. England's Mark Roe, also with a 66, was one behind. Roe logged seven birdies and needed just 23 putts. He one-putted eight of the last 10 holes. He credited this mastery to moving the ball six inches farther away from himself at address. Johnstone also led through the third round with 68—202, three strokes ahead of Smyth and seven ahead of Mouland.

Johnstone's new-found command deserted him in the final round. He could chalk up only one birdie, and struggled to a 74 that gave him a joint third with Carl Mason at 276. Mouland, meanwhile, was on a tear. He collected five birdies and an eagle in his 65. Miguel Martin, the 5-foot-1-inch Spaniard, closed hard with a 66 to take fifth on 277, one ahead of countryman Jose-Maria Olazabal, a pre-tournament favorite. Olazabal was third after two rounds, but finished 71-71 for sixth on 278.

Scandinavian Enterprise Open—£250,000
Winner: Seve Ballesteros

Maybe some master scriptwriter staged the Scandinavian Open: "OK, Ballesteros, you give the fans a quick thrill, then drop back. Parry, you lead the first round. Marsh, you get the second, and Russell, you take third. Then Ballesteros makes a big finish and wins. Got that? OK, let's go."

Ballesteros arrived at Drottningholm, near Stockholm, refreshed after a week of fishing following his British Open victory. "I have found I am too tired to play well the week after a major," he explained. Maybe everybody should take up fishing. His opening 67 left him three strokes out of the lead; a 70 in the second round, five behind; a 66 in the third, one behind, and his closing 67 gave him a five-stroke victory with 18-under-par 270. It was his second victory in two outings, his third European victory of the season, and fourth overall, counting the Westchester Classic in America. It was also his 53rd career triumph, world-wide. The giant was loose.

Starting from No. 10 in the first round, Ballesteros birdied four of the first six holes with putts of eight, 12, 15, and 20 feet. He made a Ballesteros birdie at No. 1 (his 10th hole), chipping in after hooking his tee shot almost against the pro shop wall. Then he birdied the next two holes on 15-foot putts. He was eight under par with six holes to play when he made his first error. At No. 13, he ignored his caddy's advice on the distance and ended up hitting a nine iron 20 yards over the green. "It was my fault," he said, "I relied on my eye and it it too hard." It was the first of three consecutive bogeys. "I had the course by the throat," he said, "but by the finish, the course had me by the throat." The door was open to Australian Craig Parry, age 22, Italian Open runner-up. Parry started even hotter than Ballesteros. He birdied five of the first six holes and tied the course record with an eight-under-par 64 for the first-round lead by one over Mark Davis, Eamonn Darcy, and Gordon Brand Jr.

The 36-hole leaderboard was top-heavy with Australians — Graham Marsh leading on 66-132, followed by Parry (69—133), Peter McWhinney and Peter Senior (both 68—134), and Gerard Taylor (68—135). On a day when par took a battering — there were 31 scores in the 60s — the best Ballesteros could do was a 70 for 137, five strokes off the pace. But never mind the fireworks. The show was stolen by Simon Townsend, age 24, an Englishman who had missed the 36-hole cut nine times in 10 tournaments. He left the greens in ashes. He chipped in twice and needed only eight putts on the outward nine, and 20 in all in his 64—136. (Alas, the magic died. A third-round 82 doomed him to tie for 62nd.)

It was David J. Russell's turn in the third round. He not only took the lead, he won — incredibly enough — 15 tons of steel. That was the prize for a hole-in-one at the 181-yard sixth, which Russell aced with a seven-iron. Weighing the steel against the alternative prize, money, he took the £9,000 instead. At 66—202, he also took the lead by one over Ballesteros. But that was the last of him. An outward 40 in the fourth round carried him to a 77—279 and a tie for 10th. It also opened the door to Ballesteros, who needs no invitation. Ballesteros one-putted four of the first six holes, made the turn in 34, and rushed home for a 67. The six at No. 18 was barely noticeable. His 270 was five better than Taylor, who closed with a 69.

Benson & Hedges International Open—£250,000
Winner: Peter Baker

Golf lore is jammed with spectacular finishes, but you would have to hunt far and wide to find anything to match this one: How about two eagles at the same hole within a half-hour?

That's how England's Peter Baker, a mere 20 years of age, registered his first victory in three years on the European tour in the Benson and Hedges International Open at Fulford Golf Club. And the man he beat after a head-to-head duel over the last two days was none other than the veteran Nick Faldo. First, Baker, after fighting back from a three-stroke deficit, eagled the last hole on the last day to catch Faldo. Incredibly, they had matched cards — 68-68-66-69—271, 17 under par. In the playoff, Faldo birdied the second extra hole, No. 18. But Baker eagled again.

The tournament opened with the same script, different cast. Derrick Cooper and David Williams, of England, shared the first-round lead at five-under-par 67. Cooper had six birdies and an eagle, Williams had seven birdies. They were one up on Faldo, Baker, Mark McNulty, France's Emmanuel Dussart, and Craig Parry, the young Australian. Sandy Lyle started strong, going three under par through the first six holes. But he had caught the worst of the windy weather late in the day and had to be content with a 70. Christy O'Connor, Jr., who also opened with a 70, burst into the second-round lead with a 65 that included a birdie-eagle finish. He was at 135, a stroke better than a group that included Faldo (68), who ran off four consecutive birdies from the 11th, and Baker (68), who was long and straight off the tee and who finally was rewarded by his putter.

Then Faldo and Baker surged ahead for a battle that would run for two days. Their third-round 66s put them two strokes ahead of the field. But it did seem like Faldo's week. In the final round, Baker fell behind Faldo by three strokes three times, but refused to stay put. The last time was at No. 15. Time was running out on him. But a two-stroke swing there — his birdie to Faldo's bogey — instantly brought him to within one. That's how they stood coming to No. 18, a 488-yard par-five with a slight dogleg right. A birdie would put Faldo ahead of Jose-Maria Olazabal (65) and Parry (67), who had already finished at 272. Faldo got his birdie, putting out first to turn up the pressure on Baker, who had fired his five iron second shot over the bunker to 15 feet. Baker ignored the pressure and holed the eagle. It was on to a playoff.

They halved the first hole, and went to No. 18 tee. Faldo pulled his two iron tee shot to the left, behind some trees, but rescued himself with a brilliant low, running two iron to the edge of the green. From there, he putted stiff to the hole for a sure birdie. Baker, meanwhile, had hit an excellent drive, then a five iron to 18 feet. Then he rolled it in. Faldo calmed his disappointment and paid the tribute where it was due. "It's just what we need," he said. "Peter fills the 10-year gap after people like myself, Lyle, Ballesteros, and Langer. I hope this victory will inspire the other young players."

PLM Open—£198,780
Winner: Frank Nobilo

It takes more than good golf for a man to win his first. For one thing, he has to hold up under pressure. Meet New Zealander Frank Nobilo, a fourth-year man on the European tour. He finally put it all together at the PLM Open, turned pressure-proof, and the March of the First-Timers rolled on. Nobilo was the seventh first-time winner of the season, the second in two weeks, and the third in six weeks. Under August weather at the par-70 Flommen Golf Club, at Falsterbo, Sweden, Nobilo grabbed the lead at the start and held on for a wire-to-wire victory with rounds of 63-68-71-68 for a championship record 10-under-par 270. The pressure on him was top-grade — veteran Howard Clark. Clark tightened the screws with a closing rush, but Nobilo stood his ground. And Clark, despite a fourth-round 66, fell a stroke short.

Golfers get help from all sorts of places. Nobilo may have found a first. "I want to thank my father-in-law," he said. Nobilo's putting had gone sour. His father-in-law sent him an old blade putter, the hint being, "Here, try this." It worked from the start. He had seven birdies and an eagle in the first round. He was off and running with two quick birdies, holing from 20 feet at No. 1, and from short range at No. 2 after nearly making a hole-in-one. Three more deuces and an eagle-three from 30 feet carried him to the course-record 63 and the first-round lead by one over American newcomer Peter Persons, age 25.

Clark was a distant five strokes off the first-round lead on a 68 that might have been worse but for a splendid recovery from, of all places, the Baltic Sea. Clark had to take off his shoes and socks and stand knee-deep in the Baltic to recover his tee shot off a little patch of dry land beyond the green of the par-three 12th. He made a wonderful pitch to inches, and salvaged his par. That helped save a round that was coming undone. After three birdies in the first six holes, Clark missed a birdie from three feet at No. 10 and three-putted twice for bogeys coming home.

The other challengers evaporated. Among them: 14-year British veteran Tony Charnley, seeking his first win, was second after 36 holes with 66-66 — 132, then blew to a 76 and finished tied for eighth. Persons crashed to a tie for 40th after middle rounds of 76-78. Colin Montgomerie, the promising young Scot, was sidetracked by a third-round 74 and tied for third.

Nobilo was about to put a near-lock on the PLM by the halfway point till he watered his second shot at No. 18 and took a double-bogey six. Before that, his friendly putter got him down from 10, 15 and 18 feet for three of his four birdies. The third round threw yet another test at the hopeful. Gale-force winds racked Flommen, but he held on for a sparkling 71, his only above-par round, and a 202 total. Clark was outstanding in the foul weather with a 68 to move into a tie for second at 205. Now was the time for experience to tell. Clark made his move, carding that final-round 66. But Nobilo refused to crack, and the tour had its seventh first-time winner in 21 events.

Carrolls Irish Open—£232,172
Winner: Ian Woosnam

If form charts mean anything, Ian Woosnam had as much chance of winning Carroll's Irish Open as he did of flying. But it was his time. Not only did his touch return, but he was the only one who could handle the brutal wind of the last two rounds. Look at it this way: How can a man shoot a final-round 70 and win by seven strokes? The Portmarnock scoreboard was a great wind gauge. The first two rounds, played in relatively friendly weather, were sprinkled with sub-par scores. In the third, there were only five rounds under par 72, and only one in the 60s, Roger Chapman's 69. In the fourth, again only five sub-par rounds, none in the 60s. The low was 70, one by Bob Shearer, the other by Woosnam.

This was the Woosnam who had slumped so badly after that sensational 1987 season. He righted himself long enough to win the Volvo PGA late in May, then slumped again. Then he came crashing through at Portmarnock late in August. He took the lead in the third round, returned 68-70-70-70, 10-under-par 278, and won by seven over Jose-Maria Olazabal, Des Smyth, Manuel Pinero, and Nick Faldo, all at 285.

The disappointment had to be sharp for Olazabal. He held the first-round lead with a 66 and announced, "I wish I could play like this all my life." He was out in 33, bogeyed the 10th, then ran off three consecutive birdies. He led by one over Vicente Fernandez (who was ruined by 75-80 in the middle rounds), and by two over the surprise of the tournament, Eoghan O'Connell, 20-year-old Irish amateur who plays collegiate golf in America at Wake Forest. He was tied for third at 68 in the first round, and finished strong, tied for 15th at 289. Woosnam enjoyed his best start in a long time, a 68 set up by birdies on five of his first seven holes, all from 10 feet or less.

Olazabal kept the one-stroke lead through 36 holes with 70 — 136. He had the better of the day, finishing before the foul weather arrived in the afternoon. So did Howard Clark (66 — 138), who tied for fifth with Woosnam (70). The end came for one notable — defending champion Bernhard Langer. Still troubled by both a sore back and the yips, he shot 77 — 149 and missed the 36-hole cut.

Woosnam and bad weather seemed made for each other. He took the third-round lead with 70 — 208, and Olazabal, struggling with the elements, dropped to second (74 — 210). The finale was hardly artistic. Faldo made his move with one of the best outward nines, a 34. But at the 10th, after a big drive, he left his pitch short, then three-putted. Woosnam was ripe for the catching. At the first, he hit a drive some 350 yards, to within 30 yards of the green, then dumped his second into a bunker just in front of him. At the third, he three-putted for another bogey-five.

The door was open, but Olazabal couldn't step through. He matched Woosnam's errors, three-putting the first and third. Woosnam settled himself at No. 4 with a sharp three iron that knifed through the left-to-right wind and reached the green. He got his par, then birdied the fifth and sixth with 15-foot putts. He added another birdie at No. 10, and another at No. 16. He wasn't within shouting distance now, much less striking distance. The battle for second place ended in a traffic jam, with Olazabal closing with a 75, and Smyth, Pinero, and Faldo with 73s.

German Open—£283,465
Winner: Seve Ballesteros

If anything would bring Bernhard Langer out of his deep slump, it would be the German Open. Langer, the inspiration for German golf, had won the German Open four times. Maybe it would inspire him this time. He was suffering a variety of torments — a bad back, a shriveled confidence, and worst of all, the return of the yips that had attacked him early in his career. He came into the German Open, at the Frankfurter Golf Club, having missed the 36-hole cut in six of his last seven starts. The home spectators notwithstanding, there would be no miracles here. Langer made the cut, but he was never closer to the lead than five strokes, and he finished tied for

29th at 276, 13 behind. But even a rebirth might not have mattered. Seve Ballesteros was on the prowl again.

Ballesteros never led until the final round, when he came charging up with a nine-under-par 62 — "Almost a perfect round," he said — to win his third consecutive start (British Open, Scandianavian Enterprise Open) and his fourth of the European season. Gordon Brand Jr. led him by three strokes going into the last round, and shot a 70, but couldn't outrun him. Ballesteros shot 68-68-65-62 for a 263 total, 21 under par, and a five-stroke victory over Brand. It was small consolation to Brand that Ballesteros's 62 merely tied the course record he himself had set in the third round.

But there were some new names atop the leader board before it was over. Jimmy Heggarty, a 13-year veteran from Northern Ireland looking for his first victory, joined first-time winner Mike Harwood (Portuguese Open) in the first-round lead with 65. Heggarty had seven birdies and 10 one-putt greens. He didn't go above 70 the rest of the way, but slipped to a tie for 17th with 274. Harwood's 69 in the second round got him a share of the 36-hole lead with American Bob E. Smith (67-67) at 134. Smith never went *above* 70, but had to settle for a tie for sixth with 271. Harwood dropped to a tie for 29th with a closing 74. The horror story of the tournament was written by Sam Torrance, who was struggling enough this year as it was. An opening 74 left him needing a 68 in the second round to make the 36-hole cut. But at the par-five fifth, his 14th hole, he drove into a clump of trees, took two to get out, five more to reach the green (including a bunker shot), and when he finally holed out, he had a 10. His 11-over-par 153 total missed the cut by 11.

Ballesteros was blazing in the final round, but he didn't settle things until the final nine holes. He had run off three consecutive birdies from the fifth and was out in 32 but made up only one stroke on Brand and trailed him by one. Ballesteros caught him at No. 11 with a 12-foot birdie, then took the lead for good when Brand double-bogeyed No. 13 after driving into a bunker. Brand rebounded for two birdies, but Ballesteros matched him with two of his own at the 14th and 15th. Ballesteros then settled the matter with an explosive finish — an eagle-three from 40 feet at No. 17, and a birdie-three from 20 feet at No. 18. Statistics buffs were awe-struck. Ballesteros was a cumulative 100 under par for nine completed tournaments.

Ebel European Masters-Swiss Open—£393,258
Winner: Chris Moody

It was another of those Ballesteros finishes, a run-'em-over charge that leaves them wondering what hit them. But this time, it wasn't Seve Ballesteros. The European tour's hottest golfer, seeking his fourth consecutive victory and his second in two weeks, was merely one of the astonished victims. So was Irish Open champion Ian Woosnam, seeking his second in succession, and so was Anders Forsbrand, the defending champion. The Ebel European Masters-Swiss Open fell, and fell hard, to someone few had ever heard of — a 34-year-old Briton named Chris Moody. A closing flourish that rivals anything yet seen, and the tour had its eighth first-time winner of the year.

This one was right out of Hollywood. Moody was in his 12th year on the tour. He came to the Crans-sur-Sierre course 102nd on the Order of Merit, and all but broke. His sponsors had abandoned him two years earlier. To save money, he had his girlfriend caddy for him. He had missed the 36-hole cut in eight of his previous 10 starts. And until his explosive finish, he was never closer to the lead than three strokes. All this, and he had to run the gauntlet of not only the defending champion, but two of the biggest names in the game. Moody posted 68-68-67-65 for a 20-under-par total of 268 to win by a stroke over Woosnam, Ballesteros, and Forsbrand. This on a course that took a real pounding. The 36-hole cut came in at one-under-par 143, 68 of the 72 finishers were under par 288, and only one was at 289.

Moody, three strokes off the lead in the fourth round, opened with three consecutive birdies, shook off a double-bogey six at No. 4, and added six more birdies. Coming down the stretch, he was dazzling. He swept past Ballesteros and Woosnam with birdies on four of the last five holes, including a 45-footer after a weak approach at No. 17.

Ballesteros opened his bid for a fifth victory with a nine-birdie 65 in the first round. That put him 107 under par for his European outings, but he insisted he wasn't playing the best golf of his career. In 1986, he noted, he won four tournaments in succession and six overall. Jimmy Heggarty and Bill McColl shared second with 66s. Ian Woosnam shot a 68 that would have been much better but for an embarrassing bogey-bogey finish off a fluffed chip at No. 17 and a hooked tee shot at No. 18.

Ballesteros held the lead through 36 holes at 133 with a hard-won 68. Rain flooded the course and delayed the start by over an hour, and then he and others were stranded in mid-round when fog reduced visibility to a few yards. Nick Faldo, using a new "popping" technique with his putter, returned his second 67 and joined Woosnam (66) in second place at 134. Woosnam then moved in front in the third round with 66 — 200, a stroke ahead of Ballesteros (68) as Faldo slipped away on a 71. Through all three rounds, Moody plugged away in anonymity. He was three strokes behind in each round. Then came the dynamite finish. What would the victory mean to him?

"I'll be able to pay off my overdraft now," Moody said, "and maybe buy a second-hand Ferrari."

Panasonic European Open—£300,000
Winner: Ian Woosnam

You couldn't blame Nick Faldo if he was beginning to believe that someone was sticking pins in a doll. Consider this: In the Panasonic European Open, he shot 66-65-66-66, a 17-under-par 263 — and was second by three strokes. That's one way to measure his frustration. It's also one way to measure Ian Woosnam's brilliance. For Woosnam won with 65-66-64-65 — 260, 20 under par, breaking the tournament record by six strokes over Sunningdale's Old Course. This was Woosnam at his front-running best. He trailed only once, by a stroke to Denis Durnian (64) in the first round. After battling early in the season to find the magic of 1987, Woosnam thus logged his second victory in four weeks and his third of the season. He won the Carroll's Irish Open four weeks earlier and the Volvo PGA in May. Aside from these and a second in the Ebel European Masters a week earlier, it had been a season of little more then teeth-gnashing. The same for Faldo. Aside from the French Open title, it was a season of seconds. This was his seventh, including the U.S. Open.

Judging from the scores, you would have thought the tour had stopped at a pitch-and-putt course. But they had caught par-70 Sunningdale at its agreeable best, in four days of near-perfect weather, and made the most of it. The course yielded 1,479 birdies and 66 eagles, and the 73 four-round players were a combined 255 under par at the end. Not everybody found it so sweet. The travails of Bernhard Langer ground on. There were 47 scores in the 60s for the first round, but he returned a 75, and only four out of 146 scores were higher. The 36-hole cut came in at one-over-par 141, and his second-round 74 put him out by eight strokes. Also out: the once-promising Paul Way, defending champion, on 70-72 — 142. It was his 14th miss of the year.

Woosnam made an early statement in this one, an eagle at the first hole. In the second round, his short game and his putter rescued him from some of the worst driving he's ever known. He had nine-one-putt greens, four of them to save par after escaping greenside bunkers. The patchwork 66 got him a share of the lead on 131 with Durnian (67), Mats Lanner (63), and Nick Faldo (65), who might have shot 60 but for a strange putter. His steady game got him to the green, but his putter kept leaving him short of the hole. In the third round, Woosnam (64 — 195) took the lead by two on Faldo (66), and was on his way.

Woosnam wasted no time in the final round. At No. 1, he hit a seven-iron to 12 feet and holed for an eagle-three. That set the pace. The shot that really settled him down, though, he decided, was the eight iron to five feet for a birdie at the seventh. Faldo thought the outcome turned on the 11th, where his pitch hit the flagstick and bounced 18 feet away. He got some revenge at No. 14, an eagle-three that almost was a deuce. His five-iron shot just barely missed going in. But is was too late, anyway. Only once in Woosnam's career did he fail to win when he was leading going into the final round, and that was a week ago in the Ebel European Masters. He returned to form here and had his 11th European tour victory in six years.

Lancome Trophy—£400,000
Winner: Seve Ballesteros

You know golfers. They make a 65 and say, "It should have been a 64." Seve Ballesteros is no different. "It's a pity about that runner-up place in the Swiss Open," he said with a grin, after running off with the Lancome Trophy. "Five in a row would have been a record." Well, four victories in the past five starts, and six overall, isn't bad. This one, at the par-71 St. Nom la Breteche course near Paris, was almost ridiculously easy. On 64-66-68-71, Ballesteros led by four strokes in the first round, five in the second, six in the third, and won by four with 15-under-par 269. From the second round on, Jose-Maria Olazabal (273) was the man closest in his wake.

Peugeot Spanish Open champion Mark James said it all in the first round. "Seve holed every putt he faced," James said, after a 68 left him a joint second. Ballesteros needed only 11 putts in an outward 30 and only 26 in all in his 64. He one-putted seven times in the first nine holes, and five of those were for birdies. He and Ian Woosnam (69), who won the Panasonic European Open a week earlier, were the only men in the field of 66 to go bogey-free the first day. "I like the course very much," Ballesteros said in understatement. "It is tight and long, and the greens are the best I have ever seen them."

Not everyone would agree. Nick Faldo, frustrated after "burning" the hole all day, settled for 72. Sandy Lyle missed 10 putts between eight and 12 feet, and was 11 strokes behind on 75. Woosnam, undaunted despite not getting better than a 69 out of a bogey-free round, threw down the challenge. "Five strokes are nothing over three rounds," he said. But 13 over two rounds are, and that's where he was with a 74 in the second round, after Ballesteros again rode a hot putter. "Golf is a lot of fun when you make the putts," he said. "I'm enjoying things right now." He logged six birdies in the second round, and suffered his first bogey in two days with a three-putt from 25 feet at No. 8. Olazabal was second at 135 after an up-and-down 66. He hooked into trees twice for bogeys on par-five holes, but got five birdies, including a chip-in from sand at No. 6 and three in succession at the end. Lyle returned a 63, a whopping 12-stroke improvement, and was eight strokes off at 138.

Ballesteros's big task now was to keep his concentration. "When you get so far ahead, it's hard to stay focused," he said after the third round. He recalled blowing a seven-stroke lead over the last 11 holes in a Belgian event 11 years earlier. But so far, so good. He shook off a gloomy, rainy day, adding four more birdies — three on the inward nine — and suffering only his second bogey in 54 holes. His 68 — 198 put him six ahead of Olazabal (69), who again was troubled by erratic drives.

Ballesteros's concentration finally slipped in the last round. He bogeyed the fifth, eighth, and 10th — that's five bogeys in 72 holes — but still managed a par 71. His lead was down to three at one point, but Olazabal suffered no delusions. "It was too late," he said, "and still too much against a guy like Seve."

German Masters—£286,625
Winner: Jose-Maria Olazabal

This was more than just a victory for Jose-Maria Olazabal, the young Spaniard. It also was a taste of deliverance and a sip of revenge. When he outran the field in the final round to win the German Masters at Stuttgart, one of the men he left in his wake was none other than Seve Ballesteros. The day doesn't go by when Olazabal, age 22, isn't described as either the second-best golfer in Spain or Ballesteros's heir apparent. The comparison may be flattering, but it also grows tiresome. As to revenge — Olazabal was runner-up to Ballesteros by four strokes in the Lancome Trophy just the week before, and in fact began the year tagging after him, runner-up by six strokes in the season-opening Majorca Open.

Olazabal didn't see the lead until the end. He shot 69-72-70 and trailed, respectively, by three, two, and one. A closing 68 — 279, nine under par, beat Anders Forsbrand (68) and Des Smyth (71) by two. Ballesteros, tied for the lead with Smyth and Mats Lanner going into the final round, made three double bogeys and a fell to a tie for sixth with 74 — 284. Lanner (76) dropped to a tie for 10th.

The obstacles melted away, one by one. The first-round leaderboard showed Eamonn Darcy at 66, Mark Roe at 67, and Gordon J. Brand, Tom Purtzer, and Bernhard Langer at 68. Darcy was the first to go, victim of a second-round 76. Roe fell behind with a 75, then dropped like a stone with a closing 78. Brand was 76-75, and Purtzer 72-72. And Langer's woes continued. Still fighting the putting yips, he had switched to the long "Slim Jim" type of putter in vogue on the American senior tour. After that promising 68, a second-round 75 and a closing 79 threw him back into that rut.

Smyth shot a 68 and a share of the second-round lead at 139 with the help of his career 10th hole-in-one, a seven-iron shot at the 137-yard eighth. He was tied with Lanner, who erupted for an eagle and three birdies around the turn en route to his 70. Ballesteros came into view with a 70 — 142, and a vow: "It's a pity when a 67 turns into a 70, but I am playing well and one day I feel I will kill this course." Like everyone else, Ballesteros struggled on the tricky greens. He holed for birdies at No. 8 from 25 feet and No. 9 from six. But at the 16th, he left his first putt six feet short, and at the 18th, he put it five feet past. He three-putted both holes. Olazabal, meantime, was trotting along behind. He made his move with a 70 in the third round, and was one stroke off the lead.

Ballesteros got off on the wrong foot in the final round. At No. 1, he accidentally hit the ball twice on a tap-in from 12 inches. He three-putted for a double-bogey five at No. 3 as well. A four-birdie burst got him back to within a stroke of the lead, but at No. 16, he over-hit the green and ended up in a bush. It cost him a six, his third double bogey of the day. Not that Olazabal backed into the title. He made seven birdies of his own for a 68. The heir apparent of Spain was doing fine in his own right — the German Masters, the Volvo Belgian Open, and four seconds. Not a bad year's work.

English Open—£180,000
Winner: Howard Clark

If any one thing separates the sane golfer from the other kind, it is a sense of humor. At the inaugural English Open at Royal Birkdale, even the most resilient sense of humor may have been taxed. True, the field was not as strong as it might have been. The big guns — Nick Faldo, Ian Woosnam, and Seve Ballesteros — were off preparing for the Suntory World Match Play the following week. But what the English Open lacked in marquee attraction it made up for with more bizarre stuff than most tournaments see in a decade. That doesn't include the winner, by the way. Howard Clark, who had been painfully retooling his game a la Nick Faldo — with the same guru, David Leadbetter, in Florida — surfaced in the last round for his 11th career victory and his first since the two wins of 1987. His 72-

71-67-69 — 279, nine under par, was a three-stroke win over Peter Baker, who joined the tour's small army of first-time winners in the Benson and Hedges.

England's David Ray and Paul Curry and Sweden's Magnus Persson took the lead on two-under-par 70s, but the stiff wind and the cold off the Irish Sea dominated the first round. "Yardage meant nothing," said Baker (73), whose one iron off the first tee flew out of bounds. "A stroke from 130 yards could be anything from a wedge downwind to a four iron into it." Even putting was a problem. England's Lee Jones, destined to miss the 36-hole cut after a 77 start, had to re-place his ball about 10 times on the 11th green. Ray, on the other hand, hit what he admitted was a poor approach putt at No. 17. The wind blew the ball into the hole for a birdie. Persson seemed oblivious to it all. He one-putted nine times.

The weather turned blue and balmy for the second round. It seemed to shock some. England's Jeff Hall, who opened on 81, walked in after six holes. His playing partners, Bobby Mitchell of England and Per-Arne Brostedt of Sweden, plugged away — for a while. They bailed out at their 15th hole, Mitchell being 16 over par and Brostedt 20 over. Frenchman Frederic Regard might have flirted with the notion. He opened on 84, then plunged into a wierd golfing adventure. At No. 12 green (his third hole), he chopped at a bush three times trying to get his ball out. He made six, then a seven at No. 16. Now 20 over par, he holed a three wood from 245 yards for an eagle-two at No. 18. Coming home, he strung out four birdies from the third, and shot 75. He of course missed the cut, which was at 149. Clark had something going, but droped two strokes over his last five holes for 71 — 143 and was four behind. Des Smyth took the lead on 65 — 139, but let a course record slip away. He needed only a chip-and-putt four at No. 18 for 63. But he fluffed the chip into a bunker just in front of him, and took six.

Smyth held the lead through the third round on 70 — 209, and Clark took second with 67 — 210. Then Clark moved front and center in the finale with a five-under-par run from the sixth through the 17th. A good birdie at the sixth after a poor pitch triggered it. He added a birdie-two at No. 7, shook off some poor chipping, notably two fluffs at No. 12, and was on his way.

Jersey Open—£125,000
Winner: Des Smyth

American football has the word for it: "Blindsided" — to get hit from the blind side. It's so apt that it has spread into general use. It means to fall victim to something you never saw coming. English golfer Ross McFarlane would understand even if he had never seen a Super Bowl. He got blindsided on the final hole of the Jersey Open. And that's how Des Smyth came to win it.

McFarlane, the leader entering the final round, came to Le Moye's 18th needing only a par to win, a bogey to tie. But his errant tee shot hit a spectator and bounced into a bunker. He took three strokes to get out and staggered off with a double-bogey six. If anyone was more surprised than

McFarlane himself, it was Smyth and Roger Chapman. They had already finished and were preparing their runner-up acceptance remarks. Just that suddenly, they were in a playoff. Smyth, a hero of the winning Irish team in the Dunhill Cup the week before, then added the Jersey Open, his first individual European victory in five years, with a seven-foot birdie putt at the fifth extra hole. They had tied at 15-under-par 273, Smyth with 69-68-69-67, and Chapman with 68-68-68-69. McFarlane started the final round at 202, Chapman at 204, and Smyth at 206. Chapman and Smyth never led the tournament until they had finished and McFarlane crashed at the 72nd hole.

The first-round lead was shared by a fugitive from golf burnout and a miracle-worker. The first was Chris Moody, winner of the European Masters some two months earlier. "Golf had become just a grind, and no pleasure at all," Moody said. But golf had become fun again. He had just returned from a three-day crash course with guru David Leadbetter in Florida, and the session had restored him. He returned an eight-birdie, no-bogey 64, and tied the course record set a short while earlier by the man he joined in the lead, Stephen Bennett. Bennett made 64 the fast way — with birdies on the last five holes. He also manufactured a miracle par-four at the ninth, where he missed the green wtih his approach, moved the ball only three feet with his second, then holed out from off the green.

In the second round, a 71 cost Moody a share of the lead. But Bennett held steady with a 70 — 134, 10 under par, where he was caught by a man dosed with medicine. "I had a dreadful cold for about 2½ weeks," Carl Mason said, after a 68. "Now I have another one and my legs feel very weak." Not so weak, however, that he couldn't eagle the 497-yard 11th — two woods and a 15-foot putt. They held a one-stroke lead over Moody and Tony Charnley (67). Then with Bennett fading to a 75, McFarlane jumped into the third-round lead with a 65 that included a hole-in-one with a seven-iron at the 166-yard 12th. The ace helped boost him to a 14-under-par 202 total and a one-stroke edge on Mason (69).

McFarlane, who had missed the 36-hole cut in six of his previous seven outings, broke out the champagne to celebrate his ace. The next day, he was all set to pop another cork — until he found sand at No. 18.

Volvo Masters—£350,000
Winner: Nick Faldo

The Volvo Masters — the richest event on the European tour after the British Open — ended more than just the 1988 season. It also ended the unhappy and baffling reign of the King of Second Place — Nick Faldo.

Faldo finished second an astounding eight times in 1988, three of them in playoffs, including in the U.S. Open. And as the runner-up finishes mounted one by one, the problem, some observers said, was that although he was wonderfully consistent he couldn't score those bunches of birdies it takes to win. "You don't try *not* to make birdies," the frustrated Faldo had explained many times. Then, in the last week of October, in what amounted to a summit shootout, Faldo got those birdies — a final-round surge for a come-from-behind victory over Seve Ballesteros and Sandy Lyle at tough, 7,020-yard Valderrama at Sotogrande, Spain.

"I knew something had to happen," said Faldo, who had one earlier victory, the Peugeot French Open in late June. "Two weeks ago, Seve told me to stick with it. He said I was doing everything right and would soon win. Those kind words gave me a big boost." Ballesteros probably didn't mean this soon, though. After trailing by six through the first and second rounds, Faldo opened the last round at level par, two strokes behind co-leaders Ballesteros and Lyle. Ballesteros was the first to falter, dropping two strokes over the first four holes. Faldo passed him at No. 5, chipping in from 30 feet for a birdie. Faldo then drew even with Lyle at the par-four eighth. He dropped a soft sand wedge shot 15 feet from the hole and sank the putt for a birdie to go two under par. Then he took the lead with a scrambled birdie at the 551-yard 11th — tee shot into the rough, three wood to the green, and two putts for his four and his third birdie of the day. Lyle faded with bogeys at No. 12 and No. 14. But Faldo wasn't home free yet.

A revived Ballesteros started a charge on the incoming nine with birdies at the 11th and 13th to pull within a stroke. But his move died when he lipped out birdie putts of 25 feet at No. 16 and four feet at No. 17. Faldo shot 74-71-71-68 for a four-under-par 284 total and a two-stroke victory over Ballesteros, who closed with a par 72. Lyle drifted with a 75-74 finish and was third at par — 288. But until the final round, it was a Ballesteros-Lyle show. Each had seven birdies and tied for the first-round lead at 68. Roger Chapman and Ove Sellberg, with 71s, were the only other players in the 80-man field to break par. Lyle had made a prediction: Because of the course's terrain and layout, and the slick greens, he said that the winner would come from someone who had experience on the U.S. tour. Both he and Ballesteros did. But so did Faldo (74) and, to a lesser extent, Ian Woosnam (75). Lyle, by the way, finished the first round with a three-birdie flourish. He moved into the lead with 71 — 139 through 36 holes, nudging ahead of Ballesteros (72 — 140) with a birdie from 15 feet at No. 15. Ballesteros himself contributed to Lyle's cause when his seven-iron approach missed No. 18 green and cost him a bogey.

Then it was back to a tie in the third round, through swirling winds and spiked-up greens. Some spike marks at No. 9 ultimately cost Ballesteros the solo lead. He was just three feet from a birdie, but spike marks forced his ball off line. He declined to criticize tournament officials, except to note that someone should have been pressing down the marks at the end of each hole. So Ballesteros (74) and Lyle (75) were tied at 214 going into the final round. Faldo had picked up four strokes and stood third at 216. And while Ballesteros and Lyle labored the last day, the King of Second Place made his exit and Nick Faldo, the champion, emerged in his place.

12. The African Tours

At first it seemed no more than one of those delightful aberrations that spice up golf. When was the last time a Fijian won a golf tournament outside Fiji? It happened on the Safari Tour. The man was Vijay Singh, a former caddy who had failed in his attempt at the European Tour qualifying school. He decided to take a crack at the Safari circuit anyway. What a grand entrance. He won the Nigerian Open, the first event on the 1988 schedule. And in a playoff, at that.

But Singh did more than make a footnote to history: first Fijian champion. He set the tone not only for the Safari Tour, but for the European Tour as well. It was the Year of the First-Timer. In five Safari events, there were three first-time winners. Two weeks after Singh took the Nigerian Open, a young Briton, Chris Platts, age 24, held off Mark Mouland to win the Kenya Open. And the next week, former English Amateur champion Roger Chapman wrapped up the Zimbabwe Open (by a stroke over none other than the ambitious Mr. Singh). The veteran David Llewellyn, from Wales, was to make a similar mark. He made the Zambian Open his third Safari victory, then went on to score his first-ever European victory in the Biarritz Open. He was, by the way, one of eight first-timers on the European Tour. It was a year to remember.

The turmoil was not confined to the Safari and European circuits. The fortunes of golf put a completely different face on the early segment of the 1988 Sunshine Tour. In previous years, there always was a dominant player, usually Mark McNulty. For comparison, take the early segment of 1987. McNulty won four events, and Fulton Allem and Tony Johnstone two apiece. But there was no McNulty to contend with in early 1988. Not the real one, anyway. McNulty didn't come out until the first Bloemfontein Classic early in February (there was another in November), after finally recovering from the bout with pneumonia that had knocked him out for about two months. And he was understandably weak, erratic, and rusty when he returned. And Fulton Allem was just around long enough to win once, then he was off to the American tour, where he finished 73rd on the money list. So in the January-March segment of the Sunshine Tour there were nine tournaments and nine different winners. John Bland came the closest to being the dominant figure. He warmed up with a joint second in the Bloemfontein Classic in early February, a solo second two weeks later in the AECI Charity Classic, and then a four-stroke victory in the final event, the Trustbank Tournament of Champions, in mid-March.

Allem, for years the No. 2 man behind McNulty, kicked off the Sunshine Tour in early January by winning the Palabora Classic before heading to the United States to join the American tour. Tony Johnstone stayed on a roll, taking the ICL International, his first victory of 1988 but his third dating back to late 1987. David Feherty delighted the fans at the Lexington PGA when he invented a new way to celebrate a victory. Actually, it was as much an exercise in sweet relief as anything. He nearly blew a five-stroke lead; and when he finally pulled the victory in, he fell to his face and kissed the

18th green. He also pleased himself by winning the coveted berth in the World Series of Golf, which the year before launched Allem, with runner-up winnings, onto the American tour.

The early segment was marked by a number of highlights. Wayne Westner scored his first victory, taking the Southern Sun South African Open, and Jeff Hawkes got his first, the Bloemfontein Classic, which also was the first tournament at Bloemfontein in more than a decade. But Hawkes had to survive some real heat to do it. McNulty celebrated his return from pneumonia with a Sunshine record-tying 61 in the third round. In the AECI Charity Classic, Bobby Lincoln went on a tear — a tour-record eight consecutive birdies in the final round. His reward was fitting. He won.

The scramble on the Sunshine Tour suggests that a rising tide of talent was bringing on a kind of parity, much like that gripping the American tour and the same that seems to be evolving on the European tour. The evidence, however, is too fresh and thin to be conclusive just yet. It would have been more convincing had McNulty and Allem been on the scene when all this was going on. But the best McNulty could do after his return from illness was that 61 in the first Bloemfontein and a joint second in the final early segment event, the Trustbank Tournament of Champions.

Tony Johnstone brought things back into focus when the Sunshine tour resumed later in the year. And he did it with a vengeance. He had fallen silent after taking the ICL in January, but he woke like a bear in November, winning the Minolta Copiers Match Play and the second Bloemfontein Classic back-to-back, and taking second in the Safmarine Masters and the Goodyear Classic.

As for Allem, there is no telling what he might have done had he been on hand for the entire season. But he was off to the American tour after winning the tour-opening Palabora Classic in January. He would return and, aside from a distant finish in the year-ending Goodyear Classic, wrap up the season in December the way he started it — with a victory. The biggest of his career. The man they said didn't belong in the Million Dollar Challenge justified the faith sponsors had in him with a 66-69 finish and a one-stroke victory over American Don Pooley. It was a time for rejoicing for Allem, but for gloom for Bernhard Langer. The putting yips, that enemy from early in his career, had returned with a fury at mid-season and reached their meanest point that week. His best round was a two-over-par 74. Two closing 78s left him 18 over par for four rounds and 28 strokes behind the winner.

For a lot of players, and for different reasons, 1989 was going to be a compelling year.

Nigerian Open—£52,975
Winner: Vijay Singh

You had to read the newspaper again, slowly. Who was it who won the Nigerian Open? Vijay Singh? Never heard of him. Who had?

This was Vijay Singh, a Fijian now living in Malaysia, who came from nowhere to outlast Scotland's Mike Miller at the Ikoyi Club at Lagos. January was ending and the 1988 Safari tour was just beginning, and Singh added a new dimension to the expression "surprise winner." Some in the field knew him, but slightly. "I missed the four-round qualifying cut at the PGA school at La Manga," he said, "but I'm hoping for a few European tour invites." A little biographical detail emerged: Singh, a slim six-footer and a big hitter, was a month short of his 25th birthday. He was taught the game by his father, for whom he used to caddy. His parents were living in New Zealand, and his two brothers, both golf pros, were living in Australia. Singh took a club pro job in Malaysia after finishing fourth in the 1985 Malaysian Open.

As things turned out, this race went not to the swift nor the strong, but to the steady. Doors were wildly flung open all over the place, and Singh plugged away and walked through. Miller was merely the last to step aside. Miller, the 1979 rookie of the year and a non-winner, took the first-round lead with a six-under-par 65. Bunched at 69 were four others who were about to fall victim to golf's whimsy. Jeffrey Pinsent and Ewen Murray shot 76s in the second round. Anthony Stevens, just a stroke behind Miller's lead in the second round, posted a 76 in the third, and Joe Higgins blew to 75s in the second and fourth. Fate was clearing a path for Singh.

Singh didn't come into the picture until the third round, when his 68 lifted him to a tie for second with Miller, both at three-under-par 210 and two strokes behind Paul Kent of England. Kent was yet another man marked for self-destruction. It came in the form of a 77 in the final round, dropping him to a tie for fifth. As Kent unraveled, Singh and Miller emerged. Singh was on a hit-and-miss course. He dropped shots at the fifth, 10th, and 14th, but he more than offset them with birdies at the second, 12th, 13th, and 15th. Miller was steadier, but no more productive. It came down to a tense finish.

Singh, leading by one at No. 17, bogeyed. That left it up to Miller at No. 18. He was five feet from a winning birdie. But his putt stopped just inches short, and his tap-in par left them tied at three-under-par 281 — Singh on 72-70-68-71, and Miller on 65-72-73-71. The playoff was quick. Singh made a par-five on the first extra hole, and Miller didn't.

Singh was not only a surprise winner, but a surprised one. He took one look at his trophy and grinned. "It is engraved 'Nigerian Open Champion 1987,'" he said. That year's event was canceled, but they didn't bother changing the date. Singh didn't care. He not only had his first victory, but the biggest check he had ever seen — £8,829.

Ivory Coast Open—£76,923
Winner: Gordon J. Brand

It's getting to the point that this one ought to be called "Gordon J. Brand and Friends" — meaning the "friends" are playing for second place. Brand, 32, the pleasant and self-effacing 12-year veteran, sprinted down the stretch and took the Ivory Coast Open for the third time in five years. The victory was the sixth of Brand's career, all of them on the Safari circuit. This one was no simple matter, however. The Ivory Coast Open turned on one of those things that drive golfers crazy. Losing a ball or hitting out-of-bounds is one thing. But to be high and dry and still not have a shot is something else. That's what happened to England's James Annable.

It happened in the fourth round, with Brand and Annable dueling for the lead. At the par-three 12th, Annable had an uncertain moment. Then he was relieved. His tee shot had cleared the lake. When he got to the ball, it was a new story. He was on dry land, but he found himself with an impossible lie still within the margin of the water hazard. He chose to go back and play over the lake again, but this time overshot the green. He ended up with a double-bogey five. Brand solved the hole for a par-three, and just that abruptly was three strokes clear. But, of course, it wasn't over yet.

Annable closed in, fighting back furiously for birdies on the next two holes. But Brand was no stranger to pressure. In the 1987 Dunhill Cup at St. Andrews, for one example, he was on the English team playing for the championship against those old enemies, the Scots. Perhaps little was expected of him, since his teammates were the renowned Nick Faldo and Howard Clark. But Brand more than did his bit for the English victory, crushing Sam Torrance in the final, 64-69, for a 3-1 record for the week. Now he had to respond to Annable's charge, and he did — with four consecutive birdies from No. 13. He breezed home for the title. Brand returned 68-71-67-69 — 275 at the Yamoussoukro Sporting and Golf Club, a two-stroke victory over Richard Fish. Annable's closing 72 left him two strokes further back, tied for second with Tony Stevens on 279.

Brand's victory was in some doubt earlier. He held the first-round lead with 68, a stroke ahead of Fish and Annable, then with 71—139 slipped three strokes behind in the second round to Annable's 67—136. Brand regained the lead in the third round with his best score of the week, a 67 for a 206 total and a one-stroke edge on Annable. A surprising show of strength came from Ireland's John McHenry, who came back from two 74s with two 66s for a 280 and a tie for fifth place with Joe Higgins and Vijay Singh, winner of the Nigerian Open the week before.

Kenya Open—£70,470
Winner: Chris Platts

Golfers will do anything for help — change their swings, take up good-luck pieces, get new equipment. Chris Platts got his inspiration from a far more fundamental source — desperation. Platts, 24, son of 1965 Ryder Cupper Lionel Platts, had taken a wild fling at the Safari circuit. A professional since 1981, he had to go back to the European tour qualifier five times, and in 1987 he slipped to 168th on the Order of Merit and failed again in the qualifying tournament. Undaunted and without a sponsor, he had to borrow £2,500 to play the Safari tour. His faith paid off.

Platts, withstanding a furious closing charge by Mark Mouland, shot 66-65-72-68 — 271, 13 under par at Nairobi's Muthaiga Club, to take the Kenya Open for his first big victory. He won by one stroke over Mouland (71-67-70-64 — 272).

Gordon J. Brand was the pre-tournament favorite, off his Ivory Coast Open victory the previous week. But win one week, struggle the next. He opened with a 75. Platt birdied three of the first four holes and raced to a five-under-par 66. He had six birdies in all, and except for a bogey-five at No. 18, was rarely in trouble. Ross McFarlane (68) was second.

The temperature topped 100 degrees in the second round, and Platts was hot, too. A 65 gave him the best two-round total of his career, an 11-under-par 131 that kept him two strokes clear. His chaser this time was David Jones (64—133), after McFarlane blew to a 76—144. Platts owned the par-fives. He birdied all four, even the 534-yard 18th after topping his second shot. A brilliant 100-yard pitch-and-run set up the birdie. Jones also romped on the par-fives. He birdied three, then eagled No. 18 with a 10-foot putt. Brand bounced back for a 68—143, and was fighting eye trouble. He thought it was the heat, drying out his contact lenses. "Everything was blurred," he said, "and my eyes were red and sore." But it wasn't the heat. It was an eye infection, and it would keep him from defending his Zimbabwe Open title the next week. Brand finished at 76—294, and flew home immediately.

Mouland's charge caught Platts down the stretch. Mouland exploded into the final round with five birdies in the first seven holes, sinking putts of 25 and 30 feet and holing a bunker shot to make the turn in 31. Platts went ahead by two with a birdie four at No. 10 and a birdie two from 25 feet at No. 11. But his big test was coming.

At the 15th, Platts bogeyed and Mouland birdied, and they were tied. But Platts never flinched. Mouland missed a birdie from five feet on the final hole, and it cost him a 63. Platts calmly got his birdie from 10 feet for a 68 and locked up his first big victory. One other man had reason to celebrate. The surprising Vijay Singh ducked into third place with 69—275 and jumped to the top of the Safari money list with £15,800.

Zimbabwe Open—£44,145
Winner: Roger Chapman

Squeegees and umbrellas were almost more important than golf clubs in the Zimbabwe Open. This one ought to be an "asterisk" tournament in the record books. It ended up as a 70-hole tournament, cut short in the first round when rains lashed the Chapman Club at Harare so furiously that officials had to lop off the flooded par-three third and the par-four sixth. In a marvel of coincidence, the Chapman Club was conquered by former English Amateur champion Roger Chapman, who birdied the final hole to edge out Vijay Singh for his first title in eight years as a professional. Chapman shot 63-70-71-71 — 275, six under par, for a one-stroke victory over Singh (64-68-72-72), who entered the tournament as the surprise Safari Order of Merit leader.

Appropriately enough, however, it was Richard Fish who led the storm-battered first round. He was out after the two holes were ruled unplayable and before a second storm turned greens to soggy earth and bunkers into little ponds. The course was reduced to 16 holes with a par of 65. Fish birdied three of the par fives and eagled the fourth en route to a 61, four under par for the holes played, to go two strokes clear over a group that included Chapman at 63. Fish eventualy slipped back and finished tied for ninth at 279.

All 18 holes were in play for the second round, and Singh, as had been expected, moved to the front. Singh, who won the Nigerian Open in his first African outing, was stamped as the pre-tournament favorite after Gordon

J. Brand had to withdraw and fly back to England for treatment of an eye infection. Singh rewarded his backers by taking the 36-hole lead, adding a 68 to his opening 64 for a 132, one ahead of Fish (72), Chapman (70) and Mark Roe (69). Singh twice holed 15-footers for birdies on the soggy, slow greens.

In the fourth round, Chapman escaped one threat when Carl Mason bogeyed two of the last three holes to finish two strokes behind, tied for third. Now Singh's putting set up the final test. He birdied the last two holes, from 25 and 15 feet, for his 72. Chapman needed a birdie at No. 18 to win. He faced a chip shot to a green swampy from yet another storm, so first he had to call in the squeegee crew. Then he chipped close and holed the putt for the birdie-four and the victory.

It was a long-overdue reward for the Kenya-born Chapman, 28, who lives in England. After turning pro in 1981, the former Walker Cupper was second in the Spanish Open, second twice in the Zambia Open, and second in the 1987 Kenya Open, where he lost in a playoff. In the 1987 Swiss Open, he was in second place heading into the final round, and then, he admitted, "went to pieces" after his wife called to inform him she had given birth to their first son.

Zambian Open—£75,000
Winner: David Llewellyn

For the golf fan with an eye for adventure, there were two shows going on in the Zambian Open. The first was obvious enough — David Llewellyn's running battle and one-stroke victory over Richard Fish. The other was a classic in solitary golf — a man battling himself. This was rookie John McHenry, just two weeks from his 24th birthday. McHenry, a 1987 Walker Cupper from Ireland, turned professional and won his European tour playing card in December. But barely. He tied for the 50th and last spot. In the Zambian Open at the par-73 Lusaka Golf Club, he was riding a mad pendulum: 77-71-76-66. And when have you seen a show like that? Not that he had been a threat to win. His two-under-par 290 was 10 big strokes off Llewellyn's winning 280. The point is, might this performance be a footnote to a bright career some day?

The pendulum started from the other direction for lanky Englishman Joe Higgins, 28, who failed to win his card in December. He found instant magic in a borrowed putter and raced off to a four-stroke lead with 67 in the first round on the muddy 7,200-yard course. Fish was second on 71; Llewellyn, tied for third with 72.

But the magic left that borrowed putter in the second round. Higgins soared to a 79 on his way to a 289 total. The real battle was just shaping up. Llewellyn took the 36-hole lead on 70—142, and Fish was tied for second at 72—143. Llewellyn led by three after the third round, 68—210 to Fish's 70—213. Then came a wild finish. Fish, age 29, was looking for his first victory in 11 years as a professional. Llewellyn, age 36, was a two-time winner in his 15 years as a professional. He also had teamed with Ian Woosnam to give Wales the World Cup victory over Scotland's Sandy Lyle and Sam Torrance in Hawaii in December. In fact, Llewellyn sank the winning putt.

Llewellyn led by three going into the final round, but Fish immediately trimmed that to one with two quick birdies. And almost as fast, Fish found himself four behind after he bogeyed No. 3 and Llewellyn birdied twice, No. 4 from 10 feet and No. 5 from 25. But Llewellyn wasn't safe in the barn yet. He overshot the green at No. 8 and bogeyed, and Fish rushed in again with a stunning burst — a birdie at No. 12 on a 40-foot putt, a two-putt birdie four at No. 13, and an eagle-three at No. 14 on a 20-foot putt. The awe-struck Llewellyn found himself tied.

But now experience paid off. Llewellyn had tasted such pressure in winning the 1972 Kenya Open and the 1985 Ivory Coast Open, and he held firm while Fish stumbled to a fatal bogey at No. 17, after putting his drive into the trees. Fish drove into the trees again at No. 18, but recovered brilliantly. Too late. Llewellyn locked up his third career victory with a tap-in after nearly holing his pitch-and-run. Llewellyn shot 72-70-68-70—280 to Fish's 71-72-70-68—281.

Palabora Classic—R200,000
Winner: Fulton Allem

"I know we came here to get a bit of sunshine," said Briton Andrew Chandler, "but this is ridiculous." Temperatures of over 100 degrees greeted the Palabora Classic at Han Merensky Country Club in the northeastern Transvaal in January — weather almost guaranteed to take a golfer's mind off his work.

The next order of business was putting. "A person who needs 34 putts should be selling Cokes after the first two rounds," said Fulton Allem after the first round. "I had eight birdie putts inside 10 feet, and I made only one of them. The greens got me totally confused."

The heat at the Palabora finally broke a bit, and Allem, who was seeking his third consecutive Palabora title, did not have to resort to selling Cokes. He won easily, by four strokes.

Allem, who would be leaving shortly to join the American tour, wasn't as bad off as his putter led him to believe. He was one of only 10 of the 155 starters to break the par of 72 in the first round. His 70 left him two strokes behind leaders Robbie Stewart, Steve Van Vuuren, and Wilhelm Winsnes, all with 68s. Stewart highlighted his round by holing a 50-yard approach for an eagle at No. 16. Van Vuuren's chance for the outright lead died at No. 6, where he had to waste a stroke to get his tee shot out from behind a big tree in the fairway.

Clouds mercifully lowered temperatures for most of the second day, and the scores fell with them. Winsnes, who started at No. 10, shook off three-putt bogeys at his second and fourth holes and took the halfway lead on 70—138. The other two first-round leaders backed off, Van Vuuren with a 73 and Stewart with a 72, leaving Winsnes one stroke ahead of Scotland's Ian Young (67—139). Young, also starting from No. 10, sprinted through the turn on 31. Allem scored four birdies, but dropped two strokes and settled for third on 70—140.

Young ran into trouble midway through the third round, taking a bogey at No. 9. He tripped again at the 16th, when he put his second into a dam. He finished with 73—212, two behind leaders Winsnes (72), Allem (70), and European tour regular Teddy Webber (68), all at 210.

Young's closing 69 gave him the best finish of his career, a joint second on 281 with Ireland's David Feherty, who posted a course-record 65. This, however, was Allem's day.

"When I hit a bad tee shot at the eighth, which almost went in the water, I thought that was, 'Goodnight, nurse,'" Allem said. "But I was lucky enough to stay on dry land, then almost sank my chip, and I knew this was going to be a lucky day for me."

Allem parred the first two holes, then birdied the third from about eight feet. He came up empty on an excellent birdie opportunity at the fourth, but made up for it with an eagle at No. 5 that boosted him to a 67 for an 11-under-par 277 and put him into some high company. Bobby Locke, Gary Player, and Dale Hayes were the only others to win three consecutive titles in a South African event.

ICL International—R200,000
Winner: Tony Johnstone

The 1988 ICL International might be looked back on someday as a launching point of future stars. There were, for example, Hendrik Buhrmann, 24, a third-year pro who made a strong challenge before finishing tied for eighth, and the American rookie Nolan Henke, who returned a course-record 64 in the first round on his way to a third-place finish. The 1988 ICL might also become known as the tournament that didn't begin until the third round. Note that defending champion Tony Johnstone started 66-66—132, and was no better than fourth at the halfway point.

The par-72 Zwartkops Country Club course at Pretoria, remodeled with four new holes since the 1987 ICL, was knocked silly. For the first time in Sunshine circuit history, it took better than par-144 to make the 36-hole cut. The cut figure was 143. The course had already been thrashed — 1,082 birdies and 29 eagles in the first two rounds. Buhrmann returned two 65s for a 14-under-par 130 and a one-stroke lead over Denis Durnian (66-65) and Ian Young, who tied Henke's course record with a 64 in the second round. Johnstone (66) shared fourth.

After a thunderstorm halted play on Wednesday afternoon, 42 players had to start at 6:45 a.m. on Thursday to complete their first round. "I love getting up early in the morning," said Buhrmann. "It's lovely out there." Three birdies in four holes will brighten anybody's day. A quick breakfast, and off he went again for another 65 and the best 36-hole performance of his young career. "I went into something of a mental and physical slump after failing to get my European tour card," he said. "It all feels OK now."

Ian Young, for one, wasn't ready to concede anything. "I'm ready to win," said Young, whose second in the Palabora the week before was his best ever. The 64 left him flying. "It was a dream out there, it was so easy," he said. "I just wish it was like this every day."

But it isn't. A 73 in the third round took Young out of the picture (he would finish tied for fourth), and opened the door to Johnstone. His 65 for 197 left him three strokes clear of the field after the third round. Durnian (69) and Buhrmann (70) shared second at 200. Then the fourth round turned into a Johnstone-Durnian battle.

It looked more like a runaway for a while. Johnstone took a four-stroke lead with an eagle at the 10th. "I thought that was it, and that it should be fairly comfortable from then on," he said. But his lead shrank to one when he three-putted No. 12 and No. 14 around Durnian's eagle at No. 13. They parred through to a nail-biter at No. 18. Both had birdie putts of about eight feet. Johnstone missed his, and now Durnian could tie him. But his birdie putt slipped past, and Johnstone tapped in his par for a 69, and a tournament-record 22-under-par 266. It was not only a repeat ICL title, but his first Sunshine victory of 1988 and his third dating back to November, 1987. In retrospect, maybe Johnstone found his victory in the sand. He had got up and down from bunkers eight times in the tournament.

Lexington PGA Championship—R200,000
Winner: David Feherty

You can celebrate a victory any number of ways — jump up and down, shoot a hand into the air, or dance around like a man gone slightly berserk. David Feherty found a new way when he holed the winning putt on the final hole of the Lexington PGA. Expressive Irishman that he is, he simply fell face down on the green and kissed the ground. A pilot might do something like that after a scary landing, but a golfer? Well, when you see your five-stroke lead melt to just one in the home stretch, and you still get home safely...

But there was a lot of golf to be played at the par-70 Wanderers at Johannesburg before Feherty would get to do his belly-flop.

Hendrik Buhrmann, the young South African who challenged at the ICL International the week before, zipped off to the first-round lead on a 64, and held a two-stroke lead on a group that included Eamonn Darcy, the Ryder Cup Irishman who had delighted South African PGA officials by electing to play. Feherty was well back with 69. In the second round, despite a 65, he inched up on the lead by one stroke.

That was because the second round belonged to Hugh Baiocchi, who tied the course record with a 63 for a one-stroke lead at 130 after 36 holes. "I've had a love affair with the Wanderers for a long time," Baiocchi said. His round included seven birdies and eagle-three on a 30-yard sand wedge shot at No. 5. Shortly after he finished, a severe storm halted play, leaving 57 of the 156 starters to complete their rounds the next morning. Defending champion Fulton Allem (64) was among the finishers, just a stroke off the lead. Darcy (67) stood third at 133 off a wild round of one eagle, four birdies, and three bogeys. Feherty (65) was in a group at 134.

Then Feherty made his move, flawed as it was. He was within reach of the solo lead in the third round until he bogeyed the final two holes. He shot a 66 and was caught at 200 by Baiocchi (70). Then came the final round, and St. Patrick's Day arrived on the Sunshine circuit about two months early — an all-Irish finish.

Feherty started tentatively, dropping a stroke at the first. But before long, his lead grew to a whopping five strokes at one point, and he seemed ready to coast. Then up jumped trouble.

Darcy birdied No. 13, No. 15, and No. 16, and finished at 65—268. Then Feherty bogeyed the 16th and the 17th, and his lead was down to one.

"I knew what I had to do," Feherty said, "and I hit probably my best two shots of the day to the 18th green. That left me with about a 20-foot putt, and I put my first to about a foot away — a very long foot, mind you."

Feherty covered that long foot with his next putt, and when the ball dropped, so did he — face-first. The par gave him a 67, a 267 total, and the PGA title by one stroke.

Southern Sun South African Open—R150,000
Winner: Wayne Westner

The Southern Sun South African Open was a battleground of moans, groans, and tears. Wayne Westner was the one with the tears. That was one happy fellow when he took the title. It was his first victory since 1983.

The moans came from golfers fighting the ferocious winds that battered Durban Country Club the first day and whipsawed the field over the outgoing nine. It caused some peculiar scoring. Simon Bishop, for example, posted a deceptive-looking 71: He was out 40, back in 31. But Eamonn Darcy seemed immune. He shot an eight-under-par 64 for a four-stroke lead over a logjam of 68s — American Carl Cooper, Englishman Denis Durnian, Welshman Peter Evans, and South African Derek James. Westner was a stroke back at 69.

Darcy's putter cooled in the second round, but not enough to open the door to anyone. He stayed four strokes ahead with a 70—134. Cooper, a rookie, might have closed in on him except for some awful luck. He made the turn in two under, then got burned at No. 11. His seven-iron second shot hung up high in a tree, and since he couldn't identify it, he was assessed a two-stroke penalty for a lost ball. That cost him a double-bogey six. He birdied No. 18 for 71—139, five off the lead.

Westner stayed in the hunt with 70—139, but it was a bouncy 70. He birdied the first, then three-putted for a par at the third, wasting a birdie chance. On the next four holes he missed four putts of under 12 feet. Even so, he was three under par after No. 11. Then he crashed at No. 12. His tee shot hit the green and rolled off and down the hill. He put his next over the green and down the other side. When it was all over, he had a double bogey. But he was still confident. With a little more help from his putter, he said, "I'll be there on Sunday."

Next, the groans.

Darcy was two strokes behind Westner's lead (71—275) after the third round, but he never made it to the fourth. Nor did David Feherty, who won the Lexington PGA the week before, and two Americans, Dean Prange and Chris Anderson. The starting times for the last day had been moved up for a 3 p.m. finish on television. Apparently some never got the message. All four missed their tee times and were disqualified.

In the fourth round, Westner and Ian Mosey both bogeyed the first, and Durnian birdied and took the lead — briefly. He blew up, and finished at 75—280 and a tie for third. So the stage was left to Westner and Mosey, and they practically wore it out.

After a grueling battle, they came to No. 18. Mosey needed a birdie to stay alive. And when he missed from 20 feet, Westner had the luxury of two putts from five feet for a winning par. But he holed for his birdie instead, and a two-stroke victory, 71—275 to Mosey's 71—277.

Westner admitted he almost cried coming down the last fairway. He was approaching not only the second victory of his career, but the first since the 1983 ICL International. "I honestly didn't think it would be that emotional," he said. "In fact, I still feel like I'm dreaming."

Bloemfontein City Classic—R200,000
Winner: Jeff Hawkes

It was a case of cruel and unusual punishment of a golf course. In the Bloemfontein City Classic, the first tournament there in more than a decade, par was nothing but a three-letter word. Of the 65 finishers, 59 were under the par of 288, one matched it, and only five were over. And every one of the 65 finishers broke par 72 for at least one round. There's more: Jeff Hawkes set the course record of 64 the first day, young American Jay Townsend lowered it to 63 the second, and Mark McNulty — returning to action after pneumonia sidelined him for more than two months — lowered it again the third day, this time to a breathtaking 61 that tied the Sunshine circuit low. A 61 — and he didn't win.

Despite the onslaught, Hawkes, age 34 and a professional for 12 years, was not about to be sidetracked from his first victory. He shot 64-69-66-69 — 268, 20 under par, to win by one. He was bumped from the lead only once, by Townsend's 63 in the second round. Townsend, age 25, who had to prequalify after missing the cut at the South African Open and the Lexington PGA, returned 68-63-72-66 — 269 to tie for second with John Bland (67-67-68-67).

Hawkes set not only the pace but the tone of the tournament with his opening 10-birdie, two-bogey 64. He broke from the gate like a race horse. Starting from the 10th, he roared through the turn in 30, carding seven birdies, a par, and a three-putt bogey at No. 15. That helped him to a one-stroke lead over American Andy Morse, who must have felt rejected. Morse's worst single round was a par 72, and yet he finished tied for 19th.

In the second round, Hawkes' 69 looked thin compared to Townsend's nine-birdie 63. "For the first time this year," Townsend said, "I putted like somebody with a heartbeat." What stopped him from breaking 60 was what he called a "dry spell" — a string of five pars from the ninth. By day's end, the course had been stung for more than 1,000 birdies through two rounds, and it took one-under-par 143 or less to make the 36-hole cut. Hawkes was tied for second, two strokes behind Townsend's 131. It would be the last time he would trail.

Even so, he was barely noticed in the third round, despite a 66. McNulty's rampaging 61 — he began with seven consecutive birdies — blotted out just about everything else.

It wasn't a pitch-and-putt cakewalk. McNulty had to play real golf, and also get a few breaks. His birdie at No. 2, for example: "I pulled my drive left, and had to play a low five iron under the trees to make the green,"

McNulty said. He put it to 15 feet, and made it. He missed the green at No. 3, but still birdied. At No. 4, he hit a tree with his tee shot, but it bounced back into the open, and he hit another at No. 11 and got the same break.

Ironically, McNulty had only just made the cut at 74-69 — 143. The 61 rocketed him over a small army to a tie for fifth at 204 after 54 holes, five strokes behind the leader, Jeff Hawkes (199).

Hawkes, who turned pro in 1975, finished second three times on the European tour but never better than third on the Sunshine circuit. "It's time I won," Hawkes said. "I am ready to win."

And so he was. He missed four greens on the outward nine, but each time managed to get up-and-down. He settled down coming in. After a bogey at the 13th, he played the last five holes in one under par for a 69—268. Townsend nearly tied him. At No. 17, he narrowly missed his second ace of the tournament. A 66 left him tied for second with Bland at 269. McNulty served notice that the vacation was over with four birdies in the last six holes for 68—272, a tie for sixth.

Danglo Tournament of Champions—R265,000
Winner: Mark James

In the Danglo Tournament of Champions, the attack on Germiston Country Club was awesome — 57 players broke par-72 in the first round, and 25 others matched it. Veterans Hugh Baiocchi and Mark James, and a young American, John Cyboran, led the assault with 66s. Most eyes were on pre-tournament favorite Mark McNulty. He was suffering an assortment of ills, and therefore at his most dangerous. But 71 was the best he could do.

McNulty, recently back from a 10-week layoff with pneumonia, had a sore back and a sore wrist, but declined to alibi. He simply said he wasn't putting well. He finished a solid third at 277.

This helped build the case for those who believed that Germiston was becoming a graveyard for South Africans. Back in November, 1987, Fulton Allem was set to win the Prosure Challenge, but Bobby Lincoln grabbed it away. This time it was Hugh Baiocchi on the verge of victory, and England's Mark James, who had suffered his worst year on the European tour in 1987, slipped in and filched the title. There was nothing suspect about James's two-stroke victory — 66-70-69-69 — 274, 18 under par 274.

Baiocchi and James stamped themselves as the men to beat with the opening 66s. "I've been working hard on my putting stroke, and it's starting to pay off," said Baiocchi, who had six birdies in his bogey-free round. James, age 34, who finished 32nd in Europe in 1987, said he had been tinkering with his swing. "I think I know what I'm doing now," he said. Apparently so. He carded four birdies, and an eagle at No. 2 from less than a yard.

The final battle came down to the two of them, but first there was the shaking-out process. Cyboran drifted back with a second-round 73, en route to a tie for fifth at 279. Ian Mosey moved to the top in the second round on 67—135, which was good for a one-stroke lead on Baiocchi (70), McNulty (65), and James (70), who blew a chance for the lead when he watered his tee shot at No. 18. It cost him a triple-bogey six. Meanwhile, the attack on par continued. It took even-par 144 to make the 36-hole cut, and 77 players made it. The most prominent victim was Order of Merit leader Tony Johnstone, who exited on 76—147.

James was confident, despite a third-round 69—205 that left him one behind Baiocchi (68). "I'm really looking forward to the next two days," James said, though there was only one day left. "Tomorrow I can win because I'm swinging well and my putting is good. Then on Sunday I will be back at home in Leeds."

Baiocchi started the final round with two birdies, then cooled. Two bogeys on the incoming nine sealed his fate. James locked up the win with three consecutive birdies, the last of them at No. 13 after a superb four iron to 25 feet. He bogeyed the final hole for a 69—274, and the victory by two over Baiocchi (72). It was James's first Sunshine victory in eight years, and he knew where it came from. "I didn't leave myself a second putt of more than six inches all week," he said.

AEIC Charity Classic—R150,000
Winner: Bobby Lincoln

Nobody actually gave it a name, but this was the final "McNulty Week" on the Sunshine circuit. The pneumonia was well behind him and the Masters lay dead ahead — he had received the precious invitation — and McNulty was straining to get in shape for Augusta. The AECI Charity Classic at Randpark, Johannesburg, was the last of three consecutive Sunshine tune-up tournaments since his return from the long illness layoff.

"These are the only three events I'll be teeing up in before the Masters," McNulty said of three consecutive Sunshine circuit appearances. "So it's absolutely essential that I get my game sharp here in South Africa."

Nor did McNulty intend to baby his weary body and rusty game. "After a 10-week break from golf...the last thing I need to do is take it easy," he insisted. He hadn't won, but under the circumstances, he had done well — a joint sixth at Bloemfontein and a solo third at the Danglo. So he was the man under the microscope. While everyone was watching him, the AECI opened with a surprise.

Jim Becker, a little-known American, posted a bogey-free, six-under-par 66 for a one-stroke lead in the first round. He would soar to a 75 in the second round, but still finished in a creditable tie for 11th.

Perhaps McNulty was as much of a surprise. Despite the rust and a stubborn fever, he was tied for second at 67 with Wayne Westner and John Bland.

This time, the bedeviled McNulty was suffering from tonsilitis. But he plugged away for a 71 in the second round. That got him a share — for a while — of the 36-hole lead at 138 with American Eric Booker (68) and South African Bobby Lincoln (70). But they had to wait overnight to be sure. Play was halted when a thunderstorm flooded several greens, leaving some 70 players to finish the second round the next day. Then the three "leaders" found themselves tied for third. Among the next-morning players was John Bland, and he wrapped up a 69 for a one-stroke lead with 136. Not over McNulty, et al., however, but over Wayne Player, son of Gary Player. Wayne came out that morning and finished off a 68 for 137.

Then came a wild third round. Player disappeared with a 77, the first of two. McNulty shot a 67, but Simon Hobday (67) and Desmond Terblanche (66) came from nowhere to catch him at 205. They led by one over Gavin Levenson (67—206) while Bland slipped to a 71 for 207. It was all merely prelude, however, to Lincoln's outburst.

Bland closed with a 66, McNulty with a 71, and Levenson with a 69, and they failed to dent the explosive Lincoln. Lincoln, who entered the last round three off the pace at 208, warmed up for seven holes, then roared through the pack with a Sunshine Circuit record eight consecutive birdies. The outburst carried him to a course-record 63, a 17-under-par 271 total, and a victory by two over Bland. Levenson (69) and Tony Johnstone (67) shared third on 275, and the "rusty" McNulty finished fifth at 71—276.

Helix Swazi Sun Pro-Am—R150,000
Winner: Don Levin

Fate was just hunting for new ways to vex Ian Mosey. He had missed the cut at the AECI Charity Classic the week before, and so it was a determined man who came to Royal Swazi for the Helix Swazi Sun Pro-Am. He was primed. "I have really been hard at it on the practice tee," he said. His reward was an encouraging 63 in the first round. Things were looking up. Then came fate. In the second round, darkness stranded him on the course. In the third, there was still more of the heavy rains that had swept the Mbabane area for days, this one forcing a long delay. And finally, the crucial missed putt on the 72nd green. It seemed that every time he set his teeth, something tripped him. It was a tribute to his grit that he even hung on to finish third.

The issue had to be settled in a playoff between two former American tour players, Don Levin, age 30, and Alan Pate, age 35. On this Sunshine circuit, Levin's best finish was a tie for 19th in the AECI a week earlier; Pate's a tie for 27th in the ICL International in January. They battled to a tie, and then before they could play off, rain halted play on Sunday, and darkness fell, and they had to return on Monday morning. Levin made it a quick day. He won on the first hole.

Mosey, who won the Holiday Inns tournament in 1981, got off to a flying start with a nine-birdie 63, nine under par. Royal Swazi was playing a bit soft after heavy overnight rains. Still the best anyone else could do was 66, that by Phil Harrison. Levin (68) was well astern by five strokes, and Pate (69) was setting himself up to be the surprise of the tournament.

Royal Swazi ws taking a beating. Of the 65 players who went four rounds, only four returned worse than a 72 in the second. Thus Pate (72) was shoved well back into the pack at 141, nine strokes behind Mosey's eventual 132 lead through 36 holes.

"Eventual" is the key word. Mosey was left in the dark — literally. He was on the 17th green when darkness stopped play and caught a number of players still on the course. Mosey came back the next morning and finished off a 69 that included three birdies and "13 tap-in putts for par." His 132 gave him a one-stroke lead on Levin (65) through 36 holes. Bunched at 134 were Trevor Dodds (66), Frank Edmonds (66), and Justin Hobday (65). Harrison, who also was stalled by darkness, completed a 69 in the morning and stood at 135 with John Bland (65).

The picture changed abruptly in the third round. Levin returned a 69 and Dodds a 68 to catch Mosey (70) at 14-under-par 202. And Pate came from nowhere to join the hunt, leaping a big crowd with a 64 for a tie for eighth at 205, three off the lead. He made up that deficit the next day with a 63 for a 268 total, and Levin tied him with a 66. Mosey, who led outright for the first two rounds and shared the lead in the third, had one final chance to keep pace. But he just missed a 25-foot birdie putt on the final hole, and he settled for a solo third finish at 67—269. "I hit every fairway and every green in regulation," he said, but I wasn't getting close enough. I did absolutely nothing wrong, but I just couldn't get out of third gear."

Trust Bank Tournament of Champions—R200,000
Winner: John Bland

The Sunshine circuit was coming to the end of its early-1988 segment with Mark McNulty still looking for his first victory. All-conquering just a year before, he was still struggling to regain his form after an attack of pneumonia that had put him out of action. McNulty said he was completely well, and he was looking for the boost of a victory before heading for the Masters in a month. So he came to the Kensington course in Johannesburg as the favorite in the Trust Bank Tournament of Champions. The dramatic moment was set. Except someone forgot to consult with John Bland, the Goodyear Classic winner in November, 1987 — long of tooth at age 42, but also long of determination. If anybody was conceding anything to McNulty, it sure wasn't Bland. He was a wire-to-wire winner, tied for the lead in the first round and the solo leader the rest of the way for a four-stroke victory.

Bland shot 67-66-67-68—268, 20 under par, for an almost untroubled walk over McNulty (68-67-69-68) and 26-year-old American Phil Jonas (67-69-67-69), former world junior champion, who tied for second at 272. Both went to the attack in the final round, but the flinty veteran shrugged and turned them back.

Every day, it was a different problem for Bland. He had to prove he was a pro, and he did. First, his tee shots and his iron play were just so-so. He weathered those inconveniences and returned a seven-birdie 67 in the opening round, joining five others, including Jonas, in the lead. Next, overnight rains made the demanding parkland course a grudging test. Bland shrugged that off, too, returning a six-under-par 66—133 and keeping McNulty (67—135) under wraps. Jonas slipped to third, a stroke further back on 69—136. Then came wind and rain, pummeling the golfers in the third round. It seemed tailor-made for Bland. He posted a five-under-par 67 and a 200 total. Jonas matched his 67 for a 203 total, and moved into second place, replacing McNulty, who fell to third at 69—204. Nothing seemed to bother Bland.

Finally, something did. The fourth round had been scheduled for Saturday, but heavy rains flooded the course, forcing the finale back to Monday. The tension was almost too much for Bland.

"That two-day wait took its toll on me," he said. "Mentally, I am very tired." But, obviously, not too tired.

Bland entered the final round leading Jonas by three and McNulty by four, and immediately found himself in deep trouble. Jonas made the first stab. He birdied No. 1. Bland bogeyed, and his comfortable lead had abruptly shrunk to one. But he regrouped and fired back, padding his cushion with a birdie at the third. From there, he gradually pulled away and he seemed to be coasting home. His problems were far from over, however. McNulty made a scary run at him, reeling off four successive birdies from the 11th. Then two bogeys sank him, and Bland had his 12th victory in Africa, and the 14th in his career.

Minolta Copiers Match Play—R250,000
Winner: Tony Johnstone

So far, 1988 on the Sunshine Circuit had been a year that no one was able to get a big grip on. Then up stepped Tony Johnstone, the wiry Zimbabwean who won the ICL International in January. The second segment of the 1988 tour got under way in November with the Minolta Copiers Match Play, and Johnstone swept through the field, taking not only his second title of the year, but his second consecutive Minolta championship. There was one real moment of doubt. It came on the day of the third and fourth rounds. First he ousted Ashley Roestoff in the third, 72-74, then had to go two extra holes to beat Allan Henning after they tied at par 72 in the 18 holes of regulation play. In a day of surprises, Johnstone was the only seeded player in the bottom half of the draw to survive.

"Survive" was an apt word for two rounds in dense heat and humidity. The weather whipped Denis Durnian, one of the seeded players. "This was all too much," Durnian said. "In this heat your brain just goes and your body can't take it any longer. My feet are covered in blisters and I'm exhausted." Durnian rolled to a five-stroke victory over Phil Simmons in the morning, but was sent out easily by Dale Hayes, 73-76. Fulton Allem, another seed, got to the fourth round, and was turned out by Ian Palmer, 70-71. Then a mild flap developed.

Many players complained about the format, which required those beaten in the fourth round to play off over three days for the ninth through 16th places. "There's only about £2,000 difference between the money for ninth and 16th places," one player said, "so it's like playing a three-day pro-am." Durnian and Allem departed after 10 holes of their playoff matches, complaining of knee injuries.

Johnstone won his way into the semi-finals with a 69 for a seven-stroke victory over Hayes. That put Johnstone against Palmer, whose 70 beat Swaziland's Joe Dlamini by four strokes. Wayne Westner spilled top-seeded John Bland in a lackluster match, 75-76. In the semi-finals, Westner beat Gavin Levenson, 71-73, and Johnstone edged Palmer, 69-70. Johnstone then wrapped up the title with a 71-73 victory over Westner.

Bloemfontein Classic—R250,000
Winner: Tony Johnstone

There would be no defending champion in the second Bloemfontein Classic of the 1988 (the result of a schedule move), and for the best of reasons. Jeff Hawkes, who won the first one back in February, had to go home to be with his wife for the expected arrival of their first child. But the way Tony Johnstone was playing, it might not have mattered who was in the field. Except for sharing the lead in the second round, Johnstone led all the way for his second consecutive victory in the Sunshine Circuit's late-1988 segment, and his third of the year. Johnstone returned 66-72-69-69 — 276, four under par on the par-70 Schoeman Park Golf Club, for a two-stroke victory over hot-closing Phil Harrison (66) and local assistant pro Schalk van der Merwe (70), who tied at 278.

Johnstone leaped to the front in the first round with a six-birdie, no-bogey 66, for a one-stroke lead over van der Merwe and Solly Mogare. A strong British challenge was grouping close behind. Harrison, sharp after lessons from Sam Torrance, logged two birdies and an eagle for 68, a joint fourth with Ian Mosey, who got six birdies, and Brian Evans, who joined the circuit to hone his game for the European tour school at La Manga in December. Evans got sharp in a hurry. He made two eagles. Malcolm McKenzie was at 70, and Denis Durnian, victim of the heat the week before in the Minolta Copiers Matchplay, was at 71. Heat was once again a factor, but most seemed pretty well adjusted by this time.

The field got some hope in the second round when Johnstone soared six strokes over his opening 66 and had to settle for a share of the 36-hole lead on 72-138 with Mosey (70) and van der Merwe (71). But that hope was ill-founded. That 72 was to be Johnstone's highest score of the tournament. Johnstone returned to the solo lead in the third round with a 69-207 that put him a stroke ahead of the gritty van der Merwe (70) and two ahead of European tour regular Teddy Webber (69). Mosey's bid suffered badly at the ninth, where he started with a drive into the trees and finished by two-putting from short range for a double bogey. A two-over-par 72 left him caught in a traffic jam at 210, a joint fourth that included Evans (70). Harrison, all but written off after a second-round 73, came back with a 71 and was five big strokes behind Johnstone at 212.

It would be a pressure test in the final round, the kind that club pros ordinarily don't survive. But the stubborn van der Merwe held up beautifully, returning another 70, and Harrison exploded for eight birdies and a closing 66. They tied at 278. Now it was up to Johnstone to collapse if anyone were to have a chance. But he declined to cooperate. His closing 69 was more than enough for a second consecutive victory and a strong grip on the Sunshine Tour.

Safmarine Masters—R250,000
Winner: John Bland

With three victories for the year and the last two in succession, Tony Johnstone clearly was building up a real head of steam. It was going to take a hot hand to derail him. And that's precisely what developed in the Safmarine Masters at the par-72 Stellenbosch Golf Club, Cape Town. It wasn't much of a surprise, however. The author was John Bland, who himself was enjoying a productive year. In the early segment of the Sunshine Circuit, Bland warmed up with two second places, then rushed to the Trustbank Tournament of Champions title by four strokes in mid-March, the final event before the spring-summer hiatus. The hot hand in this case was a third-round 63 that hurled him to the top of the leader board. Bland returned 69-70-63-73 for a 13-under-par 275 and a three-stroke victory over Johnstone (69-72-67-70 — 278).

In some respects, this was a third-round tournament. That's where it all happened. American Rick Hartman was the key figure in this oddity. Hartman opened with a 67 and shared the first-round lead with Wayne Westner, Nico van Rensburg, and Chris Williams by a stroke over Teddy Webber. A slight separation occurred in the second round. Westner shot 69 and Williams 70, and van Rensburg was on his way out with a 74. But Hartman came through with another 67 for a 134 total. He led Wayne Westner (69) by two, and was three ahead of Hugh Baiocchi (67) and Chris Williams (70), both at 137. Bland was a distant five strokes off the pace at 139.

Then came the third round that ripped up the field. Hartman was merely the principal victim. A 75 knocked him aside. Baiocchi took 74, Williams 73. Back in the pack, some little-known players who were in promising position through 36 holes crashed heavily. Three of them were at 139, tied with Bland, but not for long. Robert Richardson shot 74, and Peter van der Riet and Andries Oosthuizen 76 each.

Bland wasn't watching the wreckage, however. He was busy working up the 63-202 that carried him to a five-stroke lead on Wilhelm Winsnes (67) and Wayne Westner (71). But he couldn't close the gap. Winsnes finished with a 73 and Westner with a 74. If there was going to be a challenge, it would have to come from the marauding Johnstone. He tried, but it wasn't enough. Six behind going into the final round, Johnstone closed with a 70, but Bland was in such good shape that even his only over-par round, a 73, merely dented his cushion. Bland had coasted to his second Sunshine victory of 1988.

Million Dollar Challenge—US $1,650,000
Winner: Fulton Allem

They said Fulton Allem didn't belong. The eight-man field for the Million Dollar Challenge ranged from established golfers such as David Frost and Ken Green to all-conquering Ian Woosnam of 1987, the defending champion. On paper, the critics were right. Allem, fresh from a modest rookie year on the American tour (73rd on the money list), had made his name on the Sunshine Tour. Even there, he generally played second fiddle to Mark

McNulty, one of the favorites at Sun City. Nor could Allem stack up against Bernhard Langer, Chip Beck, Don Pooley, much less Woosnam. Allem himself conceded the point. "I do accept," he said, apologetically, "that out of the eight players here, I didn't have the record that matched up to everybody else's." But when it was over, he didn't have to apologize to anyone. He had not only the last laugh, but the last word. He was $1 million richer.

Allem broke out of the small pack with a surge over the last 36 holes for a 10-under-par 278 to hold off a charge by Pooley for a one-stroke victory and the $1 million prize. Allem returned 72-71-66-69 to Pooley's 67-72-74-66 at the Gary Player-designed, 7,665-yard course at the sports-and-gambling resort in Bophuthatswana. Then came Green at 280, Woosnam 283, Beck 284, Frost 285, McNulty 287, and eighth and last — suffering the worst case of yips in golf — Bernhard Langer. Langer returned 76-74-78-78 — 306 — 18 over par, 19 strokes out of seventh place, and 28 strokes off the lead.

The golf was hot and heavy, but the field lacked the sparkling names of earlier fields. The tournament threatened to become an all-American shootout from the start. Pooley and Green returned five-under-par 67s, sharing a four-stroke lead over Frost, a South African living in Dallas, and McNulty, a Zimbabwean living in Johannesburg. Pooley and Green clung to the lead through 36 holes, each with 72-139, a stroke ahead of Frost (69), while McNulty slipped with a 73. Then Allem came blasting through in the third round after a shaky start. "I had to pull myself together," he said. "Anybody who tells you he's not nervous playing for a million dollars, I think needs his head examined." Allem put together a seven-birdie, one-bogey 66, vaulting from fifth place to a share of the lead on 209 with Green, who shook off a bogey at the eighth and a double bogey at the ninth and birdied the last two holes for 70. They were two ahead of Woosnam (69-211). Pooley ran into difficulties that eventually would cost him the tournament. A third-round 74 dropped him to 213.

Pooley launched his charge in the final round, and was at nine under par and tied for the lead coming to the 18th. He was studying a birdie putt when the sound hit him. "I heard the roar from Fulton making that putt back at No. 17," Pooley said, "so I knew I'd better make my putt. I hit a good putt, but it broke more than I thought it would, and it hit the left side of the cup and stayed out." He settled for a 66. The pressure now was on Allem to hold that one-stroke lead. And confounding seers and thwarting the doubters, he did it with a par at No. 18 for a 69. He was one smiling man.

"I truly am grateful they did give me the invitation," Allem said. "I know next year there'll be no doubt."

Goodyear Classic—R250,000
Winner: Trevor Dodds

The second segment of the 1988 Sunshine Tour came to an end just before Christmas, leaving a lot of very surprised people in its wake, especially the prognosticators. Who should have won didn't; who could have won also didn't, and who didn't figure to win, did. Namely, Trevor Dodds, a third-year man who for the most part was quiet in the pack as the tournament made its way through four rounds over the testing Humewood Links at Port Elizabeth.

First, those who "should have won." Not to take anything away from Dodds, but on the early form chart the obvious favorites were Fulton Allem, who just a few weeks earlier had picked off the $1 million first prize of the Million Dollar Challenge; Tony Johnstone, who won three times, including the first two of the second segment of the tour; and John Bland, Safmarine Masters winner just two weeks earlier.

The "could have won" category consisted principally of rookie professional Ben Fouchee, former amateur whiz, and Mervyn Galant, who shared the first-round lead on four-under-par 67s. Dodds was at 70, Johnstone at 71, and Allem and Bland at 73. Fouchee, age 21, former South African amateur champion and runner-up in the British Amateur at Royal Porthcawl in June, added a 68 and shared the 36-hole lead with Wayne Westner (65) on 135. Galant slipped a bit and was third with 70-137. Dodds came in unnoticed at 68-138, sharing fourth with Johnstone (67) and three others.

At this point came a "what-might-have-been" — Dave Feherty exploding into the picture with a record eight-under-par 63. "I was putting for birdie on nearly every hole," Feherty said. He got two of them on the outward nine, and made another at No. 10, where he chipped in from 25 feet. It seemed like nothing more than a sub-par round until his blazing finish — an eagle and three birdies on the last four holes. The 63 knocked two strokes off the previous record, but that was his only consolation. Unfortunately, he had opened with a 77. He finished 74-73, well back at 287. Frustration, but of a lesser degree, was also the lot of Bland and Allem. Bland couldn't recover completely from an opening 73 and finished a joint fourth on 281; and Allem never really got going and finished at 285.

It was the third round that put Dodds' victory into sharpest perspective. He returned his third consecutive sub-par round, a fine 69, for 207 total, and faced an intimidating task. He was a joint second with Westner, Southern Sun South African Open champion in January and runner-up to Johnstone in the Minolta Copiers Matchplay in November. And together, they trailed the streaking Johnstone by two going into the final round.

Dodds didn't seem to notice. He kept his head down and closed with a 69 — 276, winning by one over Johnstone (72) and Westner (70). It would be a keener appetite he would take into the 1989 tour.

13. The Australasian Tour

Greg Norman was only in second gear for the latter part of the Australasian season, but that degree of power was enough to have him the only golfer to win more than one of the 19 top tournaments. In all he took four titles, but only the New South Wales Open was in the second half of the tour, when he was suffering the after-effects of the wrist injury sustained at the U.S. Open. Although Norman wanted to minimize the problems associated with that injury, it was noticeable when he returned for the event in Sydney, his swing was considerably shorter than before, and his coach and mentor, Charlie Earp, was concerned about what had happened. "You had the best swing in the world," he said. "Why change it?"

Norman threatened to play with consistent brilliance after he returned to the full backswing, but it will definitely require some more work, although a lot of the golf he played in the Australian Open at Royal Sydney and the Bicentennial Classic at Royal Melbourne was breathtaking. He remained the outstanding Australian golfer and, as a drawing card and role model for young people, has no peer in Australia; there are few to equal him in any sport in any part of the world. His success in recent years and his attacking approach to the game has made golf in Australia the fastest growing sport among young people.

It would be good to be able to say there were other golfers who won more than one event but, in fact, there were 14 single winners, although Curtis Strange and Ben Crenshaw surely would have had further successes had they appeared in more tournaments. Strange won well at Sanctuary Cove at the start of the tour, and Crenshaw was the leading player in the World Cup but, for brilliance and sheer excitement, first Mark Calcavecchia and then Rodger Davis were the most eye-catching in the Australian Open and Bicentennial Classic, respectively. Calcavecchia raced away from the opposition at the redesigned Royal Sydney course, winning with an astonishing 9-under-par score, six shots ahead of fellow American Mark McCumber. The following week Davis won the Bicentennial Classic at Royal Melbourne in a spine-tingling finish.

Of the one-time winners, it would be difficult to find one more popular than Wayne Grady, who claimed the PGA Championship from Norman on the fourth playoff hole at Riverside Oaks. Not everything has gone smoothly for Grady in recent years, but he has a giant-sized heart to go with his skill.

For the younger Australian brigade, Brett Ogle won his first tournament, finished third in the Bicentennial Classic and high up in several other tournaments, Ian Baker-Finch broke through for his best win in the Australian Masters at Huntingdale and Brad Hughes confirmed the promise he had been showing since turning professional when he won the Town & Country Western Australian Open. David Merriman had his first victory in the Ricky May Classic, but it would have been an even better year for the sport had one other player been able to notch more than an individual win.

A different structure within Australian golf in 1989 will see prize money estimated at around the $10 million mark, a great advance on recent years where the tour has struggled at times. This will not only be to the benefit of the professionals, but also will create even more interest with young golfers and spectators around the country.

Two American golfers, Calcavecchia and Jack Nicklaus, were responsible for mild cases of apoplexy in the corridors and watering holes at those famous clubs, Royal Sydney and Royal Melbourne respectively. Calcavecchia, with his startling par-shattering win in the Australian Open, Nicklaus for the quote which described Royal Melbourne's composite layout as a pleasant members' course.

Sanctuary Cove Classic—A$400,000
Winner: Curtis Strange

After winning the inaugural Sanctuary Cove Classic in Queensland, Curtis Strange said he thought he was just getting to the prime of his golfing life and that he was "really looking forward to the rest of the year." How right he was proven to be. There was also a touch of nostalgia about the victory because it was in Australia, 12 years earlier, that Strange had made his first sizeable check. He was second to Jack Nicklaus in the Australian Open at Kensington in 1976 and, although $17,100 is only petty cash these days, it gave him a start. "I felt rich then," he said. "Winning that amount of money really put me on my feet."

Strange needed all his determination to hold off Ian Woosnam during the 36 holes played on the final day. A third-round 67 by Strange left him a shot ahead of Woosnam and one behind Raymond Floyd, but Woosnam kept fighting back to take it right to the final hole. There, Woosnam needed to hole his chip for an eagle-three, but had to be satisfied with birdie for a 68 and 273 total, against Strange's 68 and 272. Floyd finished with 72 and 275, alone in third place.

The last day was anything but fun for the players, because of the inclement weather following the wash-out of the scheduled first day, but it was a measure of Strange's concentration and brilliant play that he didn't falter. One who did fall back was Nick Faldo, who started with 66, but then slumped with 77 in the second round and was never again able to get into contention, finishing tied for 18th place despite sub-par rounds of 71-70 on the last day.

The leading Australians, Rodger Davis and Bob Shearer, never seriously threatened the leading three overseas players, Floyd, Strange and Woosnam, who began the afternoon round on the final day respectively at 13, 12 and 11 under par. This was outstanding golf on the waterlogged fairways, with little run on the ball, and the standard remained high throughout the 18 holes.

The 17th provided the swing Strange needed over Woosnam, once Floyd had been outdistanced. Woosnam was in trouble off the tee and eventually dropped a stroke, but Strange, with a 25-foot putt to save par, judged the break perfectly. This meant Woosnam was then faced with the chip for eagle from just off the 18th green.

Strange walked away with the $72,000 winner's check but he wasn't the only happy man at the end of the day. Mark Officer, a local pro from Noosa Heads, carried off $10,000 for nearest the pin on the 290-yard par-four 16th hole. That check was $8,000 more than he had won in any tournament.

Daikyo Palm Meadows Cup—A$500,000
Winner: Greg Norman

If the rain and delays had not been enough for the golfers at Sanctuary Cove, they went through the full weather repertoire three weeks later in the first Daikyo Palm Meadows Cup, also in Queensland. All four days suffered from rain, sometimes torrential, plus thunder and lightning.

Greg Norman gave a masterly display in winning, but on the final day the main problem was whether the event could be finished. The tournament was televised by Channel Nine and, on the last afternoon, with Bernhard Langer making a charge at Norman, a cameraman filming Langer from 30 feet behind was struck by lightning on his backpack. This strike sent players, officials and cameramen scurrying for shelter, but after the lightning had disappeared, the heavy rain began again.

It was at this point Norman clinched the tournament. Tateo (Jet) Ozaki of Japan, with a third-round 65, pulled to within three shots of Greg, then on the final day was making another charge in the middle of his round. After the lightning delay, Ozaki held his game together and looked to be a real threat.

Norman had marked his ball on the 15th green, 14 feet from the hole. When he returned, he found water was starting to appear on the surface of the green. His putt needed to be a little firmer than normal, but he overdid it. He rammed the putt into the back of the hole with such force that, had it missed, he would have been faced with another 15-footer coming back. "Didn't want to be short," he said. "But it did win me the golf tournament."

Norman's rounds were 69, 66, 67 and 70 for a 272 total, one better than Ozaki and two ahead of Langer, who was alone in third place.

This event was played on a new course designed by Graham Marsh, and the fact that they were able to finish was a credit to him and others who had designed the course and drainage system. At 7,032 yards, and with a par of 72, the course was doing no one any favors, particularly in the wet conditions and with little run on the ball. Marsh himself finished at 288, and a measure of the standard of the golf played was that even par only entitled him to a share of the 48th spot.

Two of the most impressive efforts of the week came from young American players David Tentis, who finished tied for fourth with Roger Mackay at 275, and Jim Benepe, who confirmed earlier good showings with a solid four-under-par performance. But Australian Peter McWhinney went in the other direction, finishing nine strokes behind after a last round 79. McWhinney had led after two rounds and was tied for first place with Norman after three.

Mercedes Benz Australian Match Play Championship—A$100,000
Winner: Ronan Rafferty

The fact that match-play golf often highlights the drama of the game was perfectly illustrated by Ronan Rafferty's 1-up victory over Mike Clayton in the final of the Mercedes Benz Australian Match Play Championship. Rafferty was one down after the first 18 holes of the 36-hole contest, then watched in astonishment as his opponent jumped into his car and made a hectic 25-mile dash to bring a new putter from his Melbourne home. Clayton hadn't lost the original, but had snapped it across a locker-room bench in a burst of anger after his five-hole advantage had dwindled to the single hole at lunch.

The first 14 holes of the round had brought Clayton eight birdie putts in a marvellous exhibition of golf, but it wasn't good enough to save the putter which, incidentally, had been part of 28 birdies in the event up until the moment of its demise.

Neither was Clayton good enough in the end because Rafferty clung on throughout the afternoon, matching him with pars and birdies and never once letting him go more than a stroke ahead. When Rafferty won the 33rd hole and then Clayton drove wildly from the tee on the 34th, the Irishman had a 1-up lead which he held to the end to collect the winner's check for $20,000.

The final day did not provide the only drama of the weekend, because two of Australia's finest clashed bitterly in an early round, though with words rather than deeds. Ian Baker-Finch lodged an offical written complaint against the slow play of Peter Fowler, a former Australian Open champion. Baker-Finch was playing against eventual winner Rafferty in the match behind Fowler and Vaughan Somers and, after waiting several minutes to play a shot on the fourth hole, he called for the referee to intervene.

Baker-Finch said later he did not enjoy filing the complaint but would have done so even if he had been victorious over Rafferty. Fowler said, "The standard in our match wasn't very high, so we were slower than normal. But, no matter, I can handle anything now, after being stabbed in the back like this."

Blakiston Boyd Victorian Open—A$100,000
Winner: Jim Benepe

Shot-making skill is a prime requisite in golf, so too a knowledge of the psychology of the game. Knowing something about yourself as well doesn't go amiss, as young American Jim Benepe found on the fourth day at Kingston Heath, as he battled a strong wind over the final 18 holes to win the Blakiston Boyd Victorian Open.

Benepe's father is a consulting psychologist, Benepe himself a university graduate in the same subject, and he put it all to good effect on the last afternoon, even to the extent of not looking at a leaderboard until the 18th green, where he asked his caddy to tell him how he stood.

As it happened, much had been going on around him while his eyes had been glued to the ball, and the two-stroke lead the caddy was able to offer as information was excellent news, particularly as he was faced with only a 10-foot putt. Benepe won by three with a final-round 71 and 282 total. His earlier scores had been 69, 68 and 74.

Behind Benepe were Ian Baker-Finch and Peter McWhinney, who had a last-round 76, after having been five strokes ahead of Benepe through four holes. Baker-Finch finished with an even-par 72 for his 285 total.

Australian Masters—A$325,000
Winner: Ian Baker-Finch

A marvellous shot to win a golf tournament is always something to savor and Ian Baker-Finch produced it at the first hole of a playoff for the Australian Masters title, when he hit a five iron to within 18 inches of the pin. There was no doubt the adrenalin was pumping because that five iron travelled 195 yards, but he still had to watch the other two in the playoff, Craig Parry and Roger Mackay, almost hole their chip shots from just off the green.

This was a wonderful tournament with more than its share of drama, starting with the news before the event that Greg Norman was ill, and there were doubts about him being well enough to play. He spent two days in bed then, looking far from recovered, had a one-under-par 72 on the first day. "The main thing was that I was able to finish the round," he said. "I knew it was going to be a hard day and that I had to play well within myself. There are a lot of players ahead of me, but I know I can play better."

Co-leaders with 68s in the opening round were Wayne Riley, Bernhard Langer and Jim Benepe, winner of the Victorian Open the previous week, who holed his bunker shot on the eighth. Benepe, joined by Ian Baker-Finch, stayed in the lead in the second round, this time with a two-under-par 71 which featured a 32 on the very difficult back nine. Baker-Finch held the lead outright with 71-210 after the third day, Benepe falling away with a 76.

Norman shot 70 and 73 in the middle two rounds, and was on top of the leaderboard at one stage on the last day when, as he was playing the 14th, Baker-Finch and Steve Bann, each playing different holes, found themselves in trouble. However, Norman lost his touch on the greens and his challenge faded on the 16th. He finished with 69 and 284, tied for fourth place with Nick Faldo, one stroke above the playoff score. Faldo finished with a 71.

Entering the playoff were first Mackay, with a 30-foot birdie putt on the last hole, then Parry and, finally, Baker-Finch to finish at 283. Mackay's closing round was 70, Parry shot 71 and Baker-Finch, 73.

At the next-to-last hole, Baker-Finch had hit a one iron off the tee and then was faced with 225 yards to the pin. When the 17th became the first hole for the playoff, he gambled on the right-hand dogleg and hit a metal wood to set up his five-iron shot and the opportunity for his winning birdie.

ESP Open—A$250,000
Winner: Greg Norman

It was the Great White Shark at his very best, when Greg Norman launched himself at Royal Canberra with a 62 on the opening day of the ESP Open. Although Peter Senior was only four shots behind and there were another 41 players better than par, few will have been of the opinion, after Norman's scoring spree, that they had a realistic chance of winning.

"I was thinking 59 out there today," Norman said. "Particularly when I played the first nine in 30 shots, and my putter was working well. Then, although I did nothing wrong over the last five holes, I could only par them and I'm a little disappointed from that point of view, even though I'm delighted with the final score."

In past years 62s have been registered in Australia by Jack Nicklaus and the late Jim Ferrier at Manly in Sydney and twice by Gary Player in the 1965 Australian Open at Kooyonga.

Senior shot 69 and gained a stroke on Norman in the second round, to be three behind, with Langer another two strokes away, and Senior still clung on in the third round with a 70 against Norman's 69. It was too much for them, though, and Norman, on the final day, made it a walk through the park with a steady four-under-par 68 and a 269 total to win by seven strokes. Senior fell to a fourth-round 77 that cost him around $20,000, while Langer took second with a three-under-par 69, holding off Noel Ratcliffe and a young Australian player, Peter O'Malley.

Tournament Players Championship—A$300,000
Winner: Greg Norman

At the awards ceremony of the Tournament Players Championship, with Greg Norman again accepting the winner's check, there were suggestions of introducing a handicap system for future Australian tournaments in which he took part. Norman won by eight strokes and was 18 under par on a 7,000-yard course and in conditions where almost half the field finished worse than par.

Norman's scores were 67, 67, 68, 68 for a 270 total. In his last nine rounds on the Australian circuit, Norman was 41 under par, an astonishing performance, even from one of the greatest golfers.

There was a constructive side to Norman's win, when he offered some advice to the young players who finished behind him.

"The problem was in this tournament that I had most of those young players beaten before they stepped on to the first tee," Greg said. "Then, on the last day, I don't believe any of them thought they could make up the five-stroke lead I had, and that is simply a defeatist attitude. I don't ever go into a tournament thinking I am playing for second place, and I'd like to see all the young Australian pros do the same."

It was, in fact, two of the more experienced Australian pros, Peter Senior and David Graham, who finished tied for second. The best round of the tournament came on the final day from a young American, Kirk Triplett, who shot a 66. He is a graduate of the University of Nevada, with a degree in civil engineering, and is one of three golfing brothers from Palm Springs.

The New Riverside Oaks course in Cattai, New South Wales, was not completely ready for a tournament, although the layout received compliments all round, as did the potential of the course and the leisure complex. Despite having problems with the preparation, this was a very important event for the Australian Tournament Players Division, because this is the course where they will be making the home for their own event over the next 25 years.

Norman gave it the seal of approval in his four rounds, though at one stage laziness threatened to pull him back to the field during the third round. He was treating things rather casually over the first few holes and was being threatened for the lead when he hit a seven iron into the hole on the 167-yard eighth. That got him going again, he led by five strokes at the end of the day and then fired a 68 in the last round to collect $54,000.

It was a sensational performance from one who has lifted the game immeasurably in Australia by his skill and example.

Tattersall Tasmanian Open—A$100,000
Winner: Brett Ogle

Four days of appalling weather made conditions miserable for the players in the Tasmanian Open and Brett Ogle's winning score of four-under-par 284 was, under the circumstances, quite remarkable. This was Ogle's first tournament victory and his five-under 67 on the last day was a superb effort, played as it was in gale force, southwest winds with intermittent rain squalls, the type of weather which had earlier made the cut an extraordinarily high figure of 154.

Ogle was five shots behind amateur Brett Johns as the final round began and, when Ogle double-bogeyed the opening hole, his chance seemed to have gone in the atrocious conditions. Ogle then fired four successive birdies and an eagle over the next nine holes and he and Johns, playing in the same group, were tied as they came to the 16th hole. At the par-three 17th, Ogle made par and Johns bogeyed, then Ogle, with his one-shot lead, deliberately hit an enormous but risky drive over trees on the righthand side of the 18th fairway. When Ogle missed his putt, Johns had the chance to force a playoff, but his six-footer slid over the edge of the hole.

The third-round leaders, Mike Clayton, Mike Ferguson and Paul Foley, all played creditably on the last day for 72, 71, and 72 respectively, but Ogle's charge was too much for them and his first tournament win came after three years as a professional. One eye-catching performance came from Brad Hughes who, fresh from the amateur ranks, finished tied for eighth despite an opening-round 79.

Panasonic New South Wales Open—A$200,000
Winner: Greg Norman

Greg Norman won but, by his own standards, it was a scrappy effort. "Some days you play poorly and win, and that's exactly what I did out there today," Greg said after accepting the winner's check for the successful defense of his title. Peter Senior came at him with a rush and a final round of 64, with Craig Parry, one of the finest of Australia's young golfers, challenging over the last nine holes, but Norman's experience and knowledge of how to win, even when not in top form, stood him in good stead. Not that Norman had a great deal about which to complain, nor did the thousands who thronged the Concord course to watch him because, although his final round was a two-over 73, his previous scores were 66, 69 and 69, for a 277 total.

Parry, after an opening round of 64, then had 70 and two 72s to place second at 278. He received accolades from Norman at the end as being one of Australia's outstanding young golfers. "He will be carrying the flag for Australia for many years to come," Norman said. "He has an eternity of golf in front of him and he will keep on getting better and better." Parry was not at his best on the final day, and hit only one green in regulation on the opening nine holes. He might have exerted far more pressure on Norman than he did, although a three-stroke swing on the 11th gave his game some impetus.

Norman, as one might expect, was in the top three each day of the tournament, pushing his way to the front in the third round and, after birdies at the third and fourth holes on the last day, he had jumped six strokes ahead of Parry. Then frustration at the slowness of play, with a five-hour round, took its toll on Norman. He three-putted the 11th green and was in trouble on the 17th hole as well. A beautiful approach left him with a 20-foot putt for birdie and, when the ball went in the hole, he was home, barring some extraordinary disaster on the 18th.

Town & Country Western Australian Open—A$100,000
Winner: Brad Hughes

Two of Australia's most promising young golfers fought to the finish of the Town & Country Western Australian Open, played at the Lake Karrinyup Country Club in Perth, and Brad Hughes' victory came only after Ken Trimble three-putted the 72nd hole and missed the chance of a playoff. Hughes, who turned professional one month earlier, had an impressive amateur record and, with this first tournament victory, confirmed the view that in future years he will be one of Australia's best and most exciting golfers.

By coincidence, he has the same birth date as Greg Norman, whom he greatly admires and, like Norman, he strikes the ball awesome distances. With experience he will add accuracy to that attribute and, in years to come, will make many headlines in Australian golf. He was one of the top two players on the leaderboard throughout this event, but his short game troubled him on the final day as Trimble made his charge. Both young players scored brilliantly on the third day, Hughes with 67 and Trimble with 66. But Hughes, at seven under par, went into the final round with a four-stroke lead over Trimble, with New Zealander Frank Nobilo and Mark Nash the closest to them, at one under.

Trimble was in the group ahead of Hughes and, on the last hole, in being over cautious with a tricky downhill putt, left himself with a nasty six-footer for par, which he missed. This left Hughes, in the final group, needing par to win and he hit a magnificent drive to leave himself a delicate wedge to the green. He concentrated on leaving the ball below the hole, safely two-putted and pocketed the first winner's check of his career.

Australian PGA Championship—A$475,000
Winner: Wayne Grady

The Australian PGA Championship was the stuff of which sports stories are made. Greg Norman all but blew the tournament in the opening round, shot three sub-par rounds for a playoff, then lost to Wayne Grady in a four-hole comedy of missed chances. It took several heart-stopping moments for Grady to beat Norman in the playoff, with Norman taking three putts from eight feet on the second extra hole.

The Australian PGA's flagship event was played at Riverside Oaks, a year-old course in New South Wales which looked magnificent.

The first two days, with temperatures over the 100-degree mark, there was no shortage of swarms of annoying flies, then the temperature cooled, along with the tempers of some players. A neighboring farmer who disliked golf turned up his radio to full volume to distract players, one of whom, Wayne Riley, was fined for swearing during an argument with Rodger Davis, after Davis declined to allow him a free drop.

Brett Ogle set the opening-round pace with a 66 and was nine shots ahead of Norman. Grady had a 69, which he repeated in the second round.

On the third day Norman made his charge with a blistering 64, featuring some of the finest golf seen in Australia in many years. Seven birdies and an eagle had the galleries roaring, and his only lapse came where he tried to drive the 320-yard 12th hole and found the lake. All this meant Norman, going into the final day, was now tied with Ogle and Peter Senior. All were nine under par, with Grady two shots back along with Ken Trimble, Bob Shearer and Roger Mackay.

Grady's play from tee to green had been close to faultless and all he needed was a few of the putts to drop in the last round. That was exactly what happened, with Norman shooting a dashing 68, but Grady more than matched his play with a brilliant 66 to force the playoff. Grady's round included desperately-needed birdies on the 17th and 18th. Two strokes back were Senior (70) and Mackay (68), with one of the best last-day performances coming from Trimble who fired a solid 69.

Neither Grady nor Norman seemed fully settled when they began the playoff. Each parred the first hole then, on the second, came the astonishing lapses from both players, with Norman failing to capitalize on Grady's error. Norman's splendid eight-iron shot checked and spun back eight feet from the pin, Grady was 30 feet away and charged his putt 10 feet past the hole. It was still his putt and, when he missed, it seemed mere formality for Norman to take the title, but his first putt just slid by the hole and he missed a real tiddler on the way back.

Later Norman was to describe what he had done as no better than pathetic, but now he had the job of keeping Grady at bay. Wayne had refused to concede to himself he was beaten, even when Norman stood over that tiny putt. Instead, Grady asked his caddy for a new ball and kept his glove on his left hand as he watched Norman lining up. Then, after each parred the third playoff hole, he won the fourth when Norman took three to get down from the bunker.

West End South Australian Open—A$100,000
Winner: Gordon Brand Jr.

Rarely does a golfer remold his swing, walk on to the first tee of his next tournament in another country and go away with the first prize by finishing with 267, 13 under par. Gordon Brand Jr. of Scotland managed this in the West End South Australian Open, and was seven shots ahead of his nearest Australian rivals, Wayne Grady and Greg Alexander. Brand's scores were 64, 69, 69 and 65.

Bob Torrance, father of Sam, has been Brand's coach. They spent many hours on the practice tees during the 1988 European season, once Brand had decided his old swing must go. When he arrived in Australia he was under no illusions that he had solved everything, but said he was able to see real improvement and this was giving him confidence.

There is no better recipe for confidence than success, plus attention to detail; and, after Brand won and pocketed his winner's check, he made a point of asking for a copy of the videotape of the final day. "It all worked over the past four days," he said, "but I'm certain there are still small problems here and there, and I want to be able to check them out."

Brand has been no stranger to playing well in Australia, even with his old swing. He has had previous third-place finishes in the Australian Open and New South Wales PGA events. He was never really tested in Adelaide although Wayne Grady was within two shots of him at the start of the final day. Brand simply increased the pressure instead of playing safely and, by the time the players were coming down the home stretch, he had an unassailable cushion, which could have been greater but for one or two rather casual putting strokes towards the end.

Ricky May Classic—A$100,000
Winner: David Merriman

David Merriman is not a golfing name to send tremors through the field of any tournament in Australia; yet, as one of the most consistent and cheerful players on the tour, his win in the Ricky May Classic was welcomed by his fellow professionals.

The tournament was the idea of former Australian great, Jack Newton, after Ricky May died suddenly a few months earlier. Newton runs his own pro-am each year at Noosa in Queensland, and May always freely gave of his time to provide splendid entertainment. The Variety Club of Australia backed Newton's idea with the aim of providing $300,000 towards new facilities at Sydney's Prince of Wales Children's Hospital.

The rounds of golf took the usual length of time where celebrities, and some slow-playing professionals, are concerned, and Merriman sat in the clubhouse for an hour watching others attack his finishing score of 279, nine under par, which had featured a last-round 66.

He set up the victory on the same 12th hole, 321 yards, where two weeks earlier Greg Norman had found the water trying to drive the green and then had lost the playoff to Wayne Grady. Merriman desperately needing a birdie, preferably an eagle, hit his driver to within five feet of the pin and sank the putt. He was off and running and his game plan then was to make it safely to the clubhouse and have his fellow competitors fade under the pressure.

That is exactly what happened, with Mike Harwood bogeying the 17th and Paul Foley and Brett Ogle unable to make any headway. Ogle, by coincidence, had another last-round 75, as he had in the PGA Championship on the same course and in similar circumstances where he was in a winning position with one round to play.

Test Match—A$500,000
Winner: Britain

Sandy Lyle didn't want to play, didn't particularly want to fly to Australia, then finished up thinking of buying a vacation home at Port Douglas, one of the loveliest resorts in the world. Greg Norman wanted to play but, despite the searing heat, declined to allow the British players to ride on golf carts, pointing out that they were not yet in the senior ranks.

Australia wanted to win, was considered the favorite because of local knowledge and those hot and humid conditions, but the visitors stitched them up even before the final day of the inaugural Test Match at the Mirage Resort.

There was no shortage of words or controversy leading up to the golf. When all the talking had been completed, Lyle, as captain of the British team, set the pace and Australia, despite the team playing well individually, was simply wiped off the scoreboard by a margin of 11½ to 6½.

The event was sponsored by the Quintex group, television was handled by Channel 7, both of which are owned by Christopher Skase, and the magnificent new course was designed by Peter Thomson and Mike Wolveridge. They used the Ryder Cup format instead of the Dunhill Cup method of stroke-match play, which meant the matches were rarely carried though to the picturesque 18th and the clubhouse. In fact, the British team played so well that the last day was purely academic, with the Test won decisively by the visitors on the second day.

Panasonic Australian Open Championship—A$350,000
Winner: Mark Calcavecchia

Greg Norman predicted the winner would need a score between 10 and 18 under par in the Panasonic Australian Open, but Mark Calcavecchia went one better — 19-under-par 269 — with a magnificent display of golf to beat fellow American Mark McCumber by six shots. Both were enormously popular with the galleries thronging the course, not only because of their superb golf but also their warm and happy approach to the event.

Royal Sydney in its revamped form, having been redesigned by Thomson and Wolveridge, received accolades throughout the tournament. Calcavecchia set the pace with attacking golf which brought roars of approval from those on the course and millions watching on television.

Calcavecchia started one stroke off the pace with a 67, tied with Norman and on the heels of Irishman Ronan Rafferty and Australia's Peter Senior. Wayne Grady was just behind that group with 68, and David Graham, 69, and a host of players firing birdies and ensuring the half-way cut would be 148.

At the top of the leaderboard after the second day were Grady and Calcavecchia, and already the American was playing some marvellous attacking golf, moving quickly between shots and, in general, giving the impression of a thoroughly confident player. He was still a shot behind Grady, with Norman a further five strokes back and once again at odds with his putter, as was McCumber.

McCumber played immaculate golf from tee to green and was consistently placing his approaches near the flagstick, but nothing would drop for him on the putting surface. They were certainly dropping for Calcavecchia though, whose third-round 66 put him five shots ahead of Grady and six in front of McCumber, and the biggest obvious danger for him was likely to be a wavering in concentration because of the big lead.

Another danger appeared on the final morning, however, when the course and surrounding suburbs were hammered by fierce electrical storms and heavy rain. Play was delayed for almost an hour because of lightning and, with parts of the course under water, Calcavecchia knew it could be a very long day. In his favor was that his challengers had to go for birdies, and that they would need to putt at least as brilliantly as he had been doing for three days if they were to dent his lead. In the end, McCumber was unable to work any magic with his putter, nor was Grady, who had great chances for birdies at the opening two holes.

The further they went, the more assured Calcavecchia became and, when he chipped in at the fourth hole for a birdie, it all became a walk in the park and a fight for second place.

Calcavecchia said he was most delighted with his short game. "I hit one or two ugly drives during the four days, but my work around the greens was first class. In one way I was fortunate that, if I happened to be off the fairway, I didn't have too many rough lies. I'm really happy at the way it has all turned out, although my concentration did waver a little towards the end. But it wasn't a bad performance after only seeing the course in the pro-am."

McCumber matched Calcavecchia's final-round 69, as did Norman, who played well but couldn't buy a putt over the last 18 holes. Brett Ogle and the very promising Ken Trimble had the low rounds of the final day with 67 apiece. Calcavecchia's superb performance was not the lowest ever in the Australian Open, although it equalled Jack Nicklaus's score at Royal Hobart 17 years earlier. The record is held by Gary Player with an astonishing 264, 24 under par, at Kooyonga, Adelaide, in 1965.

Bicentennial Classic—A$1,500,000
Winner: Rodger Davis

Rodger Davis captured one of the year's most exciting events and pocketed half a million Australian dollars when he defeated Fred Couples at the second hole of a sudden-death playoff in the Bicentennial Classic at Royal Melbourne.

This was one of the strongest fields ever assembled for an Australian tournament, a tribute to the organizers who had worked so hard to make the week a success. Between them, 40 of the starters had won $88 million in prize money over the years and 12 of them had 36 major championships to their credit. The pairing sheets read like a Who's Who of golf, great players of the present mixed with stars of the past and, with Royal Melbourne in a benign state on all four days, the scoring was good and the excitement intense.

Five players — Davis, Couples, Brett Ogle, Ben Crenshaw and Hale Irwin — each could have won the tournament in the last hour, but the latter three fell away just when they badly needed birdies. Greg Norman came with a rush at the end to equal Irwin's course-record 64 and Ronan Rafferty, with 69 in the last round, also provided pressure for the leaders.

Couples and Davis made their mark from the first day, Couples with a magnificent 66 which had him a shot ahead of Jumbo Ozaki and Mike Colandro. Davis shot 68 and was tied with Crenshaw and Peter Senior. From then on, that group of five players gradually stretched the opposition, Crenshaw going into the second-round lead with 65 and Couples, Davis, Ogle and Irwin all shooting sub-par rounds in perfect conditions.

The third round was merely a shifting of positions, Irwin's 64 taking him to the top of the leaderboard, two shots ahead of Crenshaw, and Couples's 69, astonishingly, dropping him three places. He said ruefully after signing his card, "It's not often you can shoot three under par and drop the same number of places."

On the final day, despite Norman's charge, those five players stayed at the top of the board. Ogle, having said he needed 67 to win, went out and proved it by shooting 69 and missing the playoff by one shot, and Crenshaw and Irwin couldn't make the birdies when they were desperately needed.

Meanwhile Davis was playing brilliant golf. Couples, just as powerful off the tee and sure with the putter, matched him, but would Davis be able to handle the pressure putts at the end, or would the yips come back to haunt him? He hit a great bunker shot for birdie at the 17th and then, on the second playoff hole, was faced with a six-foot putt to win after Couples was bunkered. Davis stroked the ball confidently into the cup for his biggest-ever victory, in an event in which he and Couples, over the four days, each carded five bogeys, 46 pars, 20 birdies and an eagle.

World Cup—US$750,000
Winner: United States

After the tremendous excitement and wonderful crowds of the Bicentennial Classic the previous week, the World Cup was something of an anticlimax. The Melbourne sports public reacted to the second tournament in successive weeks by declining to make the trip to the Royal Melbourne course to watch a mixture of a few fine golfers and those who would struggle to make the cut in an ordinary professional event.

Ben Crenshaw and Mark McCumber were America's winning representatives with a score of 560, and Crenshaw took the individual prize with a 275 total. The team prize meant US $100,000 for each player and Crenshaw's individual money was US $50,000. To win Crenshaw needed to sink a tricky little three-footer on the last green, which he made for the one-stroke margin over Japan's Jet Ozaki.

If Crenshaw had missed it, the United States would have tied with Japan for the first prize because McCumber had made a complete hash of the last hole, after he and Crenshaw had a three-stroke cushion. His double-bogey six gave the Japanese pairing of Ozaki brothers, Jumbo and Jet, a glimmer of hope, and there was no shortage of nerves as Crenshaw stepped up to the ball for the final stroke.

Australia's Roger Mackay established a course record with 63, nine under par, in the second round, when a northerly wind reduced the rating of the course by three or four strokes. The wind meant that the third and eighth par-four holes were drivable, measuring 334 and 307 yards respectively.

Both Mackay and Peter Senior had been under enormous pressure because of their selection ahead of Greg Norman and Rodger Davis. They were in front after the second round, second after the third day and then couldn't hold off the United States and Japan, placing third at 562, two strokes behind.

Air New Zealand-Shell Open—NZ$200,000
Winner: Terry Gale

Bandages around the left arm and knee are not normally the trappings associated with victory on the golf circuit, but Terry Gale made light of them in winning the Air New Zealand-Shell Open at Titirangi. With his 15-year-old son Bradley caddying for him, and a rejuvenated putting touch, Gale raced away from the field with 65 on the final day for a 271 total, despite the other top six finishers all shooting 68 or better. Gale has been a consistent player around the world for the past 15 years, but wayward putting and the injuries had sapped his confidence and he was 56th on the Australasian Order of Merit prior to this tournament.

Titirangi generally is at the mercy of the golfers, but drought conditions in Auckland meant the greens were hard even before the opening drive was hit. Ian Stanley set the pace with some superb iron play for a 66, one stroke ahead of Peter Fowler, a former Australian Open champion, with Gale (69), Hale Irwin and Ossie Moore (both 68s) all issuing their challenges.

Stanley and Fowler maintained their one-two positions with 69s in the second round, while Gale and Moore also had 69s and Irwin shot 70. Last year's winner, Mike Colandro, and American star Jeff Sluman failed to make the cut. Sluman had some problems with his driving, and eight three-putt greens knocked him out of the final two rounds.

Fowler fell back in the third round with 74, and Stanley shot even-par 70 to stay one stroke ahead of Gale (68) and two in front of Moore (70) and Irwin (69). Stanley faded his opening drive of the final round over the out-of-bounds fence on the short par-four hole, took double bogey and was instantly on the defensive. A triple bogey on the 11th did nothing to retrieve the situation, and he tied for seventh with a 73.

Gale started well and his putting touch returned on the opening nine holes even though the greens were lightning fast. He had also changed his putter in the hope of being able to make some of the vital putts which had been eluding him. Moore and Irwin made a charge, Jeff Woodland was in the clubhouse with 67 and a four-round total of 275, but Gale did not falter for a moment and finished with a four-stroke advantage over Moore.

Nissan-Mobil New Zealand Open—NZ$150,000
Winner: Ian Stanley

It took 16 years but Ian Stanley finally won his first tournament in New Zealand to add to his many victories in Australia and other parts of the world. At the back of his mind over the last 18 holes was the thought that he had led going into the final round the previous week at Titirangi, but then had blown his chance with an out-of-bounds drive on the first hole, as well as subsequent lack of concentration.

Here at Paraparaumu Beach for the Nissan-Mobil New Zealand Open, Stanley worked on five hours of fierce concentration in the last round, the likes of which he hadn't experienced in years. So much so, that when interviewed later, Stanley said he would have little chance of making the cut if he were entered in another tournament the following week.

"Leading from the first day to the last shot only increases the pressure, despite what people say about it being better to be a shot ahead than a shot behind on the leaderboard," Stanley said. "There have been times when I haven't concentrated as much as I should, and I do have this reputation for being a little happy-go-lucky in my approach to the game. But when I won a tournament in similar fashion a few years ago, everyone said I was in a grumpy mood because I wasn't wisecracking with the galleries. What do you do?"

Stanley's rounds were 64-68-69-72 for a 273 total and a three-stroke victory over Mike Clayton. His five-stroke lead on the final day was certainly in no danger during the first nine holes, with his nearest challenger, Corey Pavin, double-bogeying the third hole. When Stanley walked on to the 10th tee his lead was stretched to six and then suddenly the pressure got to him. He needed to sink a tricky 12-foot putt for bogey at No. 11 and, after three-putting the 13th and 15th, the lead had dwindled to three shots with tough finishing holes to come.

Clayton had taken over Pavin's mantle as chief challenger with a blistering six-under-par 65 which put him in the clubhouse at eight under par and, for a while, he must have thought there was a chance Stanley's game would fall apart. He pulled himself together on the 16th and 17th holes, then a splendid drive on the final hole and a nine-iron to the center of the green gave him the chance to walk on to the putting surface to the cheers of the crowd.

Pavin, with an eagle on the last hole, finished third and Peter O'Malley, one of the future stars of Australian golf, came back well from a first-round 77 to hold on to fourth position with three fine rounds of 65, 67 and 69. Former Australian Open champion Peter Fowler and American David Delong were consistent throughout without being quite able to threaten the leaders on a course which allowed only nine players to better par.

14. The Asia/Japan Tour

Never in the history of professional golf had anybody seen the likes of the family affair that dominated the season in Japan in 1988. Over the years, the pro game has had its brother and sister acts in which both siblings performed with considerable success at the same time. The Wadkins, the Heberts, the Hills, the Mangrums, the Bauers of the LPGA come to mind, plus the four Henning brothers of South Africa (of whom only Harold was an especially good player), but one is hard-pressed to identify a time when three members of the same family were playing well at the same time on one of the tours around the world. Until this year in Japan on the $17 million circuit. The year of the Ozakis. Masashi, Tateo and Naomichi. Or, as known in English-speaking countries of the world — Jumbo, Jet and Joe.

It started back in the early 1970s with Masashi, who is now 42. A professional baseball player who switched to golf because of, believe this, a bad back and quickly became the No. 1 player, joined within a few years by Isao Aoki. Along came Tateo now 34, and Naomichi, now 32, late in that decade. All three have had their moments since then, but nothing to remotely compare to what they accomplished in 1988. The Ozakis won 12 of the 35 official individual tournaments scheduled for 72 holes (excluding the September regional week). That's better than a victory every three weeks all year. Jumbo had six of them, including the Japan Open Championship for the second time; Joe four and Jet two, including his second Japan PGA Championship. They had nine seconds and four thirds in those 35 events and one of the runner-up placings was a playoff loss of Naomichi.

Then, there's the money. Jumbo banked $1,082,985 and, sixth, was one of the year's seven million-dollar winners in world golf. Joe, who was second behind Jumbo on the Japan Tour money list, placed 20th in the world with $672,803 and Jet, seventh in Japan, was 33rd in the world with $536,458. That adds to family fortunes of $2,292,246. Masashi's victories came in spurts. He won the Open, Golf Digest and Bridgestone on successive October weekends, a first in Japanese golf; the Nikkei Cup and the Maruman back to back in August and the Dunlop Open in April. Naomichi's victories were in the Sapporo Tokyu, the NST Niigata, the All Nippon Airways Open and the late-season Japan Series, while Tateo put the Suntory with his PGA Championship.

The remarkable accomplishments of the Ozakis tended to obscure the exceptional season of 32-year-old Masahiro Kuramoto, the No. 4 money-winner in Japan with $506,639, who scored five victories, running his career total to 25. He won the Sendai Hoso, the Yomiuri Sapporo Beer and the Kansai PGA Championship within a five-week period in June/July, the KBC Augusta in August and the regional Chu-Shikoku at home at Hiroshima for the seventh time in nine years, in 1988 by 13 strokes. On the other hand, it was not a good year for Tsuneyuki Nakajima and 46-year-old Isao Aoki, Japan's other two superstars, both of whom went winless. Nakajima, who now plays a heavy international schedule, especially in the United States, didn't play in Japan until the end of June and was 20th on the Japan money list after his 15 starts. Holder of 39 titles in Japan, Tsuneyuki (Tommy) has won just once since 1986. Aoki's total remained at 53, now five behind Jumbo Ozaki. David Ishii, the Hawaiian who led the 1987 Japan Tour in victories and money, won just once — the Japan Match Play — but was a frequent contender and placed third in Japan and 24th on the World Money List with $682,344.

Other multiple winners in Japan in 1988 were Australians — Wayne Smith (TaylorMade Setonaikai and Kuzuha Kokusai) and Ian Baker-Finch (Pocari Sweat and Bridgestone ASO) in the "pre-season" phase of the circuit and Brian Jones, a full-time campaigner, with the Mitsubishi Galant and Tokai Classic. Jones lost two other tournaments in playoffs. Once again, the home pros, inexplicably, had little luck in the big-money events in the spring and fall. Scott Simpson, the 1987 U.S. Open champion, won his second Chunichi Crowns title in April and fellow U.S. pros Ken Green and Larry Mize won the Dunlop Phoenix and Casio, respectively, on successive weeks, while Seve Ballesteros capped his record year with his seventh victory of 1988 in the Taiheiyo Club Masters, his third win in Japan. Only Katsunari Takahashi salved national pride in the big events with his victory in the Lark Cup, a new event filling the fall slot of the old U.S. vs. Japan Matches.

A note for the future: The first of two 36-hole unofficial tournaments launching the activity in early March — the Fudosan Cup — went to Kazuya Nakajima, Tsuneyuki's 22-year-old brother.

The Asia Circuit had its usual mix of national winners, although Taiwanese golfers fared much better than the rest. Hsieh Chin Sheng was the only double winner, capturing his first two Asia Circuit tournaments at the start of the season in Hong Kong and Manila, but Lu Chien Soon, who won at Calcutta, went on to his second Asia Circuit overall championship. Hsieh Yu Shu gave the Republic of China its fourth 1988 title with his triumph in Indonesia. The big U.S. contingent claimed successive circuit wins, when Tray Tyner took the Malaysian Open and Greg Bruckner the Singapore Open two weeks after landing the non-tour Rolex Masters in Singapore. Australia's Jeff Senior (Thailand), Mexico's Carlos Espinosa (Republic of China) and The Philippines' Frankie Minoza (South Korea) claimed the other circuit titles prior to Jumbo Ozaki's win in the season closer — the Dunlop at Tokyo.

Unisys Hong Kong Open—US$150,000
Winner: Hsieh Chin Sheng

Taiwan, long dominant on the Asia Circuit, got the 1988 season off on the right foot, but from unexpected quarters in the Unisys Hong Kong Open, which launched the golfing year for the first time. Hsieh Chin Sheng, a professional for just two years, scored his initial victory in mid-February over Royal Hong Kong Golf Club's composite course at Kowloon, winning out in a tough battle down the stretch with Lu Chien Soon, his experienced countryman. Hsieh's closing 67 for 274 gave him a one-stroke victory over the five-time circuit winner and 1983 overall champion in a tournament in which he missed the cut the first time around in 1987.

The 25-year-old lingered not far off the pace as Casey Nakama of Hawaii and Ireland's David Feherty led the first day with 67, as Lu, Li Wen Shen and Burma's Han Kya Hla shared the midway margin with 136s and as Lu moved two strokes in front Saturday with 68 for 204, nine under par. Han was then runner-up at 206 with Hsieh, on rounds of 70-71-66, three back. It came down to the two Taiwanese on the back nine Sunday. Lu appeared to have victory in hand when he birdied Nos. 10, 11 and 12, but his lead dropped to two when he bogeyed the 14th and 15th. Meanwhile, Hsieh, who had an eagle, five birdies and three bogeys in the round, mustered a finishing kick. He birdied the 15th, 17th and 18th to move one in front, then watched as Lu missed his downhill birdie try on the last green in his bid for a tie and playoff. The victory was the first for a Taiwan pro in Hong Kong since Chen Tze Ming's triumph at Royal Hong Kong in 1981.

Coca Cola Philippines Open—US$120,000
Winner: Hsieh Chin Sheng

What happened at Wack Wack Golf and Country Club in the Coca Cola Philippines Open, the Asia Circuit's second stop, went against the grain. Hsieh Chin Sheng rode the momentum of his first professional victory the week before in Hong Kong to a decisive second triumph in striking contrast to the usual euphoric daze into which most first-time winners find themselves during the few weeks and often months afterward. Instead, Hsieh drew confidence from his tight win at Hong Kong and never trailed en route to a five-stroke victory. His cards: 68-69-74-72 for 283, five under par at Wack Wack, the frequent site of Asia's oldest tournament, which has survived the turmoil that has swept the nation.

With an opening 68, Hsieh shared the first-round lead with American Steve Bowman, who was to ultimately finish in second place. The Taiwanese pro moved three strokes in front Friday, shooting 69 while Chung Chun Hsin was climbing in the runner-up slot with 67 for his 140. Only five players in the field broke Wack Wack's 72 par Saturday as strong winds buffeted the course. As a result, even though posting a 74, Hsieh remained in front as Chung shaved a shot off the margin with a 73 and Bowman remained third with a 74 for 215, four back and tied with Carlos Espinosa. Despite a first-hole bogey Sunday, Hsieh opened his lead to five with a front-nine 35 as Chung faded and Bowman mounted the only challenge. The Texan was out in 36, then closed the gap to two with birdies at the 11th and 12th as the Tamsui golfer went par-bogey. However, Hsieh holed a 12-foot par putt at the 13th, birdied the 15th and was home free with a par round as Bowman slipped to 73 and 288.

Benson & Hedges Malaysian Open—US$150,000
Winner: Tray Tyner

His confidence buoyed by a strong showing in the Rolex Masters played during the Asia Circuit's off week at the end of February, Tray Tyner, a rookie pro from Texas, gave the big American contingent in the Far East its first victory in the Benson & Hedges Malaysian Open the following week. Tyner, who had just turned professional the previous July, came from two strokes off the pace with a one-under-par 71 in Sunday's final round at Saujana Golf and Country Club at Kuala Lumpur to win his first title by a single stroke with his par 288 total.

Japan's Harumitsu Hamano drew most of the attention early. After American Jerry Smith grabbed the first-day lead with 68, Hamano went to the fore with his 71-70 — 141 as Smith shot 75 for 143. Although slipping to 74 on a tough playing day, Hamano remained in front after Saturday's round, his 215 giving him a one-shot lead over Jeff Cook. Tyner was then only two behind with his 73-72-72 — 217 and stayed close on the early holes Sunday. As both Hamano and Cook struggled toward a 74 and a 76 respectively, Tyner went in front at one under par with a short birdie putt at the 15th hole, lost a stroke at the 16th, but found two closing pars enough to eke out the one-shot victory over Hamano and Hsieh Chin Sheng, who closed with 71 in his bid for a third consecutive victory on the Asia Circuit to go with his wins at Hong Kong and Manila.

The 23-year-old Tyner had finished in a three-way tie for second in the Rolex Masters in a blanket finish by Americans at Singapore Island Country Club's Bukit course. Californian Greg Bruckner was the winner with 274, three in front of Tyner, Cook and Jeff Maggert.

Singapore Open—US$220,000
Winner: Greg Bruckner

No matter where his future golfing career takes him, Greg Bruckner will always have a soft spot in his heart for Singapore, where he followed a non-tour victory two weeks later with a one-stroke triumph in the Singapore Open on the Asia Circuit, the first wins of consequence on his relatively-brief pro campaign. Bruckner's Singapore Open victory was a much tighter one than his Rolex Masters win at Singapore Island Country Club as he struggled to fend off the bid of Chung Chun Hsin, another strong newcomer out of Taiwan.

Veteran Chen Tze Ming was off and running toward a second Singapore Open title in the early going at Tanah Merah Country Club, new venue for the Singapore Open. Chen, a seven-time winner on the circuit, had a piece of the first-round lead at 69 with Chung and Canadian Danny Mijovic, then moved two ahead of Chung Friday with 68 to go seven under par with his 137 on a drizzly day. Bruckner, four back at the start of the day (72-69), bolted in front Saturday with a five-under-par 67 as Chen fell two shots off the pace with 73, joining Yuan Ching Chi at 210. The 27-year old Californian played patchy golf Sunday, but only Chung made a run at him. In fact, Bruckner had to get up and down from off the green at the last hole to avoid a playoff with the Taiwanese pro, who came from four strokes off the pace with 70. Greg's final par gave him 73 and the one-shot victory at 281. Chen had a closing 74 and placed third at 274.

Indonesia Open—US$100,000
Winner: Hsieh Yu Shu

Yet another pro from the small island nation of Taiwan joined the ranks of winners on the Asia Circuit when Hsieh Yu Shu, a 27-year-old in his sixth season on tour, ran away with the title of the Indonesia Open. Hsieh spurted from a second-round, eight-under-par 62 to a six-stroke victory in the 15-year-old tournament on the Rawamangun course of the Jakarta Golf Club. His 16-under par score of 264 was by 10 strokes the lowest of the Asia season.

After Philippine veterans Mario Siodina and Rudy Lavares opened the mid-March tournament with 65s and shared the first-round lead, the 1988 Indonesia Open was all Hsieh's. His second-round 62, following his first-day 69, moved him a stroke ahead of countryman Li Wen Shen as Lavares shot 69 and Siodina 70 that day. Hsieh's 67 the third day enabled him to develop a three-stroke lead at 198 over Siodina (66) and American Mark Aebli, who climbed high with his 64 for 201. After four front-nine birdies, the Taiwanese pro suffered three back-nine bogeys, but almost offset them with an eagle at the 15th hole. Hsieh was a bit shaky at the start in the final round, taking a bogey at the third hole, but he was solid the rest of the way, scoring five birdies for a 66 and the 264. Siodina shot 69 for 270 to be the only man even in Hsieh's vicinity. Aebli and Paul Foley, in joint third place, were 11 strokes behind the winner at 275.

Thailand Open—US$100,000
Winner: Jeff Senior

Australia got into the act when the Asia Circuit reached Bangkok for the 24th Thailand Open, the sixth stop on the 1988 tour. Jeff Senior, in his fifth season on the Asia Circuit, took advantage of a faltering Chen Liang Hsi and came from two strokes off the pace in the final round to score his initial victory in that part of the world. The 31-year-old Senior posted a closing 67 for a 12-under-par 276 and a two-shot victory over Chen at Royal Thai Army Golf Club in the US$100,000 event. It was the first win for an Aussie in Thailand since Graham Marsh won in 1973.

Chen, also a circuit non-winner, had taken the lead in the second round after Canadian Rick Gibson, Lu Chien Soon and Hsieh Yu Shu, fresh from his victory in Indonesia, opened with 68s. With his 69-68 — 137, Chen took the lead Friday, heading American Dave Tentis by a shot, and remained in front after his 70 for 207 Saturday. Hsieh jumped into second place with 66 for 208, a shot in front of Senior. Jeff kept the pressure on the Taiwanese leader with two early birdies Sunday and surged in front on the back nine when Chen three-putted three times for bogeys at the 12th, 13th and 16th holes. Senior birdied two of those holes and took the lead for good with his fifth at the 15th. Chen closed with 71 for his 278, two strokes in front of Frankie Minoza and Malaysian winner Tray Tyner.

Charminar Challenge Indian Open—US$100,000
Winner: Lu Chien Soon

Lu Chien Soon, a former Asia Circuit seasonal champion, returned to the winners circle in Calcutta, the third different Taiwanese victor of 1988 and a most decisive one. Lu, whose most recent of four wins on the circuit had been in 1985 in Indonesia, led from start to finish at Royal Calcutta Golf Club, winding up with a five-stroke victory at 281 despite a final-round, two-over-par 75.

His opening 68 gave the 29-year-old pro from Taiwan a one-stroke lead over American Jerry Smith and two over three other U.S. players, none of whom were to remain in contention. When Lu added another 68 Friday over the 7,271 yards of the par-73 Royal Calcutta course, he soared to a six-shot advantage. He birdied four of the last eight holes to open the big gap. Tracy Nakazaki, a Japanese-American, was at 142 and Kirk Triplett of the U.S. was third at 145, nine off the pace. Lu set up the cakewalk to the title with a four-birdie 70 Saturday as Triplett took over second place with a 71 but was eight strokes off the lead. Even though his putting touch betrayed him Sunday en route to the 75, Lu faced no challenge. Instead, the only battle was between Triplett and Thailand winner Jeff Senior to second place. Senior shot 68, the day's best round, and was the only other player besides Lu to score in the 60s all week, but he fell a stroke short of Triplett, who closed with 72 for 286.

Republic of China Open—US$170,000
Winner: Carolos Espinosa

The strong international aspect of the Asia Circuit emerged once again at its eighth stop as a Mexican professional captured the Republic of China Open, long the virtually exclusive possession of the island nation's strong contingent of players. Carlos Espinosa, 26, came from four strokes off the pace in the final round at Taipei's Hsin Chu Golf and Country Club to become his country's second winner in Asia, joining Rafael Alarcon, the 1984 Indian Open champion. Typical difficult weather conditions exacted their usual toll to the scoring, Espinosa winning with a five-over-par score of 293, second highest total in tournament history.

Espinosa's countryman Esteban Toledo and Japan's Hisao Inoue led the first day with even-par 72s and Craig McClellan's 36-hole total of 147 at the end of a windy second round was good enough for a one-shot lead over defending champion Mark Aebli, another American, and three Taiwanese pros — Lin Chi Hsiang, Huang Shyh Ho and 53-year-old Hsieh Yung Yo, the circuit's all-time victory leader (13). The gales continued on a hot Saturday as Lin took over first place with 73 for 221, five over par for the 54 holes. With Chen Tze Ming and Lee Wen Sheng a stroke behind, prospects looked good for a win for the Republic of China. But along came Espinosa, who had been struggling along with rounds of 76-75-74 for 225 and was lodged in seventh place. The finish was exciting. Espinosa's fourth birdie of the day gave him a solid 68, but victory came only after Lin double-bogeyed the par-five 18th hole a short time later for 73 and 294, short by a stroke.

It was the first time ever that non-Taiwanese pros won the tournament two years in a row.

Maekyung South Korean Open—US$140,000
Winner: Frankie Minoza

Frankie Minoza, currently the strongest player from The Philippines, broke Taiwan's three-year hold on the Maekyung South Korean Open, scoring a one-stroke victory in the mid-April tournament and next-to-last event on the 1988 Asia Circuit. Minoza, picking up his second circuit victory to go with his 1986 win in Indonesia, grabbed the third-round lead with a five-under-par 67 and survived a final rush by Lim Jin Han, bidding to keep the title in South Korea for the first time since amateur Kim Joo Heun won in 1982.

Canadian Rick Gibson led the first two days at Nam Seoul Country Club, a 6,860-yard, par-72 course. He opened with 69 for a one-shot lead over Minoza and Esteban Toledo and doubled the edge Friday with 71 for 140, as the Filipino followed with 72 and Lim entered contention with 68 for his 142. Minoza's 67 — 209 Saturday put him three strokes in front of South Korea's Park Yeun Tae as Gibson flailed to 75. Minoza fashioned a two-under-par 70 in the final round for 279, just enough to nip Lim, who closed with a 66 for 280. Australian Craig Parry, coming off a strong showing the previous week in Japan, closed with 67-69 for 282 and third place, Gibson getting the fourth spot in the standings with 71 for 286.

Shizuoka Open—¥$40,000,000
Winner: Toshimitsu Kai

The Japanese Tour also crowned a first-time winner when Toshimitsu Kai won the season-opening Shizuoka Open at Hamaoka, but Kai's victory came in striking contrast to Hsieh's win in Indonesia that same weekend. He went three holes of sudden death at Shizuoka Country Club's Hamaoka course before subduing Tomohiro Maruyama, another winless Japanese campaigner. The two had emerged from the pack in the final round, Maruyama completing a comeback from an opening 78 with a 66 for 283 to match Kai's total after Toshimitsu finished with 68. Maruyama birdied the last two holes of regulation play, but ultimately lost to Kai at Hamaoka's 18th hole with a bogey.

Hsieh Min Nan, who had won the Shizuoka Open 10 years earlier, opened with 70 and shared the first-round lead with Nobuo Serizawa before Seiji Ebihara took over the lead for the next two rounds. Ebihara, a three-time winner on the Japan Tour, shot 67 in the second round for 140, a stroke better than the scores of Hiroshi Makino and 22-year-old Craig Parry of Australia, playing in his second Japanese tournament. Ebihara took a 71 in the third round and clung to his one-shot lead as Parry also posted a one-under score for his 213. At that point, Kai was at 215, Maruyama at 217. Ebihara slipped to a 74 in the final round, dropping into a sixth-place tie, a shot behind Makino, Parry and Katsunari Takahashi.

In unofficial pre-season events in Japan, Kazuya Nakajima, Tsuneyuki's younger brother, won the Daiichi Fudosan Cup with 276, a one-stroke triumph at Miyazaki Kikusai Golf Club, and Katsuji Hasegawa captured a four-man playoff in the 36-hole Imperial Invitation. He, Taiijiro Tanaka, Naomichi Ozaki and Shirgeru Kawamata all shot 143s in the 36-hole event.

TaylorMade Setonaikai Open—¥40,000,000
Kuzuha Kokusai—¥18,000,000
Winner: Wayne Smith

His decision to play the "pre-season" swing of the Japan Tour paid off handsomely for Australian Wayne Smith, even though the back-to-back titles he captured in the TaylorMade Setonaikai Open and the Kuzuha Kokusai tournament do not have official status on the circuit. In winning the two events on successive Sundays, Smith collected ¥10,800,000 (US$86,400), well worth the March trip to the Land of the Rising Sun. Oddly, Katsunari Takahashi scored the same "double" in 1987.

Smith staged final-round rallies at both places. In the Setonaiki in late March, he shot a last-18, three-under-par 69 at Shito Country Club to slip past veteran Kenji Mori and post a one-shot victory over Mori, the leader over the first two rounds of the rain-shortened tournament with 65-75 — 140, and Norio Mikami, who also closed with a 69. Smith joined his illustrious countryman, Greg Norman, as a winner of the long-standing Kuzuha, an annual 36-hole event on the Kuzuha public course, a 6,238-yard, par-70 layout. Norman won there in 1977. Craig Parry, another Australian, was Smith's rally victim in the Kuzuha. Parry led the first day with 64, but Wayne, who had opened with 65, landed the title Sunday with his follow-up 66 for 131, finishing two strokes ahead of Parry (69) and Yasuhiro Funatogawa (67-66). Toru Nakamura shot 63 for 134.

Pocari Sweat Open—¥40,000,000
Winner: Ian Baker-Finch

Ian Baker-Finch maintained Australia's stranglehold in the early going of the Japanese season as the tour turned to official events with the Pocari Sweat Open at Hakuryuko Country Club near Hiroshima. Baker-Finch followed up Wayne Smith's victories the two previous Sundays with a two-stroke win at Daiwacho, his second victory in Japan. Australians blanketed the top four positions at the finish.

One of those Aussies, Craig Parry, the Kuzuha runner-up, shared the first-round lead with veteran Fujio Kobayashi at 68 on a cold and wet Thursday as Ian muddled to a 73. He got his game on track Friday, shooting a three-under-par 68 after a first-hole bogey for 141 and a one-shot lead over Graham Marsh, Australia's most successful player in Japan, and Seiiki Okuda. Then, Baker-Finch jumped his margin to four over Toshimitsu Kai, shooting a five-birdie 66 for his 207. A spotty final round dropped his margin to two at the finish. Ian had four birdies and three bogeys for 70 and 277 as Marsh finished with 67 for 279 and Brian Jones, the Aussie who plays the Japan

Tour full-time, also had a 67 for 280 and third place. Parry was fourth at 282.

Bridgestone Aso Open—¥40,000,000
Winner: Ian Baker-Finch

Ian Baker-Finch ran the Australian string of victories in Japan to four in a row when the preliminary phase of the Japan Tour reached its final stop at Asomachi for the Bridgestone Aso Open at Aso Golf Club in the national park of the same name. In contrast to his Pocari Sweat victory the previous Sunday, Baker-Finch surged from four strokes off the pace in the final round at Aso, producing a six-under-par 66 for 282 and his one-shot triumph.

Masashi (Jumbo) Ozaki, picking up where he left off in his outstanding 1987 season, shared the first-round lead with little-known Ichiro Ino at 70. Roger Mackay, yet another Australian campaigning in 1988 in Asia, was a shot back, tied with Nobuo Serizawa and Yoshikazu Yokoshima. Mackay moved in front Friday with 70 (six birdies, four bogeys) for 141, a shot in front of Yoshihisa Iwashita, who also had a 70. Ozaki dropped back into a five-way tie for third at 143. Tadami Ueno, one of the 143 shooters and a five-time winner in 15 years on tour, advanced into a first-place tie with Mackay Saturday, shooting 69 for 212 as Mackay recovered from an early double-bogey for a 71. That set the stage for the seven-birdie, one-bogey finish of the 27-year-old Baker-Finch. Ueno inched into second place with 71 for 283 as Mackay finished with 72 for 284. Ozaki tied for fourth at 285 with Yokoshima.

Dunlop International Open—¥60,000,000
Winner: Masashi Ozaki

The superior overall strength of the Japan Tour prevailed when the Asia Circuit players arrived in Japan to conclude their season in conjunction with the first important event of the season in that country. Masashi (Jumbo) Ozaki, one of the dominant figures in Japan in 1987, scored the 53rd victory of his brilliant career and no Asia Circuit player did better than Tray Tyner's seventh-place-tie finish. Lu Chien Soon tied for 10th place, wrapping up his second seasonal championship on the Asia Circuit.

Two unfamiliar names — Toru Nakayama and Shuji Tsunoda — headed the leader boards after the first round at Imamachi's Ibaraki Golf Club, posting 68s as Ozaki and six others started with 69s. Nakayama eagled the final hole for his share of the lead. They yielded the top to Chen Tze Chung (T. C. Chen to many) and Yoshiyuki Isomura Friday, Chen carding a five-birdie, one-bogey 68 and Isomura a second 69 for their 138s. Just a shot off the pace at 139, Ozaki fired into the lead Saturday with 69 for 208, taking a two-shot bulge over David Ishii, who edged him for No. 1 honors in Japan in 1987. Ishii, the Japanese-American from Hawaii, also shot 69 for 210. Nobody challenged Jumbo Sunday, his easy 70 carrying him to 278 and a three-stroke victory over Ishii, who shot 71. Taijiro Tanaka was third at 282. Nakayama, the first-round co-leader, finished fourth at 284 with Toru Nakamura.

Chunichi Crowns—¥90,000,000
Winner: Scott Simpson

Scott Simpson may well have enjoyed a greater reputation in Japan than in his home country before he climaxed his fine career by winning the 1987 U.S. Open Championship and he enhanced it a bit more when he returned to Japan in 1988. Simpson made a big name for himself in Nippon in 1984 when he won two of the Japan Tour's biggest tournaments — the Chunichi Crowns and the Dunlop Phoenix. He became Chunichi Crowns' first repeat winner since Graham Marsh in 1981 when he scored a three-stroke victory at Nagoya Country Club's Wago course on the first of May.

Scott nailed the victory the hard way, with a three-under-par 67 in the final round that brought him from three strokes off the pace to his two-under-par 278. Fellow American Mike Reid emerged from a first-round cluster at the top to take a one-stroke lead after 36 holes Friday. Reid, at that time still a highly-regarded non-winner in tour golf, shot a three-birdie, three-bogey 70 in a driving rain for 139 as Simpson, Australia's Wayne Smith, Yoshima Niizeki, Tadao Nakamura and Masashi Ozaki, winner the previous Sunday in the Dunlop, carded 140s. Saburo Fujiki took over with a hot round Saturday, firing seven birdies and taking a bogey for 64 and a one-stroke lead over Ozaki, who shot his second 69 for 209. Simpson was then at 211 with Australia's Terry Gale and Kinpachi Yoshimura. Simpson won the tournament on the front nine Sunday with birdies on the second, fourth and seventh holes, then ran off 11 straight pars for the 67 and the three-shot victory margin over Ozaki (72) and David Ishii (69).

Fuji-Sankei Classic—¥60,000,000
Winner: Ikuo Shirahama

Ten years of campaigning on the Japan Tour culminated for Ikuo Shirahama with his first professional victory in the Fuji-Sankei Classic, a tournament that has a long list of name winners through its 16-year history. The 29-year-old Shirahama came from behind in the final round at the Kawana Hotel's Fuji course to score a two-stroke victory with his four-under-par 280, frustrating two pros who were trying to end long winless streaks on the circuit.

Shinsaku Maeda and Hiroshi Makino shared the first-round lead with 68s before yielding first place to Yutaka Hagawa, Japan's star lefthander in the early 1980s who has not won since 1983. The former Japan Open champion fired a 66 for 136 Friday to take a one-stroke lead over Naomichi Ozaki (69-68) and a two-shot margin over Yasuhiro Funatogawa (70-68) on the 6,694-yard, par-71 course at Ito. Hagawa's bid was short-lived, though. On Saturday, another star of the early 1980's, Nobumitsu Yuhara, ran off five birdies, took two bogeys for 68 and grabbed a one-stroke lead at 207 over Ozaki as Hagawa slipped to 75. Larry Nelson, on a one-stop visit from the U.S., was within striking distance at 211, but Sunday belonged to Shirahama. Ikuo began the final 18 five strokes off the lead and, with the help of an eagle at the 16th, posted a 68 — 280 ahead of the other contenders and it stood up for the victory as Yuhara saw his try for his first victory in five years dissolve with a 75 that left him in the runner-up slot at 282. Ozaki, Taijiro Tanaka and Toru Nakamura were next at 283.

Japan Match Play Championship—¥50,000,000
Winner: David Ishii

Within range on a couple of earlier occasions, David Ishii, the No. 1 man on the 1987 circuit, came through the rugged Japan Match Play Championship with his first 1988 victory and, as it turned out, his last. The 33-year-old Hawaiian rolled through the five-match sequence that includes the 36-hole finals, in which he took a four-up lead over lightly-regarded Noburu Sugai on the first 18 holes and went on to a 6-and-5 victory.

David had two difficult matches en route to the title. After polishing off Terry Gale, 4 and 3, in the opening round, he captured a hard-fought, 3-and-1 victory over Toru Nakamura. He advanced to the semi-finals with a 7-and-6 rout of Koiichi Suzuki and to the finals by defeating Namio Takasu, 1 up. Sugai had no easy matches. In order, he took out Chen Tze Ming on the 20th hole, Hajime Meshiai, 3 and 1; Tateo Ozaki, 3 and 2, and Yoshitaka Yamamoto, 2 and 1, in the semi-finals. In the finals Ishii won eight holes and lost two to score his 10th victory in Japan. Takasu defeated Yamamoto in the other Sunday match for third place, 3 and 1.

Pepsi Ube—¥37,500,000
Winner: Mamoru Kondo

Bad weather made rather a shambles of the Pepsi Ube tournament, heavy rains resulting in the shortening of the event to 45 holes and reducing of the purse by one quarter to ¥37,500,000. All of this worked to the benefit of Mamoru Kondo, a 39-year-old pro who had campaigned through 14 seasons without a victory. His 34 on the nine holes played Sunday gave him a strange-sounding score of 169 and a one-stroke triumph over Masahiro Kuramoto at drenched Ube Country Club at Ajisu.

Before the rains came, Isamu Sugita, the holder of one title in nine seasons on the Japan Tour, reeled off eight birdies on his way to the lead with a 66, six under par. Four players — Isao Aoki, Toru Nakamura, Yutaka Hagawa and Kondo — had 67s. The weather then delayed the second round until Saturday, when Kondo shot 68 and Chen Tze Ming 64, a course record, to hold first place at 135. Chen had a string of four birdies and an eagle at one point in his torrid round that included three other birdies and a bogey. However, the defending champion, who holds five wins in Japan, faltered in the abbreviated session Sunday when it was decided to limit play to Ube's back nine. He dropped all the way to 10th place with a 38. Kondo had four birdies and two bogeys in his 34, while Kuramoto slipped into second place ahead of Ikuo Shirahama, the Fuji-Sankei winner, as both finished with 33s.

Mitsubishi Galant—¥56,000,000
Winner: Brian Jones

One would think that the Mitsubishi Galant is a private tournament, held just for the benefit of Brian Jones, the Australian who has lived in Japan for years and is a regular on the Japan Tour. When Jones defeated Naomichi Ozaki in the season's first playoff in this year's Mitsubishi Galant, he had his second consecutive title in the tournament and third in the last four years. So, nearly half of his seven victories in Japan have come in the Mitsubishi Galant.

Jones was in the 60s with all four of his rounds over the 7,000 yards of the Ohnuma Lake Golf Club course at Morimachi. His opening 68 left him two off the lead, set by Toru Nakayama, who shot his 66 after getting into the tournament through the Monday qualifier. Jones repeated the 68 Friday and moved into a three-way tie for the lead with David Ishii and Hiroshi Ishii (not relatives) at 136. Brian's was a steady, four-birdie round, while the other two had double-bogeys on their cards. The players were blazing Saturday. Naomichi Ozaki fired a non-bogey 65 to take a one-stroke lead at 202 over Jones (67) and Yoshikazu Yokoshima, who had eight birdies and a course-record 64. A solid, four-birdie 68 by Jones set up the tie at 271 and the playoff as Ozaki recovered from two early bogeys for 69 and his 271. Yokoshima also shot 69 and missed the playoff by a shot. The overtime work ended quickly as Jones birdied the par-five 18th, the first extra hole, while Ozaki was three-putting for par.

Sendai Hoso Classic—¥45,000,000
Winner: Masahiro Kuramoto

Maybe it took some unfavorable weather to get Masahiro's 1988 season into high gear. Little had been heard from Kuramoto until two weeks prior to the Sendai Hoso (former Tohoku) Classic when he finished second in the rain-abbreviated Pepsi Ube. The Sendai Hoso also lost a round to wet weather and the winner was . . . Masahiro Kuramoto.

Fifty-year-old Teruo Sugihara, one of whose last two victories came in the Tohoku just two years ago, stole the show in the first round when he shot 66, five under par, and shared the lead with Masashi Ozaki and Futoshi Irino at Omote Zao Kokusai Golf Club at Sendai. The rains came and washed out Friday's round. Then Kuramoto came into the picture Saturday, shooting a second 67 to move into a first-place tie with Ozaki and Irino, who had 68s, while Sugihara, who turned 51 later in the month, slipped back with 70. Kuramoto broke from the deadlock Sunday with birdies at the fourth and fifth holes and had things well in hand until he bogeyed the 16th and 18th holes, cutting his victory margin to two with 70 for 204. Irino shot 72 for 206 to nose out Ozaki, Noriichi Kawakami and David Ishii for second place.

Sapporo Tokyu Open—¥50,000,000
Winner: Naomichi Ozaki

The season's largest flurry of birdies headed Naomichi Ozaki toward his first victory of the Japan Tour season and his second in five years in the Sapporo-Tokyu Open. The youngest Ozaki wheeled in 10 birdies in the course of shooting a third-round 64 at Sapporo Kokusai Country Club. It brought him from six strokes off the pace and put him into the lead, by one stroke after that round and three at the finish. Ozaki shot 71 Sunday for 279.

Hajime Meshiai, a four-time winner on the circuit, took the first-round lead with a six-under-par 66 over the 6,949 yards of Sapporo International's Shimamatsu course. Masahiro Kuramoto, coming off his Sunday victory in the Sendai Hoso Classic, seized the lead Friday with his 68 for 138 as Meshiai took a 74. David Ishii and Katsunari Takahashi trailed then by a stroke. Ozaki took over with the 64 for 208 Saturday, entering the final round a shot in front of Yoshimi Niizeki, who shot 66 Saturday, and two ahead of Meshiai, Ishii, Ian Baker-Finch and older brother Tateo Ozaki. Naomichi slipped back into a four-way tie for the lead after bogeys at the first and fifth holes, but jumped ahead to stay when he birdied the eighth and eagled the ninth holes. Tateo Ozaki birdied the 18th for a par 72 and second place at 282, a shot ahead of Ishii and Niizeki.

Yomiuri Sapporo Beer Open—¥70,000,000
Winner: Masahiro Kuramoto

Masahiro Kuramoto and Ian Baker-Finch played volleyball with the lead in the Yomiuri Sapporo Beer Open, Kuramoto finally spiking the title with a solid finish at Yomiuri Country Club near Osaka. The four-stroke victory was Massie's second in three weeks and he was the first multiple winner of the year on the regular portion of the Japan Tour's long schedule. Kuramoto won the Sendai Hoso and tied for seventh in the Sapporo Tokyu prior to the triumph at Yomiuri.

The Japanese and the Australian traded the lead back and forth each day of the tournament. Baker-Finch had it the first day, along with Katsuji Hasegawa of Japan as both opened with 67s. The Aussie had done little since his back-to-back victories in the pre-season stretch in the Pocari Sweat and Bridgesone Aso. Kuramoto took his turn Friday, whizzing in front with 66 for 134 though bogeying his first hole of the day. Masahiro had three strokes on Tsukasa Watanabe and five on Baker-Finch (72) at that point, but gave the lead back Saturday with a shaky 74, falling a stroke behind the Australian, who posted 68 for a nine-under-par 207. Baker-Finch clung to the lead Sunday until the 14th hole. Then, at the 15th, Kuramoto birdied, Ian bogeyed and the stocky little Japanese pro put the icing on the cake with an eagle at the final hole. It was Kuramoto's 22nd victory in his eight-year pro career.

Mizuno Open—¥60,000,000
Winner: Yoshimi Niizeki

It looked like a playoff ahead in the Mizuno Open as five players shared the tournament lead at the end of 54 holes. It happened as forecast, but overtime play went on without any of those five players. Instead, Yoshimi Niizeki won the playoff and the first title of his 11-year career, defeating veteran Seiichi Kanai by rolling in a 40-foot birdie putt on the first extra hole at the Bijodai course of the Tokinodai Country Club at Hakui.

It was a good week for the veterans of the Japan Tour. Seiji Ebihara, 37, eagled the 13th hole en route to a 67 and a one-stroke lead over Yoshihisa Iwashita and ageless Shigeru Uchida, now a senior player. Fujio Kobayashi, 43, seized first place Friday, his 72-66 — 138 giving him a two-stroke lead over 51-year-old Teruo Sugihara (73-67), Uchida, Nobuo Serizawa and Jumbo Ozaki. Kobayashi and Serizawa joined Saburo Fujiki, Akira Kawamata and Tsutomu Irie at the top — 210 — in Saturday's action. Kawamata got there with the day's best score, a 66, despite an opening bogey. Of the five, Serizawa had the best round Sunday, but his 71 left him a stroke short of the playoff and in a three-way tie for third place with Hiroshi Makino and Jumbo Ozaki, who closed with a 66. Niizeki shot 69 and Kanai 68 for their 280s. The winning experience of 47-year-old Kanai — 15 victories — meant little in the face of a holed 40-footer.

Kansai PGA Championship—¥30,000,000
Winner: Masahiro Kuramoto

Masahiro Kuramoto completed an outstanding month of golf when he won the Kansai PGA Championship for the first time on July 3rd. It was his third victory since June 5th and he was seventh in one of his other two starts during the hot streak. In the Kansai (Western Japan) PGA at Sport Shinko Country Club, Kuramoto hovered just off the pace for three rounds, then grabbed a one-stroke victory with a closing 68 for 276, 12 under par.

Kuramoto's major victim at Sport Shiko was Norio Mikami, who led by three strokes with 70-67-68 — 205 entering the final round. His 72 Sunday left him in a tie for second place with Yurio Akitomi. Takeshi Kitadai and Yoichi Yamamoto had early moments of glory. Kitadai led the first day with 67 and Yamamoto took over Friday with 68-71 — 139 before Mikami staked his claim Saturday. Instead, he yielded to Kuramoto's 23rd pro victory.

Kanto PGA Championship—¥30,000,000
Winner: Tomohiro Maruyama

The circumstances were entirely different that week in the concurrent Kanto (Eastern Japan) PGA Championship. Tomohiro Maruyama, who had never captured an individual title on the Japan Tour and lost a playoff at Shizuoka earlier in the season, staked himself to a generous lead over the first two rounds at Narita Springs Country Club at Yamadamachi and held on for the victory with a 278, 10 under par over the 7,017-yard course.

Maruyama shared the first-round lead with Shigeru Kawamata at 68, then rocketed to a seven-stroke lead Friday with 66 for 134. He had birdies at both ends of the fine round and an eagle in the middle. Tomohiro lost four strokes of his margin Saturday as he shot 73 for 207. At 210 were Yoshimi Niizeki, the Mizuno Open winner the previous week, and Hiroshi Makino. Despite a wildly-fluctuating round Sunday, Maruyama clung to his three-stroke margin to the finish. His 71 included six birdies, three bogeys and a double-bogey at the 17th hole. Niizeki, with 71, and Futoshi Irino, with 69, tied for second place. The first-time winner had shared a title in the 1987 Japan Doubles.

Hiroshima Open—¥40,000,000
Winner: Hajime Matsui

Sentiment surely rode with Teruo Sugihara as the Hiroshima Open moved into its final round, but it wasn't to be. At 51, the Japanese golfing great with a like number of tour titles couldn't keep his game together through the full 72 holes and yielded the title to Hajime Matsui, who had won exactly 51 less official tournaments in his career. Matsui, who projected himself into contention with a third-round 66, closed with 68 for 274, 14 under par, and a one-stroke victory over Katsuyoshi Tomori at Hiroshima Country Club, a 6,865-yard course.

After unknown Toshiaki Sudo had his day with an opening-round 65, Sugihara took center stage for the next two days. The remarkable Teruo, who won his last two titles just two years earlier, blistered Hiroshima's Hachihonmatsu course with a 64 Friday. He had eight birdies and one-putted 15 of the 18 greens in the exciting round. With 133, he led Hisashi Nakase by two and five others by four. Sugihara managed just a par round Saturday but still led by one at 205. Matsui, with his 66, and Katsuyoshi Tomori were at 206 and Tsuneyuki Nakajima, the star pro who had just returned to Japan two weeks earlier after four months on the U.S. tour, flashed a 65 Saturday, but had to settle for 71 and a sixth-place tie Sunday. Sugihara took a 74 and dropped to 15th place.

Japan PGA Championship—¥56,000,000
Winner: Tateo Ozaki

It was not a typical major championship. Par took a beating all week at Ehime Golf Club, scene of the 1988 Japan PGA Championship, the type of event on a tour schedule that usually features a tough course, rigorously set up to avoid birdie barrages. At Ehime, Tateo Ozaki, the winner, set a PGA Championship record with his 20-under-par score of 268 and still won by only a stroke over his older brother, Masashi. The 30th player finished five under par.

Yet, the low scoring did not diminish the quality of the tournament. Both Ozakis were previous winners — Jumbo in 1971 and 1974 and Tateo (Jet) in 1985 — and three-time victor Tsuneyuki Nakajima was third at 271. Naomichi (the youngest) Ozaki was an early factor, sharing the first-round lead at 66 with Futoshi Irino and Yurio Akitomi. Jumbo Ozaki and Ikuo Shirahama, the Fuji-Sankei winner in early May, took over Friday, Ozaki with 66 and Shirahama with the day's best score of 65 for 133s and a one-shot lead over Akitomi and Nobuo Serizawa as both Naomichi Ozaki and Irino absorbed 74s.

Though taking bogeys on his first two holes Saturday, Jumbo Ozaki moved a stroke in front, coming back with five birdies on the back nine for 69 and 202. Nakajima, Serizawa, Yoshikazu Yokoshima and Toshimitsu Kai were at 203 and Tateo Ozaki, who added 66 to his earlier pair of 69s, was poised for his final-round run at 204. And run he did. He produced an eagle, seven birdies and took a bogey as he shot 64 for the 268. Jumbo Ozaki's 67 for 269 gave him two strokes on Nakajima.

NST Niigata Open—¥40,000,000
Winner: Naomichi Ozaki

Naomichi Ozaki shook off the disappointment of frittering away a good start the week before in the Japan PGA Championship and put on a fine performance in the NST Niigata Open to ring up his second victory of 1988 and the eighth of his 12-year career. Ozaki roared from four strokes off the pace after the first 18 holes with a six-under-par 66 Friday at the Niigata Sunrise Golf Course at Seiro, took a three-stroke lead and never trailed the rest of the way. He finished with 277, three strokes ahead of runner-up David Ishii.

Koichi Suzuki, Masami Morishita and Katsuyoshi Timori opened with 66s, but only the veteran Suzuki remained in contention the rest of the way. With his 136, Naomichi Ozaki built a three-shot lead over Suzuki (73), as little-known Ukyo Eimori created a stir with two eagles in a 70 round that tied him for third with Hajime Meshiai and Chen Tze Ming. Little changed Saturday as Ozaki shot 69 and Suzuki 68 to maintain their one-two positions and Ishii began his move toward second place with 67 for 208, three shots off the pace. A par round was all Naomichi needed Sunday to post his three-shot win over Ishii, who matched the 72 to slip past Suzuki (74) into second place.

Nikkei Cup—¥50,000,000
Winner: Masashi Ozaki

So, what else is new? An Ozaki won the Nikkei Cup in mid-August at Sanyo Golf Club's 7,298-yard Yoshii course. Well, an Ozaki had won the two previous tournaments on the Japan Tour and an Ozaki had won two of the three previous Nikkei Cup tournaments. This time it was Jumbo Ozaki, capturing his second tournament of the season and the Nikkei Cup for the second time. He had won it in 1986 after brother Naomichi took the inaugural in 1985. Of course, Naomichi finished second this year.

The week went like this: Yoshimi Niizeki, Yutaka Hagawa and Keiji Tejima shot 69s Thursday to lead after the first round. Naomichi moved in Friday, his 71-68 — 139 giving him a one-shot edge over Hagawa (71) and two over brother Jumbo, Niizeki, Teruo Sugihara and Eitaro Deguchi. In tough playing conditions, they bunched up at the top with the Ozakis, Hagawa and Yoshiyuki Isomura deadlocked at 215, just one under par. Isomura's 68 was the day's only sub-par round. Jumbo Ozaki had Sunday's best round, also a 68, and it resulted in his four-stroke victory, the 54th of his career, tying Isao Aoki for the all-time leadership in that department. Naomichi's 72 gave him second place at 287, a shot ahead of Hagawa (73).

Maruman Open—¥70,000,000
Winner: Masahi Ozaki

Jumbo kept his personal and the Ozaki family streaks going when the Japan Tour moved on to Higashi Matsuyama for the Maruman Open. He scored his third 1988 victory and the fourth consecutive win by one of the Ozaki brothers on the circuit, in the process becoming the winningest Japanese pro ever with his 55th triumph.

His prospects weren't particularly bright after the first round was played Friday following heavy rains that washed out the scheduled start Thursday. He shot 73 and trailed leader Seiji Ebihara by five strokes. Even his second-round 65 didn't make as big a dent as expected, since Haruo Yasuda, another of Japan's seniors still able to play well against their younger compatriots, fired a 65 too, and took the lead at 134, eight under par. Toru Nakamura shot 67 for 137 and Ozaki was next with his 138. Yasuda went in the wrong direction Sunday, opening the door for Ozaki, who won by three strokes with his 69 and 207. Hajime, Meshiai and Yoshimi Niizeki also moved up, sharing second place at 210. Yasuda shot 78 and Nakamura 75 and dropped into a three-way tie for sixth place.

KBC Augusta—¥50,000,000
Winner: Masahiro Kuramoto

Masahiro Kuramoto regained his position as Japan's most frequent winner of 1988 when he scored his fourth victory of the year in the KBC Augusta tournament and broke the Ozaki streaks as he was doing it. But, barely. All three brothers still had a shot at the title after 54 holes, sitting in a five-way tie five strokes off the pace. However, Kuramoto nursed his one-shot lead at the three-quarter mark to a two-stroke victory with a one-over-par 73 final round. Jumbo Ozaki made the strongest bid of the family, closing with 70 to join a runner-up tie in his bid for a third straight victory on the circuit.

Hajime Meshiai, who finished in that runner-up deadlock with Ozaki and Nobumitsu Yuhara at 278, was the first-round leader with 65. Then, for the second week in a row, 54-year-old Haruo Yasuda grabbed a tournament lead. Yasuda's 68-69 gave him a one-stroke edge over Kuramoto, Jumbo and Naomichi Ozaki and Pete Izumikawa. Kuramoto made his move Saturday with a bogey-free 65 over the 7,130 yards of Kyushu Shima Country Club's Keya course. His 203 gave him a one-shot margin over Izumikawa, three over Meshiai and five over the Ozakis, Tomohiro Maruyama and Katsuji

Hasegawa. Kuramoto birdied the final hole to insure his victory Sunday, the 73 giving him a 276 total, two in front of Jumbo Ozaki, Meshiai and Yuhara.

Kansai Open—¥20,000,000
Winner: Yasuo Sone

Kanto Open—¥30,000,000
Winner: Akihito Yokoyama

Kyushu Open—¥15,000,000
Winner: Katsuyoshi Tomori

Chubu Open—¥15,000,000
Winner: Teruo Nakamura

Chu-Shikoku Open—¥15,000,000
Winner: Masahiro Kuramoto

Hokkaido Open—¥10,000,000
Winner: Mamoru Takahashi

Eveywhere you looked, there was a professional golf tournament in Japan the first weekend of September. Most prominent of the six events in all parts of the country were the long-standing Kansai and Kanto Opens, the championships of Eastern and Western Japan which lack in stature because of their small purses and weak fields.

In 1988, both produced first-time winners on the Japan Tour. Akihito Yokoyama captured his first title in the Kanto Open at Edozaki Country Club in Ibaraki Prefecture. The fourth-year pro broke into the lead in the third round with a 67 after his 70-66 start, moving five strokes ahead of runner-up Katsuji Hasegawa, the second-round leader. Amazingly, Yokoyama's final-round 75 not only did not cost him the tournament but actually he found his margin open another stroke as he finished with 278 and the runners-up, Nobumitsu Yuhara and Tomohiro Maruyama, were at 284.

Yasuo Sone also won by taking the third-round lead in the Kansai Open at Kita Rokko Country Club at Kobe and carrying it the rest of the way. Although he shot a respectable 70 Sunday, his third in a row after an opening 76, Sone, in his fifth season on the pro tour, did not win as decisively. His two-under-par 286 gave him a three-shot victory over Shinsaku Maeda and four over Toru Nakamura, both veterans with many wins on their records.

The most striking win of the week, though, occurred at Hiroshima, where the hometown star, Masahiro Kuramoto, continued his remarkable domination of the Chu-Shikoku Open, a tournament he first won as an amateur just before he turned pro in 1980. Since then, he has won it six more times, missing only in 1985 and 1986. This time, he staged another rout, building a 13-stroke victory on his nine-under-par 63 in the second round at Hakuryuko Country Club. He followed with 65 and 71 for 266, the lowest 72-hole score of the year. The win, a week after he took the KBC Augusta, was his fifth in 1988.

In the other three tournaments, Katsuyoshi Tomori won the Kyushu Open by three shots with his 283, repeating his victory in the event in 1987; Teruo Nakamura ran away with his second Chubu Open title, winning by seven with his 279 at Oita Country Club; and Mamoru Takahashi scored a playoff victory over Katsunari Takahashi in the Hokkaido Open after both had finished with 280s.

Suntory Open—¥80,000,000
Winner: Tateo Ozaki

The Ozakis were back when the Japan Tour returned to full-scale action with the Suntory Open at Narashino Country Club at Inzaimachi. This time it was the middle brother who carried the family name to victory, breaking on top in the third round and going on to a three-stroke victory, his second straight 68 giving him a 14-under-par final score of 274 and his second triumph of the season. Tateo was on familiar ground, having won the Suntory in a 1985 playoff for one of his other nine victories on the circuit.

Teruo Sugihara, the indominatable 51-year-old, had another of his hot putting rounds the first day, one-putting 11 times on his way to a 66 and the lead by one over Ozaki and Shoichi Sato and by two over three others, including Masahiro Kuramoto, gunning for a third consecutive victory. Kuramoto maintained his chances of accomplishing that through the next two rounds, sharing the lead with three others after 36 holes and, with Tadami Ueno and Brian Jones, trailing Ozaki by just a stroke after 54 holes. Kuramoto had a string of four birdies on the front nine, but frittered away three of the strokes coming in. Ozaki put away the opposition early Sunday, making an eagle and three birdies on the front nine. He came home in one-over 37 for the 68. Ueno shot 70 for 277, placing second a shot ahead of Jones and Meshiai. Kuramoto finished with 72 for 279.

All Nippon Airways Open—¥70,000,000
Winner: Naomichi Ozaki

The best opening round of the season got it started, but it took a three-hole playoff for Naomichi Ozaki to wrap up his third victory of 1988 in the All Nippon Airways Open at Sapporo Golf Club at Yunicho. Oddly, the playoff amounted to a rematch, pitting Ozaki against Australia's Brian Jones, who had beaten him in overtime in the Mitsubishi Galant at the end of May.

Ozaki roared to a rare five-stroke, first-round lead Thursday when he put together a nine-under-par 63 at Sapporo, a 7,031-yard course. Brother Masashi

Ozaki had the only 68, too, making the start all the more impressive. Jumbo chopped three strokes off the lead Friday, shooting 66 while Naomichi was taking a 69 for 132. Hajime Meshiai followed Jumbo Ozaki at 137, with Jones at 138 with Kimpachi Yoshimura after his 70-68 start. Naomichi kept his shot at a wire-to-wire victory going Saturday as both he and Jumbo shot 73s, Jones and Yoshimura jumping into a tie with Jumbo at 207, four ahead of the next players in the standings. The leader shot 73 again Sunday and found himself in the playoff when Jones, shooting for his second victory of the year, closed with 71. After they matched scores on the first two playoff holes, Ozaki nailed the win with a par four at the third when Jones took a bogey.

Jun Classic—¥65,000,000
Winner: Toru Nakamura

With victories fewer and farther between lately, Toru Nakamura was taking them any way he could get them. In the case of the Jun Classic, the late-September tournament at Jun Classic Country Club in Ogawamachi, Nakamura took the third-round lead and grabbed the 24th victory of his fine career with a 35 segment when rain forced officials to cut the Sunday round to nine holes. The four-stroke victory was the first for the 37-year-old Nakamura since late 1986.

The lead bounced around the first three days. Chen Tze Chung, the respected Taiwanese pro with a U.S. Tour victory on his record, led the first round with a six-under-par 66, one stroke better than the rounds of Naomichi and Jumbo Ozaki and Brian Jones. Little-known Taisei Inagaki shot 66 Friday and took the second-round lead with 135, but the headlines went to international star Greg Norman, making his first appearance in Japan in four years. Norman fired a course-record 64, with nine birdies, and jumped into a second-place tie with Nakamura at 136, Toru shooting his second 68. Norman had fired and fell back Saturday as Nakamura went in front by three over Nobuo Serizawa as both shot 69s. Toru's 35 for 240 widened the edge to four as Serizawa managed only a par side. Norman finished with 76-37 and tied for seventh.

Tokai Classic—¥90,000,000
Winner: Brian Jones

Brian Jones rested in a four-way tie for the lead after 54 holes of the Tokai Classic with two of the game's finest players — America's current No. 1 pro Curtis Strange and fellow Australian Graham Marsh, the overseas king of Japanese golf over the years. But it didn't faze him in the least. Jones raced to his second 1988 victory on the Japan Tour with a closing, seven-under-par 65 at Miyoshi Country Club's West Course.

Chen Tze Chung, Taiwan's international star, repeated an unrewarding habit in the Tokai Classic, jumping off to the first-round lead for the second week in a row and failing to capitalize on it. Chen opened with 66 on the 7,065-yard course, taking a two-stroke lead over six players, including

Masahiro Kuramoto, a five-time winner already in 1988, and Hajime Meshiai, an almost-weekly contender on the circuit. Marsh, the 44-year-old winner of 23 titles in Japan, including the Tokai in 1985, moved into first place Friday, taking a commanding, four-stroke lead over Jones with a 65 for 134. Three solid but unspectacular rounds — 70-69-70 — lifted Strange into the third-round tie with Marsh (75), Jones (71) and Yoshitaka Yamamoto (71-68). Jones won the tournament Sunday with a strong finishing kick. He birdied five holes on the back nine, including the clinching run of three starting at the 15th hole. Koichi Suzuki had a 66 and slipped into second place at 277, four strokes behind the winner, who now holds eight titles in Japan.

Japan Open Championship—¥60,000,000
Winner: Masashi Ozaki

Few would argue that Isao Aoki, Tsuneyuki Nakajima and Masashi Ozaki constitute a modern "Big Three" in Japanese golf. Their records alone back that up. How appropriate it was, then, when they became the principal players in the 1988 Japan Open Championship in the demanding conditions of the Tokyo Golf Club at Sayama and finished one-two-three at week's end. "One" was Jumbo Ozaki, who captured his second Japan Open championship and fourth 1988 title with a four-over-par 288.

Unlike the PGA Championship, the Open provided a stern test for the players' skills over Tokyo Golf Club's 6,923 yards. Ozaki, the 1974 Japan Open champion, opened with a four-birdie 67, one of only three sub-par rounds on the rainy Thursday. Jumbo followed with 73 for 140 Friday, offsetting two early birdies with four bogeys. Norio Mikami and Kimpachi Yoshimura were one and two back respectively, but more ominous were Nakajima and Aoki, both two-time Open champions, at 143. Nakajima shot an even-par round in steady rain Saturday and took a one-stroke lead as Tokyo's heavy roughs and the wet conditions led Ozaki to a 75 and 215, putting him a shot off the pace along with Yoshimura. Aoki had 73 for 216.

Nakajima, winless in his relatively-short time on the 1988 Japan Tour, stuck to the lead Sunday until suffering a double-bogey at the 16th hole. With opportunity beckoning, Ozaki nailed down the victory when he rolled in a 40-foot birdie putt on the soggy 17th green and followed with a one-putt par at the 18th green for 73 and the 288. A bogey at the 17th cost Aoki his chance at a playoff. He shot 73 to tie Nakajima (75) at 289. Masuru Amano shot 66, the only round better than 70 Sunday, and tied for fourth with David Ishii and Katsuyoshi Tomori.

Polaroid Cup Golf Digest—¥60,000,000
Winner: Masashi Ozaki

Of his six victories in 1988, Masashi Ozaki's triumph in the Polaroid Cup Golf Digest tournament was certainly the most spectacular. What else can you say when a man goes into the final round of a tournament trailing by seven strokes and wins the title by shooting a dazzling 62 in regulation time and then wins the playoff with yet another birdie on the first extra hole? That's what Ozaki did at Tomei Country Club at Susono on the heels of his Japan Open victory the preceding Sunday.

Katsuji Hasegawa, 42, a 21-year veteran of the Japan Tour, held the Golf Digest lead for the first two days. On Thursday, he shot 66 on the par-71 Tomei course, then added 69 Friday for 135 and a one-stroke lead over Brian Jones, Kiyoshi Muroda and Kikuo Arai. At that point, Ozaki was six strokes off the pace after rounds of 69 and 72 and he fell another shot back Saturday as Jones surged into the lead with 67 for 203. The bogey-free round staked him to a three-stroke lead over Muroda. Little did he suspect that the man who would block out his bid for a third 1988 victory would come from so far back Sunday or that 69 with a three-shot lead would not be good enough. A barrage of nine birdies and two bogeys brought Ozaki roaring toward the top, but it took an eagle on the final hole to forge the tie and set a new Tomei course record in the process. Jumbo then further stunned Jones with his birdie on the first playoff hole for his year's fifth victory. Oddly, Jones had split two earlier playoffs with Ozaki's younger brother Naomichi before his victory two weeks before in the Tokai Classic.

Bridgestone—¥80,000,000
Winner: Masashi Ozaki

Despite the brilliant streaks of several of Japan's greatest players over the years, none had ever strung together three victories in a row on the Japan Tour until Masashi Ozaki did it in October of 1988. Jumbo scored another come-from-behind victory in tacking the Bridgestone title onto his wins the two previous weeks in the Japan Open and the Golf Digest tournaments.

After a lukewarm 72 start at Sodegaura Country Club on Thursday, Ozaki pulled within three strokes of the lead with another blazing round in his torrid season. His second-round 64 put him into a runner-up tie at 136 with Eitaro Deguchi and Yoshimi Niizeki. The leader was Isao Aoki, who had been suffering through a rare winless season. Aoki fashioned a 65 for his 36-hole 133, then maintained a two-stroke margin Saturday with a three-under-par 69 over Sodegaura's 7,120 yards. Ozaki shot 68 Saturday and had second place to himself. A faltering finish cost the 45-year-old Aoki his 54th world title and paved the way for Ozaki's unprecedented triple in Japan. Aoki still led by two after 14 holes, but he bogeyed the 15th, 17th and 18th holes for 73. Ozaki birdied the 16th and parred in for 69, 273 and a two-shot triumph. It was Jumbo's sixth title of 1988 and the 58th of his career.

Lark Cup—¥150,000,000
Winner: Katsunari Takahashi

It seemed like everywhere Katsunari Takahashi looked, an Ozaki was dogging him as he sought his first victory of 1988 in one of the year's two richest tournaments on the Japan Tour — the new Lark Cup — which replaced the 17-year-old U.S. vs. Japan competition on the prestigious fall schedule.

All three Ozaki brothers had a shot at the Lark Cup title and Masashi came closest, falling a stroke short in his bid for a fourth consecutive victory on the circuit, but Takahashi survived and took his 13th career victory, his first of 1988. It also was the first and only pure wire-to-wire triumph on the Japan Tour during the year.

Katsunari put together opening rounds of 65 and 66 on the par-72 ABC Golf Club course at Tojo and established a six-stroke lead. He had two eagles on the back nine Friday. The 38-year-old pro was already encountering the Ozakis. Tateo was the first-round runner-up and Masashi joined him, along with Brian Jones and Craig Parry, the Australians, in a second-place tie at 137 Friday. A par round Saturday cost Takahashi four strokes of his lead as Jumbo Ozaki shot a bogey-free 68 while he was three-putting twice during a four-bogey, four-birdie round in chilly rain. Three back-nine bogeys put Katsunari in shaky position, but Ozaki could do no better than 73 for 278, so Takahashi's 74 and 277 was just enough. Naomichi Ozaki shot 71 Sunday to take third place at 280, and brother Tateo had 74, but his 282 still landed him in fourth place. Takahashi's check was ¥27,000,000 (US$216,000).

ACOM Doubles—¥50,000,000
Winners: Bob Gilder and Doug Tewell

The small-field Acom Doubles filled a schedule hole left by the move of the Kirin Cup to Hawaii in 1988 and two Americans, arriving early for the three big Japanese tournaments to follow, Bob Gilder and Doug Tewell, picked up the unofficial victory, worth US$44,000 apiece. They shot a final-round 66 in the better-ball event for 256, 32 under par, and a one-stroke victory over Japanese pros Masanobu Kimura and Takenori Hiraishi at Chiba Springs Country Club east of Tokyo at Yamadamachi. Anders Forsbrand and Ove Sellberg of Sweden were third among the 29 teams with a final 64 for 259 to nip Britons Barry Lane and Peter Baker by a stroke.

Visa Taiheiyo Club Masters—¥100,000,000
Winner: Severiano Ballesteros

Japanese golf fans saw why Severiano Ballesteros had been the game's No. 1 international player in 1988 when he made his first visit of the year to the Land of the Rising Sun. The brilliant Spaniard, bearing the British Open crown and 1988 titles in five other countries, added Japan to his list with a decisive, three-stroke victory in the Visa Taiheiyo Club Masters on the Gotemba course in mid-November. He was seven-under-par with his 281 after four steady, solid rounds.

Brian Jones, a two-time winner earlier in the year, best handled a windy Thursday to shoot 68, but both Ballesteros and Masashi Ozaki, Japan's No. 1 player in 1988, had good field position at 71. However, when Jones slumped to 76 Friday, Yoshiyuki Isomura was the one to take over the lead, shooting a second 69 for 138 and a four-shot lead over Ballesteros and Nobumitsu Yuhara. Gotemba also claimed Ozaki (78) Friday. Seve got off his 71s with a 68 Saturday and seized the lead by a stroke over Isomura, carding six birdies and two bogeys and one-putting 10 times. Ballesteros started wobbly Sunday, yielding the lead to Isomura after bogeys at the first and fourth against Yoshiyuki's one-under-par result on those four holes. But Seve birdied the fifth and came home comfortably with three back-nine birdies for his third 71 and 281. Isomura slipped to fourth place with his 74, Yasuhiro Funatogawa taking second at 284 and Jose-Maria Olazabal third with 285, both shooting 69s.

Dunlop Phoenix—¥150,000,000
Winner: Ken Green

Not always, but the Japanese pros seem to have their problems when the Americans in sizeable numbers come to visit and play in the big fall events. Case in point: the Dunlop Phoenix, present and past. At the end of the week this November at Phoenix Country Club, the leading Japanese players were nowhere in sight as Ken Green capped his great U.S. season with his first overseas victory and led his fellow Americans to a dominating finish in one of Japan's two richest tournaments. Green nipped Fred Couples at the final hole; Jeff Sluman, the American PGA champion, was a close third and five other Yankees placed in the top 10, in which Hajime Meshiai (fifth) was the sole Japanese presence. Besides, Green was the third straight U.S. winner of the Dunlop Phoenix, and Americans have won the tournament eight of the last 11 years.

Couples was the monopolizer through the first three rounds in 1988. Fred raced to a three-stroke lead the first day with a course-record 62 — 10 birdies, no bogeys. (Miller Barber shot 63 in 1976.) Even though shooting a mere one-under-par 71 Friday, Couples built his margin to five over three of the U.S. pros — Green, the other Green, Hubert, and Sluman — at 138. It worked the other way Saturday. Couples shot a much-better 68, but lost all except one stroke of his lead as Ken Green shot 64 for 202 after being eight back after seven holes. He birdied the next five, then had four more birdies and a bogey in the finishing stretch for the 64. Sluman shot 68 and was at 203. Green moved two shots ahead on the front nine as Couples absorbed three bogeys, but Fred fought back, regaining the lead with a birdie at the 13th. However, he three-putted the 16th amid three one-putt pars by Green, taking the two even to the final hole. It was eventful. Green, playing safe with a layup second on the par-five, pitched to seven feet while Couples was reaching the edge of the green from the trees in three. Fred ran his first putt six feet past the cup and, after Green missed his birdie, flubbed his next two for a double-bogey and 74. Ken parred for 71 and 273, beating Couples by two and Sluman by three. Severiano Ballesteros, the previous week's winner, closed with 70 for 278 and fourth place. Meshiai was next at 280.

Casio World Open—¥90,000,000
Winner: Larry Mize

Even more evident case in point regarding the inability of the Japanese pros to stand off the Americans when they arrive in numbers: the Casio World Open. The rich Casio was founded in 1981 and it has yet to crown a Japanese winner. It came close in 1988 as its No. 1 player of the year, Masashi Ozaki, took a run at Larry Mize in the final round and fell one stroke short of catching the 1987 U.S. Masters champion, a non-winner since that memorable victory at Augusta. Mize, in fact, slipped to 62nd on the U.S. money list and, despite the ¥16,200,000 (US$129,600) he won in the Casio, was 56th on the World Money List.

Larry and Jumbo Ozaki lingered just off the pace the first two days as Yoshitaka Yamamoto led with 69 on a gusty Thursday — only two others, Hajime Meshiai and Shinsaku Maeda with 71s, broke par on Ibusuki Golf Club's Kaimon course at Kaimoncho — and shared first place with Spain's Jose-Maria Olazabal at 142. Mize (72-71) and Ozaki (73-70) were in third place at 143. Yamamoto maintained his pace with a 69 Saturday, but Mize replaced Olazabal at the top with a solid, four-birdie 68 for his 211. He and Yamamoto had three strokes on Olazabal and five on Jumbo and Naomichi Ozaki, Masanobu Kimura and Yasuhiro Funatogawa. Yamamoto ran out of gas and shot 79 Sunday, but Mize was equal to the task of fending off Jumbo Ozaki, even though Larry had to shake off a double-bogey at the 12th hole, where he drove out of bounds, and hole a six-foot birdie putt on the final green to avoid a playoff with Ozaki, who closed with 69 in his bid for a seventh 1989 title, making birdies on the last holes himself.

Japan Series Hitachi Cup—¥50,000,000
Winner: Naomichi Ozaki

While brothers Jumbo and Jet, along with several other Japanese stars, were competing in the big Australian Bicentennial tournament, Naomichi Ozaki carried on the family honors in the field-depleted Japan Series for the Hitachi Cup. Ozaki bested the 12 other contestants in the unique, year-end event, posting a 13-under-par 275 for a five-stroke victory over the Yomiuri Country Club courses at Osaka and Tokyo.

With only the winners of the seven designated major events and the 15 leading money-winners of the season eligible and with several of them in Australia, the Series began at Osaka's 7,030-yard course, site of the first two rounds. David Ishii, the leading money-winner in 1987 and winner of only the Japan Match Play but a healthy amount of prize money in 1988, grabbed the first-round lead Wednesday with 68, a shot better than Ozaki. Naomichi followed with 70 Thursday and deadlocked with Ikuo Shirahama (67) and Toru Nakamura (69) in first place at 139. Ishii, sputtering with bogeys on three of the par-three holes, shot 73 and tied for fourth at 141 with Katsuyoshi Tomori and Isao Aoki, with whom he shared the Series title after the 1987 "snow-out".

Ozaki moved in front to stay when the tournament resumed at Tokyo's Yomiuri. He shot 68s in both rounds, the first one giving him a one-stroke lead over Aoki and Nakamura, two over Shirahama. Two of Naomichi's five birdies in the final round came back to back at the 13th and 14th holes and he coasted home, his only bogey at the final hole merely reducing the final margin to five. In his last big chance for a 1988 victory, Aoki mustered only a par 72, placing second, a shot in front of Ishii (68) and Shirahama (72).

Daikyo Open—¥70,000,000
Winner: Saburo Fujiki

Saburo Fujiki was the one of many former winners on the Japan Tour who took advantage of the final opportunity to put a 1988 title on his record when the circuit concluded the season with a fairly-strong field for the Daikyo Open at Daikyo Country Club. Fujiki, whose last win was in the 1987 KBC Augusta, bolted into the lead on Saturday and hung on for a one-stroke victory Sunday with his 14-under-par 274, nipping Motomasa Aoki, Australian Graham Marsh and David Ishii, who failed to capitalize completely on a course-record opening round.

Ishii, who also was the first-round leader the preceding week in the Japan Series, blistered Daikyo with nine birdies Thursday for 63, yet only led Hideto Shigenobu and Koichi Suzuki by a stroke. Ishii one-putted 14 greens and had a six-birdie string in the middle of the round, outshining such superstars as Curtis Strange and Greg Norman, among the foreign standouts in the field as Masashi and Tateo Ozaki represented Japan in the World Cup in Australia. However, he and Shigenobu endured turn-around rounds Friday, David soaring to 76 and Hideto to 75. Suzuki, who also had last won in 1987, shot 67 in strong winds Friday, though, and it projected him into a six-stroke lead at 131. Tadeo Nakamura and Motomasa Aoki were at 137 and both Norman and Strange were in the picture at 138 with Marsh and four others. Fujiki then launched his finishing kick Saturday, five back-nine birdies carrying him to a 66 and a one-stroke lead at 204 over Aoki as Suzuki double-bogeyed the last hole for 75 and 206. A final-round 70 was just enough for Fujiki to land the eighth title of his career and second in the last five years. Thus, on December 11th, ended the 1988 season in Japan.

15. The LPGA Tour

If 1988 can be used as a harbinger of things to come, the days of one, two or even three players dominating the Ladies Professional Golf Association are over and more foreign players are bound to make their impact in women's golf.

Time was when Pat Bradley or Nancy Lopez or JoAnne Carner could be counted on to win four or five times, lead the money list, and with an exception or two now and then, emerge as Player-of-the-Year. Now, there's a whole host of young, aggressive players making their mark.

This past year, there were nine first-time winners — Laura Davies, Ok-Hee Ku, Sherri Turner, Mei-Chi Cheng, Shirley Furlong, Terry Jo Myers, Liselotte Neumann, Martha Nause and Patty Jordan. Eight tournaments were decided in playoffs and three of the top four in the final Rookie-of-the-Year standings were foreigners.

Oh, the old guard still had its moments as Lopez, Betsy King and Ayako Okamoto won three times each, but Rosie Jones did, too. And Turner, who had never won, did it back-to-back in the LPGA Championship and Corning Classic and went on to win the money title with $350,851.

When all was said and done, the future of the LPGA Tour may be brighter than ever despite infringement of the Senior PGA Tour into the women's television market and in the board rooms of corporate America.

Youngsters like Neumann of Sweden and Davies of England will lure other good young players from foreign countries. Neumann, in particular, seems headed for greatness. She won the U.S. Women's Open in record fashion, finished second in the Mazda Japan Classic and beat Davies by almost $30,000 for Rookie-of-the-Year honors. And the U.S. colleges are turning out more and more players ready to win right out of the gate.

"It's not going to be easy anymore to win four or five times a year, not with all these good, young players out here," said Lopez, who won Rolex Player-of-the-Year honors for the fourth time. "They're not afraid of anything. They don't blink when they get in contention. And that can only be good for the Tour."

Somebody has to replace Lopez. She's talking about retiring in a couple of years when her girls start to school. And Carner isn't getting any younger. She's won 42 tournaments, is in the Hall-of-Fame, but for the third straight year did not win a tournament and finished out of the top 20 money leaders.

Season-ending honors in 1988 went to: Turner, money winnings; Patty Sheehan, Mazda-LPGA Series; Colleen Walker, Vare Trophy, 71.26; Lopez, Rolex Player-of-the-Year and Neumann, Rookie-of-the-Year.

...ssic—$200,000
Winner: Nancy Lopez

There was the lucky coin in the pocket. There was the constant wind that served as a shield preventing her opponents from getting too close. And there was the inspiration of husband Ray following her every step around the Stonebridge Golf and Country Club in Boca Raton, Florida.

But more than anything, there was the confidence born out of the way she finished the 1987 season and the same repetitive trademark swing that churned out an assembly line-like number of pars and birdies that carried Nancy Lopez to victory in the Mazda Classic, the LPGA's first event of the 1988 season.

"I came here with a lot of confidence, a carryover from last year," said Lopez of her victory and four seconds from August through mid-September of 1987. "I thought I could play well if I did, I thought I could win."

Then there was the lucky coin, a Canadian dollar, given to her by Harold Lederman, one of her pro-am partners. "I'm superstitious anyway," Lopez said. "And after I shot 69 the first round and 68 the second, I wasn't about to let it get away."

Armed with a two-stroke lead after 36 holes, Lopez used that and a sudden cold front that brought with it crisp winds to put her game on cruise control and breeze to a two-stroke victory over Marta Figueras-Dotti, with rounds of 71 and 75 for a 283 total.

"When she took a four stroke lead into the final round, she would have had to shoot 80 the last day for anyone to really have a chance," Marta said. "And Nancy Lopez isn't going to shoot 80."

Sarasota Classic—$225,000
Winner: Patty Sheehan

It was an anxious and somewhat apprehesive Patty Sheehan who came to the Sarasota (Florida) Classic. She had won there in 1985, repeated in 1986, but chose a skiing reunion of Olympic notables over defending her title in 1987.

When she returned in 1988, Sheehan chased down Beth Daniel in the final round to win by three strokes over JoAnne Carner and Jody Rosenthal, with Daniel tying for fourth place.

"I came here with some apprehension after not defending my title last year," Sheehan said. "But they really welcomed me back. I felt like the people from Sarasota wanted me to win, and that was the best feeling I could have."

It wasn't as easy as it looked, however. Sweden's Liselotte Neumann set a blistering pace with an opening-round 64 before disappearing with 77-76-74. Daniel, in a slump of her own, whipped to the front in rounds two and three with Sheehan two behind as they headed for home.

"I felt like I had nothing to lose in the final round," Sheehan said of her closing 67 for a 282 total. "Right from the start, it was head-to-head between Beth and I. A good number was going to win."

Daniel wasn't up to it and shot 73, slipping into a tie for fourth with Sherri Turner. A five-time winner in 1982, Daniel hasn't won since 1983.

"I wasn't playing for second," Daniel said. "I look at this as a stepping stone for me. I've been humbled a great deal the last few years."

Orient Leasing Hawaiian Open—$300,000
Winner: Ayako Okamoto

It was entirely appropriate that Ayako Okamoto came out of the pack to win the LPGA's third event of the season, the Orient Leasing Hawaiian Open. After all, it had a Japanese sponsor — Itoki Corporation — and festivities were filled with speeches in both English and Japanese, and there were 12 golfers from the Japan Tour in the 144-player field.

It was on the islands of Hawaii that Okamoto first fell in love with the sport that has carried her to fame and fortune. The year was 1973 and Okamoto, then 23, was in Honolulu as a pitcher for her company softball team. "On a sightseeing tour I spotted a golf course from the hills above Pearl Harbor," Okamoto said. "I learned it was the Pearl Country Club and decided then to take up golf. It was love at first sight."

Her first victory in Hawaii, however, wasn't easy to come by. After the first round, she trailed Jan Stephenson, who opened with a 68, by a stroke and was still second after the second round to Joan Delk. Then she had to fight off JoAnne Carner in the final round. Her most anxious moment came on the last hole as Carner, needing a birdie to send the tournament to a playoff, barely missed from 12 feet.

"My heart was throbbing as her ball rolled toward the hole," said Okamoto, the LPGA's Player of the Year in 1987. "She putted it so well that my caddy and I thought that it was going to go in the hole."

Okamoto toured the 6,252-yard Arnold Palmer-managed Turtle Bay layout in three-under-par 212, one stroke better than Carner and Deb Richard, who closed with a 68.

Women's Kemper Open—$300,000
Winner: Betsy King

A gamble won and a gamble lost was the story of the LPGA's fourth stop of the year, the Women's Kemper Open at Princeville Makai Golf Club in Hawaii. And the winner felt sorry for the loser.

It was four years ago that Betsy King won for the first time on the LPGA Tour and it came in the Kemper Open, where she held off Pat Bradley and Tatusko Ohasko in the final round.

This time it was a charging King who won for the 12th time in her 12-year career, and the person she reeled in at the finish was old friend and former Furman University teammate, Beth Daniel, winning by a stroke after having trailed by as many as four as late as the 12th hole.

Daniel moved into the lead with a second-round 66 to go with her opening 72 and stretched it to three strokes with a third-round 70. Chasing her on Sunday were King, Ayako Okamoto and Amy Alcott. All but Daniel and King were gone by the 12th hole, and King's position wasn't good, being four shots back.

But Daniel bogeyed Nos. 13 and 15, King birdied No. 15 and they went to No. 18 a shot apart. No one doubted that King would go for the green in two, but few thought Daniel would gamble across the lake. King made it, Daniel tried and failed. Birdie to bogey, and victory to King.

"I feel bad for Beth," King said. "She played better than I did. It's just one of those things."

"It wasn't a hard shot, just 189 yards across the water, but I hit it thin," Daniel said.

Circle K Tucson Open—$300,000
Winner: Laura Davies

When Laura Davies elevated herself above the best in the 1987 U.S. Women's Open, the LPGA exempted her from qualifying to join their ranks. One of those who voted "aye" was Robin Walton, a member of the LPGA Player Council. And Davies, a most imposing figure from England, proved it was a worthy, though painful, vote by beating Walton with a birdie on the final hole to win the Circle K Tucson Open at Randolph North Golf Course.

Walton, winless in nine years on the LPGA Tour, had come close only once before, losing in a playoff to Jane Geddes last year in the Glendale Federal Classic. And she shouldn't have come close this time.

Davies ran off three straight birdies to start the final round and led by five strokes, but by the 10th she had given three strokes away. But nobody was making a move until Walton strung together three birdies in four holes and, when Davies bogeyed No. 17, the game was tied.

Both players were bunkered at No. 18, but Davies blasted some 50 feet to within four feet, while Walton fatted one out to 30 feet. Davies made her putt, Walton didn't. Davies' final-round 72 gave her a 278 total, while Walton shot 70 for 279.

Standard Register Turquoise Classic—$350,000
Winner: Ok-Hee Ku

The late Norm Van Brocklin, a professional football coach, once said, after getting beat by a field goal, "We need stricter immigration laws."

Most of the members of the LPGA could sympathize with Van Brocklin after the Turquoise Classic in Phoenix, Arizona. For the third time in four weeks, a foreign golfer won. This time it was Ok-Hee Ku of South Korea, following Ayako Okamoto in the Hawaiian Open and Laura Davies the week before in Tucson.

Early in the week, it seemed that Amy Alcott, as American as mom's apple pie, had this one in the bag. She opened with an eight-under 65, made four birdies in 10 holes on Friday, then hit a wall and finished with 73. Ditto on Saturday and she never again was a threat.

Ku was only one out of the lead after 36 holes, and two ahead after 54 holes, with a three-under 70.

A three-way playoff seemed in the works on Sunday with Okamoto (70) and Dottie Mochrie (69) in at 11-under 282s and Ku facing a 12-foot par putt to win.

"I was just thinking of trying to make the putt," she said. "I knew the worse that could happen was a playoff. But when I hit the putt, I felt good about the touch."

It rolled in, dead center. Ku had a final-round 72 and 281 total. It was her first LPGA victory after winning 16 times in Korea and twice in Japan.

Nabisco Dinah Shore—$500,000
Winner: Amy Alcott

There's something in the desert air that seems to bring out the best in the best each year at the Nabisco Dinah Shore in Rancho Mirage, California. The list of winners is impressive: Betsy King, Pat Bradley, Sally Little, Kathy Whitworth and Amy Alcott, now twice.

With middle rounds of 66, and 71s at the beginning and end, Alcott cruised to a two-stroke victory over Colleen Walker, and her 274 total bettered the tournament record set first by Donna Caponi in 1980 and matched by Alice Miller in 1985.

So special was her victory that Alcott and her caddy, Bill Kurre, jumped hand-in-hand into the water surrounding the huge 18th green.

In the beginning, Muffin Spencer-Devlin was on top with a great 69 in gusty breezes. Then came Alcott in a hurry. She shot 33-33 on Friday to take a one stroke lead over Colleen Walker, had another 33-33 Saturday to lead Walker by four and Rosie Jones by five.

"I hope I'm stuck on 33," Alcott said before beginning the fourth round. "It's always fun for me to play — win, lose or draw — but it's especially fun to play well here."

Alcott had only a couple of tense moments in the final round. She had back-to-back bogeys at Nos. 3 and 4, but birdied No. 5, then saved par at No. 9 with another bogey starring her in the face. Walker closed to within one at No. 11, but Alcott birdied No. 14 and carried that two-stroke lead to the victory ceremony.

The victory broke Alcott's longest winless drought — 20 months — and eased the pain of failing to win at least once a year for the first time since turning professional. "I knew it would happen sooner or later," Alcott said. "But it's especially wonderful to win again at this tournament, the one that put women's golf in the forefront of major sports."

San Diego Inamori Classic—$225,000
Winner: Ayako Okamoto

After seven weeks of flat lands and straight putts, the LPGA hit the high country — StoneRidge Country Club in San Diego. But no hill is too high for a climber, and Ayako Okamoto and Colleen Walker took San Diego golf fans to the heights in this one, with Okamoto winning for the second time in 1988.

Walker and Okamoto switched leads four times during the final 18 holes and in the end it was Walker who blinked.

Holding a one-shot lead, Walker missed a four-foot par putt at No. 16 to fall into a tie. After Okamoto hit the flagstick for a tap-in birdie at No. 17, Walker missed a four-foot birdie putt.

Walker might have won in a breeze. She opened with rounds of 68-67-69, but Okamoto turned in a blazing eight-under 63 on Saturday, using only 26 putts, just one of which was outside 20 feet, to lead by one stroke. Both finished with 69s, Okamoto having a 272 total.

"The name of the game is to get the ball in the hole quickly," Walker said. "And she must have done that to shoot 63. I shot 69 and lost six strokes. Nothing I can do about that."

Okamoto became the season's first multiple winner, and you had to go back to 1985 to find a longer period for a two-time winner to emerge. That year, it took until the 11th tournament for a repeater, Patty Sheehan.

Centinela Hospital Classic—$400,000
Winner: Nancy Lopez

The Centinela Hospital Classic was touted as the beginning of Amy Alcott's sprint into the LPGA Hall of Fame. Having reduced her magic number to three in the Nabisco Dinah Shore, Alcott now would be home at Rancho Park Golf Course in Los Angeles.

And Alcott did hit Rancho Park running, leading the first round with 69 and the second with 70, but in the end she was blown away by one already in the Hall of Fame, Nancy Lopez, who beat Spain's Marta Figueras-Dotti in a playoff.

Lopez hardly was out of Alcott's shadow in the first two rounds, shooting 71-72, and she looked like a winner when she posted a final-round 67 for a 210 total, finishing nearly an hour before Figueras-Dotti, who was playing in the final group with Alcott.

First Alcott faltered with a couple of bogeys that followed errant tee shots, but Dotti wouldn't go away. She tied Lopez with two holes to play. Both players parred the first playoff hole, but Lopez ended it on the second.

Lopez had dedicated the final round to her two-year-old daughter, Erin, who had cried over the telephone from Detroit for her mother.

Lopez left Los Angeles as the LPGA's fourth $2 million woman and its second multiple winner of the year. "I had hoped to do this last week," Lopez said of crossing the $2 million barrier, "but I'm glad I did it here, where I've won before."

USX Classic—$225,000
Winner: Rosie Jones

Rosie Jones always thought once she won for the first time on the LPGA Tour, the second one would be easier. She couldn't have been more wrong.

It took her seven years to win the first, the Rail Charity Classic in late 1987. Then she followed that with three strong challenges to open 1988, but no roses until she got to St. Petersburg, Florida, and the USX Classic.

After 72 holes, Jones was tied with 275 totals, with Kathy Postlewait, then won the championship on the same hole that got her into the playoff, No. 18.

"It's hard sometimes to win the first one. Then to play so good so many times after that and not win...and you finally get it. It kind of soothes the soul," she said.

It didn't come easily, however. Jones moved into a tie for the lead after 36 holes, moved ahead by one at the end of 54 holes, and started feeling the nerves. There was no room for error over those final 18 and she found herself down by one going to the final hole.

"I lipped out a putt at No. 17," said Jones, who finished with a two-under 70. "That was a good chance for me because I really thought everyone could birdie No. 18. I thought it was over. I was going for second."

But Jones hit the par five hole in two, two-putted for birdie, while Postlewait missed from six feet. On the playoff hole, Jones birdied again.

Sara Lee Classic—$335,000
Winner: Patti Rizzo

If ever a new tournament got off to a flying start, it was the Sara Lee Classic, held at Nashville's Hermitage Golf Course. Everyone was there and they had a blast, especially Patti Rizzo.

At the turn on the final day, three players were tied, 10 were within two shots and 16 within three. When the final putts had fallen on No. 18, four were left tied at nine-under 207.

The last of those was Rizzo, one of those can't-miss college kids from the early 1980s. She had lived up to that with victories in 1982 and 1985, but nothing since. But there on the 18th green, she rolled in a 25-foot downhill putt to tie Tammie Green, Sherri Turner and Kimberly Williams.

Back they went to the 18th tee for the playoff. Green and Williams were eliminated on the first hole, but Turner and Rizzo went down No. 1 and back up No. 9 four times before Rizzo sank a seven-foot birdie putt.

Amy Alcott led the first round with a 65. After 36 holes, Sheryl Steinhauer, Rosie Jones and Deb Richard were tied. None of those were around for the playoff.

"That putt on 18 to get into the playoff may be the most important ever to me," Rizzo said. "The drought had ended no matter what happened in the playoff."

Crestar Classic—$300,000
Winner: Juli Inkster

For the fourth straight week, it took a playoff to determine the winner of an LPGA event, but unlike the previous one, the Crestar Classic in Portsmouth, Virginia, was truly sudden death.

A week earlier, Patti Rizzo had to go five holes before emerging from a four-way logjam with her first victory in three years. This time, however, Juli Inkster made quick work of things, putting Betsy King, Rosie Jones and Nancy Lopez out of their misery on the first hole.

From 220 yards out on the 18th hole, Inkster lashed a four-wood shot that came three inches from a double-eagle.

"It was pretty much a career shot," Inkster said later.

Ironically, late in the final round Inkster was only hoping for a top-five finish. After 12 holes, she was one stroke behind Amy Alcott, Jones, Lopez, King, Missie Berteotti and overnight leader Sherri Turner. Maybe one would falter, but surely not all.

But Inkster got in first with a 69 and 209 total, then watched as one-by-one they came back to her.

On the playoff hole, Lopez put herself in trouble with a short tee shot, Jones drove it into the trees and King came up short on her eagle putt from 25 feet.

It was Inkster's first victory in 21 months. "I just haven't been patient," she said. "I kept on doing some stupid things to keep myself from winning. I'd hit 16 greens and shoot 74."

Chrysler-Plymouth Classic—$250,000
Winner: Nancy Lopez

There have been times in Nancy Lopez's career when she could take a golf tournament and turn it into her own private party. One of those was the Chrysler-Plymouth Classic in Middletown, New Jersey. It was no contest.

Lopez put together rounds of 68-70-66 for a 12-under 204 total and won by eight strokes over Jan Stephenson, the widest margin of the season. It broke the tournament record set by Kathy Whitworth in 1977, it moved her into third place on the all-time money list and she became the year's first three-time winner.

Further, it was her fourth victory in the Chrysler-Plymouth Classic, all on different courses. "I just love New Jersey," Lopez said during the award's ceremony at Navasink Country Club.

Lopez led wire-to-wire and only a strong finish by Stephenson prevented it from being worse. Stephenson, who had shot a 77 in the first round, played a bogey-less eight-birdie round of 64 that enabled her to pass 31 players on Sunday. "It was the best round of my life," she said.

Lopez led by only one over Alice Ritzman after 36 holes, but turned it on over the final nine holes with a five-under 31, while Ritzman faded badly with a closing 74.

Mazda LPGA Championship—$350,000
Winner: Sherri Turner

If ever there was a doubt that sometimes you win when you aren't even thinking about winning, Sherri Turner dispelled it in the Mazda LPGA Championship at Kings Island, Ohio.

First, this is a major, and Turner never had won anything.

Second, Turner started the final round six shots out of the lead.

And third, but more important, the player she was chasing was Amy Alcott, winner of every major but the LPGA, plus more than two dozen regular events.

But Turner did it with a final-round 67 that included birdies on three of the final four holes. Give Alcott an assist, however, as she gave way to distractions and slumped to 74 on Sunday.

As the field turned for home in the final round, Alcott and Okamoto were tied at seven under par, and Turner was four behind, then the unravelling began. Okamoto missed putts and Alcott missed fairways. Turner pulled to within two with a birdie at No. 15, saved par at No. 16, then birdied Nos. 17 and 18, for a 67 and 281 total.

"I knew I needed to birdie the last two to have a chance and I didn't think that was very likely," Turner said. "But it's like Amy told me, 'Hey, you're going to win and it will come at the most unlikely time, when you aren't even thinking about winning.' I guess she was right."

Thinking about winning is what did in Alcott. She wanted it too much. It was the only major she hadn't won. It would move her to within two victories of the LPGA Hall of Fame and with her Nabisco Dinah Shore win, would set up the possibility of a Grand Slam.

"Too many distractions," Alcott said. "Normally, I don't let those things get to me, but I couldn't control them this week."

Alcott had a chance to tie Turner with a birdie on the final hole, but her 15-foot putt never came close to going in.

Corning Classic—$325,000
Winner: Sherri Turner

In winning the LPGA Championship the week before, Sherri Turner blew out of the water the theory that you don't win for the first time in a major championship. In the Corning Classic in Corning, New York, she was at it again. You aren't supposed to play well the week after you win a major, and forget about winning.

Turner started four strokes back of Patty Sheehan, was one behind Ok-Hee Ku at the halfway point, two ahead after three rounds and held off a late-charging JoAnne Carner to win by that margin with a 273 total.

"Some of the players told me not to expect too much this week," Turner said. "They said I'd come down out of the clouds. But it worked the opposite for me. I stayed in the clouds. I came here with high expectations. I thought I could play good again."

Play well, she did, especially in the second round with a course-record tying 63. And it wasn't until after Turner took the lead with her third-round 69 that she hit the ground.

"The first three days I was able to put it in drive and go with it," she said after her victory. "But today I was real excited and nervous and I played like it."

Carner, who hadn't won since 1985, might have done it here, but an opening 74 negated her 70-65-66 finish. And Ok-Hee Ku missed her chance at victory on the greens, especially at Nos. 11, 12, 14, 15 and 17, where makeable birdie putts didn't fall.

Jamie Farr Classic—$275,000
Winner: Laura Davies

Just when it seemed at the Jamie Farr Classic that all its luck was going to be bad, along came Laura Davies to the rescue, proving again that when she's good, she's very very good.

The tournament in Toledo, Ohio, had fallen on hard times. It never had the same dates two years in a row, it never had drawn a full field of players, the clubhouse burned down, and the club and the surrounding property had been sold, and only six of the top 20 money winners played, only one (Nancy Lopez) from the top 10.

But in the final threesome on Sunday, it was Davies, Lopez and King who gave the tournament a shot in the arm. Especially Davies, the 5-10, 200-pound British lass. She posted a final-round 69, her fourth straight sub-par round, and finished with a record 11-under-par 277 to win for the second time in the year.

She was down three after the third hole, but played the ninth through 13th holes in five under par to take the lead and the tournament away from Lopez, who had led since the first round. The turning point came at the par-five 12th, where Davies chipped in for eagle.

Lopez, playing in the tournament for the third time, finished second for the second time. A final-round 73 left her three shots behind the winner. "She's just a great player and she's going to get better," Lopez said of Davies. "She has the game to dominate the tour in the future. Once she gains experience, we're all going to be in trouble."

In the four rounds, Davies had only six bogeys and a double. "I can't remember a week like that," she said.

Rochester International—$300,000
Winner: Mei-Chi Cheng

There have been longshots in all sports who have surprised both the experts and oddsmakers when it came to pressure time. One was Mei-Chi Cheng, a 28-year-old rookie from Taiwan.

Here she was on Sunday at Locust Hill Country Club in Rochester, New York, tied with Nancy Lopez and Patty Sheehan after 72 holes in the Rochester International. Given no chance at all of winning, she won on the second playoff hole.

Sheehan was the first out, bogeying the 18th hole. On the second, No. 1, Lopez was 20 feet from the hole, Cheng six feet. Lopez missed. Cheng didn't.

It might have been her first time to be in this position, but not her first under pressure. Last October, in the LPGA qualifying tournament at Sugar Land, Texas, Cheng survived a three-way playoff for the final exempt spot.

"The qualifying school was more intense. I was more nervous there than here," Cheng said. "I've played with Lopez before. She's a great player. I just said, 'Everyone is the same. Go for it.'"

Caroline Gowan led the first two rounds, but fell into a tie with Lopez and Lauri Peterson, who shot a tournament-best 65, after 54 holes. Gowan faded to an 81 in the final round and Peterson shot 79. Sheehan could have won it outright, but she made bogey on the final hole after failing to get up and down.

Cheng started the final round two strokes back and shot only 73, but Lopez had 74, to finish at 287.

Lady Keystone Open—$300,000
Winner: Shirley Furlong

Shirley Furlong added to the reputation the LPGA had achieved in 1988 of having the most depth of field in its history by winning the Lady Keystone Open at Hershey Country Club in Hershey, Pennsylvania. This wasn't one of those tournaments where the big names stayed home. Nine of the top 10 money winners were there.

Further, after 36 holes, 27 players were within five shots of the lead and 10 were just two behind. Furlong? She was three back, then ripped through the field with a closing seven-under 65 to tie Sherri Turner at 205, and won on the first playoff hole.

Though she's been around, it was Furlong's first LPGA victory and the paycheck of $45,000 was more than she had won in any event. When it was over, they were saying, "Shirley wins by a furlong." The horse-race analogy was fitting as the 28-year-old former Texas A&M All-America won it down the stretch, using five birdies over the final nine holes.

"It was almost as if I was playing with blinders on," said Furlong, going along with the racing terminlogy. "I just kept everything right in front of me, taking it one shot at a time."

After 36 holes, Ayako Okamoto, Colleen Walker and Connie Chillemi held the lead at 137, but Okamoto fell back to finish at 209, Walker held third at 208 and Chillemi remained winless in 12 seasons with a closing 75.

A sidelight of this year's event was Sandra Spuzich and her quest for a $100,000 bonus. In 1985, she aced the 160-yard fifth; in 1986 the 175-yard No. 12; in 1987 the 174-yard eighth. An ace on the 165-yard 17th would bring her the bonus. Alas, she played the hole in 3-3-3.

McDonald's Championship—$500,000
Winner: Kathy Postlewait

Kathy Postlewait came to the McDonald's Championship in Wilmington, Delaware, with few expectations, a bad back and playing against a field that included all of 1988's winners, 50 of the top 51 money winners and 91 of the top 100.

When she left, she had exceeded her expectations, still had a bad back and had beaten everyone in the field to take the $75,000 winner's share of the $500,000 purse at DuPont Country Club.

There was little to recommend Postlewait for the title. In the fourth round of the LPGA Championship, she had pulled something in her back and in the succeeding four weeks had been credited with three no-shows and one withdrawal. Her back hurt so badly she couldn't reach down and tie her shoe.

"I honestly didn't expect a whole lot," Postlewait said. "And obviously I got a whole lot more than I expected. I feel like I might have stolen one this week."

She didn't play like a thief, however. With rounds of 69-68-69-70—276, she beat Patty Sheehan by one stroke and finished two ahead of Jan Stephenson.

It's also true, however, that Sheehan might have gift-wrapped this one for Postlewait, who came in with two career victories. Sheehan led by three strokes after 36 holes, by two after 54 holes, and said, "I still feel in control."

Postlewait was three shots back after 54 holes, but tied Sheehan with three quick birdies. She took the lead with a birdie at No. 11 and held on as Sheehan failed to get up and down from just off the 18th green for a tie.

"Patty missed a number of chances today and that's not like Patty Sheehan," Postlewait said. "But I'm not going to give it back."

"I really didn't think winning this was in my stars. I didn't give winning much thought until after the second day. I was here on guts alone and whatever I got out of it, so be it."

duMaurier Classic—$400,000
Winner: Sally Little

When last we left Sally Little, the old Sally Little, she was winning tournaments left and right, and was always in the middle of those she didn't. But since 1983, there had been more bad days than even average ones. As one surgery followed another, Little at one point considered quitting the game.

Now, there's a new Sally Little, physically fit for the first time in six years. There's something about this new one, however, that reminds you of the old one, the winning part.

With a 25-foot putt on the final hole, Little won the duMaurier Classic by a stroke over Laura Davies and wiped away those years of pain and frustration.

"When that putt went in, I saw the last six years of struggle leaving me," Little said. "I had control over myself. I have started the game all over again and the struggle has been worth it ten times over."

To win, Little had to outlast the new stars of the game, Laura Davies and Sherri Turner, who finished second and third, over the Vancouver Golf Club course in Coquitlam, British Columbia. She shot 74-65-69-71—279, won $75,000 and jumped from 54th on the money list into the top 10.

"I've been struggling with my health since 1983," Little said. "I lost my confidence. I forgot how to win. I almost gave up. The turnaround was from my pride."

She moved into contention with a 65 on Friday, taking a one-shot lead into the weekend. Only once did her confidence waver, that when she bunkered her second shot at No. 17 in the final round while tied with Davies. But she got it up and down to save par.

"I was nervous and felt my concentration slip just a bit," she said. "But when I made the putt to save par, I got all my confidence back."

Mayflower Classic—$400,000
Winner: Terry-Jo Myers

The year of surprises on the LPGA Tour continued in the Mayflower Classic in Indianapolis, Indiana.

First, Mei-Chi Cheng beat Nancy Lopez and Patty Sheehan in a playoff to win the Rochester International. Then there was Shirley Furlong shooting 65 in the final round at the Lady Keystone, followed by Kathy Postlewait, bad back and all, winning at McDonalds, followed by Sally Little reappearing with wonderful golf to win the duMaurier.

Now came Terry-Jo Myers, who has been around a couple of years in obscurity, to shoot rounds of 68-69-68-71—276 and beat superstars Amy Alcott and Ayako Okamoto by one in the Mayflower.

Myers missed in her first LPGA qualifying attempt, played the Far East Tour for a year, then the Futures Tour. She finally got her card in the fall of 1985, lost it again and appeared headed in that direction again before the Mayflower, having won only $11,443.

"A lot of hard work and dedication," Myers said in explaining her sudden emergence. "Plus, I putted awfully well this week."

It wasn't until she won, however, that anybody noticed. Juli Inkster got the first day ink with a 65. Donna White was the second-day star, backing a 68 with a 67 and Okamoto took the headlines after three rounds. Terry-Jo? She was tied with Okamoto but got second-billing.

A solid even par 71 on Sunday at the Country Club of Indianpolis course took care of that oversight, and the $60,000 first place check was nice, too.

Boston Five Classic—$300,000
Winner: Colleen Walker

For 13 months, Colleen Walker wondered if she was to join that long list of golfers — male and female — who win once, then wait and wait and wait for No. 2. And it never comes.

Thus, it was with a big sigh of relief when the 31-year-old Floridian blitzed the field with rounds of 66-69-70-69—274 to win the Boston Five Classic by eight strokes.

"I have to admit it's been in the back of my mind," Walker said when asked if she wondered if she would win again. "Sometimes people win out here once, but never win again. That's why the second one is tougher to get than the first. That's why this one feels better."

No one was surprised when she won again. She won No. 1 at the Mayflower in 1987 on the way to a $190,000 year and had surpassed that coming to Boston. Plus, she has 12 top 10s, including two seconds and a third.

It was her tournament from the beginning. She shot 66 and never was out of the lead, making runner-ups of Kathryn Young, Patty Sheehan, Jane Geddes and Jan Stephenson.

"I wasn't anxious this week," Walker said. "I was hungry. I felt this should have happened before now."

Stephenson did make a little run at Walker on Saturday, wiping out a five-stroke deficit at the turn. But Walker regained four of those on the back nine. It was only one over Stephenson after eight holes on Sunday, but Jan double-bogeyed No. 9, Walker birdied it and that was the end of the ball game.

"Colleen was faltering and I thought I was going to win the tournament," Stephenson said. "Then I made a mistake and she jumped all over it."

U.S. Women's Open—$325,000
Winner: Liselotte Neumann

In 1987, Sweden's Liselotte Neumann missed the cut in the U.S. Open, but stayed around the next day and was part of Laura Davies' gallery. She then returned home, no longer satisfied with the challenge of the European women's circuit. If Davies could do it, so then could she.

From the LPGA qualifying tournament last October, Neumann made it all the way to the top of women's golf in July at Baltimore Country Club, becoming the first wire-to-wire winner of the U.S. Women's Open since Amy Alcott in 1980. She broke the record for best start with a 67, shared the record for 36- and 54-hole marks, then broke the 72-hole record of Pat Bradley, shooting a 277 total.

All of this in the face of stiff challenges from Patty Sheehan and Colleen Walker, who after 61 holes were tied for the lead with Neumann, who had four-putted. Rather than rattle her, the four-putt had an opposite effect. It calmed her. "I didn't want to show Patty any feelings," Neumann said. "I was thinking of what I would think in her place. 'This person will get frustrated and mad.' I didn't want that."

In charge of her emotions, Neumann then quickly took charge of the championship. She birdied Nos. 10, 11 and 12 to take a two-stroke lead, made it three strokes with another at No. 15, fought off a bogey at No. 16 with a 20-footer at No. 17 and it was over. "She was remarkably calm and composed," Sheehan said of Neumann. "Even when she four-putted, there was no sign of crumbling."

A national champion in Germany, Singapore, France and Sweden, and the 1986 European Open winner, Newmann became the LPGA's seventh first-time winner and the fourth straight player to make the U.S. Women's Open her first LPGA title.

"The first time, last year, when I played the Open, I guess I didn't know how big it was," she said. "This time I didn't feel any pressure. I tried to go out and have fun, and I did."

None of the experienced ones did, however. Sheehan did finish second and Walker third, but Ayako Okamoto was 11 strokes back with Nancy Lopez; JoAnne Carner had a shot until a third-round 76 did her in and finished 12 shots behind.

"At one time on our tour you could say, 'She's not going to be there after today.' I don't think you can do that anymore," said Juli Inkster. "These girls are good players. You hope you can wear them down, but it looks like some of them are able to wear us down."

Greater Washington Open—$225,000
Winner: Ayako Okamoto

The Greater Washington Open suffered growing pains in its first year on the LPGA Tour, what with a reduction in purse and small crowds, but from an artistic and suspense standpoint, it was a keeper.

Bethesda Country Club in Bethesda, Maryland, was the site of Ayako Okamoto's third victory of 1988 and for one of the few times in her career she was sitting down at the finish.

Having completed a round of four-under 67 and a 206 total, Okamoto was in the clubhouse waiting for the final group of Beth Daniel and Connie Chillemi to finish and expecting a playoff. It didn't happen.

Chillemi, a 12-year tour veteran but winless, fell out of a tie with a three-putt bogey on No. 17, although she will regret longer the double bogey at No. 12. Daniel, a 14-time winner but none since 1985, didn't succumb until the final hole. She drove into the trees, pitched out, hit over the green and made bogey.

"She was in the right place at the right time," Daniel said. "She put a number up there and let us shoot at it. There certainly was less pressure on her than on us."

Okamoto started the final round two shots behind Daniel and Chillemi, who had shot a course record 64 on Saturday. And the 1987 Player of the Year put the pressure on the leaders with a no-bogey finishing round of 67. "I never think about a certain score to win," Okamoto said. "I just try to hit fairways and greens and make putts."

Planters Pat Bradley International—$400,000
Winner: Martha Nause

With knots in her stomach and dollar signs in her eyes, Martha Nause stood close to the 18th hole at Willow Creek Country Club in High Point, North Carolina, and watched first Dot Germain and then Debbie Massey try to wrest away her day in the sun.

First, Germain failed and when Massey's 15-foot putt rolled around the hole and stayed out, Nause did a standing high jump. Victory was her's in the Planters Pat Bradley International, and so was the first-place check of $62,500.

This wasn't your basic LPGA event. Rather, the distaff side took a page from the PGA Tour and their International, the format being not stroke play but a modified version of the Stableford System, where pars get you nothing. And when it was over, Nause, a 10-year veteran had won for the first time.

Each day, beginning with 144 players, the field was cut in half until only 18 were left for Sunday's finale. Nause finished with 14 points, Massey and Judy Dickinson 13 each. Some big names never made it past the first day.

The idea in this format is to be aggressive. It was go for the flags all week.

Nause had to survive a playoff the first day when 14 players tied for the final spot with four points each. From there, she had no problems. "I told my caddy after the first-day playoff that I was going to win," she said. "I was going to be Cinderella."

On Sunday, she had six points on two birdies at the turn, ran her total to 15 points with three more coming in before losing a point with a bogey at No. 18.

Ayako Okamoto needed a birdie at No. 18 to win and failed; Nancy Lopez needed one to tie and didn't get it. Then it was left to Massey and Germain and Nause sweated them out.

Atlantic City LPGA Classic—$225,000
Winner: Juli Inkster

Juli Inkster played a game within the game and came up a double winner in the Atlantic City Classic, shooting a final-round 65 over the Sands Country Club course in Somers Point, New Jersey, to catch Beth Daniel then win on the first playoff hole.

It was a thrill for Inkster, but tore the heart out of Daniel, who after the second round had a three-shot lead on the field and was seven up on the eventual winner.

Inkster fell 10 shots behind after a bogey on the third hole. Then the game, the other game began. Inkster's caddy, John Killeen, came up with the idea: a bet. Birdies would be worth $5 to Inkster, and bogeys, $5 to Killeen. Suddenly, she makes four straight birdies. Killeen was out $20, but Inkster started thinking about maybe finishing second as she noticed other players were backing up, including Daniel.

The bet still on, Inkster birdied Nos. 10, 13 and 15 and coming behind her Daniel bogeyed Nos. 12, 13 and 15. They were tied, with the rest of the field scrambling for third place.

Inkster made gutty pars at Nos. 17 and 18, the latter of which also came out of a bet. Killeen gave her 2-to-1 odds she couldn't get up and down from a bunker. She did.

"She took me for a few bucks," Killeen said, "but it was fun."

Not for Daniel. "I just ran out of gas," said Daniel who had to play 28 holes after play was suspended in the second round and carried over. It didn't help that she was still recovering from a bout of mononucleosis. "I thought if I could shoot par, I could win. I shot one-over and that gave everybody a chance."

Nestle World Championship—$250,000
Winner: Rosie Jones

There's something about playing Nancy Lopez head-to-head, down the stretch that brings out the best in Rosie Jones.

In September of 1987, in the Rail Classic, Jones won her first LPGA event, beating Lopez with a birdie on the final hole. It happened again almost a year later as Jones birdied the 16th hole in the final round to break a deadlock with Lopez and go on to win the Nestle World Championship at Stouffer PineIsle Resort on the shores of Lake Lanier just north of Atlanta.

This one was tougher, though, much tougher for the seven-year pro who now lives on Hilton Head Island in South Carolina. The 28-year-old Jones took a five-stroke lead into the final round. But before the day was done, five golfers — Jones, Lopez, Liselotte Neumann, Patty Sheehan and Sherri Turner — had a shot at the $81,500 first-place check, richest on the circuit.

Unaccustomed as she was to having such a lead, Jones gave it all away, plus one by the eighth hole, before collecting herself late on the back nine for a final round 74 to eventually beat Neumann by a shot. Lopez, Sheehan and Turner tied for third place, two back.

The Nestle field was expanded from 12 to 16 this year, and Jones was one of the four first-timers, joining Neumann, Kathy Postlewait, Turner and France's Marie-Laure de Lorenzi Taya, a star on the European Women's Tour. Most of the pre-tournament hype was focused on the old hands, Lopez, defending champion Ayako Okamoto, Sheehan and Amy Alcott.

Predictably, Okamoto and Lopez led the first round with five-under par 67s. Alcott was a stroke back, Jan Stephenson another behind and Sheehan, Jones and Neumann close with 70s.

At the halfway mark, Lopez had given up the lead to Okamoto by a shot, while Jones surprisingly hung in, posting a 69 to move into a tie with Lopez. Sally Little was three back with Turner.

All but Jones faded after the third round. Fighting a cold and a sore toe, Jones shot a bogey-free 66 to move five up on Lopez, six in front of Sheehan and Turner.

"I've never had a five-shot lead and certainly never imagined having one here," Jones said. "But I don't feel comfortable with it."

She was even more uncomfortable after eight holes into the final round. Lopez birdied No. 2, Jones bogeyed it. Three shot lead. Lopez birdied No. 5, Jones bogeyed it. One shot lead. Lopez parred No. 8, Jones double-bogeyed it. One shot behind. Her comfort zone.

"I was not handling a five-shot lead well at all," Jones said. "I wasn't comfortable until I got one behind, which is where I usually am. Hopefully, this will be a good learning experience."

Jones finally got it going with a birdie at No. 10, but when Lopez bogeyed the 15th, those five players were tied. Then Jones got her birdie at No. 16, from 15 feet and that was that.

"I'm learning to play under pressure," Jones said, "and believe me, today was pressure like I never thought existed."

Ocean State Open—$150,000
Winner: Patty Jordan

While the LPGA's big guns were cavorting around the shores of Georgia's Lake Lanier in the elite Nestle World Championship, the elite of the future were having their fun in the sun in the Ocean State Open in Cranston, Rhode Island.

And nobody had more fun than third-year player Patty Jordan, who came from fourth place, three shots off the pace, with a final round 70 to win by two and become the LPGA's ninth first-time winner of 1988.

Joan Pitcock almost had as much fun as Jordan. The tour's youngest player at 21 charged into the second round lead with an impressive nine-under 63, four shots better than any other round in the tournament. But on payday, she shot 75 and finished tied for second with five others — Mitzi Edge, Lynn Adams, Margaret Ward, Jill Briles and Sandra Palmer.

Pitcock's fall was just what Jordan needed. She was four back early, but Pitcock went six over on an eight-hole stretch in the middle of the round and the title was up for grabs.

Jordan was a picture of stability, hitting 15 greens in regulation on a day when the wind swirled and gusted. She tied Pitcock with a birdie at No. 8 and went to the 18th with a one-shot lead. A birdie there eliminated the only two who could have caught her — Pitcock and Palmer.

The winner's check of $22,500 was the largest ever for the former Wake Forest golfer and doubled her earnings for the year.

Rail Charity Classic—$250,000
Winner: Betsy King

Betsy King had somewhat struggled with her game through much of the 1988 season before she rolled into Springfield, Illinois, for the $250,000 Rail Charity Classic at Rail Golf Club. Just the week before, in the Nestle, she had gone from red to black like a child with a coloring book before finishing at even par and 13th in the 16-player field.

But it all came together this week. She shot an opening four-under 68 and was tied for second with Vicki Fergon, Nancy Brown, Missie Berteotti and Penny Hammell, two behind Donna White.

A second straight 68 on Saturday moved her into the lead for good and she rolled to her second victory of the season on Sunday with a 71, winning by two over Margaret Ward.

"I just never could get anything going in Atlanta (for the Nestle)," King said after picking up the $37,500 winner's share of the purse. "But it didn't get me down. I came here with a good attitude, got off to a good start and really hit the ball solid."

It came as no surprise that King would be the one to finish on top. After all, she won the tournament back-to-back in 1985-86 and finished a strong third in 1987 behind Rosie Jones and Nancy Lopez.

"It's a good course for me, obviously," King said.

Cellular One-Ping Championship—$225,000
Winner: Betsy King

Hardly anybody wins two tournaments in one week. After all, hardly anyone gets such an opportunity. But Betsy King did and did. Six days after posting a two-stroke victory in the Labor Day-ending Rail Charity Classic in Springfield, Illinois, King won the Cellular One-Ping 2,000 miles away in Portland, Oregon.

In the Rail Classic, King took control of the tournament from the outset, shooting rounds of 68-68-71 — 207 and winning by two strokes over Margaret

Ward. The One-Ping triumph wasn't that easy. Susan Sanders and Colleen Walker led the first round with 68s while King had 71. But she eased in front after the second round with a 70.

"I knew it wasn't going to be easy to win this one," King said. "Those greens were as fast as anything I've ever seen. It was an exhausting day."

King lost her lead early, bogeying two of the first three after bad drives, then a three-putt bogey at No. 8 dropped her one back of Sanders. Patience won out, however, as King then birdied Nos. 14, 15 and 16 and slipped in one stroke ahead of Walker.

There were a couple of sidelights to this event. First Nancy Lopez shot 76-77 — 153 and missed the cut, her first in 116 tournaments, dating back to February of 1982. The other was the resurgence of Sandra Haynie, who won the $10,000 Ping Shootout, then tied for 11th to earn $4,421, making her the 16th LPGA member to go over the $1-million mark in career earnings.

Safeco Classic—$225,000
Winner: Juli Inkster

Most professional golfers would be happy to win a tournament one time, but Juli Inkster has now doubled her pleasure three times on the LPGA Tour, winning the Safeco Classic.

Inkster's first victory came in the Safeco in her 1983 rookie year. She's also been a double winner in the Keystone (1985-86) and the Atlantic City Classic (1986-88). This one, however, was a bit more special than any of the others.

"I can't remember playing this well on a weekend," Inkster said of her closing 65-67 that carried her to a three stroke victory over Ok-Hee Ku. "After the first round, I didn't know if I would even be around for the final two rounds."

Fighting a cold, the former three-time U.S. Women's Amateur champion opened with a four-over 76 over the 6,222-yard Meridian Valley Country Club course near Kent, Washington. But she came back with a 70 on Friday to survive the cut by four strokes.

After two rounds, Inkster found herself in a 10-way tie for 23rd, seven shots behind surprise leader Susie Redman, who didn't play well on the weekend and eventually finished tied for 11th. In the third round, Inkster shot the lowest round of the tournament, a round that included five birdies from the eighth through the 12th holes. That left her only a stroke behind defending champion Jan Stephenson.

On Sunday, Inkster grabbed the lead with a birdie on the eighth hole, fought off Ku's tie at No. 16 with another birdie and breezed in when her closest pursuer bogeyed the 17th.

Inkster's $33,750 payday left her only $16,242 short of becoming the 17th LPGA millionaire.

Santa Barbara Open—$300,000
Winner: Rosie Jones

It took Rosie Jones six years to win her first LPGA tournament, but having finally got the hang of it, she's turned 1988 into her own personal game of catch-up.

First she won the USX Classic back in the spring, then added the Nestle World Championship to her portfolio in the summer and finally became the girl for all seasons with a resounding three-stroke victory over Missie McGeorge in the autumn — the Santa Barbara Open.

Jones had to conquer two courses before this week was done, Sandpiper Golf Club in palm-tree-lined Santa Barbara and the bushy holled La Purisima course 53 miles north. No problem. She shot 70 on the coast and 70-72 in the mountains.

In 1987, La Purisima was so tough that no one broke par and only 20 of the full field escaped with scores in the 70s. Jones had a psychological advantage when the tournament moved inland from Santa Barbara. She didn't play in 1987.

"This course is a lot of fun to play," said Jones, who holed out a 118-yard nine iron for eagle at No. 18 and needed only 24 putts in her second round of 70 and a tie with McGeorge.

On Sunday, only Jones and McGeorge were in the hunt, but in the end only Jones bagged the top prize.

"I felt confident all day that I would win," Jones said.

Not bad for someone who just nine months ago wondered if she'd ever win again.

Konica San Jose Classic—$300,000
Winner: Kathy Guadagnino

With all eyes on Nancy Lopez and Sherri Turner battling for the LPGA money lead, Kathy Guadagnino finally played like Kathy Baker in the 1985 U.S. Open and stole the show.

Yes, this Mrs. Guadagino was the Miss Kathy Baker of three years ago and her first victory since Baltusrol couldn't have come at a better time. She was beginning to think it was a fluke.

"I read where one writer said that since I'd been married the only thing I'd added to my game was my name," Guadagino said. "I was beginning to believe them."

But she wiped out any doubts that married life didn't agree with her game, shooting rounds of 69-71-67 — 207 for a single stroke victory over Cathy Marino.

This was the final tournament on the American side of the Pacific and everyone was here for the bon voyage. Missie Berteotti led the first round with a 68; Juli Inkster and Missie McGeorge shared the 36-hole lead and Guadagnino was three behind.

But the winner ran off three birdies on the first three holes, grabbed the lead for good with a birdie at No. 14 and parred in for her first victory since the Open.

Lopez was a factor through nine holes on Sunday, tied for the lead, but uncharacteristically fell apart with a double-bogey and a triple-bogey on the back and finished eight behind. Turner, the leading money winner never was in it, shooting rounds of 73-72-73 — 218, 11 back.

Mazda Japan Classic—$450,000
Winner: Patty Sheehan

Patty Sheehan had seen so many opportunities evaporate midway the 1988 season that she had to wonder what it would be this time as she headed down the stretch in the LPGA's final official event of the year. As it turned out, the answer was nothing.

With a final round of 67, which included birdies on three of the final five holes, Sheehan caught U.S. Women's Open champion Liselotte Neumann, then birdied the third hole of sudden death to win the $450,000 Mazda Japan Classic.

"I was in position to win so many times this year and something would always happen. Either I'd play bad or somebody would shoot lights out," Sheehan said. "I guess the odds finally moved to my side. This is a great, great feeling."

With her victory, Sheehan won the $67,500 winner's share of the purse and the 450 Mazda bonus points and leapfroged Sherri Turner in the Mazda-LPGA Series to win the $125,000 bonus.

The LPGA gals didn't really get into this one until the second round. Round one belonged to the home team as Yuko Moriguchi, the 1987 champion, shot a five-under 67 and led Tasuko Ohasako by one and compatriot Aiko Takasu by two. Japanese heroine Ayako Okamoto was far off the pace with 73 and never really challenged.

Neumann, the winsome lass from Sweden, took control in the second round with a 66 that included her first-ever hole-in-one and led by three strokes over Moriguchi, Sheehan and Vicki Fergon.

"In this field, three strokes with a round to play isn't very safe," Neumann said. "Anything can happen Sunday."

Anything was Sheehan. She birdied Nos. 3, 8, 9 and 13, lost a shot with a bogey at No. 4, but still was only one back as Sheehan and Neumann went to 15. Birdie, birdie. The next chance came at No. 17, where Neumann could only look in wonder as Sheehan made a 30-footer to forge a tie.

"I had a chance to win it at No. 18," Sheehan said. "I had an easy putt for birdie, 20 feet right up the hill, but I read too much break into it and left it outside the hole. I really thought I was going to make it."

It was over three holes later. Faced with a similar putt, Sheehan rolled the winner into the center of the hole.

U.S. Tour

What would Jimmy Demaret have thought of this? Typical of the fitness-conscious PGA Tour, Chip Beck does his stretching exercises before practice. A previous non-winner, Beck had two victories and was second on the U.S. money list.

Third on the U.S. money list, Joey Sindelar won the Honda Classic and The International.

Steve Pate had two victories in the first six tournaments.

Often a runner-up, David Frost got out of the rough to post his first two American victories.

Veteran Lanny Wadkins also had two wins, Hawaii and Colonial.

Ben Crenshaw's sole victory was at Doral.

A Victory For Jamie

Leukemia victim Jamie Hutton received the Heritage Classic trophy from his hero, Greg Norman.

The Lighter Side

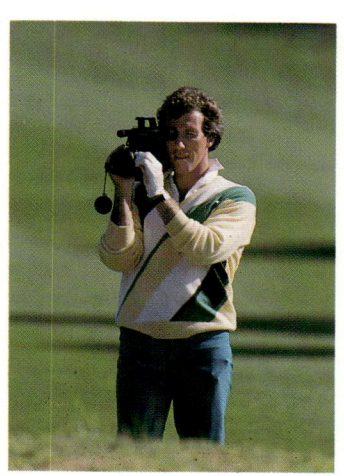

That's Mac O'Grady with a video camera, one of the tour caddys trying his hand at the game, an obviously unidentified marshal, and two gentlemen whose identity we all know, Gene Sarazen and Sam Snead, in the honorary first starting time at the Masters.

Gary Player's extraordinary season on the U.S. Senior Tour included his victory here in the U.S. Senior Open, as well as the PGA Seniors and Seniors British Open.

Senior Tour

Arnold Palmer re-entered the victory circle in the Crestar Classic.

When Gary Player was not winning, the victor often was either Orville Moody (above) or Bob Charles (right).

Sherri Turner claimed the LPGA Championship.

Michael C. Cohen

Sweden's Liselotte Neumann was winner of the U.S. Women's Open.

Amy Alcott won the Nabisco Dinah Shore title.

Rosie Jones took the Nestle World Championship.

Michael C. Cohen

Michael C. Cohen

LPGA Tour

Corinne Dibnah celebrates her triumph in the British Women's Open.

Two superstars, Nancy Lopez (bottom left) and Ayako Okamoto (right), also had tremendous seasons.

Michael C. Cohen

Despite some rainy days and missed cuts, Ian Woosnam won three events on the European circuit.

European Tour

A return of his putting difficulties left Bernhard Langer with just one victory.

The British Open was one of Seve Ballesteros' seven victories worldwide, while Spanish countryman Jose-Maria Olazabal (left) won twice.

Mark James registered two victories.

Zimbabweans Mark McNulty (above left) and Nick Price both had outstanding years.

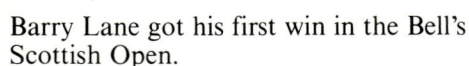

Barry Lane got his first win in the Bell's Scottish Open.

Victories in the French Open (shown here) and the Volvo Masters eased the disappointment of Nick Faldo's eight second-place finishes.

Australian Rodger Davis had one victory in Europe.

Masahiro Kuramoto was a five-time winner in Japan.

Neither Isao Aoki (left) nor Tommy Nakajima had a 1988 victory.

Asia/Japan Tours

The brothers Ozaki — Jumbo, Jet and Joe — together won 12 tournaments, led by Jumbo's six triumphs. (Above, Jet Ozaki; top right, Jumbo Ozaki.)

American David Ishii won one tournament.

Australasian Tour

Ian Baker-Finch claimed the Australian Masters title.

African Tours

Fulton Allem led off the Sunshine circuit with a win, and wrapped it up with a victory in the Million Dollar Challenge.

APPENDIXES

World Money List

This listing of the 200 leading money winners in the world of professional golf in 1988 was compiled from the results of all tournaments carried in the Appendixes of this edition, along with other non-tour and international events for which accurate figures could be obtained and in which the players competed for prize money provided by someone other than the players themselves. Skins games, shootouts and seasonal bonus money are not included. Runner-up Fulton Allem's total includes $1,000,000 from Million Dollar Challenge.

In the 23 years during which World Money Lists have been compiled, the earnings of the player in the 200th position have risen from a total of $3,326 in 1966 to $129,951 in 1988. The top 200 players in 1966 earned a total of $4,680,287. In 1988, the comparable total was $70,791,043.

Because of the fluctuating values of money throughout the world, it was necessary to determine an average value of non-American currency to U.S. money to prepare this listing. The conversion rates used for 1988 were: British pound = US $1.80; 125 Japanese yen = US$1; South African rand = US50¢; US$1 = $1.20 Australian/New Zealand/Canadian.

POS.	PLAYER, COUNTRY	TOTAL MONEY
1	Severiano Ballesteros, Spain	$1,261,275
2	Fulton Allem, South Africa	1,191,231
3	Curtis Strange, U.S.	1,184,775
4	Sandy Lyle, Scotland	1,182,438
5	Ken Green, U.S.	1,085,994
6	Masashi Ozaki, Japan	1,082,985
7	Chip Beck, U.S.	1,017,418
8	Ben Crenshaw, U.S.	992,128
9	Greg Norman, Australia	957,497
10	Nick Faldo, England	922,732
11	Joey Sindelar, U.S.	922,315
12	Fred Couples, U.S.	889,684
13	David Frost, South Africa	791,694
14	Mark Calcavecchia, U.S.	789,946
15	Bob Charles, New Zealand	778,129
16	Tom Kite, U.S.	750,474
17	Rodger Davis, Australia	747,613
18	Mark McCumber, U.S.	728,517
19	Dave Hill, U.S.	682,344
20	Naomichi Ozaki, Japan	672,803
21	Paul Azinger, U.S.	664,607
22	Jose-Maria Olazabal, Spain	656,073
23	Steve Pate, U.S.	655,853
24	David Ishii, U.S.	654,724
25	Ian Woosnam, Wales	633,144
26	Jeff Sluman, U.S.	617,938
27	Lanny Wadkins, U.S.	596,066
28	Mike Reid, U.S.	595,750
29	Payne Stewart, U.S.	595,671
30	Orville Moody, U.S.	593,025
31	Masahiro Kuramoto, Japan	559,852
32	Peter Jacobsen, U.S.	545,848

POS.	PLAYER, COUNTRY	TOTAL MONEY
33	Tateo Ozaki, Japan	536,458
34	Harold Henning, South Africa	529,915
35	Gary Player, South Africa	523,459
36	Nick Price, Zimbabwe	515,800
37	Mark O'Meara, U.S.	499,704
38	Ian Baker-Finch, Australia	498,329
39	Jay Haas, U.S.	496,449
40	Bob Tway, U.S.	489,726
41	Brian Jones, Australia	487,571
42	Mark McNulty, Zimbabwe	485,536
43	Bruce Lietzke, U.S.	483,465
44	Don Pooley, U.S.	482,937
45	Gary Koch, U.S.	469,812
46	Bruce Crampton, Australia	457,427
47	Ronan Raferty, Northern Ireland	456,556
48	Larry Nelson, U.S.	453,310
49	Chi Chi Rodriguez, U.S.	442,440
50	Isao Aoki, Japan	441,565
51	Katsunari Takahashi, Japan	440,775
52	Scott Hoch, U.S.	434,769
53	Al Geiberger, U.S.	432,732
54	Des Smyth, Ireland	425,280
55	Jodie Mudd, U.S.	420,188
56	Larry Mize, U.S.	410,798
57	Bill Glasson, U.S.	405,588
58	Miller Barber, U.S.	404,408
59	Dan Pohl, U.S.	397,566
60	Mark Wiebe, U.S.	397,086
61	Mark James, England	393,077
62	Scott Verplank, U.S.	391,646
63	Craig Stadler, U.S.	388,027
64	Tsuneyuki Nakajima, Japan	387,475
65	Peter Senior, Australia	383,242
66	Bob Gilder, U.S.	378,422
67	Dave Barr, Canada	378,133
68	Yoshimi Niizeki, Japan	376,021
69	Hajime Mashiai, Japan	374,360
70	Scott Simpson, U.S.	373,961
71	Toru Nakamura, Japan	364,959
72	Gordon Brand, Jr., Scotland	363,525
73	John Mahaffey, U.S.	356,741
74	Walter Zembriski, U.S.	353,256
75	Craig Parry, Australia	352,054
76	Billy Casper, U.S.	349,251
77	Dale Douglass, U.S.	343,133
78	Bernhard Langer, West Germany	330,161
79	Bob Lohr, U.S.	328,531
80	Arnold Palmer, U.S.	327,526
81	Jose Rivero, Spain	323,678
82	Mark Brooks, U.S.	320,655
83	Gene Sauers, U.S.	320,102
84	Larry Mowry, U.S.	319,326
85	Eamonn Darcy, Ireland	314,574
86	Don Bies, U.S.	309,652
87	Graham Marsh, Australia	298,660
88	Tom Watson, U.S.	294,156
89	Steve Jones, U.S.	292,015
90	Gil Morgan, U.S.	289,489
91	Dave Rummells, U.S.	287,175
92	Ikuo Shirahama, Japan	283,256

POS.	PLAYER, COUNTRY	TOTAL MONEY
93	Corey Pavin, U.S.	282,664
94	Doug Tewell, U.S.	279,909
95	Donnie Hammond, U.S.	277,810
96	Dan Forsman, U.S.	271,940
97	Barry Lane, England	267,243
98	Mark Mouland, Wales	265,881
99	Andrew Magee, U.S.	262,764
100	Nobuo Serizawa, Japan	262,088
101	Howard Clark, England	255,522
102	Anders Forsbrand, Sweden	252,555
103	Gene Littler, U.S.	252,000
104	Lou Graham, U.S.	250,448
105	Morris Hatalsky, U.S.	249,819
106	Clarence Rose, U.S.	244,342
107	Wayne Levi, U.S.	242,236
108	Blaine McCallister, U.S.	242,139
109	Bobby Nichols, U.S.	240,486
110	Wayne Grady, Australia	240,082
111	Peter Baker, England	238,829
112	Fuzzy Zoeller, U.S.	238,104
113	Bruce Devlin, Australia	235,270
114	Koichi Suzuki, Japan	234,922
115	Yoshikazu Yokoshima, Japan	233,879
116	John Huston, U.S.	233,551
117	Ray Floyd, U.S.	233,359
118	Jim Carter, U.S.	233,308
119	Jim Benepe, U.S.	232,961
120	Tomohiro Maruyama, Japan	229,236
121	Hale Irwin, U.S.	228,721
122	Robert Wrenn, U.S.	228,566
123	David Graham, Australia	228,191
124	Hiroshi Makino, Japan	226,875
125	Seiichi Kanai, Japan	226,124
126	Tom Purtzer, U.S.	225,833
127	Curt Byrum, U.S.	225,493
128	Andy Bean, U.S.	222,991
129	Tom Sieckmann, U.S.	215,182
130	Saburo Fujiki, Japan	214,095
131	Chen Tze Chung, Taiwan	213,793
132	Bobby Wadkins, U.S.	212,358
133	Tim Simpson, U.S.	211,414
134	Brad Faxon, U.S.	208,538
135	Roger Mackay, Australia	208,216
136	Nobumitsu Yuhara, Japan	207,841
137	Tommy Armour III, U.S.	206,765
138	Denis Durnian, England	204,480
139	Ed Fiori, U.S.	203,140
140	Tony Johnstone, Zimbabwe	200,723
141	Tsukasa Watanabe, Japan	198,658
142	D.A. Weibring, U.S.	197,301
143	Roger Chapman, England	194,904
144	Chen Tze Ming, Taiwan	193,940
145	Lee Elder, U.S.	193,198
146	Katsuyoshi Tomori, Japan	191,033
147	Charles Coody, U.S.	190,786
148	James Hallet, U.S.	188,356
149	Tadami Ueno, Japan	188,056
150	Brett Ogle, Australia	185,197
151	Roger Maltbie, U.S.	183,310
152	Tom Byrum, U.S.	180,853

POS.	PLAYER, COUNTRY	TOTAL MONEY
153	Chris Moody, England	180,428
154	Don Massengale, U.S.	179,897
155	John Cook, U.S.	179,590
156	Kenny Knox, U.S.	179,399
157	Frank Nobilo, New Zealand	177,789
158	Mike Hulbert, U.S.	171,352
159	Butch Baird, U.S.	171,153
160	Rocco Mediate, U.S.	170,136
161	Yutaka Hagawa, Japan	169,946
162	Mike Harwood, Australia	166,517
163	Ben Smith, U.S.	166,363
164	Davis Love III, U.S.	165,128
165	Steve Elkington, U.S.	164,472
166	Masanobu Kimura, Japan	161,961
167	Yoshiyuki Isomura, Japan	159,706
168	Jay Don Blake, U.S.	158,719
169	Toshimitsu Kai, Japan	158,067
170	Peter Thomson, Australia	156,129
171	Peter Fowler, Australia	155,111
172	Richard Zokol, Canada	154,685
173	Yoshitaka Yamamoto, Japan	154,172
174	Christy O'Connor Jr., Ireland	153,487
175	Calvin Peete, U.S.	152,922
176	Kinpachi Yoshimura, Japan	152,595
177	David Edwards, U.S.	151,513
178	Haruo Yasuda, Japan	151,233
179	Russ Cochran, U.S.	151,122
180	Gordon J. Brand, England	149,486
181	Wayne Riley, Australia	149,106
182	Buddy Gardner, U.S.	147,692
183	Richard Rhyan, U.S.	147,423
184	Carl Mason, England	146,733
185	Teruo Sugihara, Japan	143,974
186	Mac O'Grady, U.S.	143,153
187	Hal Sutton, U.S.	143,106
188	Lennie Clements, U.S.	142,457
189	Miguel Martin, Spain	142,406
190	Kenny Perry, U.S.	141,321
191	John Bland, South Africa	140,659
192	David Ogrin, U.S.	140,657
193	Dick Mast, U.S.	139,068
194	George Lanning, U.S.	138,400
195	Katsuji Hasegawa, Japan	137,946
196	Loren Roberts, U.S.	136,890
197	Richard Boxall, England	136,208
198	Larry Rinker, U.S.	131,796
199	Mike Donald, U.S.	131,359
200	Mike Sullivan, U.S.	129,951

The Sony Ranking

(As of December 31, 1988)

Pos.	Player	Tour	Points	1985 x1	1986 x2	1987 x4	1985-7 Total	1985-7 Minus	1988 Plus
1 (2)	Seve Ballesteros	Eur 1	1458	181	336	652	1169	–675	964
2 (1)	Greg Norman	ANZ 1	1365	85	582	564	1231	–658	792
3 (4)	Sandy Lyle	Eur 2	1297	125	126	628	879	–502	920
4 (14)	Nick Faldo	Eur 3	1103	25	82	516	623	–324	804
5 (5)	Curtis Strange	USA 1	1092	137	144	592	873	–505	724
6 (10)	Ben Crenshaw	USA 2	898	0	128	540	668	–334	564
7 (6)	Ian Woosnam	Eur 4	854	58	120	652	830	–444	468
8 (22)	David Frost	Afr 1	843	30	122	404	556	–290	580
9 (11)	Paul Azinger	USA 3	825	7	86	556	649	–328	504
10 (31)	Mark Calcavecchia	USA 4	819	0	46	408	454	–227	592
11 (18)	Masashi Ozaki	Jpn 1	781	29	202	360	591	–310	500
12 (36)	Chip Beck	USA 5	770	10	116	280	406	–208	572
13 (21)	Tom Kite	USA 6	726	71	168	324	563	–317	480
14 (8)	Lanny Wadkins	USA 7	721	127	130	440	697	–412	436
15 (3)	Bernhard Langer	Eur 5	696	184	316	612	1112	–648	232
16 (7)	Payne Stewart	USA 8	672	85	212	420	717	–401	356
17 (57)	Ken Green	USA 9	661	30	90	144	264	–147	544
18 (9)	Mark McNulty	Afr 2	645	31	206	436	673	–352	324
19 (46)	Fred Couples	USA 10	638	37	20	280	337	–187	488
20 (49)	Jose-Maria Olazabal	Eur 6	629	1	162	144	307	–154	476
21 (67)	Joey Sindelar	USA 11	599	67	90	76	233	–150	516
22 (13)	Rodger Davis	ANZ 2	589	48	226	352	626	–337	300
23 (23)	Larry Nelson	USA 12	576	31	56	464	551	–291	316
24 (25)	David Ishii	USA 13	532	27	112	376	515	–271	288
25 (26)	Mark O'Meara	USA 14	518	123	128	252	503	–313	328
26T (54T)	Mark McCumber	USA 15T	516	48	24	200	272	–160	404
26T (73)	Steve Pate	USA 15T	516	20	28	164	212	–116	420
28 (12)	Larry Mize	USA 17	511	47	110	488	645	–346	212
29 (16)	Tom Watson	USA 18	505	62	126	428	616	–339	228
30T (75)	Jeff Sluman	USA 19	503	18	22	168	208	–113	408
30T (19)	Isao Aoki	Jpn 2	503	70	214	296	580	–325	248
32 (15)	Tsuneyuki Nakajima	Jpn 3	494	125	288	204	617	–371	248
33 (17)	Scott Simpson	USA 20	493	38	50	504	592	–315	216
34 (30)	Bob Tway	USA 21	486	31	308	144	483	–257	260
35 (51)	Mike Reid	USA 22	485	29	34	224	287	–158	356
36 (29)	Dan Pohl	USA 23	473	41	154	296	491	–266	248
37 (27T)	Craig Stadler	USA 24	461	99	98	296	493	–296	264
38 (40)	Ian Baker-Finch	ANZ 3	454	49	132	184	365	–207	296
39 (27T)	Scott Hoch	USA 25	452	45	104	344	493	–269	228
40 (32)	Don Pooley	USA 26	445	22	106	304	432	–227	240
41 (47)	Nick Price	Afr 3	438	44	72	220	336	–190	292
42 (38)	Peter Senior	ANZ 4	429	10	54	316	380	–195	244
43 (56)	Jay Haas	USA 27	405	23	66	176	265	–144	284
44 (58T)	Ronan Rafferty	Eur 7	395	24	58	180	262	–143	276
45 (33)	Gordon Brand Jr.	Eur 8	387	35	70	320	425	–230	192

(   ): Figures in brackets indicate 1985-87 positions.

Pos.	Player	Tour	Points	1985 x1	1986 x2	1987 x4	1985-7 Total	1985-7 Minus	1988 Plus
46 (24)	Corey Pavin	USA 28	373	118	114	296	528	–323	168
47 (45)	Masahiro Kuramoto	Jpn 4	364	67	108	172	347	–207	224
48 (105T)	Bruce Lietzke	USA 29	360	28	56	64	148	–88	300
49 (130T)	Des Smyth	Eur 9	343	18	54	40	112	–65	296
50 (108)	Mark James	Eur 10	336	34	48	64	146	–90	280
51 (58T)	Jodie Mudd	USA 30	334	34	80	148	262	–148	220
52 (71)	Naomichi Ozaki	Jpn 5	323	34	110	80	224	–129	228
53 (74)	Tateo Ozaki	Jpn 6	313	57	110	44	211	–134	236
54 (35)	Graham Marsh	ANZ 5	312	68	112	240	420	–244	136
55T (20)	Hal Sutton	USA 31	311	93	214	272	579	–336	68
55T (41)	Howard Clark	Eur 11	311	51	122	188	361	–206	156
57 (43)	D.A. Weibring	USA 32	310	48	64	244	356	–202	156
58 (39)	Fuzzy Zoeller	USA 33	309	58	174	140	372	–215	152
59 (92)	Mark Wiebe	USA 34	305	43	74	56	173	–108	240
60 (53)	John Mahaffey	USA 35	303	79	126	72	277	–178	204
61T (62T)	Jose Rivero	Eur 12	302	28	52	160	240	–134	196
61T (65T)	Brian Jones	ANZ 6	302	24	48	164	236	–130	196
63 (37)	Ray Floyd	USA 36	294	108	188	96	392	–250	152
64 (120T)	Peter Jacobsen	USA 37	290	49	44	32	125	–87	252
65 (90T)	Dave Barr	Can 1	289	28	38	108	174	–101	216
66 (120T)	Gary Koch	USA 38	287	31	82	12	125	–78	240
67 (69T)	Fulton Allem	Afr 4	276	4	60	164	228	–116	164
68 (42)	Bobby Wadkins	USA 39	275	15	118	224	357	–186	104
69 (60)	Doug Tewell	USA 40	263	26	126	96	248	–137	152
70T (126)	Gil Morgan	USA 41	251	23	26	68	117	–70	204
70T (82T)	David Graham	ANZ 7	251	45	114	28	187	–116	180
72 (217T)	Craig Parry	ANZ 8	250	0	0	44	44	–22	228
73 (81)	Gene Sauers	USA 42	243	6	66	116	188	–97	152
74 (34)	Andy Bean	USA 43	240	47	244	132	423	–235	52
75 (72)	Donnie Hammond	USA 44	233	11	98	112	221	–116	128
76 (88)	Wayne Grady	ANZ 9	231	37	10	132	179	–108	160
77 (52)	Tze-Chung Chen	Asa 1	230	62	36	184	282	–172	120
78 (48)	Mac O'Grady	USA 45	229	44	78	196	318	–181	92
79 (78)	Anders Forsbrand	Eur 13	228	16	60	124	200	–108	136
80 (95)	Clarence Rose	USA 46	227	12	66	92	170	–91	148
81T (161)	Steve Jones	USA 47T	222	0	0	84	84	–42	180
81T (150T)	Bob Lohr	USA 47T	222	16	16	60	92	–54	184
83 (54T)	John Cook	USA 49	219	2	78	192	272	–137	84
84 (109)	Tony Johnstone	Afr 5	218	2	40	100	142	–72	148
85T (123T)	Eamonn Darcy	Eur 14	217	16	18	88	122	–69	164
85T (87)	Hajime Meshiai	Jpn 7	217	10	14	156	180	–95	132
87 (184T)	Scott Verplank	USA 50	214	25	36	0	61	–43	196
88 (132T)	Bill Glasson	USA 51	212	39	20	52	111	–75	176
89 (85T)	Toru Nakamura	Jpn 8	209	28	54	100	182	–105	132
90 (61)	Davis Love	USA 52	206	0	40	204	244	–122	84
91 (82T)	Wayne Levi	USA 53	205	41	42	104	187	–114	132
92 (187T)	Dave Rummells	USA 54	202	0	12	48	60	–30	172
93 (89)	Curt Byrum	USA 55	201	5	34	136	175	–90	116
94T (150T)	Tom Purtzer	USA 56	197	2	58	32	92	–47	152
94T (68)	Gordon J. Brand	Eur 15	197	14	130	88	232	–123	88
96 (259T)	Andrew Magee	USA 57	194	8	8	12	28	–18	184
97 (103T)	Dan Forsman	USA 58	191	23	62	64	149	–86	128
98 (50)	Calvin Peete	USA 59	190	84	196	24	304	–194	80
99 (44)	Sam Torrance	Eur 16	187	47	58	244	349	–198	36
100 (93T)	John Bland	Afr 6	186	15	64	92	171	–93	108

( ): Figures in brackets indicate 1985-87 positions.

Pos.	Player	Tour	Points	1985 x1	1986 x2	1987 x4	1985-7 Total	1985-7 Minus	1988 Plus
101 (62T)	Ken Brown	Eur 17	184	16	44	180	204	−128	72
102T (79)	Mike Hulbert	USA 60	182	0	104	92	196	−98	84
102T (99T)	Katsunari Takahashi	Jpn 9	182	39	32	92	163	−101	120
104 (130T)	Morris Hatalsky	USA 61	181	14	10	88	112	−63	132
105 (113)	Peter Fowler	ANZ 10	180	9	40	88	137	−73	116
106 (105T)	Tim Simpson	USA 62	172	28	72	48	148	−88	112
107 (391T)	Bob Gilder	USA 63	171	3	6	0	9	−6	168
108T (201T)	Hale Irwin	USA 64T	170	39	4	8	51	−45	164
108T (98)	Kenny Knox	USA 64T	170	3	84	80	167	−85	88
108T (349T)	Peter Baker	Eur 18	170	0	0	12	12	−6	164
111 (182)	Roger Chapman	Eur 19	169	21	6	36	63	−42	148
112 (517T)	Mark Brooks	USA 66	168	0	0	0	0	0	168
113T (134)	Roger Mackay	ANZ 11	166	2	12	96	110	−56	112
113T (237T)	Barry Lane	Eur 20	166	0	0	36	36	−18	148
115 (125)	Mark Mouland	Eur 21	165	6	26	88	120	−63	108
116 (76)	J.C. Snead	USA 67	163	4	42	156	202	−103	64
117 (232T)	Yoshimi Niizeki	Jpn 10	159	0	14	24	38	−19	140
118T (132T)	Robert Wrenn	USA 68	154	3	0	108	111	−57	100
118T (64)	Hugh Baiocchi	Afr 7	154	25	56	156	237	−131	48
120 (119)	Christy O'Connor, Jr.	Eur 22	153	37	34	56	127	−82	108
121 (317T)	Jim Benepe	USA 69	152	0	0	16	16	−8	144
122 (237T)	Denis Durnian	Eur 23	150	0	0	36	36	−18	132
123 (187T)	Brad Faxon	USA 70	149	2	14	44	60	−31	120
124 (244T)	Tom Sieckmann	USA 71	148	2	20	12	34	−18	132
125 (105T)	David Feherty	Eur 24	146	16	44	88	148	−82	80
126T (69T)	Roger Maltbie	USA 72	144	68	64	96	228	−148	64
126T (112)	Nobuo Serizawa	Jpn 11	144	3	0	136	139	−71	76
128 (90T)	Seiichi Kanai	Jpn 12	140	30	28	116	174	−102	68
129 (166T)	Ed Fiori	USA 73	139	22	18	36	76	−49	112
130T (128)	David Edwards	USA 74	137	0	30	84	114	−57	80
130T (93T)	Jose-Maria Canizares	Eur 25	137	33	46	92	171	−102	68
132 (517T)	Jim Carter	USA 75	136	0	0	0	0	0	136
133 (191T)	Blaine McCallister	USA 76	133	0	26	32	58	−29	104
134T (65T)	Jack Nicklaus	USA 77	130	40	152	44	236	−138	32
134T (118)	Koichi Suzuki	Jpn 13	130	15	44	72	131	−73	72
136 (101)	Keith Clearwater	USA 78	128	0	0	160	160	−80	48
137T (116T)	Buddy Gardner	USA 79T	126	24	12	96	132	−78	72
137T (217T)	Jim Hallet	USA 79T	126	0	0	44	44	−22	104
139 (77)	George Burns	USA 81	122	53	4	144	201	−127	48
140 (114T)	Hiroshi Makino	Jpn 14	119	10	22	104	136	−73	56
141T (102)	Yoshitaka Yamamoto	Jpn 15	116	20	16	120	156	−88	48
141T (172T)	Jeff Hawkes	Afr 8	116	12	4	52	68	−40	88
141T (82T)	Tze-Ming Chen	Asa 2	116	43	16	128	187	−115	44
144T (159T)	Carl Mason	Eur 26	114	18	0	68	86	−52	80
144T (296T)	Ikuo Shirahama	Jpn 16	114	0	20	0	20	−10	104
146 (154)	Tom Byrum	USA 82	113	0	18	72	90	−45	68
147T (513T)	Chris Moody	Eur 27	112	1	0	0	1	−1	112
147T (179T)	Yoshikazu Yokoshima	Jpn 17	112	0	4	60	64	−32	80
149T (184T)	Mike Harwood	ANZ 12	108	5	20	36	61	−33	80
149T (179T)	Philip Walton	Eur 28	108	0	12	52	64	−32	76

(   ): Figures in brackets indicate 1985-87 positions.

Pos.	Player	Tour	Points	1985 x1	1986 x2	1987 x4	1985-7 Total	1985-7 Minus	1988 Plus
151 (391T)	Brett Ogle	ANZ 13	107	3	6	0	9	–6	104
152T (259T)	Richard Zokol	Can 2	106	8	0	20	28	–18	96
152T (166T)	Bob Shearer	ANZ 14	106	0	64	12	76	–38	68
152T (349T)	Tommy Armour	USA 83	106	0	12	0	12	–6	100
155 (172T)	Tsukasa Watanabe	Jpn 18	104	4	20	44	68	–36	72
156T (171)	Russ Cochran	USA 84	103	18	6	48	72	–45	76
156T (127)	Manuel Pinero	Eur 29	103	45	30	40	115	–80	68
156T (221T)	Wayne Riley	ANZ 15	103	13	10	20	43	–28	88
159 (140)	Mats Lanner	Eur 30	102	0	16	84	100	–50	52
160 (114T)	Ove Sellberg	Eur 31	99	10	46	80	136	–73	36
161T (162)	Saburo Fujiki	Jpn 19	96	2	24	56	82	–42	56
161T (274T)	Steve Elkington	ANZ 16	96	0	8	16	24	–12	84
163T (221T)	Mike Clayton	ANZ 17T	95	5	10	28	43	–24	76
163T (116T)	Terry Gale	ANZ 17T	95	30	46	56	132	01	44
165T (144)	Mike Donald	USA 85	94	13	16	68	97	–55	52
165T (343T)	Miguel Martin	Eur 32	94	1	4	8	13	–7	88
165T (256T)	Frank Nobilo	ANZ 19	94	9	8	12	29	–19	84
168 (164)	Ian Mosey	Eur 33	91	2	38	40	80	–41	52
169 (123T)	Rick Fehr	USA 86	90	6	28	88	122	–64	32
170T (96)	Johnny Miller	USA 87T	89	31	18	120	169	–100	20
170T (122)	Howard Twitty	USA 87T	89	10	26	88	124	–67	32
170T (150T)	Nobumitsu Yuhara	Jpn 20	89	26	38	28	92	–59	56
173 (517T)	John Huston	USA 89	88	0	0	0	0	0	88
174 (197T)	Bill Sander	USA 90	86	8	0	44	52	–30	64
175 (85T)	Denis Watson	Afr 9	85	52	10	120	182	–117	20
176 (183)	Lyndsay Stephen	ANZ 20	83	8	22	32	62	–35	56
177T (155)	Bobby Clampett	USA 91T	82	5	12	72	89	–47	40
177T (157T)	Sam Randolph	USA 91T	82	3	0	84	87	–45	40
179T (170)	Ronnie Black	USA 93	81	0	30	44	74	–37	44
179T (156)	Ossie Moore	ANZ 21	81	14	38	36	88	–51	44
179T (204)	Yoshiyuki Isomura	Jpn 21	81	0	22	28	50	–25	56
182T (176T)	Bob Eastwood	USA 94T	80	26	8	32	66	–46	60
182T (266T)	Loren Roberts	USA 94T	80	19	0	8	27	–23	76
182T (211T)	Yasuhiro Funatogawa	Jpn 22	80	6	40	0	46	–26	60
182T (206T)	Wayne Westner	Afr 10	80	0	4	44	48	–24	56
186 (232T)	Tadami Ueno	Jpn 23	79	0	14	24	38	–19	60
187T (143)	Pat McGowan	USA 96T	78	6	44	48	98	–52	32
187T (174T)	David Ogrin	USA 96T	78	15	20	32	67	–41	52
187T (165)	David Llewellyn	Eur 34	78	19	0	60	79	–49	48
187T (176T)	Gerry Taylor	ANZ 22	78	6	12	48	66	–36	48
187T (237T)	Dick Mast	USA 96T	78	0	16	20	36	–18	60
187T (197T)	Brian Tennyson	USA 96T	78	0	0	52	52	–26	52
193T (517T)	Richard Boxall	Eur 35	76	0	0	0	0	0	76
193T (229T)	Kenny Perry	USA 100	76	0	0	40	40	–20	56
195 (148T)	Lennie Clements	USA 101	73	4	22	68	94	–49	28
196 (395T)	Jay Don Blake	USA 102	72	0	0	8	8	–4	68
197 (211T)	Masanobu Kimura	Jpn 24	71	0	14	32	46	–23	48
198T (449T)	Dave Eichelberger	USA 103T	70	0	4	0	4	–2	68
198T (110T)	Hubert Green	USA 103T	70	80	48	12	140	–110	40
198T (103T)	Gary Hallberg	USA 103T	70	25	20	104	149	–87	8

(   ): Figures in brackets indicate 1985-87 positions.

World's Winners of 1988

Spalding Invitational	Lennie Clements
MONY Tournament of Champions	Steve Pate
Bob Hope Chrysler Classic	Jay Haas
Phoenix Open	Sandy Lyle
AT&T Pebble Beach National Pro-Am	Steve Jones
Hawaiian Open	Lanny Wadkins
Shearson Lehman Hutton Andy Williams Open	Steve Pate (2)
Nissan Los Angeles Open	Chip Beck
Doral Ryder Open	Ben Crenshaw
Honda Classic	Joey Sindelar
Hertz Bay Hill Classic	Paul Azinger
The Players Championship	Mark McCumber
K-Mart Greater Greensboro Open	Sandy Lyle (2)
Masters Tournament	Sandy Lyle (3)
Deposit Guaranty Classic	Frank Conner
MCI Heritage Classic	Greg Norman (4)
USF&G Classic	Chip Beck (2)
Independent Insurance Agent Open	Curtis Strange (2)
Panasonic Las Vegas Invitational	Gary Koch
GTE Byron Nelson Classic	Bruce Lietzke
Colonial National Invitation	Lanny Wadkins (2)
Memorial Tournament	Curtis Strange (3)
Kemper Open	Morris Hatalsky
Manufacturers Hanover Westchester Classic	Seve Ballesteros (2)
U.S. Open Championship	Curtis Strange (4)
Georgia-Pacific Atlanta Classic	Larry Nelson
Beatrice Western Open	Jim Benepe (2)
Anheuser-Busch Classic	Tom Sieckmann
Hardee's Classic	Blaine McCallister
Canon Sammy Davis Jr. Hartford Open	Mark Brooks
Buick Open	Scott Verplank
Federal Express St. Jude Classic	Jodie Mudd
PGA Championship	Jeff Sluman
The International	Joey Sindelar (2)
NEC World Series of Golf	Mike Reid
Provident Classic	Phil Blackmar
Canadian Open	Ken Green
Greater Milwaukee Open	Ken Green (2)
Bank of Boston Classic	Mark Calcavecchia
B.C. Open	Bill Glasson
Southern Open	David Frost
Gatlin Brothers Southwest Classic	Tom Purtzer
Texas Open Presented By Nabisco	Corey Pavin
Pensacola Open	Andrew Magee
Walt Disney World/Oldsmobile Classic	Bob Lohr
Northern Telecom Tucson Open	David Frost (2)
Nabisco Championship	Curtis Strange (5)
Centel Classic	Bill Glasson (2)
Isuzu Kapalua International	Bob Gilder
J.C. Penney Classic	John Huston/Amy Benz
Chrysler Team Championship	George Burns/Wayne Levi
Kirin Cup	United States

EUROPEAN TOUR

Mallorca Open De Baleares	Seve Ballesteros
Torras Hostench Barcelona Open	David Whelan
AGF Biarritz Open	David Llewellyn (2)
Cannes Open	Mark McNulty
Cepsa Madrid Open	Derrick Cooper
Portuguese Open	Mike Harwood
Epson Grand Prix of Europe Match Play	Bernhard Langer
Peugeot Spanish Open	Mark James (2)
Lancia Italian Open	Greg Norman (5)
Volvo PGA Championship	Ian Woosnam
Dunhill British Masters	Sandy Lyle (4)
Wang Four Stars National Pro-Celebrity	Rodger Davis
Volvo Belgian Open	Jose-Maria Olazabal
Peugeot French Open	Nick Faldo
Monte Carlo Open	Jose Rivero
Bell's Scottish Open	Barry Lane
British Open Championship	Seve Ballesteros (3)
KLM Open	Mark Mouland
Scandinavian Enterprise Open	Seve Ballesteros (4)
Benson & Hedges International Open	Peter Baker
PLM Open	Frank Nobilo
Carrolls Irish Open	Ian Woosnam (2)
German Open	Seve Ballesteros (5)
Ebel European Masters/Swiss Open	Chris Moody
Panasonic European Open	Ian Woosnam (3)
Lancome Trophy	Seve Ballesteros (6)
German Masters	Jose-Maria Olazabal (2)
English Open	Howard Clark
Suntory World Match Play Championship	Sandy Lyle (5)
Dunhill Cup	Ireland
Jersey Open	Des Smyth
Volvo Masters	Nick Faldo (2)
Benson & Hedges Trophy Mixed Team	Mark McNulty (2)/Marie Laure de Lorenzi-Taya

AFRICAN TOURS

Nigerian Open	Vijay Singh
Ivory Coast Open	Gordon J. Brand
555 Kenya Open	Chris Platts
Zimbabwe Open	Roger Chapman
Zambian Open	David Llewellyn
Palabora Classic	Fulton Allem
ICL International	Tony Johnstone
Lexington PGA Championship	David Feherty
Southern Sun South African Open	Wayne Westner
Bloemfontein Classic	Jeff Hawkes
Danglo Tournament of Champions	Mark James
AECI Charity Classic	Bobby Lincoln
Helix Swazi Sun Classic	Don Levin
Trust Bank Tournament of Champions	John Bland
Minolta Copiers Match Play	Tony Johnstone (2)
Bloemfontein Classic	Tony Johnstone (3)
Safmarine Masters	John Bland (2)
Million Dollar Challenge	Fulton Allem (2)
Goodyear Classic	Trevor Dodds

AUSTRALIAN TOUR

Sanctuary Cove Classic	Curtis Strange
Daikyo Palm Meadows Cup	Greg Norman
Mercedes-Benz Australian Match Play	Ronan Rafferty
Blakiston Boyd Victorian Open	Jim Benepe
Australian Masters	Ian Baker-Finch
ESP Open	Greg Norman (2)
Australian Tournament Players' Championship	Greg Norman (3)
Queensland Open	Brett Officer
Tasmanian Open	Brett Ogle
Panasonic New South Wales Open	Greg Norman (6)
Town & Country Western Australian Open	Bradley Hughes
Australian PGA Championship	Wayne Grady
West End South Australian Open	Gordon Brand Jr.
Ricky May Classic	David Merriman
Test Match	Britain
Panasonic Australia Open Championship	Marck Calcavecchia (2)
Bicentennial Classic	Rodger Davis (2)
World Cup	United States / Ben Crenshaw (2)
Air New Zealand / Shell Open	Terry Gale
Nissan-Mobil New Zealand Open	Ian Stanley

ASIA/JAPAN TOUR

Unisys Hong Kong Open	Hsieh Chin Sheng
Coca Cola Philippines Open	Hsieh Chin Sheng (2)
Benson & Hedges Malaysian Open	Tray Tyner
Singapore Open	Greg Bruckner
Indonesia Open	Hsieh Yu Shu
Thailand Open	Jeff Senior
Charminar Challenge Indian Open	Lu Chien Soon
Republic of China Open	Carlos Espinosa
Maekyung South Korean Open	Frankie Minoza
Daiichi Fudosan Cup	Kazuya Nakajima
Imperial Invitation	Katsuji Hasegawa
Shizuoka Open	Toshimitsu Kai
TaylorMade Setonaikai Open	Wayne Smith
Kuzuha Kokusai	Wayne Smith (2)
Pocari Sweat Open	Ian Baker-Finch (2)
Bridgestone Aso	Ian Baker-Finch (3)
Dunlop Open	Jumbo Ozaki
Chunichi Crowns	Scott Simpson
Fuji-Sankei Classic	Ikuo Shirahama
Japan Match Play Championship	David Ishii
Pepsi Ube	Mamoru Kondo
Mitsubishi Galant	Brian Jones
Sendai Hoso Classic	Masahiro Kuramoto
Sapporo-Tokyu Open	Joe Ozaki
Yomiuri Sapporo Beer Open	Masahiro Kuromoto (2)
Mizuno Open	Yoshimi Niizeki
Kansai PGA Championship	Masahiro Kuramoto (3)
Kanto PGA Championship	Tomohiro Maruyama
Hiroshima Open	Hajime Matsui
Japan PGA Championship	Jet Ozaki
NST Niigata Open	Joe Ozaki (2)
Nikkei Cup	Jumbo Ozaki (2)
Maruman Open	Jumbo Ozaki (3)
KBC Augusta	Masahiro Kuramoto (4)
Kansai Open	Yasuo Sone
Kanto Open	Akhito Yokohama
Kyushu Open	Katsuyoshi Tomori
Chubu Open	Teruo Nakamura

Chu-Shikoku Open	Masahiro Kuramoto (5)
Hokkaido Open	Mamoru Takahashi
Suntory Open	Jet Ozaki (2)
All Nippon Airways Open	Joe Ozaki (3)
Jun Classic	Tohru Nakamura
Tokai Classic	Brian Jones (2)
Japan Open	Jumbo Ozaki (4)
Polaroid Cup Golf Digest	Jumbo Ozaki (5)
Bridgestone	Jumbo Ozaki (6)
Lark Cup	Katsunari Takahashi
ACOM Doubles	Bob Gilder (2)/Doug Tewell
VISA Taiheiyo Club Masters	Seve Ballesteros (7)
Dunlop Phoenix	Ken Green (3)
Casio World Open	Larry Mize
Japan Series Hitachi Cup	Joe Ozaki (4)
Daikyo Open	Saburo Fujiki

U.S. SENIOR TOUR

MONY Tournament of Champions	Dave Hill
First National Bank Seniors Classic	Bob Charles
General Foods PGA Seniors Championship	Gary Player
GTE Suncoast Classic	Dale Douglass
Aetna Challenge	Gary Player (2)
Vintage Chrysler Invitational	Orville Moody
GTE Classic	Harold Henning
The Pointe/Del E. Webb Arizona Classic	Al Geiberger
Fuji Electric Grand Slam Championship	Bob Charles (2)
Doug Sanders Kingwood Celebrity Classic	Chi Chi Rodriguez
Chrysler Cup	United States
Liberty Mutual Legends of Golf	Bruce Crampton/ Orville Moody (2)
Vantage At The Dominion	Billy Casper
United Hospitals Championship	Bruce Crampton (2)
NYNEX/Golf Digest Commemorative	Bob Charles (3)
Sunwest Bank/Charley Pride Classic	Bob Charles (4)
Senior Players Reunion Pro-Am	Orville Moody (3)
Mazda Tournament Players Championship	Billy Casper (2)
Northville Invitational	Don Bies
Southwestern Bell Classic	Gary Player (3)
Rancho Murieta Gold Rush	Bob Charles (5)
GTE Northwest Classic	Bruce Crampton (3)
Showdown Classic	Miller Barber
Volvo Seniors British Open	Gary Player (4)
Newport Cup	Walt Zembriski
Digital Classic	Chi Chi Rodriguez (2)
USGA Senior Open	Gary Player (5)
MONY Syracuse Classic	Dave Hill (2)
Greater Grand Rapids Open	Orville Moody (4)
Vantage Presents Bank One Classic	Bob Charles (6)
GTE North Classic	Gary Player (6)
Crestar Classic	Arnold Palmer
PaineWebber Invitational	Dave Hill (3)
Pepsi Challenge	Bob Charles (7)
Vantage Championship	Walter Zembriski (2)
General Tire Classic	Larry Mowry
Fairfield Barnett Classic	Miller Barber (2)
Gus Machado Classic	Lee Elder
GTE Kaanapali Classic	Don Bies (2)
Mauna Lani Challenge	Harold Henning
Mazda Champions	Dave Hill (4)/Colleen Walker (2)

LPGA TOUR

Mazda Classic	Nancy Lopez
Sarasota Classic	Patty Sheehan
Orient Leasing Hawaiian Open	Ayako Okamoto
Women's Kemper Open	Betsy King
Circle K Tucson Open	Laura Davies
Standard Register Turquoise Classic	Ok-Hee Ku
Nabisco Dinah Shore	Amy Alcott
San Diego Inamori Classic	Ayako Okamoto (2)
A1 Star/Centinela Hospital Classic	Nancy Lopez (2)
USX Classic	Rosie Jones
Sara Lee Classic	Patti Rizzo
Crestar Classic	Juli Inkster
Chrysler-Plymouth Classic	Nancy Lopez (3)
Mazda LPGA Championship	Sherri Turner
Corning Classic	Sherri Turner (2)
Jamie Farr Toledo Classic	Laura Davies (2)
Rochester International	Mei Chi Cheng
Lady Keystone Open	Shirley Furlong
McDonald's Championship	Kathy Postlewait
duMaurier Classic	Sally Little
Mayflower Classic	Terry-Jo Myers
Boston Five Classic	Colleen Walker
U.S. Women's Open Championship	Liselotte Neumann
Greater Washington Open	Ayako Okamoto (3)
Planters Pat Bradley International	Martha Nause
Atlantic City Classic	Juli Inkster (2)
Nestle World Championship	Rosie Jones (2)
Ocean State Open	Patty Jordan
Rail Charity Classic	Betsy King (2)
Cellular One-Ping Championship	Betsy King (3)
Safeco Classic	Juli Inkster (3)
Santa Barbara Open	Rosie Jones (3)
Konica San Jose Classic	Kathy Guadagnino
Nichirei Ladies Cup	United States
Mazda Japan Classic	Patty Sheehan (2)

Multiple Winners of 1988

PLAYER	WINS	PLAYER	WINS
Seve Ballesteros	7	Tony Johnstone	3
Bob Charles	7	Rosie Jones	3
Greg Norman	6	Betsy King	3
Jumbo Ozaki	6	Nancy Lopez	3
Gary Player	6	Ayako Okamoto	3
Masahiro Kuramoto	5	Ian Woosnam	3
Sandy Lyle	5	Fulton Allem	2
Curtis Strange	5	Miller Barber	2
Dave Hill	4	Chip Beck	2
Orville Moody	4	Jim Benepe	2
Joe Ozaki	4	Don Bies	2
Ian Baker-Finch	3	John Bland	2
Bruce Crampton	3	Mark Calcavecchia	2
Ken Green	3	Billy Casper	2
Juli Inkster	3	Ben Crenshaw	2

PLAYER	WINS	PLAYER	WINS
Laura Davies	2	Jet Ozaki	2
Rodger Davis	2	Steve Pate	2
Nick Faldo	2	Chi Chi Rodriguez	2
David Frost	2	Patty Sheehan	2
Bob Gilder	2	Hsieh Chin Sheng	2
Bill Glasson	2	Joey Sindelar	2
Harold Henning	2	Wayne Smith	2
Mark James	2	Sherri Turner	2
Brian Jones	2	Lanny Wadkins	2
David Llewellyn	2	Colleen Walker	2
Mark McNulty	2	Walter Zembriski	2
Jose-Maria Olazabal	2		

Career World Money List

The following is a listing of the 50 leading money-winners for their careers through the 1988 season. It includes active and inactive players. The World Money List from this and the 22 previous editions of this annual and a table prepared for a companion book, THE WONDERFUL WORLD OF PROFESSIONAL GOLF (Atheneum, 1973), form the basis for this compilation. Additional figures were taken from official records of major golf associations, although the shortcomings in records-keeping in professional golf outside the United States in the 1950s and 1960s and exclusions from U.S. records in a few cases during those years prevent these figures from being completely accurate. Conversions of foreign currency figures to U.S. dollars are based on average values during the particular year involved.

POS.	PLAYER, COUNTRY	TOTAL MONEY
1	Jack Nicklaus, U.S.	$6,078,922
2	Severiano Ballesteros, Spain	6,032,253
3	Tom Watson, U.S.	5,899,376
4	Greg Norman, Australia	5,024,227
5	Curtis Strange, U.S.	4,933,665
6	Lanny Wadkins, U.S.	4,900,732
7	Isao Aoki, Japan	4,803,029
8	Tom Kite, U.S.	4,796,689
9	Lee Trevino, U.S.	4,750,908
10	Raymond Floyd, U.S.	4,713,161
11	Ben Crenshaw, U.S.	4,607,264
12	Miller Barber, U.S.	4,596,464
13	Gary Player, South Africa	4,574,081
14	Billy Casper, U.S.	3,960,920
15	Gene Littler, U.S.	3,930,274
16	Masashi Ozaki, Japan	3,871,561
17	Sandy Lyle, Scotland	3,847,398
18	Hale Irwin, U.S.	3,809,559
19	Arnold Palmer, U.S.	3,806,635
20	Bernhard Langer, West Germany	3,750,352

POS.	PLAYER, COUNTRY	TOTAL MONEY
21	Johnny Miller, U.S.	3,698,391
22	Don January, U.S.	3,632,208
23	Craig Stadler, U.S.	3,590,112
24	Tsuneyuki Nakajima, Japan	3,584,618
25	Andy Bean, U.S.	3,498,615
26	Graham Marsh, Australia	3,491,381
27	David Graham, Australia	3,463,866
28	Ian Woosnam, Wales	3,328,533
29	Nick Faldo, England	3,307,585
30	Bob Charles, New Zealand	3,278,560
31	Bruce Crampton, Australia	3,150,087
32	John Mahaffey, U.S.	3,091,497
33	Larry Nelson, U.S.	3,067,811
34	Bruce Lietzke, U.S.	2,967,948
35	Payne Stewart, U.S.	2,878,008
36	Hubert Green, U.S.	2,862,004
37	Fuzzy Zoeller, U.S.	2,833,469
38	Mark O'Meara, U.S.	2,764,752
39	Chi Chi Rodriguez, U.S.	2,739,162
40	Fred Couples, U.S.	2,647,133
41	Tom Weiskopf, U.S.	2,630,667
42	Lee Elder, U.S.	2,616,328
43	Scott Simpson, U.S.	2,609,455
44	Calvin Peete, U.S.	2,533,159
45	Gil Morgan, U.S.	2,512,108
46	Hal Sutton, U.S.	2,509,911
47	Scott Hoch, U.S.	2,463,625
48	Masahiro Kuramoto, Japan	2,383,296
49	Chip Beck, U.S.	2,361,797
50	Jay Haas, U.S.	2,337,232

These 50 players have won $181,520,788 in their lifetimes playing professional tournament golf.

LPGA Money List

POS.	PLAYER	TOTAL MONEY
1	Colleen Walker	$583,116
2	Sherri Turner	373,826
3	Nancy Lopez	354,654
4	Rosie Jones	354,142
5	Patty Sheehan	352,521
6	Jan Stephenson	306,839
7	Ayako Okamoto	305,206
8	Amy Alcott	300,662
9	Betsy King	268,957
10	Juli Inkster	265,319
11	Kathy Postlewait	230,918
12	Martha Nause	199,490
13	Beth Daniel	197,635
14	Amy Benz	197,059
15	Liselotte Neumann	192,729

POS.	PLAYER	TOTAL MONEY
16	Ok-Hee Ku	$187,982
17	Laura Davies	174,232
18	Marta Figueras-Dotti	170,065
19	Judy Dickinson	163,673
20	Sally Little	162,881
21	Dotti Pepper Mochrie	150,793
22	Tammie Green	150,571
23	Debbie Massey	147,759
24	JoAnne Carner	135,301
25	Jody Rosenthal	125,839
26	Debra A. Richard	116,647
27	Mel-Chi Cheng	111,053
28	Patti Rizzo	108,960
29	Sandra Palmer	103,956
30	Nancy Brown	100,079
31	Cindy Rarick	97,212
32	Shirley Furlong	96,466
33	Myra Blackwelder	95,981
34	Michele Berteotti	95,441
35	Missie McGeorge	95,247
36	Jane Geddes	90,298
37	Heather E. Farr	89,904
38	Robin Walton	86,351
39	Donna White	85,616
40	Vicki Fergon	84,613
41	Marci Bozarth	81,440
42	Sally Quinlan	80,367
43	Terry Jo Myers	79,341
44	Lynn Adams	77,548
45	Cathy Morse	77,197
46	Cathy Marino	76,160
47	Danielle Ammaccapane	75,806
48	Kathy Guadagnino	74,074
49	Connie Chillemi	71,069
50	Janet Coles	70,715

Above list includes LPGA official money, J. C. Penney, Nikkei Cup, Mazda Champions, Spalding and several other non-tour US events.

The U.S. Tour

Spalding Invitational Pro-Amateur

Carmel Valley Country Club — Par 71
Pebble Beach Golf Links — Par 72
Carmel Valley Ranch — Par 70

December 31-January 3
purse, $250,000

Pebble Beach, California

	SCORES				TOTAL	MONEY
Lennie Clements	62	77	63	69	271	$50,000
Ken Green	69	72	65	65	271	22,333
Tim Norris	70	71	62	68	271	22,333
Dan Pohl	69	72	66	64	271	22,333
(Clements defeated Green, Norris and Pohl on first hole of playoff.)						
Jan Stephenson	67	69	65	71	272	11,000
Johnny Miller	69	70	64	71	274	9,000
Ron Stelten	73	65	71	66	275	6,250
Bob Gilder	67	67	73	68	275	6,250
Dave Barr	71	69	71	65	276	3,750
Roger Maltbie	71	69	67	69	276	3,750
Gene Sauers	72	70	70	65	277	2,900
Bobby Clampett	70	68	74	65	277	2,900
Craig Stadler	69	73	66	69	277	2,900
Bill Glasson	73	65	70	69	277	2,900
George Archer	71	70	68	69	278	2,300
Duffy Waldorf	70	71	67	70	278	2,300
Mike Reid	71	69	71	68	279	1,900
Sam Randolph	73	68	68	70	279	1,900
Mark Lye	69	75	62	73	279	1,900
Barry Jaeckel	73	70	68	69	280	1,600
Bob Lunn	68	74	68	70	280	1,600
Bob Ford	72	68	71	69	280	1,600
Steve Pate	71	70	72	68	281	1,316
John Inman	66	71	75	69	281	1,316
J.C. Snead	72	68	71	70	281	1,316
Ed Luethke	74	75	68	66	283	1,200
Val Skinner	71	73	72	68	284	1,100
Doug Tewell	78	66	70	70	284	1,100
Bruce Summerhays	74	72	70	68	284	1,100
Jay Overton	69	69	78	69	285	970
Graham Cowan	67	71	76	71	285	970
Howard Clark	65	74	74	72	285	970
Lon Hinkle	73	70	69	73	285	970
Bob Boldt	71	73	70	72	286	890
Kevin Sutherland	72	72	70	72	286	890
Rick Rhoads	72	68	76	70	286	890
Shelley Hamlin	75	70	72	69	286	890
Keith Clearwater	78	70	68	71	287	813
Cindy Rarick	74	72	67	74	287	813
Amy Alcott	70	77	70	70	287	813
Ray Vucinich	74	74	71	68	287	813
Dave Fowler	70	70	75	73	288	777
Doug Doxsie	72	70	72	74	288	777
Keith Fergus	78	66	73	71	288	777
Robert Meyer	75	72	71	70	288	777
Mark Calcavecchia	81	65	72	70	288	777
Charlie Gibson	75	72	72	69	288	777

	SCORES			TOTAL	MONEY
Rob Boldt	76	72	69	72	289	777
Gary McCord	75	70	69	76	290	747
Chuck Milne	69	77	71	73	290	747
Al Geiberger	77	74	69	70	290	747
Nathaniel Crosby	71	81	69	69	290	747

MONY Tournament of Champions

LaCosta Country Club, Carlsbad, California
Par 36-36 — 72; 7,022 yards

January 14-17
purse, $500,000

	SCORES			TOTAL	MONEY
Steve Pate	66	66	70	202	$90,000
Larry Nelson	68	67	68	203	54,000
Dave Barr	67	66	73	206	29,000
Nick Faldo	70	65	71	206	29,000
Keith Clearwater	69	67	73	209	19,000
J.C. Snead	69	69	71	209	19,000
Paul Azinger	68	73	69	210	15,062.50
Doug Tewell	69	71	70	210	15,062.50
Mark McCumber	72	68	70	210	15,062.50
Payne Stewart	68	71	71	210	15,062.50
Tom Watson	71	69	71	211	10,620
Ben Crenshaw	73	68	70	211	10,620
Tom Kite	70	70	71	211	10,620
Larry Mize	73	67	71	211	10,620
Scott Simpson	73	71	67	211	10,620
George Burns	71	67	74	212	8,266.67
Fred Couples	70	72	70	212	8,266.67
Sandy Lyle	72	72	68	212	8,266.66
Robert Wrenn	69	72	72	213	7,625
Don Pooley	71	69	73	213	7,625
Chen Tze Chung	69	71	74	214	6,760
John Cook	71	70	73	214	6,760
Johnny Miller	68	75	71	214	6,760
Curtis Strange	73	72	69	214	6,760
Sam Randolph	69	71	74	214	6,760
Jay Haas	72	71	72	215	6,100
Kenny Knox	70	71	74	215	6,100
Corey Pavin	72	70	73	215	6,100
Ken Brown	71	73	72	216	5,900
Lanny Wadkins	76	68	73	217	5,700
Davis Love III	73	72	72	217	5,700
Mac O'Grady	71	71	75	217	5,700
Mark Calcavecchia	72	75	71	218	5,450
D.A. Weibring	73	72	73	218	5,450
Gary Hallberg	72	73	74	219	5,250
Joey Sindelar	72	74	73	219	5,250
John Inman	73	73	74	220	5,100
Mike Reid	77	73	72	222	5,000

Bob Hope Chrysler Classic

Indian Wells Country Club, Palm Desert, California
Par 36-36 — 72; 6,478 yards

January 20-24
purse, $1,000,000

Bermuda Dunes Country Club, Bermuda Dunes, California
Par 36-36 — 72; 6,837 yards

LaQuinta Country Club, LaQuinta, California
Par 36-36 — 72; 6,854 yards

PGA West, Palmer Course, LaQuinta, California
Par 36-36 — 72; 6,924 yards

	SCORES					TOTAL	MONEY
Jay Haas	63	68	69	68	70	338	$180,000
David Edwards	66	71	71	65	67	340	108,000
Bob Tway	69	66	67	67	72	341	68,000
Payne Stewart	72	71	67	67	65	342	44,000
Mark O'Meara	71	66	68	68	69	342	44,000
Scott Hoch	69	66	72	68	68	343	36,000
Gil Morgan	71	67	71	67	68	344	31,166.67
Chip Beck	72	67	69	66	70	344	31,166.67
Leonard Thompson	68	66	76	70	64	344	31,166.66
Gene Sauers	69	67	69	70	70	345	26,000
Paul Azinger	67	68	65	70	75	345	26,000
Curtis Strange	74	68	66	72	66	346	21,000
Andrew Magee	65	70	68	73	70	346	21,000
Fred Couples	68	72	69	70	67	346	21,000
Brian Tennyson	67	71	72	71	66	347	17,000
Mac O'Grady	69	74	69	63	72	347	17,000
Donnie Hammond	67	67	70	70	73	347	17,000
Davis Love III	71	68	72	67	70	348	12,171.43
John Mahaffey	68	65	74	73	68	348	12,171.43
Dan Forsman	68	62	75	70	73	348	12,171.43
Peter Jacobsen	72	71	68	69	68	348	12,171.43
Tom Byrum	70	69	71	69	69	348	12,171.43
John Cook	70	68	72	67	71	348	12,171.43
Curt Byrum	67	69	73	70	69	348	12,171.42
Rocco Mediate	74	66	73	69	67	349	7,312.50
Sam Randolph	67	73	70	68	71	349	7,312.50
Mike Reid	69	69	71	70	70	349	7,312.50
Steve Pate	66	68	71	71	73	349	7,312.50
Kenny Perry	67	66	76	68	72	349	7,312.50
Buddy Gardner	71	67	68	72	71	349	7,312.50
Sandy Lyle	64	71	73	71	70	349	7,312.50
Mark Calcavecchia	70	70	70	69	70	349	7,312.50
Dave Rummells	74	72	72	65	67	350	5,062.50
David Ogrin	72	69	68	71	70	350	5,062.50
Bruce Lietzke	69	70	70	70	71	350	5,062.50
Bill Kratzert	68	70	71	69	72	350	5,062.50
Jay Don Blake	70	74	68	69	69	350	5,062.50
David Frost	68	69	72	73	68	350	5,062.50
Keith Clearwater	65	72	74	70	69	350	5,062.50
Brett Upper	69	68	67	70	76	350	5,062.50
Doug Tewell	72	69	73	67	70	351	3,500
Chris Perry	72	67	73	72	67	351	3,500
Johnny Miller	71	72	68	68	72	351	3,500
Mike Hulbert	71	70	72	69	69	351	3,500
Ray Floyd	72	66	68	72	73	351	3,500

	SCORES				TOTAL	MONEY
Ed Fiori	74	67	69	71	70	351	3,500
Lanny Wadkins	72	68	71	71	69	351	3,500
Corey Pavin	75	68	73	66	70	352	2,620
Ben Crenshaw	70	67	72	70	73	352	2,620
Bobby Wadkins	72	70	71	68	71	352	2,620

Phoenix Open

Tournament Players Club, Scottsdale, Arizona — January 28-31
Par 35-36 — 71; 6,992 yards — purse, $650,000

	SCORES				TOTAL	MONEY
Sandy Lyle	68	68	68	65	269	$117,000
Fred Couples	67	65	67	70	269	70,200
(Lyle defeated Couples on third hole of playoff)						
David Frost	67	66	70	68	271	44,200
Davis Love III	63	68	66	76	273	31,200
Ken Brown	66	71	70	67	274	22,831.25
Bob Lohr	68	70	70	66	274	22,831.25
Gil Morgan	68	66	71	69	274	22,831.25
Ken Green	70	68	67	69	274	22,831.25
Chen Tze Chung	68	68	70	69	275	17,550
Jim Carter	71	68	66	70	275	17,550
Chip Beck	66	63	75	71	275	17,550
Mark McCumber	69	71	66	70	276	14,300
Kenny Knox	72	68	68	68	276	14,300
Dave Barr	67	71	67	72	277	11,050
Larry Mize	69	72	68	68	277	11,050
Jodie Mudd	69	68	70	70	277	11,050
Tom Purtzer	68	70	68	71	277	11,050
Peter Jacobsen	70	70	66	71	277	11,050
Nick Price	71	70	68	69	278	9,100
Jay Don Blake	67	70	70	72	279	8,125
Buddy Gardner	69	68	70	72	279	8,125
John Adams	68	68	74	70	280	6,500
Scott Hoch	73	67	68	72	280	6,500
Ed Fiori	70	71	70	69	280	6,500
Gary Koch	69	70	71	70	280	6,500
Ben Crenshaw	67	69	72	73	281	4,615
Payne Stewart	70	67	70	74	281	4,615
Hal Sutton	68	66	74	73	281	4,615
Larry Rinker	69	66	72	74	281	4,615
Bill Sander	67	71	69	74	281	4,615
Corey Pavin	69	72	71	69	281	4,615
Brad Fabel	70	70	71	70	281	4,615
Leonard Thompson	68	71	71	72	282	3,434.17
Curtis Strange	71	68	73	70	282	3,434.17
Gene Sauers	74	67	72	69	282	3,434.17
Don Pooley	68	69	73	72	282	3,434.17
Jeff Sluman	67	67	76	72	282	3,434.16
Steve Jones	66	74	73	69	282	3,434.16
Ronnie Black	73	66	72	72	283	2,795
Mark Wiebe	69	66	75	73	283	2,795
Mike Reid	71	70	70	72	283	2,795
Danny Edwards	67	69	74	74	284	2,275
Bobby Wadkins	71	65	75	73	284	2,275
Steve Pate	71	68	73	72	284	2,275

	SCORES				TOTAL	MONEY
Bill Glasson	72	69	77	66	284	2,275
Wayne Levi	67	70	74	73	284	2,275
Fulton Allem	72	69	72	72	285	1,692.17
Bob Eastwood	72	67	73	73	285	1,692.17
Clarence Rose	69	69	73	74	285	1,692.17
Dan Halldorson	68	70	72	75	285	1,692.17
Fred Wadsworth	69	69	71	76	285	1,692.16
Howard Twitty	68	70	76	71	285	1,692.16

AT&T Pebble Beach National Pro-Am

Pebble Beach Golf Links
Par 36-36 — 72; 6,799 yards

February 4-7
purse, $700,000

Cypress Point Club
Par 36-36 — 72; 6,506 yards

Spyglass Hill Golf Club
Par 36-36 — 72; 6,810 yards

Pebble Beach, California

	SCORES				TOTAL	MONEY
Steve Jones	72	64	70	74	280	$126,000
Bob Tway	72	73	67	68	280	75,600
(Jones defeated Tway on second hole of playoff)						
Greg Norman	68	75	72	66	281	47,600
Jim Carter	70	71	70	71	282	27,562.50
Craig Stadler	68	70	71	73	282	27,562.50
Tom Sieckmann	69	68	75	70	282	27,562.50
Bernhard Langer	72	67	70	73	282	27,562.50
Mark Calcavecchia	67	69	75	72	283	21,700
David Canipe	70	76	68	70	284	18,900
Tom Watson	68	72	72	72	284	18,900
Mark O'Meara	69	73	71	71	284	18,900
Hale Irwin	73	70	69	73	285	13,300
Bob Gilder	71	72	74	68	285	13,300
Tommy Armour	73	69	71	72	285	13,300
Steve Pate	70	74	74	67	285	13,300
Dick Mast	72	71	68	74	285	13,300
Sandy Lyle	74	65	73	73	285	13,300
Roy Biancalana	76	70	70	70	286	9,450
Willie Wood	70	71	73	72	286	9,450
Dan Pohl	69	73	75	59	286	9,450
Andrew Magee	75	68	72	71	286	9,450
Ben Crenshaw	68	73	72	74	287	6,142.50
Dave Eichelberger	75	68	70	74	287	6,142.50
Jay Delsin	72	70	76	69	287	6,142.50
Howard Clark	70	74	72	71	287	6,142.50
Paul Azinger	72	73	73	69	287	6,142.50
Lanny Wadkins	72	71	73	71	287	6,142.50
Loren Roberts	75	72	71	69	287	6,142.50
Rocco Mediate	70	73	73	71	287	6,142.50
Jim Gallagher, Jr.	67	73	76	72	288	4,445
D.A. Weibring	76	70	69	73	288	4,445
Gene Sauers	72	71	71	74	288	4,445
Greg Ladehoff	70	74	74	70	288	4,445

	SCORES				TOTAL	MONEY
Peter Jacobsen	71	73	72	73	289	3,460
Lennie Clements	70	75	72	72	289	3,460
Robert Wrenn	71	71	75	72	289	3,460
Mark Wiebe	74	71	73	71	289	3,460
Nick Price	70	76	71	72	289	3,460
Rick Pearson	73	70	75	71	289	3,460
Bob Lohr	70	75	71	73	289	3,460
Mike Hulbert	74	74	70	72	290	2,383.50
Mike Donald	70	73	74	73	290	2,383.50
Bill Britton	72	70	73	75	290	2,383.50
Brett Upper	71	70	71	78	290	2,383.50
Joey Sindelar	75	73	70	72	290	2,383.50
Kenny Perry	74	71	72	73	290	2,383.50
Joey Rassett	70	74	72	74	290	2,383.50
Mark Lye	71	72	71	76	290	2,383.50
Bobby Wadkins	76	68	73	74	291	1,710.34
Chris Perry	73	71	74	73	291	1,710.34
Kikuo Arai	73	73	72	73	291	1,710.33
Bill Sander	70	71	77	73	291	1,710.33
David Ogrin	70	71	75	75	291	1,710.33
Larry Rinker	75	70	68	78	291	1,710.33

Hawaiian Open

Waialae Country Club, Honolulu, Hawaii
Par 36-36 — 72; 6,975 yards

February 11-14
purse, $600,000

	SCORES				TOTAL	MONEY
Lanny Wadkins	68	71	66	66	271	$108,000
Richard Zokol	66	71	65	70	272	64,800
John Huston	72	67	69	66	274	40,800
Gene Sauers	71	68	67	69	275	28,800
Fulton Allem	69	69	68	70	276	24,000
Jim Carter	69	68	71	69	277	19,425
Tom Watson	69	70	66	72	277	19,425
Loren Roberts	68	66	70	73	277	19,425
Bob Eastwood	69	69	73	66	277	19,425
J.C. Snead	70	67	73	68	278	15,000
Dave Eichelberger	75	66	69	68	278	15,000
David Ishii	70	68	69	71	278	15,000
Bill Britton	71	67	72	69	279	11,250
John Mahaffey	74	66	69	70	279	11,250
John Inman	68	68	73	70	279	11,250
Ben Crenshaw	71	67	71	70	279	11,250
Bobby Wadkins	70	73	69	68	280	8,120
Larry Nelson	70	67	75	68	280	8,120
Scott Simpson	67	72	70	71	280	8,120
Rocco Mediate	68	72	71	69	280	8,120
Jodie Mudd	66	72	71	71	280	8,120
Scott Hoch	70	68	71	71	280	8,120
Billy Andrade	69	68	71	73	281	5,340
Mark Brooks	68	70	66	77	281	5,340
Tom Sieckmann	68	67	75	71	281	5,340
Buddy Gardner	72	68	71	70	281	5,340
Hale Irwin	71	67	70	73	281	5,340
Chip Beck	69	71	70	72	282	4,440
Leonard Thompson	72	67	72	72	283	3,652.50

	SCORES				TOTAL	MONEY
Robert Wrenn	69	72	73	69	283	3,652.50
Dick Mast	71	68	71	73	283	3,652.50
Rick Pearson	69	70	70	74	283	3,652.50
Dave Rummells	72	67	70	74	283	3,652.50
Kenny Knox	73	68	72	70	283	3,652.50
Bernhard Langer	69	71	71	72	283	3,652.50
Jay Haas	72	70	68	73	283	3,652.50
Ronnie Black	70	69	71	74	284	2,760
George Archer	73	69	70	72	284	2,760
Nobuo Serizawa	72	70	69	73	284	2,760
Hajime Meshiai	71	69	73	71	284	2,760
Billy Ray Brown	71	71	73	70	285	2,100
Roy Biancalana	71	72	70	72	285	2,100
Paul Azinger	71	72	73	69	285	2,100
Mark Calcavecchia	72	68	68	77	285	2,100
Jeff Sluman	71	69	76	69	285	2,100
Calvin Peete	70	71	73	71	285	2,100
Ernie Gonzalez	73	68	71	73	285	2,100
Richard Cromwell	70	71	71	74	286	1,508
Mike Bender	71	71	73	71	286	1,508
Barry Cheesman	70	71	72	73	286	1,508
Larry Mize	72	70	71	73	286	1,508
Craig Stadler	73	69	70	74	286	1,508
Brian Tennyson	71	71	74	70	286	1,508

Shearson Lehman Hutton Andy Williams Open

Torrey Pines Golf Club, LaJolla, California
South Course: Par 36-36 — 72; 7,021 yards
North Course: Par 36-36 — 72; 6,659 yards

February 18-21
purse, $650,000

	SCORES				TOTAL	MONEY
Steve Pate	66	68	67	68	269	$117,000
Jay Haas	69	67	68	66	270	70,200
Joey Sindelar	68	67	68	68	271	37,700
Gil Morgan	74	62	67	68	271	37,700
Willie Wood	66	68	68	70	272	22,035
Roger Maltbie	67	68	68	69	272	22,035
Brad Faxon	69	65	66	72	272	22,035
Tom Kite	68	65	69	70	272	22,035
Mark Calcavecchia	66	68	70	68	272	22,035
Don Pooley	67	65	71	70	273	15,600
Gary Koch	66	68	69	70	273	15,600
Jay Don Blake	69	71	67	66	273	15,600
Fred Couples	63	71	68	71	273	15,600
Mark Wiebe	70	67	69	68	274	11,375
Mark McCumber	68	68	67	71	274	11,375
Greg Ladehoff	68	70	69	67	274	11,375
John Cook	66	68	71	69	274	11,375
Bob Tway	68	65	74	69	276	8,476
Scott Verplank	68	67	70	71	276	8,476
Mike Bender	67	70	69	70	276	8,476
Seve Ballesteros	73	67	68	68	276	8,476
Dave Barr	66	69	72	69	276	8,476
Tom Watson	65	69	69	74	277	5,346.25
Bill Sander	72	69	68	68	277	5,346.25
Jack Renner	66	71	71	69	277	5,346.25

	SCORES				TOTAL	MONEY
Scott Simpson	67	69	71	70	277	5,346.25
Ed Fiori	71	69	67	70	277	5,346.25
Bob Gilder	67	71	72	67	277	5,346.25
Curt Byrum	68	69	71	69	277	5,346.25
Mark Brooks	69	67	69	72	277	5,346.25
Hal Sutton	66	68	68	76	278	3,458
D.A. Weibring	71	65	70	72	278	3,458
Fred Wadsworth	69	69	72	68	278	3,458
Duffy Waldorf	69	70	67	72	278	3,458
Dan Pohl	70	68	70	70	278	3,458
Tim Simpson	71	67	72	68	278	3,458
Mark O'Meara	73	66	69	70	278	3,458
John Huston	68	71	69	70	278	3,458
Dan Forsman	68	67	70	73	278	3,458
Phil Blackmar	64	70	70	74	278	3,458
Tom Purtzer	71	69	72	67	279	2,470
David Peoples	72	68	71	68	279	2,470
Donnie Hammond	68	71	72	68	279	2,470
Clark Burroughs	69	70	71	69	279	2,470
Brian Tennyson	68	69	71	72	280	2,015
Bruce Lietzke	71	67	72	70	280	2,015
Mike Hulbert	69	66	71	74	280	2,015
Larry Mize	72	67	71	71	281	1,615.72
Curtis Strange	70	71	70	70	281	1,615.72
David Edwards	71	69	67	74	281	1,615.72
Gene Sauers	73	68	69	71	281	1,615.71
Buddy Gardner	70	70	69	72	281	1,615.71
Andrew Magee	70	71	68	72	281	1,615.71
George Burns	68	69	72	72	281	1,615.71

Nissan Los Angeles Open

Riviera Country Club, Pacific Palisades, California
Par 35-36 — 71; 7,029 yards

February 25-28
purse, $750,000

	SCORES				TOTAL	MONEY
Chip Beck	65	69	65	68	267	$135,000
Mac O'Grady	69	68	66	68	271	66,000
Bill Sander	70	69	66	66	271	66,000
Ed Fiori	66	68	68	70	272	33,000
Mike Reid	67	69	67	69	272	33,000
Jay Haas	65	68	69	71	273	26,062
Tom Purtzer	69	68	67	69	273	26,062
Steve Elkington	69	67	66	72	274	22,500
Donnie Hammond	66	68	73	67	274	22,500
Hal Sutton	70	68	68	69	275	20,250
Ben Crenshaw	69	64	71	72	276	18,000
Scott Simpson	70	69	69	68	276	18,000
Jim Carter	71	69	68	69	277	15,000
Jeff Sluman	67	71	71	68	277	15,000
Mark Hayes	67	70	69	72	278	13,125
Mark Calcavecchia	73	65	70	70	278	13,125
David Peoples	68	72	69	70	279	10,150
Mike Hulbert	69	68	67	75	279	10,150
Rick Fehr	67	73	68	71	279	10,150
Billy Andrade	67	71	72	69	279	10,150
Denis Watson	70	68	72	69	279	10,150

	SCORES				TOTAL	MONEY
Tom Watson	70	70	72	67	279	10,150
Jodie Mudd	72	67	70	71	280	6,321.43
Tom Kite	67	71	70	72	280	6,321.43
John Mahaffey	69	71	69	71	280	6,321.43
Nick Price	69	72	68	71	280	6,321.43
John Cook	67	70	73	70	280	6,321.43
Clarence Rose	71	69	69	71	280	6,321.43
Masashi Ozaki	65	75	69	71	280	6,321.42
Morris Hatalsky	70	69	69	73	281	4,457.15
Bob Tway	72	68	71	70	281	4,457.15
Bruce Lietzke	73	69	68	71	281	4,457.14
Larry Rinker	73	68	67	73	281	4,457.14
Roger Maltbie	70	69	73	69	281	4,457.14
Curt Byrum	72	70	70	69	281	4,457.14
Scott Verplank	66	70	71	74	281	4,457.14
*Mike Springer	69	71	71	70	281	
Ronnie Black	72	69	70	71	282	3,525
Willie Wood	69	70	72	71	282	3,525
Lanny Wadkins	70	67	71	74	282	3,525
Dan Pohl	65	72	71	75	283	3,000
Tom Byrum	70	69	72	72	283	3,000
Fred Couples	68	72	69	74	283	3,000
Payne Stewart	71	71	69	72	283	3,000
Dan Forsman	68	70	72	74	284	2,625
Pat McGowan	68	72	70	75	285	2,002.50
Rick Pearson	67	67	76	75	285	2,002.50
Peter Jacobsen	72	68	72	73	285	2,002.50
Greg Ladehoff	72	67	72	74	285	2,002.50
Scott Hoch	70	70	73	72	285	2,002.50
Steve Jones	70	71	69	75	285	2,002.50
Isao Aoki	69	72	70	74	285	2,002.50
Richard Cromwell	71	70	72	72	285	2,002.50
Mark Wiebe	70	70	72	73	285	2,002.50
Duffy Waldorf	71	69	74	71	285	2,002.50

Doral Ryder Open

Doral Hotel and Country Club, Miami, Florida
Par 36-36 — 72; 6,939 yards

March 3-6
purse, $1,000,000

	SCORES				TOTAL	MONEY
Ben Crenshaw	70	69	69	66	274	$180,000
Mark McCumber	71	68	68	68	275	88,000
Chip Beck	68	68	70	69	275	88,000
Ray Floyd	69	71	68	68	276	48,000
Larry Nelson	68	71	70	68	277	36,500
John Mahaffey	69	72	69	67	277	36,500
Joey Sindelar	71	69	69	68	277	36,500
Gil Morgan	69	69	73	67	278	29,000
Bruce Lietzke	69	71	68	70	278	29,000
Scott Hoch	72	70	68	68	278	29,000
Tom Kite	68	70	73	68	279	22,000
Ed Fiori	69	71	69	70	279	22,000
Craig Stadler	71	73	67	68	279	22,000
Robert Wrenn	70	68	72	69	279	22,000
Sandy Lyle	70	71	67	72	280	17,500
Bobby Wadkins	67	67	70	76	280	17,500

	SCORES				TOTAL	MONEY
Ken Green	72	71	70	68	281	15,500
Dan Forsman	73	69	72	67	281	15,500
Mark Lye	72	73	68	69	282	12,120
Wayne Grady	70	71	71	70	282	12,120
Fred Couples	72	72	69	69	282	12,120
Paul Azinger	71	72	69	70	282	12,120
Ken Brown	74	72	70	66	282	12,120
Wayne Levi	71	74	70	68	283	7,914.29
Mike Hulbert	77	68	70	68	283	7,914.29
Phil Blackmar	73	70	71	69	283	7,914.29
Jeff Sluman	71	70	69	73	283	7,914.29
Jack Nicklaus	68	69	71	75	283	7,914.28
Mike Reid	71	70	72	70	283	7,914.28
Mark O'Meara	71	70	74	68	283	7,914.28
Dan Pohl	77	68	69	70	284	5,671.43
Mac O'Grady	71	73	70	70	284	5,671.43
Dick Mast	74	71	66	73	284	5,671.43
Chen Tze Chung	74	72	69	69	284	5,671.43
Dave Barr	73	71	68	72	284	5,671.43
J.C. Snead	70	73	71	70	284	5,671.43
Lennie Clements	72	69	72	71	284	5,671.42
Morris Hatalsky	73	70	70	72	285	4,300
Tom Byrum	74	68	73	70	285	4,300
Steve Elkington	70	71	72	72	285	4,300
Fulton Allem	74	69	72	70	285	4,300
Tim Simpson	71	75	68	71	285	4,300
David Ogrin	75	70	70	71	286	3,045
Dave Rummells	77	69	73	67	286	3,045
Tsuneyuki Nakajima	69	74	69	74	286	3,045
Chris Perry	74	72	71	69	286	3,045
George Archer	75	70	72	69	286	3,045
Jim Gallaher, Jr.	77	68	72	69	286	3,045
David Edwards	72	70	74	70	286	3,045
Richard Zokol	71	72	71	72	286	3,045

Honda Classic

TPC at Eagle Trace, Coral Springs, Florida
Par 36-36 — 72; 7,037 yards

March 10-13
purse, $700,000

	SCORES				TOTAL	MONEY
Joey Sindelar	68	70	68	70	276	$126,000
Payne Stewart	73	71	67	67	278	52,266.67
Ed Fiori	70	67	71	70	278	52,266.67
Sandy Lyle	74	64	70	70	278	52,266.66
Jodie Mudd	70	67	72	70	279	24,587.50
Wayne Grady	72	69	70	68	279	24,587.50
Bob Lohr	73	73	66	67	279	24,587.50
Tom Byrum	70	68	71	70	279	24,587.50
Fred Couples	73	70	69	68	280	18,900
Ray Floyd	71	69	68	72	280	18,900
Ken Green	70	70	73	67	280	18,900
Tsuneyuki Nakajima	70	67	71	73	281	14,700
Mark McCumber	72	73	71	65	281	14,700
John Mahaffey	69	74	69	69	281	14,700
Paul Azinger	70	71	71	70	282	12,600
Mark Calcavecchia	75	69	70	69	283	11,200

	SCORES				TOTAL	MONEY
Mark Brooks	71	74	69	69	283	11,200
Chen Tze Chung	70	74	68	71	283	11,200
Dan Forsman	70	67	77	70	284	9,100
Buddy Gardner	74	70	70	70	284	9,100
Keith Clearwater	72	71	69	72	284	9,100
Kim Young	70	73	72	70	285	6,310
Tom Pernice Jr.	73	71	70	71	285	6,310
Larry Rinker	71	68	73	73	285	6,310
Jeff Sluman	72	68	71	74	285	6,310
Loren Roberts	70	72	73	70	285	6,310
Ronnie Black	67	74	73	71	285	6,310
Bill Buttner	73	73	69	70	285	6,310
Mark Lye	73	74	71	68	286	4,355.15
Dick Mast	73	68	75	70	286	4,355.15
Tateo Ozaki	71	71	71	73	286	4,355.14
Hajime Meshiai	70	73	69	74	286	4,355.14
Mike Sullivan	73	69	70	74	286	4,355.14
Mike Hulbert	73	71	68	74	286	4,355.14
Ken Brown	69	68	70	79	286	4,355.14
Fred Wadsworth	69	68	80	70	287	3,225.67
Aki Ohmachi	77	68	73	69	287	3,225.67
Dan Halldorson	73	72	71	71	287	3,225.67
Billy Andrade	71	75	72	69	287	3,225.67
Gary Koch	73	72	71	71	287	3,225.66
Phil Blackmar	72	74	70	71	287	3,225.66
Brian Tennyson	70	73	70	75	288	2,198
Chris Perry	76	71	70	71	288	2,198
Kenny Perry	72	69	77	70	288	2,198
Brad Faxon	70	71	77	70	288	2,198
Bruce Fleisher	74	67	74	73	288	2,198
Greg Ladehoff	74	73	72	69	288	2,198
Billy Ray Brown	73	69	74	72	288	2,198
Mike Bender	73	73	69	73	288	2,198
Tommy Armour	71	71	72	74	288	2,198

Hertz Bay Hill Classic

Bay Hill Club and Lodge, Orlando, Florida
Par 36-35 — 71; 7,103 yards

March 17-20
purse, $750,000

	SCORES				TOTAL	MONEY
Paul Azinger	66	66	73	66	271	$135,000
Tom Kite	69	68	69	70	276	81,000
Andrew Magee	66	70	73	71	280	43,500
David Frost	70	66	75	69	280	43,500
Don Pooley	68	74	73	66	281	30,000
Bruce Lietzke	69	72	71	70	282	23,475
Dave Eichelberger	72	65	71	74	282	23,475
Joey Sindelar	68	73	73	68	282	23,475
Craig Stadler	73	68	70	71	282	23,475
Payne Stewart	68	72	70	72	282	23,475
Greg Norman	73	70	73	67	283	16,500
Dave Barr	70	70	74	69	283	16,500
Ben Crenshaw	70	71	74	68	283	16,500
Griffin Rudolph	70	69	73	71	283	16,500
Sandy Lyle	68	73	70	73	284	12,375
Tom Watson	74	70	71	69	284	12,375

	SCORES				TOTAL	MONEY
Scott Verplank	70	69	72	73	284	12,375
Bobby Wadkins	68	70	73	73	284	12,375
Donnie Hammond	72	70	73	70	285	8,464.29
Tsuneyuki Nakajima	72	70	71	72	285	8,464.29
Ken Green	72	71	73	69	285	8,464.29
Ian Woosnam	70	73	70	72	285	8,464.29
Nick Price	73	69	72	71	285	8,464.28
Loren Roberts	72	69	75	69	285	8,464.28
Wayne Levi	69	71	75	70	285	8,464.28
Mike Nicolette	72	71	75	68	286	5,550
Mike Hulbert	72	71	75	68	286	5,550
Dave Rummells	71	73	70	72	286	5,550
Gary Koch	70	72	75	69	286	5,550
Buddy Gardner	70	69	73	74	286	5,550
Dan Pohl	74	68	75	70	287	4,762.50
Ray Floyd	70	74	73	70	287	4,762.50
Andy Bean	70	71	73	74	288	3,962.50
Morris Hatalsky	72	69	77	70	288	3,962.50
Brad Faxon	75	68	74	71	288	3,962.50
Scott Hoch	70	69	76	73	288	3,962.50
David Graham	72	69	76	71	288	3,962.50
Curtis Strange	68	71	76	73	288	3,962.50
Jay Don Blake	77	68	73	71	289	3,375
Rocco Mediate	69	70	78	73	290	3,075
Bob Lohr	74	71	72	73	290	3,075
Jay Haas	71	73	73	73	290	3,075
Mac O'Grady	70	72	71	78	291	2,405
Bernhard Langer	72	73	74	72	291	2,405
Larry Mize	69	71	77	74	291	2,405
Steve Jones	71	69	73	78	291	2,405
Tom Byrum	73	69	75	74	291	2,405
Fuzzy Zoeller	70	75	76	70	291	2,405
Tom Purtzer	68	76	76	72	292	1,832.50
Sam Randolph	71	72	74	75	292	1,832.50
Peter Jacobsen	69	73	73	77	292	1,832.50
John Cook	74	68	76	74	292	1,832.50
Rodger Davis	71	69	77	75	292	1,832.50
Dan Forsman	68	77	69	78	292	1,832.50

The Players Championship

TPC at Sawgrass, Ponte Vedra, Florida
Par 36-36 — 72; 6,881 yards

March 24-27
purse, $1,250,000

	SCORES				TOTAL	MONEY
Mark McCumber	65	72	67	69	273	$225,000
Mike Reid	68	69	73	67	277	135,000
David Frost	67	71	68	72	278	65,000
Fulton Allem	73	72	65	68	278	65,000
Curt Byrum	66	73	69	70	278	65,000
Lanny Wadkins	70	72	67	70	279	43,437.50
Gil Morgan	69	70	71	69	279	43,437.50
Dan Pohl	69	69	70	72	280	36,250
Payne Stewart	71	65	71	73	280	36,250
Wayne Levi	70	71	71	68	280	36,250
Mark Wiebe	71	70	71	69	281	26,500
Greg Norman	66	74	68	73	281	26,500

	SCORES				TOTAL	MONEY
Tom Kite	67	73	69	72	281	26,500
Chip Beck	73	67	69	72	281	26,500
Ben Crenshaw	69	71	69	72	281	26,500
Peter Jacobsen	69	75	69	69	282	17,535.72
Bernhard Langer	71	72	67	72	282	17,535.72
Mike Hulbert	74	69	69	70	282	17,535.72
Joey Sindelar	69	72	67	74	282	17,535.71
Gene Sauers	70	71	70	71	282	17,535.71
Calvin Peete	70	69	71	72	282	17,535.71
Gary Koch	70	72	69	71	282	17,535.71
Fuzzy Zoeller	67	74	71	71	283	11,500
Larry Rinker	75	70	68	70	283	11,500
Fred Couples	72	72	71	68	283	11,500
Ed Fiori	67	73	72	71	283	11,500
Dan Halldorson	70	71	71	72	284	9,250
John Mahaffey	67	75	69	73	284	9,250
Tsuneyuki Nakajima	73	72	67	72	284	9,250
Morris Hatalsky	70	68	71	76	285	8,125
Dick Mast	70	70	72	73	285	8,125
Paul Azinger	70	71	72	72	285	8,125
Kenny Perry	71	71	72	72	286	7,375
Jay Don Blake	70	73	72	72	287	6,907.50
Bob Eastwood	70	72	72	73	287	6,907.50
Doug Tewell	72	72	73	71	288	5,760
Donnie Hammond	68	75	73	72	288	5,760
Jodie Mudd	72	74	68	74	288	5,760
Andy Bean	72	74	70	72	288	5,760
Dave Barr	70	75	73	70	288	5,760
Buddy Gardner	72	74	70	72	288	5,760
Corey Pavin	70	76	69	74	289	4,625
Brad Fabel	72	70	74	73	289	4,625
Lennie Clements	74	71	71	73	289	4,625
Craig Stadler	74	71	73	72	290	3,875
Jeff Sluman	71	73	71	75	290	3,875
Tom Purtzer	74	72	70	74	290	3,875
Jack Renner	71	72	76	72	291	3,275
Steve Jones	73	72	72	74	291	3,275
David Edwards	73	71	71	76	291	3,275

K-Mart Greater Greensboro Open

Forest Oaks Country Club, Greensboro, North Carolina
Par 36-36 — 72; 6,984 yards

March 30-April 3
purse, $1,000,000

	SCORES				TOTAL	MONEY
Sandy Lyle	68	63	68	72	271	$180,000
Ken Green	68	67	69	67	271	108,000
(Lyle defeated Green on first hole of playoff.)						
Jeff Sluman	64	65	73	71	273	68,000
Scott Hoch	67	67	72	72	278	48,000
Gil Morgan	68	68	71	72	279	40,000
Chip Beck	70	70	72	69	281	32,375
Tom Purtzer	74	66	72	69	281	32,375
Kenny Perry	71	70	70	70	281	32,375
Donnie Hammond	67	67	73	74	281	32,375
Chen Tze Chung	66	71	75	70	282	23,000

	SCORES				TOTAL	MONEY
Bobby Clampett	74	70	67	71	282	23,000
Keith Clearwater	69	73	71	69	282	23,000
Mark Wiebe	69	71	69	73	282	23,000
Joey Sindelar	70	72	72	68	282	23,000
Ronnie Black	73	70	70	70	283	17,000
Jim Carter	70	72	72	69	283	17,000
Steve Pate	73	70	70	70	283	17,000
Larry Rinker	73	71	69	71	284	11,333.34
Rocco Mediate	68	72	72	72	284	11,333.34
Dave Rummells	75	70	68	71	284	11,333.34
George Burns	72	69	71	72	284	11,333.33
Lanny Wadkins	71	70	68	75	284	11,333.33
Mike Reid	69	71	70	74	284	11,333.33
Bob Murphy	69	66	74	75	284	11,333.33
Mark Lye	73	66	70	75	284	11,333.33
Bruce Lietzke	69	70	73	72	284	11,333.33
Robert Wrenn	70	72	68	75	285	7,400
Joe Inman	71	70	72	72	285	7,400
Wayne Levi	72	72	71	70	285	7,400
Craig Stadler	70	71	73	72	286	6,075.34
Dan Halldorson	68	70	75	73	286	6,075.34
Fred Couples	70	71	72	73	286	6,075.33
Tim Simpson	70	72	71	73	286	6,075.33
Steve Jones	74	71	71	70	286	6,075.33
Roger Maltbie	70	71	72	73	286	6,075.33
Tony Sills	73	72	69	73	287	4,506.86
Scott Verplank	74	69	72	72	287	4,506.86
Blaine McCallister	69	71	74	73	287	4,506.86
Ed Fiori	69	75	70	73	287	4,506.86
John Huston	69	71	73	74	287	4,506.86
Fred Wadsworth	72	72	73	70	287	4,506.85
Peter Jacobsen	69	74	70	74	287	4,506.85
Russ Cochran	70	71	70	77	288	3,045
Ed Dougherty	73	70	74	71	288	3,045
Morris Hatalsky	71	71	73	73	288	3,045
Ray Floyd	72	73	71	72	288	3,045
Steve Lowery	71	68	73	76	288	3,045
David Ogrin	71	72	75	70	288	3,045
Kenny Knox	71	74	71	72	288	3,045
Bill Glasson	69	73	74	72	288	3,045

Masters Tournament

Augusta National Golf Club, Augusta, Georgia
Par 36-36 — 72; 6,905 yards

April 7-10
purse, $1,000,000

	SCORES				TOTAL	MONEY
Sandy Lyle	71	67	72	71	281	$183,800
Mark Calcavecchia	71	69	72	70	282	110,200
Craig Stadler	76	69	70	68	283	69,400
Ben Crenshaw	72	73	67	72	284	48,900
Greg Norman	77	73	71	64	285	36,500
Don Pooley	71	72	72	70	285	36,500
Fred Couples	75	68	71	71	285	36,500
David Frost	73	74	71	68	286	31,000
Bernhard Langer	71	72	71	73	287	28,000
Tom Watson	72	71	73	71	287	28,000

	SCORES				TOTAL	MONEY
Seve Ballesteros	73	72	70	73	288	23,000
Ray Floyd	80	69	68	71	288	23,000
Lanny Wadkins	74	75	69	70	288	23,000
Doug Tewell	75	73	68	73	289	18,500
Nick Price	75	76	72	66	289	18,500
Dan Pohl	78	70	69	73	290	16,000
Mark McNulty	74	71	73	72	290	16,000
Fuzzy Zoeller	76	66	72	76	290	16,000
Hubert Green	74	70	75	72	291	13,500
Chen Tze Chung	76	73	72	70	291	13,500
Curtis Strange	76	70	72	74	292	11,200
Jack Nicklaus	75	73	72	72	292	11,200
Chip Beck	73	70	76	73	292	11,200
Mark McCumber	79	71	72	71	293	9,600
Payne Stewart	75	76	71	72	294	7,975
Robert Wrenn	69	75	76	74	294	7,975
Gary Koch	72	73	74	75	294	7,975
Isao Aoki	74	74	73	73	294	7,975
Rodger Davis	77	72	71	75	295	7,100
Mac O'Grady	74	73	76	73	296	6,500
Steve Jones	74	74	75	73	296	6,500
Nick Faldo	75	74	75	72	296	6,500
Tsuneyuki Nakajima	74	72	77	74	297	5,667
Larry Nelson	69	78	75	75	297	5,667
Bob Tway	74	73	74	76	297	5,667
Steve Pate	75	76	75	72	298	4,900
Andy North	74	74	75	75	298	4,900
Ken Brown	73	78	69	78	298	4,900
Joey Sindelar	79	70	74	77	300	4,400
Mark O'Meara	74	76	74	76	300	4,400
*Jay Sigel	77	72	73	78	300	
Corey Pavin	76	75	75	75	301	4,000
Gary Hallberg	73	69	80	79	301	4,000
Tom Kite	73	76	77	76	302	3,700
Jeff Sluman	80	71	78	75	304	3,400
Larry Mize	78	71	76	79	304	3,400

Out of Final 36 Holes

Sam Randolph	78	74		152
Dave Barr	77	75		152
Andy Bean	73	79		152
Kenny Knox	75	77		152
Davis Love III	73	79		152
Jay Haas	81	71		152
Scott Hoch	79	73		152
John Cook	77	76		153
Bob Eastwood	77	76		153
Gary Player	78	75		153
Mike Reid	78	76		154
Charles Coody	78	76		154
Tim Simpson	80	74		154
*David Curry	74	80		154
Roger Maltbie	76	78		154
Ian Woosnam	81	74		155
Paul Azinger	75	80		155
Keith Clearwater	82	73		155
Scott Simpson	79	76		155
*Bill Mayfair	80	75		155
George Archer	80	75		155

	SCORES				TOTAL	MONEY
Bobby Wadkins	79	76			155	
*Bill Loeffler	77	79			156	
*Len Mattiace	79	77			156	
Lennie Clements	75	81			156	
D. A. Weibring	79	77			156	
*Eric Rebmann	77	79			156	
Hal Sutton	80	77			157	
Arnold Palmer	80	77			157	
*Buddy Alexander	78	80			158	
J. C. Snead	79	79			158	
Gay Brewer	78	81			159	
*Brian Montgomery	78	81			159	
*Scott Gump	83	77			160	
*Paul Mayo	81	80			161	
Doug Ford	80	82			162	
Jodie Mudd	84	78			162	
*Stephen Ford	83	80			163	
Lee Trevino	81	83			164	
Art Wall	86	79			165	
Tommy Aaron	83	83			166	
Billy Casper	80	86			166	
*Robert Lewis	87	83			170	
Jim Thorpe	85	WD				

(Professionals who did not complete 72 holes received $1,500.)

Deposit Guaranty Classic

Hattiesburg Country Club, Hattiesburg, Mississippi   April 7-10
Par 35-35 — 70; 6,280 yards   purse, $200,000

	SCORES				TOTAL	MONEY
Frank Conner	65	70	69	63	267	$36,000
Brian Mogg	68	67	70	67	272	21,600
David Ogrin	68	69	68	68	273	13,600
Kim Young	68	70	66	70	274	7,875
Robert Thompson	72	64	69	69	274	7,875
Jeff Hart	70	68	70	66	274	7,875
John Adams	69	71	66	68	274	7,875
Rick Pearson	71	70	64	70	275	5,600
Steve Thomas	73	69	66	67	275	5,600
Lance Ten Broeck	72	64	66	73	275	5,600
Rocco Mediate	72	67	66	70	275	5,600
Tom Shaw	74	67	68	67	276	3,685.72
Lee Janzen	73	69	68	66	276	3,685.72
Jim Booros	71	70	68	67	276	3,685.72
Bruce Zabriski	68	69	70	69	276	3,685.71
Dave Eichelberger	69	69	64	74	276	3,685.71
Jim Gallagher, Jr.	71	71	67	67	276	3,685.71
Mike Bender	68	70	70	68	276	3,685.71
Mike West	70	72	70	65	277	2,600
Billy Pierot	71	70	68	68	277	2,600
David Peoples	69	69	71	68	277	2,600
Bill Glasson	68	72	68	70	278	1,856.67
Mark Maness	69	71	74	64	278	1,856.67
Brian Claar	73	70	69	66	278	1,856.67
Tommy Armour	69	73	69	67	278	1,856.67

	SCORES				TOTAL	MONEY
Roy Biancalana	69	72	67	70	278	1,856.66
Brad Bryant	70	69	67	72	278	1,856.66
Larry Ziegler	71	71	70	67	279	1,450.00
Bill Buttner	72	69	71	67	279	1,450.00
Mike Smith	72	70	70	68	280	1,162.50
Fred Wadsworth	71	68	73	68	280	1,162.50
Steve Lowery	75	67	73	65	280	1,162.50
Brian Kamm	74	68	72	66	280	1,162.50
Tom Pernice Jr.	70	71	69	70	280	1,162.50
Ed Dougherty	70	72	70	68	280	1,162.50
Billy Andrade	66	72	72	70	280	1,162.50
Rod Curl	72	72	66	70	280	1,162.50
Mike Nicolette	72	69	69	71	281	880
Tony Grimes	70	74	68	69	281	880
Jim Nelford	72	68	72	69	281	880
Bill Sander	71	69	69	72	281	880
Brandel Chamblee	68	74	71	69	282	661.15
Clark Burroughs	72	72	70	68	282	661.15
Jeffrey Lankford	73	69	71	69	282	661.14
David Jackson	72	72	65	73	282	661.14
Ernie Gonzalez	70	72	69	71	282	661.14
Vance Heafner	67	74	71	70	282	661.14
Rex Caldwell	72	66	73	71	282	661.14
James Hallet	72	72	70	69	283	512
Ray Barr, Jr.	71	69	72	71	283	512

MCI Heritage Classic

Harbour Town Golf Links, Hilton Head Island, South Carolina   April 14-17
Par 36-35 — 71; 6,657 yards   purse, $700,000

	SCORES				TOTAL	MONEY
Greg Norman	65	69	71	66	271	$126,000
Gil Morgan	71	64	69	68	272	61,600
David Frost	69	64	69	70	272	61,600
Fred Couples	68	65	68	73	274	33,600
Paul Azinger	65	70	73	68	276	26,600
David Ogrin	67	69	71	69	276	26,600
Doug Tewell	72	69	69	67	277	21,816.67
Curtis Strange	70	70	71	66	277	21,816.67
D.A. Weibring	68	71	68	70	277	21,816.66
Russ Cochran	73	68	69	68	278	17,500
Mark McCumber	72	67	69	70	278	17,500
Steve Pate	71	69	70	68	278	17,500
Curt Byrum	69	65	74	71	279	12,000
Lanny Wadkins	72	68	68	71	279	12,000
Hal Sutton	71	69	70	69	279	12,000
Larry Rinker	67	71	69	72	279	12,000
Larry Nelson	69	70	68	72	279	12,000
Jon Mahaffey	73	68	66	72	279	12,000
Sandy Lyle	70	72	67	70	279	12,000
Fred Wadsworth	74	69	69	68	280	7,583.34
Blaine McCallister	75	69	68	68	280	7,583.34
Tim Simpson	73	71	67	69	280	7,583.33
Bob Tway	70	70	70	70	280	7,583.33
Calvin Peete	70	65	73	72	280	7,583.33
Tsuneyuki Nakajima	71	66	71	72	280	7,583.33

	SCORES				TOTAL	MONEY
Bobby Wadkins	70	73	71	67	281	5,390
Brett Upper	70	70	69	72	281	5,390
Bernhard Langer	68	69	73	71	281	5,390
Ed Dougherty	73	70	70	69	282	4,451
Nick Faldo	70	69	75	68	282	4,451
Gene Sauers	72	70	67	73	282	4,451
Wayne Grady	71	67	74	70	282	4,451
Rocco Mediate	68	69	74	71	282	4,451
James Hallet	72	63	71	76	282	4,451
Billy Andrade	71	72	73	67	283	3,233
Chip Beck	67	68	70	78	283	3,233
David Graham	68	74	68	73	283	3,233
Clarence Rose	66	73	69	75	283	3,233
Leonard Thompson	69	69	72	73	283	3,233
Mike Reid	67	71	75	70	283	3,233
Jack Renner	72	72	69	70	283	3,233
Scott Hoch	68	66	75	74	283	3,233
John Cook	69	69	73	73	284	2,184
Hubert Green	75	68	68	73	284	2,184
Jay Haas	70	70	73	71	284	2,184
Danny Edwards	70	74	72	68	284	2,184
Peter Jacobsen	70	69	75	70	284	2,184
Steve Jones	73	67	72	72	284	2,184
Larry Mize	69	71	72	72	284	2,184
Bobby Clampett	72	71	77	65	285	1,764

USF&G Classic

Lakewood Country Club, New Orleans, Louisiana
Par 36-36 — 72; 7,080 yards

April 21-24
purse, $750,000

	SCORES				TOTAL	MONEY
Chip Beck	69	64	65	64	262	$135,000
Lanny Wadkins	67	65	69	68	269	81,000
Dan Forsman	68	68	70	65	271	51,000
Calvin Peete	69	70	67	66	272	36,000
Larry Mize	68	68	70	67	273	30,000
Greg Ladehoff	68	68	68	70	274	27,000
Brad Fabel	70	67	68	70	275	24,187.50
John Cook	70	70	67	68	275	24,187.50
Mark Lye	71	70	68	67	276	18,000
Russ Cochran	71	69	66	70	276	18,000
Donnie Hammond	68	71	70	67	276	18,000
Lennie Clements	69	68	68	71	276	18,000
Tom Watson	68	69	71	68	276	18,000
Robert Wrenn	68	71	68	69	276	18,000
Jodie Mudd	67	72	66	72	277	10,550
Buddy Gardner	68	69	70	70	277	10,550
Bobby Clampett	71	69	67	70	277	10,550
Jay Don Blake	71	69	71	66	277	10,550
Billy Ray Brown	70	67	69	71	277	10,550
Jeff Sluman	68	70	69	70	277	10,550
Scott Verplank	71	64	72	70	277	10,550
Hal Sutton	65	73	68	71	277	10,550
Brian Tennyson	69	70	69	69	277	10,550
Dick Mast	72	67	68	71	278	6,225
Tom Byrum	66	68	72	72	278	6,225

	SCORES				TOTAL	MONEY
Jim Carter	72	67	68	71	278	6,225
Phil Blackmar	70	69	69	70	278	6,225
Tony Sills	70	71	69	68	278	6,225
John Mahaffey	72	69	69	69	279	4,987.50
John Inman	67	72	68	72	279	4,987.50
Bob Lohr	68	70	71	70	279	4,987.50
Jim Gallagher, Jr.	70	70	70	69	279	4,987.50
Bob Proben	71	66	74	69	280	3,637.50
David Graham	68	70	71	71	280	3,637.50
Morris Hatalsky	70	69	73	68	280	3,637.50
Ed Fiori	70	70	73	67	280	3,637.50
Brad Bryant	69	71	72	68	280	3,637.50
Clarence Rose	72	68	70	70	280	3,637.50
Mark Wiebe	69	67	75	69	280	3,637.50
Ron Streck	71	69	68	72	280	3,637.50
Bill Sander	70	70	70	70	280	3,637.50
Dave Rummells	70	66	69	75	280	3,637.50
Brian Mogg	67	74	70	70	281	2,475
Tsuneyuki Nakajima	67	73	71	70	281	2,475
Mike Blackburn	67	72	72	70	281	2,475
Doug Tewell	71	67	69	74	281	2,475
Mike Sullivan	69	71	70	71	281	2,475
Chris Perry	71	67	74	70	282	1,864.29
Danny Briggs	69	71	73	69	282	1,864.29
Robert Thompson	71	67	73	71	282	1,864.29
Harry Taylor	72	69	71	70	282	1,864.29
Tom Pernice Jr.	69	70	69	74	282	1,864.28
Mike Donald	70	66	73	73	282	1,864.28
Brett Upper	69	70	69	74	282	1,864.28

Independent Insurance Agent Open

TPC at The Woodlands, The Woodlands, Texas
Par 36-36 — 72; 7,042 yards

April 28-May 1
purse, $700,000

	SCORES				TOTAL	MONEY
Curtis Strange	69	68	66	67	270	$126,000
Greg Norman	65	70	68	67	270	75,600
(Strange defeated Norman on third hole of playoff.)						
Tom Kite	69	69	66	68	272	47,600
Brian Tennyson	68	68	70	69	275	30,800
Jim Carter	71	69	68	67	275	30,800
Tim Simpson	68	70	69	69	276	25,200
Bruce Lietzke	73	68	69	68	278	22,575
Mike Donald	67	69	72	70	278	22,575
Dave Rummells	72	68	70	69	279	18,900
Jack Renner	70	70	68	71	279	18,900
Bobby Clampett	73	68	70	68	279	18,900
Hal Sutton	66	70	73	71	280	14,700
Calvin Peete	69	70	69	72	280	14,700
Ben Crenshaw	73	65	71	71	280	14,700
Jim Nelford	74	68	71	68	281	10,500
Clarence Rose	71	70	71	69	281	10,500
Chris Perry	69	69	73	70	281	10,500
Bob Proben	71	72	68	70	281	10,500
Gary Koch	73	68	67	73	281	10,500
Brad Faxon	71	69	68	73	281	10,500

	SCORES				TOTAL	MONEY
Tom Byrum	71	70	69	71	281	10,500
Davis Love III	69	71	72	70	282	6,498.34
Scott Hoch	69	73	70	70	282	6,498.34
Lance Ten Broeck	71	72	71	68	282	6,498.33
Blaine McCallister	70	70	70	72	282	6,498.33
Steve Elkington	71	67	72	72	282	6,498.33
James Hallet	71	67	71	73	282	6,498.33
Aki Ohmachi	71	68	73	71	283	4,555.15
Barry Jaeckel	75	68	69	71	283	4,555.15
Payne Stewart	69	67	74	73	283	4,555.14
Harry Taylor	69	72	72	70	283	4,555.14
John Adams	76	67	69	71	283	4,555.14
George Burns	68	72	71	72	283	4,555.14
Duffy Waldorf	68	73	70	72	283	4,555.14
Morris Hatalsky	72	69	72	71	284	3,450.80
George Archer	73	68	72	71	284	3,450.80
Mike Blackburn	74	67	71	72	284	3,450.80
Curt Byrum	71	70	70	73	284	3,450.80
Fred Couples	70	71	68	75	284	3,450.80
Mike Sullivan	68	74	70	73	285	2,590
David Peoples	69	73	74	69	285	2,590
Bob Lohr	70	68	74	73	285	2,590
Mark O'Meara	72	69	71	73	285	2,590
David Ogrin	68	70	72	75	285	2,590
Ray Floyd	65	70	76	74	285	2,590
Brad Fabel	69	71	72	73	285	2,590
Nick Price	70	72	71	73	286	1,798
Loren Roberts	72	71	71	72	286	1,798
John Inman	72	71	73	70	286	1,798
Mike Hulbert	70	68	73	75	286	1,798
Bob Gilder	72	71	71	72	286	1,798
Bill Kratzert	71	71	69	75	286	1,798
Lennie Clements	72	71	68	75	286	1,798

Panasonic Las Vegas Invitational

Las Vegas, Nevada

April 29-May 3
purse, $1,388,889

Las Vegas Country Club,
Par 36-36 — 72; 7,162 yards

Desert Inn Country Club
Par 36-36 — 72; 7,111 yards

Spanish Trail Country Club
Par 36-36 — 72; 7,088 yards

	SCORES				TOTAL	MONEY
Gary Koch	68	73	66	67	274	$250,000
Mark O'Meara	65	75	69	66	275	122,222
Peter Jacobsen	71	66	68	70	275	122,222
Curt Byrum	65	72	67	72	276	52,361.40
David Canipe	71	69	68	68	276	52,361.40
Joey Sindelar	70	72	68	66	276	52,361.40
Gene Sauers	69	71	68	68	276	52,361.40
Rick Fehr	67	74	67	68	276	52,361.40

	SCORES				TOTAL	MONEY
Payne Stewart	70	72	66	69	277	38,889
Donnie Hammond	68	75	66	68	277	38,889
Ben Crenshaw	69	69	67	73	278	29,444.40
Fuzzy Zoeller	70	72	68	68	278	29,444.40
Hal Sutton	70	71	68	69	278	29,444.40
Tony Sills	71	68	70	69	278	29,444.40
John Mahaffey	72	73	68	65	278	29,444.40
Dan Halldorson	70	71	71	67	279	19,484.15
Jay Haas	69	74	69	67	279	19,484.15
Bobby Wadkins	64	79	70	66	279	19,484.14
Calvin Peete	70	72	71	66	279	19,484.14
Rocco Mediate	69	77	69	64	279	19,484.14
Bob Lohr	66	70	72	71	279	19,484.14
Bill Glasson	69	72	70	68	279	19,484.14
Steve Pate	75	72	66	67	280	11,706.15
Steve Elkington	70	74	67	69	280	11,706.15
Mark Brooks	68	71	70	71	280	11,706.14
Dave Barr	70	72	68	70	280	11,706.14
Greg Norman	68	75	66	71	280	11,706.14
Davis Love III	70	71	67	72	280	11,706.14
Scott Hoch	72	70	67	71	280	11,706.14
Jay Don Blake	70	70	72	69	281	8,253.86
Tom Byrum	71	74	67	69	281	8,253.86
Dave Rummells	73	68	71	69	281	8,253.86
Nick Price	69	73	71	68	281	8,253.86
Ken Green	69	73	69	70	281	8,253.86
Keith Clearwater	68	70	73	70	281	8,253.85
Bill Kratzert	72	75	63	71	281	8,253.85
Mike Bender	71	69	73	69	282	5,694.45
Mike Sullivan	71	73	69	69	282	5,694.45
Tim Simpson	67	75	71	69	282	5,694.45
Brian Tennyson	69	71	72	70	282	5,694.45
Fred Couples	72	74	69	67	282	5,694.44
Scott Verplank	69	72	70	71	282	5,694.44
David Ogrin	71	73	70	68	282	5,694.44
Sam Randolph	72	73	68	69	282	5,694.44
Mike Hulbert	70	75	70	67	282	5,694.44
Mike Donald	71	70	72	70	283	3,778
Denis Watson	70	74	69	70	283	3,778
Mark Wiebe	70	75	68	70	283	3,778
Curtis Strange	73	71	69	70	283	3,778
Tom Pernice Jr.	72	70	71	70	283	3,778
James Hallet	72	70	71	70	283	3,778

GTE Byron Nelson Classic

TPC at Las Colinas Sports Club, Irving, Texas   May 12-15
Par 35-35 — 70; 6,767 yards   purse, $750,000

	SCORES				TOTAL	MONEY
Bruce Lietzke	66	69	66	70	271	$135,000
Clarence Rose	66	69	67	69	271	81,000
(Lietzke defeated Rose on first hole of playoff.)						
David Graham	68	69	67	68	272	43,500
Ben Crenshaw	66	65	70	71	272	43,500
Paul Azinger	73	68	63	69	273	27,375
Mark Calcavecchia	70	66	68	69	273	27,375

	SCORES				TOTAL	MONEY
John Cook	70	64	69	70	273	27,375
Nick Price	71	68	66	69	274	22,500
Craig Stadler	68	66	68	72	274	22,500
Tom Watson	67	73	71	64	275	18,750
David Frost	66	70	70	69	275	18,750
Fred Couples	70	71	65	69	275	18,750
Lanny Wadkins	69	69	68	70	276	12,857.15
James Hallet	72	69	68	67	276	12,857.15
Jeff Sluman	66	67	67	76	276	12,857.15
Dave Rummells	66	73	66	71	276	12,857.15
Jodie Mudd	70	69	67	70	276	12,857.14
Andrew Magee	67	70	68	71	276	12,857.14
Bob Eastwood	67	68	68	73	276	12,857.14
Dave Barr	71	66	72	68	277	8,737.50
Jay Don Blake	71	70	68	68	277	8,737.50
Mark Wiebe	64	69	72	72	277	8,737.50
Bob Lohr	73	66	67	71	277	8,737.50
Billy Andrade	69	69	72	68	278	6,075
Bobby Clampett	68	68	70	72	278	6,075
Mike Sullivan	71	70	67	70	278	6,075
Payne Stewart	66	71	68	73	278	6,075
Peter Jacobsen	66	70	69	73	278	6,075
Ray Floyd	67	71	70	70	278	6,075
Curt Byrum	66	69	71	73	279	4,657.80
Gene Sauers	72	68	68	71	279	4,657.80
Mark McCumber	71	72	67	69	279	4,657.80
Sandy Lyle	68	71	70	70	279	4,657.80
Ken Green	73	66	69	71	279	4,657.80
George Archer	66	70	71	73	280	3,618.50
Billy Ray Brown	70	70	73	67	280	3,618.50
Bob Tway	72	70	69	69	280	3,618.50
Scott Simpson	70	67	68	75	280	3,618.50
Tsuneyuki Nakajima	66	72	66	76	280	3,618.50
Dick Mast	70	69	70	71	280	3,618.50
Phil Blackmar	70	69	73	69	281	2,486.67
Richard Zokol	70	72	69	70	281	2,486.67
Tim Norris	71	72	69	69	281	2,486.67
Kenny Knox	70	72	72	67	281	2,486.67
Steve Elkington	67	73	72	69	281	2,486.67
Donnie Hammond	69	74	73	65	281	2,486.67
Tim Simpson	73	70	67	71	281	2,486.66
Bob Gilder	69	67	69	76	281	2,486.66
Mike Hammond	69	70	68	74	281	2,486.66
Bill Sander	71	67	73	71	282	1,845
Lee Trevino	69	74	66	73	282	1,845
Ed Dougherty	69	73	67	73	282	1,845

Colonial National Invitation

Colonial Country Club, Fort Worth, Texas
Par 35-35 — 70; 7,116 yards

May 19-22
purse, $750,000

	SCORES				TOTAL	MONEY
Lanny Wadkins	67	68	70	65	270	$135,000
Ben Crenshaw	69	67	68	67	271	56,000
Mark Calcavecchia	68	69	68	66	271	56,000
Joey Sindelar	71	65	67	68	271	56,000

	SCORES				TOTAL	MONEY
Clarence Rose	67	68	65	74	274	30,000
David Graham	71	66	70	68	275	25,125
Mark Wiebe	72	67	69	67	275	25,125
Scott Hoch	67	68	71	69	275	25,125
Chip Beck	71	70	69	67	277	21,000
David Frost	74	66	69	68	277	21,000
Russ Cochran	71	69	72	66	278	15,900
Ken Green	72	67	68	71	278	15,900
John Inman	67	72	67	72	278	15,900
Mark Lye	72	71	63	72	278	15,900
John Mahaffey	69	71	66	72	278	15,900
Paul Azinger	70	68	70	71	279	10,875
D.A. Weibring	71	67	72	69	279	10,875
Mark O'Meara	71	71	68	69	279	10,875
Steve Pate	69	67	71	72	279	10,875
Mac O'Grady	70	70	69	70	279	10,875
Tom Purtzer	74	68	68	69	279	10,875
John Cook	77	65	69	69	280	6,416.67
Mike Hulbert	69	68	75	68	280	6,416.67
Mike Donald	72	71	69	68	280	6,416.67
Dave Rummells	71	66	73	70	280	6,416.67
Bob Tway	70	70	70	70	280	6,416.67
Bobby Wadkins	71	71	67	71	280	6,416.67
John Huston	70	67	69	74	280	6,416.66
Lee Trevino	69	71	68	72	280	6,416.66
Payne Stewart	75	65	68	72	280	6,416.66
Mark Brooks	70	73	64	74	281	4,547.25
Ed Fiori	68	75	69	69	281	4,547.25
Doug Tewell	70	70	69	72	281	4,547.25
Scott Verplank	72	69	69	71	281	4,547.25
Tom Kite	75	70	67	70	282	3,955.50
Dave Stockton	73	69	70	70	282	3,955.50
Scott Simpson	73	68	71	71	283	3,525
Gil Morgan	70	69	68	76	283	3,525
Jodie Mudd	67	72	72	72	283	3,525
David Canipe	71	74	68	71	284	3,075
Ronnie Black	69	74	69	72	284	3,075
Jeff Sluman	75	66	73	70	284	3,075
Bob Lohr	76	69	67	73	285	2,475
Rick Fehr	70	69	70	76	285	2,475
Jim Carter	70	72	70	73	285	2,475
Kenny Knox	76	68	69	72	285	2,475
Tsuneyuki Nakajima	70	72	69	74	285	2,475
Bill Glasson	73	68	72	73	286	1,818
Andrew Magee	72	72	69	73	286	1,818
Ray Floyd	72	70	73	71	286	1,818
Buddy Gardner	68	72	73	73	286	1,818
Lennie Clements	72	72	71	71	286	1,818
Fuzzy Zoeller	76	68	69	73	286	1,818
Robert Wrenn	72	67	71	76	286	1,818
Larry Rinker	70	72	70	74	286	1,818
Corey Pavin	74	68	71	73	286	1,818
David Ogrin	77	68	69	72	286	1,818
*Bill Mayfair	73	71	72	70	286	

Memorial Tournament

Muirfield Village Golf Club, Dublin, Ohio

May 26-29
purse, $930,250

Par 36-36 — 72; 7,104 yards

	SCORES				TOTAL	MONEY
Curtis Strange	73	70	64	67	274	$160,000
Hale Irwin	70	68	68	70	276	78,220
David Frost	69	70	68	69	276	78,220
John Huston	69	70	72	71	282	39,115
Andrew Magee	70	70	68	74	282	39,115
Lanny Wadkins	79	66	71	67	283	26,880.84
Jay Haas	72	75	69	67	283	26,880.84
Payne Stewart	72	69	67	75	283	26,880.83
Greg Norman	71	74	67	71	283	26,880.83
Peter Jacobsen	68	74	72	69	283	26,880.83
Scott Hoch	74	73	64	72	283	26,880.83
Nick Price	74	67	71	72	284	18,970
Paul Azinger	72	69	71	72	284	18,970
Chip Beck	72	76	69	67	284	18,970
Tom Kite	69	70	73	73	285	15,833.34
Scott Verplank	73	69	68	75	285	15,833.33
Fred Couples	72	72	68	73	285	15,833.33
Mike Hulbert	74	71	72	69	286	14,060
Bobby Wadkins	71	76	74	66	287	12,283.34
Fuzzy Zoeller	72	70	69	76	287	12,283.33
John Mahaffey	68	73	73	73	287	12,283.33
Craig Stadler	78	71	72	67	288	8,978.34
D.A. Weibring	70	75	71	72	288	8,978.34
Mark Wiebe	75	71	70	72	288	8,978.33
Larry Mize	71	74	70	73	288	8,978.33
Steve Pate	70	74	71	73	288	8,978.33
Larry Nelson	73	69	72	74	288	8,978.33
Doug Tewell	74	73	74	68	289	6,758
Mark McCumber	74	73	75	67	289	6,758
Dave Rummells	72	70	74	73	289	6,758
Tom Purtzer	72	70	73	74	289	6,758
Mark Calcavecchia	73	75	71	70	289	6,758
Scott Simpson	71	73	69	77	290	5,862.50
Roger Maltbie	73	72	70	75	290	5,862.50
Jay Don Blake	73	76	71	71	291	5,011.67
Donnie Hammond	73	72	74	72	291	5,011.67
Gary Koch	73	75	70	73	291	5,011.67
John Cook	72	73	73	73	291	5,011.67
Hal Sutton	75	70	69	77	291	5,011.66
Ed Fiori	73	72	70	76	291	5,011.66
Robert Wrenn	74	74	72	72	292	3,837.15
J.C. Snead	72	71	76	73	292	3,837.15
Jeff Sluman	72	71	72	77	292	3,837.14
Aki Ohmachi	69	73	72	78	292	3,837.14
Clarence Rose	70	73	74	75	292	3,837.14
Bruce Lietzke	76	70	71	75	292	3,837.14
Tom Byrum	74	70	73	75	292	3,837.14
Bill Sander	76	70	73	74	293	2,977
Rocco Mediate	69	75	73	76	293	2,977
David Canipe	74	74	74	71	293	2,977
Ben Crenshaw	75	71	75	72	293	2,977
Buddy Gardner	72	73	71	77	293	2,977

Kemper Open

TPC at Avenel, Potomac, Maryland
Par 36-35 — 71; 6,867 yards

June 2-5
purse, $800,000

	SCORES				TOTAL	MONEY
Morris Hatalsky	68	66	68	72	274	$144,000
Tom Kite	67	67	71	69	274	86,400
(Hatalsky defeated Kite on second hole of playoff.)						
Craig Stadler	70	70	64	72	276	46,400
Mike Reid	69	68	67	72	276	46,400
James Hallet	68	65	72	72	277	30,400
Bob Gilder	72	65	71	69	277	30,400
Larry Mize	69	70	69	70	278	24,100
Dick Mast	72	68	68	70	278	24,100
Calvin Peete	68	70	70	70	278	24,100
John Mahaffey	68	68	68	74	278	24,100
Denis Watson	71	70	70	68	279	16,960
Roger Maltbie	71	72	70	66	279	16,960
Jay Haas	69	69	68	73	279	16,960
Tommy Armour	72	65	69	73	279	16,960
Mark Brooks	68	67	70	74	279	16,960
Fred Couples	72	69	69	70	280	13,600
Brian Tennyson	71	69	68	74	282	11,600
Dillard Pruitt	74	69	65	74	282	11,600
Bill Glasson	69	67	70	76	282	11,600
Brad Faxon	69	70	73	70	282	11,600
Howard Twitty	66	73	71	73	283	7,510
Joey Rassett	71	69	71	72	283	7,510
Joey Sindelar	74	69	65	75	283	7,510
Tony Sills	75	67	70	71	283	7,510
Jodie Mudd	72	66	70	75	283	7,510
Dan Forsman	69	72	71	71	283	7,510
Ray Barr, Jr.	71	68	73	71	283	7,510
Jay Don Blake	73	70	72	68	283	7,510
Curtis Strange	69	73	73	69	284	5,560
Brad Fabel	74	70	73	67	284	5,560
Dave Stockton	68	75	68	74	285	4,440
Buddy Gardner	73	71	71	70	285	4,440
Scott Hoch	71	72	70	72	285	4,440
Greg Ladehoff	69	72	72	72	285	4,440
Steve Jones	69	72	71	73	285	4,440
Fulton Allem	73	68	69	75	285	4,440
Chip Beck	73	71	72	69	285	4,440
Bill Britton	71	68	77	69	285	4,440
Robert Thompson	70	71	72	73	286	3,280
Bobby Wadkins	73	69	72	72	286	3,280
Webb Heintzelman	66	72	73	75	286	3,280
Dave Barr	69	71	70	76	286	3,280
Brad Bryant	68	71	70	77	286	3,280
Lanny Wadkins	71	69	74	73	287	2,560
Jack Renner	72	72	67	76	287	2,560
Tim Norris	70	68	71	78	287	2,560
Ed Fiori	71	65	75	76	287	2,560
Kenny Perry	71	69	73	75	288	2,096
Scott Simpson	72	70	74	72	288	2,096
Ken Green	67	69	73	79	288	2,096

Manufacturers Hanover Westchester Classic

Westchester Country Club, Rye, New York
Par 36-35 — 71; 6,769 yards

June 9-12
purse, $700,000

	SCORES				TOTAL	MONEY
Seve Ballesteros	72	68	69	67	276	$126,000
Greg Norman	73	69	70	64	276	52,266.67
David Frost	71	68	69	68	276	52,266.67
Ken Green	71	68	67	70	276	52,266.66
(Ballesteros defeated Norman, Frost and Green on first hole of playoff.)						
Steve Elkington	68	70	69	71	278	28,000
Loren Roberts	66	71	73	70	280	22,662.50
Dick Mast	71	68	68	73	280	22,662.50
Bob Eastwood	69	72	72	67	280	22,662.50
Brandel Chamblee	70	68	73	69	280	22,662.50
Jeff Sluman	74	70	68	69	281	18,200
Tommy Armour	73	69	71	68	281	18,200
Scott Simpson	71	69	71	71	282	13,300
J.C. Snead	68	73	70	71	282	13,300
Bill Kratzert	73	71	66	72	282	13,300
Tommy Nakajima	73	71	71	67	282	13,300
James Hallet	70	71	69	72	282	13,300
Jay Don Blake	71	72	72	67	282	13,300
Mike Reid	69	71	71	72	283	9,128
Tim Simpson	70	74	70	69	283	9,128
Payne Stewart	73	68	69	73	283	9,128
Clarence Rose	72	71	71	69	283	9,128
Russ Cochran	72	73	70	68	283	9,128
Jay Haas	70	70	72	72	284	7,000
Isao Aoki	74	70	69	71	284	7,000
Craig Stadler	71	73	71	70	285	5,460
Lance Ten Broeck	72	70	75	68	285	5,460
Don Pooley	68	76	69	72	285	5,460
David Edwards	72	72	70	71	285	5,460
Wayne Grady	75	69	71	70	285	5,460
Joey Sindelar	67	73	76	70	286	4,252.67
Jack Renner	74	68	74	70	286	4,252.67
Chris Perry	72	69	72	73	286	4,252.67
Mark McCumber	73	70	73	70	286	4,252.67
Tim Norris	70	73	74	69	286	4,252.66
Fred Couples	70	71	71	74	286	4,252.66
Leonard Thompson	74	69	73	71	287	3,084.25
Peter Senior	69	75	72	71	287	3,084.25
Howard Twitty	66	73	71	77	287	3,084.25
Johnny Miller	75	69	70	73	287	3,084.25
Bob Lohr	75	70	69	73	287	3,084.25
Dan Halldorson	70	75	68	74	287	3,084.25
Ronnie Black	72	71	73	71	287	3,084.25
Jim Carter	74	71	72	70	287	3,084.25
Bob Tway	76	68	71	73	288	2,240
Mark Lye	73	71	73	71	288	2,240
Larry Rinker	71	71	72	74	288	2,240
Bill Buttner	69	69	74	76	288	2,240
Hal Sutton	70	72	76	71	289	1,806
Wayne Levi	71	70	77	71	289	1,806
Brad Faxon	69	72	73	75	289	1,806
Brad Fabel	74	70	74	71	289	1,806

U.S. Open Championship

The Country Club, Brookline, Massachusetts
Par 35-36 — 71; 7,010 yards

June 16-19
purse, $1,000,000

	SCORES				TOTAL	MONEY
Curtis Strange	70	67	69	72	278	$180,000
Nick Faldo	72	67	68	71	278	90,000
(Strange defeated Faldo in 18-hole playoff, 71-75.)						
D.A. Weibring	71	69	68	72	280	41,370
Steve Pate	72	69	72	67	280	41,370
Mark O'Meara	71	72	66	71	280	41,370
Scott Simpson	69	66	72	74	281	25,414.50
Paul Azinger	69	70	76	66	281	25,414.50
Fuzzy Zoeller	73	72	71	66	282	20,903.50
Bob Gilder	68	69	70	75	282	20,903.50
Payne Stewart	73	73	70	67	283	17,870.50
Fred Couples	72	67	71	73	283	17,870.50
Lanny Wadkins	70	71	70	73	284	14,781.20
Dan Pohl	74	72	69	69	284	14,781.20
Larry Mize	69	67	72	76	284	14,781.20
Andy Bean	71	71	72	70	284	14,781.20
Ben Crenshaw	71	72	74	67	284	14,781.20
Joey Sindelar	76	68	70	71	285	11,981.25
Mark McNulty	73	72	72	68	285	11,981.25
Hale Irwin	71	71	72	71	285	11,981.25
Ray Floyd	73	72	73	67	285	11,981.25
Scott Hoch	71	72	71	72	286	10,344.75
Peter Jacobsen	76	70	76	64	286	10,344.75
Bob Eastwood	74	72	69	71	286	10,344.75
Chip Beck	73	72	71	70	286	10,344.75
Jay Haas	73	67	74	73	287	8,855.84
Dave Barr	73	72	72	70	287	8,855.84
Craig Stadler	70	73	71	73	287	8,855.83
Bob Tway	77	68	73	69	287	8,855.83
Mark Wiebe	75	70	73	69	287	8,855.83
Sandy Lyle	68	71	75	73	287	8,855.83
*Bill Mayfair	71	72	71	73	287	
Tommy Nakajima	74	72	69	73	288	7,726
Mark McCumber	72	72	71	73	288	7,726
Ken Green	72	70	70	76	288	7,726
Seve Ballesteros	69	74	72	73	288	7,726
Tom Watson	74	71	69	75	289	7,002.50
David Ishii	73	73	75	68	289	7,002.50
Mark Lye	75	71	71	72	289	7,002.50
Tom Kite	72	69	73	75	289	7,002.50
Lee Trevino	73	73	73	71	290	6,014.86
Nick Price	72	74	71	73	290	6,014.86
Mike Nicolette	68	73	77	72	290	6,014.86
Chip Johnson	72	72	76	70	290	6,014.86
Dan Halldorson	72	71	74	73	290	6,014.86
Clarence Rose	75	71	68	76	290	6,014.85
Danny Edwards	72	73	74	71	290	6,014.85
Kent Stauffer	72	72	78	69	291	5,119
David Graham	77	69	74	71	291	5,119
Rodger Davis	73	73	71	74	291	5,119
Dick Mast	69	75	75	73	292	4,492.25
Buddy Gardner	72	73	75	72	292	4,492.25
Isao Aoki	71	74	71	76	292	4,492.25
John Cook	73	68	78	73	292	4,492.25

	SCORES				TOTAL	MONEY
David Edwards	76	69	75	73	293	4,044
Dennis Trixler	72	73	76	73	294	3,896.50
Kenny Perry	74	71	77	72	294	3,896.50
Roger Maltbie	75	71	74	74	294	3,896.50
Jim Carter	74	72	70	78	294	3,896.50
Robert Wilkin	74	71	77	73	295	3,751.50
Steve Bowman	71	72	75	77	295	3,751.50
James Hallet	72	74	77	73	296	3,691
Larry Nelson	78	67	80	72	297	3,691
Mark Calcavecchia	74	69	78	76	297	3,691
Hal Sutton	74	72	75	77	298	3,691
Jerry Haas	73	73	73	80	299	3,691

Out of Final 36 Holes

			TOTAL
Steve Veriato	75	72	147
Jack Nicklaus	74	73	147
Mac O'Grady	75	72	147
Don Pooley	76	71	147
Steve Lowery	74	73	147
Bernhard Langer	75	72	147
Mark Brooks	74	73	147
Mike Swartz	73	75	148
George Shortridge	73	75	148
Jeff Sluman	72	76	148
Gary Koch	77	71	148
Gil Morgan	73	75	148
Ray Barr, Jr.	76	72	148
Jim Gallagher, Jr.	75	73	148
Richard Cromwell	75	73	148
Dave Stockton	76	73	149
Brian Tennyson	73	76	149
Bobby Wadkins	74	75	149
Andy North	74	75	149
Gary Player	77	72	149
Mike Reid	74	75	149
Davis Love III	75	74	149
Tom Eubank	78	71	149
Duffy Waldorf	73	77	150
Tim Simpson	77	73	150
Scott Spence	78	72	150
Blaine McCallister	75	75	150
Mark Hayes	72	78	150
Mike Hulbert	76	74	150
Mark Maness	72	79	151
Tom Inskeep	77	74	151
Brad Faxon	76	75	151
Ed Dougherty	74	77	151
Donald Dubois	77	74	151
Wayne Grady	77	74	151
David Frost	76	75	151
Bill Britton	77	74	151
Denis Watson	77	75	152
Mark Thaxton	80	72	152
Rick Schuller	78	74	152
Emlyn Aubrey	76	76	152
Steve Chapman	76	76	152
Chen Tze Chung	73	79	152
Mike White	79	74	153
Andrew Magee	76	77	153

	SCORES		TOTAL	MONEY
Billy Andrade	79	74	153	
Greg Loosigian	77	76	153	
William Hamilton	78	75	153	
Mike Hammond	75	78	153	
Bob Lohr	78	75	153	
Lennie Clements	76	77	153	
David Thore	79	75	154	
Brett Upper	77	77	154	
Jerry Smith	76	78	154	
Charles Bolling	80	74	154	
Cary Hungate	75	79	154	
Robert Friend	77	77	154	
J.C. Anderson	78	76	154	
Bob Boyd	80	75	155	
George Burns	77	78	155	
Al Morton	74	81	155	
Masashi Ozaki	77	78	155	
Hubert Green	76	79	155	
Webb Heintzelman	79	76	155	
Glen Barrett	79	76	155	
Brad Bell	78	77	155	
Douglas Wherry	78	78	156	
Corey Pavin	78	78	156	
*Thomas Tolles	77	79	156	
Jim Thorpe	75	81	156	
Steve Haskins	77	80	157	
*Pat Duncan	82	75	157	
Rick Dalpos	80	77	157	
Clark Dennis	83	74	157	
*Steven Rintoul	82	76	158	
James Moodie	77	81	158	
Dave Erickson	75	83	158	
Robert Singletary	80	78	158	
Tom Woodard	82	77	159	
Mark Mielke	82	77	159	
Hunt Gilliland	81	78	159	
Woody Blackburn	81	79	160	
Mike McGee	76	84	160	
Darrell Kestner	83	77	160	
Pat Stephens	82	78	160	
Lee Chill	81	80	161	
Baker Maddera	83	79	162	
Charles Bowles	80	85	165	
John Fleischer	85	82	167	
Greg Norman	74	WD		
Dave Rummels	80	WD		

(All professionals who did not complete 72 holes received $1,000.)

Georgia-Pacific Atlanta Classic

Atlanta Country Club, Marietta, Georgia
Par 36-36 — 72; 7,007 yards

June 23-26
purse, $700,000

	SCORES				TOTAL	MONEY
Larry Nelson	63	66	66	63	268	$126,000
Chip Beck	67	66	70	66	269	75,600
Paul Azinger	66	67	66	71	270	47,600
Lanny Wadkins	69	68	70	65	272	28,933.34
Bobby Wadkins	64	69	68	71	272	28,933.33
Dave Rummells	67	69	67	69	272	28,933.33
Nick Price	68	71	68	66	273	22,575
Clarence Rose	68	71	66	68	273	22,575
Scott Hoch	70	65	68	71	274	20,300
Wayne Levi	68	69	68	70	275	18,200
Mark Calcavecchia	67	71	67	70	275	18,200
Larry Rinker	66	69	67	74	276	14,700
Steve Elkington	71	69	66	70	276	14,700
Dave Barr	70	66	70	70	276	14,700
Tim Simpson	68	72	67	70	277	11,550
Blaine McCallister	70	70	68	69	277	11,550
Dan Pohl	69	71	69	68	277	11,550
Ray Floyd	72	69	67	69	277	11,550
Brian Tennyson	71	70	67	70	278	8,190
Loren Roberts	70	68	70	70	278	8,190
Bob Gilder	72	69	68	69	278	8,190
Bill Glasson	68	71	72	67	278	8,190
Hubert Green	70	71	65	72	278	8,190
Brad Fabel	66	72	70	70	278	8,190
Fuzzy Zoeller	71	69	69	70	279	5,460
Larry Mize	69	72	68	70	279	5,460
Davis Love III	73	69	67	70	279	5,460
Kenny Knox	68	71	67	73	279	5,460
Ray Barr, Jr.	67	69	73	70	279	5,460
Bob Tway	69	70	72	69	280	4,550
Tommy Brannon	65	74	68	73	280	4,550
Mark Brooks	70	71	69	70	280	4,550
Steve Jones	68	70	69	74	281	3,867.50
Morris Hatalsky	69	70	70	72	281	3,867.50
Mike Hulbert	70	71	70	70	281	3,867.50
Brian Claar	73	69	69	70	281	3,867.50
Tim Norris	72	69	73	68	282	2,940
Rick Pearson	74	68	67	73	282	2,940
Calvin Peete	69	69	70	74	282	2,940
Tom Garner	67	70	73	72	282	2,940
John Inman	66	73	73	70	282	2,940
Ronnie Black	68	70	71	73	282	2,940
Jay Don Blake	69	67	75	71	282	2,940
Antonio Cerda	69	69	73	71	282	2,940
Brett Upper	71	68	68	76	283	2,002
Mac O'Grady	70	71	72	70	283	2,002
Rocco Mediate	71	68	71	73	283	2,002
Gene Sauers	69	70	74	70	283	2,002
Keith Fergus	72	70	70	71	283	2,002
Ed Fiori	68	70	71	74	283	2,002

Beatrice Western Open

Butler National Golf Club, Oak Brook, Illinois

Par 36-36 — 72; 7,097 yards

June 30-July 3

purse, $900,000

	SCORES				TOTAL	MONEY
Jim Benepe	71	68	69	70	278	$162,000
Peter Jacobsen	70	65	69	75	279	97,200
Brad Faxon	71	69	71	69	280	52,200
Isao Aoki	71	73	67	69	280	52,200
D.A. Weibring	70	71	69	71	281	34,200
Dan Forsman	68	69	71	73	281	34,200
Hale Irwin	73	69	69	71	282	27,112.50
Bill Glasson	69	73	71	69	282	27,112.50
Morris Hatalsky	66	79	68	69	282	27,112.50
Mark Calcavecchia	71	71	67	73	282	27,112.50
J.C. Snead	72	69	70	72	283	17,325
Tom Watson	72	69	70	72	283	17,325
Wayne Levi	73	68	72	70	283	17,325
Dan Halldorson	72	71	69	71	283	17,325
Dave Eichelberger	73	67	68	75	283	17,325
Fulton Allem	68	73	73	69	283	17,325
Ben Crenshaw	75	70	65	73	283	17,325
Bill Britton	70	71	67	75	283	17,325
Doug Tewell	70	73	70	71	284	9,787.50
Tom Sieckmann	67	72	74	71	284	9,787.50
Corey Pavin	71	72	68	73	284	9,787.50
Rocco Mediate	69	70	78	67	284	9,787.50
Kenny Perry	74	71	70	69	284	9,787.50
Bob Gilder	74	72	67	71	284	9,787.50
Ed Fiori	70	67	76	71	284	9,787.50
Mark Brooks	72	73	73	66	284	9,787.50
Mike Sullivan	72	72	71	70	285	6,390
Dan Pohl	72	71	73	69	285	6,390
Mark McCumber	71	71	75	68	285	6,390
David Ogrin	74	69	70	72	285	6,390
Dick Mast	71	71	72	71	285	6,390
Jeff Sluman	71	74	69	72	286	4,670
Dave Rummells	69	75	72	70	286	4,670
Bob Tway	69	72	76	69	286	4,670
Robert Thompson	71	69	73	73	286	4,670
Larry Nelson	71	69	74	72	286	4,670
Aki Ohmachi	73	70	72	71	286	4,670
John Mahaffey	72	68	71	75	286	4,670
Danny Edwards	70	71	71	74	286	4,670
Wayne Grady	71	73	69	73	286	4,670
Scott Verplank	70	71	75	71	287	3,150
Clarence Rose	70	71	72	74	287	3,150
Joey Sindelar	70	69	78	70	287	3,150
Lee Trevino	74	68	74	71	287	3,150
Nick Price	73	69	74	71	287	3,150
Steve Lowery	77	69	73	68	287	3,150
Steve Elkington	73	73	72	69	287	3,150
Scott Simpson	70	74	72	72	288	2,262
Brian Mogg	66	75	72	75	288	2,262
Kenny Knox	73	71	67	77	288	2,262
Brad Fabel	71	69	75	73	288	2,262
Billy Andrade	70	73	69	76	288	2,262
John Cook	71	72	74	71	288	2,262

Anheuser-Busch Classic

Kingsmill Golf Club, Williamsburg, Virginia
Par 36-35 — 71; 6,746 yards

July 7-10
purse, $650,000

	SCORES				TOTAL	MONEY
Tom Sieckmann	69	66	66	69	270	$117,000
Mark Wiebe	68	70	64	68	270	70,200
(Sieckmann defeated Wiebe on second hole of playoff.)						
Gene Sauers	68	71	67	66	272	37,700
Kenny Knox	67	69	65	71	272	37,700
Jeff Sluman	70	67	72	64	273	24,700
Mark McCumber	68	69	69	67	273	24,700
Fuzzy Zoeller	67	68	69	70	274	19,581.25
Tim Simpson	69	71	69	65	274	19,581.25
Peter Jacobsen	67	65	69	73	274	19,581.25
Jeff Coston	75	67	65	67	274	19,581.25
Joey Sindelar	70	70	69	66	275	14,950
Chris Kite	67	73	65	70	275	14,950
Tom Byrum	65	73	70	67	275	14,950
Richard Zokol	71	67	68	70	276	10,075
Robert Wrenn	70	69	68	69	276	10,075
Clarence Rose	69	68	69	70	276	10,075
Curtis Strange	68	67	69	72	276	10,075
Jerry Pate	66	68	71	71	276	10,075
David Peoples	72	69	69	66	276	10,075
Bob Lohr	71	67	68	70	276	10,075
Scott Hoch	67	68	69	72	276	10,075
Larry Rinker	66	72	70	69	277	6,240
Brad Fabel	69	67	72	69	277	6,240
Blaine McCallister	68	69	72	68	277	6,240
Steve Elkington	69	69	67	72	277	6,240
Bill Glasson	69	68	69	71	277	6,240
Kenny Perry	69	68	75	66	278	4,420
Calvin Peete	71	66	68	73	278	4,420
Danny Edwards	68	69	71	70	278	4,420
John Adams	74	66	71	67	278	4,420
Billy Ray Brown	68	70	66	74	278	4,420
Clark Burroughs	66	70	71	71	278	4,420
Russ Cochran	68	71	68	71	278	4,420
Sam Randolph	67	70	71	71	279	3,428.75
Tom Purtzer	65	69	72	73	279	3,428.75
Steve Lowery	72	67	70	70	279	3,428.75
Charles Bolling	66	70	72	71	279	3,428.75
Bobby Wadkins	71	67	71	71	280	2,730
Rick Pearson	70	71	68	71	280	2,730
Bob Proben	70	68	74	68	280	2,730
David Ogrin	72	68	68	72	280	2,730
Mike Donald	71	71	73	65	280	2,730
Bill Buttner	65	70	71	74	280	2,730
Loren Roberts	71	68	72	70	281	2,210
John Cook	73	67	72	69	281	2,210
Howard Twitty	71	70	68	73	282	1,842.75
D.A. Weibring	71	70	74	67	282	1,842.75
John Inman	67	71	73	71	282	1,842.75
Lennie Clements	69	72	68	73	282	1,842.75
Tom Pernice Jr.	72	70	71	70	283	1,545.15
Ed Dougherty	67	70	77	69	283	1,545.15
Larry Ziegler	70	72	68	73	283	1,545.14
Billy Andrade	71	69	69	74	283	1,545.14
Dewey Arnette	71	71	70	71	283	1,545.14

	SCORES				TOTAL	MONEY
Bill Britton	68	72	72	71	283	1,545.14
Bobby Clampett	67	69	71	76	283	1,545.14

Hardee's Classic

Oakwood Country Club, Coal Valley, Illinois
Par 35-35 — 70; 6,606 yards

July 14-17
purse, $600,000

	SCORES				TOTAL	MONEY
Blaine McCallister	68	62	63	68	261	$108,000
Dan Forsman	64	66	67	67	264	64,800
Sam Randolph	64	67	69	66	266	40,800
Brad Fabel	67	66	67	67	267	24,800
Steve Jones	67	69	67	64	267	24,800
Scott Hoch	69	65	67	66	267	24,800
Bob Lohr	68	68	66	66	268	19,350
Russ Cochran	66	64	69	69	268	19,350
Tom Sieckmann	67	67	69	66	269	15,600
Jim Dent	66	68	68	67	269	15,600
Dave Barr	69	67	67	66	269	15,600
Ray Barr, Jr.	66	67	70	66	269	15,600
David Ogrin	67	68	69	66	270	12,600
Gene Sauers	62	73	70	66	271	11,100
John Huston	68	69	65	69	271	11,100
Kim Young	66	67	71	68	272	7,620
Tim Simpson	70	68	66	68	272	7,620
David Peoples	67	68	70	67	272	7,620
Jeff Sluman	67	65	73	67	272	7,620
Dan Pohl	68	64	68	72	272	7,620
Mike Donald	66	68	71	67	272	7,620
Mark Brooks	65	70	67	70	272	7,620
Billy Ray Brown	65	68	67	72	272	7,620
Curt Byrum	68	70	70	64	272	7,620
Brian Claar	67	79	68	68	272	7,620
Tom Purtzer	65	68	72	68	273	4,170
Ray Stewart	70	67	65	71	273	4,170
Ron Streck	67	65	70	71	273	4,170
Dillard Pruitt	69	67	70	67	273	4,170
Jim Gallagher, Jr.	69	66	67	71	273	4,170
Mark Maness	65	67	69	72	273	4,170
Mark Hayes	68	69	67	69	273	4,170
Rod Curl	69	70	66	68	273	4,170
Bruce Soulsby	69	67	70	68	274	2,965.72
John Adams	68	67	70	69	274	2,965.72
Clark Burroughs	70	68	68	68	274	2,965.72
Lance Ten Broeck	65	68	74	67	274	2,965.71
Barry Jaeckel	68	65	72	69	274	2,965.71
Hale Irwin	66	67	69	72	274	2,965.71
Gil Morgan	68	66	74	66	274	2,965.71
Robert Thompson	69	70	67	69	275	2,280
Bob Gilder	68	69	67	71	275	2,280
Bill Glasson	67	69	70	69	275	2,280
Donnie Hammond	69	69	66	71	275	2,280
Tony Sills	66	70	71	69	276	1,602
Gary Hallberg	66	72	69	69	276	1,602
Ernie Gonzalez	65	67	75	69	276	1,602
Rick Dalpos	68	71	68	69	276	1,602

	SCORES				TOTAL	MONEY
Danny Briggs	66	67	69	74	276	1,602
David Edwards	67	71	68	70	276	1,602
Bob Eastwood	71	68	67	70	276	1,602
Keith Clearwater	68	70	71	67	276	1,602
Rick Rehr	64	71	70	71	276	1,602
John Cook	68	70	71	67	276	1,602

Canon Sammy Davis Jr — Hartford Open

TPC of Connecticut, Cromwell, Connecticut
Par 36-35 — 71; 6,786 yards

July 21-24
purse, $700,000

	SCORES				TOTAL	MONEY
Mark Brooks	66	65	69	69	269	$126,000
Joe Sindelar	65	72	67	65	269	61,600
Dave Barr	69	67	70	63	269	61,600
(Brooks won playoff, defeating Sindelar on first extra hole, Barr on second.)						
Ronnie Black	66	69	65	70	270	30,800
Mark Calcavecchia	67	66	67	70	270	30,800
Brett Upper	67	66	69	69	271	24,325
Roger Maltbie	64	68	72	67	271	24,325
Blaine McCallister	68	66	69	69	272	19,600
Brad Faxon	65	69	69	69	272	19,600
Lennie Clements	68	70	68	66	272	19,600
George Archer	70	66	67	69	272	19,600
Kenny Perry	67	68	68	70	273	15,400
Mark Hayes	67	69	69	68	273	15,400
Bob Lohr	67	71	69	67	274	11,900
Gene Sauers	68	68	69	69	274	11,900
Steve Lowery	66	72	70	66	274	11,900
Rocco Mediate	69	70	67	68	274	11,900
Fulton Allem	67	68	67	72	274	11,900
Dave Rummells	69	69	69	68	275	7,365.56
Rick Pearson	69	69	70	67	275	7,365.56
Jay Delsing	66	73	70	66	275	7,365.56
Curt Byrum	69	70	69	67	275	7,365.56
Tom Byrum	70	69	70	66	275	7,365.56
Steve Thomas	69	69	68	69	275	7,365.56
Lee Trevino	67	69	74	65	275	7,365.55
Tony Sills	70	67	67	71	275	7,365.55
Clark Burroughs	66	66	74	69	275	7,365.55
Wayne Levi	67	67	74	68	276	4,865
Danny Edwards	69	67	69	71	276	4,865
Tommy Armour	69	66	68	73	276	4,865
Paul Azinger	69	71	67	69	276	4,865
Tim Norris	70	66	70	71	277	4,051.50
Ken Green	66	70	71	70	277	4,051.50
Jim Gallagher, Jr.	68	71	69	69	277	4,051.50
Billy Andrade	71	66	69	71	277	4,051.50
Brian Tennyson	69	71	69	69	278	3,013.78
Doug Tewell	68	71	69	70	278	3,013.78
Gil Morgan	67	70	69	72	278	3,013.78
Harry Taylor	68	72	69	69	278	3,013.78
Dillard Pruitt	69	71	66	72	278	3,013.78
John Cook	70	69	68	71	278	3,013.78
Brad Bryant	69	71	71	67	278	3,013.78
Hubert Green	70	65	73	70	278	3,013.77

	SCORES				TOTAL	MONEY
John Inman	69	66	72	71	278	3,013.77
Clarence Rose	69	71	69	70	279	2,002
Gary McCord	68	68	74	69	279	2,002
Bob Gilder	71	69	72	67	279	2,002
John Adams	68	71	69	71	279	2,002
Mike Bender	70	70	68	71	279	2,002
Roy Biancalana	71	69	70	69	279	2,002

Buick Open

Warwick Hills Country Club, Grand Blanc, Michigan
Par 36-36 — 72; 7,014 yards

July 28-31
purse, $700,000

	SCORES				TOTAL	MONEY
Scott Verplank	66	66	70	66	268	$126,000
Doug Tewell	68	70	68	64	270	75,600
Fred Couples	66	69	71	65	271	47,600
Tim Norris	69	66	71	66	272	33,600
Ben Crenshaw	70	71	66	67	274	26,600
James Hallet	67	69	69	69	274	26,600
Gene Sauers	68	71	68	68	275	20,370
Jack Renner	68	72	68	67	275	20,370
Dave Rummells	68	71	66	70	275	20,370
Kenny Knox	69	68	69	69	275	20,370
Scott Hoch	66	72	68	69	275	20,370
Wayne Grady	69	68	70	69	276	14,175
Tommy Armour	69	68	70	69	276	14,175
Greg Powers	69	72	65	70	276	14,175
Tom Sieckmann	69	67	71	69	276	14,175
Brad Faxon	71	69	71	66	277	9,820
Dave Eichelberger	69	68	67	73	277	9,820
Tom Purtzer	69	72	69	67	277	9,820
Tim Simpson	66	70	70	71	277	9,820
Jodie Mudd	72	70	69	66	277	9,820
Mark O'Meara	71	70	67	69	277	9,820
Mike Hulbert	75	67	66	69	277	9,820
Ken Green	68	70	65	75	278	6,440
Jim Carter	69	70	70	69	278	6,440
Robert Wrenn	72	68	69	69	278	6,440
Howard Twitty	69	65	68	76	278	6,440
Steve Elkington	68	67	67	77	279	4,760
Dan Forsman	70	68	74	67	279	4,760
Mark Brooks	71	70	70	68	279	4,760
Fuzzy Zoeller	71	69	68	71	279	4,760
Mike Sullivan	67	68	72	72	279	4,760
Tom Kite	71	71	69	68	279	4,760
Peter Jacobsen	70	71	69	69	279	4,760
George Archer	66	72	69	73	280	3,692
Kim Young	69	72	70	69	280	3,692
Jeff Sluman	69	70	68	73	280	3,692
Rocco Mediate	68	70	71	71	280	3,692
David Graham	69	70	70	72	281	3,010
John Adams	68	73	71	69	281	3,010
Ron Streck	69	69	73	70	281	3,010
J.C. Snead	72	70	69	70	281	3,010
Davis Love III	69	73	74	65	281	3,010
Bob Eastwood	73	69	69	71	282	2,184

	SCORES				TOTAL	MONEY
Bill Britton	70	70	71	71	282	2,184
Clark Burroughs	73	69	72	68	282	2,184
Tom Byrum	71	69	73	69	282	2,184
Ray Stewart	74	67	71	70	282	2,184
Dillard Pruitt	73	69	74	66	282	2,184
Barry Jaeckel	69	70	71	72	282	2,184
Mike Donald	71	70	69	73	283	1,664
Bob Estes	68	73	71	71	283	1,664
Buddy Gardner	73	68	74	68	283	1,664
Fulton Allem	71	68	72	72	283	1,664
Michael Bradley	74	68	70	71	283	1,664
Bobby Wadkins	72	68	70	73	283	1,664
Bruce Lietzke	70	72	71	70	283	1,664

Federal Express St. Jude Classic

Colonial Country Club, Cordova, Tennessee
Par 36-36 — 72; 7,282 yards

August 4-7
purse, $953,842

	SCORES				TOTAL	MONEY
Jodie Mudd	68	68	67	70	273	$171,692
Nick Price	73	64	71	66	274	83,938
Peter Jacobsen	68	68	72	66	274	83,938
Dave Rummells	70	69	66	71	276	39,425.34
Larry Mize	70	68	70	68	276	39,425.33
Tim Simpson	68	68	68	72	276	39,425.33
Curtis Strange	69	71	67	70	277	30,761.50
Tom Kite	71	69	67	70	277	30,761.50
Fulton Allem	69	69	71	69	278	27,661
Richard Zokol	71	70	73	65	279	21,143.17
Larry Nelson	73	70	66	70	279	21,143.17
Loren Roberts	70	72	72	65	279	21,143.17
Scott Hoch	71	68	69	71	279	21,143.17
Howard Twitty	70	69	69	71	279	21,143.16
Tommy Armour	69	69	74	67	279	21,143.16
Davis Love III	70	73	68	69	280	15,261.34
Hal Sutton	72	69	69	70	280	15,261.33
Trevor Dodds	72	68	71	69	280	15,261.33
Sam Randolph	72	67	74	68	281	11,970.75
Doug Tewell	66	73	69	73	281	11,970.75
Bruce Soulsby	70	69	69	73	281	11,970.75
Ken Brown	73	70	70	68	281	11,970.75
Bob Tway	70	72	71	69	282	8,775.50
Jeff Sluman	72	68	70	72	282	8,775.50
John Huston	71	73	68	70	282	8,775.50
Bill Britton	71	71	70	70	282	8,775.50
Payne Stewart	69	70	69	75	283	6,772.20
Tim Norris	72	68	71	72	283	6,772.20
David Jackson	70	69	76	68	283	6,772.20
Mike Hulbert	73	66	72	72	283	6,772.20
Brad Fabel	70	72	73	68	283	6,772.20
Jack Renner	73	70	72	69	284	5,521
David Ogrin	71	72	70	71	284	5,521
Gil Morgan	70	71	72	71	284	5,521
John Adams	71	70	73	70	284	5,521
Fuzzy Zoeller	72	69	72	72	285	4,299
Denis Watson	72	72	71	70	285	4,299

	SCORES				TOTAL	MONEY
Clarence Rose	76	68	72	69	285	4,299
Mark Lye	71	70	71	73	285	4,299
John Inman	72	72	70	71	285	4,299
Andy Bean	73	70	69	73	285	4,299
Ronnie Black	72	71	72	70	285	4,299
Harry Taylor	72	70	73	71	286	3,243
Bill Glasson	71	70	71	74	286	3,243
Ed Fiori	66	71	76	73	286	3,243
Jay Don Blake	70	72	72	72	286	3,243
Larry Rinker	70	72	78	67	287	2,483.17
Robert Wrenn	69	75	73	70	287	2,483.17
Steve Lowery	69	75	70	73	287	2,483.17
Clark Burroughs	69	73	75	70	287	2,483.17
Buddy Gardner	70	71	72	74	287	2,483.16
Ed Dougherty	72	69	74	72	287	2,483.16

PGA Championship

Oak Tree Golf Club, Edmond, Oklahoma
Par 36-35 — 71; 7,015 yards

August 11-14
purse, $1,000,000

	SCORES				TOTAL	MONEY
Jeff Sluman	69	70	68	65	272	$160,000
Paul Azinger	67	66	71	71	275	100,000
Tommy Nakajima	69	68	74	67	278	70,000
Tom Kite	72	69	71	67	279	45,800
Nick Faldo	67	71	70	71	279	45,800
Dave Rummells	73	64	68	75	280	32,500
Bob Gilder	66	75	71	68	280	32,500
Dan Pohl	69	71	70	71	281	28,000
Mark O'Meara	70	71	70	71	282	21,500
Greg Norman	68	71	72	71	282	21,500
Payne Stewart	70	69	70	73	282	21,500
Ray Floyd	68	68	74	72	282	21,500
Kenny Knox	72	69	68	73	282	21,500
Steve Jones	69	68	72	73	282	21,500
Craig Stadler	68	73	75	67	283	16,500
John Mahaffey	71	71	70	71	283	16,500
Richard Zokol	70	70	74	70	284	11,500
Nick Price	74	70	67	73	284	11,500
Jay Overton	68	66	76	74	284	11,500
Corey Pavin	71	70	75	68	284	11,500
Mark McNulty	73	70	67	74	284	11,500
David Graham	70	67	73	74	284	11,500
Mark Calcavecchia	73	69	70	72	284	11,500
Ben Crenshaw	70	71	69	74	284	11,500
Lanny Wadkins	74	69	70	72	285	6,666.67
Scott Hoch	74	69	68	74	285	6,666.67
Jay Don Blake	71	73	72	69	285	6,666.67
David Edwards	71	69	77	68	285	6,666.67
Blaine McCallister	73	67	75	70	285	6,666.66
Ronnie Black	71	71	70	73	285	6,666.66
Curtis Strange	72	72	73	69	286	4,842.86
Gary Koch	72	65	78	71	286	4,842.86
Rocco Mediate	68	74	70	74	286	4,842.86
Donnie Hammond	72	72	73	69	286	4,842.86
Steve Elkington	73	70	74	69	286	4,842.86

	SCORES				TOTAL	MONEY
Tom Watson	72	68	74	72	286	4,842.85
Chip Beck	67	72	73	74	286	4,842.85
James Hallet	72	68	74	73	287	3,211.12
Calvin Peete	74	66	74	73	287	3,211.11
Mark Wiebe	74	68	73	72	287	3,211.11
David Ishii	73	71	74	69	287	3,211.11
Hale Irwin	74	70	72	71	287	3,211.11
Jay Haas	73	71	71	72	287	3,211.11
Larry Nelson	70	71	76	70	287	3,211.11
Isao Aoki	73	71	70	73	287	3,211.11
Tommy Brannon	70	71	74	72	287	3,211.11
Peter Jacobsen	73	68	75	72	288	2,400.00
Bob Tway	71	71	70	77	289	2,231.25
Denis Watson	70	70	79	70	289	2,231.25
Dave Stockton	70	69	75	75	289	2,231.25
John Cook	67	69	76	77	289	2,231.25
Robert Wrenn	72	68	73	77	290	2,092.50
D.A. Weibring	72	72	73	73	290	2,092.50
Jodie Mudd	70	73	77	70	290	2,092.50
Scott Bess	74	69	73	74	290	2,092.50
Ed Fiori	71	69	76	74	290	2,092.50
Rodger Davis	73	69	76	72	290	2,092.50
Peter Senior	68	73	74	76	291	1,990
Don Pooley	72	69	73	77	291	1,990
John Inman	73	69	75	74	291	1,990
Bob Makoski	69	72	72	78	291	1,990
Bruce Lietzke	70	72	76	74	292	1,930
Steve Pate	71	72	72	77	292	1,930
Mike Reid	68	71	79	75	293	1,900
Gibby Gilbert	72	72	74	76	294	1,880
Hal Sutton	69	74	75	77	295	1,840
Bobby Wadkins	75	69	76	75	295	1,840
Jim Carter	73	68	76	78	295	1,840
Andrew Magee	71	73	74	79	297	1,800
Doug Tewell	70	68	81	79	298	1,800
Dick Mast	71	72	72	85	300	1,800
Hubert Green	74	69	WD			

Out of Final 36 Holes

Dave Barr	74	71	145
Jim Benepe	71	74	145
Curt Byrum	79	66	145
Tom Byrum	73	72	145
Fred Couples	74	71	145
Scott Simpson	74	72	146
Tim Simpson	72	74	146
Mac O'Grady	70	76	146
Bob Lohr	75	71	146
Brad Faxon	78	68	146
Seve Ballesteros	71	75	146
Gary Hallberg	73	73	146
Fuzzy Zoeller	74	73	147
Gene Sauers	74	73	147
Joey Sindelar	74	73	147
Tom Sieckmann	73	74	147
Clarence Rose	73	74	147
Fulton Allem	73	74	147
Ken Brown	74	73	147
Ken Green	74	73	147

	SCORES		TOTAL	MONEY
Bob Eastwood	75	72	147	
Bob Groff	72	75	147	
Lee Trevino	77	71	148	
David Thore	78	70	148	
Andy North	74	74	148	
Gil Morgan	76	72	148	
Sam Randolph	73	75	148	
David Frost	75	73	148	
Scott Verplank	77	72	149	
Tom Purtzer	75	74	149	
Ralph Landrum	75	74	149	
Andy Bean	78	71	149	
Morris Hatalsky	76	73	149	
Woody Fitzhugh	74	75	149	
Tom Wargo	78	72	150	
Arnold Palmer	74	76	150	
Larry Mize	73	77	150	
Mike Hulbert	73	77	150	
Wayne Grady	76	74	150	
Jim Weeden	75	76	151	
Jack Nicklaus	72	79	151	
Mark McCumber	76	75	151	
Bob Mann	78	73	151	
Keith Clearwater	77	74	151	
Bernhard Langer	74	77	151	
Mike Donald	75	76	151	
Lonnie Nielsen	78	74	152	
Mike Malaska	77	75	152	
Jim Albus	80	72	152	
Russ Cochran	76	76	152	
Jim Dickson	74	78	152	
Gregg Jones	76	76	152	
Benny Passons	78	75	153	
Dana Quigley	79	74	153	
Michael Burke Jr.	78	75	153	
Bob Lendzion	78	75	153	
Gene Fieger	75	78	153	
Mike Lawrence	79	75	154	
Bob Menne	77	77	154	
Darrell Kestner	78	76	154	
Bill Brodell	79	75	154	
Mark Brooks	80	74	154	
Mark Gurnow	78	78	156	
Jay Lumpkin	74	82	156	
Ray Freeman	75	81	156	
Mike San Filippo	80	77	157	
David Glenz	79	78	157	
John Paesani	79	78	157	
Lynn Janson	77	80	157	
Bob Klein	81	77	158	
Jim Sobb	78	80	158	
Carl Poche	80	79	159	
Jeff Roth	77	82	159	
Rick Vershure	78	81	159	
Don Brigham	79	83	162	
Dwight Nevil	81	84	165	
Ian Woosnam	78	WD		
Bill Glasson	WD			

(All players who did not complete 72 holes received $1,000.)

The International

Castle Pines Golf Club, Castle Rock, Colorado

August 17-21

Par 36-36 — 72; 7,503 yards

purse, $1,115,280

WEDNESDAY QUALIFIERS

11 Mike Reid, $10,000.
8 Ian Baker-Finch, $7,500.
7 Bobby Clampett, Nick Price, Sam Randolph, J.C. Snead, $1,875.
6 Andy Bean, Billy Ray Brown, Steve Pate.
5 Isao Aoki, Larry Rinker, Donnie Hammond, Roger Maltbie, Gene Sauers.
4 Raymond Floyd, Mike McCullough, Dick Mast, Jodie Mudd, Doug Tewell.
3 Danny Edwards, Paul Azinger, Bill Sander, Antonio Cerda, Jack Nicklaus, Joey Sindelar.
2 Ronnie Black, David Ishii, Bruce Soulsby, Andrew Magee, Ken Green, Tom Kite, Bob Tway, D.A. Weibring, Fuzzy Zoeller.
1 Jose Rivero, Curt Byrum, Bill Glasson, Bruce Lietzke, Bob Eastwood.

THURSDAY QUALIFIERS

10 Ben Crenshaw, Mark O'Meara, $8,750.
9 Billy Andrade, Fred Couples, Steve Jones.
7 Ken Brown, Mark Calcavecchia, Kenny Perry, Don Pooley, Robert Wrenn.
6 Russ Cochran, Willie Wood, Dan Pohl.
5 Loren Roberts, Rocco Mediate, Jack Renner, Ray Stewart, David Frost, Jeff Sluman, Miguel Martin.
4 Anders Forsbrand, Clarence Rose, Bill Britton, Jim Carter, Steve Elkington, Mark Hayes, Aki Ohmachi, Corey Pavin, Tom Byrum, Mark McCumber, Chip Beck.
3 Brian Tennyson, Ove Sellberg, Taijiro Tanaka, Robert Thompson, Davis Love, III.
2 David Ogrin, Richard Zokol, Mark Wiebe.

FRIDAY QUALIFIERS

11 Couples, Sindelar, Weibring, $7,500 each.
9 K. Green, Jones, Lietzke, Maltbie, Pate, Tewell, Wrenn, $357 each.
8 K. Brown, Carter, Floyd, Nicklaus, Ogrin, Price, Wiebe.
7 Aoki, Beck, Love, Pavin, Randolph, R. Stewart.
6 Glasson, Hayes, Pohl, Sauers.
5 Calcavecchia, T. Byrum, Cerda, Danny Edwards, Pooley, Sellberg, Zokol.
4 Cochran, Crenshaw, Elkington, Hammond, McCumber, O'Meara.
3 Bean, Britton, Ishii.
2 Kite, Magee, McCullough, Mudd, Rose, Sluman, Tway, Wood.
1 Reid, Martin, Perry.

SATURDAY QUALIFIERS

14 Lietzke, $10,000.
13 Crenshaw, Mudd, $6,250 each.
11 Beck, Kite, Randolph, $833 each.
10 Magee, Wiebe.
9 Bean, Tewell.
8 Love, Pohl.
7 Britton, Pate, Sindelar.
6 Reid, Glasson, Zokol.

FINAL ROUND

17 Sindelar, $180,000.
13 Pohl, Pate, $88,000 each.
12 Wiebe, $48,000.

11   Beck, $40,000.
 9   Love, $36,000.
 8   Crenshaw, $33,500.
 6   Lietzke, $31,000 each.
 5   Glasson, $29,000.
 3   Kite, $27,000.
 2   Magee, Reid, Randolph, $23,000 each.
 1   Mudd, $19,000.
 0   Britton, Tewell, $17,500.
-2   Bean, Zokol, $15,500.

NEC World Series of Golf

Firestone Country Club, Akron, Ohio   August 25-28
Par 35-35 — 70; 7,136 yards   purse, $900,000

	SCORES				TOTAL	MONEY
Mike Reid	70	65	71	69	275	$162,000
Tom Watson	74	69	64	68	275	97,200
(Reid defeated Watson on first hole of playoff.)						
Ian Baker-Finch	68	67	71	71	277	52,200
Larry Nelson	70	70	66	71	277	52,200
Sandy Lyle	69	67	71	71	278	36,000
Chip Beck	71	69	69	70	279	31,350
Steve Pate	74	67	74	64	279	31,350
Ben Crenshaw	73	67	68	72	280	28,100
Jay Haas	69	73	69	70	281	25,300
Bruce Lietzke	70	69	72	70	281	25,300
Jeff Sluman	71	73	71	67	282	22,600
Greg Norman	72	71	69	71	283	20,800
Mark McCumber	70	71	66	77	284	19,100
Anders Forsbrand	75	72	70	68	285	15,850
Morris Hatalsky	75	69	69	72	285	15,850
Scott Verplank	75	70	68	72	285	15,850
Joey Sindelar	71	76	70	68	285	15,850
Isao Aoki	74	75	64	73	286	13,600
Lanny Wadkins	71	66	73	77	287	11,260
Steve Jones	71	71	73	72	287	11,260
Blaine McCallister	67	73	76	71	287	11,260
Jodie Mudd	74	69	73	71	287	11,260
Craig Stadler	76	71	70	70	287	11,260
David Ishii	71	73	72	72	288	10,100
Keith Clearwater	72	77	72	68	289	9,500
Doug Tewell	75	69	68	77	289	9,500
Tom Sieckmann	70	73	71	75	289	9,500
Curtis Strange	71	73	69	76	289	9,500
Mark Brooks	68	70	77	74	289	9,500
Paul Azinger	72	71	72	75	290	8,700
Jim Benepe	71	71	75	73	290	8,700
Scott Simpson	71	69	72	78	290	8,700
David Feherty	70	68	78	77	293	8,400
Wayne Westner	77	73	73	71	294	8,300
Ken Brown	69	77	75	77	298	8,150
Gary Hallberg	74	75	72	77	298	8,150
John Inman	73	72	78	77	300	8,000
Paul Way	77	70	74	80	301	7,850
Gary Koch	74	80	72	75	301	7,850
Hsieh Chin Sheng	76	72	78	77	303	7,700
Jay Lumpkin	76	78	76	77	307	7,600

Provident Classic

Valleybrook Golf and Country Club, Hixson, Tennessee   August 25-28
Par 35-35 — 70; 6,641 yards   purse, $450,000

	SCORES				TOTAL	MONEY
Phil Blackmar	66	64	69	65	264	$81,000
Payne Stewart	65	67	67	65	264	48,600
(Blackmar defeated Stewart on first hole of playoff.)						
Mark Hayes	70	69	63	67	269	23,400
Billy Ray Brown	69	69	65	66	269	23,400
Jim Dent	66	66	67	70	269	23,400
Leonard Thompson	66	67	69	68	270	13,612.50
Bill Glasson	68	69	68	65	270	13,612.50
James Hallet	67	65	69	69	270	13,612.50
Bill Bergin	69	67	65	69	270	13,612.50
Bill Britton	63	70	66	71	270	13,612.50
Russ Cochran	66	69	67	68	270	13,612.50
Bob Wolcott	67	70	67	67	271	9,112.50
Mike Sullivan	68	68	68	67	271	9,112.50
Harry Taylor	68	67	69	67	271	9,112.50
Roger Maltbie	69	69	66	67	271	9,112.50
Duffy Waldorf	69	67	67	69	272	6,975
Joey Rassett	66	69	68	69	272	6,975
Mark Lye	69	65	67	71	272	6,975
John Adams	70	67	69	66	272	6,975
Loren Roberts	71	66	70	66	273	4,875
Ray Barr, Jr.	68	68	68	69	273	4,875
Roy Biancalana	63	71	67	72	273	4,875
David Canipe	68	71	66	68	273	4,875
Antonio Cerda	69	68	68	68	273	4,875
Brian Claar	69	66	68	70	273	4,875
Greg Twiggs	70	67	70	67	274	2,999.30
Howard Twitty	69	68	69	68	274	2,999.30
Jack Renner	65	68	70	71	274	2,999.30
Billy Pierot	65	73	64	72	274	2,999.30
Dan Halldorson	69	68	68	69	274	2,999.30
David Peoples	67	68	71	68	274	2,999.30
Rocco Mediate	67	72	67	68	274	2,999.30
Mike Bender	67	69	68	70	274	2,999.30
Ed Dougherty	66	68	72	68	274	2,999.30
Danny Briggs	68	68	72	66	274	2,999.30
Bruce Zabriski	67	66	74	68	275	2,028.15
Tim Norris	71	65	70	69	275	2,028.15
Dillard Pruitt	67	69	67	72	275	2,028.14
Mike Nicolette	66	73	66	70	275	2,028.14
Kenny Perry	64	67	73	71	275	2,028.14
Andrew Magee	71	67	68	69	275	2,028.14
Jim Gallagher Jr.	69	67	69	70	275	2,028.14
Stan Utley	69	70	72	65	276	1,370.25
Tony Sills	73	66	66	71	276	1,370.25
Ted Schulz	67	70	68	71	276	1,370.25
Ron Streck	68	71	67	70	276	1,370.25
Phil Hancock	71	64	71	70	276	1,370.25
Tom Pernice Jr.	70	68	69	69	276	1,370.25
Brian Fogt	66	72	69	69	276	1,370.25
Tommy Armour	67	71	71	67	276	1,370.25

Canadian Open

Glen Abbey Golf Club, Oakville, Ontario
Par 35-37 — 72; 7,102 yards

September 1-4
purse, $750,000

	SCORES				TOTAL	MONEY
Ken Green	70	65	68	72	275	$135,000
Scott Verplank	69	70	67	70	276	66,000
Bill Glasson	70	71	68	67	276	66,000
Mike Sullivan	71	70	69	67	277	33,000
Dave Barr	72	68	71	66	277	33,000
Mark Wiebe	72	69	70	67	278	27,000
Gordon Smith	71	71	70	67	279	22,593.75
Larry Rinker	77	65	65	72	279	22,593.75
Wayne Grady	69	72	68	70	279	22,593.75
Jay Delsing	70	67	68	74	279	22,593.75
Bob Tway	71	69	66	74	280	17,250
John Huston	70	73	64	73	280	17,250
Larry Mize	66	71	71	72	280	17,250
Tim Simpson	68	72	71	70	281	13,500
Jodie Mudd	75	67	70	69	281	13,500
Tom Byrum	68	68	73	72	281	13,500
Robert Thompson	71	74	69	68	282	9,487.50
D.A. Weibring	72	67	68	75	282	9,487.50
David Ogrin	71	72	69	70	282	9,487.50
Greg Powers	74	69	66	73	282	9,487.50
Johnny Miller	69	70	74	69	282	9,487.50
James Hallet	69	70	73	70	282	9,487.50
Bruce Lietzke	73	71	71	67	282	9,487.50
Barry Jaeckel	68	72	67	75	282	9,487.50
Steve Jones	69	75	67	72	283	6,125
Bill Britton	66	75	71	71	283	6,125
Billy Ray Brown	75	69	70	69	283	6,125
Don Pooley	70	73	66	75	284	4,575
Gene Sauers	72	69	72	71	284	4,575
Mark McCumber	75	70	70	69	284	4,575
Greg Ladehoff	74	70	73	67	284	4,575
Bob Lohr	72	66	74	72	284	4,575
Scott Hoch	69	71	71	73	284	4,575
Jay Don Blake	70	73	69	72	284	4,575
Brad Bryant	72	69	74	69	284	4,575
Dan Forsman	71	71	72	70	284	4,575
Curt Byrum	72	69	70	73	284	4,575
Duffy Waldorf	71	72	69	73	285	3,000
Brian Tennyson	69	74	69	73	285	3,000
Nick Price	72	69	71	73	285	3,000
Joey Rassett	72	70	72	71	285	3,000
Jeff Sluman	64	71	73	77	285	3,000
Mark O'Meara	73	69	70	73	285	3,000
Jack Nicklaus	68	74	76	67	285	3,000
Donnie Hammond	71	69	72	73	285	3,000
Lance Ten Broeck	75	69	69	73	286	1,976.25
David Tentis	72	71	72	71	286	1,976.25
Davis Love III	72	72	72	70	286	1,976.25
Tim Norris	70	68	74	74	286	1,976.25
Bob Gilder	73	66	73	74	286	1,976.25
Rocco Mediate	72	73	70	71	286	1,976.25
Kenny Perry	72	72	69	73	286	1,976.25
George Archer	72	72	71	71	286	1,976.25

Greater Milwaukee Open

Tuckaway Country Club, Franklin, Wisconsin
Par 36-36 — 72; 7,030 yards

September 8-11
purse, $700,000

	SCORES				TOTAL	MONEY
Ken Green	70	69	61	68	268	$126,000
Dan Pohl	70	72	66	66	274	46,200
Donnie Hammond	68	69	68	69	274	46,200
Jim Gallagher, Jr.	67	67	72	68	274	46,200
Mark Calcavecchia	71	68	69	66	274	46,200
Nick Price	70	71	67	67	275	25,200
Corey Pavin	66	72	70	68	276	21,816.67
Tim Simpson	70	70	70	66	276	21,816.67
David Ogrin	70	66	70	70	276	21,816.66
Dave Barr	66	68	68	75	277	18,900
Dave Eichelberger	69	73	68	68	278	15,400
Pat McGowan	70	69	69	70	278	15,400
Billy Andrade	69	69	67	73	278	15,400
Barry Cheesman	70	69	72	67	278	15,400
Bob Tway	74	67	68	70	279	11,550
Lance Ten Broeck	70	69	69	71	279	11,550
David Frost	71	71	67	70	279	11,550
John Adams	75	65	70	69	279	11,550
Tom Byrum	73	70	72	65	280	6,949.10
Bobby Wadkins	73	68	70	69	280	6,949.09
Payne Stewart	73	69	68	70	280	6,949.09
Steve Pate	70	72	70	68	280	6,949.09
Wayne Levi	74	69	68	69	280	6,949.09
Dan Forsman	72	68	67	73	280	6,949.09
Ray Floyd	71	70	68	71	280	6,949.09
Mike Nicolette	70	70	70	70	280	6,949.09
Scott Hoch	73	67	69	71	280	6,949.09
Gary Hallberg	70	72	69	69	280	6,949.09
Ray Barr, Jr.	72	69	68	71	280	6,949.09
Tom Sieckmann	68	70	72	71	281	4,068.75
Larry Rinker	72	67	73	69	281	4,068.75
Tony Sills	72	67	73	69	281	4,068.75
Scott Verplank	71	69	70	71	281	4,068.75
Bob Gilder	75	67	64	75	281	4,068.75
Steve Elkington	73	68	71	69	281	4,068.75
Mike Bender	68	69	74	70	281	4,068.75
Brian Claar	68	70	72	71	281	4,068.75
Ron Streck	69	74	68	71	282	2,870
Clarence Rose	72	71	69	70	282	2,870
Joey Rassett	74	67	69	72	282	2,870
Hubert Green	71	71	68	72	282	2,870
Rick Fehr	69	71	73	69	282	2,870
Bill Kratzert	70	71	72	69	282	2,870
Brad Bryant	69	72	69	72	282	2,870
Ray Stewart	74	69	68	72	283	1,773.34
David Tentis	74	68	70	71	283	1,773.34
Duffy Waldorf	70	72	74	67	283	1,773.34
Joey Sindelar	69	74	68	72	283	1,773.34
Jay Haas	72	71	70	70	283	1,773.34
Mike Sullivan	69	68	71	75	283	1,773.33
Bruce Soulsby	70	72	72	69	283	1,773.33
Jack Renner	71	70	69	73	283	1,773.33
Morris Hatalsky	70	69	73	71	283	1,773.33
Tim Norris	72	69	70	72	283	1,773.33

	SCORES				TOTAL	MONEY
Mark Lye	70	71	74	68	283	1,773.33
Greg Ladehoff	74	68	69	72	283	1,773.33
Chip Beck	70	67	69	77	283	1,773.33
Jim Benepe	73	67	72	71	283	1,773.33
Jim Carter	71	71	70	71	283	1,773.33

Bank of Boston Classic

Pleasant Valley Country Club, Sutton, Massachusetts
Par 36-35 — 71; 7,110 yards

September 15-18
purse, $600,000

	SCORES				TOTAL	MONEY
Mark Calcavecchia	71	67	70	66	274	$108,000
Don Pooley	75	68	69	63	275	64,800
Fuzzy Zoeller	68	69	69	70	276	31,200
Dave Rummells	70	69	70	67	276	31,200
John Mahaffey	70	69	70	67	276	31,200
Steve Pate	68	68	69	72	277	20,100
Wayne Levi	71	67	69	70	277	20,100
Wayne Grady	71	68	69	69	277	20,100
Duffy Waldorf	71	70	69	68	278	14,400
D.A. Weibring	68	68	69	73	278	14,400
Clarence Rose	71	70	71	66	278	14,400
Roger Maltbie	71	71	66	70	278	14,400
Donnie Hammond	67	73	71	67	278	14,400
Blaine McCallister	73	69	70	66	278	14,400
Gene Sauers	75	67	68	69	279	9,300
J.C. Snead	72	71	64	72	279	9,300
Bob Proben	78	65	68	68	279	9,300
Dan Forsman	72	72	67	68	279	9,300
Ian Baker-Finch	73	72	65	69	279	9,300
Rex Caldwell	72	71	69	67	279	9,300
Loren Roberts	72	71	69	68	280	6,720
Jodie Mudd	71	73	71	65	280	6,720
Chris Kite	71	69	70	70	280	6,720
Mark Wiebe	75	68	70	68	281	4,642.50
Mike Sullivan	72	68	71	70	281	4,642.50
Sam Randolph	71	73	66	71	281	4,642.50
Bobby Wadkins	71	69	72	69	281	4,642.50
Larry Rinker	68	72	65	76	281	4,642.50
Bill Britton	70	75	65	71	281	4,642.50
Tom Byrum	70	69	70	72	281	4,642.50
Keith Clearwater	72	71	70	68	281	4,642.50
Bill Sander	73	66	68	75	282	3,180
Joey Sindelar	70	69	71	72	282	3,180
David Ogrin	70	73	70	69	282	3,180
Nick Price	69	74	68	71	282	3,180
Curtis Strange	71	70	72	69	282	3,180
Brad Faxon	74	68	71	69	282	3,180
David Frost	67	70	70	75	282	3,180
John Adams	72	72	72	66	282	3,180
Robert Wrenn	76	68	71	68	283	2,460
Ed Fiori	72	71	71	69	283	2,460
Mark Brooks	71	67	73	72	283	2,460
Bruce Zabriski	73	72	72	67	284	1,872
Ray Stewart	69	73	72	70	284	1,872
Jim Gallagher Jr.	73	69	73	69	284	1,872

	SCORES				TOTAL	MONEY
Jim Nelford	75	69	71	69	284	1,872
Chip Beck	72	69	73	70	284	1,872
Mike Blackburn	73	71	69	71	284	1,872
Jay Don Blake	74	69	72	69	284	1,872
Lee Trevino	73	72	71	69	285	1,494
Grant Waite	72	72	73	68	285	1,494

B. C. Open

En Joie Golf Club, Endicott, New York
Par 37-34 — 71; 6,966 yards

September 22-25
purse, $500,000

	SCORES				TOTAL	MONEY
Bill Glasson	66	68	65	69	268	$90,000
Bruce Lietzke	68	71	67	64	270	44,000
Wayne Levi	66	71	66	67	270	44,000
Jeff Sluman	68	70	68	65	271	22,000
Don Pooley	67	66	70	68	271	22,000
Ken Green	66	70	72	65	273	16,750
Brad Bryant	68	68	67	70	273	16,750
Fred Couples	70	67	69	67	273	16,750
Joey Sindelar	67	65	70	72	274	12,500
Lance Ten Broeck	66	69	68	71	274	12,500
Kenny Perry	69	70	66	69	274	12,500
Kenny Knox	68	70	68	68	274	12,500
Ian Baker-Finch	69	68	67	70	274	12,500
Mike Sullivan	67	69	74	65	275	9,250
Steve Pate	68	72	68	67	275	9,250
Rick Pearson	71	67	71	67	276	8,000
Roger Maltbie	65	68	72	71	276	8,000
George Archer	68	71	70	67	276	8,000
Dave Rummells	65	70	70	72	277	6,275
Davis Love III	68	69	69	71	277	6,275
Bill Mayfair	67	71	72	67	277	6,275
Jay Haas	67	71	73	66	277	6,275
Mark Wiebe	66	71	71	70	278	3,925
Loren Roberts	73	67	68	70	278	3,925
Ron Streck	69	71	68	70	278	3,925
Bobby Wadkins	71	70	69	68	278	3,925
Pat McGowan	70	69	72	67	278	3,925
Mark Lye	69	68	70	71	278	3,925
Brian Mogg	70	65	71	72	278	3,925
Blaine McCallister	69	70	68	71	278	3,925
Mike Hammond	71	68	69	70	278	3,925
Billy Andrade	70	71	69	68	278	3,925
Howard Twitty	67	73	68	71	279	2,641.67
Corey Pavin	70	71	68	70	279	2,641.67
Andrew Magee	69	69	69	72	279	2,641.67
Danny Briggs	69	69	70	71	279	2,641.67
Steve Thomas	68	69	72	70	279	2,641.66
Rocco Mediate	69	66	72	72	279	2,641.66
Duffy Waldorf	68	69	72	71	280	2,000
Brad Faxon	73	68	69	70	280	2,000
Dick Mast	71	69	69	71	280	2,000
Mark Brooks	70	71	70	69	280	2,000
Bill Buttner	70	67	68	75	280	2,000
Bobby Clampett	70	66	74	70	280	2,000

	SCORES				TOTAL	MONEY
Richard Zokol	72	69	69	71	281	1,600
Mike Nicolette	68	71	71	71	281	1,600
Larry Rinker	67	71	71	73	282	1,301.67
Dan Halldorson	72	67	71	72	282	1,301.67
Rick Fehr	67	73	71	71	282	1,301,67
Ken Brown	70	69	71	72	282	1,301.67
Jim Simons	65	71	77	69	282	1,301.66
Ed Daugherty	65	67	77	73	282	1,301.66

Southern Open

Green Island Country Club, Columbus, Georgia
Par 35-35 — 70; 6,791 yards

September 29-October 2
purse, $400,000

	SCORES				TOTAL	MONEY
David Frost	70	68	65	67	270	$72,000
Bob Tway	71	66	66	67	270	43,200
(Frost defeated Tway on first hole of playoff.)						
Dan Forsman	67	66	69	69	271	20,800
George Archer	70	66	70	65	271	20,800
Dave Barr	72	68	61	70	271	20,800
Mike Hulbert	67	66	69	70	272	14,400
Lance Ten Broeck	68	65	69	71	273	12,050
Jeff Sluman	63	67	74	69	273	12,050
Corey Pavin	69	70	66	68	273	12,050
Mike Donald	67	70	71	65	273	12,050
Larry Mize	70	67	68	69	274	9,200
David Peoples	69	68	71	66	274	9,200
Russ Cochran	68	68	68	70	274	9,200
Leonard Thompson	69	63	71	72	275	6,400
Tim Simpson	70	72	67	66	275	6,400
Harry Taylor	69	69	68	69	275	6,400
Larry Rinker	68	70	68	69	275	6,400
Chris Perry	68	73	67	67	275	6,400
Mark Lye	71	71	65	68	275	6,400
Jim Booros	72	67	67	69	275	6,400
Robert Wrenn	70	66	72	68	276	3,653.34
Griffin Rudolph	68	73	68	67	276	3,653.34
Larry Nelson	70	67	70	69	276	3,653.34
Payne Stewart	73	65	68	70	276	3,653.33
Steve Lowery	68	67	69	72	276	3,653.33
Ed Fiori	68	70	68	70	276	3,653.33
Brad Fabel	67	71	65	73	276	3,653.33
Ray Barr, Jr.	70	70	67	69	276	3,653.33
Bobby Clampett	68	68	69	71	276	3,653.33
Ray Stewart	67	68	73	69	277	2,228
Gene Sauers	74	68	69	66	277	2,228
Kenny Knox	70	68	71	68	277	2,228
Johnny Miller	72	65	69	71	277	2,228
Gary Koch	66	69	70	72	277	2,228
Jim Gallagher Jr.	71	70	68	68	277	2,228
Gibby Gilbert	72	67	69	69	277	2,228
Hale Irwin	67	70	69	71	277	2,228
Bob Estes	71	64	70	72	277	2,228
Lennie Clements	73	66	71	67	277	2,228
Bill Sander	71	66	71	70	278	1,560
John Huston	70	66	70	72	278	1,560

	SCORES				TOTAL	MONEY
Mike Bender	73	68	69	68	278	1,560
Antonio Cerda	70	70	73	65	278	1,560
Andy Dillard	69	71	68	70	278	1,560
Larry Ziegler	69	72	70	68	279	1,121.15
Scott Hoch	73	68	70	68	279	1,121.15
Joey Sindelar	69	71	70	69	279	1,121.14
Blaine McCallister	72	68	68	71	279	1,121.14
Buddy Gardner	70	72	67	70	279	1,121.14
Jim Dent	71	68	70	70	279	1,121.14
Billy Ray Brown	71	67	71	70	279	1,121.14

Gatlin Brothers Southwest Classic

Fairways Oaks Golf and Racquet Club, Abilene, Texas
Par 36-36 — 72; 7,166 yards

October 6-9
purse, $400,000

	SCORES				TOTAL	MONEY
Tom Purtzer	64	72	69	64	269	$72,000
Mark Brooks	64	68	70	67	269	43,200
(Purtzer defeated Brooks on first hole of playoff.)						
Buddy Gardner	69	68	69	65	271	27,200
Dan Pohl	70	69	66	67	272	17,600
Brad Bryant	66	68	68	70	272	17,600
Mark O'Meara	71	70	68	64	273	12,950
Tommy Armour	71	70	64	68	273	12,950
Paul Azinger	66	70	69	68	273	12,950
Dave Barr	69	67	68	69	273	12,950
Howard Twitty	68	68	70	68	274	10,400
Davis Love III	73	65	70	66	274	10,400
Tim Norris	70	70	66	69	275	8,400
Kenny Knox	72	69	68	66	275	8,400
Ben Crenshaw	69	66	70	70	275	8,400
Steve Pate	70	72	68	66	276	6,800
George Archer	71	69	68	68	276	6,800
Bobby Clampett	64	72	72	68	276	6,800
Mark Calcavecchia	71	71	66	69	277	4,868.58
Bob Tway	72	68	69	68	277	4,868.57
Payne Stewart	71	70	67	69	277	4,868.57
Leonard Thompson	73	67	65	72	277	4,868.57
Barry Jaeckel	69	70	69	69	277	4,868.57
Jim Booros	68	69	70	70	277	4,868.57
Billy Ray Brown	69	68	71	69	277	4,868.57
David Peoples	67	75	69	67	278	2,988.58
D.A. Weibring	72	67	67	72	278	2,988.57
Sam Randolph	71	69	69	69	278	2,988.57
Hubert Green	67	69	71	71	278	2,988.57
Mike Hulbert	71	66	73	68	278	2,988.57
Billy Andrade	71	66	72	69	278	2,988.57
Brian Claar	68	67	71	72	278	2,988.57
Duffy Waldorf	70	70	69	70	279	2,264
Paul Trittler	71	67	67	74	279	2,264
Tom Pernice Jr.	70	70	71	68	279	2,264
Dan Forsman	73	68	69	69	279	2,264
Ken Brown	68	71	70	70	279	2,264
Bruce Zabriski	71	68	71	70	280	1,760
Gary Koch	70	71	67	72	280	1,760
Mike Blackburn	74	66	70	70	280	1,760

	SCORES				TOTAL	MONEY
Terrance Dill	70	69	71	70	280	1,760
David Edwards	70	68	72	70	280	1,760
Antonio Cerda	70	69	69	72	280	1,760
Harry Taylor	70	68	72	71	281	1,360
Clarence Rose	67	72	72	70	281	1,360
John Adams	72	64	72	73	281	1,360
Barry Cheesman	69	69	71	72	281	1,360
Robert Thompson	72	70	70	70	282	1,027.43
Greg Powers	67	73	72	70	282	1,027.43
Jim Nelford	69	70	73	70	282	1,027.43
Jim Gallagher Jr.	68	70	71	73	282	1,027.43
Clark Dennis	69	67	72	74	282	1,027.43
Steve Elkington	70	72	70	70	282	1,027.43
Keith Clearwater	66	69	74	73	282	1,027.42

Texas Open Presented By Nabisco

Oak Hills Country Club, San Antonio, Texas
Par 35-35 — 70; 6,576 yards

October 13-16
purse, $500,000

	SCORES				TOTAL	MONEY
Corey Pavin	64	63	66	66	259	$108,000
Robert Wrenn	69	68	68	62	267	64,800
Pat McGowan	68	68	67	65	268	40,800
Tom Kite	67	64	69	69	269	28,800
Bobby Wadkins	64	71	69	66	270	20,340
Mike Sullivan	63	67	77	63	270	20,340
Payne Stewart	69	65	68	68	270	20,340
Tom Pernice Jr.	65	66	67	72	270	20,340
Roger Maltbie	68	67	68	67	270	20,340
Don Pooley	67	69	69	66	271	14,400
Jodie Mudd	68	66	70	67	271	14,400
Ben Crenshaw	67	65	69	70	271	14,400
Jay Haas	66	65	73	67	271	14,400
Gary McCord	72	66	67	67	272	10,500
Brad Faxon	70	68	68	66	272	10,500
Russ Cochran	66	70	68	68	272	10,500
Steve Elkington	68	70	68	66	272	10,500
Scott Verplank	69	67	72	65	273	7,824
Duffy Waldorf	65	69	72	67	273	7,824
Jeff Sluman	68	69	73	63	273	7,824
Bob Lohr	68	69	70	66	273	7,824
Hubert Green	66	71	67	69	273	7,824
Willie Wood	68	68	72	66	274	5,190
Hale Irwin	68	69	71	66	274	5,190
Loren Roberts	70	67	68	69	274	5,190
David Ogrin	71	66	71	66	274	5,190
Blaine McCallister	66	68	71	69	274	5,190
Ed Fiori	69	63	77	65	274	5,190
Hal Sutton	69	69	69	68	275	3,732.86
Tom Watson	66	70	72	67	275	3,732.86
Andrew Magee	69	70	70	66	275	3,832.86
John Cook	66	67	73	69	275	3,732.86
Mike Hulbert	69	70	68	68	275	3,732.86
Bruce Zabriski	66	72	68	69	275	3,732.85
David Canipe	69	65	71	70	275	3,732.85
Lanny Wadkins	71	66	71	68	276	3,015

	SCORES				TOTAL	MONEY
Sam Randolph	68	69	69	70	276	3,015
Steve Pate	68	71	70	68	277	2,580
John Huston	69	69	69	70	277	2,580
David Frost	65	68	70	74	277	2,580
Bill Buttner	67	72	69	69	277	2,580
Antonio Cerda	68	69	74	66	277	2,580
Bruce Soulsby	69	70	70	69	278	1,722.55
Aki Ohmachi	68	68	72	70	278	1,722.55
Tom Sieckmann	67	67	76	68	278	1,722.55
John Mahaffey	66	68	77	67	278	1,722.55
Billy Ray Brown	66	71	71	70	278	1,722.55
Bobby Clampett	69	67	75	67	278	1,722.55
Greg Ladehoff	65	72	71	70	278	1,722.54
Rick Pearson	66	66	75	71	278	1,722.54
Dave Rummells	69	70	66	73	278	1,722.54
Bob Murphy	69	70	69	70	278	1,722.54
Jay Delsing	68	69	67	74	278	1,722.54

Pensacola Open

Tiger Point Golf Club, Gulf Breeze, Florida
Par 36-36 — 72; 7,033 yards

October 20-23
purse, $400,000

	SCORES				TOTAL	MONEY
Andrew Magee	70	68	67	66	271	$72,000
Ken Green	68	68	69	67	272	29,866.67
Tom Byrum	72	64	65	71	272	29,866.67
Bruce Lietzke	71	67	67	67	272	29,866.66
Dan Pohl	66	71	70	67	274	16,000
Bobby Wadkins	70	68	68	69	275	13,900
James Hallet	72	70	68	65	275	13,900
Ray Stewart	71	66	68	71	276	12,400
Dave Rummells	70	70	69	68	277	9,600
Scott Hoch	68	67	74	68	277	9,600
Mike McCullough	68	72	70	67	277	9,600
Billy Andrade	66	73	69	69	277	9,600
Jay Don Blake	72	68	69	68	277	9,600
Lennie Clements	69	71	69	68	277	9,600
Gene Sauers	68	75	70	65	278	6,200
Loren Roberts	68	70	73	67	278	6,200
Kenny Perry	66	72	70	70	278	6,200
Kenny Knox	70	68	74	66	278	6,200
Ray Barr, Jr.	69	70	68	71	278	6,200
John Cook	67	68	71	72	278	6,200
Hal Sutton	67	71	70	71	279	3,755
Mark Wiebe	69	71	71	68	279	3,755
Rick Pearson	70	70	68	71	279	3,755
Robert Wrenn	67	71	69	72	279	3,755
Howard Twitty	69	68	74	68	279	3,755
Mark Hayes	66	69	73	71	279	3,755
John Mahaffey	72	69	70	68	279	3,755
Fred Couples	70	68	72	69	279	3,755
Ron Streck	69	72	70	69	280	2,435
Tony Sills	68	71	67	74	280	2,435
Dick Mast	70	69	69	72	280	2,435
Rocco Mediate	69	72	74	65	280	2,435
Donnie Hammond	71	71	70	68	280	2,435

	SCORES				TOTAL	MONEY
Buddy Gardner	72	68	70	70	280	2,435
Jodie Mudd	71	69	69	71	280	2,435
Jim Benepe	72	68	70	70	280	2,435
Tim Norris	71	69	74	67	281	1,760
Dave Eichelberger	69	69	74	69	281	1,760
Bob Lohr	72	70	68	71	281	1,760
John Huston	70	74	68	69	281	1,760
Brad Fabel	70	72	71	68	281	1,760
Barry Cheesman	68	71	71	71	281	1,760
Joey Rassett	72	71	70	69	282	1,320
Dan Halldorson	67	72	73	70	282	1,320
Mike Nicolette	75	67	71	69	282	1,320
Bill Britton	69	71	72	70	282	1,320
Curt Byrum	67	69	71	75	282	1,320
Bruce Soulsby	75	68	72	68	283	1,032
Steve Jones	69	75	72	67	283	1,032
Bob Gilder	69	75	70	69	283	1,032
Mike Donald	72	71	70	70	283	1,032

Walt Disney World/Oldsmobile Classic

Walt Disney World, Lake Buena Vista, Florida
Magnolia Course: Par 36-36 — 72; 7,190 yards
Palm Course: Par 36-36 — 72; 6,967 yards
Lake Buena Vista Course: Par 36-36 — 72; 6,706 yards

October 27-30
purse, $700,000

	SCORES				TOTAL	MONEY
Bob Lohr	62	67	66	68	263	$126,000
Chip Beck	66	68	63	66	263	75,600
(Lohr defeated Beck on fifth hole of playoff.)						
Fuzzy Zoeller	64	69	66	70	269	40,600
Bruce Lietzke	69	67	65	68	269	40,600
Dan Pohl	68	68	68	66	270	25,550
Paul Azinger	67	68	62	73	270	25,550
Mike Donald	68	67	70	65	270	25,550
Robert Wrenn	66	66	71	68	271	19,600
Gene Sauers	69	67	67	68	271	19,600
Mark Wiebe	69	67	68	67	271	19,600
Larry Nelson	72	63	67	69	271	19,600
Tom Kite	66	68	66	72	272	15,400
Ken Green	70	64	68	70	272	15,400
Mark O'Meara	69	68	65	71	273	12,250
Morris Hatalsky	71	67	69	66	273	12,250
Mark Calcavecchia	65	71	68	69	273	12,250
David Canipe	68	67	69	69	273	12,250
Bobby Wadkins	70	68	66	70	274	9,128
Rick Pearson	66	68	71	69	274	9,128
John Mahaffey	68	69	66	71	274	9,128
Tim Norris	68	68	70	68	274	9,128
Steve Elkington	71	65	68	70	274	9,128
Tom Purtzer	69	67	69	70	275	5,900
Hal Sutton	74	68	66	67	275	5,900
Donnie Hammond	67	68	74	66	275	5,900
David Peoples	68	69	67	71	275	5,900
Dan Halldorson	68	68	68	71	275	5,900
Hubert Green	70	70	67	68	275	5,900
David Edwards	66	69	71	69	275	5,900

	SCORES				TOTAL	MONEY
Brett Upper	68	71	67	70	276	4,347.20
Dave Rummells	70	70	66	70	276	4,347.20
Davis Love III	70	69	67	70	276	4,347.20
Larry Mize	75	66	64	71	276	4,347.20
Wayne Levi	70	68	66	72	276	4,347.20
Payne Stewart	69	69	72	67	277	3,161.56
Brad Fabel	70	72	67	68	277	3,161.56
Russ Cochran	67	70	70	70	277	3,161.56
Buddy Gardner	72	68	66	71	277	3,161.56
Dave Eichelberger	74	67	67	69	277	3,161.56
Tim Simpson	68	70	65	74	277	3,161.55
Mark McCumber	65	72	72	68	277	3,161.55
Gil Morgan	68	66	72	71	277	3,161.55
Steve Pate	71	70	66	70	277	3,161.55
Lance Ten Broeck	70	69	69	70	278	1,895.84
Mike McCullough	69	68	67	74	278	1,895.84
Corey Pavin	73	66	66	73	278	1,895.84
Dan Forsman	69	71	67	71	278	1,895.84
Joey Sindelar	71	74	66	67	278	1,895.83
Robert Thompson	69	68	70	71	278	1,895.83
Bob Tway	68	70	69	71	278	1,895.83
Howard Twitty	70	69	70	69	278	1,895.83
Jodie Mudd	74	68	68	68	278	1,895.83
Ed Fiori	71	71	68	68	278	1,895.83
Ernie Gonzalez	70	70	68	70	278	1,895.83
Fred Couples	68	69	72	69	278	1,895.83

Northern Telecom Tucson Open

TPC at Starpass, Tucson, Arizona
Par 36-36 — 72; 7,010 yards

November 3-6
purse, $600,000

	SCORES				TOTAL	MONEY
David Frost	66	66	67	67	266	$108,000
Mark O'Meara	67	69	65	70	271	52,800
Mark Calcavecchia	66	73	63	69	271	52,800
Mark Wiebe	73	65	61	73	272	26,400
Ken Green	71	66	67	68	272	26,400
Andrew Magee	68	73	67	65	273	21,600
D.A. Weibring	68	69	67	70	274	17,460
Don Pooley	70	65	68	71	274	17,460
Tom Kite	68	73	67	66	274	17,460
Curt Byrum	68	68	65	73	274	17,460
Jim Carter	71	68	64	71	274	17,460
Corey Pavin	66	70	68	71	275	12,600
Payne Stewart	66	73	70	66	275	12,600
James Hallet	68	74	67	66	275	12,600
Bob Tway	71	67	68	70	276	10,200
Howard Twitty	71	65	70	70	276	10,200
Russ Cochran	65	65	71	75	276	10,200
Hale Irwin	69	65	69	74	277	7,824
Tommy Armour	71	70	67	69	277	7,824
Fred Couples	69	68	70	70	277	7,824
Mark Brooks	72	69	69	67	277	7,824
John Cook	67	68	73	69	277	7,824
Curtis Strange	68	68	69	73	278	5,760
Chip Beck	71	68	69	70	278	5,760

	SCORES				TOTAL	MONEY
Bill Britton	71	69	67	71	278	5,760
Blaine McCallister	69	72	70	68	279	4,620
Peter Jacobsen	68	75	68	68	279	4,620
Ronnie Black	73	70	66	70	279	4,620
Robert Wrenn	70	66	71	73	280	3,990
Ray Stewart	72	71	64	73	280	3,990
Donnie Hammond	69	71	72	68	280	3,990
Wayne Levi	67	71	74	68	280	3,990
Richard Zokol	72	68	71	70	281	3,315
Dan Halldorson	67	73	66	75	281	3,315
Steve Jones	71	71	65	74	281	3,315
Mike Donald	72	69	69	71	281	3,315
Tom Sieckmann	72	71	68	71	282	2,820
Steve Lowery	72	66	73	71	282	2,820
Homero Blancas	68	71	70	73	282	2,820
Fuzzy Zoeller	69	69	70	75	283	2,280
Mike Reid	69	70	70	74	283	2,280
Chris Perry	69	71	68	75	283	2,280
Ron Streck	69	70	70	74	283	2,280
Paul Trittler	70	69	74	70	283	2,280
JIm Gallagher, Jr.	69	70	71	73	283	2,280
Greg Powers	70	73	69	72	284	1,663.20
Mike Hulbert	68	72	70	74	284	1,663.20
John Adams	69	71	70	74	284	1,663.20
Bob Eastwood	74	70	69	71	284	1,663.20
Jim Booros	71	73	69	71	284	1,663.20
*Robert Gamez	71	72	71	70	284	

Nabisco Championship

Pebble Beach Golf Links, Pebble Beach, California
Par 36-36 — 72; 6,799 yards

November 10-13
purse, $2,000,000

	SCORES				TOTAL	MONEY
Curtis Strange	64	71	70	74	279	$360,000
Tom Kite	72	65	70	72	279	216,000
(Strange defeated Kite on second hole of playoff.)						
Mark Calcavecchia	70	71	65	74	280	104,666.67
Payne Stewart	73	70	64	73	280	104,666.67
Ken Green	67	70	69	74	280	104,666.66
Peter Jacobsen	71	70	67	73	281	72,000
Fred Couples	75	67	67	73	282	68,000
Gary Koch	71	72	68	74	285	55,800
Bruce Lietzke	69	68	70	78	285	55,800
Jodie Mudd	70	71	68	76	285	55,800
Mike Reid	72	72	68	73	285	55,800
Bob Tway	69	70	71	75	285	55,800
Scott Verplank	69	70	72	74	285	55,800
Mark McCumber	73	70	70	73	286	44,266.67
Lanny Wadkins	72	70	67	77	286	44,266.67
Jay Haas	69	71	70	76	286	44,266.66
Paul Azinger	73	70	69	75	287	39,600
David Frost	69	71	70	77	287	39,600
Sandy Lyle	72	71	68	76	287	39,600
Steve Pate	70	72	69	76	287	39,600
Ben Crenshaw	72	71	69	76	288	37,200
Joey Sindelar	68	73	67	80	288	37,200

	SCORES				TOTAL	MONEY
Dan Pohl	72	69	71	78	290	36,000
Chip Beck	71	69	73	79	292	34,800
Mark Wiebe	76	64	74	78	292	34,800
Larry Nelson	75	69	73	76	293	33,400
Jeff Sluman	72	75	71	75	293	33,400
Scott Hoch	70	76	70	78	294	32,800
Mark O'Meara	70	73	77	79	299	32,400
Greg Norman	75	76	74	79	304	32,000

Centel Classic

Killearn Golf and Country Club, Tallahassee, Florida
Par 36-36 — 72; 7,124 yards

November 10-13
purse, $500,000

	SCORES				TOTAL	MONEY
Bill Glasson	67	69	68	68	272	$90,000
Tommy Armour	70	71	65	68	274	54,000
Bob Lohr	69	67	68	71	275	29,000
Chris Perry	67	71	66	71	275	29,000
Kenny Perry	69	66	69	72	276	18,250
Mike Donald	70	66	70	70	276	18,250
Buddy Gardner	68	69	70	69	276	18,250
Jay Overton	68	70	73	66	277	14,500
Bernhard Langer	66	70	71	70	277	14,500
George Archer	68	69	70	70	277	14,500
Kenny Knox	67	71	69	71	278	12,500
Dick Mast	69	69	67	74	279	9,800
Rocco Mediate	67	71	74	67	279	9,800
Brad Faxon	69	71	68	71	279	9,800
Dan Halldorson	71	68	69	71	279	9,800
Tom Byrum	68	70	70	71	279	9,800
Loren Roberts	67	71	70	72	280	7,000
John Mahaffey	68	72	69	71	280	7,000
Bill Sander	68	67	74	71	280	7,000
Beau Baugh	66	75	71	68	280	7,000
Bill Britton	73	67	71	69	280	7,000
Bob Gilder	73	71	67	70	281	5,000
David Canipe	68	74	70	69	281	5,000
Barry Cheesman	73	66	69	73	281	5,000
Brian Claar	71	71	68	71	281	5,000
Larry Ziegler	69	70	71	72	282	3,700
Ron Steck	70	68	72	72	282	3,700
John Huston	72	66	72	72	282	3,700
Antonio Cerda	69	71	73	69	282	3,700
Brad Fabel	68	70	73	71	282	3,700
Robert Thompson	69	74	70	70	283	3,031.25
Leonard Thompson	73	71	67	72	283	3,031.25
Mark Pfeil	72	70	67	74	283	3,031.25
David Edwards	70	73	70	70	283	3,031.25
Lance Ten Broeck	65	76	69	74	284	2,309.38
Jim Gallagher, Jr.	70	70	72	72	284	2,309.38
Dan Forsman	73	70	70	71	284	2,309.38
Brad Bryant	72	72	69	71	284	2,309.38
Tony Sills	72	68	76	68	284	2,309.37
Danny Briggs	69	71	69	75	284	2,309.37
Lennie Clements	69	71	69	75	284	2,309.37
Richard Cromwell	69	69	70	76	284	2,309.37

	SCORES				TOTAL	MONEY
Mark Gurnow	70	73	69	73	285	1,603.34
Bob Eastwood	70	70	72	73	285	1,603.34
Mike Smith	71	73	70	71	285	1,603.33
Ernie Gonzalez	76	68	69	72	285	1,603.33
Clark Burroughs	71	73	72	69	285	1,603.33
Brandel Chamblee	69	72	74	70	285	1,603.33
Victor Regalado	72	70	71	73	286	1,247.50
Bill Mayfair	73	71	75	67	286	1,247.50
Phil Blackmar	67	76	73	70	286	1,247.50
Jim Booros	69	71	72	74	286	1,247.50

Isuzu Kapalua International

Kapalua Golf Club, Bay Course, Kapalua, Maui, Hawaii
Par 36-36 — 72; 6,879 yards

November 23-26
purse, $600,000

	SCORES				TOTAL	MONEY
Bob Gilder	65	64	71	66	266	$150,000
John Mahaffey	65	64	73	66	268	84,000
Corey Pavin	67	67	67	71	272	53,000
Mark O'Meara	67	69	69	68	273	34,000
Steve Pate	69	67	69	68	273	34,000
Ben Crenshaw	68	69	70	68	275	23,000
Joey Sindelar	69	71	68	68	276	15,666.67
Jodie Mudd	70	65	71	70	276	15,666.67
Jim Carter	68	71	66	71	276	15,666.66
Mac O'Grady	66	70	71	70	277	12,000
Dave Barr	70	69	72	67	278	8,138.89
Don Pooley	67	74	68	69	278	8,138.89
James Hallet	68	72	69	69	278	8,138.89
Hale Irwin	66	72	72	68	278	8,138.89
Dave Rummells	69	67	70	72	278	8,138.89
Steve Jones	69	68	73	68	278	8,138.89
Bob Lohr	69	67	73	69	278	8,138.89
Blaine McCallister	69	73	68	68	278	8,138.89
Bill Glasson	64	69	69	76	278	8,138.88
Mark Brooks	70	72	70	68	280	6,125
Lennie Clements	71	70	72	67	280	6,125
Mark Calcavecchia	73	64	75	69	281	5,500
Donnie Hammond	70	70	69	72	281	5,500
Morris Hatalsky	70	75	67	69	281	5,500
Peter Jacobsen	68	73	69	72	282	4,375
Billy Andrade	72	71	69	70	282	4,375
Jim Benepe	69	76	65	72	282	4,375
Curt Byrum	70	73	71	68	282	4,375
Anders Forsbrand	70	70	75	67	282	4,375
Tom Sieckmann	72	72	71	67	282	4,375
Ed Fiori	73	71	72	67	283	3,500
Roger Maltbie	70	70	71	73	284	3,125
Gary McCord	73	71	67	73	284	3,125
Bobby Clampett	71	73	73	68	285	2,550
Lee Trevino	70	71	75	69	285	2,550
Greg Meyer	71	70	71	73	285	2,550
Tom Purtzer	70	71	73	72	286	2,300
Andy Bean	71	69	74	72	286	2,300
Calvin Peete	72	70	74	70	286	2,300
Kenny Knox	67	71	75	74	287	2,200

	SCORES				TOTAL	MONEY
Bruce Lietzke	70	74	72	72	288	2,150
Keith Clearwater	70	73	75	74	292	2,050
John Cook	72	67	78	75	292	2,050
Mark Rolfing	74	73	79	72	298	2,000

J. C. Penney Classic

Bardmoor Country Club, Largo, Florida   December 1-4
Par 36-36 — 72; 6,882 yards — men   purse, $800,000
6,434 yards — women

	SCORES				TOTAL	MONEY (Each)
John Huston/Amy Benz	69	68	65	67	269	$80,000
Larry Mize/Martha Nause	66	68	67	70	271	50,000
Scott Hoch/Beth Daniel	67	69	67	69	272	26,000
Rocco Mediate/Missie Berteotti	71	69	67	65	272	26,000
Mark Brooks/Heather Farr	69	68	66	70	273	14,083.34
Buddy Gardner/Debbie Massey	68	73	65	67	273	14,083.33
Roger Maltbie/Joanne Carner	68	71	71	63	273	14,083.33
Mike Sullivan/Sally Little	68	66	68	72	274	9,100
Jay Haas/Patty Sheehan	65	69	72	68	274	9,100
Mike Hulbert/Lori Garbacz	71	65	65	73	274	9,100
Kenny Knox/Jan Stephenson	70	70	66	68	274	9,100
Dick Mast/Lynn Adams	69	71	66	68	274	9,100
David Canipe/Cathy Morse	70	72	65	68	275	6,325
Brad Faxon/Jody Rosenthal	67	67	72	69	275	6,325
Larry Rinker/Laurie Rinker	66	71	68	70	275	6,325
John Mahaffey/Chris Johnson	67	69	67	72	275	6,325
Dave Eichelberger/Sandra Palmer	70	72	66	68	276	5,300
Gary Hallberg/Vicki Fergon	70	69	70	67	276	5,300
Donnie Hammond/Tammie Green	70	68	69	69	276	5,300
Morris Hatalsky/Donna White	68	64	71	73	276	5,300
Jim Carter/Danille Ammaccapanne	72	67	67	71	277	4,700
Clarence Rose/Shirley Furlong	70	66	73	68	277	4,700
Calvin Peete/Liselotte Neumann	69	73	72	64	278	4,000
Robert Wrenn/Rosie Jones	70	71	68	69	278	4,000
Steve Jones/Jane Crafter	67	72	70	69	278	4,000
Gary Koch/Deb Richard	70	66	70	72	278	4,000
D.A. Weibring/Colleen Walker	71	68	67	72	278	4,000
Bill Glasson/Nancy Brown	71	68	68	72	279	3,233.34
Gene Sauers/Judy Dickinson	72	68	70	69	279	3,233.33
J.C. Snead/Kathy Postlewaite	69	71	70	69	279	3,233.33
Brad Fabel/Marta Figueras-Dotti	75	68	69	68	280	3,000
Tom Byrum/Laura Davies	69	71	69	72	281	2,850
Mike Donald/Margaret Ward	75	69	67	70	281	2,850
Keith Clearwater/Cindy Rarick	69	70	70	73	282	2,700
Jim Dent/Jerilyn Britz	72	67	72	72	283	2,500
Dan Forsman/Dottie Mochrie	69	72	71	71	283	2,500
Brian Tennyson/Marci Bozarth	69	72	70	72	283	2,500
Bobby Clampett/Kathy Baker-Guadagnino	72	71	67	74	284	2,162.50
Russ Cochran/Myra Blackwelder	71	73	74	66	284	2,162.50
Richard Zokol/Kathy Whitworth	74	65	71	74	284	2,162.50
Wayne Levi/Dale Eggeling	71	71	72	70	284	2,162.50
James Hallet/Sally Quinlan	74	69	69	73	285	1,975
Tom Purtzer/Juli Inkster	73	75	70	67	285	1,975

	SCORES				TOTAL	MONEY
Blaine McCallister/Sherri Turner	72	72	73	68	285	1,975
Jay Don Blake/Connie Chillemi	75	68	73	70	286	1,925
Kenny Perry/Jo Myers	74	73	71	70	288	1,900
Tommy Armour/Missie McGeorge	73	74	70	72	289	1,850
Bill Britton/Cathy Marino	71	72	73	73	289	1,850
David Ogrin/Robin Walton	72	76	70	71	289	1,850
Dave Stockton/Donna Caponi	72	73	74	72	291	1,800

Chrysler Team Championship

Palm Beach Polo and Country Club   December 8-11
Cypress course: Par 36-36 — 72; 7,080 yards   purse, $600,000
Wellington course: Par 36-36 — 72; 6,850 yards
Dunes course: Par 36-36 — 72; 7,050 yards

West Palm Beach Florida

	SCORES				TOTAL	MONEY (Each)
George Burns/Wayne Levi	63	67	63	59	252	$50,000
Mike Hulbert/Bob Tway	61	64	64	63	252	28,500
(Burns/Levi defeated Hulbert/Tway on first hole of playoff.)						
Jim Rutledge/Mike Smith	64	60	62	67	253	17,500
Clarence Rose/Tim Simpson	64	65	64	62	255	10,666.67
Mark Brooks/Doug Higgins	64	62	66	63	255	10,666.67
Bobby Clampett/Bill Glasson	60	63	64	68	255	10,666.66
Paul Azinger/Andy Bean	64	66	62	64	256	8,600
John Adams/Bill Sander	65	67	61	64	257	7,250
Gary Hallberg/Scott Hoch	63	64	64	66	257	7,250
Dan Pohl/Greg Powers	65	67	58	67	257	7,250
Jim Hallet/Brian Tennyson	63	62	64	68	257	7,250
Billy Andrade/Robert Wrenn	65	65	64	64	258	4,857.15
Jim Gallagher/Mark Pfeil	64	66	62	66	258	4,857.15
Brad Faxon/Denny Hepler	61	68	65	64	258	4,857.14
Bob Lohr/Chris Perry	66	67	62	63	258	4,857.14
Mark Hayes/Mike Sullivan	61	65	64	68	258	4,857.14
Jay Don Blake/Don Shirey	66	63	61	68	258	4,857.14
Jim Carter/Rocco Mediate	63	65	67	63	258	4,857.14
Clark Burroughs/Lance Ten Broeck	61	65	67	66	259	3,625
Curt Byrum/Tom Byrum	66	65	63	65	259	3,625
John Huston/Gene Sauers	64	65	61	70	260	3,250
Greg Ladehoff/Dave Rummells	64	64	66	67	261	2,750
Buddy Gardner/Roger Maltbie	61	68	65	67	261	2,750
Charlie Epps/Blaine McCallister	64	64	62	71	261	2,750
Billy Ray Brown/Robert Thompson	65	69	61	67	262	2,250
Dan Halldorson/Denis Watson	65	67	62	69	263	1,800
Brad Bryant/Ernie Gonzalez	66	64	65	68	263	1,800
Bobby Nichols/Craig Nichols	66	65	64	68	263	1,800
Dick Mast/David Peoples	66	66	63	70	265	1,400

Kirin Cup World Championship of Golf

Kapalua Resort, Kapalua, Maui, Hawaii   December 14-17
Par 36-36 — 72; 6,761 yards   purse, $1,000,000

WEDNESDAY

EUROPE defeated JAPAN, 9—3.
Ronan Rafferty (Europe) and Isao Aoki (Japan) tied, 69—69.
Gordon Brand Jr. (Europe) defeated Yoshimi Niizeki, 72—74.
Nobuo Serizawa (Japan) defeated Mark Mouland, 71—78.
Anders Forsbrand (Europe) defeated Hiroshi Makino, 73—77.
Jose Rivero (Europe) defeated Masahiro Kuramoto, 69—70.
Mark James (Europe) defeated Tsuneyuki Nakajima, 70—74.

UNITED STATES defeated AUSTRALIA/NEW ZEALAND, 10—2.
Joey Sindelar (U.S.) defeated Peter Senior, 69—71.
Chip Beck (U.S.) defeated Brian Jones, 66—71.
Mike Reid (U.S.) defeated Craig Parry, 69—70.
Steve Pate (U.S.) defeated Graham Marsh, 68—72.
Ben Crenshaw (U.S.) defeated Ian Baker-Finch, 66—70.
Rodger Davis (A/NZ) defeated Curtis Strange, 67—68.

THURSDAY

JAPAN defeated AUSTRALIA/NEW ZEALAND, 7—5.
Senior (A/NZ) defeated Nakajima, 67—69.
Makino (Japan) and Marsh (A/NZ) tied, 72—72.
Parry (A/NZ) defeated Niizeki, 71—73.
Serizawa (Japan) defeated Jones, 74—76.
Kuramoto (Japan) defeated Baker-Finch, 67—71.
Aoki (Japan) defeated Davis, 70—72.

UNITED STATES defeated EUROPE, 10—2.
Beck (U.S.) and Rafferty (Europe) tied, 66—66.
Sindelar (U.S.) defeated James, 67—69.
Pate (U.S.) defeated Brand, 64—74.
Reid (U.S.) defeated Rivero, 65—72.
Crenshaw (U.S.) and Forsbrand (Europe) tied, 68—68.
Strange (U.S.) defeated Mouland, 68—73.

FRIDAY

AUSTRALIA/NEW ZEALAND defeated EUROPE, 7—5.
Mouland (Europe) defeated Davis, 69—70.
Rafferty (Europe) defeated Baker-Finch, 70—72.
Jones (A/NZ) defeated Brand, 69—70.
Forsbrand (Europe) and Marsh (A/NZ) tied, 71—71.
Parry (A/NZ) defeated James, 69—75.
Senior (A/NZ) defeated Rivero, 69—72.

UNITED STATES defeated JAPAN, 9—3.
Strange (U.S.) and Nakajima (Japan) tied, 69—69.
Crenshaw (U.S.) defeated Niizeki, 67—75.
Reid (U.S.) defeated Serizawa, 71—72.
Makino (Japan) defeated Pate, 70—73.
Beck (U.S.) defeated Kuramoto, 69—71.
Sindelar (U.S.) defeated Aoki, 68—70.

   THREE-ROUND RESULTS: United States 29, Europe 16, Australia/New Zealand 14, Japan 13.

SATURDAY

PLAYOFF FOR THIRD-FOURTH PLACE

AUSTRALIA/NEW ZEALAND defeated JAPAN, 8—4.
Nakajima (Japan) defeated Davis, 69—71.
Baker-Finch (A/NZ) defeated Niizeki, 71—74.
Jones (A/NZ) defeated Serizawa, 74—75.
Marsh (A/NZ) defeated Makino, 70—72.
Kuramoto (Japan) defeated Parry, 67—73.
Senior (A/NZ) defeated Aoki, 68—77.

FINALS

UNITED STATES defeated EUROPE, 8—4.
Strange (U.S.) defeated Mouland, 70—71.
Sindelar (U.S.) defeated Rafferty, 68—70.
Rivero (Europe) defeated Reid, 72—76.
Forsbrand (Europe) defeated Pate, 70—71.
Crenshaw (U.S.) defeated Brand, 70—71.
Beck (U.S.) defeated James, 69—73.

   PRIZE MONEY: Each U.S. player received $60,000; European $35,000; Australian/New Zealander $30,000; Japanese $25,000.

The U.S. Senior Tour

MONY Senior Tournament of Champions

LaCosta Country Club, Carlsbad, California   January 14-17
Par 36-36 — 72; 6,815 yards   purse, $100,000

Fourth round cancelled, rain

	SCORES			TOTAL	MONEY
Dave Hill	68	72	71	211	$30,000
Miller Barber	69	72	71	212	14,000
Al Geiberger	73	69	70	212	14,000
Bob Charles	73	71	70	214	8,000
Orville Moody	69	73	72	214	8,000
Bruce Crampton	74	69	72	215	5,500
Larry Mowry	76	68	74	218	4,500
Billy Casper	68	75	76	219	4,000
Don January	73	74	74	221	3,000
Gene Littler	76	71	77	224	3,000
Gary Player	77	71	76	224	3,000
Chi Chi Rodriguez	74	77	73	224	3,000

First National Bank Seniors Classic

Houghton Golf Club, Johannesburg, South Africa
Par 37-35 — 72; 7,320 yards

February 5-7
purse, R300,000

	SCORES			TOTAL	MONEY
Bob Charles	70	71	65	206	R90,000
Bruce Devlin	66	70	71	209	47,000
Bruce Crampton	72	71	70	213	27,500
Harold Henning	70	71	72	213	27,500
Orville Moody	69	73	72	214	22,000
Billy Casper	75	73	68	216	19,000
Butch Baird	72	69	75	216	19,000
Peter Thomson	74	70	76	220	17,000
Doug Sanders	79	73	69	221	16,000
Denis Hutchinson	78	74	74	226	15,000

General Foods PGA Seniors Championship

PGA National Golf Club, Palm Beach Gardens, Florida
Par 36-36 — 72; 6,530 yards

February 11-14
purse, $350,000

	SCORES				TOTAL	MONEY
Gary Player	69	73	72	70	284	$63,000
Chi Chi Rodriguez	70	72	71	74	287	37,800
Miller Barber	73	75	70	70	288	20,300
Al Geiberger	69	71	73	75	288	20,300
Arnold Palmer	72	69	76	72	289	13,300
Orville Moody	69	71	74	75	289	13,300
Bruce Devlin	73	72	69	77	291	11,287.50
Harold Henning	69	75	78	69	291	11,287.50
Walter Zembriski	73	71	74	74	292	9,800
Larry Mowry	69	76	74	73	292	9,800
Bob Charles	67	73	78	78	293	8,400
Bruce Crampton	74	73	74	72	293	8,400
Tommy Aaron	69	73	75	78	295	7,000
Lee Elder	70	76	74	75	295	7,000
Art Silvestrone	76	71	74	75	296	6,125
Al Chandler	72	75	76	73	296	6,125
Bill Collins	74	71	79	74	298	5,425
Charles Coody	72	76	72	78	298	5,425
Gene Borek	74	74	72	79	299	4,550
Gay Brewer	71	77	75	76	299	4,550
Tony Morosco	76	75	74	74	299	4,550
Roland Stafford	73	73	76	78	300	3,360
Jim King	72	75	75	78	300	3,360
Joe Lopez	77	73	76	74	300	3,360
Don Massengale	72	75	76	77	300	3,360
Jay Hyon	77	73	74	76	300	3,360
Joe Jimenez	71	80	72	78	301	2,485
George Lanning	69	79	75	78	301	2,485
Bob Brue	73	78	72	78	301	2,485
El Collins	72	72	83	74	301	2,485
Mike Fetchick	75	73	76	77	301	2,485
Art Wall	74	76	81	71	302	2,071.67
Ken Still	72	80	76	74	302	2,071.67
Bobby Nichols	73	77	76	76	302	2,071.66
Howie Johnson	74	77	80	72	303	1,803.34

	SCORES				TOTAL	MONEY
Mike Souchak	79	74	76	74	303	1,803.33
Dale Douglass	76	73	75	79	303	1,803.33
Gordon Waldespuhl	76	76	77	75	304	1,575
Robert Boldt	75	77	74	78	304	1,575
Billy Maxwell	75	75	76	78	304	1,575

GTE Suncoast Classic

Tampa Palms Country Club, Tampa, Florida　　　　　February 18-21
Par 36-36 — 72; 6,631 yards　　　　　purse, $300,000

	SCORES			TOTAL	MONEY
Dale Douglass	67	69	74	210	$45,000
Orville Moody	69	76	67	212	26,000
Gary Player	70	71	72	213	21,500
Bob Charles	72	69	73	214	13,400
Al Geiberger	73	70	71	214	13,400
Don Massengale	69	75	70	214	13,400
Doug Dalziel	75	69	70	214	13,400
Bob Erickson	74	70	72	216	9,250
Larry Mowry	72	73	72	217	7,245
Charles Coody	71	73	73	217	7,245
Don Bies	72	73	72	217	7,245
George Lanning	71	75	71	217	7,245
Bob Brue	72	68	77	217	7,245
Fred Hawkins	71	77	71	219	5,200
Arnold Palmer	70	71	78	219	5,200
Tommy Aaron	73	75	71	219	5,200
Dave Hill	71	76	72	219	5,200
Jim King	71	75	73	219	5,200
John Frillman	73	73	74	220	3,850
Bobby Nichols	71	71	78	220	3,850
Bob Toski	72	73	75	220	3,850
Chick Evans	74	76	70	220	3,850
Gene Littler	74	72	74	220	3,850
Walter Zembriski	75	75	71	221	3,200
Richard Rhyan	78	72	71	221	3,200
Harold Henning	74	72	75	221	3,200
Don January	77	73	72	222	2,900
Chi Chi Rodriguez	73	74	76	223	2,675
Billy Casper	74	77	72	223	2,675
Charles Sifford	74	74	76	224	2,412.50
Bill Collins	75	73	76	224	2,412.50
Bruce Devlin	70	82	73	225	2,175
Jim Ferree	73	75	77	225	2,175
Ben Smith	75	75	76	226	1,975
Jack Fleck	73	73	80	226	1,975
Joe Lopez	77	77	73	227	1,587.50
Bruce Crampton	82	73	72	227	1,587.50
Gay Brewer	73	81	73	227	1,587.50
John Brodie	75	74	78	227	1,587.50
Charles Owens	77	75	75	227	1,587.50
Jerry Barber	72	76	79	227	1,587.50
Robert Rawlins	79	74	74	227	1,587.50
Dick Howell	72	81	74	227	1,587.50

Aetna Challenge

The Club at Pelican Bay, Naples, Florida
Par 36-36 — 72; 6,719 yards

February 25-28
purse, $300,000

	SCORES			TOTAL	MONEY
Gary Player	70	70	67	207	$45,000
Dave Hill	68	73	67	208	26,000
Harold Henning	71	69	70	210	21,500
Bob Charles	69	70	72	211	18,000
Bobby Nichols	75	66	72	213	14,500
Walter Zembriski	73	71	70	214	10,550
Gay Brewer	71	71	72	214	10,550
Bruce Devlin	69	72	74	215	8,168.75
Chi Chi Rodriguez	74	68	73	215	8,168.75
Don Bies	79	69	67	215	8,168.75
Gene Littler	74	73	68	215	8,168.75
Al Kelley	78	70	69	217	6,400
Orville Moody	73	70	74	217	6,400
Ben Smith	73	73	72	218	5,500
George Lanning	76	74	68	218	5,500
Joe Jimenez	79	71	68	218	5,500
Dale Douglass	72	74	73	219	4,450
Agim Bardha	74	75	70	219	4,450
Charles Coody	77	72	70	219	4,450
Don Massengale	69	76	74	219	4,450
Charles Sifford	77	75	68	220	3,800
Jim Ferree	76	73	72	221	3,200
Jim King	80	69	72	221	3,200
Billy Maxwell	74	73	74	221	3,200
Doug Ford	81	69	71	221	3,200
Gardner Dickinson	78	70	73	221	3,200
Al Chandler	75	75	71	221	3,200
Bruce Crampton	77	70	74	221	3,200
Miller Barber	74	73	75	222	2,412.50
Mike Fetchick	74	74	74	222	2,412.50
Joe Lopez	78	73	71	222	2,412.50
Larry Mowry	71	78	73	222	2,412.50
Doug Dalziel	75	77	71	223	2,025
Butch Baird	75	72	76	223	2,025
Roland Stafford	73	76	74	223	2,025
Gene Borek	78	73	73	224	1,737.50
Art Silvestrone	77	74	73	224	1,737.50
Gordon Jones	71	80	73	224	1,737.50
J.C. Goosie	78	73	73	224	1,737.50
Joe Campbell	80	71	74	225	1,296.88
Howie Johnson	75	74	76	225	1,296.88
Ray Montgomery	74	75	76	225	1,296.88
John Brodie	75	74	76	225	1,296.88
Paul Harney	76	70	79	225	1,296.87
Richard Rhyan	80	72	73	225	1,296.87
Billy Casper	74	78	73	225	1,296.87
Tommy Aaron	78	75	72	225	1,296.87

The Vintage Chrysler Invitational

The Vintage Club, Indian Wells, California
Mountain Course: Par 36-36 — 72; 6,907 yards
Desert Course: Par 36-36 — 72; 6,240 yards

March 3-6
purse, $320,000

	SCORES				TOTAL	MONEY
Orville Moody	64	66	70	63	263	$48,000
Al Geiberger	67	69	67	71	274	26,000
Harold Henning	70	75	65	64	274	26,000
Larry Mowry	68	66	74	69	277	19,500
Miller Barber	71	71	66	70	278	13,750
Ben Smith	72	71	67	68	278	13,750
Butch Baird	73	72	68	66	279	10,500
Dale Douglass	67	73	68	71	279	10,500
Bob Charles	71	68	67	75	281	8,200
Don Bies	68	73	71	69	281	8,200
Gary Player	69	72	70	70	281	8,200
Chi Chi Rodriguez	72	72	68	70	282	7,000
Arnold Palmer	72	70	71	69	282	7,000
Dave Hill	70	72	70	71	283	6,066.67
Rafe Botts	71	77	65	70	283	6,066.67
Bruce Devlin	69	74	69	71	283	6,066.66
Don January	76	69	70	70	285	5,400
Charles Sifford	69	72	74	70	285	5,400
Roberto de Vicenzo	75	69	69	72	285	5,400
John Brodie	69	71	71	75	286	4,800
Gene Littler	66	79	70	71	286	4,800
Bobby Nichols	71	74	76	65	286	4,800
George Lanning	75	69	73	70	287	4,300
Tommy Aaron	72	75	66	74	287	4,300
Ken Still	75	71	74	70	290	3,600
Bob Brue	71	76	73	70	290	3,600
Jimmy Powell	72	73	71	74	290	3,600
Lee Elder	70	74	71	75	290	3,600
Jim Ferree	74	75	71	70	290	3,600
Walter Zembriski	74	72	74	71	291	2,900
Charles Coody	69	77	71	74	291	2,900
Dow Finsterwald	70	74	75	73	292	2,500
Bob Toski	70	71	78	73	292	2,500
Don Massengale	69	75	75	74	293	2,200
Charles Owens	74	72	70	78	294	1,950
J.C. Goosie	72	73	76	73	294	1,950
Gordon Jones	76	76	72	71	295	1,800
Doug Sanders	72	77	73	74	296	1,600
Gay Brewer	76	72	73	75	296	1,600
Bruce Crampton	73	75	71	77	296	1,600

GTE Classic

Wood Ranch Golf Club, Simi Valley, California
Par 36-36 — 72; 6,727 yards

March 10-13
purse, $275,000

	SCORES			TOTAL	MONEY
Harold Henning	68	73	73	214	$41,250
Bruce Crampton	74	72	71	217	21,725
Dale Douglass	72	73	72	217	21,725
Walter Zembriski	69	77	72	218	12,187.50

	SCORES			TOTAL	MONEY
Don Bies	73	69	76	218	12,187.50
Butch Baird	73	70	75	218	12,187.50
Orville Moody	71	72	75	218	12,187.50
Chi Chi Rodriguez	73	71	75	219	7,825
Miller Barber	74	70	75	219	7,825
Larry Mowry	72	69	78	219	7,825
Shigeru Uchida	72	72	76	220	6,500
Bobby Nichols	78	74	71	223	5,837.50
Charles Coody	75	76	72	223	5,837.50
Howie Johnson	75	74	75	224	5,325
Al Geiberger	79	72	74	225	4,475
Billy Maxwell	74	78	73	225	4,475
Doug Sanders	77	74	74	225	4,475
Bob Charles	70	78	77	225	4,475
Tommy Aaron	74	76	75	225	4,475
Gay Brewer	79	73	74	226	3,275
Ben Smith	73	74	79	226	3,275
Roland Stafford	77	75	74	226	3,275
Robert Boldt	76	70	80	226	3,275
Agim Bardha	75	80	71	226	3,275
Jim King	76	80	70	226	3,275
Chick Evans	74	73	80	227	2,562.50
John Brodie	74	77	76	227	2,562.50
Doug Dalziel	77	77	73	227	2,562.50
Dave Hill	79	74	74	227	2,562.50
Al Kelley	79	73	76	228	2,250
J.C. Goosie	76	71	82	229	2,075
Roberto de Vicenzo	72	81	76	229	2,075
Fred Haas	74	76	80	230	1,912.50
Mike Fetchick	74	77	79	230	1,912.50
George Lanning	78	75	78	231	1,687.50
Jay Hyon	75	76	80	231	1,687.50
Gene Littler	77	76	78	231	1,687.50
Joe Jimenez	80	77	74	231	1,687.50
Jerry Barber	77	75	80	232	1,278.58
George Bayer	82	76	74	232	1,278.57
Art Silvestrone	76	76	80	232	1,278.57
Don Massengale	77	75	80	232	1,278.57
Bill Johnston	79	75	78	232	1,278.57
Denny Felton	81	75	76	232	1,278.57
Gordon Waldespuhl	76	79	77	232	1,278.57

The Pointe/Del E. Webb Arizona Classic

Hillcrest Golf Club, Sun City West, Arizona
Par 36-36 — 72; 6,672 yards

March 17-20
purse, $225,000

	SCORES			TOTAL	MONEY
Al Geiberger	63	69	67	199	$33,750
Orville Moody	68	67	65	200	19,250
Dave Hill	67	67	67	201	15,850
Gay Brewer	68	68	68	204	11,950
Harold Henning	68	68	68	204	11,950
Roland Stafford	69	69	68	206	8,050
Miller Barber	68	69	70	207	7,475
Gene Littler	70	67	71	208	6,075
Don Massengale	69	71	68	208	6,075

	SCORES			TOTAL	MONEY
Bobby Nichols	72	69	67	208	6,075
Walter Zembriski	67	70	71	208	6,075
Bob Brue	69	68	72	209	4,330
Bob Charles	71	71	67	209	4,330
Doug Dalziel	71	69	69	209	4,330
Roberto de Vicenzo	67	73	69	209	4,330
Jim King	70	71	68	209	4,330
Butch Baird	71	72	67	210	3,400
Billy Casper	70	71	69	210	3,400
Jim Ferree	73	69	68	210	3,400
Agim Bardha	66	73	72	211	2,575
Charles Coody	70	70	71	211	2,575
Bruce Crampton	69	74	68	211	2,575
Bruce Devlin	70	70	71	211	2,575
Dale Douglass	71	70	70	211	2,575
Quinton Gray	66	75	70	211	2,575
Peter Thomson	70	70	71	211	2,575
John Frillman	68	72	72	212	2,050
George Lanning	70	71	71	212	2,050
Doug Sanders	69	71	72	212	2,050
Lee Elder	70	72	71	213	1,706.25
Joe Jimenez	72	69	72	213	1,706.25
Larry Mowry	72	69	72	213	1,706.25
Ben Smith	73	73	67	213	1,706.25
Ken Still	69	70	75	214	1,433.34
Rafe Botts	74	70	70	214	1,433.33
Jimmy Powell	70	72	72	214	1,433.33
George Bayer	71	73	71	215	1,300
Fred Hawkins	69	71	75	215	1,300
J.C. Goosie	73	73	70	216	1,200
Art Silvestrone	73	73	70	216	1,200

Fuji Electric Grand Slam Championship

Oak Hills Country Club, Narita, Japan
Par 36-36 — 72; 6,660 yards

March 25-27
purse, $360,000

(Saturday's second round cancelled, rain.)

	SCORES		TOTAL	MONEY
Bob Charles	67	69	136	$75,000
Larry Mowry	73	64	137	41,000
Billy Casper	68	69	137	41,000
Arnold Palmer	70	68	138	25,500
Teruo Sugihara	70	69	139	18,250
Charles Coody	69	70	139	18,250
Kanehiko Uchida	68	72	140	11,666
Orville Moody	74	66	140	11,666
Harold Henning	72	68	140	11,666
Gene Littler	71	70	141	7,500
Ichirou Togawa	68	75	143	5,700
Don Massengale	68	75	143	5,700
Bob Toski	71	72	143	5,700
Agim Bardha	70	73	143	5,700
Miller Barber	74	71	145	4,325
Don January	74	71	145	4,325
Bob Brue	72	73	145	4,325

	SCORES		TOTAL	MONEY
Shigeru Uchida	73	72	145	4,325
Jean Garaialde	75	71	146	3,633
Toshiaki Sekimuzu	72	74	146	3,633
Tadashi Kitsuta	72	74	146	3,633
Peter Butler	73	74	147	3,300
Yuji Ogawa	73	74	147	3,300
Lu Liang Huan	72	75	147	3,300
Hideo Jibiki	74	74	148	3,000
Tommy Aaron	76	72	148	3,000
Seiichi Sato	73	75	148	3,000
Tomoo Ishii	75	74	149	2,750
Ichio Satuo	75	74	149	2,750
Chin Sei Ha	74	76	150	2,550
Dow Finsterwald	73	77	150	2,500
Peter Thomson	75	76	151	2,000
Hiroshi Gunji	76	77	153	2,000
Kouichi Ishikawa	77	76	153	2,000
Fumio Sakurai	77	76	153	2,000
Hideyo Sugimoto	79	76	155	2,000
Minuro Nakamura	76	79	155	2,000
Yoshiaki Kitanaka	81	76	156	2,000
Chuck Campbell	81	77	158	2,000
Yasuhiro Yamamoto	78	82	160	2,000

Doug Sanders Kingwood Celebrity Classic

Deerwood Club, Houston, Texas
Par 36-36 — 72; 6,564 yards

April 15-17
purse, $250,000

	SCORES			TOTAL	MONEY
Chi Chi Rodriguez	70	69	69	208	$37,500
Miller Barber	71	69	70	210	20,625
John Brodie	69	68	73	210	20,625
Gay Brewer	73	71	67	211	15,625
Bob Charles	71	72	69	212	12,500
Harold Henning	70	72	71	213	9,375
Gene Littler	72	70	72	214	8,437
Arnold Palmer	70	72	72	214	8,437
Bobby Nichols	69	69	77	215	7,500
Gary Player	75	72	69	216	6,300.34
Lee Elder	72	72	72	216	6,300.33
Jim Ferree	73	70	73	216	6,300.33
Butch Baird	72	73	72	217	4,666.67
Bruce Crampton	71	73	73	217	4,666.67
Al Geiberger	73	73	71	217	4,666.67
Ben Smith	72	73	72	217	4,666.67
Bruce Devlin	72	71	74	217	4,666.66
Water Zembriski	71	70	76	217	4,666.66
Joe Jimenez	70	78	70	218	3,625
Orville Moody	72	74	72	218	3,625
Billy Casper	77	71	71	219	3,250
Dave Hill	74	75	71	220	3,125
Tommy Aaron	76	69	77	222	2,812.50
Bob Brue	79	70	73	222	2,812.50
Lou Graham	78	72	72	222	2,812.50
Charles Owens	74	74	74	222	2,812.50
George Bayer	70	75	78	223	2,250

	SCORES			TOTAL	MONEY
Don Bies	78	74	71	223	2,250
Bob Erickson	77	76	70	223	2,250
Dow Finsterwald	76	74	73	223	2,250
J.C. Goosie	72	74	77	223	2,250
Howie Johnson	75	77	72	224	1,781.25
Jim King	77	75	72	224	1,781.25
George Lanning	76	73	75	224	1,781.25
Doug Sanders	82	71	71	224	1,781.25
Homero Blancas	75	75	75	225	1,531.25
Gordon Jones	74	76	75	225	1,531.25
Don Massengale	80	73	72	225	1,531.25
Bob Toski	78	69	78	225	1,531.25
Mike Fetchick	76	76	74	226	1,344
Jack Fleck	74	79	73	226	1,344

Chrysler Cup

Tournament Players Club at Prestancia, Sarasota, Florida   April 21-24
Par 36-36 — 72; 6,763 yards   purse, $600,000

FINAL RESULT: United States 55, International 45

FIRST ROUND
Four-Ball Match

Billy Casper-Al Geiberger (U.S.) defeated Roberto de Vicenzo-Bruce Devlin, 1 up.
Arnold Palmer-Chi Chi Rodriguez (U.S.) defeated Gary Player-Bob Charles, 1 up.
Orville Moody-Miller Barber (U.S.) defeated Bruce Crampton-Harold Henning, 2 and 1.
Dale Douglass-Gene Littler (U.S.) defeated Peter Thomson-Christy O'Connor, 2 and 1.

STANDINGS: United States 16, International 0.

SECOND ROUND
Singles Match

Moody (U.S.) defeated Devlin, 1 up.
Rodriguez (U.S.) defeated Henning, 1 up.
Littler (U.S.) defeated O'Connor, 5 and 4.
Crampton (Int.) defeated Palmer, 2 and 1.
Thomson (Int.) defeated Casper, 2 and 1.
Barber (U.S.) defeated de Vicenzo, 7 and 5.
Geiberger (U.S.) defeated Charles, 2 and 1.
Player (Int.) defeated Douglass, 5 and 4.

STANDINGS: United States 26, International 6.

THIRD ROUND
Four-Ball Stroke

Player-Charles (Int.) defeated Casper-Douglass, 66-67.
Crampton-Henning (Int.) defeated Barber-Palmer, 64-65.
Geiberger-Littler (U.S.) defeated de Vicenzo-O'Connor, 65-66.
Moody-Rodriguez (U.S.) defeated Thomson-Devlin, 61-66.

STANDINGS: United States 40, International 20.

FOURTH ROUND
Singles Stroke

Charles (Int.) defeated Moody, 67-70.
Littler (U.S.) defeated Thomson, 70-71.
Henning (Int.) defeated Douglass, 70-71.
Casper (U.S.) defeated O'Connor, 72-73.
Player (Int.) defeated Palmer, 72-74.
Crampton (Int.) defeated Barber, 72-74.
Devlin (Int.) defeated Geiberger, 72-73.
Rodriguez (U.S.) defeated de Vicenzo, 69-70.

Each member of the United States team received $50,000; each member of the
International team received $25,000.

Liberty Mutual Legends of Golf

Onion Creek Country Club, Austin, Texas
Par 35-35 — 70; 6,367 yards

April 28-May 1
purse, $670,000
(unofficial)

	SCORES				TOTAL	MONEY (Team)
Bruce Crampton/Orville Moody	67	64	61	62	254	$120,000
Tommy Aaron/Lou Graham	64	64	64	62	254	65,000
(Crampton/Moody defeated Aaron/Graham on sixth hole of playoff.)						
Bob Charles/Bruce Devlin	63	62	66	64	255	44,000
Peter Thomson/Harold Henning	65	64	62	64	255	44,000
Arnold Palmer/Miller Barber	65	65	61	65	256	29,000
Billy Casper/Gay Brewer	65	64	64	64	257	22,500
Jim Ferree/Charles Coody	68	63	62	64	257	22,500
Bobby Nichols/Butch Baird	63	63	66	66	258	18,000
Dale Douglass/Dow Finsterwald	67	66	63	64	260	15,000
Bill Collins/Billy Maxwell	64	65	67	65	261	14,000
Don January/Gene Littler	67	67	64	64	262	12,500
Gardner Dickinson/Don Massengale	70	64	62	66	262	12,500
Doug Sanders/Dave Hill	67	65	67	64	263	11,000
Al Geiberger/Deane Beman	67	67	63	67	264	10,000
Homero Blancas/Phil Rodgers	66	67	65	70	268	10,000
Jack Burke/Paul Harney	67	66	66	70	269	10,000
Chi Chi Rodriguez/Lee Elder	67	69	65	69	270	10,000
Tommy Jacobs/Ken Still	69	66	70	68	273	10,000
Bob Goalby/Charles Owens	71	72	64	67	274	10,000
Johnny Pott/George Knudson	68	71	71	67	277	10,000

SUPER SENIORS

Roberto de Vicenzo/Charles Sifford	63	67	65	67	262	$40,000
Mike Souchak/Joe Jimenez	70	65	65	65	265	30,000
Fred Haas/Fred Hawkins	64	64	69	69	266	14,000
Tommy Bolt/Art Wall	69	68	67	63	267	13,000
Sam Snead/Howie Johnson	66	67	69	66	268	12,000
Bob Toski/Mike Fetchick	70	69	67	63	269	11,000
Doug Ford/Jerry Barber	65	70	70	68	273	10,000
Ted Kroll/Kel Nagle	65	71	66	71	273	10,000
Julius Boros/George Bayer	68	71	67	71	277	10,000
Lionel Hebert/Jay Hebert	71	69	70	69	279	10,000

Vantage At The Dominion

Dominion Country Club, San Antonio, Texas
Par 36-36 — 72; 6,814 yards

May 6-8
purse, $250,000

	SCORES			TOTAL	MONEY
Billy Casper	70	68	67	205	$37,500
Chi Chi Rodriguez	71	67	68	206	21,500
Don January	72	67	68	207	17,800
Gene Littler	71	71	67	209	11,933.34
Bruce Crampton	71	71	67	209	11,933.33
Dale Douglass	73	65	71	209	11,933.33
Peter Thomson	72	73	65	210	7,105
Dave Hill	73	68	69	210	7,105
Don Bies	71	72	67	210	7,105
Bobby Nichols	68	71	71	210	7,105
Walter Zembriski	69	73	68	210	7,105
Orville Moody	75	67	69	211	5,091.67
Harold Henning	72	69	70	211	5,091.67
Al Geiberger	69	70	72	211	5,091.66
Larry Mowry	72	69	71	212	4,550
Charles Coody	71	68	74	213	4,175
Mike Fetchick	72	70	71	213	4,175
Miller Barber	73	68	73	214	3,365
Lou Graham	71	71	72	214	3,365
Jimmy Powell	70	72	72	214	3,365
Ben Smith	72	68	74	214	3,365
Joe Jimenez	70	74	70	214	3,365
Tommy Aaron	70	75	70	215	2,650
Roland Stafford	71	71	73	215	2,650
Gordon Jones	71	71	73	215	2,650
Gay Brewer	74	70	71	215	2,650
Jim King	69	77	69	215	2,650
Fred Hawkins	73	72	71	216	2,150
Bob Charles	74	72	70	216	2,150
Bob Erickson	73	72	71	216	2,150
Don Massengale	71	73	73	217	1,862.50
Dick Howell	73	75	69	217	1,862.50
Bob Brue	73	75	70	218	1,675
Lee Elder	72	76	70	218	1,675
Doug Ford	71	72	75	218	1,675
Robert Boldt	72	74	74	220	1,487.50
Billy Maxwell	76	71	73	220	1,487.50
Gardner Dickinson	72	75	74	221	1,350
Jim Ferree	71	77	73	221	1,350
Bob Toski	77	74	71	222	1,175
Bill Collins	73	71	78	222	1,175
Doug Dalziel	70	77	75	222	1,175
Phil Rodgers	73	78	71	222	1,175
Bill Johnston	73	78	71	222	1,175

United Hospitals Championship

Chester Valley Golf Club, Malvern, Pennsylvania
Par 35-35 — 70; 6,406 yards

May 13-15
purse, $225,000

	SCORES			TOTAL	MONEY
Bruce Crampton	71	65	69	205	$33,750
Billy Casper	70	67	68	205	19,250
(Crampton defeated Casper on first hole of playoff.)					
Lou Graham	70	67	69	206	15,850
Lee Elder	70	68	71	209	13,250
Miller Barber	72	66	72	210	10,650
Orville Moody	71	72	68	211	8,050
Robert Boldt	72	72	68	212	6,625
Jim Cochran	73	71	68	212	6,625
Bill Collins	70	70	72	212	6,625
Richard Rhyan	69	74	69	212	6,625
Gay Brewer	71	74	68	213	4,615
Bob Brue	73	70	70	213	4,615
Gene Littler	71	73	69	213	4,615
Chi Chi Rodriguez	71	72	70	213	4,615
Ben Smith	71	71	71	213	4,615
Don Bies	74	70	70	214	3,625
Charles Coody	74	69	71	214	3,625
Harold Henning	73	70	71	214	3,625
Bruce Devlin	69	73	73	215	3,062.50
Peter Thomson	76	69	70	215	3,062.50
Walter Zembriski	72	73	71	216	2,800
Ray Beallo	73	71	73	217	2,506.25
J.C. Goosie	73	71	73	217	2,506.25
Jay Hyon	72	72	73	217	2,506.25
Jimmy Powell	74	69	74	217	2,506.25
Quinton Gray	67	78	73	218	2,150
Dave Hill	71	71	76	218	2,150
Dick Howell	73	75	70	218	2,150
Butch Baird	76	72	71	219	1,900
Homero Blancas	75	72	72	219	1,900
Fred Hawkins	73	74	73	220	1,545.84
Robert Rawlins	72	74	74	220	1,545.84
Doug Ford	75	75	70	220	1,545.83
Bobby Nichols	69	77	74	220	1,545.83
Roland Stafford	74	72	74	220	1,545.83
Ken Still	73	73	74	220	1,545.83
Jerry Barber	74	76	71	221	1,200
Bill Bishop	73	73	75	221	1,200
Al Chandler	75	73	73	221	1,200
Chick Evans	77	71	73	221	1,200
Joe Jimenez	76	72	73	221	1,200
Ralph Terry	75	73	73	221	1,200

Nynex/Golf Digest Commemorative

Sleepy Hollow Country Club, Scarborough, New York
Par 35-35 — 70; 6,545 yards

May 20-22
purse, $300,000

	SCORES			TOTAL	MONEY
Bob Charles	63	67	67	196	$45,000
Don Massengale	68	65	67	200	23,750

	SCORES			TOTAL	MONEY
Harold Henning	67	67	66	200	23,750
Bruce Crampton	67	68	66	201	18,000
Larry Mowry	65	70	67	202	14,500
Charles Coody	66	70	67	203	11,100
Dale Douglass	69	71	65	205	9,258.34
Dave Hill	69	67	69	205	9,258.33
Don Bies	72	67	66	205	9,258.33
Lou Graham	72	66	68	206	7,800
Chi Chi Rodriguez	71	68	68	207	6,850
Doug Dalziel	69	69	69	207	6,850
Gene Littler	70	70	68	208	5,833.34
Gardner Dickinson	69	69	70	208	5,833.33
Butch Baird	69	70	69	208	5,833.33
Miller Barber	68	68	73	209	5,200
Joe Jimenez	73	72	65	210	4,208.34
Ken Still	69	72	69	210	4,208.34
Jim Cochran	71	70	69	210	4,208.33
Orville Moody	73	68	69	210	4,208.33
Jim King	69	69	72	210	4,208.33
Bob Brue	76	65	69	210	4,208.33
J.C. Goosie	70	68	73	211	3,200
Jimmy Powell	71	70	70	211	3,200
Al Kelley	71	71	69	211	3,200
Lee Elder	71	68	72	211	3,200
Rafe Botts	75	69	67	211	3,200
Ben Smith	75	67	70	212	2,420.84
Robert Boldt	73	71	68	212	2,420.84
Chick Evans	66	75	71	212	2,420.83
Jim Ferree	67	71	74	212	2,420.83
John Frillman	70	72	70	212	2,420.83
Tommy Aaron	72	69	71	212	2,420.83
Gordon Waldespuhl	72	71	70	213	1,855
Walter Zembriski	71	75	67	213	1,855
Fred Hawkins	71	72	70	213	1,855
Agim Bardha	75	69	69	213	1,855
Gene Borek	75	69	69	213	1,855
Kel Nagle	68	72	74	214	1,512.50
Charles Owens	73	71	70	214	1,512.50
Art Silvestrone	68	77	69	214	1,512.50
Roland Stafford	73	72	69	214	1,512.50

Sunwest Bank/Charley Pride Classic

Four Hills Country Club, Albuquerque, New Mexico
Par 36-36 — 72; 6,722 yards

May 27-29
purse, $250,000

	SCORES			TOTAL	MONEY
Bob Charles	69	68	69	206	$41,250
Orville Moody	69	67	72	208	23,850
Rafe Botts	74	69	69	212	17,975
Don Bies	72	69	71	212	17,975
Ben Smith	69	73	71	213	10,800
Bob Brue	74	72	67	213	10,800
Tommy Aaron	74	72	67	213	10,800
Art Wall	71	72	71	214	6,710.72
Lou Graham	69	73	72	214	6,710.72
Ray Beallo	75	71	68	214	6,710.72

	SCORES			TOTAL	MONEY
Charles Sifford	71	71	72	214	6,710.71
Robert Boldt	73	69	72	214	6,710.71
Don Massengale	70	71	73	214	6,710.71
Gene Mitchell	74	67	73	214	6,710.71
Al Geiberger	72	74	69	215	4,750
Bobby Nichols	70	70	75	215	4,750
Jimmy Powell	74	70	71	215	4,750
Bob Erickson	70	72	74	216	4,062.50
Gene Torres	75	71	70	216	4,062.50
Phil Rodgers	74	72	71	217	3,425
Art Silvestrone	74	70	73	217	3,425
Jerry Barber	71	72	74	217	3,425
Pat Schwab	74	68	75	217	3,425
Jim Cochran	72	73	73	218	2,900
Harold Henning	72	71	75	218	2,900
Chick Evans	73	74	71	218	2,900
Al Chandler	75	70	74	219	2,437.50
Larry Mowry	72	75	72	219	2,437.50
Charles Mehok	73	70	76	219	2,437.50
Joe Jimenez	73	73	73	219	2,437.50
Agim Bardha	76	71	73	220	2,125
Alton Duhon	74	71	76	221	1,912.50
Howie Johnson	76	75	70	221	1,912.50
Peter Thomson	69	75	77	221	1,912.50
Dick Howell	70	71	80	221	1,912.50
Homero Blancas	77	74	71	222	1,537.50
Fred Hawkins	72	71	79	222	1,537.50
Gordon Jones	71	79	72	222	1,537.50
George Lanning	76	77	69	222	1,537.50
Charles Owens	77	77	68	222	1,537.50
George Bayer	71	74	77	222	1,537.50

Senior Players Reunion Pro-Am

Bent Tree Country Club, Dallas, Texas
Par 36-36 — 72; 6,804 yards

June 3-5
purse, $250,000

	SCORES			TOTAL	MONEY
Orville Moody	70	70	66	206	$37,500
Bobby Nichols	69	69	68	206	18,033.34
Bob Charles	68	68	70	206	18,033.33
Don Massengale	68	71	67	206	18,033.33
(Moody won playoff, defeating Nichols, Charles and Massengale on first extra hole.)					
Charles Coody	69	69	69	207	9,800
Harold Henning	69	69	69	207	9,800
Gary Player	70	71	66	207	9,800
Homero Blancas	69	69	70	208	7,400
Al Geiberger	71	70	67	208	7,400
Larry Mowry	70	68	71	209	6,162.50
Walter Zembriski	69	70	70	209	6,162.50
Miller Barber	65	74	71	210	5,091.67
Charles Owens	70	69	71	210	5,091.67
Bruce Crampton	72	71	67	210	5,091.66
Bob Brue	71	70	70	211	4,300
Doug Dalziel	75	70	66	211	4,300
Dale Douglass	72	70	69	211	4,300
Gay Brewer	70	74	69	213	3,365

	SCORES			TOTAL	MONEY
Richard Rhyan	73	71	69	213	3,365
Chi Chi Rodriguez	74	68	71	213	3,365
Doug Sanders	72	69	72	213	3,365
Peter Thomson	69	71	73	213	3,365
Jerry Barber	70	72	73	215	2,712.50
Lee Elder	70	71	74	215	2,712.50
Don January	69	72	74	215	2,712.50
Ben Smith	74	72	69	215	2,712.50
Butch Baird	72	70	74	216	2,212.50
Jim Cochran	73	72	71	216	2,212.50
Bruce Devlin	77	70	69	216	2,212.50
Charles Sifford	73	73	70	216	2,212.50
Chick Evans	73	71	73	217	1,675
Mike Fetchick	69	76	72	217	1,675
Bill Johnston	72	74	71	217	1,675
Gordon Jones	70	75	72	217	1,675
Al Kelley	70	75	72	217	1,675
George Lanning	73	73	71	217	1,675
Ralph Terry	73	70	74	217	1,675
Roland Stafford	74	75	69	218	1,375
Tommy Aaron	75	72	72	219	1,300
Bob Erickson	74	74	71	219	1,300

Mazda Senior Tournament Players Championship

TPC at Sawgrass, Valley Course, Ponte Verdra, Florida
Par 36-36 — 72; 6,646 yards

June 9-12
purse, $400,000

	SCORES				TOTAL	MONEY
Billy Casper	69	68	74	67	278	$60,000
Al Geiberger	70	72	68	70	280	35,000
Miller Barber	73	68	68	72	281	24,200
Don January	74	72	65	70	281	24,200
Gary Player	72	71	67	71	281	24,200
Bob Charles	67	73	71	71	282	14,150
Bruce Crampton	71	68	72	71	282	14,150
Lou Graham	71	70	71	71	283	12,000
Orville Moody	75	72	70	66	283	12,000
Charles Coody	70	68	73	73	284	10,050
Larry Mowry	71	70	73	70	284	10,050
Gene Littler	75	70	73	67	285	8,800
Don Bies	75	74	68	69	286	8,000
Dale Douglass	72	75	69	70	286	8,000
Gardner Dickinson	70	69	76	72	287	7,200
Bobby Nichols	71	73	71	72	287	7,200
Charles Owens	75	73	68	72	288	6,400
Roland Staford	74	72	67	75	288	6,400
Walter Zembriski	73	71	71	74	289	5,433.34
Jim Ferree	70	73	76	70	289	5,433.33
Charles Sifford	73	69	73	74	289	5,433.33
Jim Cochran	70	75	75	70	290	4,600
Bob Erickson	71	74	74	71	290	4,600
Don Massengale	73	73	73	71	290	4,600
Ken Still	68	75	74	73	290	4,600
Bob Brue	71	74	77	69	291	3,900
Dave Hill	68	75	76	72	291	3,900
Chi Chi Rodriguez	74	76	67	74	291	3,900

	SCORES				TOTAL	MONEY
Bill Collins	72	68	74	78	292	3,300
Bruce Devlin	71	73	75	73	292	3,300
Jim King	76	71	71	74	292	3,300
Butch Baird	74	76	72	71	293	2,775
Bob Goalby	66	75	78	74	293	2,775
Arnold Palmer	73	75	70	75	293	2,775
Robert Rawlins	68	72	76	77	293	2,775
Doug Sanders	75	71	73	74	293	2,775
Dick Howell	77	71	72	74	294	2,325
Joe Jimenez	72	78	71	73	294	2,325
Howie Johnson	75	75	69	75	294	2,325
Ralph Terry	73	72	74	75	294	2,325

Northville Invitational

Meadow Brook Club, Jericho, New York   June 17-19
Par 36-36 — 72; 6,595 yards   purse, $350,000

	SCORES			TOTAL	MONEY
Don Bies	69	67	66	202	$52,500
Bob Charles	70	68	66	204	30,000
Lou Graham	70	70	66	206	22,000
Dave Hill	69	68	69	206	22,000
Gene Littler	71	68	68	207	15,500
Harold Henning	67	69	71	207	15,500
Bruce Crampton	68	70	71	209	12,000
Bob Brue	74	69	67	210	10,500
Dale Douglass	71	67	72	210	10,500
Bobby Nichols	67	73	71	211	8,500
Don Massengale	73	71	67	211	8,500
George Lanning	72	70	69	211	8,500
Orville Moody	71	70	71	212	7,500
Jim Cochran	71	73	69	213	6,500
Doug Dalziel	71	72	70	213	6,500
Bruce Devlin	66	73	74	213	6,500
Ben Smith	71	73	70	214	5,250
Charles Owens	70	73	71	214	5,250
Homero Blancas	72	72	71	215	4,316.67
Charles Coody	74	71	70	215	4,316.67
Jim Ferree	72	73	70	215	4,316.67
Larry Mowry	73	71	71	215	4,316.67
Roberto de Vincenzo	73	69	73	215	4,316.66
Ken Still	72	72	71	215	4,316.66
Butch Baird	74	73	69	216	3,750
Billy Casper	73	70	73	216	3,750
Bob Goalby	72	74	72	218	3,450
Jim King	73	74	71	218	3,450
Gene Borek	73	71	74	218	3,450
Bob Erickson	73	73	72	218	3,450
Rafe Botts	75	75	69	219	3,050
John Brodie	73	74	72	219	3,050
Al Chandler	75	73	71	219	3,050
Lee Elder	74	73	72	219	3,050
Dick Howell	70	79	71	220	2,800
Doug Sanders	73	74	74	221	2,650
Walter Zembriski	71	77	73	221	2,650
Roland Stafford	74	74	74	222	2,450

	SCORES			TOTAL	MONEY
Paul Harney	77	73	72	222	2,450
Agim Bardha	72	74	78	224	2,200
Robert Boldt	75	73	76	224	2,200
Billy Maxwell	75	75	74	224	2,200

Southwestern Bell Classic

Quail Creek Golf and Country Club, Oklahoma City, Oklahoma   June 24-26
Par 36-36 — 72; 6,708 yards   purse, $250,000

	SCORES			TOTAL	MONEY
Gary Player	69	68	66	203	$37,500
Harold Henning	69	66	68	203	21,500
(Player defeated Henning on first hole of playoff.)					
Gene Littler	68	70	68	206	17,800
Ben Smith	69	70	68	207	13,350
Bobby Nichols	68	70	69	207	13,350
Chi Chi Rodriguez	68	71	70	209	8,075
Miller Barber	71	71	67	209	8,075
Lou Graham	74	67	68	209	8,075
Bruce Crampton	70	68	71	209	8,075
Charles Sifford	71	69	70	210	5,520
Walter Zembriski	71	70	69	210	5,520
Don Bies	73	68	69	210	5,520
Bob Charles	72	68	70	210	5,520
Roberto de Vicenzo	70	69	71	210	5,520
Orville Moody	69	70	73	212	3,925
Butch Baird	71	70	71	212	3,925
Doug Dalziel	74	69	69	212	3,925
Dale Douglass	74	70	68	212	3,925
Al Geiberger	71	68	73	212	3,925
J.C. Goosie	73	72	67	212	3,925
Richard Rhyan	70	70	73	213	2,775
Don Massengale	69	70	74	213	2,775
Robert Boldt	71	70	72	213	2,775
Rafe Botts	70	73	70	213	2,775
Jim Cochran	73	68	72	213	2,775
Dave Hill	69	71	73	213	2,775
Joe Jimenez	72	70	71	213	2,775
Charles Owens	71	72	71	214	2,087.50
Billy Casper	73	71	70	214	2,087.50
Al Chandler	72	69	73	214	2,087.50
Chick Evans	70	73	71	214	2,087.50
Deray Simon	75	69	71	215	1,825
Jimmy Powell	74	72	70	216	1,600
Homero Blancas	71	70	75	216	1,600
Jim King	71	74	71	216	1,600
Charles Coody	73	72	71	216	1,600
John Frillman	74	69	73	216	1,600
George Lanning	75	72	70	217	1,325
Bob Goalby	70	71	76	217	1,325
Gordon Jones	77	70	70	217	1,325

Rancho Murieta Gold Rush

Rancho Murieta Country Club, Rancho Murieta, California   July 2-4
Par 36-36 — 72; 6,657 yards   purse, $350,000

	SCORES			TOTAL	MONEY
Bob Charles	69	69	69	207	$52,500
Gary Player	68	71	70	209	30,000
Peter Thomson	66	74	70	210	18,750
Orville Moody	72	68	70	210	18,750
Al Geiberger	69	72	69	210	18,750
Lou Graham	68	68	74	210	18,750
Dave Hill	70	69	73	212	12,000
Jimmy Powell	72	72	69	213	10,000
Miller Barber	67	72	74	213	10,000
Roberto de Vicenzo	69	76	68	213	10,000
Bobby Nichols	69	71	74	214	8,300
Charles Sifford	70	75	70	215	7,300
Homero Blancas	70	71	74	215	7,300
Bruce Crampton	70	71	74	215	7,300
Ken Still	74	68	74	216	6,300
Butch Baird	69	71	77	217	5,550
Jim Ferree	70	72	75	217	5,550
Billy Maxwell	68	75	75	218	4,700
J.C. Goosie	72	70	76	218	4,700
Doug Dalziel	75	77	67	219	4,200
Bob Erickson	70	75	74	219	4,200
Harold Henning	73	73	73	219	4,200
Richard Rhyan	75	73	72	220	3,450
Walter Zembriski	74	73	73	220	3,450
Charles Owens	71	75	74	220	3,450
Chi Chi Rodriguez	75	71	74	220	3,450
Charles Coody	73	75	72	220	3,450
George Lanning	73	74	73	220	3,450
Bruce Devlin	75	72	73	220	3,450
Gene Littler	73	71	76	220	3,450
Tommy Aaron	73	77	71	221	2,950
Mike Fetchick	71	74	76	221	2,950
Al Kelley	71	80	71	222	2,750
Larry Mowry	73	73	76	222	2,750
Joe Campbell	71	72	80	223	2,500
Arnold Palmer	70	80	73	223	2,500
Don Massengale	74	72	77	223	2,500
Jerry Barber	75	74	75	224	2,150
Gay Brewer	71	76	77	224	2,150
Bob Brue	72	75	77	224	2,150
Joe Lopez	73	77	74	224	2,150

GTE Northwest Classic

Inglewood Country Club, Kenmore, Washington   July 8-10
Par 37-35 — 72; 6,501 yards   purse, $300,000

	SCORES			TOTAL	MONEY
Bruce Crampton	69	68	70	207	$45,000
Don Bies	71	67	70	208	23,750
Bruce Devlin	69	70	69	208	23,750
Chi Chi Rodriguez	69	70	70	209	16,250

	SCORES			TOTAL	MONEY
Harold Henning	71	68	70	209	16,250
Larry Mowry	66	72	72	210	11,100
Agim Bardha	70	70	71	211	9,625
Bob Brue	67	75	69	211	9,625
Robert Rawlins	71	72	69	212	8,162.50
Arnold Palmer	71	71	70	212	8,162.50
Jim Ferree	71	74	69	214	6,633.34
Bobby Nichols	73	71	70	214	6,633.33
Al Geiberger	72	73	69	214	6,633.33
Orville Moody	70	73	72	215	5,500
Dick Hendrickson	71	70	74	215	5,500
Dave Hill	73	70	72	215	5,500
John Brodie	69	74	74	217	4,320
Jim King	73	74	70	217	4,320
Charles Coody	71	74	72	217	4,320
Lee Elder	75	72	70	217	4,320
J.C. Goosie	70	73	74	217	4,320
Jimmy Powell	74	71	73	218	3,125
Walter Zembriski	76	67	75	218	3,125
Ralph Terry	70	77	71	218	3,125
Peter Thomson	73	73	72	218	3,125
Dick Howell	74	74	70	218	3,125
Joe Jimenez	73	71	74	218	3,125
George Lanning	73	71	74	218	3,125
Joe Lopez	78	69	71	218	3,125
Roland Stafford	71	76	72	219	2,139.29
Doug Dalziel	76	72	71	219	2,139.29
Al Kelley	73	73	73	219	2,139.29
Bob Erickson	74	72	73	219	2,139.29
Phil Rodgers	72	72	75	219	2,139.28
Charles Sifford	73	73	73	219	2,139.28
Tommy Aaron	71	72	76	219	2,139.28
Art Wall	72	75	73	220	1,700
Butch Baird	74	70	76	220	1,700
Quinton Gray	75	72	73	220	1,700
Ken Still	72	75	74	221	1,362.50
Charles Owens	75	73	73	221	1,362.50
Jerry Barber	71	75	75	221	1,362.50
Miller Barber	73	74	74	221	1,362.50
Billy Maxwell	71	74	76	221	1,362.50
Gordon Jones	77	74	70	221	1,362.50

Showdown Classic

Jeremy Ranch Country Club, Park City, Utah
Par 36-36 — 72; 7,103 yards

July 15-17
purse, $350,000

	SCORES			TOTAL	MONEY
Miller Barber	70	67	70	207	$52,500
Richard Rhyan	72	67	70	209	24,666.67
Orville Moody	71	68	70	209	24,666.67
Ben Smith	66	67	76	209	24,666.66
Bruce Crampton	73	67	70	210	17,000
Charles Coody	71	68	72	211	14,000
Robert Rawlins	70	71	71	212	11,500
Al Geiberger	75	69	68	212	11,500
Walter Zembriski	72	69	72	213	9,500

	SCORES			TOTAL	MONEY
Jim Cochran	68	69	76	213	9,500
Charles Owens	71	70	73	214	8,050
Bob Goalby	72	71	71	214	8,050
Gordon Waldespuhl	71	68	76	215	7,050
Don Bies	70	69	76	215	7,050
Gene Littler	71	71	74	216	6,050
Peter Thomson	69	75	72	216	6,050
George Lanning	71	77	69	217	4,550
Ralph Terry	72	73	72	217	4,550
Bobby Nichols	73	68	76	217	4,550
Tommy Aaron	74	70	73	217	4,550
Doug Dalziel	72	72	73	217	4,550
Bob Erickson	75	74	68	217	4,550
Billy Maxwell	71	72	75	218	3,750
Rafe Botts	73	74	71	218	3,750
Homero Blancas	69	75	75	219	3,500
Joe Jimenez	73	74	72	219	3,500
Quinton Gray	72	73	74	219	3,500
Agim Bardha	75	73	72	220	3,150
Robert Boldt	74	72	74	220	3,150
Jim Ferree	77	73	70	220	3,150
Larry Mowry	73	78	69	220	3,150
Jim O'Hern	76	72	73	221	2,850
Kel Nagle	76	71	74	221	2,850
Deray Simon	73	71	78	222	2,400
Bob Brue	77	71	74	222	2,400
Dick Hendrickson	72	72	78	222	2,400
Jim King	73	72	77	222	2,400
Joe Lopez	78	72	72	222	2,400
J.C. Goosie	76	72	74	222	2,400
Jimmy Powell	73	76	73	222	2,400

Volvo Seniors British Open

Ailsa Course, Turnberry, Scotland
Par 35-35 — 70; 6,480 yards

July 21-24
purse, £150,000

	SCORES				TOTAL	MONEY
Gary Player	65	66	72	69	272	£25,000
Billy Casper	68	65	72	68	273	16,400
Harold Henning	70	68	68	68	274	9,150
Bob Charles	70	69	68	70	277	7,350
Jim O'Hern	70	70	68	73	281	6,150
Arnold Palmer	69	70	73	71	283	4,720
Neil Coles	70	65	69	79	283	4,720
Bruce Devlin	69	70	76	69	284	3,610
George Will	70	73	73	70	286	3,057.50
Christy O'Connor	70	73	71	72	286	3,057.50
Terry Westbrook	70	70	71	76	287	2,635
Art Silvestrone	72	70	69	76	287	2,635
Hedley Muscroft	73	74	75	69	291	2,430
David Butler	74	69	76	74	293	2,310
Peter Gill	74	75	73	72	294	2,093.33
Lu Liang Huan	74	71	74	75	294	2,093.33
Ramon Sota	76	73	69	76	294	2,093.33
Paddy Skerritt	75	76	73	72	296	1,797.50
Ernie Jones	75	71	75	75	296	1,797.50

	SCORES				TOTAL	MONEY
Mohamed Moussa	72	76	70	78	296	1,797.50
Lou Garrison	68	72	76	80	296	1,797.50
Jim McAlister	71	77	73	76	297	1,660
Paul Kelly	74	76	74	74	298	1,540
Derek Strachan	72	73	76	77	298	1,540
Tony Grubb	74	74	73	77	298	1,540
Kyle Burton	76	76	69	77	298	1,540
Hugh Boyle	73	74	73	78	298	1,540
Maurice Moir	75	74	75	75	299	1,420
Derek Craik	76	73	76	75	300	1,380
Denis Hutchinson	74	72	79	76	301	1,300
*Colin McLachlan	75	73	76	77	301	
Austin Skerritt	76	70	78	77	301	1,300
Fred Boobyer	78	74	71	78	301	1,300
John Goodwin	79	71	78	74	302	1,160
Jack Wilkshire	78	71	77	76	302	1,160
Al Johnston	78	74	74	76	302	1,160
Gordon Cunningham	75	70	78	79	302	1,160
Joe Hardwick	75	71	76	81	303	1,040
Joe Hunter	77	71	74	81	303	1,040
Michael Murphy	74	74	80	76	304	907
Geoff Hunt	75	78	74	77	304	907
Norman Drew	74	73	77	80	304	907
David Snell	75	75	74	80	304	907
Ross Whitehead	71	74	77	82	304	907
*William Buckley	75	74	76	80	305	

Newport Cup

Newport Country Club, Newport, Rhode Island
Par 36-36 — 72; 6,566 yards

July 22-24
purse, $250,000

(Final round rained out; reverted to 36 holes.)

	SCORES		TOTAL	MONEY
Walt Zembriski	67	65	132	$37,500
Charles Coody	67	67	134	21,500
Lee Elder	67	68	135	18,000
Orville Moody	71	66	137	15,000
Larry Mowry	68	70	138	9,481.25
Charles Owens	69	69	138	9,481.25
George Lanning	65	73	138	9,481.25
Lou Graham	68	70	138	9,481.25
Gay Brewer	70	69	193	7,275
Chi Chi Rodriguez	68	72	140	6,116.67
Miller Barber	71	69	140	6,116.67
Joe Jimenez	71	69	140	6,116.66
Charles Sifford	72	69	141	4,750
John Brodie	70	71	141	4,750
Jimmy Powell	72	69	141	4,750
Bruce Crampton	72	69	141	4,750
Bill Johnston	71	70	141	4,750
Ralph Terry	69	73	142	3,487.50
Peter Thomson	73	69	142	3,487.50
Dale Douglass	71	71	142	3,487.50
Bob Erickson	68	74	142	3,487.50
Bob Goalby	70	72	142	3,487.50

	SCORES		TOTAL	MONEY
Billy Maxwell	71	71	142	3,487.50
Mike Fetchick	72	71	143	2,912.50
Roland Stafford	71	72	143	2,912.50
Al Chandler	72	72	144	2,537.50
Bill Collins	71	73	144	2,537.50
Doug Sanders	73	71	144	2,537.50
Jim Ferree	76	68	144	2,537.50
Richard Rhyan	74	71	145	2,075
Jim Cochran	74	71	145	2,075
Ben Smith	71	74	145	2,075
Dick Howell	70	75	145	2,075
Art Wall	73	73	146	1,691.67
Phil Rodgers	72	74	146	1,691.67
Gardner Dickinson	75	71	146	1,691.67
Don Massengale	75	71	146	1,691.67
Doug Dalziel	74	72	146	1,691.66
Billy Farrell	72	74	146	1,691.66
Jerry Barber	74	73	147	1,425
Fred Hawkins	74	73	147	1,425
Jim King	74	73	147	1,425

Digital Classic

Nashawtuc Country Club, Concord, Massachusetts
Par 36-36 — 72; 6,649 yards

July 29-31
purse, $300,000

	SCORES			TOTAL	MONEY
Chi Chi Rodriguez	68	65	69	202	$45,000
Bob Charles	71	65	67	203	26,000
Don Bies	70	69	66	205	21,500
Dale Douglass	75	64	68	207	16,250
Al Geiberger	68	70	69	207	16,250
Arnold Palmer	70	69	69	208	10,550
Larry Mowry	73	67	68	208	10,550
Harold Henning	69	68	72	209	8,887.50
Butch Baird	71	68	70	209	8,887.50
Doug Dalziel	69	68	73	210	7,800
Gene Littler	70	70	71	211	6,240
Joe Jimenez	69	77	65	211	6,240
Bobby Nichols	67	71	73	211	6,240
Bob Brue	71	71	69	211	6,240
J.C. Goosie	71	70	70	211	6,240
Don Massengale	73	70	69	212	4,600
Bruce Crampton	73	71	68	212	4,600
Lee Elder	70	71	71	212	4,600
Jim Ferree	71	68	73	212	4,600
Bob Goalby	72	71	69	212	4,600
Deray Simon	72	72	69	213	3,500
Roland Stafford	72	72	69	213	3,500
Lou Graham	70	71	72	213	3,500
Homero Blancas	69	71	73	213	3,500
Bruce Devlin	74	73	66	213	3,500
Phil Rodgers	72	72	70	214	2,559.38
Miller Barber	76	69	69	214	2,559.38
Gordon Jones	72	74	68	214	2,559.38
Bob Erickson	75	69	70	214	2,559.38
Kel Nagle	70	70	74	214	2,559.37

	SCORES			TOTAL	MONEY
Ken Still	71	72	71	214	2,559.37
Charles Owens	72	69	73	214	2,559.37
George Lanning	71	70	73	214	2,559.37
Peter Thomson	70	76	69	215	1,975
Tommy Aaron	69	70	76	215	1,975
Doug Sanders	75	69	72	216	1,775
Howie Johnson	75	71	70	216	1,775
John Frillman	71	72	73	216	1,775
Buck Adams	73	73	71	217	1,587.50
Jack Fleck	73	70	74	217	1,587.50

USGA Senior Open

Medinah Country Club, Medinah, Illinois   August 4-8
Par 36-36 — 72; 6,881 yards   purse, $325,000

	SCORES				TOTAL	MONEY
Gary Player	74	70	71	73	288	$65,000
Bob Charles	75	70	70	73	288	32,500
(Player defeated Charles in 18-hole playoff, 68-70.)						
Bruce Crampton	73	74	70	72	289	21,285
Orville Moody	72	73	72	73	290	13,877.50
Peter Thomson	72	73	72	73	290	13,877.50
Chi Chi Rodriguez	73	76	75	67	291	10,042
Harold Henning	70	73	76	72	291	10,042
Al Geiberger	73	71	77	71	292	8,259.50
Lou Graham	72	71	73	76	292	8,259.50
Butch Baird	73	75	73	73	294	7,060.50
Billy Casper	69	71	76	78	294	7,060.50
Don Bies	77	71	76	71	295	6,121.67
Gene Borek	73	75	75	72	295	6,121.67
Gene Littler	73	72	76	74	295	6,121.66
Dave Hill	73	74	75	74	296	5,293
J.C. Goosie	75	72	74	75	296	5,293
Walter Zembriski	69	75	74	78	296	5,293
Charles Coody	76	74	74	73	297	4,831
Doug Dalziel	72	73	80	73	298	4,618
Dale Douglass	80	73	72	74	299	4,370.50
Homero Blancas	78	74	70	77	299	4,370.50
Paul Moran	83	70	73	75	301	4,016.34
Bob Brue	76	78	72	75	301	4,016.33
Arnold Palmer	75	74	75	77	301	4,016.33
*Robert Housen	77	76	75	74	302	
Don Massengale	77	74	76	75	302	3,712.50
Ken Still	78	74	74	76	302	3,712.50
Gay Brewer	75	79	78	71	303	3,392
Dean Sheetz	75	77	76	75	303	3,392
Dick Hendrickson	77	74	75	77	303	3,392
Jim Ferree	75	75	73	80	303	3,392
John Frillman	77	78	74	75	304	3,016.60
Tommy Aaron	75	78	76	75	304	3,016.60
Bobby Nichols	78	75	75	76	304	3,016.60
Gordon Jones	77	76	75	76	304	3,016.60
Jim King	76	79	72	77	304	3,016.60
*Richard Sucher	75	77	74	78	304	
Earl Puckett	78	75	79	73	305	2,766.50
Bob Goalby	73	78	75	79	305	2,766.50
Billy Maxwell	74	72	80	80	306	2,660

Mony Syracuse Classic

Lafayette Country Club, Jamesville, New York
Par 36-36 — 72; 6,540 yards

August 12-14
purse, $250,000

	SCORES			TOTAL	MONEY
Dave Hill	68	64	68	200	$37,500
Bobby Nichols	70	67	68	205	19,650
Butch Baird	69	67	69	205	19,650
Bob Charles	70	68	68	206	13,350
Doug Dalziel	65	70	71	206	13,350
Harold Henning	70	68	69	207	8,408.34
Ben Smith	69	67	71	207	8,408.33
George Lanning	67	69	71	207	8,408.33
Bruce Devlin	69	68	71	208	6,762.50
Lou Graham	66	72	70	208	6,762.50
Gary Player	72	66	71	209	5,450
Larry Mowry	71	72	66	209	5,450
Bruce Crampton	68	69	72	209	5,450
Walter Zembriski	69	71	70	210	4,425
Ray Beallo	71	70	69	210	4,425
Homero Blancas	72	67	71	210	4,425
Rafe Botts	70	68	72	210	4,425
Kel Nagle	71	68	72	211	3,800
Gordon Waldespuhl	74	73	65	212	3,425
Ken Still	69	72	71	212	3,425
Gordon Jones	73	66	74	213	2,837.50
Jim King	73	68	72	213	2,837.50
Chi Chi Rodriguez	70	72	71	213	2,837.50
Roland Stafford	74	69	70	213	2,837.50
Richard Rhyan	71	73	69	213	2,837.50
Al Chandler	70	72	71	213	2,837.50
Charles Sifford	72	71	71	214	2,275
Billy Maxwell	74	70	70	214	2,275
Jim Cochran	70	71	73	214	2,275
De Ray Simon	71	73	71	215	1,875
Ralph Terry	68	72	75	215	1,875
Tommy Aaron	73	68	74	215	1,875
Joe Jimenez	70	74	71	215	1,875
Jim O'Hern	72	71	73	216	1,600
James Hatfield	66	76	74	216	1,600
Bob Erickson	73	73	70	216	1,600
Joe Lopez	71	72	74	217	1,383.34
Phil Rodgers	71	70	76	217	1,383.33
Robert Boldt	71	74	72	217	1,383.33
Lee Elder	72	70	76	218	1,250
J.C. Goosie	74	73	71	218	1,250

Greater Grand Rapids Open

Elks Country Club, Grand Rapids, Michigan
Par 36-35 — 71; 6,453 yards

August 19-21
purse, $250,000

	SCORES			TOTAL	MONEY
Orville Moody	68	65	70	203	$37,500
Gary Player	70	68	66	204	18,033.34

	SCORES			TOTAL	MONEY
Chi Chi Rodriguez	66	68	70	204	18,033.33
Chick Evans	67	70	67	204	18,033.33
Dave Hill	69	72	64	205	8,840
Harold Henning	67	67	71	205	8,840
Bruce Devlin	70	68	67	205	8,840
James Hatfield	68	70	67	205	8,840
J.C. Goosie	68	69	68	205	8,840
Joe Jimenez	67	73	66	206	6,162.50
Billy Casper	68	67	71	206	6,162.50
Homero Blancas	67	71	69	207	5,091.67
Jim Cochran	71	68	68	207	5,091.67
Jim King	68	69	70	207	5,091.66
Bobby Nichols	67	69	72	208	4,175
Walter Zembriski	73	68	67	208	4,175
Ken Still	71	71	66	208	4,175
Gay Brewer	68	70	70	208	4,175
Richard Rhyan	67	71	71	209	3,050
Kel Nagle	70	69	70	209	3,050
Roland Stafford	70	72	67	209	3,050
Ray Beallo	69	72	68	209	3,050
Robert Boldt	71	71	67	209	3,050
Doug Dalziel	69	72	68	209	3,050
Mike Fetchick	70	69	70	209	3,050
Art Wall	72	67	71	210	2,275
Al Chandler	67	73	70	210	2,275
Gardner Dickinson	71	69	70	210	2,275
Jim Ferree	68	67	75	210	2,275
Dick Hendrickson	69	71	70	210	2,275
Ben Smith	73	70	68	211	1,750
Howie Johnson	73	73	65	211	1,750
John Brodie	70	73	68	211	1,750
Denny Felton	67	73	71	211	1,750
Don Massengale	72	71	68	211	1,750
Butch Baird	68	72	72	212	1,335.72
Gordon Jones	75	67	70	212	1,335.72
Bob Goalby	72	70	70	212	1,335.72
Phil Rodgers	75	69	68	212	1,335.71
Miller Barber	71	74	67	212	1,335.71
Dow Finsterwald	73	66	73	212	1,335.71
Lou Graham	72	68	72	212	1,335.71

Vantage Presents Bank One Classic

Griffin Gate Country Club, Lexington, Kentucky
Par 35-35 — 70; 6,595 yards

August 26-28
purse, $250,000

	SCORES			TOTAL	MONEY
Bob Charles	63	66	71	200	$37,500
Dick Hendrickson	64	65	72	201	21,500
Gary Player	65	68	70	203	12,400
Walter Zembriski	68	70	65	203	12,400
Miller Barber	68	65	70	203	12,400
Dale Douglass	68	68	67	203	12,400
Bob Erickson	67	65	71	203	12,400
Gene Littler	68	69	67	204	7,083.34
Robert Boldt	65	69	70	204	7,083.33

	SCORES			TOTAL	MONEY
Billy Casper	67	68	69	204	7,083.33
Lou Graham	68	66	71	205	5,450
Don Bies	68	68	69	205	5,450
Harold Henning	66	72	67	205	5,450
Gordon Jones	69	68	69	206	4,425
Larry Mowry	70	64	72	206	4,425
Bobby Nichols	66	70	70	206	4,425
Charles Coody	68	70	68	206	4,425
Richard Rhyan	73	65	69	207	3,800
Gay Brewer	68	73	68	209	3,333.34
Dave Hill	73	68	68	209	3,333.33
James Hatfield	71	69	69	209	3,333.33
Charles Owens	71	69	70	210	2,775
Don Massengale	71	70	69	210	2,775
J.C. Goosie	66	70	74	210	2,775
Jim Cochran	68	72	70	210	2,775
Bruce Devlin	70	68	72	210	2,775
Jim King	70	73	68	211	2,275
Jack Fleck	67	74	70	211	2,275
John Frillman	71	68	72	211	2,275
Al Chandler	68	72	72	212	1,875
Joe Lopez	68	73	71	212	1,875
Bill Collins	66	71	75	212	1,875
Charles Mehok	72	72	68	212	1,875
Phil Rodgers	72	68	73	213	1,525
Ben Smith	70	71	72	213	1,525
Butch Baird	72	71	70	213	1,525
Doug Dalziel	69	74	70	213	1,525
Chick Evans	71	75	67	213	1,525
Kel Nagle	70	71	73	214	1,250
Homero Blancas	71	70	73	214	1,250
Gardner Dickinson	69	71	74	214	1,250
Bob Goalby	67	74	73	214	1,250

GTE North Classic

Broadmoor Country Club, Indianapolis, Indiana
Par 36-36 — 72; 6,690 yards

September 8-10
purse, $350,000

	SCORES			TOTAL	MONEY
Gary Player	70	65	66	201	$52,500
Dave Hill	70	68	65	203	30,000
Orville Moody	68	68	68	204	20,333.34
Miller Barber	71	65	68	204	20,333.33
Dale Douglass	67	68	69	204	20,333.33
Bob Charles	72	67	66	205	12,333.34
J.C. Goosie	68	68	69	205	12,333.33
Harold Henning	70	69	66	205	12,333.33
Walter Zembriski	70	68	68	206	9,500
Richard Rhyan	67	69	70	206	9,500
Bob Erickson	69	68	70	207	8,300
Don Bies	69	72	67	208	7,300
Jim Cochran	70	69	69	208	7,300
Bruce Devlin	73	66	69	208	7,300
Don Massengale	73	65	71	209	5,550
Homero Blancas	69	72	68	209	5,550

	SCORES			TOTAL	MONEY
Charles Coody	66	71	72	209	5,550
Doug Dalziel	69	72	68	209	5,550
Chi Chi Rodriguez	70	71	69	210	4,300
Billy Casper	72	69	69	210	4,300
Al Chandler	68	70	72	210	4,300
Gene Littler	72	70	68	210	4,300
Charles Owens	74	68	69	211	3,700
Arnold Palmer	70	70	71	211	3,700
Lou Graham	74	69	68	211	3,700
Bobby Nichols	70	68	74	212	3,450
Ken Still	67	70	75	212	3,450
Gay Brewer	71	70	72	213	3,250
George Lanning	71	72	70	213	3,250
Art Wall	72	70	72	214	3,000
Robert Boldt	69	71	74	214	3,000
Larry Mowry	72	70	72	214	3,000
Tommy Aaron	75	70	70	215	2,800
Ben Smith	73	70	73	216	2,600
Butch Baird	74	66	76	216	2,600
Jim Ferree	75	70	71	216	2,600
Gene Borek	71	72	74	217	2,250
Lee Elder	68	70	79	217	2,250
Mike Fetchick	71	71	75	217	2,250
John Frillman	74	71	72	217	2,250

Crestar Classic

Hermitage Country Club, Richmond, Virginia
Par 36-36 — 72; 6,644 yards

September 16-18
purse, $325,000

	SCORES			TOTAL	MONEY
Arnold Palmer	65	68	70	203	$48,750
Larry Mowry	68	71	68	207	23,716.67
Lee Elder	68	69	70	207	23,716.67
Jim Ferree	69	69	69	207	23,716.66
Gene Littler	67	72	69	208	12,187.50
George Lanning	71	73	64	208	12,187.50
Bob Charles	68	72	68	208	12,187.50
Dale Douglass	69	70	69	208	12,187.50
Gardner Dickinson	68	70	71	209	9,250
Gay Brewer	71	73	66	210	8,150
J.C. Goosie	72	68	70	210	8,150
Walter Zembriski	70	66	75	211	6,225
Don Massengale	67	72	72	211	6,225
Chi Chi Rodriguez	70	70	71	211	6,225
Don Bies	73	70	68	211	6,225
Bruce Crampton	75	68	68	211	6,225
Dick Hendrickson	70	70	71	211	6,225
Bobby Nichols	67	69	76	212	4,543.75
Roland Stafford	70	71	71	212	4,543.75
Miller Barber	73	69	70	212	4,543.75
Dave Hill	69	71	72	212	4,543.75
Homero Blancas	73	71	69	213	3,687.50
Billy Casper	73	71	69	213	3,687.50
Harold Henning	72	68	73	213	3,687.50
John Frillman	70	69	74	213	3,687.50

	SCORES			TOTAL	MONEY
Charles Owens	69	73	72	214	3,225
Ralph Terry	68	71	75	214	3,225
Gary Player	74	72	69	215	2,455.56
Ken Still	75	69	71	215	2,455.56
Richard Rhyan	73	73	69	215	2,455.56
Gene Borek	69	77	69	215	2,455.56
Doug Dalziel	74	72	69	215	2,455.56
Ben Smith	74	69	72	215	2,455.55
Tommy Aaron	69	70	76	215	2,455.55
Joe Jimenez	74	69	72	215	2,455.55
Bob Goalby	70	72	73	215	2,455.55
Bob Brue	72	74	70	216	1,691.67
Billy Maxwell	72	73	71	216	1,691.67
Chick Evans	75	71	70	216	1,691.67
Lou Graham	71	74	71	216	1,691.67
Jim Cochran	71	73	72	216	1,691.66
Jim King	71	73	72	216	1,691.66

PaineWebber Invitational

Quail Hollow Country Club, Charlotte, North Carolina
Par 36-36 — 72; 6,819 yards

September 23-25
purse, $350,000

	SCORES			TOTAL	MONEY
Dave Hill	68	68	70	206	$45,000
Bruce Crampton	70	71	66	207	27,000
Arnold Palmer	72	66	70	208	22,500
Bobby Nichols	69	68	72	209	16,875
Don Massengale	67	71	71	209	16,875
Don Bies	71	70	69	210	10,500
John Brodie	70	69	71	210	10,500
Gene Littler	69	70	71	210	10,500
Walter Zembriski	71	69	71	211	8,625
Bob Charles	71	66	74	211	8,625
Dale Douglass	74	66	72	212	7,575
Homero Blancas	69	74	70	213	6,318.75
Larry Mowry	71	68	74	213	6,318.75
Bob Erickson	72	70	71	213	6,318.75
Orville Moody	70	71	72	213	6,318.75
Harold Henning	72	70	72	214	5,400
Gay Brewer	75	73	67	215	4,800
Chi Chi Rodriguez	72	70	73	215	4,800
Lou Graham	71	74	70	215	4,800
Butch Baird	68	76	72	216	3,780
Ben Smith	75	69	72	216	3,780
Charles Coody	74	70	72	216	3,780
J.C. Goosie	73	75	68	216	3,780
George Lanning	70	76	70	216	3,780
Bert Yancey	70	70	77	217	3,300
Charles Owens	71	72	75	218	3,150
Miller Barber	71	77	71	219	2,925
Gary Player	71	70	78	219	2,925
Roberto De Vicenzo	76	71	73	220	2,625
Jim Ferree	72	72	76	220	2,625
Bob Brue	71	75	75	221	2,231.25
Chick Evans	74	70	77	221	2,231.25

	SCORES			TOTAL	MONEY
Bob Goalby	74	74	73	221	2,231.25
Dick Hendrickson	77	75	69	221	2,231.25
Doug Dalziel	75	76	71	222	1,966.67
Bruce Devlin	72	75	75	222	1,966.67
Robert Boldt	73	74	75	222	1,966.66
Jerry Barber	73	71	79	223	1,737.50
Doug Ford	76	75	72	223	1,737.50
Doug Sanders	77	70	76	223	1,737.50
Jim King	77	72	74	223	1,737.50

Pepsi Challenge

Horseshoe Bend Country Club, Roswell, Georgia
Par 36-36 — 72; 6,702 yards

September 30-October 2
purse, $300,000

(Final round rained out.)

	SCORES		TOTAL	MONEY
Bob Charles	70	69	139	$45,000
Bert Yancey	68	72	140	21,833.34
Harold Henning	72	68	140	21,833.33
Dick Hendrickson	68	72	140	21,833.33
George Lanning	68	73	141	11,866.67
Lou Graham	73	68	141	11,866.67
Doug Sanders	69	72	141	11,866.66
Dean Sheetz	71	71	142	8,887.50
Gary Player	71	71	142	8,887.50
Walter Zembriski	70	73	143	6,500
Dave Hill	72	71	143	6,500
Jim King	71	72	143	6,500
Orville Moody	74	69	143	6,500
Charles Coody	71	72	143	6,500
Jack Fleck	74	69	143	6,500
Joe Jimenez	70	74	144	5,050
Bob Erickson	72	72	144	5,050
Charles Owens	71	74	145	3,554.55
Gene Littler	71	74	145	3,554.55
Paul Moran	76	69	145	3,554.55
Peter Thomson	75	70	145	3,554.55
Don Bies	76	69	145	3,554.55
Bill Byars	71	74	145	3,554.55
Larry Mowry	74	71	145	3,554.54
Charles Sifford	73	72	145	3,554.54
Don Massengale	73	72	145	3,554.54
Homero Blancas	74	71	145	3,554.54
Mike Fetchick	71	74	145	3,554.54
Ken Still	72	74	146	2,355
Phil Rodgers	71	75	146	2,355
Doug Dalziel	73	73	146	2,355
Bruce Devlin	74	72	146	2,355
Dale Douglass	75	71	146	2,355
Jimmy Powell	71	76	147	1,855
Butch Baird	75	72	147	1,855
Roberto de Vicenzo	74	73	147	1,855
Doug Ford	73	74	147	1,855
Al Geiberger	76	71	147	1,855

	SCORES				TOTAL	MONEY
Bobby Nichols	77	71			148	1,512.50
Dick Howell	76	72			148	1,512.50
Bill Johnston	73	75			148	1,512.50
John Frillman	72	76			148	1,512.50

Vantage Championship

Tanglewood Park, Clemmons, North Carolina
Par 35-35 — 70; 6,606 yards

October 6-9
purse, $900,000

	SCORES				TOTAL	MONEY
Walter Zembriski	73	68	67	70	278	$135,000
Dave Hill	68	72	72	69	281	68,116.67
Al Geiberger	71	72	69	69	281	68,116.67
Richard Rhyan	69	68	72	72	281	68,116.66
Dale Douglass	73	71	70	69	283	44,800
Larry Mowry	73	72	69	70	284	33,550
Arnold Palmer	72	71	70	72	285	29,050
Chi Chi Rodriguez	75	73	70	67	285	29,050
Jimmy Powell	72	70	69	74	285	29,050
Bert Yancy	71	72	71	72	286	22,600
Lou Graham	68	69	70	79	286	22,600
Chick Evans	69	70	73	74	286	22,600
Miller Barber	71	72	73	72	288	18,700
Bob Charles	76	69	72	71	288	18,700
George Lanning	73	70	70	76	289	15,100
Dick Hendrickson	70	72	72	75	289	15,100
Bob Brue	78	66	74	71	289	15,100
Harold Henning	73	73	74	69	289	15,100
Bruce Crampton	72	73	76	68	289	15,100
Bobby Nichols	73	74	72	71	290	11,950
Gary Player	75	72	72	71	290	11,950
Ben Smith	69	71	74	77	291	11,050
Peter Thomson	71	72	72	77	292	9,925
Robert Boldt	75	74	70	73	292	9,925
Roberto de Vicenzo	73	75	72	72	292	9,925
Jim Ferree	72	71	71	78	292	9,925
Orville Moody	70	73	77	73	293	8,350
Agim Bardha	72	69	74	78	293	8,350
Doug Dalziel	74	70	73	76	293	8,350
Ken Still	74	73	74	73	294	6,550
Tommy Aaron	73	72	75	74	294	6,550
Don Bies	72	76	73	73	294	6,550
Gay Brewer	73	73	77	71	294	6,550
Charles Coody	75	67	76	76	294	6,550
John Frillman	73	73	74	74	294	6,550
Don Massengale	78	71	72	74	295	5,200
Gene Littler	75	73	75	72	295	5,200
John Brodie	72	74	74	75	295	5,200
Bob Erickson	76	73	75	71	295	5,200
Jack Fleck	74	73	74	74	295	5,200

General Tire Classic

Desert Inn Country Club, Las Vegas, Nevada   October 28-30
Par 36-36 — 72; 6,810 yards   purse, $250,000

	SCORES			TOTAL	MONEY
Larry Mowry	68	65	71	204	$37,500
Bobby Nichols	68	69	69	206	20,625
Bob Charles	67	66	73	206	20,625
Dave Hill	68	68	72	208	15,625
Bruce Crampton	71	73	65	209	10,208.34
Joe Jimenez	72	66	71	209	10,208.33
Orville Moody	68	68	73	209	10,208.33
Gary Player	72	69	69	210	7,812.50
Lou Graham	69	72	69	210	7,812.50
Walter Zembriski	69	69	73	211	6,593.50
Harold Henning	70	69	72	211	6,593.50
Ben Smith	70	70	72	212	5,625
Al Geiberger	74	71	67	212	5,625
Miller Barber	69	74	70	213	4,512.60
Don Bies	72	71	70	213	4,512.60
Bob Erickson	73	73	67	213	4,512.60
Jim Ferree	68	72	73	213	4,512.60
Arnold Palmer	72	66	75	213	4,512.60
Chi Chi Rodriguez	74	70	70	214	3,325
Billy Casper	75	68	71	214	3,325
George Lanning	74	71	69	214	3,325
Doug Sanders	76	70	68	214	3,325
Charles Sifford	71	75	68	214	3,325
Jim King	72	71	72	215	2,875
Dale Douglass	74	69	73	216	2,687.50
Lee Elder	75	69	72	216	2,687.50
John Brodie	73	73	71	217	2,312.50
Bob Rosburg	71	76	70	217	2,312.50
Peter Thomson	72	70	75	217	2,312.50
Dow Finsterwald	74	70	73	217	2,312.50
Tommy Aaron	76	74	68	218	1,795
Butch Baird	72	74	72	218	1,795
Ray Beallo	72	74	72	218	1,795
Ken Still	74	71	73	218	1,795
Don Massengale	71	78	69	218	1,795
Homero Blancas	78	71	70	219	1,543.50
Gay Brewer	74	75	70	219	1,543.50
Jerry Barber	73	77	71	221	1,387.67
Gene Littler	73	75	73	221	1,387.67
Doug Ford	73	74	74	221	1,387.66

Fairfield Barnett Classic

Suntree Country Club, Melbourne, Florida   November 11-13
Par 36-36 — 72; 6,590 yards   purse, $225,000

	SCORES			TOTAL	MONEY
Miller Barber	64	65	68	197	$33,750
Homero Blancas	66	68	68	202	19,250
Dave Hill	68	68	70	206	15,850

	SCORES			TOTAL	MONEY
Walter Zembriski	68	68	73	209	11,950
Larry Mowry	67	72	70	209	11,950
Ben Smith	70	72	68	210	7,187.50
Jimmy Powell	70	72	68	210	7,187.50
Butch Baird	71	67	72	210	7,187.50
Bruce Crampton	70	71	69	210	7,187.50
Dale Douglass	70	69	72	211	5,537.50
Al Geiberger	70	71	70	211	5,537.50
Bobby Nichols	73	67	72	212	4,096.43
Arnold Palmer	70	69	73	212	4,096.43
Jim Cochran	67	73	72	212	4,096.43
Doug Dalziel	75	69	68	212	4,096.43
Bruce Devlin	70	70	72	212	4,096.43
Lee Elder	73	70	69	212	4,096.43
Doug Sanders	75	70	67	212	4,096.42
Jim King	69	69	75	213	2,830
Al Kelley	73	71	69	213	2,830
Charles Mehok	73	69	71	213	2,830
Rafe Botts	67	72	74	213	2,830
Jim Ferree	70	72	71	213	2,830
Charles Sifford	69	74	71	214	2,350
Joe Lopez	74	70	70	214	2,350
Lou Graham	74	71	69	214	2,350
Roland Stafford	73	71	71	215	1,766.67
Bobby Greenwood	69	73	73	215	1,766.67
John Brodie	72	70	73	215	1,766.67
Dick Howell	73	73	69	215	1,766.67
Chick Evans	70	72	73	215	1,766.67
John Frillman	71	73	71	215	1,766.67
J.C. Goosie	71	74	70	215	1,766.66
Bob Brue	70	74	71	215	1,766.66
Bob Erickson	72	74	69	215	1,766.66
Richard Rhyan	72	73	71	216	1,300
Billy Maxwell	71	75	70	216	1,300
Auggie Navarro	77	69	70	216	1,300
Harold Henning	72	71	73	216	1,300

Gus Machado Classic

Links at Key Biscayne, Key Biscayne, Florida
Par 35-36 — 71; 6,715 yards

November 18-20
purse, $300,000

	SCORES			TOTAL	MONEY
Lee Elder	67	70	65	202	$45,000
Al Geiberger	70	74	63	207	26,000
Bob Charles	71	70	68	209	18,000
Lou Graham	70	69	70	209	18,000
Harold Henning	68	70	71	209	18,000
Miller Barber	69	72	69	210	11,100
Butch Baird	72	67	72	211	9,625
Dale Douglass	73	69	69	211	9,625
Charles Owens	70	73	69	212	7,808.34
Ben Smith	70	73	69	212	7,808.33
Arnold Palmer	71	72	69	212	7,808.33
George Lanning	71	73	69	213	6,200
Gene Littler	70	72	71	213	6,200

	SCORES			TOTAL	MONEY
Roland Stafford	73	68	72	213	6,200
Larry Mowry	69	73	72	214	5,350
Charles Coody	70	72	72	214	5,350
Bruce Crampton	74	68	73	215	4,600
Doug Dalziel	74	70	71	215	4,600
Bruce Devlin	71	75	69	215	4,600
Jimmy Powell	73	71	72	216	3,816.67
Joe Jimenez	77	69	70	216	3,816.67
Doug Sanders	70	71	75	216	3,816.66
Chi Chi Rodriguez	75	71	71	217	2,978.13
Homero Blancas	71	75	71	217	2,978.13
Bob Brue	72	75	70	217	2,978.13
Billy Casper	75	71	71	217	2,978.13
Tommy Aaron	74	76	67	217	2,978.12
Don Bies	70	75	72	217	2,978.12
Joe Lopez	69	76	72	217	2,978.12
Paul Harney	75	70	72	217	2,978.12
Ken Still	72	74	72	218	2,181.25
Bill Collins	72	72	74	218	2,181.25
Gordon Jones	72	76	70	218	2,181.25
Bill Johnston	77	72	69	218	2,181.25
Gay Brewer	72	75	72	219	1,775
Bobby Nichols	73	73	73	219	1,775
Bob Erickson	76	72	71	219	1,775
Richard Rhyan	72	75	72	219	1,775
John Frillman	69	81	69	219	1,775
Dick McNeill	77	71	72	220	1,475
Al Kelley	73	75	72	220	1,475
Jim King	73	73	74	220	1,475

GTE Kaanapali Classic

Royal Kaanapali Country Club, Maui, Hawaii
Par 36-36 — 72; 6,704 yards

December 2-4
purse, $300,000

	SCORES			TOTAL	MONEY
Don Bies	68	67	69	204	$45,000
Don January	66	68	71	205	26,000
Dave Hill	68	68	70	206	21,500
Jimmy Powell	68	68	71	207	16,250
Billy Casper	69	69	69	207	16,250
Harold Henning	67	68	73	208	11,100
Al Kelley	71	68	71	210	9,258.34
Chi Chi Rodriguez	68	70	72	210	9,258.33
Lee Elder	66	74	70	210	9,258.33
Butch Baird	71	71	69	211	7,450
Al Geiberger	73	68	70	211	7,450
Gene Littler	71	71	70	212	6,025
Larry Mowry	70	71	71	212	6,025
Charles Sifford	69	72	71	212	6,025
Lou Graham	68	70	74	212	6,025
Allan Yamamoto	70	72	71	213	4,466.67
Don Massengale	70	72	71	213	4,466.67
Bob Erickson	70	75	68	213	4,466.67
Joe Jimenez	69	71	73	213	4,466.67
Orville Moody	66	71	76	213	4,466.66

	SCORES			TOTAL	MONEY
Bruce Crampton	66	78	69	213	4,466.66
Miller Barber	71	71	72	214	3,650
Ben Smith	74	68	73	215	3,200
Ken Still	68	71	76	215	3,200
John Brodie	65	76	74	215	3,200
Bob Charles	71	70	74	215	3,200
Jim King	70	73	72	215	3,200
Robert Boldt	71	70	75	216	2,608.34
Roland Stafford	69	76	71	216	2,608.33
Dale Douglass	70	74	72	216	2,608.33

Mauna Lani Challenge

Mauna Lani Golf Club, Waikoloa, Hawaii
Par 36-36 — 72; 6,682 yards

December 9-11
purse, $300,000

	SCORES			TOTAL	MONEY
Harold Henning	66	66	70	202	$45,000
Bob Erickson	69	69	68	206	20,000
Don January	68	69	70	207	11,250
Billy Casper	69	70	68	207	11,250
Al Geiberger	72	66	69	207	11,250
Dave Hill	64	72	71	207	11,250
Dale Douglass	69	70	69	208	6,000
Rafe Botts	73	66	69	208	6,000
Ben Smith	67	70	71	208	6,000
Lou Graham	68	67	73	208	6,000
Bob Charles	70	66	72	208	6,000
Don Massengale	67	69	73	209	4,650
Bob Rawlins	68	71	71	210	4,066.67
George Lanning	71	68	71	210	4,066.67
Gay Brewer	66	70	74	210	4,066.66
Lee Elder	70	72	69	211	3,600
Tommy Aaron	71	68	73	212	3,400
Bob Brue	67	72	74	213	2,860
Jim Ferree	71	70	72	213	2,860
Jerry Barber	71	72	70	213	2,860
Butch Baird	74	70	69	213	2,860
Larry Mowry	71	73	69	213	2,860
Charles Sifford	71	72	71	214	2,525
Mike Fetchick	68	75	71	214	2,525
Al Kelley	68	75	72	215	2,425
Doug Sanders	69	72	74	215	2,425
John Brodie	73	66	78	217	2,350
Jim King	68	73	78	219	2,275
Gordon Jones	71	73	75	219	2,275
Kyle Burton	71	77	72	220	2,200

Mazda Champions

Hyatt-Dorado Beach, East Course, Dorado Beach, Puerto Rico
Par 36-36 — 72; 6,740 yards - men
               6,265 yards - women

December 16-18
purse, $850,000

	SCORES			TOTAL	MONEY (Each)
Dave Hill/Colleen Walker	60	62	64	186	$250,000
Chi Chi Rodriguez/Jan Stephenson	74	61	65	190	50,000
Orville Moody/Tammy Green	63	66	62	191	25,000
Harold Henning/Nancy Lopez	66	65	62	193	20,000
Al Geiberger/Juli Inkster	66	63	65	194	17,000
Arnold Palmer/Kathy Postlewait	67	69	59	195	14,000
Bruce Crampton/Betsy King	68	64	65	197	12,000
Gary Player/Sherri Turner	67	69	63	199	10,000
Gene Littler/Ok Hee Ku	67	66	67	200	7,500
Don Bies/Amy Alcott	68	68	64	200	7,500
Bob Charles/Patty Sheehan	66	69	66	201	6,250
Miller Barber/Rosie Jones	69	66	68	203	5,750

The European Tour

Mallorca Open De Baleares

Santa Ponsa Golf Club, Mallorca, Spain
Par 36-36 — 72; 7,150 yards

March 10-13
purse, £200,000

	SCORES				TOTAL	MONEY
Severiano Ballesteros	70	68	67	67	272	£33,330
Jose-Maria Olazabal	68	73	64	73	278	22,200
Gordon Brand Jr.	76	68	70	66	280	12,520
Ronan Rafferty	73	70	70	70	283	8,490
Barry Lane	71	73	67	72	283	8,490
Martin Poxon	72	72	69	70	283	8,490
John Jacobs	71	73	68	72	284	6,000
Des Smyth	73	71	72	69	285	5,000

	SCORES				TOTAL	MONEY
Mark James	73	70	71	72	286	3,646.67
Manuel Pinero	72	71	74	69	286	3,646.67
Peter Jones	72	72	71	71	286	3,646.67
Peter Baker	71	73	70	72	286	3,646.67
John Slaughter	68	72	73	73	286	3,646.67
Craig McClellan	71	73	73	69	286	3,646.67
Juan Anglada	74	75	66	72	287	2,760
Neil Hansen	71	66	71	79	287	2,760
Andrew Murray	74	72	72	69	287	2,760
Armando Saavedra	71	72	73	71	287	2,760
Jose Rivero	71	71	72	74	288	2,344
Christy O'Connor Jr.	76	71	71	70	288	2,344
Denis Durnian	76	68	74	70	288	2,344
David Williams	72	73	69	74	288	2,344
David Gilford	75	70	70	73	288	2,344
Eamonn Darcy	74	70	75	70	289	1,840
David Feherty	72	75	72	70	289	1,840
Antonio Garrido	74	73	70	72	289	1,840
Brian Waites	73	76	69	71	289	1,840
Jose Gervas	75	71	74	69	289	1,840
Miguel Martin	69	75	76	69	289	1,840
Richard Boxall	72	70	75	72	289	1,840
Jamie Howell	77	71	68	73	289	1,840
Mats Hallberg	76	69	69	75	289	1,840
Johan Rystrom	76	70	73	70	289	1,840
Jerry Haas	72	71	70	76	289	1,840
Calvin Peete	74	71	71	73	289	1,840
Philip Walton	76	73	67	74	290	1,500
Mike Miller	74	73	69	74	290	1,500
Ross McFarlane	73	73	76	69	291	1,280
Ian Woosnam	71	78	71	71	291	1,280
Frederic Regard	74	74	72	71	291	1,280
Emilio Rodriguez	68	74	77	72	291	1,280
Mariano Aparicio	77	72	72	70	291	1,280
Roger Chapman	71	73	76	71	291	1,280
Jerry Anderson	73	74	75	69	291	1,280
Ian Young	74	72	71	74	291	1,280
Anders Forsbrand	72	72	72	75	291	1,280
David J. Russell	76	72	71	73	292	920
Eduardo Romero	73	74	72	73	292	920
Bryan Norton	73	70	75	74	292	920
Magnus Persson	74	73	74	71	292	920
Ross Drummond	75	73	72	72	292	920
Andrew Sherborne	74	75	73	70	292	920
Philip Parkin	75	73	75	69	292	920
Manuel Calero	72	74	77	69	292	920
Tom Sieckman	71	76	73	72	292	920

Torras Hostench Barcelona Open

Real Club de Golf el Prat, Barcelona, Spain
Par 35-37 — 72; 6,492 yards

March 17-20
purse, £200,000

	SCORES				TOTAL	MONEY
David Whelan	68	65	74	69	276	£33,330
Mark Mouland	71	68	69	68	276	14,906.66
Nick Faldo	66	68	71	71	276	14,906.66

	SCORES				TOTAL	MONEY
Barry Lane	71	69	67	69	276	14,906.66

(Whelan won playoff, defeating Faldo and Mouland on first hole, Lane on fourth hole.)

Johan Rystrom	70	69	68	71	278	8,470
Sam Torrance	75	68	68	68	279	7,000
David Gilford	68	73	68	71	280	4,433.33
Malcolm MacKenzie	72	68	68	72	280	4,433.33
Philip Harrison	71	68	73	68	280	4,433.33
Christy O'Connor Jr.	72	69	71	68	280	4,433.33
Peter Teravainen	68	71	69	72	280	4,433.33
Peter Baker	75	69	70	66	280	4,433.33
Michael Allen	66	73	70	72	281	2,948
Jose-Maria Olazabal	69	69	73	70	281	2,948
Denis Durnian	74	69	69	69	281	2,948
Jerry Anderson	73	71	70	67	281	2,948
Andrew Murray	75	68	68	70	281	2,948
Eamonn Darcy	72	70	70	70	282	2,320
Howard Clark	69	72	69	72	282	2,320
Ian Mosey	70	70	72	70	282	2,320
Stephen Bennett	71	71	70	70	282	2,320
Philip Walton	71	72	67	72	282	2,320
Armando Saavedra	74	69	72	67	282	2,320
Jim Rutledge	73	67	71	71	282	2,320
Magnus Persson	70	71	68	73	282	2,320
Tony Charnley	71	71	67	74	283	1,920
Gordon J. Brand	70	69	70	74	283	1,920
Peter Jones	70	72	69	72	283	1,920
Mark James	73	71	70	69	283	1,920
Magnus Jonsson	70	69	71	73	283	1,920
Mariano Aparicio	75	69	70	70	284	1,582.50
Simon Bishop	70	69	73	72	284	1,582.50
David Williams	71	73	74	66	284	1,582.50
Peter McWhinney	72	72	71	69	284	1,582.50
Bob E. Smith	71	70	73	70	284	1,582.50
John McHenry	73	70	72	69	284	1,582.50
Mitch Adcock	73	68	71	72	284	1,582.50
John Morgan	74	69	72	69	284	1,582.50
David Llewellyn	71	72	73	69	285	1,380
Eduardo Romero	72	72	71	70	285	1,380
Jacob Rasmussen	76	68	73	69	286	1,280
Emmanuel Dussart	75	69	74	68	286	1,280
Juan Quiros	72	71	72	71	286	1,280
Jeremy Bennett	71	72	70	74	287	1,120
Peter Mitchell	75	69	72	71	287	1,120
Paul Thomas	72	72	70	73	287	1,120
John Jacobs	70	73	71	73	287	1,120
Colin Montgomerie	71	72	73	71	287	1,120
Antonio Garrido	72	72	72	72	288	900
Craig Laurence	69	72	77	70	288	900
David A. Russell	74	69	73	72	288	900
Alberto Binaghi	72	69	78	69	288	900
Jose Davila	74	70	73	71	288	900
Ross McFarlane	71	72	75	70	288	900

AGF Biarritz Open

Biarritz Golf Club, Biarritz, France
Par 34-34 — 68; 5,878 yards

March 31-April 3
purse, £142,146

	SCORES				TOTAL	MONEY
David Llewellyn	64	69	60	65	258	£23,691.07
Christy O'Connor Jr.	66	66	65	68	265	15,787.73
Barry Lane	71	65	63	67	266	8,002.85
Jose Rivero	67	63	69	67	266	8,002.85
Mark James	67	69	65	66	267	4,705.05
Gordon Brand Jr.	64	69	68	66	267	4,705.05
Michael Allen	67	66	69	65	267	4,705.05
Philip Walton	65	66	67	69	267	4,705.05
Simon Bishop	64	70	68	66	268	2,771.86
Neil Hansen	68	66	66	68	268	2,771.86
Jim Rutledge	66	67	66	69	268	2,771.86
Eamonn Darcy	63	71	67	67	268	2,771.86
Howard Clark	71	64	67	67	269	2,179.58
Malcolm MacKenzie	68	68	65	68	269	2,179.58
Mike Clayton	67	68	67	67	269	2,179.58
Emanuele Bolognesi	71	67	68	64	270	1,687.24
John Morgan	68	69	67	66	270	1,687.24
Anders Forsbrand	69	69	61	71	270	1,687.24
Peter Jones	70	64	70	66	270	1,687.24
Magnus Persson	69	66	67	68	270	1,687.24
Ron Commans	68	67	67	68	270	1,687.24
David Whelan	67	68	69	66	270	1,687.24
Grant Turner	69	69	65	67	270	1,687.24
Robert Richardson	69	67	69	65	270	1,687.24
Miguel Martin	71	65	71	63	270	1,687.24
Jose-Maria Olazabal	67	67	68	68	270	1,687.24
Antonio Garrido	70	66	69	66	271	1,321.96
David Ray	66	67	68	70	271	1,321.96
Philip Harrison	70	65	70	66	271	1,321.96
Roger Chapman	67	70	66	68	271	1,321.96
Santiago Luna	66	67	67	71	271	1,321.96
Des Smyth	67	70	67	68	272	1,108.74
David Gilford	69	69	68	66	272	1,108.74
Derrick Cooper	67	66	72	67	272	1,108.74
Gery Watine	69	68	66	69	272	1,108.74
Martin Poxon	69	69	66	68	272	1,108.74
Olivier Leglise	68	68	70	66	272	1,108.74
Christian Bonardi	67	69	68	68	272	1,108.74
Bryan Norton	70	66	66	71	273	909.74
Frank Nobilo	72	65	67	69	273	909.74
Juan Anglada	70	66	67	70	273	909.74
Gordon J. Brand	65	68	70	70	273	909.74
Ronan Rafferty	68	70	67	68	273	909.74
Jose Davila	69	69	68	67	273	909.74
Chris Moody	67	71	68	67	273	909.74
Tony Stevens	71	67	68	68	274	767.59
Magnus Sunesson	69	68	69	68	274	767.59
Paul Thomas	69	69	67	69	274	767.59
Johan Rystrom	65	68	70	72	275	710.73
Wayne Riley	69	69	67	71	276	653.87
Jeremy Bennett	69	68	69	70	276	653.87
Jerry Anderson	69	65	71	71	276	653.87

Cannes Open

Cannes Mougins Golf Club, Cannes, France
Par 36-36 — 72; 6,786 yards

April 14-17
purse, £189,555

	SCORES				TOTAL	MONEY
Mark McNulty	72	71	70	66	279	£31,588.82
Ron Commans	70	68	72	72	282	16,453.11
Joey Sindelar	69	74	69	70	282	16,453.11
Denis Durnian	72	69	74	70	285	9,477.59
Tony Charnley	71	75	74	66	286	7,330.92
Jim Rutledge	72	75	71	68	286	7,330.92
Howard Clark	70	72	73	72	287	5,686.56
Philip Walton	71	73	68	76	288	4,065.89
Jose-Maria Olazabal	74	69	72	73	288	4,065.89
Ove Sellberg	71	77	70	70	288	4,065.89
Juan Anglada	72	74	71	71	288	4,065.89
Wayne Riley	68	75	75	71	289	3,156.04
Michael Allen	71	73	76	69	289	3,156.04
David Llewellyn	75	74	70	71	290	2,843.28
Neil Hansen	72	73	75	70	290	2,843.28
Manuel Pinero	75	73	71	72	291	2,382.94
Sam Torrance	76	72	72	71	291	2,382.94
Mike Harwood	70	77	73	71	291	2,382.94
Mike Smith	75	72	74	70	291	2,382.94
Manuel Calero	76	72	73	70	291	2,382.94
Paul Way	76	73	75	67	291	2,382.94
Peter Fowler	75	75	71	70	291	2,382.94
Andrew Murray	77	72	72	71	292	1,905
Tony Johnstone	73	72	73	74	292	1,905
Ross Drummond	77	69	76	70	292	1,905
Frederic Regard	78	68	76	70	292	1,905
Ronan Rafferty	74	70	72	76	292	1,905
Gordon J. Brand	71	75	72	74	292	1,905
Miguel Martin	75	74	67	76	292	1,905
Mark Mouland	75	73	74	70	292	1,905
Richard Boxall	76	69	71	77	293	1,578.02
John Jacobs	74	71	75	73	293	1,578.02
Eamonn Darcy	71	74	73	75	293	1,578.02
Glenn Ralph	73	73	75	72	293	1,578.02
Magnus Sunesson	73	74	73	74	294	1,364.77
Jeff Hall	75	75	70	74	294	1,364.77
Emanuele Bolognesi	73	68	76	77	294	1,364.77
Antonio Garrido	75	74	73	72	294	1,364.77
Andrew Sherborne	74	75	73	72	294	1,364.77
Luis Carbonetti	73	74	73	74	294	1,364.77
Barry Lane	69	80	74	71	294	1,364.77
Wayne Westner	76	73	72	74	295	1,156.27
Johan Rystrom	75	72	75	73	295	1,156.27
Derrick Cooper	72	74	71	78	295	1,156.27
Neil Coles	75	75	73	72	295	1,156.27
Martin Poxon	72	78	73	73	296	947.76
Anders Forsbrand	71	75	75	75	296	947.76
David Whelan	71	77	69	79	296	947.76
Ian Mosey	76	72	77	71	296	947.76
Ronald Stelten	78	71	75	72	296	947.76
Emmanuel Dussart	76	72	75	73	296	947.76
Frederic Martin	75	74	74	73	296	947.76

Cepsa Madrid Open

Real Club de la Puerta de Hierro, Madrid, Spain
Par 36-36 — 72; 6,938 yards

April 21-24
purse, £200,000

	SCORES				TOTAL	MONEY
Derrick Cooper	70	68	69	68	275	£33,330
Manuel Pinero	69	69	67	71	276	17,360
Miguel Martin	69	69	68	70	276	17,360
Severiano Ballesteros	69	68	69	72	278	10,000
Howard Clark	69	76	71	64	280	6,190
Mark McNulty	71	67	71	71	280	6,190
John Morgan	68	72	68	72	280	6,190
Mark James	71	70	69	70	280	6,190
Bernard Gallacher	69	71	70	70	280	6,190
Ignacio Gervas	65	69	73	74	281	3,840
David Ray	72	73	69	67	281	3,840
Sam Torrance	75	70	66	71	282	2,965.71
Ossie Moore	70	71	70	71	282	2,965.71
Jose Rivero	68	73	72	69	282	2,965.71
Eamonn Darcy	73	67	70	72	282	2,965.71
Jose-Maria Olazabal	74	70	69	69	282	2,965.71
Mike Harwood	71	68	70	73	282	2,965.71
Mark Mouland	71	69	69	73	282	2,965.71
Chris Moody	69	73	68	73	283	2,375
Mike Clayton	69	72	69	73	283	2,375
David Llewellyn	71	71	72	69	283	2,375
Juan Angalda	68	73	70	72	283	2,375
*Yago Beamonte	69	66	72	76	283	
Ronan Rafferty	74	71	68	71	284	2,130
Ron Commans	76	67	70	71	284	2,130
Manuel Calero	70	74	71	69	284	2,130
John De Forest	69	69	72	74	284	2,130
Roger Chapman	73	72	68	72	285	1,950
Peter Fowler	71	69	71	74	285	1,950
Wayne Riley	71	71	69	75	286	1,632
Ian Young	68	74	72	72	286	1,632
Ove Sellberg	73	70	72	71	286	1,632
Emilio Rodriguez	73	70	72	71	286	1,632
Miguel Jimenez	74	71	72	69	286	1,632
John Slaughter	69	75	72	70	286	1,632
Carl Mason	70	75	75	66	286	1,632
Tony Johnstone	68	71	70	77	286	1,632
Richard Boxall	72	68	75	71	286	1,632
Anders Forsbrand	66	69	74	77	286	1,632
Eduardo Romero	73	68	72	74	287	1,300
John Bland	71	74	70	72	287	1,300
Rodger Davis	68	73	73	73	287	1,300
Steen Tinning	67	74	73	73	287	1,300
Brian Marchbank	70	72	72	73	287	1,300
Manuel Sanchez	73	70	69	75	287	1,300
Philip Walton	71	69	75	73	288	1,020
Stephen Bennett	73	69	74	72	288	1,020
Armando Saavedra	74	71	73	70	288	1,020
Simon Bishop	71	71	76	70	288	1,020
Glenn Ralph	69	74	74	71	288	1,020
Jeff Hall	68	75	73	72	288	1,020
Andrew Sherborne	74	70	72	72	288	1,020
Christy O'Connor Jr.	74	70	70	74	288	1,020
*Borja Queipo de Llano	71	71	72	74	288	

Portuguese Open

Quinta do Lago Golf Club, Almancil, Algarve, Portugal
Par 36-36 — 72; 7,091 yards

April 28-May 1
purse, £200,000

	SCORES				TOTAL	MONEY
Mike Harwood	73	70	68	69	280	£33,330
Eamonn Darcy	69	70	72	70	281	22,200
Peter Baker	74	68	67	73	282	11,260
Des Smyth	70	74	68	70	282	11,260
Peter Fowler	71	68	73	71	283	8,470
Ignacio Gervas	74	70	69	71	284	7,000
Philip Harrison	69	73	73	70	285	5,500
Jose Rivero	73	72	71	69	285	5,500
Richard Boxall	74	71	69	72	286	3,646.67
Gordon J. Brand	73	73	73	67	286	3,646.67
Tony Johnstone	72	71	71	72	286	3,646.67
Malcolm MacKenzie	74	70	70	72	286	3,646.67
Ronan Rafferty	71	71	70	74	286	3,646.67
Wayne Westner	74	70	73	69	286	3,646.67
Derrick Cooper	68	75	74	70	287	2,820
Emilio Rodriguez	72	71	69	75	287	2,820
John Slaughter	69	72	73	73	287	2,820
John Bland	69	71	73	75	288	2,320
John Jacobs	73	68	72	75	288	2,320
Colin Montgomerie	72	69	74	73	288	2,320
Christy O'Connor Jr.	72	73	68	75	288	2,320
David Ray	69	74	71	74	288	2,320
Johan Rystrom	69	75	72	72	288	2,320
Mike Smith	73	73	70	72	288	2,320
Sam Torrance	71	74	72	71	288	2,320
Stephen Bennett	69	70	72	78	289	1,920
Simon Bishop	74	71	68	76	289	1,920
Carl Mason	70	75	72	72	289	1,920
Peter Mitchell	72	75	70	72	289	1,920
Keith Waters	74	69	72	74	289	1,920
Denis Durnian	75	72	72	71	290	1,665
Chris Moody	75	69	73	73	290	1,665
Ian Roberts	69	75	71	75	290	1,665
Peter Teravainen	73	74	72	71	290	1,665
Michael Allen	73	74	73	71	291	1,380
Jerry Anderson	77	69	71	74	291	1,380
Jeremy Bennett	72	75	74	70	291	1,380
Jose-Maria Canizares	76	71	73	71	291	1,380
Antonio Garrido	74	69	74	74	291	1,380
David Gilford	69	76	71	75	291	1,380
Jeff Hawkes	73	71	73	74	291	1,380
Gavin Levenson	69	74	74	74	291	1,380
Martin Poxon	74	70	70	77	291	1,380
Jim Rutledge	71	74	71	75	291	1,380
Roger Chapman	71	74	73	74	292	1,060
John De Forest	73	73	71	75	292	1,060
Bernard Gallacher	75	72	70	75	292	1,060
David Llewellyn	74	72	72	74	292	1,060
Wayne Riley	73	73	71	75	292	1,060
Armando Saavedra	75	71	73	73	292	1,060

Epson Grand Prix of Europe Match Play Championship

St. Pierre Golf and Country Club, Chepstow, England
Par 35-36 — 71; 6,873 yards

May 5-8
purse, £275,000

FIRST ROUND

Ken Brown defeated Magnus Persson, 2 and 1.
Des Smyth defeated Jeff Hawkes, 5 and 4.
Christy O'Connor Jr. defeated Mark Mouland, 3 and 2.
Rodger Davis defeated Paul Way, 1 up.
Denis Durnian defeated Noel Ratcliffe, 5 and 3.
Glenn Ralph defeated Barry Lane, 1 up.
Bill Longmuir defeated Ove Sellberg, 1 up, 19 holes.
Brian Marchbank defeated Rick Hartmann, 4 and 2.
Tony Johnstone defeated Jose Rivero, 1 up.
Anders Forsbrand defeated Bill Malley, 3 and 1.
John Morgan defeated Tony Charnley, 3 and 2.
Gordon J. Brand defeated David Llewellyn, 3 and 1.
Antonio Garrido defeated Mark James, 1 up, 19 holes.
Carl Mason defeated John O'Leary, 4 and 2.
Robert Lee defeated Eamonn Darcy, 5 and 3.
Howard Clark defeated Jose-Maria Olazabal, 2 up.
Mark Roe defeated Gavin Levenson, 3 and 1.
Miguel Martin defeated Hugh Baiocchi, 3 and 1.
Philip Walton defeated John Bland, 1 up, 19 holes.
Peter Fowler defeated Jose Maria Canizares, 2 and 1.
Ian Mosey defeated Sam Torrance, 3 and 2.
David A. Russell defeated Ronan Rafferty, 1 up.
David J. Russell defeated David Feherty, 1 up, 20 holes.
Roger Chapman defeated Manuel Pinero, 1 up.
(All first-round losers received £1,715.)

SECOND ROUND

Ian Woosnam defeated Brown, 2 and 1.
Smyth defeated O'Connor, 1 up, 21 holes.
Davis defeated Durnian, 1 up.
Ralph defeated Mats Lanner, 1 up.
Bernhard Langer defeated Longmuir, 1 up, 19 holes.
Johnstone defeated Marchbank, 1 up, 19 holes.
Morgan defeated Forsbrand, 5 and 3.
Gordon J. Brand defeated Gordon Brand Jr., 2 and 1.
Garrido defeated Nick Faldo, 2 and 1.
Mason defeated Lee, 2 and 1.
Clark defeated Roe, 2 and 1.
Martin defeated Peter Senior, 3 and 2.
Masahiro Kuramoto defeated Walton, 1 up.
Mosey defeated Fowler, 1 up.
David J. Russell defeated David A. Russell, 1 up.
Mark McNulty defeated Chapman, 3 and 2.
(All second-round losers received £3,000.)

THIRD ROUND

Smyth defeated Woosnam, 2 and 1.
Davis defeated Ralph, 4 and 3.
Langer defeated Johnstone, 2 and 1.
Morgan defeated Gordon J. Brand, 1 up, 19 holes.
Mason defeated Garrido, 1 up, 20 holes.
Clark defeated Martin, 4 and 2.
Kuramoto defeated Mosey, 1 up, 20 holes.

McNulty defeated David J. Russell, 5 and 4.
(All third-round losers received £4,750.)

QUARTER-FINALS

Davis defeated Smyth, 3 and 1.
Langer defeated Morgan, 1 up.
Clark defeated Mason, 5 and 4.
McNulty defeated Kuramoto, 3 and 2.
(All quarter-final losers received £9,100.)

SEMI-FINALS

McNulty defeated Clark, 3 and 2.
Langer defeated Davis, 1 up.

PLAYOFF FOR THIRD-FOURTH PLACE

Davis defeated Clark, 3 and 2.
(Davis received £17,190, Clark £13,750.)

FINALS

Langer defeated McNulty, 4 and 2.
(Langer received £50,000, McNulty £30,500.)

Peugeot Spanish Open

Real Golf de Pedrena, Santander, Spain
Par 35-35 — 70; 6,438 yards

May 12-15
purse, £166,230

	SCORES				TOTAL	MONEY
Mark James	63	68	63	68	262	£27,703.63
Nick Faldo	68	67	62	68	265	18,456.42
Richard Boxall	63	64	70	69	266	10,406.08
Gordon J. Brand	70	66	64	68	268	7,677.51
Christy O'Connor Jr.	67	66	69	66	268	7,677.51
Eamonn Darcy	71	68	67	64	270	4,986.94
Jose-Maria Olazabal	71	66	65	68	270	4,986.94
Miguel Martin	70	67	65	68	270	4,986.94
Gordon Brand Jr.	69	68	68	66	271	3,241.51
Derrick Cooper	69	71	63	68	271	3,241.51
David Williams	67	66	69	69	271	3,241.51
Colin Montgomerie	69	64	70	68	271	3,241.51
Bill Malley	69	71	64	68	272	2,552.05
Wayne Riley	71	67	61	73	272	2,552.05
Jose Cabo	73	63	68	68	272	2,552.05
Peter Senior	68	68	71	66	273	2,341.49
Severiano Ballesteros	72	67	67	68	274	1,990.62
Ken Brown	67	66	69	72	274	1,990.62
Jose-Maria Canizares	71	70	66	67	274	1,990.62
Barry Lane	70	70	69	65	274	1,990.62
Peter Fowler	68	67	73	66	274	1,990.62
Mike Clayton	68	65	70	71	274	1,990.62
Philip Harrison	69	66	70	69	274	1,990.62
David Gilford	72	64	70	68	274	1,990.62
Anders Forsbrand	69	68	71	67	275	1,720.50
Jose Rivero	67	70	70	68	275	1,720.50
Stephen Bennett	69	65	69	73	276	1,545.95
David Llewellyn	69	71	67	69	276	1,545.95
Mark Roe	72	68	69	67	276	1,545.95

	SCORES				TOTAL	MONEY
Glenn Ralph	66	71	69	70	276	1,545.95
Juan Quiros	70	69	68	69	276	1,545.95
Antonio Garrido	71	67	70	69	277	1,329.85
Mike Miller	68	69	66	74	277	1,329.85
Alberto Binaghi	72	67	74	64	277	1,329.85
Michel Tapia	66	69	74	68	277	1,329.85
Armando Saavedra	69	71	66	71	277	1,329.85
Michael Allen	73	67	68	70	278	1,196.87
Emilio Rodriguez	73	66	71	68	278	1,196.87
Paul Thomas	68	68	70	72	278	1,196.87
Mike Harwood	73	68	72	66	279	1,080.50
Mariano Aparicio	69	72	71	67	279	1,080.50
David Ray	70	71	71	67	279	1,080.50
Jose M. Carriles	69	70	64	76	279	1,080.50
Mark Davis	69	71	70	70	280	964.14
David Jones	69	68	72	71	280	964.14
Ross McFarlane	73	68	67	72	280	964.14
Miguel Jimenez	69	70	70	72	281	864.40
Paul Curry	72	66	70	73	281	864.40
Luis Carbonetti	70	65	74	72	281	864.40
Manuel Pinero	68	70	76	68	282	664.93
Ignacio Gervas	71	69	70	72	282	664.93
David A. Russell	68	73	70	71	282	664.93
Ian Mosey	69	70	73	70	282	664.93
Per-Arne Brostedt	72	69	73	68	282	664.93
Andrew Sherborne	71	70	69	72	282	664.93
Jimmy Heggarty	72	68	71	71	282	664.93

Lancia Italian Open

Monticello Golf Course, Como, Italy
Par 36-36 — 72; 6,966 yards

May 19-22
purse, £212,000

(Course shortened to par 69, 6,157 yards for first round because of rain.)

	SCORES				TOTAL	MONEY
Greg Norman	69	68	63	70	270	£35,319.06
Craig Parry	65	68	67	71	271	23,531.91
Ronan Rafferty	66	70	67	69	272	13,271.15
Denis Durnian	67	70	68	68	273	9,794.36
Roger Chapman	66	68	69	70	273	9,794.36
Gordon Brand Jr.	67	68	70	69	274	6,889.97
Ian Woosnam	68	68	69	69	274	6,889.97
Philip Parkin	65	72	68	70	275	5,024.38
Peter Senior	70	69	67	69	275	5,024.38
David Whelan	63	71	70	72	276	4,070.38
Bob Shearer	67	70	71	68	276	4,070.38
Barry Lane	67	69	71	70	277	3,354.89
Colin Montgomerie	68	71	68	70	277	3,354.89
Rodger Davis	65	74	69	69	277	3,354.89
Jose Rivero	66	68	71	72	277	3,354.89
Wayne Riley	67	69	75	67	278	2,861.99
Jeff Hawkes	66	74	70	68	278	2,861.99
Juan Anglada	70	65	70	73	278	2,861.99
Giuseppe Cali	64	72	72	71	279	2,323.51
John Slaughter	65	75	70	69	279	2,323.51
Vicente Fernandez	63	71	71	74	279	2,323.51

	SCORES				TOTAL	MONEY
David Gilford	64	70	71	74	279	2,323.51
Luis Carbonetti	66	72	69	72	279	2,323.51
Hugh Baiocchi	69	71	69	70	279	2,323.51
Ron Commans	69	63	70	77	279	2,323.51
Mats Hallberg	68	69	72	70	279	2,323.51
Johan Rystrom	66	71	71	71	279	2,323.51
Philip Walton	70	70	69	70	279	2,323.51
Tony Johnstone	67	71	67	75	280	1,848.63
Mike Clayton	69	69	72	70	280	1,848.63
Steen Tinning	65	69	73	73	280	1,848.63
Howard Clark	65	72	75	68	280	1,848.63
David Feherty	64	70	74	72	280	1,848.63
Rick Hartmann	70	70	72	69	281	1,611.19
Keith Waters	69	70	71	71	281	1,611.19
Eduardo Romero	68	71	70	72	281	1,611.19
Richard Boxall	68	71	71	71	281	1,611.19
Tony Stevens	68	71	72	70	281	1,611.19
Mark Litton	71	67	75	69	282	1,420.39
Emmanuel Dussart	68	70	72	72	282	1,420.39
Bill McColl	62	74	74	72	282	1,420.39
Peter Mitchell	66	74	71	71	282	1,420.39
David Ray	68	67	72	76	283	1,229.60
Ossie Moore	66	71	74	72	283	1,229.60
Lyndsay Stephen	71	69	72	71	283	1,229.60
Jimmy Heggarty	67	73	70	73	283	1,229.60
Geralamo Delfino	65	71	74	73	283	1,229.60
Ross Drummond	66	73	74	71	284	1,102.40
Oliver Eckstein	65	73	78	69	285	954
Eamonn Darcy	69	70	72	74	285	954
Alessandro Rogato	68	71	75	71	285	954
Ross McFarlane	68	70	74	73	285	954
David Williams	67	71	73	74	285	954
Bryan Norton	69	71	73	72	285	954

Volvo PGA Championship

The Wentworth Club, West Course, Virgina Water, Surrey, England
Par 35-37 — 72; 6,945 yards

May 27-30
purse, £300,000

	SCORES				TOTAL	MONEY
Ian Woosnam	67	70	70	67	274	£50,000
Severiano Ballesteros	67	68	71	70	276	26,040
Mark James	68	72	68	68	276	26,040
Roger Chapman	70	71	71	66	278	13,850
Mark McNulty	67	71	69	71	278	13,850
Jeff Hawkes	67	70	70	72	279	10,500
John Bland	72	70	69	69	280	7,740
Bernhard Langer	67	66	74	73	280	7,740
Sandy Lyle	70	76	68	66	280	7,740
Nick Faldo	71	70	71	69	281	6,000
Jose-Maria Canizares	69	68	70	75	282	5,340
Jose-Maria Olazabal	68	66	78	70	282	5,340
Stephen Bennett	71	71	71	70	283	4,710
Des Smyth	70	70	72	71	283	4,710
Howard Clark	70	71	71	72	284	3,980
Eamonn Darcy	75	70	69	70	284	3,980
Rodger Davis	68	72	75	69	284	3,980

	SCORES				TOTAL	MONEY
Mike Miller	66	74	74	70	284	3,980
Christy O'Connor Jr.	71	70	69	74	284	3,980
Ronan Rafferty	68	71	74	71	284	3,980
Tommy Armour III	73	70	72	70	285	3,420
Tony Johnstone	73	72	71	69	285	3,420
Emilio Rodriguez	76	67	74	68	285	3,420
Brian Marchbank	70	69	73	74	286	3,060
Mark Mouland	71	73	68	74	286	3,060
Andrew Oldcorn	65	73	76	72	286	3,060
Manuel Pinero	72	71	70	73	286	3,060
Peter Senior	74	71	73	68	286	3,060
Ian Baker-Finch	72	74	69	72	287	2,700
John Morgan	73	71	75	68	287	2,700
Magnus Persson	71	68	73	75	287	2,700
Richard Boxall	73	69	69	77	288	2,430
Denis Durnian	72	70	75	71	288	2,430
Miguel Martin	73	73	70	72	288	2,430
Teddy Webber	70	71	78	69	288	2,430
Simon Bishop	72	70	74	73	289	2,040
Neil Hansen	73	73	74	69	289	2,040
Barry Lane	70	75	72	72	289	2,040
Ossie Moore	70	70	77	72	289	2,040
Jose Rivero	65	78	75	71	289	2,040
Mark Roe	70	76	70	73	289	2,040
Jim Rutledge	73	72	72	72	289	2,040
Andrew Sherborne	73	73	71	72	289	2,040
Greg J. Turner	72	71	74	72	289	2,040
Clive Tucker	71	74	74	71	290	1,710
Brian Waites	73	72	72	73	290	1,710
David Jones	73	70	74	74	291	1,530
Malcolm Mackenzie	76	70	73	72	291	1,530
Chris Moody	67	73	82	69	291	1,530
Wayne Riley	67	69	78	77	291	1,530

Dunhill British Masters

Woburn Golf and Country Club, Duke's Course, Bow Brickhill, England June 2-5
Par 34-38 — 72; 6,913 yards purse, £250,000

	SCORES				TOTAL	MONEY
Sandy Lyle	66	68	68	71	273	£41,660
Nick Faldo	72	67	67	69	275	21,705
Mark McNulty	69	69	72	65	275	21,705
Jose-Maria Olazabal	69	68	71	68	276	12,500
Ronan Rafferty	72	67	71	69	279	10,600
Mark James	68	75	71	67	281	8,125
Philip Walton	73	68	71	69	281	8,125
Jose-Maria Canizares	74	71	69	68	282	6,250
Ken Brown	74	67	74	68	283	4,875
Rodger Davis	70	71	70	72	283	4,875
Bob Shearer	70	71	71	71	283	4,875
Lee Trevino	69	75	70	69	283	4,875
Jerry Anderson	72	72	72	68	284	3,757.50
Christy O'Connor Jr.	73	73	70	68	284	3,757.50
Peter Senior	68	70	72	74	284	3,757.50
Des Smyth	70	70	74	70	284	3,757.50
Hugh Baiocchi	72	70	72	71	285	3,175

	SCORES				TOTAL	MONEY
Andrew Murray	70	69	72	74	285	3,175
Jose Rivero	70	71	72	72	285	3,175
Ian Woosnam	71	73	74	67	285	3,175
Jeff Hawkes	69	71	74	72	286	2,887.50
Wayne Riley	72	74	69	71	286	2,887.50
Tony Charnley	67	73	73	74	287	2,700
Eamonn Darcy	71	70	74	72	287	2,700
Magnus Persson	73	70	76	68	287	2,700
Gordon Brand Jr.	72	72	73	71	288	2,362.50
Neil Coles	71	71	75	71	288	2,362.50
Mats Lanner	71	76	72	69	288	2,362.50
Robert Lee	73	71	73	71	288	2,362.50
Ossie Moore	68	69	75	76	288	2,362.50
Magnus Sunesson	73	69	71	75	288	2,362.50
Ron Commans	74	72	70	73	289	2,050
Manuel Pinero	70	73	76	70	289	2,050
Johan Rystrom	71	71	72	75	289	2,050
Michael Allen	74	73	71	72	290	1,725
Ian Baker-Finch	74	72	71	73	290	1,725
Derrick Cooper	71	72	77	70	290	1,725
Anders Forsbrand	73	72	71	74	290	1,725
Barry Lane	72	70	74	74	290	1,725
Malcolm Mackenzie	68	75	74	73	290	1,725
Bill Malley	76	71	70	73	290	1,725
Miguel Martin	71	69	76	74	290	1,725
Ove Sellberg	69	75	72	74	290	1,725
Lyndsay Stephen	72	71	75	72	290	1,725
David Feherty	73	74	71	73	291	1,325
Mike Harwood	74	73	71	73	291	1,325
Tony Johnstone	73	72	72	74	291	1,325
Frank Nobilo	74	70	78	69	291	1,325
Gerry Taylor	69	75	73	74	291	1,325
David Williams	76	70	74	71	291	1,325

Wang Four Stars National Pro-Celebrity

Moor Park Golf Club, Rickmansworth, England
Par 37-35 — 72; 6,817 yards

June 9-12
purse, £201,600

	SCORES				TOTAL	MONEY
Rodger Davis	69	63	71	72	275	£30,000
Jose-Maria Canizares	69	67	69	71	276	16,350
Eamonn Darcy	67	68	69	72	276	16,350
David Ray	67	69	69	74	279	9,300
Mike Harwood	69	70	70	72	281	7,300
Barry Lane	71	69	69	72	281	7,300
Gordon Brand Jr.	69	70	71	72	282	4,284
Emmanuel Dussart	70	74	67	71	282	4,284
Mark Roe	72	71	66	73	282	4,284
John Slaughter	68	73	71	70	282	4,284
Des Smyth	71	71	71	69	282	4,284
Roger Chapman	71	69	72	71	283	2,745.71
David Jones	73	65	73	72	283	2,745.71
Brian Marchbank	70	71	69	73	283	2,745.71
Chris Moody	73	69	73	68	283	2,745.71
John Morgan	72	69	70	72	283	2,745.71
David J. Russell	71	67	70	75	283	2,745.71

	SCORES				TOTAL	MONEY
Ronald Stelten	70	71	68	74	283	2,745.71
Michael Allen	71	67	69	77	284	2,260
Wayne Riley	72	70	70	72	284	2,260
Lyndsay Stephen	74	66	71	73	284	2,260
Jerry Anderson	72	67	71	75	285	2,040
Malcolm Mackenzie	74	70	74	67	285	2,040
John McHenry	68	73	72	72	285	2,040
Richard Boxall	72	67	72	75	286	1,800
Ian Mosey	74	71	69	72	286	1,800
Frank Nobilo	77	68	70	71	286	1,800
Jim Rutledge	74	66	72	74	286	1,800
Grant Turner	72	72	73	69	286	1,800
Paul Curry	73	71	74	69	287	1,500
David Feherty	71	72	73	71	287	1,500
Bernard Gallacher	74	69	72	72	287	1,500
Rick Hartmann	68	73	71	75	287	1,500
John Jacobs	71	67	75	74	287	1,500
Ossie Moore	73	68	74	72	287	1,500
David A. Russell	71	72	70	74	287	1,500
Wayne Westner	73	68	74	75	287	1,500
Stephen Bennett	71	72	71	74	288	1,260
Tony Charnley	69	74	72	73	288	1,260
Howard Clark	74	73	68	73	288	1,260
Brian Waites	72	71	70	75	288	1,260
Juan Anglada	71	71	71	76	289	1,060
Derrick Cooper	74	70	73	72	289	1,060
Bobby Mitchell	73	73	69	74	289	1,060
Martin Poxon	80	70	66	73	289	1,060
Keith Waters	74	70	71	74	289	1,060
David Williams	69	71	73	76	289	1,060
Mike Clayton	70	75	72	73	290	860
Ron Commans	69	72	72	77	290	860
Vaughan Somers	73	75	68	74	290	860
Lee Trevino	77	68	71	74	290	860

Volvo Belgian Open

Bercuit Golf Club, Brussels, Belgium
Par 35-36 — 71; 6,543 yards

June 16-19
purse, £200,000

	SCORES				TOTAL	MONEY
Jose-Maria Olazabal	67	69	64	69	269	£33,330
Mike Smith	67	73	63	70	273	22,200
Gordon J. Brand	69	70	67	71	277	11,260
Ove Sellberg	68	71	70	68	277	11,260
Peter Baker	68	73	67	70	278	8,470
Eduardo Romero	72	69	71	67	279	5,620
Tony Johnstone	69	68	71	71	279	5,620
Ronan Rafferty	68	70	69	72	279	5,620
Stephen Bennett	71	72	69	67	279	5,620
Mats Lanner	73	69	68	70	280	3,840
Carl Mason	69	68	73	70	280	3,840
Gordon Brand Jr.	71	66	74	70	281	3,240
Wayne Riley	68	69	71	73	281	3,240
Tommy Armour III	68	72	71	70	281	3,240
Juan Anglada	68	76	70	68	282	2,880
Frank Nobilo	72	68	67	75	282	2,880

	SCORES				TOTAL	MONEY
Paul Kent	67	73	69	74	283	2,298.18
Christy O'Connor Jr.	71	73	72	67	283	2,298.18
Neal Briggs	69	72	74	68	283	2,298.18
Roger Chapman	69	72	70	72	283	2,298.18
Sam Torrance	70	68	71	74	283	2,298.18
Glenn Ralph	68	72	75	68	283	2,298.18
Ian Mosey	71	70	71	71	283	2,298.18
Denis Durnian	70	72	67	74	283	2,298.18
Brett Ogle	73	67	72	71	283	2,298.18
Anders Sorensen	68	73	70	72	283	2,298.18
Peter McWhinney	70	67	70	76	283	2,298.18
John Morgan	71	72	71	70	284	1,830
Peter Mitchell	70	74	69	71	284	1,830
Manuel Calero	73	71	70	70	284	1,830
Anders Forsbrand	73	72	72	67	284	1,830
Mark Davis	70	71	72	72	285	1,640
Alberto Binaghi	73	71	72	69	285	1,640
Mike Clayton	70	68	75	72	285	1,640
Ignacio Gervas	72	68	72	74	286	1,500
Jamie Howell	73	67	71	75	286	1,500
James Spence	69	70	71	76	286	1,500
Brian Marchbank	73	70	73	70	286	1,500
Howard Clark	72	72	72	71	287	1,360
Carl Magnus Stroemberg	69	75	71	72	287	1,360
Jerry Anderson	69	76	71	71	287	1,360
Wayne Smith	71	73	72	72	288	1,200
Bill Malley	68	69	75	76	288	1,200
Tony Charnley	74	71	72	71	288	1,200
Richard Boxall	72	71	75	70	288	1,200
Martin Poxon	75	68	69	76	288	1,200
Bryan Lewis	71	74	73	71	289	960
Jeremy Bennett	73	70	75	71	289	960
Ossie Moore	71	73	72	73	289	960
Magnus Sunesson	71	73	72	73	289	960
Mitch Adcock	69	71	75	74	289	960
Bob E. Smith	67	74	70	78	289	960
Andrew Oldcorn	73	72	71	73	289	960

Peugeot French Open

Chantilly Golf Club, Chantilly, France
Par 35-35 — 70; 7,173 yards

June 23-26
purse, £283,420

	SCORES				TOTAL	MONEY
Nick Faldo	71	67	68	68	274	£47,236.66
Denis Durnian	65	68	69	74	276	24,600.85
Wayne Riley	72	67	67	70	276	24,600.85
Ossie Moore	71	69	69	69	278	13,084.56
David Feherty	72	70	66	70	278	13,084.56
Peter Senior	70	69	68	72	279	9,919.70
Ronan Rafferty	73	69	74	64	280	7,794.05
David Williams	73	67	69	71	280	7,794.05
Malcolm Mackenzie	72	70	68	72	282	5,525.69
Sam Torrance	69	73	70	70	282	5,526.69
Miguel Martin	75	68	65	74	282	5,526.69
Anders Forsbrand	72	72	67	71	282	5,526.69
Curtis Strange	70	73	70	70	283	4,563.06

THE EUROPEAN TOUR / 441

	SCORES				TOTAL	MONEY
Roger Chapman	69	71	74	70	284	3,996.22
Severiano Ballesteros	72	71	69	72	284	3,996.22
Jerry Anderson	71	72	71	70	284	3,996.22
Paul Curry	73	73	71	67	284	3,996.22
Andrew Murray	74	67	70	73	284	3,996.22
Peter Baker	72	71	71	72	286	3,106.28
Philip Harrison	71	74	68	73	286	3,106.28
John DeForest	75	70	70	71	286	3,106.28
Jose-Maria Olazabal	74	67	73	72	286	3,106.28
Andrew Chandler	73	72	70	71	286	3,106.28
Richard Boxall	66	73	75	72	286	3,106.28
Ken Brown	70	72	75	69	286	3,106.28
Mark Roe	69	74	71	72	286	3,106.28
Ian Mosey	72	71	72	71	286	3,106.28
Carl Mason	72	73	69	72	286	3,106.28
Keith Waters	66	75	72	74	287	2,437.41
Peter Mitchell	76	70	72	69	287	2,437.41
Jim Rutledge	71	73	71	72	287	2,437.41
Antonio Garrido	74	69	71	73	287	2,437.41
Marc Antonio Farry	72	70	73	72	287	2,437.41
Eamonn Darcy	73	73	73	68	287	2,437.41
Bill Malley	75	71	69	73	288	2,097.31
Santiago Luna	72	74	71	71	288	2,097.31
Gordon J. Brand	74	71	73	70	288	2,097.31
Brian Marchbank	69	75	73	71	288	2,097.31
Mark Mouland	67	74	75	72	288	2,097.31
Christy O'Connor Jr.	71	74	72	72	289	1,785.55
Mats Hallberg	72	71	71	75	289	1,785.55
Jose-Maria Canizares	72	69	76	72	289	1,785.55
Mitch Adcock	76	70	68	75	289	1,785.55
Tony Charnley	73	73	75	68	289	1,785.55
Brian Watts	71	73	73	72	289	1,785.55
Mike Clayton	74	69	76	71	290	1,473.78
Glenn Ralph	74	70	72	74	290	1,473.78
John Bland	73	71	77	69	290	1,473.78
Martin Poxon	73	70	70	77	290	1,473.78
Jimmy Heggarty	75	71	72	72	290	1,473.78

Monte Carlo Open

Mont Agel Golf Club, La Turbie, Monte Carlo
Par 34-35 — 69; 6,198 yards

June 29-July 2
purse, £210,084

	SCORES				TOTAL	MONEY
Jose Rivero	65	64	67	65	261	£35,013.37
Mark McNulty	66	62	68	67	263	23,342.25
Severiano Ballesteros	65	66	67	68	266	13,151.26
Lyndsay Stephen	72	68	62	66	268	10,504.20
Hugh Baiocchi	67	68	67	68	270	8,887.51
Nick Faldo	71	65	69	67	272	7,352.94
Jeff Hawkes	66	70	71	66	273	5,777.31
Bob E. Smith	71	67	68	67	273	5,777.31
Gavin Levenson	67	66	70	71	274	4,445.67
Peter Senior	70	68	67	69	274	4,445.67
Michael Allen	69	71	70	65	275	3,209.03
Antonio Garrido	68	68	68	71	275	3,209.03
Bob Shearer	73	67	65	70	275	3,209.03

	SCORES				TOTAL	MONEY
Craig Parry	68	65	68	74	275	3,209.03
Manuel Calero	69	67	71	68	275	3,209.03
Andrew Sherborne	65	69	72	69	275	3,209.03
Peter Teravainen	72	64	68	71	275	3,209.03
Magnus Persson	68	69	65	73	275	3,209.03
Emilio Rodriguez	69	64	73	70	276	2,429.97
Costantino Rocca	73	67	68	68	276	2,429.97
Colin Montgomerie	69	68	72	67	276	2,429.97
Richard Boxall	68	69	70	69	276	2,429.97
Jerry Haas	67	69	69	71	276	2,429.97
Wayne Stephens	74	66	70	66	276	2,429.97
Mitch Adcock	66	75	67	69	277	2,016.81
Jim Rutledge	70	66	69	72	277	2,016.81
Mark Mouland	68	68	67	74	277	2,016.81
Frederic Regard	70	66	67	74	277	2,016.81
Manuel Pinero	74	64	70	69	277	2,016.81
Ian Baker-Finch	71	68	68	70	277	2,016.81
Philip Parkin	73	67	69	68	277	2,016.81
Paul Kent	72	69	67	70	278	1,701.68
Glenn Ralph	69	69	72	68	278	1,701.68
Miguel Martin	72	67	70	69	278	1,701.68
Anders Sorensen	67	69	70	72	278	1,701.68
Jerry Anderson	71	70	69	69	279	1,554.62
Grant Turner	72	68	68	71	279	1,554.62
Silvio Grappasonni	69	69	66	75	279	1,554.62
Mike Harwood	72	67	70	71	280	1,386.55
Joe Higgins	66	71	71	72	280	1,386.55
Ian Roberts	71	69	69	71	280	1,386.55
Philip Walton	70	71	69	70	280	1,386.55
David Williams	67	70	72	71	280	1,386.55
Glyn Davies	67	73	67	74	281	1,239.50
John Slaughter	74	67	70	70	281	1,239.50
Gery Watine	68	70	74	70	282	1,113.45
Ron Commans	70	71	69	72	282	1,113.45
Paul Curry	67	68	74	73	282	1,113.45
Derrick Cooper	71	69	70	72	282	1,113.45
Wraith Grant	74	67	71	71	283	945.38
Benoit Ducoulombier	69	68	72	74	283	945.38
Bryan Norton	71	69	71	72	283	945.38
Craig McClellan	70	67	72	74	283	945.38

Bell's Scottish Open

Gleneagles Hotel, King's Course, Gleneagles, Scotland
Par 35-36 — 71; 6,745 yards

July 6-9
purse, £250,000

	SCORES				TOTAL	MONEY
Barry Lane	70	67	66	68	271	£41,660
Jose Rivero	64	70	72	68	274	21,705
Sandy Lyle	68	69	69	68	274	21,705
Roger Chapman	68	68	67	72	275	12,500
Peter Fowler	71	63	69	73	276	10,600
Jose-Maria Olazabal	71	70	67	69	277	8,125
Mats Lanner	71	71	72	63	277	8,125
David Gilford	69	70	70	69	278	5,362.50
Rodger Davis	74	66	68	70	278	5,362.50
Russell Weir	66	72	67	73	278	5,362.50

	SCORES				TOTAL	MONEY
David Graham	71	69	70	68	278	5,362.50
Mark O'Meara	70	69	67	73	279	4,046.67
Mike Harwood	68	65	75	71	279	4,046.67
Ian Woosnam	68	71	71	69	279	4,046.67
Fred Couples	64	68	72	76	280	3,521.67
Stephen Bennett	69	65	76	70	280	3,521.67
Denis Durnian	70	67	71	72	280	3,521.67
Anders Forsbrand	71	71	68	71	281	3,062.50
Wayne Smith	67	72	67	75	281	3,062.50
Mark James	74	69	69	69	281	3,062.50
Howard Clark	70	69	73	69	281	3,062.50
Bill McColl	72	70	70	70	282	2,700
Hugh Baiocchi	69	72	71	70	282	2,700
Noel Ratcliffe	68	71	69	74	282	2,700
Ian Baker-Finch	70	67	75	70	282	2,700
Payne Stewart	68	70	71	73	282	2,700
Craig Parry	70	68	73	72	283	2,437.50
Peter Senior	69	72	71	71	283	2,437.50
David Feherty	69	72	70	73	284	2,150
Brian Marchbank	74	68	73	69	284	2,150
Carl Mason	73	68	69	74	284	2,150
Tommy Armour III	72	69	71	72	284	2,150
Gordon Brand Jr.	71	72	69	72	284	2,150
Colin Montgomerie	69	72	72	71	284	2,150
John De Forest	72	69	75	69	285	1,875
Frank Nobilo	69	73	74	69	285	1,875
Peter Mitchell	72	71	71	71	285	1,875
Mike Clayton	72	69	75	69	285	1,875
Mats Hallberg	65	76	70	75	286	1,625
Robert Lee	69	71	71	75	286	1,625
Sam Torrance	68	72	73	73	286	1,625
Emmanuel Dussart	74	68	70	74	286	1,625
Michael Allen	70	71	71	74	286	1,625
Vaughan Somers	71	70	72	73	286	1,625
Jose-Maria Canizares	70	71	74	72	287	1,325
Des Smyth	70	72	74	71	287	1,325
Tony Charnley	68	69	75	75	287	1,325
Peter Teravainen	70	72	70	75	287	1,325
Philip Parkin	71	69	74	73	287	1,325
Andrew Sherborne	71	67	73	76	287	1,325

British Open Championship

Royal Lytham and St. Annes Golf Club, Lytham St. Annes, England   July 14-17
Par 35-36 — 71; 6,857 yards   purse, £704,100

	SCORES				TOTAL	MONEY
Severiano Ballesteros	67	71	70	65	273	£80,000
Nick Price	70	67	69	69	275	60,000
Nick Faldo	71	69	68	71	279	47,000
Fred Couples	73	69	71	68	281	33,500
Gary Koch	71	72	70	68	281	33,500
Peter Senior	70	73	70	69	282	27,000
David Frost	71	75	69	68	283	21,000
Payne Stewart	73	75	68	67	283	21,000
Isao Aoki	72	71	73	67	283	21,000
Sandy Lyle	73	69	67	74	283	21,000

	SCORES				TOTAL	MONEY
David J. Russell	71	74	69	70	284	16,500
Brad Faxon	69	74	70	71	284	16,500
Eduardo Romero	72	71	69	73	285	14,000
Larry Nelson	73	71	68	73	285	14,000
Curtis Strange	79	69	69	68	285	14,000
Ben Crenshaw	73	73	68	72	286	10,500
Jose Rivero	75	69	70	72	286	10,500
Don Pooley	70	73	69	74	286	10,500
Andy Bean	71	70	71	74	286	10,500
Tom Kite	75	71	73	68	287	7,000
Bob Tway	71	71	72	73	287	7,000
Gordon Brand Jr.	72	76	68	71	287	7,000
Bob Charles	71	74	69	73	287	7,000
Rodger Davis	76	71	72	68	287	7,000
Jack Nicklaus	75	70	75	68	288	5,500
Ian Woosnam	76	71	72	69	288	5,500
Mark O'Meara	75	69	75	70	289	5,200
James Benepe	75	72	70	73	290	4,600
Mark McNulty	73	73	72	72	290	4,600
Tom Watson	74	72	72	72	290	4,600
Chip Beck	72	71	74	73	290	4,600
Tommy Armour III	73	72	72	73	290	4,600
Howard Clark	71	72	75	72	290	4,600
Wayne Riley	72	71	72	76	291	4,150
Lanny Wadkins	73	71	71	76	291	4,150
Jose-Maria Olazabal	73	71	73	75	292	3,950
Gordon J. Brand	73	74	72	73	292	3,950
Brian Marchbank	73	74	73	73	293	3,455.56
Jay Haas	71	76	78	68	293	3,455.56
Corey Pavin	74	73	71	75	293	3,455.56
Noel Ratcliffe	70	77	76	70	293	3,455.56
Ken Brown	75	72	75	71	293	3,455.56
David A. Russell	72	73	72	76	293	3,455.56
Ronan Rafferty	74	74	71	74	293	3,455.56
Graham Marsh	75	73	71	74	293	3,455.56
Wayne Grady	69	76	72	76	293	3,455.56
Sam Torrance	74	74	75	71	294	3,050
Mark McCumber	75	71	72	76	294	3,050
Paul Kent	74	70	79	71	294	3,050
Andy North	77	68	74	75	294	3,050
Paul Azinger	72	75	73	74	294	3,050
Philip Walton	72	74	75	74	295	2,800
Peter Fowler	72	72	78	73	295	2,800
Fuzzy Zoeller	72	74	76	73	295	2,800
Hubert Green	74	73	73	75	295	2,800
Johnny Miller	75	73	72	75	295	2,800
Mike Smith	75	71	76	74	296	2,625
Carl Mason	75	69	77	75	296	2,625
*Paul Broadhurst	73	73	74	76	296	
Gary Player	72	76	73	76	297	2,525
Craig Stadler	72	68	81	76	297	2,525
Simon Bishop	77	71	73	77	298	2,400
Mark James	71	77	74	76	298	2,400
Andrew Sherborne	71	72	76	79	298	2,400
Manuel Pinero	75	73	77	74	299	2,300
Paul Carman	77	71	80	73	301	2,250
Greg Bruckner	72	74	80	76	302	2,175
Hsieh Chin Sheng	74	73	73	82	302	2,175
Bernhard Langer	73	75	75	80	303	2,100
Gary Stafford	76	72	78	79	305	2,050

	SCORES				TOTAL	MONEY
Peter Mitchell	73	75	79	81	308	2,000

Out of the final 36 holes

			TOTAL
Hajime Meshiai	75	74	149
Lee Trevino	75	74	149
Ian Baker-Finch	76	73	149
Larry Mize	72	77	149
David Ishii	78	71	149
Craig Parry	75	75	150
Scott Verplank	72	78	150
Mats Lanner	75	75	150
Andrew Chandler	75	75	150
Joe Higgins	74	76	150
Christy O'Connor Jr.	75	75	150
Andrew Magee	72	78	150
John Bland	76	74	150
Alberto Binaghi	74	76	150
Davis Love III	80	71	151
Russell Weir	77	74	151
Mike Reid	78	73	151
Roger Chapman	73	78	151
Tony Johnstone	76	75	151
Jamie Howell	77	74	151
Derrick Cooper	74	77	151
Mark Roe	76	75	151
Gerry Taylor	76	75	151
Magnus Persson	79	73	152
Richard Thompson	77	75	152
Clive Tucker	78	74	152
Ove Sellberg	79	73	152
Eamonn Darcy	78	74	152
Teddy Webber	79	73	152
Robert Lee	75	77	152
Johan Rystrom	74	78	152
Lucien Tinkler	77	75	152
David Williams	77	76	153
Raymond Floyd	76	77	153
Denis Durnian	76	77	153
Peter Baker	76	77	153
Ron Commans	73	80	153
Peter McWhinney	76	77	153
Hugh Baiocchi	79	74	153
*James Cook	77	76	153
*Trevor Foster	74	79	153
John Morgan	78	76	154
David Armstrong	80	74	154
Hal Sutton	76	78	154
David Gilford	78	76	154
*A. C. Nash	75	79	154
*Christian Hardin	77	77	154
Jose-Maria Canizares	77	78	155
Gordon Townhill	78	77	155
David Jones	78	77	155
Lindsay Mann	81	75	156
James White	77	79	156
Neil Burke	80	76	156
Peter Akakasiaka	77	79	156
Ed Sneed	79	77	156
Mike Harwood	79	77	156

	SCORES			TOTAL	MONEY
David Thore	78	78		156	
Leif Hederstrom	79	77		156	
Anders Forsbrand	79	78		157	
Ged Furey	80	77		157	
Lu Chien Soon	78	79		157	
Andrew Rogers	82	75		157	
Michael Allen	83	75		158	
Steve Pate	80	78		158	
Chris Moody	81	77		158	
Steen Tinning	76	82		158	
Tony Jacklin	80	79		159	
Roger Mackay	80	80		160	
David Graham	79	81		160	
Mark Calcavecchia	76	84		160	
Mark Mouland	76	84		160	
Andrew Cotton	77	83		160	
Jose Cabo	79	81		160	
Sandy Stephen	82	78		160	
*Charles Rymer	83	77		160	
David Whelan	81	80		161	
Alan McCloskey	83	78		161	
Neil Hansen	80	82		162	
Robert Richardson	82	81		163	
Barry Lane	78	85		163	
*Darren Prosser	81	82		163	
Wayne Smith	81	WD			

(All professionals who did not complete 72 holes received £450.)

KLM Open

Hilversum Golf Club, Hilversum, Holland
Par 36-36 — 72; 6,673 yards

July 21-24
purse, £250,000

	SCORES				TOTAL	MONEY
Mark Mouland	72	68	69	65	274	£41,660
Des Smyth	71	67	67	70	275	27,760
Carl Mason	69	69	72	66	276	14,075
Tony Johnstone	68	66	68	74	276	14,075
Miguel Martin	71	72	68	66	277	10,600
Jose-Maria Olazabal	69	67	71	71	278	8,125
Craig Parry	70	70	67	71	278	8,125
Andrew Murray	65	76	67	71	279	5,616.67
David Williams	68	71	68	72	279	5,616.67
Mark McNulty	70	69	67	73	279	5,616.67
Luis Carbonetti	70	72	69	69	280	4,185
Mark Roe	69	66	73	72	280	4,185
Magnus Persson	70	69	69	72	280	4,185
David Graham	73	70	69	68	280	4,185
Andrew Sherborne	72	73	68	68	281	3,378
Michael King	70	69	71	71	281	3,378
Ross McFarlane	72	67	71	71	281	3,378
Roger Chapman	68	74	67	72	281	3,378
Ian Mosey	68	69	70	74	281	3,378
Jimmy Heggarty	68	73	73	68	282	2,887.50
Tony Charnley	72	70	70	70	282	2,887.50
Ronan Rafferty	70	73	68	71	282	2,887.50

	SCORES				TOTAL	MONEY
Richard Boxall	70	75	65	72	282	2,887.50
Denis Durnian	67	76	73	67	283	2,475
David Gilford	76	69	71	67	283	2,475
Peter Baker	74	68	70	71	283	2,475
David A. Russell	66	72	73	72	283	2,475
Eduardo Romero	73	70	68	72	283	2,475
Philip Parkin	69	69	72	73	283	2,475
Vicente Fernandez	68	71	70	74	283	2,475
Gordon J. Brand	71	73	71	69	284	2,081.25
Stephen McAllister	73	71	69	71	284	2,081.25
John Jacobs	67	74	70	73	284	2,081.25
David J. Russell	69	68	72	75	284	2,081.25
Grant Turner	70	70	72	73	285	1,850
Michael Allen	72	72	72	69	285	1,850
Manuel Calero	68	77	71	69	285	1,850
Graham Marsh	73	70	67	75	285	1,850
Andy Bean	70	73	66	76	285	1,850
*Constant Smits Van Waesberghe	71	71	76	67	285	
Barry Lane	73	70	74	69	286	1,500
Noel Ratcliffe	73	71	72	70	286	1,500
Colin Montgomerie	72	73	70	71	286	1,500
Magnus Jonsson	73	70	71	72	286	1,500
Anders Sorensen	72	71	71	72	286	1,500
Ruud Bos	74	70	70	72	286	1,500
Philip Harrison	69	73	71	73	286	1,500
Keith Waters	71	72	69	74	286	1,500
Ossie Moore	69	75	68	74	286	1,500
Lyndsay Stephen	70	72	74	71	287	1,100
Chris Moody	71	72	73	71	287	1,100
Glenn Ralph	67	73	75	72	287	1,100
David Jones	72	72	70	73	287	1,100
Neil Hansen	66	75	72	74	287	1,100
Juan Anglada	66	72	74	75	287	1,100

Scandinavian Enterprise Open

Drottningholm Golf Club, Stockholm, Sweden
Par 36-36 — 72; 6,747 yards

July 28-31
purse, £250,000

	SCORES				TOTAL	MONEY
Severiano Ballesteros	67	70	66	67	270	£41,660
Gerry Taylor	67	68	71	69	275	27,760
Graham Marsh	66	66	77	67	276	14,075
Peter Senior	66	68	72	70	276	14,075
Kyi Hla Han	68	69	69	71	277	9,675
Gordon Brand Jr.	65	71	68	73	277	9,675
Craig Stadler	68	69	69	72	278	6,450
Craig Parry	64	69	73	72	278	6,450
Richard Boxall	72	66	68	72	278	6,450
Brett Ogle	73	67	69	70	279	4,480
Peter McWhinney	66	68	78	67	279	4,480
Ronan Rafferty	70	68	72	69	279	4,480
David J. Russell	68	68	66	77	279	4,480
Mark James	69	74	71	66	280	3,522
Stephen McAllister	72	70	68	70	280	3,522
Craig McClellan	68	72	71	69	280	3,522
John Morgan	69	69	71	71	280	3,522

	SCORES				TOTAL	MONEY
Paul Curry	71	68	72	69	280	3,522
Magnus Persson	71	66	72	72	281	2,891.67
Sam Torrance	70	71	71	69	281	2,891.67
Jesper Parnevik	71	69	70	71	281	2,891.67
Eamonn Darcy	65	72	73	71	281	2,891.67
Malcolm MacKenzie	71	68	72	70	281	2,891.67
Colin Montgomerie	71	72	71	67	281	2,891.67
Jerry Haas	71	69	70	72	282	2,475
Mark Davis	65	77	68	72	282	2,475
Bill Longmuir	68	73	72	69	282	2,475
Paul Kent	70	72	74	66	282	2,475
Eduardo Romero	70	67	72	73	282	2,475
Mikael Karlsson	69	73	71	70	283	2,175
Andrew Murray	69	67	75	72	283	2,175
Philip Harrison	66	70	76	71	283	2,175
Christy O'Connor Jr.	70	70	72	72	284	1,975
David Jones	70	72	72	70	284	1,975
Michael Allen	69	69	78	68	284	1,975
David R. Jones	69	71	73	71	284	1,975
Ignacio Gervas	71	71	67	76	285	1,700
John Jacobs	68	71	74	72	285	1,700
Teddy Webber	68	72	72	73	285	1,700
Frank Nobilo	70	72	74	69	285	1,700
Manuel Calero	70	67	74	74	285	1,700
Vicente Fernandez	67	74	70	74	285	1,700
Anders Sorensen	71	69	75	70	285	1,700
Magnus Jonsson	71	72	69	74	286	1,350
Joe Higgins	73	68	71	74	286	1,350
Santiago Luna	69	72	77	68	286	1,350
Mats Lanner	69	68	73	76	286	1,350
Daniel Westermark	72	70	73	71	286	1,350
Derrick Cooper	73	70	75	68	286	1,350
David Whelan	67	74	71	74	286	1,350

Benson & Hedges International Open

Fulford Golf Club, York, England
Par 36-36 — 72; 6,809 yards

August 4-7
purse, £250,000

	SCORES				TOTAL	MONEY
Peter Baker	68	68	66	69	271	£41,660
Nick Faldo	68	68	66	69	271	27,760
(Baker defeated Faldo on second hole of playoff.)						
Jose-Maria Olazabal	70	71	66	65	272	14,075
Craig Parry	68	68	69	67	272	14,075
Mark James	72	69	68	65	274	10,600
Sandy Lyle	70	67	69	69	275	8,750
Christy O'Connor Jr.	70	65	71	70	276	7,500
Howard Clark	72	70	68	67	277	5,362.50
Emmanuel Dussart	68	71	69	69	277	5,362.50
Des Smyth	70	70	65	72	277	5,362.50
Mark McNulty	68	68	68	73	277	5,362.50
Denis Durnian	75	69	70	64	278	3,866
Hugh Baiocchi	71	69	71	67	278	3,866
Jerry Anderson	72	69	70	67	278	3,866
Philip Walton	71	70	68	69	278	3,866
Graham Marsh	71	68	69	70	278	3,866

	SCORES				TOTAL	MONEY
Peter Senior	76	68	70	65	279	3,375
Paul Kent	70	72	72	66	280	2,939.29
Andrew Sherborne	73	72	69	66	280	2,939.29
Peter Fowler	73	72	69	66	280	2,939.29
David J. Russell	72	70	70	68	280	2,939.29
John Bland	72	72	67	69	280	2,939.29
David A. Russell	71	68	71	70	280	2,939.29
David Williams	67	69	72	72	280	2,939.29
Vicente Fernandez	72	71	72	66	281	2,512.50
Gordon J. Brand	71	72	71	67	281	2,512.50
Gavin Levenson	73	67	71	70	281	2,512.50
Malcolm MacKenzie	72	66	72	71	281	2,512.50
Carl Mason	72	68	70	72	282	2,287.50
Richard Boxall	75	69	69	69	282	2,287.50
Manuel Pinero	70	69	72	72	283	2,055
David Llewellyn	70	72	70	71	283	2,055
Manuel Calero	75	68	71	69	283	2,055
Miguel Martin	72	73	71	67	283	2,055
Jeff Hawkes	75	70	74	64	283	2,055
Derrick Cooper	67	73	70	74	284	1,850
Eamonn Darcy	71	72	71	70	284	1,850
Peter Teravainen	72	70	75	67	284	1,850
Barry Lane	73	71	72	69	285	1,700
Peter Mitchell	73	71	67	74	285	1,700
Gordon Brand Jr.	70	70	72	73	285	1,700
Ove Sellberg	71	73	72	70	286	1,400
Santiago Luna	73	72	73	68	286	1,400
Tony Johnstone	70	71	75	70	286	1,400
Bill Malley	70	73	67	76	286	1,400
Frank Nobilo	73	72	71	70	286	1,400
Neil Coles	70	70	75	71	286	1,400
Simon Bishop	73	69	73	71	286	1,400
Gary Webb	74	70	70	72	286	1,400
Michael King	75	69	70	72	286	1,400

PLM Open

Flommen Golf Club, Falsterbo, Sweden
Par 36-34 — 70; 6,511 yards

August 11-14
purse, £198,780

	SCORES				TOTAL	MONEY
Frank Nobilo	63	68	71	68	270	£33,126.72
Howard Clark	68	69	68	66	271	22,064.60
Peter Fowler	65	69	72	70	276	10,267.00
Anders Forsbrand	67	66	72	71	276	10,267.00
Colin Montgomerie	66	67	74	69	276	10,267.00
Ove Sellberg	69	68	72	69	278	6,957.31
Anders Sorensen	69	68	71	71	279	5,963.41
Craig Parry	67	67	76	70	280	4,094.87
Tony Charnley	66	66	76	72	280	4,094.87
Magnus Persson	68	71	72	69	280	4,094.87
Stephen Bennett	72	69	67	72	280	4,094.87
Mark Mouland	68	74	69	69	280	4,094.87
Steen Tinning	72	68	74	67	281	3,200.36
Matts Hallberg	67	67	73	75	282	2,802.80
Gordon J. Brand	70	69	74	69	282	2,802.80
Jerry Anderson	65	73	76	68	282	2,802.80

	SCORES				TOTAL	MONEY
Andrew Murray	70	71	71	70	282	2,802.80
Vaughan Somers	70	72	71	69	282	2,802.80
Philip Harrison	69	70	75	69	283	2,299.29
David Gilford	67	75	68	73	283	2,299.29
Richard Boxall	69	70	76	68	283	2,299.29
Denis Durnian	66	72	71	74	283	2,299.29
Bill Malley	68	74	73	68	283	2,299.29
Ronan Rafferty	72	69	73	69	283	2,299.29
*Olle Karlsson	71	69	78	65	283	
Wayne Riley	68	68	75	73	284	2,027.56
Mats Lanner	67	68	77	72	284	2,027.56
Simon Bishop	68	69	75	72	284	2,027.56
David A. Russell	66	71	76	72	285	1,789.02
Peter Dahlberg	69	70	75	71	285	1,789.02
Brett Ogle	70	70	75	70	285	1,789.02
Mikael Karlsson	72	70	73	70	285	1,789.02
Magnus Sunesson	70	68	75	72	285	1,789.02
Paul Carrigill	67	70	76	73	286	1,610.12
Johan Rystrom	66	72	77	71	286	1,610.12
Jeremy Robinson	69	67	80	71	287	1,470.97
Alberto Binaghi	72	70	69	76	287	1,470.97
Paul Kent	70	72	73	72	287	1,470.97
Paul Curry	71	69	78	69	287	1,470.97
Martin Poxon	70	70	77	70	287	1,470.97
Costantino Rocca	67	72	78	71	288	1,113.17
Barry Lane	71	68	75	74	288	1,113.17
Simon Townend	70	71	75	72	288	1,113.17
Peter Persons	64	76	78	70	288	1,113.17
Rudd Bos	71	70	77	70	288	1,113.17
Keith Waters	71	71	76	70	288	1,113.17
Clas Hultman	70	71	75	72	288	1,113.17
Per-Arne Brostedt	69	73	72	74	288	1,113.17
Ross Drummond	69	70	78	71	288	1,113.17
Magnus Grankvist	71	71	74	72	288	1,113.17
Andrew Sherborne	72	70	74	72	288	1,113.17
Mark Roe	71	69	75	73	288	1,113.17
John Hawksworth	71	71	74	72	288	1,113.17

Carrolls Irish Open

Portmarnock Golf Club, Dublin, Ireland
Par 36-36 — 72; 7,109 yards

August 18-21
purse, £232,172

	SCORES				TOTAL	MONEY
Ian Woosnam	68	70	70	70	278	£38,689.88
Jose-Maria Olazabal	66	70	74	75	285	15,443.62
Des Smyth	68	73	71	73	285	15,443.62
Manuel Pinero	69	68	75	73	285	15,443.62
Nick Faldo	71	68	73	73	285	15,443.62
Eamonn Darcy	69	68	75	74	286	6,102.82
Philip Walton	69	68	75	74	286	6,102.82
Bob Shearer	69	70	77	70	286	6,102.82
Martin Sludds	70	72	71	73	286	6,102.82
Roger Chapman	73	71	69	73	286	6,102.82
Peter Mitchell	70	70	74	73	287	4,004.97
Mark Roe	71	70	75	71	287	4,004.97
Mark James	75	69	71	72	287	4,004.97

	SCORES				TOTAL	MONEY
Marc Pendaries	76	69	72	71	288	3,590.38
Gordon J. Brand	70	69	73	77	289	3,383.09
Craig Parry	71	71	74	73	289	3,383.09
*Eoghan O'Connell	68	73	76	72	289	
Tony Charnley	69	73	75	73	290	3,043.12
Sandy Lyle	69	71	73	77	290	3,043.12
Curtis Strange	71	72	73	74	290	3,043.12
Andrew Oldcorn	73	73	72	72	290	3,043.12
Derrick Cooper	69	72	76	74	291	2,520.73
Keith Waters	69	76	75	71	291	2,520.73
Neil Hansen	69	76	73	73	291	2,520.73
Howard Clark	72	66	78	75	291	2,520.73
Ian Mosey	72	73	74	72	291	2,520.73
Mark Mouland	73	69	72	77	291	2,520.73
John McHenry	76	67	76	72	291	2,520.73
Mike Clayton	71	69	76	76	292	1,966.10
Richard Boxall	71	69	78	74	292	1,966.10
Grant Turner	72	72	74	74	292	1,966.10
Vaughan Somers	73	72	72	75	292	1,966.10
Anders Sorensen	73	71	74	74	292	1,966.10
Brian Marchbank	73	72	72	75	292	1,966.10
David Williams	74	68	76	74	292	1,966.10
Bill Longmuir	75	70	73	74	292	1,966.10
Jimmy Heggarty	75	71	73	73	292	1,966.10
Mike Smith	69	76	72	76	293	1,558.87
Carl Mason	69	70	81	73	293	1,558.87
Glenn Ralph	70	71	74	78	293	1,558.87
Hugh Baiocchi	71	74	72	76	293	1,558.87
Andrew Stubbs	71	75	75	72	293	1,558.87
Ian Young	72	72	72	77	293	1,558.87
Michael Allen	73	71	75	74	293	1,558.87
Wayne Riley	70	75	76	73	294	1,335.00
Malcolm MacKenzie	71	70	76	77	294	1,335.00
Vicente Fernandez	67	75	80	73	295	1,160.86
Paul Leonard	70	75	74	76	295	1,160.86
Ossie Moore	72	70	79	74	295	1,160.86
Gordon Brand Jr.	73	72	76	74	295	1,160.86
Steven Bottomley	75	69	77	74	295	1,160.86

German Open

Frankfurter Golf Club, Frankfurt, Germany
Par 35-36 — 71; 6,749 yards

August 25-28
purse, £283,465

	SCORES				TOTAL	MONEY
Severiano Ballesteros	68	68	65	62	263	£47,244.09
Gordon Brand Jr.	67	69	62	70	268	31,464.57
Mike Clayton	68	68	68	65	269	15,959.06
Bill Longmuir	71	67	67	64	269	15,959.06
Mark James	71	69	65	65	270	12,000.00
Richard Boxall	68	69	62	72	271	7,965.36
Des Smyth	66	69	69	67	271	7,965.36
Carl Mason	67	71	66	67	271	7,965.36
Bob E. Smith	67	67	69	68	271	7,965.36
Peter Senior	67	69	66	70	272	5,253.54
Frank Nobilo	67	68	69	68	272	5,253.54
Mike Smith	71	66	67	68	272	5,253.54

	SCORES				TOTAL	MONEY
Craig Parry	67	71	67	68	273	4,266.14
Jeff Hawkes	68	70	71	64	273	4,266.14
Denis Durnian	67	70	65	71	273	4,266.14
Bryan Norton	70	65	71	67	273	4,266.14
Philip Walton	71	70	70	63	274	3,394.49
Wayne Riley	67	67	70	70	274	3,394.49
Jimmy Heggarty	65	70	69	70	274	3,394.49
Eamonn Darcy	66	69	68	71	274	3,394.49
Ronan Rafferty	71	68	68	67	274	3,394.49
Tony Charnley	69	70	67	68	274	3,394.49
Mark Roe	70	69	68	67	274	3,394.49
Brett Ogle	66	70	69	69	274	3,394.49
John Bland	70	69	67	69	275	2,848.82
Colin Montgomerie	69	70	66	70	275	2,848.82
Tony Johnstone	71	70	70	64	275	2,848.82
Mark McNulty	69	72	64	70	275	2,848.82
Mike Harwood	65	69	68	74	276	2,551.18
Bernhard Langer	72	67	68	69	276	2,551.18
Andrew Oldcorn	69	71	67	69	276	2,551.18
Paul Curry	69	73	68	67	277	2,352.76
Vicente Fernandez	70	70	71	66	277	2,352.76
Gavin Levenson	73	69	69	67	278	2,182.68
Juan Anglada	69	71	68	70	278	2,182.68
Manuel Pinero	70	71	69	68	278	2,182.68
Teddy Webber	74	68	69	67	278	2,182.68
Christy O'Connor Jr.	66	70	70	73	279	1,984.25
Howard Clark	69	69	74	67	279	1,984.25
Stephen Bennett	68	72	70	69	279	1,984.25
John Slaughter	67	70	69	74	280	1,644.09
David A. Russell	70	70	73	67	280	1,644.09
Manuel Calero	71	71	70	68	280	1,644.09
Martin Poxon	72	69	71	68	280	1,644.09
John Morgan	71	70	70	69	280	1,644.09
Andrew Murray	69	71	69	71	280	1,644.09
Andrew Sherborne	67	74	71	68	280	1,644.09
Chris Moody	72	68	71	69	280	1,644.09
Peter Mitchell	72	69	72	67	280	1,644.09
Jerry Haas	69	73	69	70	281	1,162.21
Jim Rutledge	70	71	74	66	281	1,162.21
Ronald Stelten	68	74	68	71	281	1,162.21
Philip Harrison	72	67	72	70	281	1,162.21
Bob Shearer	68	72	69	72	281	1,162.21
David Williams	68	74	73	66	281	1,162.21
Michael McLean	68	73	70	70	281	1,162.21
Tony Stevens	73	67	68	73	281	1,162.21

Ebel European Masters—Swiss Open

Crans-sur-Sierre Golf Club, Sierre, Switzerland
Par 36-36 — 72; 6,811 yards

September 1-4
purse, £393,258

	SCORES				TOTAL	MONEY
Chris Moody	68	68	67	65	268	£65,543.07
Ian Woosnam	68	66	66	69	269	29,312.11
Severiano Ballesteros	65	68	68	68	269	29,312.11
Anders Forsbrand	67	71	67	64	269	29,312.11
Peter Senior	70	68	64	68	270	16,651.69

	SCORES				TOTAL	MONEY
Ronan Rafferty	70	66	69	67	272	13,764.04
Gordon Brand Jr.	70	68	67	68	273	9,107.87
David Frost	70	68	72	63	273	9,107.87
Jose-Maria Olazabal	73	69	65	66	273	9,107.87
Brett Ogle	73	68	65	67	273	9,107.87
Nick Faldo	67	67	71	68	273	9,107.87
Mark Mouland	68	70	72	64	274	6,221.91
Philip Walton	71	69	66	68	274	6,221.91
Ian Baker-Finch	71	71	68	64	274	6,221.91
Frank Nobilo	67	72	67	68	274	6,221.91
Carl Mason	68	71	70	66	275	5,426.03
Barry Lane	67	68	70	70	275	5,426.03
David Feherty	67	74	70	65	276	4,974.72
Mike Harwood	68	70	69	69	276	4,974.72
Jim Rutledge	68	71	69	69	277	4,483.15
Gordon J. Brand	69	68	71	69	277	4,483.15
Sandy Lyle	76	67	65	69	277	4,483.15
David Williams	73	67	66	71	277	4,483.15
Jose-Maria Canizares	67	73	69	68	277	4,483.15
Jimmy Heggarty	66	72	67	73	278	3,893.26
Andrew Chandler	70	68	70	70	278	3,893.26
Ian Young	73	70	69	66	278	3,893.26
Antonio Garrido	71	71	68	68	278	3,893.26
Armando Saavedra	67	73	68	70	278	3,893.26
Wayne Riley	67	73	69	70	279	3,241.57
Andrew Sherborne	70	72	67	70	279	3,241.57
Vicente Fernandez	71	69	69	70	279	3,241.57
Bob Shearer	69	72	67	71	279	3,241.57
Miguel Martin	72	70	67	70	279	3,241.57
Mitch Adcock	68	70	70	71	279	3,241.57
Martin Poxon	70	69	69	71	279	3,241.57
Wayne Smith	69	71	73	67	280	2,752.81
David J. Russell	68	71	72	69	280	2,752.81
Bill McColl	66	72	73	69	280	2,752.81
Mark Roe	76	65	70	69	280	2,752.81
Des Smyth	69	72	69	70	280	2,752.81
Bill Longmuir	71	68	77	65	281	2,398.88
Andrew Murray	70	73	70	68	281	2,398.88
Eduardo Romero	71	68	71	71	281	2,398.88
Jerry Haas	69	74	73	65	281	2,398.88
Manuel Calero	68	75	69	70	282	1,808.99
John Jacobs	70	68	72	72	282	1,808.99
Grant Turner	69	74	71	68	282	1,808.99
Frederic Regard	70	71	70	71	282	1,808.99
Colin Montgomerie	68	72	69	73	282	1,808.99
Michael Allen	71	69	68	74	282	1,808.99
Ian Mosey	74	66	69	73	282	1,808.99
Jeff Hawkes	70	72	73	67	282	1,808.99
Jose Rivero	73	69	72	68	282	1,808.99
Rodger Davis	71	71	69	71	282	1,808.99
Magnus Sunesson	72	68	72	70	282	1,808.99

Panasonic European Open

Sunningdale Golf Club, Old Course, London, England
Par 35-35 — 70; 6,580 yards

September 8-11
purse, £300,000

	SCORES				TOTAL	MONEY
Ian Woosnam	65	66	64	65	260	£50,000
Nick Faldo	66	65	66	66	263	33,300
Jose-Maria Olazabal	65	70	64	67	266	15,493.33
Sandy Lyle	69	65	67	65	266	15,493.33
Mark James	66	70	63	67	266	15,493.33
Gordon Brand Jr.	65	70	67	65	267	10,500
Craig Parry	68	70	67	63	268	9,000
Jose Rivero	68	65	66	70	269	7,500
Brett Ogle	71	68	66	65	270	6,360
Peter Baker	67	68	66	69	270	6,360
Denis Durnian	64	67	69	71	271	5,170
Mark McNulty	67	66	70	68	271	5,170
Mats Lanner	68	63	69	71	271	5,170
Ronan Rafferty	67	74	64	67	272	4,410
Mike Harwood	66	67	70	69	272	4,410
David Williams	68	68	64	72	272	4,410
Teddy Webber	67	71	68	67	273	3,642.86
Jose-Maria Canizares	70	69	66	68	273	3,642.86
Michael King	71	66	67	69	273	3,642.86
Tony Charnley	68	70	67	68	273	3,642.86
Mike Smith	72	68	65	68	273	3,642.86
John Bland	67	68	63	75	273	3,642.86
Eduardo Romero	70	68	66	69	273	3,642.86
Christy O'Connor Jr.	68	64	70	72	274	3,195
Jerry Haas	69	66	71	68	274	3,195
Frank Nobilo	69	70	70	66	275	2,925
Stephen Bennett	71	67	66	71	275	2,925
Peter Mitchell	72	67	66	70	275	2,925
Barry Lane	66	74	68	67	275	2,925
Mike Clayton	66	70	70	70	276	2,538
Noel Ratcliffe	67	73	67	69	276	2,538
Richard Boxall	66	71	67	72	276	2,538
Carl Mason	70	70	64	72	276	2,538
Bill Mayfair	66	72	69	69	276	2,538
Rodger Davis	70	71	68	68	277	2,160
Andrew Sherborne	73	67	70	67	277	2,160
Philip Walton	69	71	69	68	277	2,160
Gordon J. Brand	70	71	67	69	277	2,160
Roger Chapman	69	66	72	70	277	2,160
Jeff Hawkes	69	66	71	71	277	2,160
Wayne Riley	68	67	69	73	277	2,160
Santiago Luna	70	68	70	70	278	1,830
Ross Drummond	70	69	70	69	278	1,830
John Jacobs	71	70	71	66	278	1,830
Andrew Murray	69	71	68	70	278	1,830
Magnus Jonsson	71	65	71	72	279	1,530
Neal Briggs	72	67	67	73	279	1,530
Ossie Moore	70	68	69	72	279	1,530
Ian Young	67	66	74	72	279	1,530
Gary Koch	68	71	69	71	279	1,530
Bob Shearer	70	70	69	70	279	1,530

Lancome Trophy

St. Nom-la-Breteche Golf Club, Paris, France
Par 35-36 — 72; 6,722 yards

September 15-18
purse, £400,000

	SCORES				TOTAL	MONEY
Severiano Ballesteros	64	66	68	71	269	£66,660
Jose-Maria Olazabal	69	66	69	69	273	44,440
Greg Norman	71	72	68	67	278	22,520
Sandy Lyle	75	63	68	72	278	22,520
Ronan Rafferty	71	70	75	63	279	16,940
Rodger Davis	71	73	71	65	280	14,000
Jose Rivero	74	68	69	70	281	8,220
Peter Baker	70	67	74	70	281	8,220
Chris Moody	71	68	72	70	281	8,220
John Bland	71	69	69	72	281	8,220
Christy O'Connor Jr.	72	72	70	67	281	8,220
Tony Johnstone	74	71	67	69	281	8,220
Richard Boxall	70	77	69	65	281	8,220
Jeff Hawkes	75	68	67	71	281	8,220
Marc Pendaries	69	76	69	68	282	5,520
Mark James	68	72	72	70	282	5,520
Eamonn Darcy	72	68	72	70	282	5,520
David Feherty	72	71	71	68	282	5,520
Mark Mouland	72	70	71	70	283	4,688
Carl Mason	75	73	70	65	283	4,688
Sam Torrance	71	68	71	73	283	4,688
Denis Durnian	70	70	72	71	283	4,688
Gordon J. Brand	70	73	69	71	283	4,688
Miguel Martin	70	73	71	70	284	4,140
Tony Charnley	75	67	70	72	284	4,140
Mark Roe	72	72	70	70	284	4,140
Ian Woosnam	69	74	69	72	284	4,140
Jim Thorpe	73	67	70	75	285	3,600
Philip Walton	72	71	75	67	285	3,600
Andrew Murray	72	72	69	72	285	3,600
Gordon Brand Jr.	72	70	71	72	285	3,600
Nick Faldo	72	72	73	68	285	3,600
Roger Chapman	69	77	69	71	286	3,160
Frank Nobilo	71	71	71	73	286	3,160
Michael Allen	70	74	73	69	286	3,160
Howard Clark	72	72	67	75	286	3,160
Craig Parry	68	71	72	76	287	2,760
Frederic Regard	73	70	74	70	287	2,760
Eduardo Romero	74	74	69	70	287	2,760
Mark McNulty	74	64	70	79	287	2,760
Peter Senior	72	74	72	69	287	2,760
Mike Clayton	74	67	75	71	287	2,760
Stephen Bennett	73	70	74	71	288	2,280
Jim Rutledge	74	75	71	68	288	2,280
Jose-Maria Canizares	72	71	70	75	288	2,280
David Williams	73	71	73	71	288	2,280
Derrick Cooper	74	71	69	74	288	2,280
David Whelan	71	75	68	74	288	2,280
David J. Russell	69	76	74	71	290	2,000
Mike Harwood	75	71	69	76	291	1,840
Colin Montgomerie	70	72	76	73	291	1,840
Des Smyth	71	73	72	75	291	1,840

German Masters

Stuttgarter Golf Club, Stuttgart, West Germany
Par 36-36 — 72; 6,809 yards

September 21-25
purse, £286,625

	SCORES				TOTAL	MONEY
Jose-Maria Olazabal	69	72	70	68	279	$47,770.70
Anders Forsbrand	75	68	70	68	281	24,878.99
Des Smyth	71	68	71	71	281	24,878.99
Tom Purtzer	68	72	72	70	282	13,232.49
Mark McNulty	69	72	71	70	282	13,232.49
Ronan Rafferty	75	69	72	68	284	9,315.29
Severiano Ballesteros	72	70	68	74	284	9,315.29
Jeff Hawkes	78	70	69	68	285	6,793.00
Jose Rivero	71	71	72	71	285	6,793.00
Philip Walton	70	71	75	70	286	5,503.19
Mats Lanner	69	70	71	76	286	5,503.19
Eamonn Darcy	66	76	71	74	287	4,772.30
Nick Faldo	73	71	72	71	287	4,772.30
Sandy Lyle	69	75	72	72	288	4,213.38
David Feherty	73	69	70	76	288	4,213.38
Ian Mosey	70	72	72	74	288	4,213.38
Jerry Anderson	71	72	70	76	289	3,707.01
Ian Woosnam	72	70	73	74	289	3,707.01
Paul Way	74	72	72	71	289	3,707.01
Miguel Martin	75	71	70	74	290	3,396.50
Sam Torrance	74	71	71	74	290	3,396.50
Denis Durnian	71	74	74	72	291	3,181.53
Juan Anglada	73	69	73	76	291	3,181.53
Mark Roe	67	75	71	78	291	3,181.53
Gordon J. Brand	68	76	75	73	292	2,794.59
Andrew Oldcorn	74	70	74	74	292	2,794.59
John Slaughter	70	72	74	76	292	2,794.59
Robert Lee	76	72	75	69	292	2,794.59
Malcolm MacKenzie	73	74	75	70	292	2,794.59
Paul Thomas	76	71	74	71	292	2,794.59
David Jones	72	72	71	78	293	2,417.20
Peter Teravainen	71	73	74	75	293	2,417.20
Bernhard Langer	68	75	71	79	293	2,417.20
Carl Mason	74	72	72	76	294	2,178.34
Bernard Gallacher	75	72	74	73	294	2,178.34
Gordon Brand Jr.	76	73	70	75	294	2,178.34
Andrew Murray	74	71	77	72	294	2,178.34
Jim Rutledge	70	75	75	74	294	2,178.34
Ian Young	71	73	76	75	295	1,891.72
Carlo Knauss	74	72	76	73	295	1,891.72
Antonio Postiglione	74	73	75	73	295	1,891.72
Magnus Persson	70	73	74	78	295	1,891.72
Peter Baker	77	70	74	74	295	1,891.72
Chris Moody	73	73	76	74	296	1,633.76
David A. Russell	75	73	75	73	296	1,633.76
Andrew Sherborne	71	75	75	75	296	1,633.76
Magnus Sunesson	74	72	78	72	296	1,633.76
Emmanuel Dussart	73	76	77	71	297	1,318.47
Ove Sellberg	74	71	75	77	297	1,318.47
Derrick Cooper	71	78	75	73	297	1,318.47
Manuel Pinero	71	75	75	76	297	1,318.47
Christy O'Connor Jr.	74	75	78	70	297	1,318.47
Torsten Giedeon	76	73	74	74	297	1,318.47
Steen Tinning	75	72	75	75	297	1,318.47

English Open

Royal Birkdale Golf Club, Southport, England
Par 35-37 — 72; 7,022 yards

September 29-October 2
purse, £180,000

	SCORES				TOTAL	MONEY
Howard Clark	72	71	67	69	279	£30,000
Peter Baker	73	70	69	70	282	20,000
Des Smyth	74	65	70	74	283	10,150
Peter McWhinney	75	67	74	67	283	10,150
Stephen McAllister	73	69	73	69	284	7,000
Miguel Martin	74	71	72	67	284	7,000
David J. Russell	74	70	70	71	285	5,400
Tony Charnley	74	73	69	70	286	4,130
Bill Longmuir	74	70	72	70	286	4,130
Richard Boxall	74	71	76	66	287	3,300
Mark Mouland	75	73	70	69	287	3,300
Mark James	74	68	75	70	287	3,300
Martin Poxon	76	70	72	70	288	2,575
Bernard Gallacher	72	73	72	71	288	2,575
Marc Pendaries	74	74	72	68	288	2,575
Andrew Murray	79	70	70	69	288	2,575
Derrick Cooper	74	73	71	70	288	2,575
Chris Moody	72	68	72	76	288	2,575
Philip Walton	77	69	71	71	288	2,575
Andrew Sherborne	72	74	69	73	288	2,575
David Feherty	76	70	75	68	289	2,040
Paul Curry	70	74	74	71	289	2,040
Peter Fowler	71	77	71	70	289	2,040
Ian Mosey	75	71	71	72	289	2,040
David A. Russell	73	71	74	71	289	2,040
Roger Chapman	75	68	76	71	290	1,645.71
Denis Durnian	76	71	72	71	290	1,645.71
Michael McLean	73	73	73	71	290	1,645.71
Gordon J. Brand	74	72	73	71	290	1,645.71
Brian Waites	76	73	71	70	290	1,645.71
Gordon Brand Jr.	74	69	77	70	290	1,645.71
Russell Weir	74	68	74	74	290	1,645.71
Peter Mitchell	75	73	71	72	291	1,440
David Ray	70	77	73	71	291	1,440
Philip Harrison	73	73	71	74	291	1,440
Jerry Anderson	74	73	76	69	292	1,260
Kyi Hla Han	73	72	78	69	292	1,260
Andrew Chandler	72	73	74	73	292	1,260
David Williams	74	68	78	72	292	1,260
Magnus Persson	70	75	79	68	292	1,260
Mark Roe	76	72	72	72	292	1,260
Andrew Oldcorn	78	71	72	72	293	1,020
Bryan Norton	73	71	74	75	293	1,020
Colin Montgomerie	75	72	75	71	293	1,020
Ross Drummond	77	70	76	70	293	1,020
Paul Way	76	71	74	72	293	1,020
John McHenry	76	73	74	70	293	1,020
Ross McFarlane	76	71	74	73	294	840
Mike Miller	73	70	77	74	294	840
Glenn Ralph	76	69	77	72	294	840

Suntory World Match Play Championship

Wentworth Club, West Course,
Virginia Water, Surrey, England
Par 434 534 444 — 35; 345 434 455 — 37 — 72;
6,945 yards

October 6-10
purse, £265,000

FIRST ROUND

Jeff Sluman defeated Nobuo Serizawa, 6 and 5

Sluman	W35	434	444	X	345	433	444	34	X
Serizawa	C34	523	545	X	336	43C	456	X	X

Sluman leads, 4 up

Sluman	535	424	454	36	245	4
Serizawa	535	443	44C	X	355	4

Joey Sindelar defeated Barry Lane, 5 and 4

Sindelar	434	525	444	35	244	424	455	34	69
Lane	535	544	444	38	344	434	455	36	74

Sindelar leads, 4 up

Sindelar	524	446	444	37	354	43
Lane	535	534	444	37	245	53

Nick Price defeated Rodger Davis, 2 and 1

Price	434	534	444	35	343	335	444	33	68
Davis	434	535	444	36	345	434	455	37	73

Price leads, 4 up

Price	535	633	445	38	344	434	54
Davis	435	634	344	36	354	433	45

Mark McCumber defeated Mark McNulty, 1 hole

McCumber	435	534	444	36	345	423	444	33	69
McNulty	435	433	444	34	445	C34	544	X	X

McCumber leads, 3 up

McCumber	535	434	445	37	345	534	344	35	72
McNulty	534	534	444	36	344	425	444	34	70

SECOND ROUND

Ian Woosnam defeated Jeff Sluman, 7 and 6

Woosnam	424	433	435	32	354	436	444	37	69
Sluman	334	534	434	33	445	444	445	38	71

Woosnam leads, 3 up

Woosnam	435	424	444	34	344
Sluman	533	643	534	36	455

Nick Faldo defeated Joey Sindelar, 5 and 4

Faldo	435	534	444	36	344	434	444	34	70
Sindelar	536	434	435	37	345	435	444	36	73

Faldo leads, 3 up

Faldo	335	334	445	34	345	43
Sindelar	435	434	434	34	345	54

Sandy Lyle defeated Nick Price, 3 and 2

Lyle	335	534	443	34	335	345	544	36	70
Price	435	434	333	32	445	434	444	36	68

Price leads, 2 up

Lyle	555	434	344	37	245	334	3
Price	434	535	446	38	346	435	3

Seve Ballesteros defeated Mark McCumber at 37th hole

Ballesteros	445	533	444	36	345	435	544	37	73
McCumber	535	433	444	35	244	534	444	34	69

McCumber leads, 4 up

Ballesteros	434	436	534	36	345	434	554	37	73
McCumber	534	534	454	37	355	445	554	40	77

Match all-square

Ballesteros	3
McCumber	4

SEMI-FINALS

Sandy Lyle defeated Seve Ballesteros, 7 and 6

Lyle	335	424	434	32	235	433	453	32	64
Ballesteros	424	524	454	34	345	333	444	33	67

Lyle leads, 2 up

Lyle	334	432	544	32	334
Ballesteros	535	433	544	36	435

Nick Faldo defeated Ian Woosnam, 1 hole

Faldo	434	444	445	36	335	434	345	34	70
Woosnam	434	434	544	35	344	324	455	34	69

Woosnam leads, 1 up

Faldo	435	434	454	36	334	434	444	33	69
Woosnam	434	433	545	35	345	534	354	36	71

FINAL

Sandy Lyle defeated Nick Faldo, 2 and 1

Lyle	434	444	434	34	344	524	334	32	66
Faldo	444	434	443	34	344	524	444	34	68

Lyle leads, 2 up

Lyle	445	434	444	36	435	423	34
Faldo	434	434	444	34	344	435	35

NOTE: Playoff between Seve Ballesteros and Ian Woosnam for third and fourth place was cancelled due to rain and the players shared the prize money.

PRIZE MONEY: Lyle £75,000; Faldo £40,000; Ballesteros, Woosnam £25,000 each; Sluman, Sindelar, Price, McCumber £15,000 each; Serizawa, Lane, Davis, McNulty £10,000 each.

LEGEND: C—conceded hole to opponent; W—won hole by concession without holing out; X—no total score.

Dunhill Cup

Old Course, St. Andrews, Scotland
Par 36-36 — 72; 6,933 yards

October 11-16
purse, US$1,018,000

PRELIMINARY ROUND

ZIMBABWE DEFEATED ARGENTINA, 2-1
Morgan Shumba (Z) defeated Eduardo Romero, 73-75; Anthony Edwards (Z) defeated Miguel Fernandez, 73-75; Vincente Fernandez (A) defeated Tim Price, 72-75.

SWEDEN DEFEATED SINGAPORE, 3-0
Magnus Persson (Swed.) defeated Madasamy Murugiah, 74-77; Anders Forsbrand

(Swed.) defeated Bill Fung, 76-80; Ove Sellberg (Swed.) defeated Swee Wah Lim, 71-78.

(Each member of each losing team received US $3,000.)

FIRST ROUND

UNITED STATES DEFEATED PHILIPPINES, 3-0
Curtis Strange (US) defeated Eddie Bagtas, 70-75; Chip Beck (US) defeated Rudy Lavares, 68-81; Mark McCumber (US) defeated Frankie Minoza, 72-75.

IRELAND DEFEATED CANADA, 2-1
Dave Barr (C) defeated Ronan Rafferty, 67-69; Eamonn Darcy (I) defeated Dan Halldorson, 69-72; Des Smyth (I) defeated Richard Zokol, 69-76.

SPAIN DEFEATED ZIMBABWE, 3-0
Severiano Ballesteros (S) defeated Price, 72-74; Jose Rivero (S) defeated Edwards, 68-72; Jose-Maria Olazabal (S) defeated Shumba, 74-78.

AUSTRALIA DEFEATED BRAZIL, 3-0
Rodger Davis (A) defeated Rafael Navarro, 69-73; David Graham (A) defeated Carlos Dluosh, 68-79; Greg Norman (A) defeated Priscillo Diniz, 71-73.

ENGLAND DEFEATED FRANCE, 3-0
Mark James (E) defeated Frederic Regard, 66-75; Barry Lane (E) defeated Michel Tapia, 70-75; Nick Faldo (E) defeated Emmanuel Dussart, 65-70.

SCOTLAND DEFEATED THAILAND, 3-0
Gordon Brand Jr. (S) defeated Boonchu Ruangkit, 74-76; Colin Montgomerie (S) defeated Suthep Meesawad, 72-80; Sandy Lyle (S) defeated Somsakdi Srinsangar, 70-73.

JAPAN DEFEATED DENMARK, 3-0
Naomichi Ozaki (J) defeated Jacob Rasmussen, 69-77; Tateo Ozaki (J) defeated Steen Tinning, 68-69; Hajime Meshiai (J) defeated Anders Sorensen, 72-75.

WALES DEFEATED SWEDEN, 3-0
David Llewellyn (W) defeated Persson, 72-75; Mark Mouland (W) defeated Sellberg, 70-71; Ian Woosnam (W) defeated Forsbrand, 69-75.

(Each member of each losing team received US$7,500.)

QUARTER-FINALS

AUSTRALIA DEFEATED WALES, 2-1
Graham (A) defeated Mouland, 67-76; Davis (A) defeated Llewellyn, 69-70; Woosnam (W) defeated Norman, 71-73.

IRELAND DEFEATED UNITED STATES, 2½-½
Rafferty (I) defeated McCumber, 71-72; Smyth (I) halved with Beck, 71-71; Darcy (I) defeated Strange, 66-68.

SPAIN DEFEATED JAPAN, 3-0
Ballesteros (S) defeated N. Ozaki, 72-74; Rivero (S) defeated Meshiai, 65-68; Olazabal (S) defeated T. Ozaki, 68-69.

ENGLAND DEFEATED SCOTLAND, 2-1
Brand (S) defeated Lane, 71-73; James (E) defeated Montgomerie, 69-71; Faldo (E) defeated Lyle, 67-68.

(Each member of each losing team received US$15,000.)

SEMI-FINALS

AUSTRALIA DEFEATED SPAIN, 2-1
Norman (A) defeated Ballesteros, 67-69; Davis (A) defeated Rivero, 71-72; Olazabal (S) defeated Graham, 69-73.

IRELAND DEFEATED ENGLAND, 2-1
Lane (E) defeated Rafferty, 65-68; Smyth (I) defeated Faldo, 69-70; Darcy (I) defeated James, 68-72.

PLAYOFF—THIRD-FOURTH PLACES

SPAIN DEFEATED ENGLAND, 2-1
Faldo (E) defeated Olazabal, 66-67; Ballesteros (S) defeated Lane, 71-72; Rivero (S) defeated James, 69-70.

(Each Spanish player received US$36,666; each English player received US$26,666.)

FINALS

IRELAND DEFEATED AUSTRALIA, 2-1
Smyth (I) defeated Davis, 71-73; Rafferty (I) defeated Graham, 69-74; Norman (A) defeated Darcy, 63-71.

(Each Irish player received US$100,000; each Australian player received US$50,000.)

Jersey Open

La Moye Golf Club, Jersey
Par 36-36 — 72; 6,734 yards

October 20-23
purse, £122,000

	SCORES				TOTAL	MONEY
Des Smyth	69	68	69	67	273	£20,330
Roger Chapman	68	68	68	69	273	13,540
(Smyth defeated Chapman on fifth hole of playoff.)						
Carl Mason	66	68	69	71	274	5,795
Paul Way	71	69	65	69	274	5,795
Ross McFarlane	67	70	65	72	274	5,795
Neil Hansen	68	69	69	68	274	5,795
David Whelan	71	68	68	68	275	3,660
Christy O'Connor Jr.	66	71	69	70	276	2,887
Chris Moody	64	71	69	72	276	2,887
Steven Bottomley	68	70	70	69	277	2,265
Steen Tinning	68	69	71	69	277	2,265
David Gilford	71	70	68	68	277	2,265
Mark Roe	69	69	68	72	278	1,990
Tony Charnley	68	67	71	73	279	1,890
Derrick Cooper	70	74	69	67	280	1,648
Denis Durnian	67	72	72	69	280	1,648
Mats Hallberg	71	72	65	72	280	1,648
Mats Lanner	69	73	70	68	280	1,648
Michael King	71	69	68	72	280	1,648
Martin Poxon	73	71	70	67	281	1,440
Eduardo Romero	68	71	71	71	281	1,440
Eamonn Darcy	69	71	72	69	281	1,440
Bernard Gallacher	68	72	72	69	281	1,440
Colin Montgomerie	66	73	72	71	282	1,260
Bill Longmuir	72	71	71	68	282	1,260

	SCORES				TOTAL	MONEY
Peter Fowler	67	74	73	68	282	1,260
Paul Broadhurst	74	71	66	71	282	1,260
John Morgan	71	73	68	70	282	1,260
David Williams	69	72	75	67	283	1,060
Brian Marchbank	68	69	71	75	283	1,060
Stephen Bennett	64	70	75	74	283	1,060
David J. Russell	70	75	70	68	283	1,060
Paul Curry	73	72	70	68	283	1,060
Anders Sorensen	69	70	74	71	284	878
Andrew Oldcorn	66	71	74	73	284	878
Ross Drummond	68	69	76	71	284	878
Barry Lane	70	68	72	74	284	878
Ian Mosey	66	71	75	72	284	878
Frederic Regard	73	67	72	73	285	770
Gordon J. Brand	68	74	70	73	285	770
Neal Briggs	71	74	68	72	285	770
David Ray	65	75	71	74	285	770
Anders Forsbrand	70	73	72	70	285	770
David A. Russell	70	73	72	71	286	680
Ronan Rafferty	71	68	73	74	286	680
Grant Turner	75	70	71	70	286	680
Bill Malley	71	72	74	69	286	680
Andrew Murray	68	71	69	79	287	610
John McHenry	70	72	73	72	287	610
Ian Young	68	72	76	71	287	610

Volvo Masters

Valderrama Club Course, Sotogrande, Spain
Par 36-36 — 72; 7,020 yards

October 27-30
purse, £351,690

	SCORES				TOTAL	MONEY
Nick Faldo	74	71	71	68	284	£58,330
Severiano Ballesteros	68	72	74	72	286	38,860
Sandy Lyle	68	71	75	74	288	21,910
Ian Woosnam	75	74	70	70	289	17,500
Roger Chapman	71	77	70	75	293	13,540
Eamonn Darcy	74	71	74	74	293	13,540
Mats Lanner	77	70	74	73	294	8,522.50
Anders Sorensen	76	67	76	75	294	8,522.50
Peter Fowler	77	71	71	75	294	8,522.50
Christy O'Connor Jr.	78	73	70	73	294	8,522.50
Jose-Maria Canizares	76	76	67	76	295	6,230
Neil Hansen	77	72	75	71	295	6,230
Howard Clark	73	73	74	76	296	5,490
Manuel Pinero	74	71	81	70	296	5,490
Neil Coles	78	76	72	71	297	5,140
Peter Baker	72	74	75	77	298	4,628.75
Manuel Calero	77	73	73	75	298	4,628.75
Ove Sellberg	71	74	76	77	298	4,628.75
Jose-Maria Olazabal	78	74	69	77	298	4,628.75
Simon Bishop	74	72	79	74	299	4,095
Tony Charnley	74	72	75	78	299	4,095
Des Smyth	73	81	71	74	299	4,095
David J. Russell	74	79	74	73	300	3,780
Carl Mason	75	72	79	74	300	3,780
Barry Lane	74	75	75	76	300	3,780

	SCORES				TOTAL	MONEY
Michael Allen	73	76	76	76	301	3,206.88
David Whelan	76	74	77	74	301	3,206.88
Mark James	73	76	75	77	301	3,206.88
Ronan Rafferty	77	76	71	77	301	3,206.88
Vicente Fernandez	78	76	76	71	301	3,206.88
Derrick Cooper	74	76	73	78	301	3,206.88
Gordon J. Brand	78	76	71	76	301	3,206.88
David Gilford	77	76	74	74	301	3,206.88
Denis Durnian	73	75	75	79	302	2,730
Mark McNulty	75	79	71	77	302	2,730
Eduardo Romero	79	70	77	76	302	2,730
Ignacio Gervas	82	71	79	71	303	2,485
David Williams	74	76	76	77	303	2,485
Richard Boxall	78	72	79	74	303	2,485
Paul Way	74	78	76	75	303	2,485
Ross McFarlane	79	73	80	73	305	2,170
Johan Rystrom	75	77	78	75	305	2,170
Malcolm MacKenzie	73	80	75	77	305	2,170
Bernard Gallacher	76	72	84	73	305	2,170
Jimmy Heggarty	77	76	75	77	305	2,170
Bill Longmuir	75	76	83	72	306	1,925
Paul Curry	79	71	78	78	306	1,925
Juan Anglada	75	77	76	79	307	1,785
David Feherty	77	77	72	81	307	1,785
David Llewellyn	73	76	78	81	307	1,785

Benson & Hedges Trophy Mixed Team Tournament

La Moraleja Club, Madrid, Spain
Par 36-36 — 72; 6,547 yards

November 10-13
purse, £120,000

	SCORES				TOTAL	MONEY
Mark McNulty/Marie Laure de Lorenzi-Taya	69	68	67	72	276	£20,000
Jose Maria Canizares/Tania Abitbol	67	76	68	66	277	15,000
Bill Longmuir/Florence Descampe	71	70	70	67	278	10,250
Andrew Stubbs/Suzanne Strudwick	66	69	73	70	278	10,250
Derrick Cooper/Peggy Conley	74	67	66	73	280	6,500
Andrew Sherborne/Katrina Douglas	70	72	70	68	280	6,500
Manuel Pinero/Marta Figueras-Dotti	72	71	70	69	282	4,500
Jose Rivero/Xonia Wunsch Ruiz	71	71	71	69	282	4,500
Mats Lanner/Marie Wennersten	72	69	67	74	282	4,500
Simon Bishop/Debbie Dowling	74	73	68	69	284	3,500
Carl Mason/Caroline Griffiths	70	72	71	73	286	3,000
Steven Bottomley/Frederica Dassu	68	74	72	73	287	2,600
Keith Waters/Barbara Helbig	70	70	69	78	287	2,600
Paul Thomas/Jane Connachan	73	71	72	71	287	2,600
David Jones/Cathy Panton	75	72	72	69	288	2,250
Tommy Horton/Sophia Gronberg	72	70	79	68	289	2,100
*Yago Beamonte/Maria Orueta	73	71	73	72	289	
Paul Carrigill/Diana Heinicke	75	70	70	75	290	1,950
Glenn Ralph/Dale Reid	72	76	72	72	292	1,750
Mike Miller/Muriel Thomson	74	71	76	71	292	1,750
Jerry Anderson/Majorie Jones	74	78	72	69	293	1,462.50
David Ray/Ann Jones	73	75	75	70	293	1,462.50
Ignacio Gervas/Beverley New	75	70	72	76	293	1,462.50

The African Tours

Nigerian Open

Ikoyi Club, Lagos, Nigeria
Par 36-35 — 71; 6,389 yards

January 28-31
purse, £52,975

	SCORES				TOTAL	MONEY
Vijay Singh	72	70	68	71	281	£8,829.24
Mike Miller	65	72	73	71	281	5,886.16
(Singh defeated Miller on first hole of playoff.)						
Malcolm Gregson	73	71	69	71	284	2,982.52
Peter Akakasiaka	72	70	70	72	284	2,982.52
Paul Kent	70	70	68	77	285	2,050.15
James Lebbie	70	73	71	71	285	2,050.15
John Morgan	70	78	68	71	287	1,366.67
Anthony Stevens	69	69	76	73	287	1,366.67
David Wood	70	74	73	70	287	1,366.67
Andrew Cotton	71	71	76	70	288	949.44
Jeffrey Pinsent	69	76	71	72	288	949.44
Ewen Murray	69	76	71	72	288	949.44
David Owoyemi	76	70	71	71	288	949.44
Glyn Davies	74	70	73	72	289	809.94
Joe Higgins	69	75	71	75	290	778.15
Mikael Krantz	72	73	72	74	291	746.37
David R. Jones	74	75	72	71	292	698.69
Peter Cowen	74	71	72	75	292	698.69
Tommy Horton	71	74	70	78	293	612.51
Frederic Regard	72	77	69	75	293	612.51
Tunde Raimi	73	77	72	71	293	612.51
Bello Seibidor	70	75	78	70	293	612.51
Philip Talbot	72	74	72	75	293	612.51
Tony Uduimoh	78	71	72	72	293	612.51
Garry Harvey	73	74	71	76	294	516.22
Paul Hoad	70	72	75	77	294	516.22
David Blakeman	71	77	75	71	294	516.22
Jones Esioyibo	71	74	71	78	294	516.22
Jacob Omoruah	73	74	72	75	294	516.22
D. Sakata	71	72	75	76	294	516.22

Ivory Coast Open

President Golf Club, Yamoussoukro, Ivory Coast
Par 36-36 — 72; 6,476 yards

February 4-7
purse, £76,923

	SCORES				TOTAL	MONEY
Gordon J. Brand	68	71	67	69	275	£12,819.23
Richard Rish	69	73	67	68	277	8,538.46
James Annable	69	67	71	72	279	4,330.77
Tony Stevens	70	69	72	68	279	4,330.77
Joe Higgins	71	70	67	72	280	2,752.56
John McHenry	74	74	66	66	280	2,752.56

	SCORES				TOTAL	MONEY
Vijay Singh	72	70	69	69	280	2,752.56
John Morgan	70	72	70	69	281	1,923.08
Emmanuel Dussart	74	68	71	69	282	1,723.08
Wraith Grant	70	76	70	67	283	1,425.64
Mike Miller	71	70	70	72	283	1,425.64
David Blakeman	76	69	69	69	283	1,425.64
Wayne Stephens	67	74	73	70	284	1,157.69
Andrew Stubbs	71	76	67	70	284	1,157.69
David Wood	72	74	69	69	284	1,157.69
David Jagger	69	76	71	68	284	1,157.69
Martin Poxon	76	68	70	71	285	1,015.39
Chris Platts	74	71	72	68	285	1,015.39
Garry Harvey	68	76	73	69	286	938.47
Craig Laurence	77	70	70	69	286	938.47
Jeffrey Pinsent	69	74	73	71	287	900
Colin Montgomerie	72	74	72	70	288	842.31
Peter Akakasiaka	71	68	71	78	288	842.31
Peter Cowen	72	75	70	71	288	842.31
Chris Gray	71	76	71	70	288	842.31
Jean Lamaison	80	72	68	69	289	784.62
Steven Bottomley	75	77	69	69	290	750
Thierry Abbas	74	75	72	69	290	750
Grant Turner	77	72	71	71	291	703.85
Philip Talbot	74	71	71	75	291	703.85

555 Kenya Open

Muthaiga Golf Club, Nairobi, Kenya
Par 36-35 — 71; 6,765 yards

February 11-14
purse, £70,470

	SCORES				TOTAL	MONEY
Chris Platts	66	65	72	68	271	£11,442.95
Mark Mouland	71	67	70	64	272	7,751.68
Vijay Singh	71	68	67	69	275	4,328.86
Peter Harrison	69	71	70	66	276	3,406.04
Paul Kent	72	69	68	69	278	2,885.91
David James	72	64	72	71	279	1,850.33
Craig Laurence	73	70	66	70	279	1,850.33
Carl Mason	69	72	67	71	279	1,850.33
Ross McFarlane	68	76	67	68	279	1,850.33
Andrew Stubbs	71	68	71	69	279	1,850.33
Roger Chapman	71	69	70	70	280	1,165.10
Jose Gervas	71	70	69	70	280	1,165.10
David Jones	69	64	73	74	280	1,165.10
Frederic Regard	69	68	71	72	280	1,165.10
Chris Gray	69	70	69	72	280	1,165.10
James Spence	71	73	66	71	281	978.19
Tony Stevens	69	70	71	71	281	978.19
Emmanuel Dussart	75	68	70	70	283	875.84
Malcolm Gregson	70	71	74	68	283	875.84
David Llewellyn	73	70	66	74	283	875.84
Magnus Persson	71	72	69	71	283	875.84
Wraith Grant	73	73	69	69	284	732.89
Stephen Hamill	72	72	68	72	284	732.89
John McHenry	72	72	68	72	284	732.89
David Williams	72	72	71	70	284	732.89
David Jagger	72	69	72	71	284	732.89

	SCORES				TOTAL	MONEY
Steve Cipa	71	67	75	72	285	596.83
Joe Higgins	72	71	69	73	285	596.83
Stephen McAllister	70	73	72	70	285	596.83
Colin Montgomerie	74	65	70	76	285	596.83
Mark Roe	72	71	72	70	285	596.83
David Blakeman	73	70	69	73	285	596.83
Anthony Edwards	73	68	75	69	285	596.83

Zimbabwe Open

Chapman Golf Club, Harare, Zimbabwe
Par 36-36 — 72; 6,521 yards

February 18-21
purse, £44,145

	SCORES				TOTAL	MONEY
Roger Chapman	63	70	71	71	275	£7,356.44
Vijay Singh	64	68	72	72	276	4,901.90
Carl Mason	65	70	71	71	277	2,280.91
Colin Montgomerie	66	72	66	73	277	2,280.91
David Williams	66	70	67	74	277	2,280.91
Joe Higgins	64	72	71	71	278	1,324.40
Mark Mouland	64	74	68	72	278	1,324.40
Mark Roe	64	69	74	71	278	1,324.40
Richard Fish	61	72	71	75	279	935.09
Bill Longmuir	67	71	68	73	279	935.09
Garry Harvey	63	76	71	70	280	767.60
David Llewellyn	66	71	72	71	280	767.60
Tony Stevens	66	72	70	72	280	767.60
John McHenry	65	71	69	76	281	668.41
David Jagger	63	76	73	69	281	668.41
Peter Barber	63	72	74	73	282	583.64
Paul Carrigill	67	70	76	69	282	583.64
Steve Cipa	63	78	77	64	282	583.64
Peter Cowen	67	73	72	70	282	583.64
John Morgan	64	72	77	70	283	540.22
Peter Harrison	65	74	73	72	284	519.13
Andrew Sherborne	64	74	74	72	284	519.13
Jose Gervas	68	73	72	73	286	476.79
Paul Kent	66	71	71	78	286	476.79
Mike Miller	69	70	73	74	286	476.79
Jacob Rasmussen	67	70	73	76	286	476.79
Emmanuel Dussart	68	78	70	71	287	420.29
Martin Poxon	68	70	79	70	287	420.29
Glenn Ralph	66	74	71	76	287	420.29
Andrew Stubbs	67	72	74	74	287	420.29

Zambian Open

Lusaka Golf Club, Lasaka, Zambia
Par 35-38 — 73; 7,217 yards

February 25-28
purse, £75,000

	SCORES				TOTAL	MONEY
David Llewellyn	72	70	68	70	280	£12,500
Richard Fish	71	72	70	68	281	8,320
Glenn Ralph	72	73	71	71	287	4,690

	SCORES				TOTAL	MONEY
Jeffrey Pinsent	72	73	74	70	289	3,460
Joe Higgins	67	79	70	73	289	3,460
John McHenry	77	71	76	66	290	2,435
Chris Platts	72	74	71	73	290	2,435
Steve Cipa	73	70	73	75	291	1,875
John Morgan	76	71	75	70	292	1,680
Grant Turner	73	76	74	70	293	1,440
Vijay Singh	76	74	72	71	293	1,440
Mikael Krantz	75	72	73	74	294	1,250
John Vingoe	73	73	75	73	294	1,250
Mike Miller	73	73	75	74	295	1,125
Ewen Murray	79	69	75	72	295	1,125
James Spence	77	75	71	73	296	1,013.33
Peter Harrison	75	73	73	75	296	1,013.33
Jose Gervas	75	74	72	75	296	1,013.33
Colin Montgomerie	76	74	76	71	297	903.33
Andrew Clapp	75	73	77	72	297	903.33
Michael Ingham	74	72	73	78	297	903.33
Paul Kent	75	78	72	73	298	831.67
Bernard Gallacher	75	74	74	75	298	831.67
Peter Cowen	74	76	73	75	298	831.67
Malcolm Gregson	78	73	76	72	299	777.50
Frederic Regard	74	74	78	73	299	777.50
Phil Golding	75	74	74	77	300	708.75
Wraith Grant	76	71	74	79	300	708.75
David Blakeman	74	73	73	80	300	708.75
Anthony Edwards	75	78	74	73	300	708.75

Palabora Classic

Hans Merensky Golf Club, Phalaborwa
Par 36-36 — 72; 6,727 yards

January 6-9
purse, R200,000

	SCORES				TOTAL	MONEY
Fulton Allem	70	70	70	67	277	R32,000
David Feherty	75	72	69	65	281	18,500
Ian Young	72	67	73	69	281	18,500
Ron McCann	70	72	71	69	282	7,900
Tony Johnstone	74	68	69	71	282	7,900
Teddy Webber	70	72	68	72	282	7,900
Wilhelm Winsnes	68	70	72	72	282	7,900
Malcolm McKenzie	75	71	71	67	284	5,000
John Bland	73	71	72	69	285	3,600
Bob E. Smith	72	72	71	70	285	3,600
Derek James	74	71	69	71	285	3,600
Neil Hansen	73	73	69	70	285	3,600
Chris Williams	76	69	69	71	285	3,600
Robbie Stewart	68	74	60	73	285	3,600
Phil Simmons	74	70	74	68	286	2,900
Jeff Hawkes	71	74	74	68	287	2,750
Nolan Henke	76	69	70	72	287	2,750
Simon Hobday	73	72	73	70	288	2,416
Hugh Biaocchi	72	73	72	71	288	2,416
Jack Ferenz	74	69	73	72	288	2,416
Gavin Levenson	81	69	67	71	288	2,416
Craigen Pappas	72	72	70	74	288	2,416
Jeremy Robinson	76	73	72	69	290	2,050

	SCORES				TOTAL	MONEY
Don Levin	74	74	72	70	290	2,050
Bobby Lincoln	76	72	71	71	290	2,050
Len O'Kennedy	77	73	68	72	290	2,050
Andries Oosthuizen	73	76	69	72	290	2,050
Kevin Stone	76	72	69	73	290	2,050
Brian Evans	74	75	74	68	291	1,755
Alan Pate	73	74	72	72	291	1,755
Ian Palmer	74	72	70	75	291	1,755
Peter van der Riet	75	72	67	77	291	1,755

ICL International

Zwartkops Country Club, Pretoria
Par 36-36 — 72; 7,125 yards

January 13-16
purse, R200,000

	SCORES				TOTAL	MONEY
Tony Johnstone	66	66	65	69	266	R32,000
Denis Durnian	65	66	69	67	267	23,000
Nolan Henke	67	70	68	66	268	14,000
Fulton Allem	70	66	69	66	271	9,200
Ian Young	67	64	73	67	271	9,200
Simon Hobday	69	67	71	65	272	6,600
Jeff Hawkes	71	65	69	67	272	6,600
Hugh Biaocchi	69	67	69	68	273	4,700
Hendrick Burhmann	65	65	70	73	273	4,700
David Feherty	69	68	68	69	274	4,000
Trevor Dodds	72	68	69	66	275	3,300
Ashley Roestoff	66	70	71	68	275	3,300
Rick Hartman	65	67	73	70	275	3,300
Jeffrey Roth	68	69	69	69	275	3,300
Wayne Westner	74	69	68	65	276	2,850
John Bland	71	66	70	69	276	2,850
Hugh Royer	69	72	67	69	277	2,650
Wilhelm Winsnes	69	68	71	69	277	2,650
Robert Richardson	71	69	72	66	278	2,370
Chris Williams	70	70	70	68	278	2,370
Mark James	69	67	71	71	278	2,370
John Riegger	69	69	68	72	278	2,370
Phil Simmons	68	70	71	70	279	2,170
Richard Kaplan	72	67	68	72	279	2,170
Steven Burnett	72	71	70	67	280	2,050
Jannie Le Grange	68	71	72	69	280	2,050
Brian Evans	73	70	73	65	281	1,742.22
Jay Townsend	71	70	71	69	281	1,742.22
Desmond Terblanche	73	70	69	69	281	1,742.22
Andries Oosthuizen	71	71	70	69	281	1,742.22
Alan Pate	71	69	71	70	281	1,742.22
Don Robertson	70	68	72	71	281	1,742.22
Wayne Bradley	70	69	71	71	281	1,742.22
Eamonn Darcy	68	72	70	71	281	1,742.22
John Cyboran	70	67	70	74	281	1,742.22

Lexington PGA Championship

Wanderers Golf Club, Johannesburg
Par 35-35 — 70; 6,960 yards

January 20-23
purse, R200,000

	SCORES				TOTAL	MONEY
David Feherty	69	65	66	67	267	R32,000
Eamonn Darcy	66	67	70	65	268	23,000
Trevor Dodds	67	68	67	69	271	14,000
Hugh Biaocchi	67	63	70	72	272	10,000
Teddy Webber	68	67	69	69	273	8,400
Jack Ferenz	69	68	71	66	274	6,600
Gavin Levenson	68	70	67	69	274	6,600
Jeff Hawkes	70	69	69	67	275	4,700
Hugh Royer	69	65	71	70	275	4,700
John Bland	70	72	68	66	276	3,440
Phil Simmons	67	71	70	68	276	3,440
Stuart Smith	72	69	66	69	276	3,440
John Cyboran	66	68	72	60	276	3,440
Hendrik Buhrmann	64	70	71	71	276	3,440
Frank Edmonds	72	67	70	68	277	2,700
Tony Johnstone	67	67	73	70	277	2,700
Mike White	71	67	69	70	277	2,700
John Riegger	69	69	68	71	277	2,700
Fulton Allem	67	64	73	73	277	2,700
Simon Hobday	69	72	70	67	278	2,233.33
Jannie Le Grange	70	70	69	69	278	2,233.33
Chris Williams	70	69	69	70	278	2,233.33
Ian Palmer	69	72	66	71	278	2,233.33
Denis Durnian	67	69	70	72	278	2,233.33
Rick Hartman	69	68	68	73	278	2,233.33
Greg McDonald	69	66	74	70	279	1,960
Ian Mosey	67	70	71	71	279	1,960
Andre Cruse	70	67	69	73	279	1,960
Mark James	69	70	73	68	280	1,780
Bobby Lincoln	69	72	68	71	280	1,780
Wayne Westner	72	69	66	73	280	1,780

Southern Sun South African Open Championship

Durban Country Club, Durban
Par 36-36 — 72; 6,558 yards

January 28-31
purse, R150,000

	SCORES				TOTAL	MONEY
Wayne Westner	69	70	65	71	275	R24,150
Ian Mosey	71	69	66	71	277	17,400
Richard Kaplan	74	70	69	67	280	8,250
Denis Durnian	68	70	67	75	280	8,250
Tony Johnstone	75	69	68	68	280	8,250
Malcolm McKenzie	72	70	71	68	281	5,100
John Bland	72	69	67	73	281	5,100
Carl Cooper	68	71	68	76	283	3,500
Derek James	68	72	69	74	283	3,500
Chris Moody	73	74	64	72	283	3,500
Andrew Morse	73	70	72	69	284	2,850
Jack Ferenz	71	74	74	68	287	2,443.75
Marty Schiene	70	70	73	74	287	2,443.75
Ashley Roestoff	73	69	71	74	287	2,443.75

	SCORES				TOTAL	MONEY
Hugh Biaocchi	72	72	69	74	287	2,443.75
Craigen Pappas	70	74	74	70	288	2,125
Paul Way	71	72	74	71	288	2,125
Robert Richardson	72	71	70	75	288	2,125
Harold Henning	74	70	72	73	289	1,937.50
Bob E. Smith	72	71	71	75	289	1,937.50
John Cyboran	72	74	70	74	290	1,725
Trevor Dodds	74	73	68	75	290	1,725
Simon Hobday	74	69	71	76	290	1,725
Nick Godin	73	69	71	77	290	1,725
Len O'Kennedy	71	72	70	77	290	1,725
Jeff Hawkes	72	70	76	73	291	1,522.50
Chris Williams	73	74	70	74	291	1,522.50
Phil Harrison	72	72	73	74	291	1,522.50
Mike Worroll	74	72	71	74	291	1,522.50
Ron McCann	70	76	74	72	292	1,310
Chip Johnson	74	73	73	72	292	1,310
Alan Pate	74	72	73	73	292	1,310
Eric Booker	72	71	75	74	292	1,310
Don Levin	69	75	70	78	292	1,310
Brian Evans	69	73	77	74	293	1,150
Roger Wessels	75	72	72	74	293	1,150
Desmond Terblanche	74	71	72	76	293	1,150
Tom Lehman	73	74	69	77	293	1,150
Mike White	74	72	68	79	293	1,150
Andrew Chandler	75	70	74	75	294	1,042.50
Jeffrey Roth	77	69	73	75	294	1,042.50
Jim Becker	71	73	74	77	295	965
Steve Van Vuuren	72	74	71	78	295	965
Teddy Webber	73	73	70	79	295	965
Graeme Oliver	76	70	77	73	296	860
Andy Zullo	73	74	73	76	296	860
Hugh Inggs	70	75	76	75	296	860
John Fourie	74	72	72	78	296	860
Wayne Bradley	71	76	74	76	297	770
Michael Green	75	72	75	75	297	770

Bloemfontein Classic

Schoeman Park Golf Club, Bloemfontein
Par 35-35 — 70; 6,706 yards

February 10-13
purse, R200,000

	SCORES				TOTAL	MONEY
Jeff Hawkes	64	69	66	69	268	R32,000
Jay Townsend	68	63	72	66	269	18,500
John Bland	67	67	68	67	269	18,500
Ian Palmer	67	66	67	70	270	10,000
Hendrik Buhrmann	68	65	71	67	271	8,400
Tony Johnston	66	70	69	67	272	6,066.67
Mark McNulty	74	69	61	68	272	6,066.67
Hugh Biaocchi	71	66	67	68	272	6,066.67
Trevor Dodds	67	67	71	68	273	4,200
Teddy Webber	71	66	69	67	273	4,200
Robert Lee	71	69	66	68	274	3,600
Wilhelm Winsnes	71	70	66	68	275	3,300
Gavin Levenson	66	71	68	70	275	3,300
Allan Henning	69	72	66	69	276	3,000

	SCORES				TOTAL	MONEY
Ian Mosey	72	71	67	67	277	2,800
Wayne Bradley	68	70	70	69	277	2,800
Tom Lehman	69	70	68	70	277	2,800
Craigen Pappas	70	71	69	68	278	2,600
Simon Hobday	72	71	71	65	279	2,208.89
J. C. Anderson	74	69	69	67	279	2,208.89
Ashley Roestoff	76	66	70	67	279	2,208.89
Carl Cooper	70	69	70	70	279	2,208.89
Ron McCann	70	70	68	71	279	2,208.89
Andrew Morse	65	71	71	72	279	2,208.89
Bobby Lincoln	69	72	67	71	279	2,208.89
Schalk van der Merwe	72	69	66	72	279	2,208.89
Tom Sutter	72	66	68	73	279	2,208.89
Jim Becker	68	74	71	67	280	1,760
Mark Wiltshire	75	68	69	68	280	1,760
Bob E. Smith	73	68	70	69	280	1,760
Mike White	69	71	70	70	280	1,760
Steven Burnett	72	68	69	71	280	1,760
Justin Hobday	72	69	68	71	280	1,760

Danglo Tournament of Champions

Germiston Golf Club, Germiston
Par 36-35 — 71; 7,127 yards

February 17-20
purse, R265,000

	SCORES				TOTAL	MONEY
Mark James	66	60	69	69	274	R40,400
Hugh Biaocchi	66	70	68	72	276	29,037.50
Mark McNulty	71	65	70	71	277	17,675
Robert Friend	73	70	67	68	278	12,625
Ron McCann	72	71	69	67	279	9,847.50
John Cyboran	66	73	69	71	279	9,847.50
Stuart Smith	71	69	72	68	280	5,555
Paul Way	69	69	74	68	280	5,555
Ian Mosey	68	67	76	69	280	5,555
Denis Durnian	70	71	67	72	280	5,555
John Bland	70	71	68	71	280	5,555
Chris Williams	72	67	68	73	280	5,555
Ashley Roestoff	70	68	77	66	281	3,686.50
Gavin Levenson	74	67	73	67	281	3,686.50
Robert Richardson	71	71	72	67	281	3,686.50
Justin Hobday	67	77	70	67	281	3,686.50
Rick Hartman	72	70	66	73	281	3,686.50
Hendrik Buhrman	71	73	70	68	282	2,838.10
Andries Oosthuizen	71	72	70	69	282	2,838.10
Craigen Pappas	68	72	73	69	282	2,838.10
Clarke Dennis	72	72	69	69	282	2,838.10
J. C. Anderson	75	67	69	71	282	2,838.10
Michael King	70	71	70	71	282	2,838.10
Brad Worthington	69	70	71	72	282	2,838.10
Trevor Dodds	68	71	71	72	282	2,838.10
Nolan Henke	71	71	68	72	282	2,838.10
Robert Lee	72	65	70	75	282	2,838.10
Richard Kaplan	68	72	73	70	283	2,285.13
Wilhelm Winsnes	72	65	75	71	283	2,285.13
Ian Young	69	68	74	72	283	2,285.13
Phil Jonas	73	69	69	72	283	2,285.13

AECI Charity Classic

Rand Park Golf Club, Johannesburg
Par 72; 7,320 yards

February 24-27
purse, R150,000

	SCORES				TOTAL	MONEY
Bobby Lincoln	68	70	70	63	271	R24,000
John Bland	67	69	71	66	273	17,250
Gavin Levenson	68	71	67	69	275	9,000
Tony Johnstone	68	71	69	67	275	9,000
Mark McNulty	67	71	67	71	276	6,300
Trevor Dodds	69	70	69	69	277	4,950
Simon Hobday	69	69	67	72	277	4,950
Teddy Webber	71	70	71	66	278	3,350
Rick Hartman	71	72	66	69	278	3,350
Ron McCann	67	71	70	70	278	3,350
Phillip Hatchett	70	70	69	70	279	2,625
Jim Becker	66	75	68	70	279	2,625
Gert Von Biljon	74	70	69	67	280	2,150
John Lew	68	70	73	69	280	2,150
Marty Schiene	73	68	69	70	280	2,150
Eric Booker	70	68	71	71	280	2,150
J. C. Anderson	68	72	68	72	280	2,150
Desmond Terblanche	68	71	66	75	280	2,150
Whilhelm Winsnes	72	69	74	66	281	1,777.50
Mike White	74	70	69	68	281	1,777.50
Don Levin	71	68	72	70	281	1,777.50
Wayne Westner	67	75	68	71	281	1,777.50
Hendrik Buhrmann	74	68	73	67	282	1,492.50
Don Robertson	71	71	73	67	282	1,492.50
Phil Harrison	69	70	75	68	282	1,492.50
Frank Edmonds	75	68	70	69	282	1,492.50
Paul Van Zyl	68	73	72	69	282	1,492.50
Peter Mathews	72	72	68	70	282	1,492.50
Chris Anderson	72	70	69	71	282	1,492.50
Brian Evans	69	71	69	73	282	1,492.50

Helix Swazi Sun Classic

Royal Swazi Sun Country Club, Mbabane, Swaziland
Par 36-36 — 72; 6,708 yards

March 3-6
purse, R150,000

	SCORES				TOTAL	MONEY
Don Levin	68	65	69	66	268	R24,000
Alan Pate	69	72	64	63	268	17,250
(Levin defeated Pate in playoff.)						
Ian Mosey	63	69	70	67	269	10,500
John Bland	70	65	69	67	271	7,500
Phil Harrison	66	69	70	67	272	5,850
Frank Edmonds	68	66	69	69	272	5,850
Trevor Dodds	68	66	68	71	273	4,500
Jay Townsend	67	70	67	70	274	3,525
Justin Hobday	69	65	70	70	274	3,525
Phil Jonas	68	68	72	67	275	2,750
Andries Oosthuizen	71	71	67	66	275	2,750
Robert Richardson	67	69	69	70	275	2,750
Wayne Bradley	69	66	71	70	276	2,325
Bobby Verwey Jr.	70	69	68	69	276	2,325

	SCORES				TOTAL	MONEY
Hugh Biaocchi	71	70	69	67	277	1,987.50
Douglas Wherry	71	68	70	68	277	1,987.50
David Glenz	68	69	72	68	277	1,987.50
Jack Ferenz	68	71	69	69	277	1,987.50
J. C. Anderson	73	69	66	69	277	1,987.50
Jim Becker	70	69	68	70	277	1,987.50
Steve Van Vuuren	71	67	73	67	278	1,672.50
Mike White	69	72	70	67	278	1,672.50
Wilhelm Winsnes	71	67	72	68	278	1,672.50
Brad Worthington	71	71	68	68	278	1,672.50
Ian Palmer	67	69	76	67	279	1,447.50
Jannie Le Grange	67	74	68	70	279	1,447.50
Hendrik Buhrmann	71	70	67	71	279	1,447.50
David Armor	69	71	68	71	279	1,447.50
Chris Williams	70	70	67	72	279	1,447.50
Marty Schiene	69	68	70	72	279	1,447.50

Trust Bank Tournament of Champions

Kensington Golf Club, Johannesburg
Par 35-37 — 72; 6,716 yards

March 9-12
purse, R200,000

	SCORES				TOTAL	MONEY
John Bland	67	66	67	68	268	R32,000
Phil Jonas	67	69	67	69	272	18,500
Mark McNulty	68	67	69	68	272	18,500
Tony Johnstone	68	68	73	70	279	10,000
Nolan Henke	68	71	71	70	280	7,800
Jeff Hawkes	69	69	69	73	280	7,800
Richard Kaplan	76	69	70	67	282	5,500
Teddy Webber	67	73	74	68	282	5,500
Bobby Lincoln	71	67	71	75	284	4,200
Wilhelm Winsnes	67	69	70	78	284	4,200
Tertius Claassens	71	72	75	67	285	3,500
Schalk van der Merwe	72	71	68	74	285	3,500
Don Robertson	72	71	70	73	286	3,100
Ron McCann	69	73	70	74	286	3,100
Mike White	74	73	73	67	287	2,800
Hugh Baiocchi	75	70	72	70	287	2,800
John Cyboran	71	73	68	75	287	2,800
David Glenz	73	74	71	70	288	2,455
Wayne Westner	68	72	75	73	288	2,455
Trevor Dodds	73	70	71	74	288	2,455
Don Mashego	69	76	68	75	288	2,455
Allan Henning	73	73	72	71	289	2,140
Stuart Smith	74	71	72	72	289	2,140
Peter Mkata	70	74	73	72	289	2,140
Mark Johnson	71	73	72	73	289	2,140
Gert Von Biljon	72	70	72	75	289	2,140
Phillip Hatchett	73	73	75	69	290	1,813.33
Eric Booker	74	72	74	70	290	1,813.33
Brian Evans	75	73	72	70	290	1,813.33
Richard Parker	73	70	75	72	290	1,813.33
Brad Worthington	71	71	75	73	290	1,813.33
Frank Edmonds	67	75	72	76	290	1,813.33

Minolta Copiers Match Play Tournament

Gary Player Country Club, Sun City, Bophuthatswana
Par 36-36 — 72; 7,665 yards

November 7-12
purse, R250,000

SEMI-FINALS

Wayne Westner defeated Gavin Levenson, 71-73
Tony Johnstone defeated Ian Palmer, 69-70

PLAYOFFS FOR PLACES 5-8

John Bland defeated Bobby Lincoln, 65-75
Dale Hayes defeated Joe Dlamini, 71-75

PLAYOFFS FOR PLACES 9-12

Don Robertson defeated Des Terblanche, 71-77
Allan Henning defeated Malcolm McKenzie, 72-72, 19 holes

PLAYOFFS FOR PLACES 13-16

Fulton Allem defeated Denis Burnian, 70-74
Kevin Stone defeated Simon Hobday, 73-77

FINALS

Johnstone defeated Westner, 71-73 (Johnston, R40,000; Westner, R28,750)

PLAYOFF FOR 3RD PLACE

Palmer defeated Levenson, 71-78 (Palmer, R17,500; Levenson, R12,500)

PLAYOFF FOR 5TH PLACE

Hayes defeated Bland, 72-73 (Hayes, R10,500; Bland, R9,000)

PLAYOFF FOR 7TH PLACE

Dlamini defeated Lincoln, 72-78 (Dlamini, R7,500; Lincoln, R6,270)

PLAYOFF FOR 9TH PLACE

Robertson defeated Henning, 76-78 (Robertson, R5,500; Henning, R5,000)

PLAYOFF FOR 11TH PLACE

Terblanche defeated McKenzie, no score (Terblanche, R4,550; McKenzie, R4,250)

PLAYOFF FOR 13TH PLACE

Allem defeated Stone, 76-77 (Allem, R4,000; Stone, R3,750)

PLAYOFF FOR 15TH PLACE

Durnian defeated Hobday, 75-76 (Durnian, R3,500; Hobday, R3,250)

Bloemfontein Classic

Schoeman Park Golf Club, Bloemfontein
Par 35-35 — 70; 6,706 yards

November 16-19
purse, R250,000

	SCORES				TOTAL	MONEY
Tony Johnstone	66	72	69	69	276	R40,000
Phil Harrison	68	73	71	66	278	23,125
Schalk van der Merwe	67	71	70	70	278	23,125
Kevin Stone	70	71	73	65	279	10,666.67
Wayne Westner	76	69	65	69	279	10,666.67
Teddy Webber	74	66	69	70	279	10,666.67
Brian Evans	68	72	70	71	281	6,875
Bobby Lincoln	70	70	70	71	281	6,875

	SCORES				TOTAL	MONEY
Carl Cooper	69	73	71	70	283	4,650
Robert Richardson	75	72	66	70	283	4,650
Gary Gilchrist	70	74	68	71	283	4,650
Ian Mosey	68	70	72	73	283	4,650
John Bland	74	69	69	71	283	4,650
Desmond Terblanche	70	70	70	74	284	3,687.50
Gavin Levenson	71	72	67	74	284	3,687.50
Steven Burnett	74	73	69	70	286	3,250
Denis Durnian	71	72	72	71	286	3,250
Solly Mogare	67	76	71	72	286	3,250
Mark Wiltshire	69	71	72	74	286	3,250
Chris Williams	73	71	66	76	286	3,250
Don Robertson	73	72	76	66	287	2,825
Andries Oosthuizen	73	72	72	70	287	2,825
Richard Kaplan	74	71	71	71	287	2,825
Hugh Baiocchi	73	72	74	69	288	2,487.50
Allan Henning	71	72	74	71	288	2,487.50
Ian Hutchings	72	72	73	71	288	2,487.50
Justin Hobday	74	72	71	71	288	2,487.50
Rick Hartman	72	74	71	71	288	2,487.50
Steve Van Vuuren	76	69	67	76	288	2,487.50
Peter Mkata	71	73	71	74	289	2,225

Safmarine Masters

Stellenbosch Golf Club, Cape Town
Par 37-35 — 72; 7,036 yards

November 23-26
purse, R250,000

	SCORES				TOTAL	MONEY
John Bland	69	70	63	73	275	R40,000
Tony Johnstone	69	72	67	70	278	28,750
Denis Durnian	71	68	70	70	279	17,500
Gavin Levenson	72	70	70	68	280	10,666.67
Phil Harrison	72	67	69	72	280	10,666.67
Wilhelm Winsnes	71	69	67	73	280	10,666.67
Rick Hartman	67	67	75	72	281	6,875
Wayne Westner	67	69	71	74	281	6,875
Nico van Rensburg	67	74	73	68	282	5,250
Hugh Baiocchi	70	67	74	71	282	5,250
Derek James	71	70	72	70	283	4,025
Jim Thorpe	72	69	71	71	283	4,025
Simon Hobday	73	68	70	72	283	4,025
Brian Evans	73	72	67	71	283	4,025
Chris Williams	67	70	73	73	283	4,025
Carl Cooper	74	70	69	71	284	3,437.50
Chris Moody	71	71	69	73	284	3,437.50
Dale Hayes	73	72	71	69	285	3,068.75
Malcolm McKenzie	73	71	71	70	285	3,068.75
Teddy Webber	68	72	72	73	285	3,068.75
Allan Henning	71	71	70	73	285	3,068.75
Steve Van Vuuren	74	72	70	70	286	2,750
Peter van der Riet	71	68	76	71	286	2,750
Phil Simmons	69	73	70	74	286	2,750
Robert Richardson	71	68	74	74	287	2,600
John Fourie	71	71	75	71	288	2,412.50
Marvyn Galant	73	72	71	72	288	2,412.50
Bob Smith	73	71	70	74	288	2,412.50

	SCORES				TOTAL	MONEY
Don Robertson	75	74	66	73	288	2,412.50
Bobby Lincoln	75	71	75	68	289	2,079.17
Desmond Terblanche	77	69	72	71	289	2,079.17
Etienne Groenewald	73	71	73	72	289	2,079.17
Steven Burnett	72	74	71	72	289	2,079.17
Jeremy Robinson	73	74	69	73	289	2,079.17
Andries Oosthuizen	71	68	76	74	289	2,079.17

Million Dollar Challenge

Gary Player Country Club, Sun City, Bophuthatswana
Par 36-36 — 72; 7,665 yards

December 1-4
purse, $1,650,000

	SCORES				TOTAL	MONEY
Fulton Allem	72	71	66	69	278	$1,000,000
Don Pooley	67	72	74	66	279	200,000
Ken Green	67	72	70	71	280	100,000
Ian Woosnam	72	70	69	72	283	90,000
Chip Beck	74	70	68	72	284	80,000
David Frost	71	69	72	73	285	70,000
Mark McNulty	71	73	71	72	287	60,000
Bernhard Langer	76	74	78	78	306	50,000

Goodyear Classic

Humewood Golf Club, Port Elizabeth
Par 35-35 — 70; 6,454 yards

December 15-18
purse, R250,000

	SCORES				TOTAL	MONEY
Trevor Dodds	70	68	69	69	276	R40,000
Tony Johnstone	71	67	67	72	277	23,125
Wayne Westner	70	65	72	70	277	23,125
Jeff Hawkes	72	72	70	67	281	9,875
John Bland	73	69	70	69	281	9,875
Chris Moody	75	70	66	70	281	9,875
Mark Wiltshire	70	69	70	72	281	9,875
Schalk van der Merwe	73	71	68	70	282	5,875
Ian Palmer	70	67	73	72	282	5,875
Wayne Player	70	70	75	68	283	4,750
Ben Fouches	67	68	77	71	283	4,750
Denis Durnian	75	71	68	70	284	4,000
Rob Richardson	70	69	73	72	284	4,000
Justin Hobday	69	69	72	74	284	4,000
Rick Hartman	72	74	72	67	285	3,437.50
Malcolm McKenzie	75	68	71	71	285	3,437.50
Fulton Allem	73	72	67	73	285	3,437.50
Richard Kaplan	71	71	68	75	285	3,437.50
Dale Hayes	73	71	75	67	286	2,879.17
Wilhelm Winsnes	73	70	73	70	286	2,879.17
Phil Harrison	74	70	71	71	286	2,879.17
Gavin Levenson	73	72	68	73	286	2,879.17
Derek James	73	68	72	73	286	2,879.17
Glenn James	70	71	72	73	286	2,879.17
Mervyn Galant	67	70	78	72	287	2,450

	SCORES				TOTAL	MONEY
Sean Pappas	73	74	69	71	287	2,450
Carl Cooper	73	68	72	74	287	2,450
David Feherty	77	63	74	73	287	2,450
Chris Williams	72	67	73	75	287	2,450
John Fourie	75	68	75	70	288	2,079.17
Bobby Lincoln	73	73	72	70	288	2,079.17
Vincent Tshabalala	73	73	71	71	288	2,079.17
Bob Smith	74	67	72	75	288	2,079.17
Hendrik Buhrmann	77	68	70	73	288	2,079.17
Teddy Webber	69	69	72	78	288	2,079.17

The Australasian Tour

Sanctuary Cove Classic

Sanctuary Cove, Queensland
Par 36-36 — 72; 6,689 yards

January 7-10
purse, A$400,000

	SCORES				TOTAL	MONEY
Curtis Strange	67	70	67	68	272	A$72,000
Ian Woosnam	69	66	70	68	273	43,200
Ray Floyd	69	67	67	72	275	27,600
Rodger Davis	67	74	70	67	278	18,280
Bob Shearer	71	68	71	68	278	18,280
Grant Waite	70	70	71	68	279	15,280
Mike Ferguson	69	72	68	71	280	12,800
Ossie Moore	69	66	72	73	280	12,800
Simon Owen	69	72	68	72	281	8,900
David Graham	72	69	68	72	281	8,900
David Ishii	69	71	66	75	281	8,900
Brad King	70	73	68	70	281	8,900
Paul Foley	75	69	68	70	282	6,560
Mark K. Nash	69	71	76	67	283	5,460
Tim Elliott	77	64	71	71	283	5,460
Ian Roberts	72	68	74	69	283	5,460
Mike Clayton	71	66	70	76	283	5,460
Jeff Senior	67	74	71	72	284	4,416
Ian Baker-Finch	68	72	70	74	284	4,416
Craig Parry	69	70	72	73	284	4,416
Nick Faldo	66	77	71	70	284	4,416
Peter O'Malley	69	73	72	70	284	4,416
Mike Harwood	70	71	70	74	285	3,760
Jerry Anderson	72	68	70	75	285	3,760
David Tentis	70	69	70	76	285	3,760
Arnold Palmer	74	67	73	72	286	3,120
Roger Mackay	71	69	72	74	286	3,120
Lyndsay Stephen	71	74	72	69	286	3,120
Peter Senior	70	69	73	74	286	3,120
Lucien Tinkler	68	68	73	77	286	3,120

Daikyo Palm Meadows Cup

Palm Meadows, Gold Coast, Queensland
Par 36-36 — 72; 7,032 yards

January 28-31
purse, A$500,000

	SCORES				TOTAL	MONEY
Greg Norman	69	66	67	70	272	A$90,000
Tateo Ozaki	68	72	65	68	273	54,000
Bernhard Langer	70	68	67	69	274	34,500
Roger Mackay	65	70	67	73	275	22,850
David Tentis	68	67	70	70	275	22,850
Anthony Painter	71	69	67	71	278	18,100
Mark O'Meara	68	71	68	71	278	18,100
Hajime Meshiai	72	70	67	70	279	14,200
Masahiro Kuramoto	71	69	67	72	279	14,200
Brian Jones	71	70	70	69	280	9,320
Peter Jones	69	68	72	71	280	9,320
Yokoshima Yoshikazo	71	67	70	72	280	9,320
Mike Ferguson	66	71	71	72	280	9,320
Gordon Brand Jr.	68	70	67	75	280	9,320
Rodger Davis	72	70	71	68	281	5,937.50
Ronan Rafferty	68	76	69	68	281	5,937.50
Anders Forsbrand	70	67	74	70	281	5,937.50
Masashi Ozaki	74	70	67	70	281	5,937.50
Peter Senior	73	69	67	72	281	5,937.50
Ian Woosnam	71	68	68	74	281	5,937.50
Wayne Riley	70	69	68	74	281	5,937.50
Peter McWhinney	70	66	66	79	281	5,937.50
Lucien Tinkler	70	69	72	71	282	4,800
Jim Rutledge	71	68	70	73	282	4,800
David Graham	69	72	72	70	283	4,300
Wayne Smith	73	67	70	73	283	4,300
Yutaka Hagawa	67	73	70	73	283	4,300
Katsuji Hasegawa	67	73	73	71	284	3,625
Greg Turner	71	72	69	72	284	3,625
Jim Benepe	68	71	73	72	284	3,625
Terry Gale	72	66	70	76	284	3,625

Mercedes-Benz Australian Match Play Championship

Kingston Heath Golf Club, Melbourne, Victoria
Par 36-36 — 72; 7,428 yards

February 5-7
purse, A$100,000

FIRST ROUND

Gerry Taylor defeated Anders Forsbrand, 5 and 4
Mike Clayton defeated Peter Jones, 4 and 2
Wayne Riley defeated Ian Stanley, 4 and 2
Peter O'Malley defeated Frank Nobilo, 1 up
Gordon Brand defeated Ossie Moore, 2 up
Peter Fowler defeated Jeff Senior, 2 and 1
*Brett Johns defeated Bob Shearer, 1 up, 19 holes
Stewart Ginn defeated Jim Benepe, 4 and 3
(Each losing player received A$1,000.)

SECOND ROUND

Ian Baker-Finch defeated Stewart Ginn, 4 and 2
Ronan Raffety defeated *Brett Johns, 7 and 6

Peter Fowler defeated Rodger Davis, 3 and 2
Vaughan Somers defeated Gordon Brand, 2 and 1
Peter O'Malley defeated Peter Senior, 4 and 3
Craig Parry defeated Wayne Riley, 1 up
Mike Clayton defeated Roger Mackay, 3 and 2
Mike Colandro defeated Gerry Taylor, 6 and 4
(Each losing player received A$2,500.)

QUARTER-FINALS

Rafferty defeated Baker-Finch, 4 and 2
Somers defeated Fowler, 2 up
Parry defeated O'Malley, 5 and 4
Clayton defeated Colandro, 2 up
(Each losing player received A$3,500.)

SEMI-FINALS

Rafferty defeated Somers, 3 and 2
Clayton defeated Parry, 5 and 4

THIRD-FOURTH PLACE PLAYOFF

Parry defeated Somers, 5 and 4

FINAL

Rafferty defeated Clayton, 1 up
(Rafferty received A$20,000, Clayton A$15,000, Parry A$10,000,
Somers A$8,000.)

Blakiston Boyd Victorian Open

Kingston Heath Golf Club, Melbourne, Victoria
Par 36-36 — 72; 7,428 yards

February 11-14
purse, A$100,000

	SCORES			TOTAL	MONEY
Jim Benepe	69	68	74	71	282	A$18,000
Ian Baker-Finch	70	69	74	72	285	8,850
Peter McWhinney	68	70	71	76	285	8,850
Lyndsay Stephen	74	71	68	73	286	4,980
Peter Fowler	67	71	77	72	287	3,800
Jeff Woodland	71	72	71	73	287	3,800
Mike Colandro	72	69	70	76	287	3,800
Peter Senior	74	68	75	71	288	2,980
Bob Shearer	72	70	73	74	289	2,700
Noel Ratcliffe	70	74	75	71	290	1,864
Peter O'Malley	71	71	73	75	290	1,864
Brad King	67	72	74	77	290	1,864
Roger Mackay	73	67	73	77	290	1,864
Brett Officer	69	70	73	78	290	1,864
Ossie Moore	67	69	80	77	293	1,360
Mike Harwood	73	70	73	77	293	1,360
*Matthew King	68	72	75	78	293	
Kirk Triplett	73	74	76	71	294	1,230
Wayne Case	73	66	78	77	294	1,230
Russell Swanson	74	72	77	72	295	1,100
Rob McNaughton	74	71	73	77	295	1,100
Brett Ogle	68	72	76	79	295	1,100
John Clifford	73	74	76	73	296	920
Andrew Gutteridge	71	74	76	75	296	920

	SCORES				TOTAL	MONEY
David Smith	70	74	76	76	296	920
Jason Deep	74	73	73	76	296	920
Peter Jones	74	72	72	78	296	920
Tom Oyama	73	70	73	80	296	920
*Shane Robinson	71	71	79	75	296	
Richard Gilkey	73	73	79	72	297	740
Graeme Trew	70	74	79	74	297	740
Simon Owen	72	71	74	80	297	740

Australian Masters

Huntingdale Golf Club, Melbourne, Victoria
Par 37-36 — 73; 6,955 yards

February 18-21
purse, A$325,000

	SCORES				TOTAL	MONEY
Ian Baker-Finch	69	70	71	73	283	A$58,500
Craig Parry	69	73	70	71	283	28,762.50
Roger Mackay	69	75	69	70	283	28,762.50
(Baker-Finch defeated Parry and Mackay on first hole of playoff.)						
Greg Norman	72	70	73	69	284	14,852.50
Nick Faldo	70	71	72	71	284	14,852.50
Peter Fowler	73	74	69	69	285	12,415
Steve Bann	71	72	74	69	286	10,400
Stewart Ginn	70	74	71	71	286	10,400
Ian Woosnam	73	73	74	67	287	7,691.66
David Smith	73	76	69	69	287	7,691.66
Jeff Senior	70	76	69	72	287	7,691.66
Rick Gibson	74	73	74	67	288	4,355
Lyndsay Stephen	71	75	74	68	288	4,355
David Feherty	75	70	73	70	288	4,355
Wayne Riley	68	81	69	70	288	4,355
Rodger Davis	75	74	69	70	288	4,355
Gerry Taylor	72	75	70	71	288	4,355
Frank Nobilo	72	74	70	72	288	4,355
Graham Marsh	71	74	72	71	288	4,355
David Tentis	73	74	66	75	288	4,355
Bernhard Langer	68	73	71	76	288	4,355
Anthony Gilligan	71	73	75	70	289	3,120
Wayne Smith	75	74	70	70	289	3,120
Brett Officer	70	72	76	71	289	3,120
Jim Benepe	68	71	76	74	289	3,120
Simon Owen	74	72	74	70	290	2,535
Ronan Rafferty	71	71	77	71	290	2,535
Mike Ferguson	72	74	73	71	290	2,535
Peter Senior	72	73	73	72	290	2,535
Jeff Woodland	71	71	69	79	290	2,535

ESP Open

Royal Canberra Golf Club, Canberra, ACT
Par 36-36 — 72; 6,914 yards

February 25-28
purse, A$250,000

	SCORES				TOTAL	MONEY
Greg Norman	62	70	69	68	269	A$45,000
Bernhard Langer	68	69	70	69	276	27,000
Noel Ratcliffe	72	70	66	70	278	17,250
Peter O'Malley	71	70	67	71	279	12,450
Mike Ferguson	71	68	74	67	280	9,975
Kel Devlin	71	71	68	70	280	9,975
Jon Evans	73	71	68	69	281	7,162.50
Ian Baker-Finch	73	71	67	70	281	7,162.50
Mike Colandro	68	69	74	70	281	7,162.50
Jim Benepe	73	68	68	72	281	7,162.50
Wayne Riley	72	71	68	71	282	4,350
David Tentis	68	69	73	72	282	4,350
Jim Rutledge	68	70	71	73	282	4,350
Peter Senior	66	69	70	77	282	4,350
Peter Fowler	72	70	71	70	283	3,160
Gerry Taylor	68	75	69	71	283	3,160
Taijiro Tanaka	67	72	73	71	283	3,160
John Clifford	70	69	71	73	283	3,160
Rick Gibson	71	67	72	73	283	3,160
Ken Trimble	72	70	71	71	284	2,700
George Serhan	71	73	66	74	284	2,700
Ian Stanley	72	69	72	72	285	2,350
Yoshikazu Yokoshima	71	71	71	72	285	2,350
Bruce Soulsby	69	71	73	72	285	2,350
Terry Gale	69	70	72	74	285	2,350
Anders Sorensen	70	68	73	74	285	2,350
Brett Officer	70	71	74	71	286	1,950
Larry Canning	72	71	72	71	286	1,950
David Graham	73	70	72	71	286	1,950
*David Ecob	72	70	70	74	286	

Tournament Players' Championship

Riverside Oaks PGA National, Cattai, New South Wales
Par 36-36 — 72; 6,902 yards

March 3-6
purse, A$300,000

	SCORES				TOTAL	MONEY
Greg Norman	67	67	68	68	270	A$54,000
Peter Senior	67	72	70	69	278	26,550
David Graham	69	69	70	70	278	26,550
Kirk Triplett	71	73	69	66	279	13,710
Roger Mackay	70	68	72	69	279	13,710
Rodger Davis	70	70	71	69	280	10,860
Graham Marsh	71	69	67	73	280	10,860
Peter Fowler	70	71	71	71	283	8,940
Anthony Gilligan	72	68	75	69	284	6,675
Wayne Riley	67	74	73	70	284	6,675
Mike Harwood	74	71	67	72	284	6,675
Anders Forsbrand	69	68	70	77	284	6,675
Larry Canning	70	74	72	69	285	4,150
David Smith	70	69	75	71	285	4,150
Gerry Taylor	72	71	70	72	285	4,150

	SCORES				TOTAL	MONEY
Grant Waite	69	70	73	73	285	4,150
Brett Ogle	70	67	74	74	285	4,150
Ian Baker-Finch	74	68	69	74	285	4,150
Richard Gilkey	73	73	70	70	286	3,180
Glenn Joyner	71	73	70	72	286	3,180
Ossie Moore	71	71	72	72	286	3,180
Lucien Tinkler	67	75	71	73	286	3,180
Kel Devlin	72	71	69	74	286	3,180
Mike Colandro	70	70	78	68	287	2,580
Frank Nobilo	69	73	73	72	287	2,580
Ian Roberts	72	71	72	72	287	2,580
Brad King	71	72	72	72	287	2,580
Peter McWhinney	71	70	70	76	287	2,580
Vaughan Somers	72	72	73	71	288	2,085
Ray Picker	72	71	74	71	288	2,085
Stewart Ginn	74	72	71	71	288	2,085
Leif Hederstrom	67	70	75	76	288	2,085

Tattersall Tasmanian Open

Tasmania Golf Club, Hobart, Tasmania
Par 37-35 — 72; 6,794 yards

October 13-16
purse, A$100,000

	SCORES				TOTAL	MONEY
Brett Ogle	74	71	72	67	284	A$18,000
*Brett Johns	70	70	72	73	285	
Mike Clayton	72	75	67	72	286	10,800
Mike Ferguson	70	76	70	71	287	6,900
Paul Foley	72	72	72	72	288	4,980
Ossie Moore	74	71	72	72	289	4,160
Anthony Painter	75	72	71	73	291	3,820
Mike Colandro	73	76	73	70	292	3,033.33
Greg Alexander	75	72	73	72	292	3,033.33
Brad Hughes	79	70	69	74	292	3,033.33
Bob Shearer	70	75	76	72	293	1,960
Ray Picker	72	74	74	73	293	1,960
Anthony Gilligan	73	78	70	72	293	1,960
Lucien Tinkler	71	71	78	73	293	1,960
Mike Harwood	70	75	74	75	294	1,480
Craig Warren	71	79	73	72	295	1,326.66
David Ecob	72	73	76	74	295	1,326.66
John Clifford	77	72	70	76	295	1,326.66
Phillip Glass	75	76	75	70	296	1,200
Brett Officer	75	74	74	74	297	1,100
Lyndsay Stephen	72	75	74	76	297	1,100
John Erickson	71	72	75	79	297	1,100
Mark K. Nash	72	80	74	72	298	980
Ken Collins	71	77	72	78	298	980
Russell Swanson	72	77	71	78	298	980
Stuart Holmes	77	75	72	75	299	880
George Serhan	72	75	75	77	299	880
Glenn Joyner	78	74	77	71	300	744
Peter Jones	76	70	78	76	300	744
Steve Wilson	70	81	72	77	300	744
David Smith	76	70	76	78	300	744
Ian Stanley	75	71	72	82	300	744

Panasonic New South Wales Open

Concord Golf Club, Sydney, New South Wales
Par 35-36 — 71; 6,660 yards

October 20-23
purse, A$200,000

	SCORES				TOTAL	MONEY
Greg Norman	66	69	69	73	277	A$36,000
Craig Parry	64	70	72	72	278	21,600
Peter Senior	71	73	72	64	280	13,800
Lyndsay Stephen	64	73	73	71	281	9,140
John Clifford	72	68	70	71	281	9,140
Frank Nobilo	74	68	68	72	282	7,240
Anthony Gilligan	69	71	69	73	282	7,240
Glenn Joyner	72	67	73	71	283	5,680
Vaughan Somers	69	73	69	72	283	5,680
Mike Clayton	73	71	71	69	284	3,573.33
Steve Rintoul	71	74	69	70	284	3,573.33
Ossie Moore	73	69	70	72	284	3,573.33
Wayne Case	69	67	74	74	284	3,573.33
Bob Shearer	67	74	68	75	284	3,573.33
Jeff Woodland	73	71	66	74	284	3,573.33
Brad Hughes	69	71	74	71	285	2,460
Paul Foley	71	70	71	73	285	2,460
Mike Colandro	72	69	72	72	285	2,460
Noel Ratcliffe	73	70	70	72	285	2,460
John Price	76	71	70	70	287	2,120
George Serhan	69	71	75	72	287	2,120
Mike Ferguson	70	72	69	76	287	2,120
Wayne Riley	71	68	76	73	288	1,920
Gerry Taylor	75	66	72	75	288	1,920
Lucien Tinkler	70	75	75	69	289	1,720
Greg Hohnen	68	72	75	74	289	1,720
Ken Trimble	68	72	74	75	289	1,720
Bruce P. Smith	73	69	75	73	290	1,560
*Steve Conran	74	72	68	76	290	
Peter Lonard	70	71	77	73	291	1,440
David Smith	70	71	72	78	291	1,440

Town & Country Western Australian Open

Lake Karrinyup Country Club, Perth, Western Australia
Par 36-36 — 72; 6,644 yards

October 27-30
purse, A$100,000

	SCORES				TOTAL	MONEY
Brad Hughes	71	71	67	75	284	A$18,000
Ken Trimble	74	73	66	72	285	10,800
Frank Nobilo	71	74	70	71	286	4,965
Mark K. Nash	76	70	69	71	286	4,965
Bob Shearer	73	72	71	70	286	4,965
Jeff Woodland	73	72	72	69	286	4,965
Lyndsay Stephen	73	73	70	71	287	3,420
Stuart Holmes	73	70	75	70	288	2,680
Brett Officer	75	72	72	69	288	2,680
Mike Clayton	73	74	70	71	288	2,680
Anthony Painter	74	73	70	72	289	2,040
Tim Elliott	73	74	74	70	291	1,640

		SCORES			TOTAL	MONEY
Gerry Taylor	77	70	70	74	291	1,640
Greg Turner	72	75	69	75	291	1,640
Craig Warren	72	72	76	72	292	1,326.66
Andrew La'Brooy	73	72	74	73	292	1,326.66
Wayne Case	73	74	71	74	292	1,326.66
Ossie Moore	73	74	74	72	293	1,200
Phillip Glass	73	75	76	70	294	1,060
Robert Stephens	74	73	75	72	294	1,060
Peter Jones	74	71	75	74	294	1,060
Brad King	71	77	72	74	294	1,060
Ken Collins	76	73	70	75	294	1,060
Paul Hiskey	75	72	78	70	295	920
Cameron Howell	74	77	70	74	295	920
*Stephen Leaney	78	69	76	72	295	
Glenn Joyner	74	75	75	72	296	820
David Ecob	74	76	72	74	296	820
Greg Alexander	74	71	74	77	296	820
Timothy Petrovic	74	76	78	69	297	706.66
Trevor Downing	75	73	75	74	297	706.66
John Clifford	76	73	74	74	297	706.66

Australian PGA Championship

Riverside Oaks PGA National, Cattai, New South Wales
Par 36-36 — 72; 6,950 yards

November 3-6
purse, A$475,000

		SCORES			TOTAL	MONEY
Wayne Grady	69	69	71	66	275	A$85,500
Greg Norman	75	68	64	68	275	51,300
(Grady defeated Norman on fourth hole of playoff.)						
Roger Mackay	71	69	69	68	277	28,215
Peter Senior	71	67	69	70	277	28,215
Ken Trimble	69	72	68	69	278	19,760
Brett Ogle	66	70	71	75	282	18,145
Frank Nobilo	69	71	73	70	283	13,608.75
Terry Price	75	69	68	71	283	13,608.75
Graham Marsh	71	66	74	72	283	13,608.75
Lyndsay Stephen	70	71	70	72	283	13,608.75
Wayne Smith	70	70	74	70	284	8,265
Wayne Riley	73	71	69	71	284	8,265
Jason Deep	72	66	74	72	284	8,265
Bob Shearer	70	68	71	75	284	8,265
Ossie Moore	74	71	70	70	285	6,301.66
Rodger Davis	75	67	70	73	285	6,301.66
Richard Boxall	73	70	68	74	285	6,301.66
David Graham	74	74	70	68	286	5,244
Kel Devlin	69	78	69	70	286	5,244
Robert Stephens	73	72	70	71	286	5,244
Simon Owen	75	71	67	73	286	5,244
George Serhan	68	70	73	75	286	5,244
Mark K. Nash	72	68	75	72	287	4,560
Mike Ferguson	73	71	70	73	287	4,560
Mike Colandro	74	72	73	69	288	3,895
Ray Picker	70	74	74	70	288	3,895
Anthony Gilligan	70	70	77	71	288	3,895
Paul Foley	75	71	71	71	288	3,895

	SCORES				TOTAL	MONEY
Peter Fowler	70	67	75	76	288	3,895
Craig Parry	75	70	72	72	289	3,182.50
Andrew La'Brooy	71	72	73	73	289	3,182.50
Ian Baker-Finch	74	70	72	73	289	3,182.50
Mike Harwood	74	70	70	75	289	3,182.50

West End South Australian Open

The Grange Golf Club, Adelaide, South Australia
Par 37-33 — 70; 6,457 yards

November 9-12
purse, A$100,000

	SCORES				TOTAL	MONEY
Gordon Brand Jr.	64	69	69	65	267	A$18,000
Greg Alexander	68	69	68	69	274	8,850
Wayne Grady	68	69	67	70	274	8,850
Craig Parry	73	69	69	64	275	4,980
Frank Nobilo	73	70	62	71	276	4,160
Mike Harwood	71	69	71	66	277	3,620
Jeff Woodland	74	68	69	66	277	3,620
Ronan Rafferty	72	71	70	66	279	2,680
Brad Hughes	73	70	67	69	279	2,680
Lyndsay Stephen	71	68	67	73	279	2,680
Mike Colandro	74	72	68	66	280	1,920
David Merriman	71	73	67	69	280	1,920
Howard Clark	74	67	73	67	281	1,506.66
Brett Officer	71	69	70	71	281	1,506.66
Wayne Smith	70	71	66	74	281	1,506.66
Ray Picker	74	72	69	67	282	1,230
Simon Owen	71	75	69	67	282	1,230
Noel Ratcliffe	70	68	76	68	282	1,230
Jack Larkin	68	74	70	70	282	1,230
David Graham	69	72	73	69	283	1,060
David Smith	71	71	72	69	283	1,060
Ian Stanley	72	72	69	70	283	1,060
Lucien Tinkler	74	69	74	67	284	940
Anthony Painter	75	67	69	73	284	940
Bob Shearer	69	72	73	70	284	940
Peter Senior	71	73	73	68	285	780
Jason Deep	71	66	78	70	285	780
Richard Boxall	72	68	73	72	285	780
George Serhan	69	71	71	74	285	780
Anthony Gilligan	70	71	68	76	285	780

Ricky May Classic

Riverside Oaks PGA National, Cattai, New South Wales
Par 36-36 — 72; 6,950 yards

November 17-20
purse, A$100,000

	SCORES				TOTAL	MONEY
David Merriman	76	69	68	66	279	A$18,000
Mike Harwood	68	69	74	70	281	10,800
Paul Foley	70	74	66	72	282	5,940

	SCORES				TOTAL	MONEY
Brett Ogle	69	70	68	75	282	5,940
John Clifford	69	75	71	68	283	3,990
Mike Colandro	75	71	68	69	283	3,990
Jon Evans	70	71	75	68	284	2,420
Ken Trimble	72	72	72	68	284	2,420
Paul Powell	75	69	71	69	284	2,420
Gerry Taylor	70	74	71	69	284	2,420
Jeff Woodland	69	72	71	72	284	2,420
Craig Warren	72	70	70	72	284	2,420
Larry Canning	66	72	70	76	284	2,420
Ray Picker	73	69	73	70	285	1,440
Greg Turner	71	69	69	76	285	1,440
David Sheather	70	71	76	69	286	1,157.14
Wayne Riley	74	71	72	69	286	1,157.14
Bob Shearer	76	71	69	70	286	1,157.14
Lyndsay Stephen	68	75	72	71	286	1,157.14
Tony Stevens	72	75	67	72	286	1,157.14
Robert McNamara	69	71	73	73	286	1,157.14
Vaughan Somers	75	71	67	73	286	1,157.14
David Smith	78	68	72	69	287	920
Peter Jones	72	69	73	73	287	920
Simon Owen	73	74	68	72	287	920
Mark K. Nash	69	73	71	74	287	920
Kevin Burton	71	72	72	73	288	780
Brad Hughes	76	71	67	74	288	780
Anthony Painter	70	72	70	76	288	780
Brett Griffiths	73	70	76	70	289	650
Steve Rintoul	74	72	73	70	289	650
Anders Sorensen	72	71	74	72	289	650
Roger Stephens	71	72	73	73	289	650
Stuart Holmes	71	75	70	73	289	650
George Serhan	71	73	71	74	289	650

Test Match

Mirage Resort, Port Douglas, Queensland
Par 36-36 — 72; 6,871 yards

November 18-20
purse, A$500,000

FINAL SCORE: Britain 11½, Australia 6½

FRIDAY

Foursomes
Ronan Rafferty and Howard Clark (UK) defeated Steve Elkington and David Graham, 2 up.
Mark James and Ian Woosnam (UK) defeated Rodger Davis and Peter Senior, 2 and 1.
Sandy Lyle and Gordon Brand Jr. (UK) halved with Greg Norman and Craig Parry.

Fourball
Norman and Graham (A) defeated Woosnam and James, 6 and 4.
Rafferty and Clark (UK) defeated Senior and Elkington, 3 and 1.
Parry and Davis (A) defeated Lyle and Brand Jr., 1 up.
UNITED KINGDOM LEADS, 3½ - 2½.

SATURDAY

Fourball
Clark and Rafferty (UK) defeated Senior and Graham, 2 and 1.

Lyle and Woosnam (UK) defeated Norman and Elkington, 4 and 2.
James and Brand Jr. (UK) defeated Parry and Davis, 2 and 1.

Foursomes
Lyle and Woosnam (UK) defeated Davis and Parry, 2 and 1.
Brand Jr. and James (UK) defeated Elkington and Graham, 3 and 2.
Clark and Rafferty (UK) defeated Norman and Senior, 2 and 1.
UNITED KINGDOM LEADS, 9½ - 2½.

SUNDAY

Singles
Davis (A) defeated Brand Jr., 5 and 4.
Elkington (A) defeated Woosnam, 4 and 2.
Clark (UK) defeated Graham, 4 and 3.
Parry (A) defeated James, 6 and 4.
Senior (A) defeated Rafferty, 2 and 1.
Lyle (UK) defeated Norman, 2 and 1.

PRIZE MONEY: Britain A$350,000, Australia A$150,000.

Panasonic Australian Open Championship

Royal Sydney Golf Club, Sydney, New South Wales
Par 36-36 — 72; 6,807 yards

November 24-27
purse, A$350,000

	SCORES				TOTAL	MONEY
Mark Calcavecchia	67	67	66	69	269	A$63,000
Mark McCumber	68	70	68	69	275	37,800
Wayne Grady	68	65	72	71	276	24,150
David Graham	69	70	68	71	278	15,995
Ronan Rafferty	66	72	70	70	278	15,995
Greg Norman	67	72	73	69	281	12,670
Rodger Davis	71	70	70	70	281	12,670
Brett Ogle	74	72	69	67	282	9,940
Craig Warren	71	71	71	69	282	9,940
Anthony Gilligan	70	69	69	75	283	7,700
Mark James	67	72	69	75	283	7,700
Greg Turner	70	74	67	73	284	6,020
Peter McWhinney	71	71	72	70	284	6,020
Bob Shearer	74	73	68	70	285	4,777.50
Gordon Brand Jr.	71	73	70	71	285	4,777.50
Ian Stanley	68	72	74	71	285	4,777.50
Ken Trimble	69	77	72	67	285	4,777.50
Des Smyth	68	68	73	77	286	3,937.50
Mike Harwood	74	68	68	76	286	3,937.50
Howard Clark	72	72	71	71	286	3,937.50
Ian Woosnam	75	73	67	71	286	3,937.50
Craig Parry	71	73	70	73	287	3,220
Jeff Woodland	72	69	71	75	287	3,220
Mike Ferguson	70	75	70	72	287	3,220
Steen Tinning	70	72	72	73	287	3,220
Peter Senior	66	74	76	71	287	3,220
Wayne Smith	74	70	72	71	287	3,220
Brad Hughes	70	75	72	71	288	2,450
Brad King	75	72	71	70	288	2,450
Brett Officer	71	71	74	72	288	2,450
John Cook	71	70	75	72	288	2,450

	SCORES				TOTAL	MONEY
David Merriman	73	73	69	73	288	2,450
Tod Power	73	73	69	73	288	2,450
Jon Evans	70	73	74	72	289	2,170
Brett Griffiths	71	74	76	69	290	1,995
Steve Elkington	70	73	77	70	290	1,995
Ian Baker-Finch	70	73	70	77	290	1,995
Terry Gale	70	70	74	76	290	1,995
Frank Nobilo	73	74	71	73	291	1,785
Greg Carroll	75	71	70	75	291	1,785
George Serhan	74	74	72	72	292	1,540
*Lester Peterson	70	74	74	74	292	
Vaughan Somers	72	75	72	73	292	1,540
Mike Clayton	76	72	70	74	292	1,540
Ossie Moore	74	72	71	75	292	1,540
Robert Stephens	75	72	72	73	292	1,540
Ken Collins	73	75	72	73	293	1,225
Peter O'Malley	71	76	74	72	293	1,225
Mark K. Nash	72	70	75	76	293	1,225
Stewart Ginn	73	73	73	74	293	1,225

Bicentennial Classic

Royal Melbourne Golf Club, Composite Course,
  Melbourne, Victoria, Australia
Par 35-37 — 72; 6,977 yards

December 1-4
purse, A$1,500,000

	SCORES				TOTAL	MONEY
Rodger Davis	68	67	68	68	271	A$500,000
Fred Couples	66	69	69	67	271	165,000
(Davis defeated Couples on second hole of playoff.)						
Brett Ogle	70	67	66	69	272	90,000
Ben Crenshaw	68	65	70	70	273	55,000
Hale Irwin	69	67	65	72	273	55,000
Greg Norman	73	66	73	64	276	35,750
Ronan Rafferty	70	67	70	69	276	35,750
Hajime Meshiai	70	66	73	69	278	27,500
John Cook	72	72	68	66	278	27,500
Peter Senior	68	69	70	71	278	27,500
Howard Clark	70	68	70	71	279	24,000
Craig Parry	71	71	70	69	281	22,000
Scott Simpson	71	68	73	69	281	22,000
Tateo Ozaki	74	73	69	65	281	22,000
Jeff Sluman	72	69	76	66	283	18,500
Scott Verplank	70	74	71	68	283	18,500
Masashi Ozaki	67	72	71	73	283	18,500
Mark McCumber	71	68	73	71	283	18,500
Bob Shearer	74	69	70	71	284	14,600
Craig Stadler	70	69	73	72	284	14,600
Graham Marsh	70	68	74	72	284	14,600
Jack Nicklaus	75	69	74	66	284	14,600
Jim Benepe	69	70	69	75	284	14,600
Frank Nobilo	77	71	70	68	286	12,000
Ken Trimble	72	72	72	70	286	12,000
Lyndsay Stephen	73	70	72	71	286	12,000
Peter Fowler	72	69	75	70	286	12,000
Steve Elkington	72	73	69	72	286	12,000
Ian Baker-Finch	70	69	73	75	287	9,860

	SCORES				TOTAL	MONEY
Mike Harwood	72	70	73	72	287	9,860
Mike Reid	70	71	76	70	287	9,860
Paul Foley	71	71	72	73	287	9,860
Wayne Grady	74	68	71	74	287	9,860
Brad Hughes	70	72	74	72	288	9,100
Dan Pohl	71	69	74	74	288	9,100
David Graham	73	72	73	71	289	8,700
Mark Calcavecchia	76	74	70	69	289	8,700
Gordon Brand Jr.	74	70	75	71	290	8,300
Mike Colandro	67	76	71	76	290	8,300
Wayne Riley	74	69	76	72	291	8,000
Roger Mackay	73	75	73	73	294	7,900
Ossie Moore	74	69	74	78	295	7,750
Terry Gale	74	72	76	73	295	7,750
Peter Thomson	74	75	74	73	296	7,600
Johnny Miller	74	72	75	76	297	7,400
Brian Jones	80	69	76	72	297	7,400
Jeff Woodland	74	79	71	73	297	7,400
Bruce Devlin	75	74	78	75	302	7,200
Mike Ferguson	77	77	77	72	303	7,100
Kel Nagle	79	77	81	79	316	7,000

World Cup

Royal Melbourne Golf Club, Composite Course,
  Melbourne, Victoria, Australia
Par 35-37 — 72; 6,977 yards

December 8-11
purse, US$750,000

	INDIVIDUAL SCORES				TOTAL
UNITED STATES (560) — $200,000					
Ben Crenshaw	68	67	66	74	275
Mark McCumber	71	70	71	73	285
JAPAN (561) — US$110,000					
Tateo Ozaki	68	69	67	72	276
Masashi Ozaki	70	71	71	73	285
AUSTRALIA (562) — US$80,000					
Peter Senior	70	68	70	70	278
Roger Mackay	73	63	72	76	284
CANADA (569) — US$65,000					
Dave Barr	70	67	65	75	277
Brent Franklin	74	72	75	71	292
SCOTLAND (570) — US$41,000					
Gordon Brand Jr.	71	66	73	69	279
Colin Montgomerie	69	74	76	72	291
NEW ZEALAND (571) — US$30,000					
Frank Nobilo	67	69	70	78	284
Greg Turner	72	71	70	74	287
SPAIN (572) — US$20,000					
Jose Rivero	67	70	71	78	286
Manuel Pinero	72	70	68	76	286
ARGENTINA (576) — US$16,000					
Eduardo Romero	75	72	68	70	285
Jorge Soto	70	74	75	72	291

CHINESE TAIPEI (580) — US$7,666

Sheng-San Hsu	74	71	73	78	296
Wan-Sheng Li	69	66	75	74	284

IRELAND (580) — US$7,666

Ronan Rafferty	71	70	68	75	284
Des Smyth	71	74	74	77	296

ITALY (580) — US$7,666

Costantino Rocca	73	72	71	74	290
Giuseppe Cali	74	71	71	74	290

DENMARK (582) — US$5,000

Anders Sorensen	73	71	68	73	285
Steen Tinning	72	73	73	79	297

WALES (582) — US$5,000

Mark Mouland	73	72	67	75	287
David Llewellyn	77	70	71	77	295

BRAZIL (583) — US$5,000

Priscillo Diniz	69	73	76	86	304
Rafael Navarro	71	74	66	68	279

ENGLAND (589) — US$5,000

Mark James	69	74	69	80	292
Barry Lane	73	75	73	76	297

THAILAND (589) — US$5,000

Somsakdi Srisangar	72	71	76	75	294
Boonchu Ruangkit	77	75	68	75	295

MEXICO (591) — US$5,000

Rafael Alarcon	69	72	67	75	283
Enrique Serna	80	73	72	83	308

COLUMBIA (592) — US$5,000

Rogelio Gonzales	73	78	75	79	305
Eduardo Herrera	70	74	70	73	287

FRANCE (597) — US$5,000

Emmanuel Dussart	76	72	75	76	299
Marc Pendaries	77	71	72	78	298

SWEDEN (597) — US$5,000

Anders Forsbrand	76	77	76	75	304
Johan Rystrom	70	74	72	77	293

SOUTH KOREA (598) — US$5,000

Nam Sin Park	69	77	73	73	292
Sang Ho Choi	77	76	73	80	306

FINLAND (606) — US$5,000

Timo Sipponen	74	75	76	76	301
Markku Louhio	73	82	77	73	305

PHILIPPINES (610) — US$5,000

Mario Siodina	73	75	74	76	298
Rudy Labares	78	77	72	85	312

INDIA (615) — US$5,000

Rohtas Singh	74	79	73	77	303
Basad Ali	77	79	74	82	312

VENEZUELA (616) — US$5,000

Ramon Munoz	75	75	70	80	300
Julian Santana	76	80	75	85	316

WEST GERMANY (617) — US$5,000

Carlo Knauss	79	79	76	78	312
Wolfgang John	77	73	75	80	305

ZIMBABWE (620) — US$5,000

Anthony Edwards	74	78	78	81	311
Tim Price	77	77	76	79	309

SWITZERLAND (622) — US$5,000

Karim Baradie	70	75	77	85	307
Helmuth Schumacher	73	82	81	79	315

MALAYSIA (625) — US$5,000

Sahabudin Yusof	75	77	77	90	319
Barrie Buluah	77	76	73	80	306

HONG KONG (629) — US$5,000

Yau Sui Ming	78	78	79	81	316
Alex Tang	80	78	76	79	313

INDONESIA (637) — US$5,000

Gimin Suwirjo	78	75	84	82	319
Kasiadi	79	79	79	81	318

HOLLAND (640) — US$5,000

Willem Swart	82	77	85	80	324
Kees Borst	78	80	77	81	316

INTERNATIONAL TROPHY

WINNER — Crenshaw - 275 - US$50,000. ORDER OF FINISH: Tateo Ozaki - 276; Barr - 277; Senior - 278; Brand Jr., Navarro - 279; Alarcon - 283; Nobilo, Li, Mackay, Rafferty - 284; Sorensen, Romero, McCumber, Masashi Ozaki - 285; Rivero, Pinero - 286; Herrera, Mouland, Turner - 287; Rocca, Cali - 290; Montgomerie, Soto - 291; Franklin, James, Park - 292; Rystrom - 293; Srisangar - 294; Ruangkit, Llewellyn - 295; Smyth, Hsu - 296; Lane, Tinning - 297; Pendaries, Siodina - 298; Dussart - 299; Munoz - 300; Sipponen - 301; Singh - 303; Forsbrand, Diniz - 304; Louhio, John, Gonzales - 305; Buluah, Choi - 306; Baradie - 307; Serna - 308; Price - 309; Edwards - 311; Ali, Knauss, Labares - 312; Tang - 313; Schumacher - 315; Santana, Borst, Ming - 316; Kasiadi - 318; Suwirjo, Yusof - 319; Swart - 324.

Air New Zealand/Shell Open

Titirangi Golf Club, Auckland
Par 35-35 — 70; 6,311 yards

December 8-11
purse, NZ$200,000

	SCORES				TOTAL	MONEY
Terry Gale	69	69	68	65	271	NZ$36,000
Ossie Moore	68	69	70	68	275	15,120
Jeff Woodland	68	71	69	67	275	15,120
Hale Irwin	68	70	69	68	275	15,120
Rodger Davis	71	70	69	66	276	8,320
Steve Rintoul	71	69	68	69	277	7,640
Peter Fowler	67	69	74	68	278	6,400
Ian Stanley	66	69	70	73	278	6,400
Kirk Triplett	69	74	69	67	279	5,400
David Delong	71	74	69	66	280	4,133.33
Vaughan Somers	74	70	69	67	280	4,133.33
Simon Owen	72	68	70	70	280	4,133.33
Ray Picker	73	70	72	66	281	3,280

	SCORES				TOTAL	MONEY
Noel Ratcliffe	76	70	70	67	283	2,730
David Smith	72	74	70	67	283	2,730
Mike Clayton	71	72	71	69	283	2,730
Peter O'Malley	71	71	68	73	283	2,730
Craig Warren	74	68	74	68	284	2,250
Bruce Soland	70	73	73	68	284	2,250
Craig Mann	72	72	70	70	284	2,250
Mike Harwood	72	70	70	72	284	2,250
Jeff Wagner	69	75	73	68	285	1,800
Jon Diggetts	69	70	77	69	285	1,800
Grant Waite	74	72	67	72	285	1,800
Jack Larkin	74	73	69	69	285	1,800
James Varnam	65	78	71	71	285	1,800
Phillip Glass	72	70	72	71	285	1,800
Richard Gilkey	71	73	70	71	285	1,800
Russell Swanson	72	72	72	70	286	1,390
Brad Hughes	69	74	72	71	286	1,390
Philip Baird	73	72	70	71	286	1,390
Tony Brigstock	71	72	70	73	286	1,390

Nissan-Mobil New Zealand Open

Paraparaumu Beach Golf Club, Paraparaumu
Par 35-36 — 71; 6,492 yards

December 15-18
purse, NZ$150,000

	SCORES				TOTAL	MONEY
Ian Stanley	64	68	69	72	273	NZ$27,000
Mike Clayton	73	68	70	65	276	16,200
Corey Pavin	69	69	68	71	277	10,350
Peter O'Malley	77	65	67	69	278	7,470
Peter Fowler	72	69	70	68	279	5,985
David Delong	69	72	68	70	279	5,985
John Clifford	69	76	67	70	282	4,550
Frank Nobilo	71	67	70	74	282	4,550
Ian Roberts	69	68	71	74	282	4,550
Simon Owen	71	68	68	77	284	3,540
Vaughan Somers	72	74	63	76	285	2,880
Darren Cole	66	73	69	77	285	2,880
David Smith	72	69	71	74	286	2,340
Greg Alexander	72	74	67	73	286	2,340
David Merriman	71	72	69	75	287	2,040
Brett Officer	75	70	68	74	287	2,040
Wayne Case	73	70	74	71	288	1,890
*Philip Tataurangi	72	73	70	73	288	
Kirk Triplett	72	75	72	70	289	1,625
Mike Harwood	74	70	69	76	289	1,625
Russell Swanson	73	70	71	75	289	1,625
Stuart Holmes	73	71	69	76	289	1,625
Ray Picker	72	69	72	76	289	1,625
Richard Gilkey	72	67	73	77	289	1,625
Jack Oliver	73	71	71	75	290	1,320
John Brellenthin	71	75	70	74	290	1,320
Martin Gates	72	72	72	74	290	1,320
Steve Rintoul	67	70	76	77	290	1,320
Steven Aisbett	75	68	74	74	291	1,110
Ossie Moore	74	69	73	75	291	1,110
Philip Baird	72	71	68	80	291	1,110

The Asia/Japan Tour

Unisys Hong Kong Open

Royal Hong Kong Golf Club, Composite Course, Kowloon
Par 36-35 — 71; 6,722 yards

February 11-14
purse, US$150,000

	SCORES				TOTAL	MONEY
Hsieh Chin Sheng	70	71	66	67	274	US$25,000
Lu Chien Soon	69	67	68	71	275	16,660
Greg Bruckner	71	70	70	66	277	9,390
Esteban Toledo	70	67	72	69	278	7,500
Li Wen Shen	69	67	71	72	279	6,360
Frankie Minoza	73	70	71	66	280	3,750
Chen Tze Ming	69	72	69	70	280	3,750
David Feherty	67	72	70	71	280	3,750
Yau Sui Ming	72	71	70	68	281	3,360
Kyi Hla Han	68	68	70	75	281	3,360
Greg Turner	72	72	71	67	282	2,700
Pat Horgan	73	73	69	67	282	2,700
Ho Ming Chung	68	76	72	67	283	2,100
Greg Twiggs	74	70	68	71	283	2,100
Chen Liang Hsi	69	72	70	72	283	2,100
Lu Hsi Chuen	73	68	69	73	283	2,100
Mike Cunning	73	69	67	74	283	2,100
Jeff Maggert	72	76	66	70	284	1,930
Mark Trauner	70	69	73	72	284	1,930
Dave Tentis	72	65	74	73	284	1,930
Choi Yoon Soo	72	72	71	70	285	1,710
Craig McClellan	71	74	70	70	285	1,710
Shen Chung Shyan	73	69	72	71	285	1,710
Hsieh Min Nan	71	71	69	74	285	1,710
Hung Wen Neng	71	71	73	71	286	1,590
Hsieh Yu Shu	72	75	66	73	286	1,590
Lassales Laurent	75	73	70	69	287	1,330
Bill Israelson	70	77	70	70	287	1,330
Casey Nakama	67	72	76	72	287	1,330
Hikaru Emoto	72	71	71	73	287	1,330
Harumitsu Hamano	74	69	71	73	287	1,330
Hsu Chi San	71	71	71	74	287	1,330

Coca Cola Philippines Open

Wack Wack Golf and Country Club, East Course, Manila
Par 36-36 — 72; 7,090 yards

February 18-21
purse, US$120,000

	SCORES				TOTAL	MONEY
Hsieh Chin Sheng	68	69	74	72	283	US$19,992
Steve Bowman	68	73	74	73	288	13,332
Carlos Espinosa	69	73	73	74	289	6,756
Lu Ho Tsai	73	74	71	71	289	6,756

	SCORES				TOTAL	MONEY
Lu Hsi Chuen	72	73	76	69	290	3,972
Tray Tyner	72	73	74	71	290	3,972
Steve Veriato	73	76	69	72	290	3,972
Yuan Ching Chi	69	75	76	70	290	3,972
Emlyn Aubrey	74	71	73	73	291	2,214
Chung Chun Hsin	73	67	73	78	291	2,214
Jeff Cook	75	72	73	71	291	2,214
Ian Doig	72	75	73	71	291	2,214
Jay Nichols	75	67	78	71	291	2,214
Mario Siodina	78	70	74	69	291	2,214
Rudy Lavares	73	72	74	73	292	1,788
Choi Yoon Soo	71	71	77	74	293	1,578
Lu Chien Soon	70	71	69	73	293	1,578
Lin Chie Hsiang	71	73	75	74	293	1,578
Mike Standly	73	76	74	70	293	1,578
Mark Aebli	69	73	74	78	294	1,370.40
Mike Cunning	75	71	74	74	294	1,370.40
Kuo Chi Hsiung	74	73	69	78	294	1,370.40
Eleuterio Nival	73	72	72	77	294	1,370.40
Robert Pactoleren	72	71	74	77	294	1,370.40
Greg Bruckner	75	74	75	71	295	1,218
Hsieh Yu Shu	72	76	75	72	295	1,218
Ted Schulz	72	75	76	72	295	1,218
Mark Trayner	78	71	73	73	295	1,218
Jim Blair	74	73	72	77	296	1,060.80
Barry Conser	74	74	75	73	296	1,060.80
Yau Sui Ming	75	71	75	75	296	1,060.80
Danny Mijovic	74	72	77	73	296	1,060.80
Graig McClellan	72	73	77	74	296	1,060.80

Benson & Hedges Malaysian Open

Saujana Golf and Country Club, Kuala Lumpur, Malaysia
Par 72

March 3-6
purse, US$150,000

	SCORES				TOTAL	MONEY
Tray Tyner	73	72	72	71	288	US$25,000
Harumitsu Hamano	71	70	74	74	289	13,028
Hsieh Chin Sheng	73	75	70	71	289	13,028
Casey Nakama	76	73	70	72	291	7,500
Lin Chie Hsiang	69	76	75	72	292	5,370
Jeff Cook	72	73	71	76	292	5,370
Todd Hamilton	73	74	73	72	292	5,370
Kouji Morisaki	74	74	74	72	294	3,102
Lai Chung Jen	72	80	69	73	294	3,102
Emlyn Aubrey	74	77	70	73	294	3,102
Jeff Maggert	72	73	79	70	294	3,102
Don Walsworth	74	74	75	71	294	3,102
Danny Mijovic	72	74	74	75	295	2,235
Kuo Chi Hsiung	74	74	74	73	295	2,235
Lu Chien Soon	72	77	74	72	295	2,235
Robert Huxtable	73	72	74	76	295	2,235
Ian Doig	76	74	75	70	295	2,235
Kim Hak Shu	71	75	77	73	296	1,766
Chen Tze Ming	78	73	74	71	296	1,766
Li Wen Shen	75	74	75	72	296	1,766
Barry Conser	77	74	71	74	296	1,766

	SCORES				TOTAL	MONEY
Rick Dalpos	74	75	73	74	296	1,766
Mark Trauner	72	71	77	76	296	1,766
Craig McClellan	75	73	76	72	296	1,766
Frankie Minoza	73	75	73	76	297	1,523
Steve Bowman	71	74	74	78	297	1,523
Greg Bruckner	76	71	78	72	297	1,523
Pat Hogan	71	75	76	75	297	1,523
Kyi Hla Han	72	77	74	75	298	1,305
Noriichi Kawakami	71	77	76	74	298	1,305
Tsao Chien Teng	76	76	73	73	298	1,305
Bob Lendzion	74	76	71	77	298	1,305
Jerry Smith	68	75	76	79	298	1,305
Steve Veriato	74	73	76	75	298	1,305

Singapore Open

Tanah Merah Country Club, Singapore
Par 36-36 — 72; 7,070 yards

March 10-13
purse, US$220,000

	SCORES				TOTAL	MONEY
Greg Bruckner	72	69	67	73	281	US$36,652
Chung Chun Hsin	69	70	73	70	282	24,442
Chen Tze Ming	69	68	73	74	284	13,772
Ted Schulz	77	71	69	68	285	11,000
Mark Aebli	73	71	70	72	286	8,514
Rick Gibson	73	70	70	73	286	8,514
Lin Chie Hsiang	71	74	69	73	287	6,600
Peter Fowler	74	75	71	68	288	4,730
Tray Tyner	72	77	70	69	288	4,730
Wayne Smith	74	70	75	69	288	4,730
Yuan Ching Chi	70	70	70	78	288	4,730
Noriichi Kawakami	73	74	69	74	290	3,644
David Smith	72	72	72	74	290	3,644
Steve Jurgensen	71	71	73	75	290	3,644
Rick Dalpos	75	74	71	71	291	2,821
Fung Hee Kwan	76	73	70	72	291	2,821
Dave Tentis	75	73	71	72	291	2,821
Bill Israelson	74	72	72	73	291	2,821
Lin Chia	72	73	73	73	291	2,821
Rudy Lavares	73	70	75	73	291	2,821
Stewart Ginn	70	70	75	76	291	2,821
Wayne Riley	71	74	69	77	291	2,821
Kuo Chi Hsiung	75	71	73	73	292	2,359
Jim Benepe	73	73	72	74	292	2,359
Pat Horgan	73	73	72	74	292	2,359
Chen Liang Hsi	71	72	73	76	292	2,359
Choi Yoon Soo	73	75	75	70	293	2,101
Harumitsu Hamano	74	73	74	72	293	2,101
Steve Chapman	75	71	75	72	293	2,101
Barry Conser	75	73	70	75	293	2,101

Indonesia Open

Jakarta Golf Club, Rawamangun Course, Jakarta, Indonesia   March 16-19
Par 70   purse, US$100,000

	SCORES				TOTAL	MONEY
Hsieh Yu Shu	69	62	67	66	264	US$16,600
Mario Siodina	65	70	66	69	270	11,110
Paul Foley	68	68	71	68	275	5,630
Mark Aebli	68	69	64	74	275	5,630
Li Wen Shen	66	66	72	72	276	3,870
Jeff Cook	69	67	68	72	276	3,870
Rudy Lavares	65	69	68	75	277	3,000
Jerry Smith	66	69	70	73	278	2,246
Dave Tentis	73	65	72	68	278	2,246
Jeff Maggert	75	64	71	68	278	2,246
Yuan Ching Chi	70	68	67	74	279	1,664
Kyi Hla Han	71	72	65	71	279	1,664
Mark Trauner	70	68	74	67	279	1,664
Mike Cunning	69	69	72	69	279	1,664
Jeff Senior	72	68	69	70	279	1,664
Greg Bruckner	73	68	70	69	280	1,365
Jim Benepe	72	69	67	72	280	1,365
Bradley King	68	70	71	72	281	1,177
Kuo Chi Hsiung	72	68	69	72	281	1,177
Lai Chung Jen	71	68	69	73	281	1,177
Peter O'Malley	71	72	69	69	281	1,177
Kirk Triplett	68	73	70	70	281	1,177
Tsao Chien Teng	69	70	69	73	281	1,177
Ted Lehman	72	70	69	70	281	1,177
Barry Conser	67	72	71	72	282	958
Paterno Braza	70	72	72	68	282	958
Sumarno	69	67	73	73	282	958
Junji Hasizoe	71	70	75	66	282	958
Don Walsworth	68	70	73	71	282	958
Carlos Espinosa	69	72	72	69	282	958
Robert Michael	71	70	72	69	282	958
Thaworn Wiratchant	71	72	68	71	282	958

Thailand Open

Royal Thai Army Golf Club, Bangkok, Thailand   March 24-27
Par 72; 6,865 yards   purse, US$100,000

	SCORES				TOTAL	MONEY
Jeff Senior	72	69	68	67	276	US$16,660
Chen Liang Hsi	69	68	70	71	278	11,110
Frankie Minoza	73	67	70	70	280	5,630
Tray Tyner	70	71	70	69	280	5,630
Rick Gibson	68	73	73	67	281	3,870
Chen Tze Ming	74	70	71	66	281	3,870
Hsieh Yu Shu	68	74	66	74	282	2,580
Dave Tentis	70	68	74	70	282	2,580
Somsak Srisanga	72	71	69	70	282	2,580
Bonchu Ruengkit	70	69	71	74	284	2,000
Paul Foley	74	72	69	70	285	1,664
Hsieh Chin Sheng	73	72	71	69	285	1,664
Lu Chien Soon	68	72	74	71	285	1,664

	SCORES				TOTAL	MONEY
Lu Hsi Chuen	72	69	73	71	285	1,664
Jerry Smith	71	71	70	73	285	1,664
Paterno Braza	73	72	69	72	286	1,400
Noriichi Kawakami	70	72	71	74	287	1,211.43
Chung Chun Hsin	71	73	73	70	287	1,211.43
Jim Benepe	70	74	70	73	287	1,211.43
Steve Bowman	71	73	71	72	287	1,211.43
Jeff Cook	78	68	72	69	287	1,211.43
Steve Veriato	69	74	73	71	287	1,211.43
Don Walsworth	74	73	70	70	287	1,211.43
Peter O'Malley	73	72	72	71	288	1,000
Kyi Hla Han	70	74	70	74	288	1,000
Rudy Lavares	73	69	71	75	288	1,000
Kuo Chi Hsiung	72	73	73	70	288	1,000
Lu Ho Tsai	71	73	72	72	288	1,000
Craig McClellan	72	70	71	75	288	1,000
Thaworn Wiratchant	74	70	72	72	288	1,000

Charminar Challenge Indian Open

Royal Calcutta Golf Club, Calcutta, India
Par 36-37 — 73; 7,271 yards

March 31-April 3
purse, US$100,000

	SCORES				TOTAL	MONEY
Lu Chien Soon	68	68	70	75	281	US$16,660
Kirk Triplett	72	71	71	72	286	11,110
Jeff Senior	75	75	69	68	287	6,260
Tracy Nakazaki	70	72	74	72	288	5,000
Toshiya Shibutani	74	75	72	70	291	3,870
Thaworn Wiratchant	71	74	71	75	291	3,870
Anthony Gilligan	73	73	71	75	292	3,000
Firoz Ali	74	76	72	71	293	2,500
James Harper	73	74	75	72	294	2,033
Mark Aebli	75	72	72	75	294	2,033
Tray Tyner	78	74	70	72	294	2,033
Lu Ho Tsai	75	76	73	71	295	1,615
Rick Dalpos	71	77	73	74	295	1,615
Todd Hamilton	76	73	72	74	295	1,615
Ted Lehmann	75	74	74	72	295	1,615
Peter O'Malley	74	72	79	71	296	1,340
Ken Trimble	71	78	73	74	296	1,340
Bob Lendzion	72	73	77	74	296	1,340
Noriichi Kawakami	73	76	71	77	297	1,220
Per Arne Brostedt	73	79	74	71	297	1,220
Bradley King					298	1,071
David Smith		Round			298	1,071
Kyi Hla Han					298	1,071
Carlos Espinosa		by			298	1,071
Lu Hsi Chuen					298	1,071
Barry Conser		Round			298	1,071
Jeff Cook					298	1,071
David O'Kelly		Scores			298	1,071
Kousei Miyata					299	898
Arjin Sophon		Unavailable			299	898
Emlyn Aubrey					299	898
Kyle Coody					299	898

Republic of China Open

Hsin Chu Golf and Country Club, Taipei, Taiwan
Par 36-36 — 72; 6,825 yards

April 7-10
purse, US$170,000

	SCORES				TOTAL	MONEY
Carlos Espinosa	76	75	74	68	293	US$28,000
Lin Chi Hsiang	73	75	73	73	294	17,766.67
Lee Wen Sheng	77	74	71	73	295	10,016.67
Rick Gibson	80	72	75	69	296	7,461.10
Chen Liang Hsi	74	80	73	69	296	7,461.10
Yu Chin Han	76	74	73	73	296	7,461.10
David Smith	79	76	73	69	297	3,557.23
Hsieh Min Nan	74	75	76	72	297	3,557.23
Craig McClellan	74	73	78	72	297	3,557.23
Richard Foreman	76	80	69	72	297	3,557.23
Tsao Chien Teng	76	74	75	72	297	3,557.23
Lu Chien Soon	75	75	74	73	297	3,557.23
Esteban Toledo	72	79	76	71	298	2,517.77
David Tentis	75	75	76	72	298	2,517.77
Huang Shyh Ho	73	75	76	74	298	2,517.77
Hsieh Yu Shu	74	78	77	70	299	2,144.43
Mark Aebli	75	73	78	73	299	2,144.43
Hsieh Yung Yo	73	75	78	73	299	2,144.43
Ted Schulz	78	76	76	70	300	1,925.57
Jim Benepe	76	78	75	71	300	1,925.57
Chen Tze Ming	76	76	70	78	300	1,925.57
Hikaru Emoto	78	77	76	70	301	1,800
Bob Lendzion	75	78	78	70	301	1,800
Chen Chien Chin	78	76	78	70	302	1,648
Kuo Chi Hsiung	77	74	77	74	302	1,648
Hsieh Chin Sheng	76	75	77	74	302	1,648
Jeff Maggert	76	79	73	74	302	1,648
Wong Teh Chong	74	82	75	71	302	1,648
*Chen Yun Shin	77	77	79	69	302	
Shen Chung Shyan	76	79	75	73	303	1,369.03
Kirk Triplett	82	74	78	69	303	1,369.03
Steve Bowman	77	75	77	74	303	1,369.03
Hsu Tien Lai	76	77	76	74	303	1,369.03
Tray Tyner	78	76	78	71	303	1,369.03
Ho Ming Chung	75	77	75	76	303	1,369.03
Hisao Inoue	72	79	80	72	303	1,369.03
*Lu Wen Teh	76	76	77	74	303	

Maekyung South Korean Open

Nam Seoul Country Club, Seoul, South Korea
Par 36-36 — 72; 6,860 yards

April 14-17
purse, US$140,000

	SCORES				TOTAL	MONEY
Frankie Minoza	70	72	67	70	279	US$23,000
Lim Jin Han	74	68	72	66	280	15,000
Craig Parry	74	72	67	69	282	8,700
Rick Gibson	69	71	75	71	286	7,000
Li Wen Shen	76	71	67	73	287	5,900
Park Yeun Tae	72	71	69	76	288	3,700
Park Nam Sin	74	72	71	71	288	3,700

	SCORES				TOTAL	MONEY
Kwon Oh Chul	73	72	73	70	288	3,700
Lee Myung Ha	78	72	68	70	288	3,700
Choi Sang Ho	75	71	72	70	288	3,700
Andrew Labrooy	79	69	73	68	289	2,443
Hsieh Yu Shu	74	73	72	70	289	2,443
Choi Youn Soo	75	73	72	69	289	2,443
Esteban Toledo	70	73	72	75	290	1,965
Lin Chie Hsiang	73	73	72	72	290	1,965
Lu Hsi Chuen	75	74	70	71	290	1,965
Rick Dalpos	72	75	72	71	290	1,965
Lu Chien Soon	76	73	71	71	291	1,710
Jeff Maggert	72	76	71	72	291	1,710
Kim Suk Chong	71	74	76	70	291	1,710
Kwak Heung Soo	74	76	72	69	291	1,710
Shimon Takamatsu	74	76	71	71	292	1,516
Chen Liang Hsi	74	70	72	76	292	1,516
Kim Duk Woon	74	71	74	73	292	1,516
Lin Chia	76	74	71	71	292	1,516
Yoshio Fumiyama	75	70	73	75	293	1,154
Toru Hiyami	78	70	74	71	293	1,154
Hisao Inoue	76	71	72	74	293	1,154
Akira Suzuki	74	73	74	72	293	1,154
Chen Chien Chen	74	75	73	71	293	1,154
Chung Chun Hsin	76	73	72	72	293	1,154
Ho Ming Chung	73	75	74	71	293	1,154
Tadao Nakamura	75	71	73	74	293	1,154
Cho Bum Soo	71	74	73	75	293	1,154
Kim Yung Il	71	75	71	76	293	1,154

Daiichi Fudosan Cup

Miyazaki Kikusai Golf Club
Par 72; 6,266 yards

March 3-6
purse, ¥60,000,000

	SCORES				TOTAL	MONEY
Kazuya Nakajima	66	73	65	72	276	¥10,800,000
Masahiro Shiota	72	72	67	66	277	4,320,000
Hsieh Min Nan	69	71	70	67	277	4,320,000
Naomichi Ozaki	70	70	67	70	277	4,320,000
Shuuichi Sano	69	70	70	69	278	2,055,000
Hikaru Emoto	69	71	67	71	278	2,055,000
Yutaka Hagawa	68	70	71	69	278	2,055,000
Shigeru Kawamata	73	68	69	68	278	2,055,000
Fujio Kobayashi	72	67	70	70	279	1,470,000
Katsuyoshi Tomori	71	69	63	76	279	1,470,000
Toshimitsu Kai	72	72	71	65	280	912,000
Saburo Fujiki	67	71	72	70	280	912,000
Seiji Ebihara	69	71	68	72	280	912,000
Seiichi Kanai	74	67	67	72	280	912,000
Katsuji Hasegawa	70	72	71	67	280	912,000
Yoshihisa Iwashita	68	71	71	70	280	912,000
Isamu Sugita	73	69	67	71	280	912,000
Norio Adachi	72	70	66	72	280	912,000
Isao Isozaki	73	67	69	72	281	566,000
Nobuo Serizawa	71	68	70	72	281	566,000
Tsutomu Irie	70	72	68	71	281	566,000
Tomohiro Maruyama	71	71	68	71	281	566,000

	SCORES			TOTAL	MONEY
Hiromichi Namiki	71	70	70	70	281	566,000
Haruo Yasuda	75	69	68	69	281	566,000

Imperial Invitation

Seve Ballesteros Golf Course
Par 72; 6,920 yards

March 12-13
purse, ¥35,000,000

	SCORES		TOTAL	MONEY
Katsuji Hasegawa	68	75	143	¥6,300,000
Taiijiro Tanaka	72	71	143	2,520,000
Naomichi Ozaki	72	71	143	2,520,000
Shigeru Kawamata	70	73	143	2,520,000
(Hasegawa won playoff.)				
Katsuyoshi Tomori	71	73	144	1,198,750
Toshimitsu Kai	75	69	144	1,198,750
Yoshihisa Iwashita	73	71	144	1,198,750
Toshiaki Sudo	75	69	144	1,198,750
Koiichi Uehara	73	72	145	764,750
Kikuo Arai	73	72	145	764,750
Hiroshi Ishii	69	76	145	764,750
Takahiro Takeyasu	75	70	145	764,750
Norio Mikami	75	71	146	546,000
Mike Thomas	71	75	146	546,000
Futoshi Irie	73	73	146	546,000
Nobumitsu Yuhara	75	72	147	361,666
Motomasa Aoki	74	73	147	361,666
Tomohiro Maruyama	74	73	147	361,666
Yoshimi Watanabe	74	73	147	361,666
Hiroshi Goda	75	72	147	361,666
Satoshi Higashi	76	71	147	361,666
Yurio Akitomi	74	73	147	361,666
Namio Takasu	75	72	147	361,666
Ikuo Shirahama	72	75	147	361,666

Shizuoka Open

Shizuoka Country Club, Hamaoka Course, Hamaoka
Par 72; 6,919 yards

March 17-20
purse, ¥40,000,000

	SCORES				TOTAL	MONEY
Toshimitsu Kai	71	72	72	68	283	¥7,200,000
Tomohiro Maruyama	78	72	67	66	283	4,000,000
(Kai defeated Maruyama on third hole of playoff.)						
Katsunari Takahashi	74	70	72	68	284	2,080,000
Hiroshi Makino	71	70	72	71	284	2,080,000
Craig Parry	72	69	71	72	284	2,080,000
Seeiji Ebihara	73	67	71	74	285	1,360,000
Yoshimi Niizeki	76	71	68	70	285	1,360,000
Norio Adachi	73	74	68	72	287	1,040,000
Nobuo Serizawa	70	72	74	71	287	1,040,000
Teruo Sugihara	73	75	68	71	287	1,040,000
Osamu Watanabe	75	72	70	71	288	736,000
Noboru Sugai	74	71	70	73	288	736,000

	SCORES				TOTAL	MONEY
Koiichi Suzuki	75	71	71	71	288	736,000
Hsieh Min Nan	70	73	75	71	289	600,000
Haruo Yasuda	78	70	69	72	289	600,000
Satoshi Higashi	77	72	70	71	290	454,400
Yoshihisa Iwashita	74	71	71	74	290	454,400
Harumitsu Hamano	74	72	74	70	290	454,400
Saburo Fujiki	74	76	72	68	290	454,400
Yoshikazu Yokoshima	71	71	73	75	290	454,400
Masayuki Imai	76	71	72	72	291	356,800
Seiichi Kanai	74	72	73	72	291	356,800
Atsushi Murota	72	76	73	70	291	356,800
Yasuhiro Funatogawa	76	75	69	71	291	356,800
Katsui Hasegawa	75	70	75	71	291	356,800
Yoshitaka Yamamoto	72	72	72	76	292	312,000
Pete Izumikawa	71	74	75	72	292	312,000
Keiji Tejima	74	72	72	74	292	312,000
Shinsaku Maeda	75	72	75	70	292	312,000
Hisashi Suzumura	72	75	72	73	292	312,000

Taylormade Setonaikai Open

Shito Country Club
Par 72; 6,335 yards

March 24-27
purse, ¥40,000,000

(Shortened to 54 holes, rain.)

	SCORES			TOTAL	MONEY
Wayne Smith	71	73	69	213	¥7,200,000
Norio Mikami	72	73	69	214	3,360,000
Kenji Mori	65	75	74	214	3,360,000
Motomasa Aoki	71	75	69	215	1,920,000
Toshimitsu Kai	68	76	72	216	1,520,000
Yoshihisa Takasaka	72	74	70	216	1,520,000
Minoru Hatsumi	70	75	72	217	1,220,000
Harry Taylor	69	75	73	217	1,220,000
Shigeru Kawamata	73	73	72	218	833,600
Tsutomu Irie	69	77	72	218	833,600
Hiromichi Namiki	71	74	73	218	833,600
Tadao Nakamura	75	72	71	218	833,600
Yutaka Suzuki	73	75	70	218	833,600
Akihito Yokoyama	71	75	73	219	552,000
Fujio Kobayashi	73	75	71	219	552,000
Hiroshi Goda	70	72	77	219	552,000
Masanobu Kimura	70	73	76	219	552,000
Craig Parry	77	71	72	220	403,200
Koichi Uehara	73	75	72	220	403,200
Yasuo Sone	73	75	72	220	403,200
Kenji Sogame	69	78	73	220	403,200
Masaru Amano	72	75	73	220	403,200

Kuzuha Kokusai

Kuzuha Public Course, Kuzuha
Par 70; 6,238 yards

April 2-3
purse, ¥18,000,000

	SCORES		TOTAL	MONEY
Wayne Smith	65	66	131	¥3,600,000
Craig Parry	64	69	133	1,512,000
Yasuhiro Funatogawa	67	66	133	1,512,000
Toru Nakamura	71	63	134	864,000
Brett Ogle	70	65	135	648,000
Taiichiro Kanaya	67	68	135	648,000
Kinpachi Yoshimura	69	66	135	648,000
David Ishii	66	70	136	468,000
Katsuji Hasegawa	68	68	136	468,000
Kazuo Kanayama	70	66	136	468,000
Joji Furuki	66	71	137	255,111
Norio Suzuki	67	70	137	255,111
Fujio Kobayashi	70	67	137	255,111
Yoshitaka Yamamoto	71	66	137	255,111
Kikuo Arai	71	66	137	255,111
Seiichi Kanai	67	70	137	255,111
Shozo Miyamoto	72	65	137	255,111
Tomoo Inoue	68	69	137	255,111
Hiroshi Ishii	67	70	137	255,111
Nobuo Serizawa	69	69	138	176,500
Koichi Uehara	70	68	138	176,500
Shinsaku Shimada	68	70	138	176,500
Hideto Shigenobu	67	71	138	176,500

Pocari Sweat Open

Hakuryuko County Club, Diawacho
Par 71; 6,780 yards

April 7-10
purse, ¥40,000,000

	SCORES				TOTAL	MONEY
Ian Baker-Finch	73	68	66	70	277	¥7,200,000
Graham Marsh	71	71	70	67	279	4,000,000
Brian Jones	72	72	69	67	280	2,720,000
Craig Parry	68	76	68	70	282	1,920,000
Norio Adachi	74	71	69	69	283	1,520,000
Seiiki Okuda	72	70	72	69	283	1,520,000
Tsutomu Irie	74	74	68	68	284	1,100,000
Yoshimi Niizeki	72	76	67	69	284	1,100,000
Roger Mackay	73	76	66	69	284	1,100,000
David Ishii	73	73	67	71	284	1,100,000
Kikuo Arai	75	72	69	69	285	656,000
Hiroshi Makino	72	72	74	67	285	656,000
Toshimitsu Kaii	74	71	66	74	285	656,000
Saburo Fujiki	75	71	69	70	285	656,000
Yoshikazu Yokoshima	76	73	69	67	285	656,000
Naomichi Ozaki	74	74	66	71	285	656,000
Seiichi Koizumi	74	75	64	73	286	392,000
Norio Mikami	73	71	73	69	286	392,000
Kinpachi Yoshimura	74	71	68	73	286	392,000
Yasuhiro Funatogawa	73	73	70	70	286	392,000
Hideki Kase	73	70	77	66	286	392,000
Tateo Ozaki	74	73	69	70	286	392,000

	SCORES				TOTAL	MONEY
Seiichi Kanai	73	74	69	70	286	392,000
Nobumitsu Yuhara	74	72	70	70	286	392,000
Ikuo Shirahama	76	72	67	71	286	392,000
Hideto Shigenobu	76	73	70	68	287	308,000
Mike Ferguson	71	76	69	71	287	308,000
Katsuji Hasegawa	72	74	71	70	287	308,000
Yurio Akitomi	72	75	74	66	287	308,000
Tsukasa Watanabe	75	71	70	71	287	308,000
Taijiro Tanaka	72	74	71	70	287	308,000

Bridgestone Aso

Aso Golf Club, Aso, Kumamoto
Par 72; 7,037 yards

April 14-17
purse, ¥40,000,000

	SCORES				TOTAL	MONEY
Ian Baker-Finch	75	73	68	66	282	¥7,200,000
Tadami Ueno	72	71	69	71	283	4,000,000
Roger Mackay	71	70	71	72	284	2,720,000
Masashi Ozaki	70	73	74	68	285	1,760,000
Yoshikazu Yokoshima	71	75	67	72	285	1,760,000
Yoshihisa Iwashita	72	70	77	69	288	1,440,000
Tomohiro Maruyama	77	72	72	68	289	1,220,000
Katsunari Takahashi	75	72	71	71	289	1,220,000
Yoshinori Mizushima	74	72	70	74	290	874,000
Naomichi Ozaki	72	71	72	75	290	874,000
Nobuo Serizawa	71	74	73	72	290	874,000
Hsieh Min Nan	72	71	72	75	290	874,000
Masaru Amano	73	76	71	71	291	554,666
Motomasa Aoki	72	71	73	75	291	554,666
David Ishii	76	74	70	71	291	554,666
Brian Jones	75	74	70	72	291	554,666
Teruo Sugihara	73	72	75	71	291	554,666
Nobumitsu Yuhara	75	73	71	72	291	554,666
Satoshi Higashi	74	71	71	76	292	371,428
Yoshiyuki Isomura	74	76	73	69	292	371,428
Brett Ogle	74	74	71	73	292	371,428
Hiroshi Makino	79	71	72	70	292	371,428
Peter Senior	75	74	74	69	292	371,428
Chen Tze Ming	76	72	72	72	292	371,428
Yasuo Sone	79	73	72	68	292	371,428
Atsushi Murota	78	74	67	74	293	320,000
Kazuya Nakajima	77	73	72	71	293	320,000
Yoshitaka Yamamoto	74	73	75	71	293	320,000
Hajime Meshiai	75	71	74	74	294	284,800
Masahiro Kuramoto	74	78	73	69	294	284,800
Eitaro Deguchi	77	70	71	76	294	284,800
Takenori Hiraishi	75	74	72	73	294	284,800
Yutaka Hagawa	75	74	75	70	294	284,800
Taisei Inagaki	78	71	73	72	294	284,800

Dunlop International Open

Ibaraki Golf Club, Inamachi
Par 72; 7,163 yards

April 21-24
purse, ¥60,000,000

	SCORES				TOTAL	MONEY
Masashi Ozaki	69	70	69	70	278	¥10,800,000
David Ishii	71	70	69	71	281	6,000,000
Taijiro Tanaka	73	68	72	69	282	4,080,000
Toru Nakamura	74	69	68	73	284	2,640,000
Tohru Nakayama	68	72	74	70	284	2,640,000
Kinpachi Yoshimura	75	71	70	69	285	2,160,000
Hajime Meshiai	70	75	70	71	286	1,740,000
Tray Tyner	72	71	70	73	286	1,740,000
Emlyn Aubery	75	69	73	69	286	1,740,000
Lu Chien Soon	72	71	72	72	287	1,082,000
Rick Dalpos	70	73	71	73	287	1,082,000
Isamu Sugita	73	69	70	75	287	1,082,000
Graham Marsh	73	74	70	70	287	1,082,000
Craig Parry	72	70	73	72	287	1,082,000
David Smith	72	69	73	73	287	1,082,000
Hiroshi Makino	73	73	71	71	288	681,600
Masahiro Kuramoto	71	76	70	71	288	681,600
David Tentis	73	69	79	67	288	681,600
Ian Baker-Finch	76	71	69	72	288	681,600
Rick Gibson	70	74	72	72	288	681,600
Masanobu Kimura	69	71	73	76	289	552,000
Peter Senior	70	72	77	70	289	552,000
Jeff Senior	74	73	73	69	289	552,000
Satoshi Sudo	71	69	75	75	290	486,000
Li Wen Sheng	72	71	76	71	290	486,000
Lin Chia	69	74	73	74	290	486,000
Seiji Ebihara	73	70	72	75	290	486,000
Kirk Triplett	69	73	74	74	290	486,000
Kikuo Arai	73	71	74	72	290	486,000

Chunichi Crowns

Nagoya Country Club, Wago Course, Nagoya
Par 70; 6,491 yards

April 28-May 1
purse, ¥90,000,000

	SCORES				TOTAL	MONEY
Scott Simpson	71	69	71	67	278	¥16,200,000
David Ishii	71	72	69	69	281	7,560,000
Masashi Ozaki	71	69	69	72	281	7,560,000
Yoshimi Niizeki	68	72	74	69	283	3,720,000
Haruo Yasuda	71	75	66	71	283	3,720,000
Mike Reid	69	70	73	71	283	3,720,000
Terry Gale	68	73	70	73	284	2,745,000
Saburo Fujiki	70	74	64	76	284	2,745,000
Ian Baker-Finch	73	74	71	67	285	2,205,000
Masahiro Kuramoto	74	69	75	67	285	2,205,000
Peter Senior	72	73	70	71	286	1,728,000
Teruo Sugihara	78	71	69	68	286	1,728,000
Kinpachi Yoshimura	70	71	70	76	287	1,404,000
Naomichi Ozaki	72	71	70	74	287	1,404,000
Graham Marsh	72	73	73	69	287	1,404,000
Tadao Nakamura	71	69	72	76	288	996,000

	SCORES				TOTAL	MONEY
Wayne Smith	68	72	74	74	288	996,000
Hiroshi Makino	70	75	72	71	288	996,000
Koichi Suzuki	74	70	72	72	288	996,000
Yoshikazu Yokoshima	75	70	68	75	288	996,000
Norio Mikami	71	74	69	74	288	996,000
Katsuji Hasegawa	70	76	72	71	289	758,571
Shinsaku Maeda	69	74	73	73	289	758,571
Tsukasa Watanabe	74	74	69	72	289	758,571
Masaji Kusakabe	76	70	72	71	289	758,571
Isao Aoki	75	69	74	71	289	758,571
Seiichi Kanai	74	74	72	69	289	758,571
Lu Liang Huan	73	73	74	69	289	758,571
Ikuo Shirahama	69	77	70	74	290	675,000
Teruo Nakamura	74	73	73	70	290	675,000

Fuji Sankei Classic

Kawana Hotel, Fuji Course, Ito
Par 71; 6,694 yards

May 5-8
purse, ¥60,000,000

	SCORES				TOTAL	MONEY
Ikuo Shirahama	71	71	70	68	280	¥10,800,000
Nobumitsu Yuhara	70	69	68	75	282	6,000,000
Taijiro Tanaka	72	70	69	72	283	3,120,000
Tohru Nakamura	70	71	70	72	283	3,120,000
Naomichi Ozaki	69	68	71	75	283	3,120,000
Wayne Smith	69	70	71	74	284	1,845,000
David Ishii	71	71	73	69	284	1,845,000
Hiroshi Makino	68	73	73	70	284	1,845,000
Yasuhiro Funatogawa	70	68	72	74	284	1,845,000
Yutaka Hagawa	70	66	75	74	285	1,290,000
Chen Tze Ming	75	71	69	70	285	1,290,000
Tateo Ozaki	72	70	71	73	286	940,800
Masashi Ozaki	73	67	74	72	286	940,800
Larry Nelson	72	70	69	75	286	940,800
Saburo Fujiki	70	75	69	72	286	940,800
Seiji Ebihara	70	75	72	69	286	940,800
Tsutomu Irie	72	74	70	71	287	672,000
Brian Jones	77	71	69	70	287	672,000
Haruo Yasuda	71	71	71	74	287	672,000
Shinsaku Maeda	68	73	75	72	288	554,400
Seiki Okuda	71	71	71	75	288	554,400
Tadao Nakamura	73	73	71	71	288	554,400
Kikuo Arai	73	72	70	73	288	554,400
Graham Marsh	72	71	73	72	288	554,400
Teruo Nakamura	74	69	75	72	290	504,000
Kazuo Kanayama	73	71	71	76	291	480,000
Tomohiro Maruyama	73	67	78	73	291	480,000
Tadami Ueno	72	74	71	74	291	480,000
Roger Mackay	74	71	73	74	292	438,000
Lu Chien Soon	72	73	72	75	292	438,000
Koichi Suzuki	72	75	72	73	292	438,000

Japan Match Play Championship

Green Academy Country Club, Ishikawa
Par 72; 7,019 yards

May 12-15
purse, ¥50,000,000

FIRST ROUND

David Ishii defeated Terry Gale, 4 and 3
Toru Nakamura defeated Tadao Nakamura, 3 and 2
Kinpachi Yoshimura defeated Hiroshi Makino, 3 and 2
Koiichi Suzuki defeated Nobuo Serizawa, 1 up
Hsieh Min Nan defeated Teruo Nakamura, 3 and 2
Namio Takasu defeated Tsukasa Watanabe, 1 up
Isao Aoki defeated Isamu Sugita, 1 up
Naomichi Ozaki defeated Yoshikazu Yokoshima, 2 and 1
Masashi Ozaki defeated Nobumitsu Yuhara, 5 and 4
Saburo Fujiki defeated Katsunari Takahashi, 2 and 1
Masanobu Kimura defeated Brian Jones, 1 up
Yoshitaka Yamamoto defeated Ian Baker-Finch, 1 up, 19 holes
Hajime Meshiai defeated Lu Liang Huan, 6 and 4
Noburu Sugai defeated Chen Tze Ming, 1 up, 20 holes
Graham Marsh defeated Seiji Ebihara, 3 and 2
Tateo Ozaki defeated Seiichi Kanai, 1 up
(Each first-round loser received ¥250,000)

SECOND ROUND

Ishii defeated Nakamura, 3 and 1
Suzuki defeated Yoshimura, 4 and 2
Takasu defeated Hsieh, 1 up
Naomichi Ozaki defeated Aoki, 2 and 1
Fujiki defeated Masashi Ozaki, 4 and 3
Yamamoto defeated Kimura, 1 up, 19 holes
Sugai defeated Meshiai, 3 and 1
Tateo Ozaki defeated Marsh, 6 and 5
(Each second-round loser received ¥500,000)

QUARTER-FINALS

Ishii defeated Suzuki, 7 and 6
Takasu defeated Naomichi Ozaki, 3 and 2
Yamamoto defeated Fujiki, 1 up
Sugai defeated Tateo Ozaki, 3 and 2
(Each quarter-finals loser received ¥1,000,000

SEMI-FINALS

Ishii defeated Takasu, 1 up
Sugai defeated Yamamoto, 2 and 1

THIRD-FOURTH PLACE PLAYOFF

Takasu defeated Yamamoto, 3 and 1
(Takasu received ¥3,500,000; Yamamoto ¥2,500,000)

FINAL

Ishii defeated Sugai, 6 and 5
(Ishii received ¥14,000,000; Sugai ¥7,000,000

Pepsi Ube

Ube Country Club, Ajisu   May 19-22
Par 72; 6,595 yards   purse, ¥37,500,000

(Second round rained out; final round shortened to nine holes)

	SCORES			TOTAL	MONEY
Mamoru Kondo	67	68	34	169	¥6,750,000
Masahiro Kuramoto	69	68	33	170	3,750,000
Ikuo Shirahama	68	70	33	171	2,550,000
Seiichi Kanai	68	69	35	172	1,318,750
Isao Aoki	67	69	36	172	1,318,750
Isamu Sugita	66	71	35	172	1,318,750
Teruo Nakamura	70	66	36	172	1,318,750
Shigeru Kawamata	70	70	32	172	1,318,750
Haruo Yasuda	70	67	35	172	1,318,750
Chen Tze Ming	71	64	38	173	806,250
Toru Nakamura	67	71	35	173	806,250
Teruo Sugihara	71	67	36	174	588,000
Seiji Ebihara	71	68	35	174	588,000
Koichi Suzuki	69	68	37	174	588,000
Chuken Kaneko	74	69	31	174	588,000
Takenori Hiraishi	70	69	35	174	588,000
Toshiaki Sudo	71	69	35	175	390,000
Tadao Nakamura	68	71	36	175	390,000
Yoshikazu Yokoshima	70	71	34	175	390,000
Kikuo Arai	70	69	36	175	390,000
Tateo Ozaki	71	70	34	175	390,000
Eiji Kobayashi	71	70	34	175	390,000
Tadami Ueno	72	73	31	176	315,000
Keiji Tejima	73	68	35	176	315,000
Masashi Ozaki	74	68	34	176	315,000
Hideyuki Sato	74	71	31	176	315,000
Futoshi Irino	68	70	38	176	315,000
Hajime Meshiai	69	70	38	177	281,250
Katsuyoshi Tomori	71	73	33	177	281,250
Nozomi Kamatsu	71	71	35	177	281,250
Hiroshi Makino	71	68	38	177	281,250

Mitsubishi Galant

Ohnuma Lake Golf Club, Morimachi   May 26-29
Par 72; 7,000 yards   purse, ¥56,000,000

	SCORES				TOTAL	MONEY
Brian Jones	68	68	67	68	271	¥10,080,000
Naomichi Ozaki	68	69	65	69	271	5,600,000
(Jones defeated Ozaki on first hole of playoff.)						
Yoshikazu Yokoshima	73	66	64	69	272	3,808,000
David Ishii	69	67	69	71	276	2,314,666
Isao Aoki	68	69	70	69	276	2,314,666
Toru Nakamura	72	68	67	69	276	2,314,666
Hiroshi Ishii	68	68	74	67	277	1,792,000
Shigeru Kawamata	70	71	68	69	278	1,624,000
Katsunari Takahashi	71	70	68	71	280	1,456,000
Ikuo Shirahama	71	70	68	72	281	1,204,000
Toshimitsu Kai	74	69	68	70	281	1,204,000

	SCORES			TOTAL	MONEY
Motomasa Aoki	74	71	68	69	282	948,000
Tateo Ozaki	74	68	70	70	282	948,000
Katsuji Hasegawa	70	72	71	69	282	948,000
Haruo Yasuda	73	72	72	66	283	806,400
Takeshi Kitashiro	69	70	74	71	284	636,160
Atsushi Murota	72	70	71	71	284	636,160
Kikuo Arai	75	70	65	74	284	636,160
Kinpachi Yoshimura	73	69	70	72	284	636,160
Hsieh Min Nan	76	66	73	69	284	636,160
Tohru Nakayama	66	72	75	72	285	486,400
Masaru Yamano	73	67	71	74	285	486,400
Norio Mikami	72	70	71	72	285	486,400
Hiroshi Makino	73	70	71	71	285	486,400
Yoshiyuki Isomura	67	74	72	72	285	486,400
Seiichi Kanai	70	70	69	76	285	486,400
Koiichi Uehara	70	73	69	73	285	486,400
Minoru Hatsumi	77	67	71	71	286	404,160
Yoshitake Yamamoto	72	69	76	69	286	404,160
Futoshi Irino	73	70	73	70	286	404,160
Lu Hsi Cheun	71	71	73	71	286	404,160
Gregory Mayer	72	71	72	71	286	404,160
Joji Furuki	69	74	74	69	286	404,160
Chuken Kaneko	71	71	72	72	286	404,160

Sendai Hoso Classic

Omote Zao Kokusai Country Club, Sendai
Par 71; 6,950 yards

June 2-5
purse, ¥45,000,000

(Second round rained out)

	SCORES			TOTAL	MONEY
Masahiro Kuramoto	67	67	70	204	¥6,075,000
Futoshi Irino	66	68	72	206	3,375,000
Masashi Ozaki	66	68	73	207	1,755,000
Noriichi Kawakami	67	68	72	207	1,755,000
David Ishii	70	68	69	207	1,755,000
Teruo Sugihara	66	70	72	208	1,037,812
Seiiji Ebihara	70	68	70	208	1,037,812
Yoshimi Niizeki	70	65	73	208	1,037,812
Takeshi Yoneyama	69	69	70	208	1,037,812
Toshiaki Nakagawa	67	72	70	209	776,250
Koiichi Suzuki	69	68	73	210	648,000
Haruo Yasuda	67	69	74	210	648,000
Shinsaku Maeda	70	70	71	211	486,000
Minoru Hatsumi	67	72	72	211	486,000
Keiji Tejima	72	68	71	211	486,000
Kazuo Kanayama	69	73	69	211	486,000
Tsukasa Watanabe	69	69	73	211	486,000
Hsieh Min Nan	75	69	68	212	321,468
Chen Tze Ming	72	72	68	212	321,468
Eitaro Deguchi	69	72	71	212	321,468
Yutaka Hagawa	73	68	71	212	321,468
Naomichi Ozaki	72	71	69	212	321,468
Nobumitsu Yuhara	67	74	71	212	321,468
Norihiko Matsumoto	72	69	71	212	321,468
Taiijiro Tanaka	72	69	71	212	321,468
Brian Jones	69	70	74	213	259,875

	SCORES			TOTAL	MONEY
Craig Parry	69	69	75	213	259,875
Hajim Meshiai	70	70	73	213	259,875
Kikuo Arai	69	71	73	213	259,875
Lu Hsi Chuen	72	72	69	213	259,875
Shoichi Sato	67	74	72	213	259,875

Sapporo-Tokyu Open

Sapporo Kokusai Country Club, Hiroshimacho   June 9-12
Par 72; 6,949 yards   purse, ¥50,000,000

	SCORES				TOTAL	MONEY
Naomichi Ozaki	70	74	64	71	279	¥9,000,000
Tateo Ozaki	71	70	69	72	282	5,000,000
David Ishii	69	70	71	73	283	2,900,000
Yoshimi Niizeki	72	71	66	74	283	2,900,000
Katsuyoshi Timori	70	72	70	73	285	1,900,000
Koichi Suzuki	70	72	69	74	285	1,900,000
Ian Baker-Finch	73	72	65	76	286	1,525,000
Masahiro Kuramoto	70	68	74	74	286	1,525,000
Gregory Mayer	68	74	70	75	287	1,150,000
Atsushi Murota	72	71	71	73	287	1,150,000
Satoshi Furuyama	73	68	71	75	287	1,150,000
Katsunari Takahashi	70	69	72	77	288	880,000
Hajime Meshiai	66	74	70	78	288	880,000
Masashiro Shiota	74	72	67	76	289	664,000
Tadao Nakamura	72	75	67	75	289	664,000
Tsukasa Watanabe	74	66	76	73	289	664,000
Graham Marsh	71	73	72	73	289	664,000
Norio Adachi	72	72	70	75	289	664,000
Toru Nakamura	74	71	71	74	290	464,285
Namio Takasu	72	74	73	71	290	464,285
Eitaro Deguchi	70	76	73	71	290	464,285
Ikuo Shirahama	72	73	73	72	290	464,285
Seiichi Kanai	69	74	75	72	290	464,285
Brian Jones	72	73	71	74	290	464,285
Takeshi Kitashiro	74	73	67	76	290	464,285
Kinpachi Yoshimura	77	70	72	72	291	405,000
Futoshi Irino	70	72	70	79	291	405,000
Ichiro Teramoto	73	73	73	73	292	365,333
Seiichi Koizumi	74	73	72	73	292	365,333
Chen Tze Ming	71	73	74	74	292	365,333
Seiiki Okuda	70	73	75	74	292	365,333
Niromichi Namiki	72	74	73	73	292	365,333
Yoshihisa Takasaka	74	72	70	76	292	365,333

Yomiuri Sapporo Beer Open

Yomiuri Country Club, Nishinomiya   June 16-19
Par 72; 7,023 yards   purse, ¥70,000,000

	SCORES				TOTAL	MONEY
Masahiro Kuramoto	68	66	74	69	277	¥12,600,000
Yoshikazu Yokoshima	69	72	70	70	281	5,040,000

	SCORES				TOTAL	MONEY
Ian Baker-Finch	67	72	68	74	281	5,040,000
Tsukawa Watanabe	70	67	71	73	281	5,040,000
Seiichi Kanai	71	69	72	70	282	2,520,000
Nobuo Serizawa	68	74	69	71	282	2,520,000
Graham Marsh	71	70	72	69	282	2,520,000
Chen Tze Ming	69	76	69	69	283	1,925,000
Masahiro Shiota	72	69	70	72	283	1,925,000
Satoshi Higashi	73	72	70	70	285	1,610,000
Masaru Amano	69	74	67	76	286	964,727
Tohru Nakamura	72	74	71	69	286	964,727
Kazuhiro Takami	71	74	68	73	286	964,727
Shinsaku Maeda	70	72	72	72	286	964,727
Katsunari Takahashi	73	71	70	72	286	964,727
Hajime Meshiai	72	71	69	74	286	964,727
Yoshihisa Takasaka	74	72	68	72	286	964,727
Taisei Inagaki	72	71	71	72	286	964,727
Toshiaki Sudo	72	72	70	72	286	964,727
Katsuji Hasegawa	67	72	74	73	286	964,727
Eitaro Deguchi	70	72	72	72	286	964,727
Ichiro Teramoto	76	68	74	69	287	590,000
Kinpachi Yoshimura	71	73	73	70	287	590,000
Teruo Sugihara	71	72	72	72	287	590,000
Hiroshi Makino	72	71	73	71	287	590,000
Haruo Yasuda	73	72	75	67	287	590,000
Tomohiro Maruyama	68	73	72	74	287	590,000
Ikuo Shirahama	75	69	70	73	287	590,000
Yoshihisa Iwashita	71	74	72	71	288	498,400
Taiichi Nakagawa	70	74	71	73	288	498,400
Naomichi Ozaki	70	71	73	74	288	498,400
Seiiki Okuda	75	66	72	75	288	498,400
Yoshimi Niizeki	70	72	73	73	288	498,400
Kenji Tokuyama	69	73	73	73	288	498,400

Mizuno Open

Tokinodai Country Club, Hakui
Par 72; 6,766 yards

June 23-26
purse, ¥60,000,000

	SCORES				TOTAL	MONEY
Yoshimi Niizeki	69	74	68	69	280	¥10,800,000
Seiichi Kanai	69	72	71	68	280	6,000,000
(Niizeki defeated Kanai on first hole of playoff.)						
Hiroshi Makino	70	73	68	70	281	3,120,000
Masashi Ozaki	70	70	75	66	281	3,120,000
Nobuo Serizawa	70	70	70	71	281	3,120,000
Shigeru Kawamata	69	73	69	71	282	2,040,000
Akira Kawamata	71	73	66	72	282	2,040,000
Fujio Kobayashi	72	66	72	73	283	1,396,800
Hajime Meshiai	69	74	70	70	283	1,396,800
David Ishii	71	72	68	72	283	1,396,800
Atsushi Murota	71	72	70	70	283	1,396,800
Teruo Sugihara	73	67	72	71	283	1,396,800
Shinsaku Maeda	70	71	72	71	284	1,008,000
Yoshikazu Yokoshima	74	73	69	69	285	796,800
Ian Baker-Finch	71	74	70	70	285	796,800
Yoshitaka Yamamoto	72	71	69	73	285	796,800
Tsuneyuki Nakajima	71	70	75	69	285	796,800

	SCORES				TOTAL	MONEY
Tsutomu Irie	71	71	68	75	285	796,800
Satoshi Higashi	70	71	74	71	286	624,000
Shigeru Uchida	68	72	72	75	287	554,400
Katsuji Hasegawa	71	71	74	71	287	554,400
Lu Chien Soon	73	69	70	75	287	554,400
Saburo Fujiki	69	72	69	77	287	554,400
Chen Tze Ming	73	73	73	68	287	554,400
Osamu Watanabe	76	72	70	70	288	498,000
Eitaro Deguchi	69	74	72	73	288	498,000
Yoshihisa Takasaka	73	74	72	70	289	456,000
Norio Mikami	72	74	72	71	289	456,000
Ikuo Shirahama	71	73	69	76	289	456,000
Taiichi Nakagawa	73	74	70	72	289	456,000
Kazuo Kanayama	76	72	71	70	289	456,000

Kansai PGA Championship

Sport Shinko Country Club, Kiwanishi
Par 72; 6,850 yards

June 30-July 3
purse, ¥30,000,000

	SCORES				TOTAL	MONEY
Masahiro Kuramoto	71	69	68	68	276	¥5,400,000
Yurio Akitomi	73	68	70	66	277	2,520,000
Norio Mikami	70	67	68	72	277	2,520,000
Tadao Nakamura	72	66	70	70	278	1,440,000
Toshimitsu Kai	68	70	71	70	279	1,140,000
Thoru Nakamura	71	71	67	70	279	1,140,000
Toyotake Nakao	70	70	71	70	281	870,000
Teruo Nakamura	71	66	74	70	281	870,000
Katsuyoshi Tomori	73	73	69	66	281	870,000
Kinpachi Yoshimura	72	72	70	68	282	645,000
Yoichi Yamamoto	69	67	73	73	282	645,000
Takeshi Kitashiro	70	68	72	73	283	508,000
Eitaro Deguchi	67	73	69	74	283	508,000
Yoshitaka Yamamoto	68	71	73	71	283	508,000
Takayoshi Nishikawa	74	69	70	71	284	381,000
Tsutomu Irie	69	74	70	71	284	381,000
Tatsuya Shiraishi	75	69	69	71	284	381,000
Hatsutoshi Sakai	70	70	72	72	284	381,000
Hisashi Terada	76	70	70	69	285	288,000
Kazuo Kanayama	71	71	73	70	285	288,000
Yasuo Sone	71	73	69	72	285	288,000
Keiji Tejima	69	70	72	74	285	288,000
Shozo Miyamoto	74	71	70	70	285	288,000
Isamu Sugita	69	68	74	75	286	240,000
Yoshiyuki Isomura	70	74	70	72	286	240,000
Teruo Suzuki	74	73	69	70	286	240,000
Masayuki Kawamura	73	71	70	72	286	240,000
Shinsaku Maeda	74	71	71	70	286	240,000
Teruo Sugihara	73	71	73	69	286	240,000
Takamasa Sakai	74	71	70	71	286	240,000

Kanto PGA Championship

Narita Springs Country Club, Yamadamachi
Par 72; 7,017 yards

June 30-July 3
purse, ¥40,000,000

	SCORES				TOTAL	MONEY
Tomohiro Maruyama	68	66	73	71	278	¥7,200,000
Futoshi Irino	71	72	69	69	281	3,360,000
Yoshimi Niizeki	70	73	67	71	281	3,360,000
Shigeru Kawamata	68	73	70	71	282	1,920,000
Tsuneyuki Nakajima	74	72	68	69	283	1,600,000
Hideyuki Sato	73	72	74	65	284	1,440,000
Seiji Ebihara	70	73	69	73	285	1,160,000
Chen Tze Ming	70	75	68	72	285	1,160,000
Hajime Meshiai	73	69	72	71	285	1,160,000
Satoshi Higashi	71	70	74	72	287	782,000
Masaji Kusakabe	71	73	70	73	287	782,000
Haruo Yasuda	69	76	72	70	287	782,000
Hiroshi Makino	69	72	69	77	287	782,000
Ikuo Shirahama	72	76	70	70	288	600,000
Saburo Fujiki	72	73	68	75	288	600,000
Tateo Ozaki	71	78	71	69	289	454,400
Yoshinori Mizumaki	72	70	73	74	289	454,400
Yoshikzu Yokoshima	76	71	73	69	289	454,400
Takahiro Sekine	74	71	73	71	289	454,400
Ichiro Ino	70	73	73	73	289	454,400
Masashi Ozaki	70	79	70	71	290	368,000
Minoru Hatsumi	74	76	69	71	290	368,000
Eiichi Itai	70	72	75	73	290	368,000
Koichi Suzuki	72	75	74	70	291	332,000
Katsunari Takahashi	75	73	74	69	291	332,000
Noboru Sugai	71	76	73	71	291	332,000
Yoshinori Kaneko	72	73	69	77	291	332,000
Koji Nakajima	73	76	74	69	292	304,000
Naomichi Ozaki	71	73	73	75	292	304,000
Shuichi Sano	73	74	74	71	292	304,000

Hiroshima Open

Hiroshima Golf Club, Hiroshima
Par 72; 6,865 yards

July 7-10
purse, ¥40,000,000

	SCORES				TOTAL	MONEY
Hajime Matsui	69	71	66	68	274	¥7,200,000
Katsuyoshi Tomori	70	67	69	69	275	4,000,000
Tadao Nakamura	68	69	70	69	276	2,720,000
Shigeru Kawamata	70	71	68	68	277	1,760,000
Yoshimi Niizeki	71	70	70	66	277	1,760,000
Futoshi Irie	73	69	69	67	278	963,555
Toshimitsu Kai	70	68	70	70	278	963,555
Yoshihisa Iwashita	72	68	67	71	278	963,555
Tadami Ueno	68	69	71	70	278	963,555
Akira Yabe	70	69	68	71	278	963,555
Hiroshi Makino	69	68	70	71	278	963,555
Tommy Nakajima	72	70	65	71	278	963,555
Yoshikazu Yokoshima	67	71	69	71	278	963,555
Kinpachi Yoshimura	71	69	70	68	278	963,555
Masanobu Kimura	70	72	72	65	279	552,000

	SCORES				TOTAL	MONEY
Teruo Sugihara	69	64	72	74	279	552,000
Toshiaki Sudo	65	73	72	70	280	448,000
Atsushi Murota	73	70	69	68	280	448,000
Katsunari Takahashi	72	68	69	71	280	448,000
Seiiki Okuda	72	67	69	73	281	354,000
Yoshitaka Yamamoto	71	72	71	67	281	354,000
Joji Furuki	72	71	65	73	281	354,000
Yoshihisa Takasaka	69	73	70	69	281	354,000
Tateo Ozaki	73	70	70	68	281	354,000
Eiichi Itai	68	71	71	71	281	354,000
Tsukasa Watanabe	70	73	68	70	281	354,000
Takeshi Shibata	72	72	67	70	281	354,000
Seiichi Kanai	68	72	70	72	282	288,685
Teruo Nakamura	69	69	72	72	282	288,685
Yutaka Hagawa	68	74	68	72	282	288,685
Takayoshi Nishikawa	73	68	70	71	282	288,685
Noamichi Ozaki	68	71	74	69	282	288,685
Kazuo Kanayama	72	71	69	70	282	288,685
Nobuo Serizawa	72	71	71	68	282	288,685

Japan PGA Championship

Ehime Golf Course, Uchiko   July 21-24
Par 36-36 — 72; 7,010 yards   purse, ¥56,000,000

	SCORES				TOTAL	MONEY
Tateo Ozaki	69	69	66	64	268	¥11,700,000
Masashi Ozaki	67	66	69	67	269	6,500,000
Tsuneyuki Nakajima	67	68	68	68	271	4,420,000
Ikuo Shirahama	68	65	72	67	272	2,860,000
Toshimitsu Kai	68	68	67	69	272	2,860,000
Tomohiro Maruyama	72	66	68	68	274	2,340,000
Yoshikazu Yokoshima	68	70	65	72	275	2,080,000
Minoru Hatsumi	71	68	70	67	276	1,592,500
Haruo Yasuda	70	69	69	68	276	1,592,500
Masanobu Kimura	67	71	71	67	276	1,592,500
Nobuo Serizawa	67	67	69	73	276	1,592,500
Hiroshi Makino	71	69	74	63	277	1,144,000
Yurio Akitomi	66	68	72	71	277	1,144,000
Yoshiyuki Isomura	71	70	71	66	278	897,000
Tadami Ueno	72	68	67	71	278	897,000
Katsunari Takahashi	71	68	70	69	278	897,000
Toru Nakamura	72	69	67	70	278	897,000
Keiji Tejima	68	68	72	71	279	684,666
Hajime Meshiai	71	70	71	67	279	684,666
Teruo Nakamura	70	68	70	71	279	684,666
David Ishii	71	70	70	69	280	588,250
Katsuyoshi Tomori	69	71	71	69	280	588,250
Kazushige Kono	69	73	70	68	280	588,250
Shuichi Sano	75	67	70	68	280	588,250
Ian Baker-Finch	67	72	71	71	281	546,000
Koichi Suzuki	68	71	70	73	282	526,500
Kiyoshi Muroda	67	74	73	68	282	526,500
Futoshi Irino	66	74	72	71	283	481,000
Yoshitaka Yamamoto	67	73	72	71	283	481,000
Motomasa Aoki	67	73	68	75	283	481,000
Seiichi Kanai	68	71	72	72	283	481,000
Tsukasa Watanabe	73	69	69	72	283	481,000

NST Niigata Open

Niigata Sunrise Golf Course, Seiro
Par 36-36 — 72; 7,190 yards

July 28-31
purse, ¥40,000,000

	SCORES				TOTAL	MONEY
Naomichi Ozaki	70	66	69	72	277	¥7,200,000
David Ishii	69	72	67	72	280	4,000,000
Koichi Suzuki	66	73	68	74	281	2,720,000
Hajime Meshiai	72	68	72	71	283	1,920,000
Pete Izumikawa	74	67	69	74	284	1,600,000
Masahiro Kuramoto	72	70	71	72	285	1,168,000
Takeru Shibata	73	68	73	71	285	1,168,000
Kiyoshi Muroda	72	73	73	67	285	1,168,000
Taisei Inagaki	70	74	72	69	285	1,168,000
Seiji Ebihara	71	71	70	73	285	1,168,000
Saburo Fujiki	72	72	74	68	286	736,000
Eitaro Deguchi	73	71	74	68	286	736,000
Nobuo Serizawa	70	71	73	72	286	736,000
Katsuji Hasegawa	68	76	73	70	287	552,000
Chen Tze Ming	69	71	75	72	287	552,000
Tsukasa Watanabe	74	73	73	67	287	552,000
Yoshihisa Iwashita	68	79	69	71	287	552,000
Kazuo Kanayama	71	71	74	72	288	448,000
Kinpachi Yoshimura	70	74	74	71	289	371,428
Tadao Nakamura	71	76	69	73	289	371,428
Tadami Ueno	73	71	74	71	289	371,428
Akira Yabe	71	75	71	72	289	371,428
Shuichi Sano	72	71	74	72	289	371,428
Kikuo Arai	74	72	72	71	289	371,428
Yoshiyuki Isomura	71	72	74	72	289	371,428
Yoshikazu Yokoshima	70	76	74	70	290	312,000
Yoshimi Niizeki	71	71	75	73	290	312,000
Tateo Ozaki	69	75	77	69	290	312,000
Noboru Sugai	71	76	71	72	290	312,000
Satoshi Furuyama	72	75	70	73	290	312,000

Nikkei Cup

Sanyo Golf Club, Yoshii Course, Yoshii
Par 36-36 — 72; 7,298 yards

August 11-14
purse, ¥50,000,000

	SCORES				TOTAL	MONEY
Masashi Ozaki	72	71	72	68	283	¥9,000,000
Naomichi Ozaki	71	68	76	72	287	5,000,000
Yutaka Hagawa	69	71	75	73	288	3,400,000
Harumitsu Hamano	72	73	73	73	291	2,066,666
Yoshiyuki Isomura	76	71	68	76	291	2,066,666
Yoshimi Niizeki	69	74	77	71	291	2,066,666
Junji Matsuzawa	73	72	73	74	292	1,600,000
Akira Yabe	77	70	74	72	293	1,300,000
Yoshinori Kaneko	76	75	72	70	293	1,300,000
Tateo Ozaki	72	74	74	73	293	1,300,000
Fujio Kobayashi	74	73	76	71	294	1,000,000
Joji Furuki	71	73	75	76	295	846,666
Teruo Sugihara	71	72	76	76	295	846,666
Shizuo Mori	72	77	77	69	295	846,666
Isamu Sugita	71	73	77	75	296	562,500

	SCORES				TOTAL	MONEY
Nobuo Serizawa	75	73	73	75	296	562,500
Yoshitaka Yamamoto	71	74	75	76	296	562,500
Hisayuki Sasaki	73	76	73	74	296	562,500
Toru Nakamura	73	75	77	71	296	562,500
Yurio Akitomi	74	75	72	75	296	562,500
Shuichi Sano	72	72	78	74	296	562,500
Masakatsu Sano	81	66	77	72	296	562,500
Saburo Fujiki	74	74	76	73	297	410,000
Kazushige Kono	75	74	72	76	297	410,000
Hisashi Terada	73	74	73	77	297	410,000
Minoru Hatsumi	76	70	75	76	297	410,000
Katsunari Takahashi	75	72	78	72	297	410,000
Masaji Kusakabe	75	74	76	72	297	410,000
Eitaro Deguchi	73	70	76	78	297	410,000
Teruo Nakamura	77	73	73	75	298	347,000
Hiroshi Ueda	75	72	76	75	298	347,000
Mitoshi Tomita	72	74	78	74	298	347,000
Futoshi Irino	76	74	76	72	298	347,000
Katsuji Hasegawa	72	75	75	76	298	347,000
Katsuyoshi Tomori	77	73	77	71	298	347,000

Maruman Open

Higashi Matsuyama Country Club, Higashi Matsuyama
Par 71; 6,624 yards

August 18-21
purse, ¥70,000,000

(First round cancelled, rain.)

	SCORES			TOTAL	MONEY
Masashi Ozaki	73	65	69	207	¥9,450,000
Hajime Meshiai	71	73	66	210	4,410,000
Yoshimi Niizeki	69	73	68	210	4,410,000
Satoru Nishikawa	70	76	65	211	2,310,000
Masahiro Kuramoto	71	72	68	211	2,310,000
Haruo Yasuda	69	65	78	212	1,697,500
Toru Nakamura	70	67	75	212	1,697,500
Seiji Ebihara	68	72	72	212	1,697,500
Hiroshi Makino	74	68	71	213	1,286,250
Ikuo Shirahama	70	70	73	213	1,286,250
Namio Takasu	73	70	71	214	894,600
Katsuyoshi Tomori	70	76	68	214	894,600
Chen Tze Ming	71	73	70	214	894,600
Yoshitaka Yamamoto	71	75	68	214	894,600
Pete Izumikawa	73	73	68	214	894,600
Nobuo Serizawa	71	71	73	215	596,400
Eiichi Itai	70	73	72	215	596,400
Terry Gale	70	74	71	215	596,400
Shuichi Sano	70	75	70	215	596,400
Yutaka Hagawa	74	72	69	215	596,400
Masanobu Kimura	72	70	74	216	444,500
Futoshi Irino	74	70	72	216	444,500
Kiminori Kato	73	72	71	216	444,500
Shinsaku Maeda	71	74	71	216	444,500
Tsutomu Irie	69	77	70	216	444,500
Katsuji Hasegawa	72	73	71	216	444,500
Kazuo Kanayama	71	74	71	216	444,500
Akira Yabe	71	73	72	216	444,500

	SCORES			TOTAL	MONEY
Eitaro Deguchi	76	69	71	216	444,500
Masaji Kusakabe	70	74	73	217	351,400
Katsunari Takahashi	72	71	74	217	351,400
Yoshiyuki Isomura	75	68	74	217	351,400
Hiroaki Uenishi	71	72	74	217	351,400
Noboru Sugai	73	73	71	217	351,400
Takeru Shibata	73	70	74	217	351,400
Isao Isozaki	72	71	74	217	351,400
Keiji Tejima	73	72	72	217	351,400
Naomichi Ozaki	73	70	74	217	351,400

KBC Augusta

Kyushu Shima Country Club, Shima
Par 72; 7,130 yards

August 25-28
purse, ¥50,000,000

	SCORES				TOTAL	MONEY
Masahiro Kuramoto	67	71	65	73	276	¥9,000,000
Hajime Meshiai	65	75	66	72	278	3,600,000
Nobumitsu Yuhara	71	70	68	69	278	3,600,000
Masashi Ozaki	70	68	70	70	278	3,600,000
Chen Tze Ming	71	70	69	69	279	1,900,000
Tateo Ozaki	70	70	68	71	279	1,900,000
Yoshikazu Yokoshima	74	71	69	66	280	1,450,000
Katsuji Hasegawa	72	68	68	72	280	1,450,000
Tomohiro Maruyama	69	71	68	72	280	1,450,000
Pete Izumikawa	66	72	66	77	281	1,075,000
Naomichi Ozaki	68	70	70	73	281	1,075,000
Yoshitaka Yamamoto	71	70	68	73	282	880,000
Yutaka Hagawa	70	72	72	68	282	880,000
Katsunari Takahashi	72	68	73	70	283	750,000
Toru Nakamura	73	70	70	70	283	750,000
Norio Mikami	73	71	69	71	284	630,000
Brian Jones	72	71	71	70	284	630,000
Nobuo Serizawa	71	70	71	73	285	526,666
Tadami Ueno	70	71	68	76	285	526,666
Seiji Ebihara	71	73	70	71	285	526,666
Haruo Yasuda	68	69	73	76	286	480,000
Lu Liang Huan	71	75	68	73	287	421,428
Ikuo Shirahama	71	73	72	71	287	421,428
Kazuo Kanayama	72	70	70	75	287	421,428
Namio Takasu	73	71	75	68	287	421,428
Shigeru Kawamata	69	71	75	72	287	421,428
Koichi Suzuki	74	70	70	73	287	421,428
Masayuki Kawamura	73	73	68	73	287	421,428
Norihiko Matsumoto	73	69	76	70	288	365,000
Tsutomu Irie	70	73	72	73	288	365,000
Shizuo Mori	70	75	69	74	288	365,000
Katsuyoshi Tomori	72	72	70	74	288	365,000

Kansai Open

Kita Rokko Country Club, Kobe
Par 72

September 1-4
purse, ¥20,000,000

	SCORES				TOTAL	MONEY
Yasuo Sone	76	70	70	70	286	¥5,000,000
Shinsaku Maeda	75	75	70	69	289	2,500,000
Toru Nakamura	75	70	73	72	290	1,300,000
Osamu Watanabe	76	74	70	72	292	1,000,000
Teruo Sugihara	76	73	71	72	292	1,000,000
Takenori Hiraishi	73	73	75	73	294	700,000
Keiichi Kobayashi	77	73	74	70	294	700,000
Yuzou Oyama	78	72	72	72	294	700,000
Yoshitaka Yamamoto	75	74	75	71	295	550,000
Kazuo Kanayama	73	73	75	75	296	500,000
Shozo Miyamoto	74	74	76	73	297	400,000
Masakatsu Sano	77	74	74	72	297	400,000
Tatsuo Nakagami	73	79	73	72	297	400,000
Yoichi Yamamoto	76	72	71	79	298	275,000
Yoshiyuki Isomura	78	75	73	72	298	275,000
Toshimitsu Kai	80	73	71	75	299	200,000
Mikio Nakamatsu	74	72	78	75	299	200,000
Hisashi Terada	72	77	78	73	300	200,000
Toshiaki Nakagawa	75	75	80	71	301	186,666
Yoshio Ichikawa	79	73	75	74	301	186,666
Hiroya Kamide	78	74	76	73	301	186,666
Kosaku Shimada	80	74	75	73	302	160,000
Toshiya Shibutani	74	74	78	76	302	160,000
Mitsuhiro Kitsuta	78	75	74	75	302	160,000
Takeshi Matsukawa	76	77	76	74	303	160,000
Masaaki Shiraishi	76	78	78	72	304	130,000
Hisao Inoue	78	71	77	78	304	130,000
Koki Idori	74	74	78	78	304	130,000

Kanto Open

Edozaki Country Club, Ibaraki Prefecture
Par 70; 6,869 yards

September 1-4
purse, ¥30,000,000

	SCORES				TOTAL	MONEY
Akihito Yokoyama	70	66	67	75	278	¥6,000,000
Nobumitsu Yuhara	69	73	70	72	284	2,400,000
Tomohiro Maruyama	72	72	69	71	284	2,400,000
Seiichi Kanai	72	73	69	71	285	1,200,000
Koichi Suzuki	70	70	71	75	286	862,500
Seiji Ebihara	75	72	67	72	286	862,500
Hajime Meshiai	73	71	71	71	286	862,500
Katsuji Hasegawa	70	65	73	78	286	862,500
Yutaka Hagawa	66	74	74	73	287	700,000
Naomichi Ozaki	70	70	72	76	288	625,000
Haruo Yasuda	72	71	73	72	288	625,000
Yoshinori Mizumaki	69	76	71	73	289	570,000
Seiichi Koizumi	73	74	70	73	290	540,000
Hiroshi Makino	67	74	72	78	291	495,000
Akira Yabe	72	72	74	73	291	495,000
Yoshimi Watanabe	75	74	72	71	292	412,000
Kiyoshi Muroda	75	72	71	74	292	412,000

	SCORES				TOTAL	MONEY
Junji Matsuzawa	68	73	73	78	292	412,000
Hsieh Min Nan	73	76	70	73	292	412,000
Hideki Kase	75	72	72	73	292	412,000
Shigeru Kawamata	76	72	73	72	293	345,000
Harumitsu Hamano	71	70	77	75	293	345,000
Takao Kage	76	74	71	72	293	345,000
Saburo Fujiki	71	71	72	79	293	345,000
Fujio Kobayashi	73	73	75	72	293	345,000
Tsukasa Watanabe	71	72	75	75	293	345,000
Pete Izumikawa	72	75	76	71	294	305,000
Tateo Ozaki	77	72	73	72	294	305,000
Kikuo Arai	70	73	74	78	295	265,000
Toshiaki Sudo	72	73	75	75	295	265,000
Yoshio Fumiyama	75	75	73	72	295	265,000
Toru Nakayama	76	69	74	76	295	265,000
Yoshikazu Yokoshima	74	71	73	77	295	265,000
Akira Kawamata	71	69	75	80	295	265,000

Kyushu Open

Oita Country Club
Par 72

September 1-4
purse, ¥15,000,000

	SCORES				TOTAL	MONEY
Katsuyoshi Tomori	71	70	70	72	283	¥4,000,000
(Unidentified amateur)	72	76	64	74	286	
Misao Yamamoto	71	70	70	78	289	1,025,000
Kinpachi Yoshimura	70	74	73	72	289	1,025,000
Keiji Tejima	71	74	69	76	290	650,000
Isamu Sugita	74	76	70	73	293	550,000
Atsushi Ikehara	76	70	67	81	294	400,000
Yurio Akitomi	74	70	72	78	294	400,000
Yoshinori Onishi	71	76	70	77	294	400,000
Shinji Kuraoka	76	72	75	72	295	300,000
Chikara Nagata	74	72	75	75	296	200,000
Yoshihiro Hori	72	75	74	75	296	200,000
Tadashige Kusano	75	73	74	74	296	200,000
Kuniharu Nakagawahara	77	76	70	73	296	200,000
Toshiomi Inaga	73	76	74	74	297	155,000
Kosei Sakai	72	76	73	76	297	155,000
Tsugiomi Takita	72	72	77	77	298	140,000
Norikazu Kawakami	81	71	69	78	299	108,333
Yoshihito Murayama	77	74	72	76	299	108,333
Mineyuki Yoshimatsu	71	74	79	75	299	108,333
Sadatoshi Makimura	71	75	76	77	299	108,333

Chubu Open

Myoshi Country Club, Nagoya
Par 72

September 1-4
purse, ¥15,000,000

	SCORES				TOTAL	MONEY
Teruo Nakamura	66	72	69	72	279	¥4,000,000
Akimitsu Tokita	71	70	73	72	286	1,600,000

	SCORES				TOTAL	MONEY
Masahiro Shioda	71	72	71	72	286	1,600,000
Yutaka Suzuki	73	74	68	73	288	683,333
Kakuji Matsui	72	74	71	71	288	683,333
Masami Ito	67	72	76	73	288	683,333
Hisashi Suzumura	72	72	71	75	290	425,000
Tadao Nakamura	72	75	71	72	290	425,000
Mitsuaki Kondo	71	73	71	76	291	350,000
Takuo Terashima	73	74	70	75	292	275,000
Hiroaki Uenishi	72	78	70	72	292	275,000
Hideaki Yamashita	71	73	74	77	295	193,333
Kazumasa Tamura	69	75	76	75	295	193,333
Koichi Inoue	72	73	75	75	295	193,333
Tomio Araki	70	77	73	76	296	160,000
Takeru Shibata	75	71	75	75	296	160,000
Eitaro Deguchi	74	76	76	70	296	160,000
Tetsuro Yoshikawa	73	76	73	75	297	125,000
Hiroshi Ishii	77	73	72	75	297	125,000
Yoshihisa Kosaka	73	68	77	79	297	125,000
Chen Chien Chin	73	72	72	80	297	125,000
Muneyoshi Nakayama	75	73	72	78	298	110,000
Koji Ota	77	74	75	72	298	110,000
Norihiko Matsumoto	72	72	77	78	299	110,000
Mitsuo Hirukawa	76	75	74	74	299	110,000
Kazutomo Niwa	75	75	74	76	300	100,000
Saburo Hayashi	78	73	75	74	300	100,000
Shoichi Yamamoto	74	75	74	77	300	100,000
Motoi Nakamura	72	74	76	79	301	96,666
Masamitsu Oguri	73	74	80	74	301	96,666
Jun Hattori	77	73	72	79	301	96,666

Chu-Shikoku Open

Hakuryuko Country Club, Hiroshima
Par 72

September 1-4
purse, ¥15,000,000

	SCORES				TOTAL	MONEY
Masahiro Kuramoto	67	63	65	71	266	¥4,000,000
Tadami Ueno	70	72	72	65	279	2,000,000
Takashi Miyoshi	69	72	70	69	280	1,200,000
Seiki Okuda	72	68	69	72	281	800,000
Takafumi Ogawa	67	72	71	72	282	562,500
Kiminori Kato	69	70	70	73	282	562,500
Tsukasa Watanabe	69	73	68	72	282	562,500
Norio Mikami	74	66	69	73	282	562,500
Hideto Shigenobu	71	73	70	69	283	375,000
Hideo Hashimoto	67	73	70	73	283	375,000
Yoshihiro Miyanaka	73	71	71	69	284	265,000
Nobuhiro Yoshino	72	73	69	70	284	265,000
Kazuki Nagao	71	70	73	72	286	190,000
Koji Inaba	68	71	73	74	286	190,000
Mitoshi Tomita	73	74	70	69	286	190,000
Nobuo Sato	66	72	74	75	287	160,000
Kenji Sogame	74	70	72	71	287	160,000
Takeshi Nakaya	73	71	73	70	287	160,000
Masami Seto	68	74	74	72	288	140,000
Yasuhiro Daio	71	74	72	72	289	130,000
Katsumi Hara	72	70	74	74	290	120,000

	SCORES				TOTAL	MONEY
Naoki Kotani	74	69	72	77	292	120,000
Mitsuhiko Masuda	73	75	70	74	292	120,000
Yoshikazu Sakamoto	72	74	74	73	293	110,000
Kazuo Yamamoto	73	74	71	75	293	110,000
Masami Nishiyama	74	73	71	75	293	110,000
Yasuyuki Sawai	72	70	80	71	293	110,000
Tsuyoshi Sato	71	74	75	74	294	100,000
Kosei Miyata	75	70	78	72	295	100,000
Seiichi Suzuki	76	70	78	71	295	100,000

Hokkaido Open

Sapporo Elm Country Club
Par 72

September 2-4
purse, ¥10,000,000

	SCORES				TOTAL	MONEY
Mamoru Takahashi	72	70	71	67	280	¥3,000,000
Katsunari Takahashi	69	70	68	73	280	1,500,000
(Mamoru Takahashi defeated Katsunari Takahashi in playoff.)						
Shoichi Sato	71	68	71	71	281	1,000,000
Koichi Uehara	70	75	71	69	285	600,000
Akihiko Kojima	73	75	67	71	286	450,000
Namio Takasu	72	72	70	73	287	400,000
Toshinori Horiki	75	71	74	71	291	250,000
Hiroshi Yamada	73	73	73	74	293	210,000
Kesahiko Uchida	72	76	71	74	293	210,000
Kazuhiro Takami	74	74	74	74	296	180,000
Yoshiyuki Omori	72	76	72	77	297	130,000
Fumio Tanaka	75	74	76	72	297	130,000
Masaaki Fujii	72	76	76	73	297	130,000
Kenji Takeda	78	73	73	73	297	130,000
Hiroshi Todate	75	77	71	75	298	130,000
Mitsuyoshi Goto	75	73	78	73	299	100,000
Toshiaki Nakamura	76	73	76	75	300	100,000
Susumu Mori	73	74	74	79	300	100,000
Masaaki Shiraishi	72	75	78	76	301	100,000
Shinji Kubota	77	76	77	72	302	100,000
Yasutomo Ishii	74	71	78	79	302	100,000
Yoshiharu Takai	77	75	73	78	303	100,000
Kanae Nobechi	77	74	74	79	304	100,000
Saoshi Sudo	72	79	77	76	304	100,000
Ryoichi Takamoto	76	75	73	80	304	100,000
Masaru Sato	79	72	80	74	305	100,000
Masaaki Yamamoto	76	77	80	73	306	100,000
Kenji Noma	79	71	74	82	306	100,000
Noritaka Shiraishi	80	75	77	74	306	100,000
Kazumi Takai	73	78	80	77	308	100,000
Masami Hashimoto	79	71	79	79	308	100,000

Suntory Open

Narashino Country Club, Inzaimachi
Par 72; 7,100 yards

September 8-11
purse, ¥80,000,000

	SCORES				TOTAL	MONEY
Tateo Ozaki	67	71	68	68	274	¥14,400,000
Tadami Ueno	69	68	70	70	277	8,000,000
Brian Jones	70	68	69	71	278	4,640,000
Hajime Meshiai	69	68	71	70	278	4,640,000
Masahiro Kuramoto	68	69	70	72	279	3,200,000
Pete Izumikawa	70	70	73	68	281	2,720,000
Seiichi Kanai	71	70	70	70	281	2,720,000
Nobumitsu Yuhara	70	74	66	72	282	2,320,000
Chen Tze Chung	73	66	73	71	283	1,748,000
Naomichi Ozaki	70	69	71	73	283	1,748,000
Teruo Sugihara	66	77	69	71	283	1,748,000
Yutaka Hagawa	69	68	73	73	283	1,748,000
Hisao Inoue	70	72	72	71	285	1,248,000
Toshimitsu Kai	71	73	71	70	285	1,248,000
Toru Nakamura	69	73	71	72	285	1,248,000
Shoichi Sato	67	73	69	77	286	970,666
Isao Aoki	75	69	70	72	286	970,666
Larry Mize	73	69	73	71	286	970,666
Kiyoshi Muroda	72	70	70	75	287	784,000
Taichiro Kanatani	73	71	70	73	287	784,000
Eitaro Deguchi	72	72	69	74	287	784,000
Takenori Hiraishi	68	71	72	76	287	784,000
Tsuyoshi Yoneyama	76	68	73	71	288	664,000
Keiji Tejima	71	70	71	76	288	664,000
Yurio Akitomi	73	70	74	71	288	664,000
Norio Mikami	71	73	72	72	288	664,000
David Ishii	72	70	73	73	288	664,000
Masashi Ozaki	70	72	69	77	288	664,000
Masanobu Kimura	68	71	73	77	289	592,000
Shuichi Sano	71	73	67	78	289	592,000
Yoshitaka Yamamoto	72	70	75	72	289	592,000

All Nippon Airways Open

Sapporo Golf Club, Yunicho
Par 72; 7,031 yards

September 15-18
purse, ¥70,000,000

	SCORES				TOTAL	MONEY
Naomichi Ozaki	63	69	73	73	278	¥12,600,000
Brian Jones	70	68	69	71	278	7,000,000
(Ozaki defeated Jones on third hole of playoff.)						
Masashi Ozaki	68	66	73	72	279	4,760,000
Kinpachi Yoshimura	71	67	69	73	280	3,360,000
Tsuneyuki Nakajima	73	68	70	72	283	2,660,000
David Ishii	69	70	72	72	283	2,660,000
Namio Takasu	70	74	72	69	285	2,240,000
Yoshikazu Yokoshima	72	69	76	70	287	2,030,000
Satoshi Higashi	73	73	70	72	288	1,610,000
Yoshiyuki Isomura	69	73	73	73	288	1,610,000
Kiyoshi Maita	70	72	76	70	288	1,610,000
Nobumitsu Yuhara	71	74	71	73	289	1,288,000
Shinsaku Maeda	72	75	72	71	290	1,040,400

	SCORES				TOTAL	MONEY
Noboru Sugai	73	72	71	74	290	1,040,400
Koichi Suzuki	73	74	71	72	290	1,040,400
Eduardo Herrera	72	70	75	73	290	1,040.400
Taichiro Kanatani	71	70	72	77	290	1,040,400
Hiroshi Makino	75	70	76	70	291	717,500
Masanobu Kimura	71	70	75	75	291	717,500
Haruo Yasuda	72	75	72	72	291	717,500
Eitaro Deguchi	72	76	70	73	291	717,500
Chen Tze Chung	74	74	73	71	292	620,666
Saburo Fujiki	72	72	76	72	292	620,666
Tomohiro Maruyama	72	71	75	74	292	620,666
Toru Nakamura	74	72	74	73	293	553,000
Yoshio Fumiyama	69	75	75	74	293	553,000
Chen Tze Ming	70	74	73	76	293	553,000
Tateo Ozaki	77	70	76	70	293	553,000
Yoshimi Niizeki	70	73	75	75	293	553,000
Hajime Meshiai	69	68	75	81	293	553,000

Jun Classic

Jun Classic Country Club, Ogawamachi
Par 72; 7,087 yards

September 22-25
purse, ¥65,000,000

(Final round shortened to nine holes - rain)

	SCORES				TOTAL	MONEY
Toru Nakamura	68	68	69	35	240	¥11,700,000
Nobuo Serizawa	70	69	69	36	244	6,500,000
Hiroshi Makino	70	68	74	34	246	4,420,000
Masahiro Kuramoto	70	72	71	34	247	2,860,000
Chen Tze Ming	72	67	73	35	247	2,860,000
Naomichi Ozaki	67	72	73	36	248	2,340,000
Takeru Shibata	70	71	72	36	249	1,690,000
Taisei Inagaki	69	66	77	37	249	1,690,000
Isao Aoki	69	70	74	36	249	1,690,000
Greg Norman	72	64	76	37	249	1,690,000
Tadao Nakamura	70	71	73	35	249	1,690,000
Yoshinori Kaneko	71	70	72	37	250	1,144,000
David Ishii	69	71	73	37	250	1,144,000
Hsieh Min Nan	71	73	71	36	251	897,000
Nobumitsu Yuhara	73	74	71	33	251	897,000
Masashi Ozaki	67	71	76	37	251	897,000
Satoshi Higashi	72	71	73	35	251	897,000
Terry Gale	72	73	69	38	252	702,000
Koichi Suzuki	73	70	71	38	252	702,000
Brian Jones	67	71	76	39	253	611,000
Isamu Sugita	68	71	77	37	253	611,000
Chen Tze Chung	66	73	73	41	253	611,000
Masanobu Kimura	74	72	71	36	253	611,000
Toshimitsu Kai	73	72	72	37	254	559,000
Seiji Ebihara	72	71	72	40	255	507,000
Namio Takasu	70	73	74	38	255	507,000
Hideto Shigenobu	70	72	76	37	255	507,000
Yutaka Hagawa	72	72	76	35	255	507,000
Kikuo Arai	72	72	74	37	255	507,000
Tsuneyuki Nakajima	73	70	70	42	255	507,000
Ikuo Shirahama	71	72	74	38	255	507,000

Tokai Classic

Miyoshi Country Club, West Course, Miyoshicho
Par 72; 7,065 yards

September 29-October 2
purse, ¥90,000,000

	SCORES				TOTAL	MONEY
Brian Jones	69	69	71	65	274	¥10,800,000
Koichi Suzuki	68	73	70	66	277	6,000,000
Curtis Strange	70	69	70	70	279	4,080,000
Yutaka Hagawa	68	72	70	71	281	2,640,000
Graham Marsh	69	65	75	72	281	2,640,000
Yoshitaka Yamamoto	71	68	70	74	283	1,940,000
Chen Tze Chung	66	74	72	71	283	1,940,000
David Ishii	70	72	70	71	283	1,940,000
Tsukasa Watanabe	73	74	66	71	284	1,560,000
Katsunari Takahashi	71	70	71	73	285	1,380,000
Taisei Inagaki	76	70	70	70	286	1,062,000
Tom Kite	72	67	73	74	286	1,062,000
Yoshinori Kaneko	71	74	72	69	286	1,062,000
Masahiro Kuramoto	68	72	74	72	286	1,062,000
Teruo Sugihara	69	72	73	73	287	828,000
Akihito Yokoyama	73	69	74	71	287	828,000
Seiichi Kanai	73	72	75	68	288	696,000
Nobumitsu Yuhara	71	73	72	72	288	696,000
Taichiro Kanatani	71	73	71	74	289	576,000
Tadami Ueno	72	74	71	72	289	576,000
Saburo Fujiki	71	71	76	71	289	576,000
Teruo Nakamura	73	73	71	72	289	576,000
Hsieh Min Nan	73	67	74	75	289	576,000
Masashi Ozaki	73	68	77	72	290	492,000
Koichi Uehara	71	75	75	69	290	492,000
Naomichi Ozaki	74	73	75	68	290	492,000
Haruo Yasuda	71	72	75	72	290	492,000
Hiroshi Ishii	73	72	76	69	290	492,000
Masanobu Kimura	70	75	74	72	291	438,000
Katsuji Hasegawa	68	75	75	73	291	438,000
Kiyoshi Maita	71	71	75	74	291	438,000
Toshiki Matsui	71	74	74	72	291	438,000

Japan Open

Tokyo Golf Club, Sayama
Par 71; 6,923 yards

October 6-9
purse, ¥60,000,000

	SCORES				TOTAL	MONEY
Masashi Ozaki	67	73	75	73	288	¥10,000,000
Isao Aoki	74	69	73	73	289	5,000,000
Tsuneyuki Nakajima	75	68	71	75	289	5,000,000
Masaru Amano	75	73	76	66	290	2,566,666
Katsuyoshi Tomori	74	70	72	74	290	2,566,666
David Ishii	73	70	74	73	290	2,566,666
Katsunari Takahashi	72	76	72	71	291	1,900,000
Eitaro Deguchi	79	71	69	72	291	1,900,000
Koichi Uehara	75	71	71	75	292	1,450,000
Naomichi Ozaki	77	69	73	73	292	1,450,000
Tomohiro Maruyama	75	72	73	72	292	1,450,000
Yoshinori Kaneko	74	75	70	73	292	1,450,000
Norio Mikami	73	68	77	75	293	1,150,000

	SCORES				TOTAL	MONEY
Ikuo Shirahama	77	73	72	71	293	1,150,000
Hiromichi Namiki	71	72	76	75	294	950,000
Tom Kite	72	73	79	70	294	950,000
Toru Nakayama	76	75	73	71	295	750,000
Hideki Kase	74	73	74	74	295	750,000
Greg Bruckner	74	73	79	71	297	575,000
Seiichi Kanai	76	73	75	73	297	575,000
Chen Tze Ming	75	76	72	74	297	575,000
Hideto Shigenobu	78	68	75	76	297	575,000
Kinpachi Yoshimura	69	73	73	82	297	575,000
Toru Nakamura	75	72	76	74	297	575,000
Taisei Inagaki	76	75	73	74	298	485,000
Toshiaki Sudo	73	77	77	71	298	485,000
Masahiro Kuramoto	73	74	73	78	298	485,000
Akihito Yokoyama	77	70	74	77	298	485,000
Tadao Nakamura	73	72	75	79	299	455,000
Frankie Minoza	75	73	75	76	299	455,000
Haruo Yasuda	73	74	77	76	300	435,000
Fujio Kobayashi	75	77	78	70	300	435,000
Carlos Espinosa	76	75	75	75	301	385,000
Yoshikazu Yokoshima	78	72	78	73	301	385,000
Hsieh Yu Shu	74	78	71	78	301	385,000
Brian Jones	78	74	75	74	301	385,000
Shinjiro Tanaka	74	73	78	76	301	385,000
Teruo Nakamura	75	77	75	74	301	385,000
Roger Mackay	79	72	75	75	301	385,000
Hatsutoshi Sakai	78	72	71	80	301	385,000
Koichi Suzuki	74	71	75	82	302	325,000
Nobumitsu Yuhara	76	76	75	75	302	325,000
Akimitsu Tokita	80	71	75	76	302	325,000
Teruo Sugihara	77	74	75	76	302	325,000
Minoru Hatsumi	75	74	82	72	303	280,000
Yoshiyuki Isomura	79	72	74	78	303	280,000
Seiji Ebihara	74	75	77	77	303	280,000
Hajime Meshiai	75	77	75	76	303	280,000
Shoichi Sato	76	76	78	73	303	280,000
Hsieh Min Nan	77	74	78	74	303	280,000

Polaroid Cup Golf Digest

Tomei Country Club, Susono
Par 71; 6,770 yards

October 13-16
purse, ¥60,000,000

	SCORES				TOTAL	MONEY
Masashi Ozaki	69	72	69	62	272	¥10,800,000
Brian Jones	69	67	67	69	272	6,000,000
(Ozaki defeated Jones on first hole of playoff.)						
Katsunari Takahashi	67	70	70	67	274	4,080,000
Nobuo Serizawa	72	70	66	68	276	2,640,000
Katsuji Hasegawa	66	69	72	69	276	2,640,000
Isao Aoki	69	70	71	67	277	1,940,000
Koichi Suzuki	69	69	72	67	277	1,940,000
Ian Baker-Finch	69	69	71	68	277	1,940,000
Toru Nakamura	72	69	69	68	278	1,470,000
Kiyoshi Muroda	69	67	70	72	278	1,470,000
Scott Simpson	72	71	68	68	279	1,104,000
Isamu Sugita	68	72	71	68	279	1,104,000

	SCORES				TOTAL	MONEY
Yutaka Hagawa	67	70	71	71	279	1,104,000
Yoshiyuki Isomura	74	67	70	69	280	828,000
Satsuki Takahashi	72	70	70	68	280	828,000
Masaji Kusakabe	68	69	70	73	280	828,000
D.A. Weibring	72	70	72	66	280	828,000
Hiromichi Namiki	70	70	71	70	281	672,000
Teruo Sugihara	70	71	73	68	282	566,000
Seiichi Kanai	69	69	74	70	282	566,000
Pete Izumikawa	67	71	74	70	282	566,000
Shinsaku Maeda	72	70	71	69	282	566,000
Nobumitsu Yuhara	70	68	73	71	282	566,000
Takeru Shibata	72	71	69	70	282	566,000
Kikuo Arai	69	67	74	73	283	474,000
Yoshihisa Iwashita	71	72	68	72	283	474,000
Yoshikazu Yokoshima	71	66	72	74	283	474,000
Seiji Ebihara	70	67	73	73	283	474,000
Futoshi Irino	72	72	69	70	283	474,000
Teruo Nakamura	72	71	72	68	283	474,000

Bridgestone

Sodegaura Country Club, Chiba
Par 72; 7,120 yards

October 20-23
purse, ¥80,000,000

	SCORES				TOTAL	MONEY
Masashi Ozaki	72	64	68	69	273	¥14,400,000
Isao Aoki	68	65	69	73	275	8,000,000
Yoshimi Niizeki	69	67	69	73	278	5,440,000
Masanobu Kimura	72	70	68	69	279	3,520,000
Chen Tze Chung	70	73	67	69	279	3,520,000
Ian Baker-Finch	68	72	70	70	280	2,880,000
Toru Nakamura	68	69	72	72	281	2,560,000
Yoshitaka Yamamoto	76	64	73	69	282	1,862,400
Yoshiyuki Isomura	74	69	70	69	282	1,862,400
Kazushige Kouno	73	68	70	71	282	1,862,400
Katsuji Hasegawa	67	72	71	72	282	1,862,400
Hsieh Yu Shu	70	69	74	69	282	1,862,400
Noboru Sugai	73	71	70	69	283	1,344,000
Yoshikazu Yokoshima	73	71	69	71	284	1,200,000
Hajime Meshiai	73	71	71	69	284	1,200,000
Masahiro Kuramoto	67	73	73	72	285	970,666
Akihito Yokoyama	72	69	74	70	285	970,666
Yutaka Hagawa	68	74	70	73	285	970,666
Kiyoshi Muroda	72	71	69	74	286	754,666
Isamu Sugita	70	74	69	73	286	754,666
Teruo Sugihara	71	73	70	72	286	754,666
Yoshinori Kaneko	75	69	69	73	286	754,666
Tsukasa Watanabe	71	72	73	70	286	754,666
Katsunari Takahashi	68	73	75	70	286	754,666
Bernhard Langer	69	73	69	76	287	648,000
David Ishii	74	72	71	70	287	648,000
Hiroshi Ishii	72	73	72	70	287	648,000
Eitaro Deguchi	69	67	76	75	287	648,000
Tateo Ozaki	70	74	73	71	288	584,000
Sandy Lyle	71	74	71	72	288	584,000
Motomasa Aoki	72	74	68	74	288	584,000
Kazuo Kanayama	73	73	69	73	288	584,000

Lark Cup

ABC Golf Club, Tojo
Par 72; 7,156 yards

October 27-30
purse, ¥150,000,000

	SCORES				TOTAL	MONEY
Katsunari Takahashi	65	66	72	74	277	¥27,000,000
Masashi Ozaki	70	67	68	73	278	15,000,000
Naomichi Ozaki	71	69	69	71	280	10,200,000
Tateo Ozaki	67	70	71	74	282	7,200,000
Craig Parry	70	67	75	71	283	5,400,000
Brian Jones	69	68	73	73	283	5,400,000
Ikuo Shirahama	68	70	74	71	283	5,400,000
Hajime Meshiai	71	70	73	70	284	4,350,000
Chen Tze Ming	72	70	72	71	285	3,450,000
Bob Gilder	68	71	73	73	285	3,450,000
David Ishii	70	68	76	71	285	3,450,000
Terry Gale	70	73	70	73	286	2,640,000
Wayne Smith	70	72	69	75	286	2,640,000
Wayne Grady	71	72	73	71	287	1,920,000
Nobumitsu Yuhara	72	72	74	69	287	1,920,000
Satoshi Higashi	69	71	72	75	287	1,920,000
Tsukasa Watanabe	73	75	72	67	287	1,920,000
Roger Mackay	71	68	74	74	287	1,920,000
Tsuneyuki Nakajima	75	71	71	70	287	1,920,000
Seiichi Kanai	71	74	72	71	288	1,386,000
Masanobu Kimura	71	68	76	73	288	1,386,000
Taisei Inagaki	68	70	74	76	288	1,386,000
Kinpachi Yoshimura	68	75	72	73	288	1,386,000
Isao Sugita	71	71	74	72	288	1,386,000
Haruo Yasuda	72	76	70	71	289	1,155,000
Nobuo Serizawa	69	71	77	72	289	1,155,000
Eitarou Deguchi	68	73	76	72	289	1,155,000
Eiichi Itai	73	68	77	71	289	1,155,000
Doug Tewell	70	72	74	73	289	1,155,000
Hsieh Min Nan	73	68	74	74	289	1,155,000
Teruo Sugihara	72	72	71	74	289	1,155,000
Yoshikazu Yokoshima	71	75	72	71	289	1,155,000

VISA Taiheiyo Club Masters

Taiheiyo Club, Gotemba Course, Gotemba
Par 71; 7,072 yards

November 10-13
purse, ¥100,000,000

	SCORES				TOTAL	MONEY
Seve Ballesteros	71	71	68	71	281	¥18,000,000
Yasuhiro Funatogawa	73	75	67	69	284	10,000,000
Jose-Maria Olazabal	72	72	72	69	285	5,800,000
Yoshiyuki Isomura	69	69	73	74	285	5,800,000
Katsunari Takahashi	75	73	68	70	286	3,600,000
David Ishii	73	73	70	70	286	3,600,000
Scott Simpson	72	74	70	70	286	3,600,000
Yutaka Hagawa	74	74	66	73	287	2,750,000
Tsuneyuki Nakajima	74	71	69	73	287	2,750,000
Doug Tewell	72	73	73	70	288	2,046,666
Don Pooley	72	72	70	74	288	2,046,666
Masaji Kusakabe	71	74	70	73	288	2,046,666
Masashi Ozaki	71	78	68	72	289	1,560,000

	SCORES				TOTAL	MONEY
Hsieh Min Nan	73	72	71	73	289	1,560,000
Toru Nakamura	71	72	73	73	289	1,560,000
Curt Byrum	75	71	72	72	290	1,080,000
Nobuo Serizawa	69	76	76	69	290	1,080,000
Nobumitsu Yuhara	69	73	74	74	290	1,080,000
Kikuo Arai	75	74	68	73	290	1,080,000
Masahiro Kuramoto	72	72	75	71	290	1,080,000
Katsuji Hasegawa	73	75	71	71	290	1,080,000
Tadami Ueno	73	74	71	72	290	1,080,000
Roger Mackay	73	74	72	72	291	850,000
Kazuo Kanayama	72	74	72	73	291	850,000
Brian Jones	68	76	76	71	291	850,000
Satoshi Hitashi	74	72	73	72	291	850,000
Terry Gale	75	76	72	69	292	800,000
Masanobu Kimura	74	75	72	72	293	760,000
Graham Marsh	72	76	72	73	293	760,000
Chen Tze Chung	75	72	73	73	293	760,000
Futoshi Irino	73	73	74	74	294	660,525
Kouichi Suzuki	73	74	67	80	294	660,525
Fujio Kobayashi	73	75	73	73	294	660,525
Yoshikazu Yokoshima	74	76	71	73	294	660,525
Saburou Fujiki	74	74	73	73	294	660,525
Haruo Yasuda	74	75	75	70	294	660,525
Yoshitaka Yamamoto	72	74	74	74	294	660,525
Hajime Meshiai	71	73	77	73	294	660,525
Shigeru Kawamata	73	70	78	74	295	564,000
Isao Sugita	77	73	72	73	295	564,000
Tateo Ozaki	79	65	76	75	295	564,000
Norio Suzuki	74	72	72	77	295	564,000
Hiroshi Makino	73	75	73	75	296	500,000
Akihito Yokoyama	74	76	72	74	296	500,000
Ian Baker-Finch	73	76	76	71	296	500,000
Isao Aoki	72	74	73	77	296	500,000
Blaine McCallister	75	71	72	79	297	452,000
Bobby Wadkins	77	74	71	75	297	452,000
Tadao Nakamura	74	73	72	78	297	452,000
Teruo Nakamura	77	74	75	72	298	436,000
Chen Tze Ming	72	77	73	76	298	436,000
Peter Baker	72	75	72	79	298	436,000

Dunlop Phoenix

Phoenix Country Club, Miyazaki
Par 72; 6,993 yards

November 17-20
purse, ¥150,000,000

	SCORES				TOTAL	MONEY
Ken Green	70	68	64	71	273	¥27,000,000
Fred Couples	62	71	68	74	275	15,000,000
Jeff Sluman	70	68	65	73	276	10,200,000
Seve Ballesteros	72	69	67	70	278	7,200,000
Hajime Meshiai	67	72	67	74	280	6,000,000
Johnny Miller	69	73	68	71	281	5,400,000
Hubert Green	68	70	71	74	283	4,350,000
Larry Mize	70	72	74	67	283	4,350,000
Jose-Maria Olazabal	69	73	68	73	283	4,350,000
Scott Simpson	71	71	67	75	284	3,225,000
Larry Nelson	66	73	72	73	284	3,225,000

	SCORES				TOTAL	MONEY
Graham Marsh	72	68	74	71	285	2,640,000
Seiichi Kanai	72	72	71	70	285	2,640,000
Ian Baker-Finch	72	72	72	70	286	2,250,000
Masanobu Kimura	72	71	70	73	286	2,250,000
Teruo Nakamura	75	70	68	74	287	1,582,500
Tsukasa Watanabe	71	75	71	70	287	1,582,500
Roger Mackay	70	69	72	76	287	1,582,500
Chen Tze Chung	65	75	71	76	287	1,582,500
Tom Watson	72	75	69	71	287	1,582,500
Bob Tway	69	71	68	79	287	1,582,500
Masashi Ozaki	71	75	73	68	287	1,582,500
Craig Stadler	69	74	69	75	287	1,582,500
Jay Haas	71	74	73	70	288	1,215,000
Toru Nakamura	70	74	75	69	288	1,215,000
Isao Aoki	72	75	73	68	288	1,215,000
Mike Reid	71	74	72	71	288	1,215,000
Katsunari Takahashi	68	72	76	72	288	1,215,000
Bobby Wadkins	70	75	71	72	288	1,215,000
Scott Verplank	71	71	76	71	289	1,095,500
Nobumitsu Yahara	72	70	71	76	289	1,095,500
Nobuo Serizawa	73	76	68	73	290	1,038,000
Scott Hoch	75	73	71	71	290	1,038,000
Norio Mikami	72	75	72	72	291	966,000
Tadami Ueno	72	75	73	71	291	966,000
Masaji Kusakabe	71	72	74	74	291	966,000
Mark Wiebe	71	72	74	74	291	966,000
Teruo Sugihara	71	75	76	70	292	906,000
Tsuneyuki Nakajima	68	74	75	76	293	798,000
Saburou Fujiki	69	74	72	78	293	798,000
Hideto Shigenobu	70	75	73	75	293	798,000
Tomohiro Maruyama	74	73	71	75	293	798,000
Tsutomu Irie	72	73	73	75	293	798,000
Kouichi Suzuki	70	72	72	79	293	798,000
Kazushige Kouno	73	69	74	77	293	798,000
David Ishii	73	72	75	73	293	798,000
Hsieh Min Nan	71	73	75	75	294	690,000
Lim Jin Han	70	74	78	73	295	668,000
Naomichi Ozaki	73	74	77	71	295	668,000
Brian Jones	68	76	76	75	295	668,000

Casio World Open

Ibusuki Golf Club, Kaimoncho
Par 72; 6,985 yards

November 24-27
purse, ¥90,000,000

	SCORES				TOTAL	MONEY
Larry Mize	72	71	68	73	284	¥16,200,000
Masashi Ozaki	73	70	73	69	285	9,000,000
Tsukasa Watanabe	74	72	74	68	288	6,120,000
Tsuneyuki Nakajima	79	73	68	69	289	4,320,000
Brian Jones	72	74	75	69	290	2,934,000
Scott Simpson	74	71	75	70	290	2,934,000
Chen Tze Chung	75	71	73	71	290	2,934,000
Yoshitaka Yamamoto	69	73	69	79	290	2,934,000
Jose-Maria Olazabal	73	69	72	76	290	2,934,000
Hajime Meshiai	71	74	73	73	291	1,935,000
Ken Green	76	70	74	71	291	1,935,000

	SCORES				TOTAL	MONEY
Mark Wiebe	77	72	71	72	292	1,524,000
Shinsaku Maeda	71	75	72	74	292	1,524,000
Scott Hoch	76	70	76	70	292	1,524,000
Kinpachi Yoshimura	76	69	73	75	293	1,143,000
Yasuhiro Funatogawa	74	69	73	77	293	1,143,000
Isao Aoki	74	72	72	75	293	1,143,000
Mark Brooks	76	74	72	71	293	1,143,000
Fred Couples	82	71	72	69	294	882,000
Koichi Suzuki	80	70	76	68	294	882,000
Toshimitsu Kai	73	75	74	72	294	882,000
Masanobu Kimura	74	72	70	78	294	882,000
Naomichi Ozaki	76	71	69	79	295	783,000
Seiichi Kanai	75	71	74	75	295	783,000
Katsuji Hasegawa	76	74	75	71	296	747,000
David Ishii	77	76	71	72	296	747,000
Teruo Sugihara	78	70	72	77	297	685,800
Tadami Ueno	76	74	73	74	297	685,800
Ove Sellberg	78	73	74	72	297	685,800
Graham Marsh	74	73	71	79	297	685,800
Hidehito Shigenobu	76	77	71	73	297	685,800
Yoshikazu Yokoshima	73	75	76	74	298	615,600
Kazuo Kanayama	79	75	75	69	298	615,600
Hubert Green	77	70	75	76	298	615,600
Tadao Nakamura	75	77	72	75	299	565,200
Yoshinori Kaneko	74	74	73	78	299	565,200
Yoshimi Niizeki	77	77	71	74	299	565,200
Peter Baker	75	71	79	74	299	565,200
Nobumitsu Yuhara	76	74	76	74	300	507,600
Futoshi Irino	77	71	75	77	300	507,600
Katsuyoshi Tomori	77	69	75	79	300	507,600
Akihito Yokoyama	78	73	75	74	300	507,600
Scott Verplank	78	74	72	77	301	471,600
Shuichi Sano	80	71	76	75	302	450,000
Jeff Sluman	77	72	79	74	302	450,000
Namio Takasu	76	73	74	80	303	408,960
Chen Tze Ming	77	76	75	75	303	408,960
Hsieh Min Nan	76	75	77	75	303	408,960
Norio Mikami	77	76	74	76	303	408,960
Saburo Fujiki	83	71	75	74	303	408,960

Japan Series Hitachi Cup

Yomiuri Country Club, Osaka
Par 72; 7,030 yards

November 30-December 4
purse, ¥50,000,000

Yomiuri Country Club, Tokyo
Par 72; 7,071 yards

	SCORES				TOTAL	MONEY
Naomichi Ozaki	69	70	68	68	275	¥14,000,000
Isao Aoki	71	70	67	72	280	7,500,000
Ikuo Shirahama	72	67	70	72	281	4,100,000
David Ishii	68	73	72	68	281	4,100,000
Toru Nakamura	70	69	69	74	282	2,800,000
Katsuyoshi Tomori	71	70	71	72	284	2,300,000
Tomohiro Maruyama	70	73	69	73	285	2,000,000
Akihito Yokoyama	73	73	71	71	288	1,600,000

	SCORES				TOTAL	MONEY
Masahiro Kuramoto	73	77	69	69	288	1,600,000
Yoshimi Niizeki	72	74	71	71	288	1,600,000
Yoshikazu Yokoshima	72	71	73	74	290	1,400,000
Katsunari Takahashi	73	72	72	75	292	1,300,000
Koichi Suzuki	75	73	76	70	294	1,200,000

Daikyo Open

Daikyo Country Club, Onna, Okinawa
Par 72; 6,273 yards

December 8-11
purse, ¥70,000,000

	SCORES				TOTAL	MONEY
Saburo Fujiki	66	72	66	70	274	¥12,600,000
Motomasa Aoki	65	72	68	70	275	5,040,000
David Ishii	63	76	69	67	275	5,040,000
Graham Marsh	70	68	68	69	275	5,040,000
Toru Nakamura	69	69	69	70	277	2,800,000
Tsukasa Watanabe	68	72	70	68	278	2,380,000
Seiichi Kanai	69	70	70	69	278	2,380,000
Yutaka Hagawa	69	69	70	71	279	1,629,600
Ian Baker-Finch	69	70	70	70	279	1,629,600
Tadao Nakamura	68	69	72	70	279	1,629,600
Greg Norman	69	69	72	69	279	1,629,600
Koichi Suzuki	64	67	75	73	279	1,629,600
Hiroshi Makino	68	73	72	68	281	1,092,000
Nobumitsu Yuhara	67	77	68	69	281	1,092,000
Norikazu Kawakami	72	68	71	70	281	1,092,000
Keiji Tejima	72	69	70	71	282	849,333
Masanobu Kimura	70	72	72	68	282	849,333
Kikuo Arai	68	70	70	74	282	849,333
Tsuneyuki Nakajima	71	69	69	74	283	700,000
Eitaro Deguchi	68	72	71	72	283	700,000
Curtis Strange	71	67	71	74	283	700,000
Katsuyoshi Tomori	70	72	73	69	284	620,666
Hideto Shigenobu	64	75	75	70	284	620,666
Ikuo Shirahama	66	76	70	72	284	620,666
Joji Furuki	70	73	71	71	285	560,000
Tomohiro Maruyama	68	76	70	71	285	560,000
Isao Isozaki	69	71	73	72	285	560,000
Naomichi Ozaki	66	75	72	72	285	560,000
Ichiro Teramoto	67	76	75	67	285	560,000
Eiichi Itai	74	69	72	71	286	518,000

The LPGA Tour

Mazda Classic

Stonebridge Golf and Country Club, Boca Raton, Florida
Par 36-36 — 72; 6,368 yards

February 4-7
purse, $200,000

	SCORES				TOTAL	MONEY
Nancy Lopez	69	68	71	75	283	$30,000
Marta Figueras-Dotti	70	70	72	73	286	18,500
Juli Inkster	74	71	75	68	288	8,434
Heather Farr	70	74	73	71	288	8,434
Jan Stephenson	72	71	71	74	288	8,433
Patty Sheehan	71	72	71	74	288	8,433
Amy Benz	69	72	73	74	288	8,433
Martha Foyer	71	70	72	75	288	8,433
Lauri Peterson	72	75	71	71	289	4,054
Kathy Postlewait	70	73	73	73	289	4,054
Amy Alcott	70	73	72	74	289	4,053
Patti Rizzo	67	72	76	74	289	4,053
Rosie Jones	71	72	76	71	290	3,007
Deedee Lasker	71	75	72	72	290	3,007
Janet Coles	74	69	73	74	290	3,007
Beverly Klass	71	73	71	75	290	3,007
Julie Cole	71	75	74	71	291	2,407
Nina Foust	76	72	71	72	291	2,407
Colleen Walker	72	70	76	73	291	2,407
Muffin Spencer-Devlin	70	73	73	75	291	2,407
Betsy King	71	68	77	75	291	2,407
JoAnne Carner	74	71	76	71	292	1,926
Kathy Baker-Guadagnino	71	73	76	72	292	1,926
Cathy Morse	73	72	74	73	292	1,925
Laurie Rinker	72	74	72	74	292	1,925
Deb Richard	74	70	72	76	292	1,925
Cathy Marino	70	74	70	78	292	1,925
M. J. Smith	74	74	74	71	293	1,617
Kelly Leadbetter	75	72	75	71	293	1,617
Ok-Hee Ku	71	72	77	73	293	1,617
Dawn Coe	72	68	78	75	293	1,617

Sarasota Classic

Bent Tree Country Club, Sarasota, Florida
Par 36-36 — 72; 6,170 yards

February 11-14
purse, $225,000

	SCORES				TOTAL	MONEY
Patty Sheehan	71	72	72	67	282	$33,750
JoAnne Carner	70	74	73	68	285	18,000
Jody Rosenthal	71	70	74	70	285	17,999
Sherri Turner	69	74	73	70	286	10,687
Beth Daniel	68	73	72	73	286	10,687
Cathy Morse	73	74	72	68	287	7,256
Juli Inkster	72	75	72	68	287	7,256
Penny Hammel	70	78	70	71	289	5,850
Jan Stephenson	68	78	73	71	290	5,006
Colleen Walker	72	73	71	74	290	5,006

	SCORES				TOTAL	MONEY
Marta Figueras-Dotti	73	74	74	70	291	3,620
Jane Geddes	74	72	73	72	291	3,620
Amy Alcott	74	69	76	72	291	3,619
Liselotte Neumann	64	77	76	74	291	3,619
Beth Solomon	72	74	70	75	291	3,619
Shelley Hamlin	72	75	68	76	291	3,619
Myra Blackwelder	76	74	73	69	292	2,814
Rosie Jones	69	77	76	70	292	2,813
Nancy Lopez	73	74	73	72	292	2,813
Cathy Marino	75	75	74	69	293	2,291
Martha Nause	73	75	74	71	293	2,291
Amy Benz	70	74	78	71	293	2,291
Kim Shipman	73	74	72	74	293	2,291
Lori Garbacz	76	70	73	74	293	2,291
Donna White	71	73	74	75	293	2,291
Cathy Johnston	70	72	75	76	293	2,290
Missie McGeorge	72	77	75	70	294	1,753
Sherrie Steinhauer	71	76	77	70	294	1,753
Dottie Mochrie	71	72	77	74	294	1,753
Dot Germain	71	72	77	74	294	1,753
Janet Anderson	76	73	70	75	294	1,753
Nancy Scranton Brown	72	76	71	75	294	1,753
Laurel Kean	69	75	73	77	294	1,753
Muffin Spencer-Devlin	70	73	74	77	294	1,752

Orient Leasing Hawaiian Open

Turtle Bay Resort, Oahu, Hawaii
Par 36-36 — 72; 6,252 yards

February 25-27
purse, $300,000

	SCORES			TOTAL	MONEY
Ayako Okamoto	69	72	72	213	$45,000
Deb Richard	73	73	68	214	24,000
Jo Anne Carner	70	71	73	214	24,000
Beth Daniel	70	73	72	215	13,000
Kathy Postlewait	70	73	72	215	13,000
Jan Stephenson	68	75	72	215	13,000
Marci Bozarth	73	72	71	216	7,500
Patty Sheehan	73	72	71	216	7,500
Cathy Gerring	71	72	73	216	7,500
Joan Delk	71	69	76	216	7,500
Lisa Young	77	73	67	217	4,981
Lenore Rittenhouse	75	72	70	217	4,980
Tatsuko Ohsako	74	71	72	217	4,980
Juli Inkster	72	73	72	217	4,980
Pat Bradley	75	69	73	217	4,980
Lynn Adams	75	71	72	218	4,050
Dottie Mochrie	77	74	68	219	3,600
Missie McGeorge	79	69	71	219	3,600
Deborah McHaffie	76	71	72	219	3,600
Rosie Jones	74	72	73	219	3,600
Anne-Marie Palli	71	71	77	219	3,600
Martha Nause	78	73	69	220	3,083
Sherri Turner	77	73	70	220	3,082
Colleen Walker	76	75	70	221	2,552
Nancy Brown	76	74	71	221	2,552
Missie Berteotti	75	75	71	221	2,552

	SCORES			TOTAL	MONEY
Vicki Fergon	73	75	73	221	2,552
Shirley Furlong	70	77	74	221	2,552
Susie Redman	75	71	75	221	2,552
Sandra Palmer	72	73	76	221	2,551
Judy Dickinson	71	73	77	221	2,551
Sally Quinlan	70	73	78	221	2,551

Women's Kemper Open

Princeville Makai Golf Course, Sauai, Hawaii
Par 36-36 — 72; 6,237 yards

March 3-6
purse, $300,000

	SCORES				TOTAL	MONEY
Betsy King	73	72	66	69	280	$45,000
Beth Daniel	72	66	70	73	281	27,750
Tammie Green	70	71	73	68	282	20,250
Ayako Okamoto	71	71	69	72	283	15,750
Amy Alcott	70	71	70	73	284	12,750
Alice Ritzman	73	68	73	72	286	9,675
Colleen Walker	70	71	72	73	286	9,675
Mei Chi Cheng	73	74	71	69	287	6,421
Heather Farr	73	74	70	70	287	6,420
JoAnne Carner	70	71	74	72	287	6,420
Rosie Jones	70	73	70	74	287	6,420
Marci Bozarth	68	71	72	76	287	6,420
Cindy Figg-Currier	76	71	70	71	288	4,800
Nancy Brown	73	72	70	73	288	4,800
Shirley Furlong	72	71	74	72	289	4,013
Shelley Hamlin	70	73	73	73	289	4,013
Marta Figueras-Dotti	72	70	73	74	289	4,012
Kim Shipman	71	73	70	75	289	4,012
Barb Bunkowsky	72	75	75	68	290	3,303
Janet Coles	74	73	72	71	290	3,303
Patti Rizzo	70	75	74	71	290	3,303
Jerilyn Britz	75	73	70	72	290	3,303
Vicki Fergon	69	73	75	73	290	3,303
Cathy Morse	71	74	73	73	291	2,820
Chris Johnson	69	74	75	73	291	2,820
Kim Bauer	73	72	68	78	291	2,820
Myra Blackwelder	71	73	77	71	292	2,418
Meg Mallon	73	72	74	73	292	2,418
Deedee Lasker	72	73	73	74	292	2,418
Laurie Rinker	71	72	73	76	292	2,417
Martha Nause	73	72	69	78	292	2,417
Elaine Crosby	73	71	69	79	292	2,417

Circle K Tucson Open

Randolph North Golf Course, Tucson, Arizona
Par 35-37 — 72; 6,243 yards

March 17-20
purse, $300,000

	SCORES				TOTAL	MONEY
Laura Davies	63	74	69	72	278	$45,000
Robin Walton	69	64	76	70	279	27,750

	SCORES				TOTAL	MONEY
Patty Sheehan	68	68	72	72	280	20,250
Jan Stephenson	73	69	68	71	281	15,750
Marci Bozarth	73	70	69	70	282	12,750
Rosie Jones	70	70	72	71	283	10,500
Sherri Turner	72	66	73	73	284	8,850
Colleen Walker	75	70	73	67	285	6,421
Nancy Lopez	71	73	71	70	285	6,420
Ok-Hee Ku	72	69	71	73	285	6,420
Heather Farr	71	70	71	73	285	6,420
Janet Coles	72	66	74	73	285	6,420
Jody Rosenthal	73	72	71	70	286	4,950
Karin Mundinger	72	76	71	69	288	4,500
Deb Richard	69	73	73	73	288	4,500
Marta Figueras-Dotti	75	71	72	71	289	3,750
Nancy Rubin	74	70	74	71	289	3,750
Anne-Marie Palli	74	72	70	73	289	3,750
Vicki Fergon	78	69	67	75	289	3,750
Mary Murphy	71	69	74	75	289	3,750
Cathy Marino	74	74	70	72	290	3,155
Missie Berteotti	74	74	69	73	290	3,155
Susan Sanders	70	72	71	77	290	3,155
Hollis Stacy	73	71	77	70	291	2,685
Missie McGeorge	75	72	72	72	291	2,685
Dottie Mochrie	77	69	73	72	291	2,685
Patti Rizzo	72	71	76	72	291	2,685
Val Skinner	76	71	71	73	291	2,685
Connie Chillemi	70	75	73	73	291	2,685
Nina Foust	73	74	75	70	292	2,285
Jill Briles	75	73	73	71	292	2,285
Sandra Palmer	73	71	76	72	292	2,285

Standard Register Turquoise Classic

Moon Valley Country Club, Phoenix, Arizona
Par 36-37 — 73; 6,404 yards

March 24-27
purse, $350,000

	SCORES				TOTAL	MONEY
Ok-Hee Ku	71	68	70	72	281	$52,500
Dottie Mochrie	70	72	71	69	282	28,000
Ayako Okamoto	71	71	70	70	282	28,000
Amy Alcott	65	73	73	73	284	16,625
Colleen Walker	67	71	73	73	284	16,625
Chris Johnson	70	76	70	69	285	10,559
Heather Farr	74	69	71	71	285	10,558
Juli Inkster	72	71	70	72	285	10,558
Nancy Brown	74	69	75	69	287	6,840
Sherri Turner	75	73	68	71	287	6,840
Jane Geddes	73	74	68	72	287	6,840
Danielle Ammaccapane	70	72	71	74	287	6,840
Rosie Jones	70	71	70	76	287	6,840
Mary Beth Zimmerman	69	75	77	67	288	5,100
Penny Hammel	73	72	71	72	288	5,100
Liselotte Neumann	74	70	71	73	288	5,100
Betsy King	73	72	73	71	289	4,400
Connie Chillemi	70	73	74	72	289	4,400
Laura Davies	75	70	70	74	289	4,400
Patti Rizzo	73	72	74	71	290	3,651

	SCORES				TOTAL	MONEY
Jody Rosenthal	71	72	76	71	290	3,651
Jan Stephenson	72	75	72	71	290	3,650
Barb Bunkowsky	71	73	74	72	290	3,650
Amy Benz	74	71	71	74	290	3,650
Kathy Postlewait	72	71	72	75	290	3,650
Tammie Green	76	68	75	72	291	3,000
JoAnne Carner	71	75	72	73	291	3,000
Cindy Figg-Currier	70	75	73	73	291	3,000
Terry-Jo Myers	72	73	72	74	291	3,000
Hollis Stacy	73	73	71	74	291	3,000

Nabisco Dinah Shore

Mission Hills Country Club, Rancho Mirage, California
Par 36-36 — 72; 6,308 yards

March 31-April 3
purse, $500,000

	SCORES				TOTAL	MONEY
Amy Alcott	71	66	66	71	274	$80,000
Colleen Walker	73	65	69	69	276	42,000
Rosie Jones	73	67	68	71	279	26,000
*Caroline Keggi	75	71	66	69	281	
Nancy Lopez	74	69	70	69	282	18,000
Marta Figueras-Dotti	70	69	70	73	282	18,000
Dottie Mochrie	76	71	70	67	284	14,431
Jane Geddes	75	73	66	70	284	14,431
Dawn Coe	77	67	70	70	284	14,430
Debbie Massey	72	68	73	72	285	10,643
Jan Stephenson	69	72	70	74	285	10,643
Juli Inkster	74	73	70	69	286	7,941
Jo Anne Carner	73	72	72	69	286	7,941
Muffin Spencer-Devlin	68	76	72	70	286	7,941
Mary Beth Zimmerman	74	67	74	71	286	7,940
Cathy Morse	72	69	73	72	286	7,940
Ok-Hee Ku	78	70	70	69	287	6,338
Sherri Turner	79	69	67	72	287	6,338
Jody Rosenthal	77	69	71	71	288	5,860
Kathy Postlewait	75	69	73	71	288	5,859
Janet Coles	75	75	69	70	289	5,148
Laura Davies	78	69	72	70	289	5,148
Martha Nause	79	70	68	72	289	5,148
Robin Walton	75	69	72	73	289	5,148
Barb Thomas	76	73	73	68	290	4,353
Jerilyn Britz	72	74	75	69	290	4,353
Lauri Peterson	74	73	73	70	290	4,353
Missie Berteotti	74	71	72	73	290	4,353
Bonnie Lauer	74	68	74	74	290	4,352
Kathy Baker-Guadagnino	76	71	74	70	291	3,650
Patti Rizzo	75	73	71	72	291	3,650
Jane Crafter	74	70	75	72	291	3,650
Judy Dickinson	79	69	70	73	291	3,649
Donna White	74	70	74	73	291	3,649
Myra Blackwelder	72	77	74	69	292	2,801
Cindy Rarick	80	70	72	70	292	2,801
Ayako Okamoto	71	72	77	72	292	2,801
Hollis Stacy	75	75	69	73	292	2,801
Tammie Green	75	73	70	74	292	2,801
Betsy King	77	70	71	74	292	2,801

	SCORES				TOTAL	MONEY
Chris Johnson	71	76	71	74	292	2,800
Kim Shipman	75	69	74	74	292	2,800
Deb Richard	75	70	72	75	292	2,800
Alice Ritzman	77	69	77	70	293	2,153
Denise Strebig	77	71	73	72	293	2,152
Nancy Brown	76	71	71	75	293	2,152
Sally Quinlan	75	72	76	71	294	1,605
Marci Bozarth	76	74	72	72	294	1,605
Mindy Moore	76	74	72	72	294	1,605
Amy Benz	75	74	73	72	294	1,605
Vicki Fergon	72	75	75	72	294	1,605
Barb Bunkowsky	71	75	76	72	294	1,605
Lori Garbacz	78	72	71	73	294	1,604
Janet Anderson	73	74	73	74	294	1,604
Laurie Rinker	74	72	74	74	294	1,604
*Kathleen Scrivner	73	73	72	76	294	

San Diego Inamori Classic

Stone Ridge Country Club, San Diego, California   April 7-10
Par 35-36 — 71; 6,042 yards   purse, $225,000

	SCORES				TOTAL	MONEY
Ayako Okamoto	69	71	63	69	272	$33,750
Colleen Walker	68	67	69	69	273	20,812
Judy Dickinson	68	71	68	67	274	15,187
Nancy Lopez	70	68	72	68	278	11,812
Martha Nause	71	71	69	68	279	8,719
Ok-Hee Ku	68	70	69	72	279	8,718
Mindy Moore	71	70	71	69	281	5,625
Amy Alcott	72	70	67	72	281	5,625
Dot Germain	69	72	68	72	281	5,625
Patty Sheehan	67	71	69	74	281	5,624
Betsy King	71	71	71	69	282	3,983
Mei Chi Cheng	78	66	68	70	282	3,983
Janet Coles	72	67	70	73	282	3,982
Cindy Mackey	70	71	75	67	283	3,113
Marci Bozarth	74	71	68	70	283	3,113
Shirley Furlong	70	70	73	70	283	3,113
Sally Little	74	69	69	71	283	3,112
Kris Monaghan	71	71	69	72	283	3,112
Cathy Morse	72	72	71	69	284	2,539
Liselotte Neumann	73	72	68	71	284	2,539
Chris Johnson	68	73	71	72	284	2,539
Allison Finney	68	72	70	74	284	2,539
Sherri Turner	71	74	68	72	285	2,230
Lenore Rittenhouse	65	71	72	77	285	2,229
Sandra Palmer	68	73	77	68	286	1,988
Robin Walton	71	73	71	71	286	1,988
Nina Foust	74	69	72	71	286	1,988
Jackie Bertsch	73	71	70	72	286	1,988
Danielle Ammaccapane	72	70	70	74	286	1,987
Missie McGeorge	73	71	74	69	287	1,693
Therese Hession	73	73	71	70	287	1,692
Caroline Gowan	70	72	73	72	287	1,692
Kim Bauer	71	69	72	75	287	1,692

Al Star/Centinela Hospital Classic

Rancho Park Golf Course, Los Angeles, California
Par 37-35 — 72; 6,191 yards

April 15-17
purse, $400,000

	SCORES			TOTAL	MONEY
Nancy Lopez	71	72	67	210	$60,000
Marta Figueras-Dotti	70	70	70	210	37,000
(Lopez defeated Figueras-Dotti on second hole of playoff.)					
Colleen Walker	73	71	67	211	27,000
Kim Shipman	73	70	69	212	19,000
Amy Alcott	69	70	73	212	19,000
Martha Nause	73	75	65	213	11,400
Amy Benz	73	72	68	213	11,400
Sherri Turner	72	68	73	213	11,400
Juli Inkster	70	70	73	213	11,400
Penny Hammel	74	71	69	214	7,160
Hollis Stacy	71	73	70	214	7,160
Robin Hood	73	70	71	214	7,160
Nancy Ledbetter	72	71	71	214	7,160
Sally Quinlan	73	68	73	214	7,160
Cathy Morse	75	73	67	215	5,467
Ayako Okamoto	72	72	71	215	5,467
Debbie Massey	72	71	72	215	5,466
Sandra Palmer	71	76	69	216	4,256
Mitzi Edge	74	72	70	216	4,256
Marci Bozarth	74	71	71	216	4,256
Janet Anderson	72	73	71	216	4,256
Missie Berteotti	71	74	71	216	4,256
Deb Richard	72	72	72	216	4,255
Heather Farr	74	69	73	216	4,255
Connie Chillemi	75	67	74	216	4,255
Lynn Adams	70	70	76	216	4,255
Deedee Lasker	75	71	71	217	3,115
Bonnie Lauer	73	72	72	217	3,115
Kathy Postlewait	73	71	73	217	3,115
Dottie Mochrie	72	72	73	217	3,115
Dot Germain	73	70	74	217	3,115
Jane Geddes	71	72	74	217	3,115
Judy Dickinson	73	69	75	217	3,115
Shirley Furlong	71	71	75	217	3,115

USX Classic

Pasadena Yacht and Country Club, St. Petersburg, Florida
Par 36-36 — 72; 6,013 yards

April 21-24
purse, $225,000

	SCORES				TOTAL	MONEY
Rosie Jones	67	69	69	70	275	$33,750
Kathy Postlewait	68	69	69	69	275	20,812
(Jones defeated Postlewait on first hole of playoff.)						
Barb Bunkowsky	71	70	67	69	277	15,187
Connie Chillemi	70	70	71	67	278	10,687
Donna White	68	68	71	71	278	10,687
Lynn Connelly	70	75	70	65	280	6,413
Vicki Fergon	68	70	74	68	280	6,412
Carolyn Hill	71	68	70	71	280	6,412
Trish Johnson	71	69	68	72	280	6,412

	SCORES				TOTAL	MONEY
Dottie Mochrie	71	72	71	67	281	4,028
Jan Stephenson	73	71	69	68	281	4,028
JoAnne Carner	73	69	71	68	281	4,028
Heather Drew	66	72	73	70	281	4,028
Jane Crafter	71	70	68	72	281	4,028
Sue Ertl	72	70	72	68	282	3,076
Tina Tombs Purtzer	67	71	71	73	282	3,076
Sherrin Smyers	69	70	69	74	282	3,075
Robin Walton	73	71	70	69	283	2,757
Gina Hull	71	73	68	71	283	2,757
Anne Kelly	70	71	74	69	284	2,476
Cindy Hill	71	72	69	72	284	2,476
Susan Sanders	70	70	70	74	284	2,476
Nina Foust	71	73	72	69	285	2,153
Allison Finney	74	71	69	71	285	2,152
Terry-Jo Myers	72	74	67	72	285	2,152
Jerilyn Britz	71	72	70	72	285	2,152
Laurie Rinker	71	73	73	69	286	1,914
Nancy Taylor	73	69	71	73	286	1,913
Kathy Baker-Guadagnino	70	70	70	76	286	1,913
Stephanie Farwig	74	72	72	69	287	1,686
Sally Little	70	74	73	70	287	1,685
Susan Tonkin	69	71	76	71	287	1,685
Becky Pearson	74	72	68	73	287	1,685

Sara Lee Classic

Hermitage Golf Club, Nashville, Tennessee
Par 36-36 — 72; 6,242 yards

April 29-May 1
purse, $335,000

	SCORES			TOTAL	MONEY
Patti Rizzo	70	70	67	207	$50,250
Tammie Green	70	71	66	207	23,729
Sherri Turner	71	69	67	207	23,729
Kim Williams	69	71	67	207	23,728
(Rizzo won playoff, defeating Green and Williams on first hole, Turner on fifth hole.)					
Nancy Brown	72	69	67	208	11,139
Judy Dickinson	70	68	70	208	11,139
Rosie Jones	69	68	71	208	11,139
Deb Richard	71	66	71	208	11,138
Amy Alcott	65	74	70	209	7,454
Kathy Postlewait	72	67	70	209	7,453
Mei-Chi Cheng	72	72	66	210	5,562
Ok-Hee Ku	70	73	67	210	5,562
Lauri Peterson	70	73	67	210	5,562
Amy Benz	69	70	71	210	5,561
Lisa Walters	69	69	72	210	5,561
Dale Eggeling	72	71	68	211	4,189
Laurel Kean	74	69	68	211	4,188
Marta Figueras-Dotti	71	71	69	211	4,188
Janet Coles	72	69	70	211	4,188
Heather Farr	70	70	71	211	4,188
Jerilyn Britz	68	75	69	212	3,122
Jane Crafter	73	70	69	212	3,122
Martha Foyer	71	71	70	212	3,121
Jane Geddes	70	71	71	212	3,121
Juli Inkster	74	67	71	212	3,121

	SCORES			TOTAL	MONEY
Marci Bozarth	69	71	72	212	3,121
Penny Hammel	69	71	72	212	3,121
Donna Cusano-Wilkins	68	72	72	212	3,121
Kathy Baker-Guadagnino	69	70	73	212	3,121
Sherri Steinhauer	66	71	75	212	3,121

Crestar Classic

Portsmouth Sleepy Hole Golf Club, Portsmouth, Virginia
Par 36-36 — 72; 6,126 yards

May 6-8
purse, $300,000

	SCORES			TOTAL	MONEY
Juli Inkster	70	70	69	209	$45,000
Rosie Jones	73	66	70	209	21,250
Nancy Lopez	71	68	70	209	21,250
Betsey King	69	68	72	209	21,250
(Inkster defeated Jones, Lopez and King on first hole of playoff.)					
Amy Alcott	71	70	69	210	10,700
Missie Berteotti	68	69	73	210	10,700
Sherri Turner	68	68	74	210	10,700
Heather Farr	72	68	71	211	7,800
Allison Finney	72	71	69	212	6,352
Colleen Walker	69	73	70	212	6,352
Lynn Adams	70	71	71	212	6,351
Janet Coles	73	71	69	213	4,805
Judy Dickinson	71	72	70	213	4,805
Trish Johnson	71	72	70	213	4,805
Hollis Stacy	70	70	73	213	4,805
Connie Chillemi	71	74	69	214	3,755
Debbie Massey	70	75	69	214	3,755
Sherri Steinhauer	71	73	70	214	3,755
Myra Blackwelder	71	71	72	214	3,755
Jody Rosenthal	69	73	72	214	3,755
Martha Foyer	70	73	72	215	3,099
Sally Little	71	71	73	215	3,099
Donna White	70	72	73	215	3,099
Kim Shipman	65	74	76	215	3,098
Nina Foust	73	71	72	216	2,735
Sandra Palmer	70	73	73	216	2,735
Tammie Green	72	69	75	216	2,735
Nancy Brown	71	74	72	217	2,465
Tina Tombs Purtzer	72	72	73	217	2,465
Cathy Reynolds	70	73	74	217	2,465

Chrysler-Plymouth Classic

Navesink Country Club, Middletown, New Jersey
Par 37-35 — 72; 6,232 yards

May 13-15
purse, $250,000

	SCORES			TOTAL	MONEY
Nancy Lopez	68	70	66	204	$37,500
Jan Stephenson	77	71	64	212	23,125
Margaret Ward	71	74	68	213	15,000
Alice Ritzman	68	71	74	213	15,000
Marta Figueras-Dotti	70	70	74	214	10,625

	SCORES			TOTAL	MONEY
Ok-Hee Ku	71	75	69	215	7,542
Sherri Turner	73	72	70	215	7,542
Marci Bozarth	73	70	72	215	7,541
Colleen Walker	71	74	71	216	5,074
Jody Rosenthal	73	71	72	216	5,074
Janet Coles	69	74	73	216	5,074
Kay Cockerill	72	70	74	216	5,074
Kris Monaghan	72	74	71	217	3,898
Sally Quinlan	72	73	72	217	3,898
Mei Chi Cheng	70	74	73	217	3,898
Tammie Green	73	75	70	218	3,273
Mindy Moore	75	72	71	218	3,273
Barb Bunkowsky	72	74	72	218	3,273
Shelley Hamlin	70	77	72	219	2,721
Missie McGeorge	75	72	72	219	2,721
Mary Murphy	75	72	72	219	2,721
Kathy Baker-Guadagnino	72	74	73	219	2,721
Penny Hammel	73	73	73	219	2,721
Jackie Bertsch	71	73	75	219	2,720
Jo Ann Washam	74	76	70	220	2,261
Sue Ertl	77	72	71	220	2,261
Shirley Furlong	74	74	72	220	2,260
Val Skinner	73	73	74	220	2,260
Barb Thomas	74	75	72	221	1,964
Cindy Figg-Currier	73	75	73	221	1,964
Deedee Lasker	72	74	75	221	1,963
Sherri Steinhauer	72	74	75	221	1,963

Mazda LPGA Championship

Jack Nicklaus Sports Center, Kings Island, Ohio
Par 36-36 — 72; 6,389 yards

May 19-22
purse, $350,000

	SCORES				TOTAL	MONEY
Sherri Turner	70	71	73	67	281	$52,500
Amy Alcott	68	71	69	74	282	32,375
Marta Figueras-Dotti	74	70	71	69	284	15,890
Kathy Postlewait	74	69	69	72	284	15,890
Sally Little	72	71	69	72	284	15,890
Ayako Okamoto	71	71	69	73	284	15,890
Amy Benz	70	71	69	74	284	15,890
Missie Berteotti	74	70	68	73	285	9,100
Sally Quinlan	69	68	79	70	286	7,415
Jane Geddes	73	70	70	73	286	7,414
Judy Dickinson	74	69	69	74	286	7,414
Lynn Adams	73	71	73	70	287	5,793
Marci Bozarth	72	70	73	72	287	5,793
Dot Germain	72	69	71	75	287	5,793
Jan Stephenson	71	73	71	73	288	4,802
Mei Chi Cheng	72	70	72	74	288	4,801
Danielle Ammaccapane	74	68	71	75	288	4,801
JoAnne Carner	73	72	73	71	289	4,218
Laurel Kean	74	70	73	72	289	4,218
Vicki Fergon	71	73	71	74	289	4,218
Lenore Rittenhouse	74	72	74	70	290	3,699
Donna White	71	74	72	73	290	3,699
Lisa Walters	68	77	70	75	290	3,698

	SCORES				TOTAL	MONEY
Betsy King	74	75	71	71	291	3,203
Cathy Morse	75	70	74	72	291	3,203
Nancy Lopez	72	73	74	72	291	3,203
Connie Chillemi	74	69	72	76	291	3,203
Sherrin Smyers	68	71	76	76	291	3,203
Dawn Coe	78	71	72	71	292	2,735
Deb Richard	73	74	72	73	292	2,735
Jane Crafter	73	73	72	74	292	2,735
Colleen Walker	71	71	72	78	292	2,734
Debbie Massey	67	75	78	73	293	2,459
Tammie Green	72	76	71	74	293	2,459
Shelley Hamlin	77	72	76	69	294	2,153
Cathy Marino	75	70	75	74	294	2,153
Rosie Jones	75	73	71	75	294	2,153
Alice Ritzman	73	72	73	76	294	2,153
Nina Foust	68	72	76	78	294	2,152
Sandra Palmer	72	77	71	75	295	1,847
Tina Tombs Purtzer	75	73	71	76	295	1,846
Laura Hurlbut	72	67	82	75	296	1,663
Barb Bunkowsky	74	74	70	78	296	1,663
Muffin Spencer-Devlin	70	72	76	78	296	1,663
Dottie Mochrie	76	71	76	74	297	1,453
Heather Farr	75	72	75	75	297	1,453
Terry-Jo Myers	76	71	74	76	297	1,453
Cindy Rarick	77	72	75	74	298	1,213
Martha Nause	74	75	75	74	298	1,212
Val Skinner	77	71	75	75	298	1,212
Jerilyn Britz	75	75	72	76	298	1,212

Corning Classic

Corning Country Club, Corning, New York
Par 36-36 — 72; 6,062 yards

May 26-29
purse, $325,000

	SCORES				TOTAL	MONEY
Sherri Turner	71	63	69	70	273	$48,750
JoAnne Carner	74	70	65	66	275	26,000
Ok-Hee Ku	69	64	71	71	275	25,999
Patty Sheehan	67	70	73	69	279	17,062
Jerilyn Britz	70	71	69	70	280	13,812
Martha Foyer	72	70	70	70	282	11,375
Sally Quinlan	71	73	70	69	283	8,558
Kathryn Young	73	66	74	70	283	8,558
Mei Chi Cheng	73	69	71	70	283	8,558
Laurel Kean	70	73	69	72	284	6,035
Debbie Massey	77	68	67	72	284	6,035
Dottie Mochrie	74	70	68	72	284	6,035
Betsy King	69	69	70	76	284	6,034
Trish Johnson	74	69	73	69	285	4,621
Vicki Fergon	78	69	68	70	285	4,620
Jan Stephenson	69	72	72	72	285	4,620
Rosie Jones	71	67	72	75	285	4,620
Patti Rizzo	69	70	77	70	286	3,689
Amy Alcott	70	70	76	70	286	3,689
Alice Ritzman	76	69	69	72	286	3,689
Lori Garbacz	72	74	68	72	286	3,689
Lauri Peterson	68	73	71	74	286	3,688

	SCORES				TOTAL	MONEY
Colleen Walker	71	69	71	75	286	3,688
Sandra Spuzich	74	73	72	68	287	3,085
Lynn Connelly	77	71	70	69	287	3,085
Sherri Steinhauer	67	75	72	73	287	3,084
Donna White	75	71	73	69	288	2,695
Amy Benz	72	71	75	70	288	2,695
Deb Richard	76	72	69	71	288	2,695
Denise Strebig	74	73	70	71	288	2,695
Shirley Furlong	73	70	73	72	288	2,694

Jamie Farr Toledo Classic

Glengarry Country Club, Toledo, Ohio
Par 36-36 — 72; 6,235 yards

June 2-5
purse, $275,000

	SCORES				TOTAL	MONEY
Laura Davies	69	70	69	69	277	$41,250
Nancy Lopez	68	70	69	73	280	25,437
Jan Stephenson	70	72	70	71	283	16,500
Betsy King	72	69	68	74	283	16,499
Myra Blackwelder	74	71	70	71	286	11,687
Nancy Taylor	71	69	73	74	287	9,625
Tammie Green	73	74	72	69	288	8,112
Lynn Adams	74	72	75	69	290	6,806
Sarah LeVeque	75	76	67	72	290	6,806
Heather Farr	75	71	75	71	292	5,513
Amy Read	73	74	72	73	292	5,513
Patty Jordan	75	72	71	75	293	4,838
Janice Gibson	76	75	73	70	294	4,041
Laurie Rinker	77	73	74	70	294	4,041
Patti Rizzo	76	73	71	74	294	4,041
Lauri Peterson	77	71	72	74	294	4,040
Janet Coles	69	76	75	74	294	4,040
Joan Pitcock	73	78	73	71	295	3,326
Mindy Moore	76	76	70	73	295	3,326
Amy Benz	73	76	73	73	295	3,325
Kim Williams	75	77	72	72	296	2,982
Robin Walton	78	72	72	74	296	2,981
Deedee Lasker	78	77	71	71	297	2,407
Allison Finney	80	75	70	72	297	2,407
M. J. Smith	77	74	74	72	297	2,406
Jane Geddes	79	75	70	73	297	2,406
Sandra Spuzich	77	75	72	73	297	2,406
Sandra Palmer	74	73	77	73	297	2,406
Meg Mallon	73	74	77	73	297	2,406
Martha Nause	76	77	70	74	297	2,406
Donna White	76	70	76	75	297	2,406
Mei Chi Cheng	76	72	73	76	297	2,406

Rochester International

Locust Hill Country Club, Pittsford, New York
Par 35-37 — 72; 6,216 yards

June 9-12
purse, $300,000

	SCORES				TOTAL	MONEY
Mei Chi Cheng	71	77	66	73	287	$45,000
Patty Sheehan	73	71	69	74	287	24,000
Nancy Lopez	72	69	71	75	287	24,000
(Cheng won playoff, defeating Sheehan on first extra hole, Lopez on second extra hole.)						
Nancy Brown	73	72	72	71	288	15,750
Cindy Rarick	73	70	72	74	289	11,625
Danielle Ammaccapane	68	72	75	74	289	11,625
Dottie Mochrie	77	69	74	70	290	8,325
Judy Dickinson	73	74	71	72	290	8,325
Lauri Peterson	72	75	65	79	291	7,050
Marta Figueras-Dotti	75	74	72	71	292	6,001
Cathy Morse	73	73	71	75	292	6,000
Alice Ritzman	76	73	73	71	293	4,525
Missie McGeorge	78	73	70	72	293	4,525
Sherri Turner	73	78	69	73	293	4,525
Kathy Whitworth	74	75	68	76	293	4,525
Sherri Steinhauer	68	76	73	76	293	4,525
Caroline Gowan	67	72	73	81	293	4,525
Cathy Johnston	74	74	77	69	294	3,311
Cindy Figg-Currier	74	77	70	73	294	3,311
Vicki Fergon	75	73	73	73	294	3,311
Cathy Marino	73	71	77	73	294	3,311
Deb Richard	75	71	74	74	294	3,311
Kristi Albers	73	72	75	74	294	3,310
Martha Foyer	74	74	70	76	294	3,310
Janice Gibson	76	73	74	72	295	2,550
Juli Inkster	77	75	69	74	295	2,550
Susan Tonkin	76	68	76	75	295	2,550
Connie Chillemi	73	75	71	76	295	2,550
Alice Miller	76	71	72	76	295	2,550
Kim Williams	73	72	74	76	295	2,550
Jody Rosenthal	70	77	71	77	295	2,550

Lady Keystone Open

Hershey Country Club, Hershey, Pennsylvania
Par 36-36 — 72; 6,348 yards

June 17-19
purse, $300,000

	SCORES			TOTAL	MONEY
Shirley Furlong	68	72	65	205	$45,000
Sherri Turner	73	65	67	205	27,750
(Furlong defeated Turner on first hole of playoff.)					
Val Skinner	71	69	67	207	20,250
Sherri Steinhauer	69	70	69	208	13,000
Sandra Palmer	69	69	70	208	13,000
Colleen Walker	68	69	71	208	13,000
Betsy King	68	71	70	209	7,900
Marci Bozarth	68	70	71	209	7,900
Ayako Okamoto	67	70	72	209	7,900
Juli Inkster	67	73	70	210	6,001
Patty Jordan	69	70	71	210	6,000

	SCORES			TOTAL	MONEY
Patty Sheehan	72	71	68	211	5,100
Lynn Adams	71	68	72	211	5,100
Cindy Rarick	71	73	68	212	4,238
Tammie Green	70	73	69	212	4,238
Jan Stephenson	70	72	70	212	4,237
Connie Chillemi	68	69	75	212	4,237
Liselotte Neumann	72	71	70	213	3,525
Danielle Ammaccapane	71	71	71	213	3,525
Dale Eggeling	73	69	71	213	3,525
Debbie Massey	70	72	71	213	3,525
LeAnn Cassaday	75	70	69	214	2,974
Sally Little	74	69	71	214	2,974
Lori West	72	71	71	214	2,974
Marta Figueras-Dotti	72	70	72	214	2,973
Janet Anderson	71	76	68	215	2,421
Mei Chi Cheng	75	71	69	215	2,421
Kim Bauer	74	71	70	215	2,421
Laura Davies	70	74	71	215	2,421
Mitzi Edge	74	70	71	215	2,421
Sandra Spuzich	70	74	71	215	2,420
Amy Alcott	72	70	73	215	2,420
Sue Ertl	72	70	73	215	2,420

McDonald's Championship

Du Pont Country Club, Wilmington, Delaware
Par 35-36 — 71; 6,366 yards

June 23-26
purse, $500,000

	SCORES				TOTAL	MONEY
Kathy Postlewait	69	68	69	70	276	$75,000
Patty Sheehan	68	66	69	74	277	46,250
Jan Stephenson	71	70	68	69	278	27,084
Nancy Lopez	71	66	72	69	278	27,083
Dottie Mochrie	70	67	68	73	278	27,083
Jody Rosenthal	70	72	70	68	280	15,084
Colleen Walker	71	70	69	70	280	15,083
Judy Dickinson	70	69	71	70	280	15,083
Tammie Green	75	71	67	68	281	10,126
Amy Alcott	70	71	71	69	281	10,125
Vicki Fergon	73	68	69	71	281	10,125
Lori Garbacz	69	72	69	71	281	10,125
Jane Crafter	75	71	70	66	282	7,125
Allison Finney	71	73	69	69	282	7,125
Deedee Lasker	69	71	73	69	282	7,125
Marlene Floyd	71	69	72	70	282	7,125
Lenore Rittenhouse	72	68	71	71	282	7,125
Dot Germain	68	71	71	72	282	7,125
Sally Quinlan	71	74	72	66	283	5,396
Betsy King	69	73	71	70	283	5,396
Ayako Okamoto	71	70	72	70	283	5,396
Deb Richard	72	68	73	70	283	5,396
Joe Ann Washam	69	74	69	71	283	5,396
Donna White	70	68	74	71	283	5,395
Robin Hood	72	72	74	66	284	4,250
Myra Blackwelder	74	69	72	69	284	4,250
Val Skinner	69	72	74	69	284	4,250
Juli Inkster	67	72	76	69	284	4,250

	SCORES				TOTAL	MONEY
Denise Strebig	75	70	68	71	284	4,250
Jo Anne Carner	70	70	71	73	284	4,250
Sherri Steinhauer	71	68	72	73	284	4,250

duMaurier Classic

Vancouver Golf Club, Coquitlam, British Columbia   June 30-July 3
Par 35-37 — 72; 6,361 yards   purse, $500,000

	SCORES				TOTAL	MONEY
Sally Little	74	65	69	71	279	$75,000
Laura Davies	69	71	70	70	280	46,250
Sherri Turner	68	72	70	72	282	33,750
Nancy Brown	72	74	71	68	285	19,938
Deb Richard	72	72	71	70	285	19,938
Jan Stephenson	70	72	73	70	285	19,937
Amy Alcott	72	70	71	72	285	19,937
Rosie Jones	72	71	71	72	286	13,000
Ok-Hee Ku	74	72	71	70	287	10,148
Colleen Walker	73	68	73	73	287	10,148
Patti Rizzo	73	70	70	74	287	10,147
Debbie Massey	72	68	73	74	287	10,147
Amy Benz	75	71	73	69	288	7,795
Ayako Okamoto	73	73	69	73	288	7,795
Sherri Steinhauer	69	72	74	73	288	7,795
Cindy Rarick	71	73	73	72	289	6,545
Juli Inkster	75	72	69	73	289	6,545
Dawn Coe	72	70	74	73	289	6,545
Betsy King	76	71	75	69	291	5,670
Judy Dickinson	74	72	73	72	291	5,670
Mei Chi Cheng	69	73	76	73	291	5,670
Val Skinner	73	73	71	74	291	5,670
Hollis Stacy	76	73	74	69	292	4,524
Marci Bozarth	75	75	72	70	292	4,523
Lynn Adams	72	72	76	72	292	4,523
Jerilyn Britz	74	76	69	73	292	4,523
Lori Garbacz	73	73	73	73	292	4,523
Alice Ritzman	69	74	75	74	292	4,523
Lenore Rittenhouse	74	71	70	77	292	4,523
Patty Sheehan	73	69	73	77	292	4,523
Tina Tombs Purtzer	76	74	74	69	293	3,658
Vicki Fergon	71	77	72	73	293	3,658
Jody Rosenthal	76	69	74	74	293	3,657
Gail Lee Hirata	73	71	74	75	293	3,657
Cathy Morse	74	76	74	70	294	3,158
Dottie Mochrie	71	71	79	73	294	3,158
Shirley Furlong	74	72	73	75	294	3,157
Lauri Peterson	71	73	74	76	294	3,157
Pat Bradley	73	76	75	71	295	2,558
Caroline Gowan	71	78	74	72	295	2,558
Pam Allen	76	74	72	73	295	2,558
Chris Johnson	74	75	73	73	295	2,557
Robin Walton	69	72	81	73	295	2,557
Mary Beth Zimmerman	72	73	75	75	295	2,557
Mindy Moore	74	74	74	74	296	2,145
Nancy Lopez	77	73	70	76	296	2,145
Beth Daniel	79	71	75	72	297	1,895

	SCORES				TOTAL	MONEY
Trish Johnson	73	75	76	73	297	1,895
Kay Cockerill	77	71	75	74	297	1,895
Heather Farr	75	75	75	73	298	1,545
Jo Ann Washam	73	77	73	75	298	1,545
Karin Mundinger	75	72	76	75	298	1,545
Sally Quinlan	73	73	77	75	298	1,545
Shelley Hamlin	73	70	78	77	298	1,545

Mayflower Classic

Country Club of Indianapolis, Indianapolis, Indiana   July 7-10
Par 36-35 — 71; 6,124 yards   purse, $400,000

	SCORES				TOTAL	MONEY
Terry-Jo Myers	68	69	68	71	276	$60,000
Amy Alcott	71	65	71	70	277	32,000
Ayako Okamoto	70	68	67	72	277	32,000
Judy Dickinson	71	69	70	70	280	19,000
Sherri Turner	70	67	71	72	280	19,000
Missie McGeorge	73	66	72	70	281	14,000
Val Skinner	72	69	73	68	282	10,534
Amy Benz	70	73	69	70	282	10,533
Tammie Green	68	71	73	70	282	10,533
Juli Inkster	65	72	74	72	283	7,667
Danielle Ammaccapane	71	69	70	73	283	7,667
Donna White	68	67	74	74	283	7,666
Lenore Rittenhouse	69	71	77	67	284	5,700
Lynn Connelly	71	69	75	69	284	5,700
Sally Quinlan	68	76	67	73	284	5,700
Kathy Postlewait	72	67	71	74	284	5,700
Colleen Walker	68	73	68	75	284	5,700
Jerilyn Britz	70	70	67	77	284	5,700
Cindy Rarick	71	74	70	70	285	4,600
Robin Walton	74	70	71	70	285	4,600
Betsy King	68	71	71	75	285	4,600
Cindy Figg-Currier	72	74	71	69	286	3,775
Marta Figueras-Dotti	71	72	74	69	286	3,775
Nancy Taylor	69	76	71	70	286	3,774
Mitzi Edge	74	69	73	70	286	3,774
Carol French	72	70	74	70	286	3,774
Deb Richard	70	72	73	71	286	3,774
Dot Germain	70	69	72	75	286	3,774
Sandra Spuzich	70	73	77	67	287	3,000
Allison Finney	69	70	78	70	287	3,000
Caroline Gowan	71	67	79	70	287	3,000
Connie Chillemi	75	69	71	72	287	3,000
Jill Briles	70	73	72	72	287	3,000
Sandra Palmer	73	70	71	73	287	3,000

Boston Five Classic

Sheraton Tara Hotel at Ferncroft Village, Danvers, Massachusetts
Par 35-37 — 72; 6,008 yards

July 14-17
purse, $300,000

	SCORES				TOTAL	MONEY
Colleen Walker	66	69	70	69	274	$45,000
Kathryn Young	71	69	75	67	282	19,125
Patty Sheehan	77	68	67	70	282	19,125
Jane Geddes	71	71	69	71	282	19,125
Jan Stephenson	71	69	69	73	282	19,125
Betsy King	71	69	70	73	283	10,500
Dale Eggeling	74	71	73	66	284	7,500
Sally Quinlan	69	73	72	70	284	7,500
Cathy Marino	70	70	72	72	284	7,500
Cindy Rarick	70	70	72	72	284	7,500
Deedee Lasker	74	71	71	69	285	5,301
Liselotte Neumann	72	72	70	71	285	5,300
Beth Daniel	71	71	72	71	285	5,300
Lenore Rittenhouse	74	70	70	72	286	4,238
Sally Little	70	73	71	72	286	4,238
Becky Pearson	67	73	73	73	286	4,237
Pam Allen	74	68	69	75	286	4,237
Marta Figueras-Dotti	74	74	70	69	287	3,600
Myra Blackwelder	75	68	73	71	287	3,600
Robin Walton	73	70	70	74	287	3,600
Jody Rosenthal	74	73	72	69	288	3,155
Martha Foyer	72	74	73	69	288	3,155
Laura Davies	74	72	71	71	288	3,155
Joan Pitcock	70	75	71	73	289	2,910
Elaine Crosby	73	73	74	70	290	2,775
Lisa Walters	74	71	74	71	290	2,775
Susie Redman	75	74	73	69	291	2,460
Mindy Moore	72	78	71	70	291	2,460
Amy Read	76	70	74	71	291	2,460
Dot Germain	72	74	72	73	291	2,460
Heather Drew	69	72	75	75	291	2,460

U.S. Women's Open Championship

Baltimore Country Club, Baltimore, Maryland
Par 35-36 — 71; 6,232 yards

July 21-24
purse, $400,000

	SCORES				TOTAL	MONEY
Liselotte Neumann	67	72	69	69	277	$70,000
Patty Sheehan	70	72	68	70	280	35,000
Dottie Mochrie	70	69	76	68	283	21,679
Colleen Walker	70	74	68	71	283	21,679
Jan Stephenson	72	72	71	69	284	14,393
Missie Berteotti	75	71	68	71	285	11,826
Amy Benz	70	72	71	72	285	11,826
Kristi Albers	73	70	72	71	286	9,726
Juli Inkster	71	68	75	72	286	9,726
Vicki Fergon	70	71	75	71	287	8,315
Beth Daniel	77	71	66	73	287	8,315
Betsy King	76	74	71	67	288	7,038
Ayako Okamoto	75	73	71	69	288	7,038
Kris Hanson	73	72	73	70	288	7,038

	SCORES				TOTAL	MONEY
Nancy Lopez	72	74	71	71	288	7,038
JoAnne Carner	69	73	76	71	289	5,954
Nancy Brown	71	73	72	73	289	5,954
Kay Cockerill	73	70	72	74	289	5,954
Mei Chi Cheng	74	76	70	70	290	5,070
Chris Johnson	73	74	73	70	290	5,070
Rosie Jones	74	70	74	72	290	5,070
Marta Figueras-Dotti	77	71	69	73	290	5,070
Tammie Green	71	70	71	78	290	5,070
Robin Hood	77	72	71	71	291	4,310
Deedee Lasker	73	71	74	73	291	4,310
Judy Dickinson	71	76	71	73	291	4,310
Sally Quinlan	69	75	74	73	291	4,310
Donna White	72	70	73	76	291	4,310
*Carol Semple Thompson	79	71	70	72	292	
Kathy Guadagnino	72	72	75	73	292	3,820
Sherrie Turner	73	72	73	74	292	3,820
Jody Rosenthal	74	73	71	74	292	3,820
Shelley Hamlin	74	74	73	72	293	3,468
Patti Rizzo	78	71	71	73	293	3,468
Debbie Massey	74	73	73	73	293	3,468
Alice Ritzman	73	74	70	76	293	3,468
Shirley Furlong	70	75	72	76	293	3,468
Cathy Morse	73	74	73	74	294	3,132
Sally Little	71	75	72	76	294	3,132
Janet Coles	72	71	74	77	294	3,132
Amy Alcott	76	74	74	71	295	2,882
Jane Geddes	74	76	73	72	295	2,882
Dale Eggeling	76	72	72	75	295	2,882
Meg Mallon	78	71	75	72	296	2,632
*Brandie Burton	74	75	73	74	296	
Dawn Coe	74	72	74	76	296	2,632
Sue Ertl	74	72	73	77	296	2,632
Val Skinner	75	72	78	72	297	2,424
Heather Farr	72	75	72	78	297	2,424
Robin Walton	73	75	72	78	298	2,257
Laura Davies	72	73	75	78	298	2,257

Greater Washington Open

Bethesda Country Club, Bethesda, Maryland
Par 36-35 — 71; 6,250 yards

July 29-31
purse, $225,000

	SCORES			TOTAL	MONEY
Ayako Okamoto	69	70	67	206	$33,750
Beth Daniel	68	69	70	207	18,000
Connie Chillemi	72	64	71	207	17,999
Susan Sanders	68	73	67	208	11,812
Debbie Massey	73	70	66	209	8,719
Judy Dickinson	67	74	68	209	8,718
Amy Benz	71	72	67	210	4,927
Amy Alcott	70	71	69	210	4,927
Dawn Coe	70	70	70	210	4,927
Juli Inkster	71	69	70	210	4,927
Liselotte Neumann	71	68	71	210	4,926
Mary Beth Zimmerman	69	70	71	210	4,926
Jan Stephenson	68	69	73	210	4,926

	SCORES			TOTAL	MONEY
Janet Coles	68	70	73	211	3,508
Elaine Crosby	70	75	67	212	2,850
Cathy Marino	72	73	67	212	2,850
Deb Richard	72	70	70	212	2,849
Jill Briles	70	71	71	212	2,849
Mei Chi Cheng	69	72	71	212	2,849
Rosie Jones	72	69	71	212	2,849
Gina Hull	71	70	71	212	2,849
Myra Blackwelder	73	71	69	213	2,290
Marta Figueras-Dotti	70	74	69	213	2,289
Penny Hammel	72	68	73	213	2,289
Tammie Green	71	73	70	214	2,035
Chris Johnson	71	71	72	214	2,035
Cindy Mackey	73	69	72	214	2,034
Susie Redman	72	70	72	214	2,034
*Tina Barrett	70	71	73	214	
Amy Read	79	67	69	215	1,768
Anne Kelly	71	73	71	215	1,767
Lynn Adams	69	74	72	215	1,767
Vicki Fergon	72	67	76	215	1,767

Planters Pat Bradley International

Willow Creek Golf Club, High Point, North Carolina August 4-7
Par 36-36 — 72; 6,260 yards purse, $400,000

FIRST ROUND QUALIFIERS

19	Amy Benz, Janet Anderson, Kim Bauer.
15	Kathy Whitworth, Val Skinner, Cindy Rarick.
14	Juli Inkster.
13	Laurie Rinker.
12	Ayako Okamoto, Nancy Lopez.
11	Kristl Albers, Mei-Chi Cheng, Beth Daniel, Robin Walton, Tammie Green, Therese Hession, Sherri Steinhauer.
10	Robin Hood, Danielle Ammaccapane, Pam Allen, Dawn Coe, Jane Geddes, Judy Dickinson, Loretta Alderette, Lynn Adams.
9	Patty Sheehan, Jody Rosenthal.
8	Margaret Ward, Cindy Currier, Alice Miller, Betsy King, Amy Alcott, Sally Quinlan, Julie Kintz.
7	Deb Skinner, Donna White, Jane Crafter, Marci Bozarth, Sherri Turner, Laura Hurlbut, Cindy Ferro, Jerilyn Britz, Sharon Barrett.
6	Becky Pearson, Deb Richard, Caroline Gowan, Dot Germain, Pat Bradley, JoAnne Carner, Kelly Leadbetter, Allison Finney, Karin Mundinger.
5	Chris Johnson, Shirley Furlong, Elaine Crosby, Mary Murphy, Mary Beth Zimmerman, Heather Farr, Kris Monaghan, Susan Tonkin, Deedee Lasker, Kim Shipman.
4	Dale Eggeling, Cathy Morse, Martha Nause, Kim Williams, Kris Tschetter, Rebecca Ward, Debbie Massey, Joan Delk, JoAnn Washam, Missie McGeorge.

(Each qualifier received $2,000.)

SECOND ROUND QUALIFIERS

22	Richard, $8,000.
18	Okamoto, $3,000.
15	Inkster, Quinlan, McGeorge.

14   Crafter, White, Rosenthal, Benz.
12   Bradley.
11   Eggeling, Dickinson, Whitworth, Cheng.
10   Tschetter, Turner, Anderson.
9   Britz, Rinker, Skinner.
8   Alcott, Steinhauer.
7   Delk, Carner, Massey, Germain, Adams, Lopez.
6   Zimmerman, Farr, Nause, Hession.
5   Johnson, Sheehan, Albers, Allen.

THIRD ROUND QUALIFIERS

15   Germain, Bradley, Rosenthal, $5,000 each.
14   Farr, Massey, Quinlan.
13   Inkster.
12   Johnson, Britz.
11   Nause, Dickinson, Okamoto.
9   Richard, Alcott, Zimmerman.
8   Allen, Lopez.
7   Anderson.

FINAL ROUND

14   Nause, $62,500.
13   Massey, Dickinson, $35,000 each.
12   Okamoto, $20,000.
11   Lopez, $10,500.
10   Germain, Britz, $8,500 each.
9   Alcott, Anderson, Rosenthal, $6,750 each.
7   Inkster, $5,250.
6   Allen, $4,750.
5   Zimmerman, $4,250.
4   Farr, $4,000.
3   Bradley, Quinlan, $3,625 each.
2   Johnson, $3,250.
-2   Richard, $3,000.

Atlantic City Classic

Sands Country Club, Somers Point, New Jersey   August 19-21
Par 36-35 — 71; 6,020 yards   purse, $225,000

	SCORES			TOTAL	MONEY
Juli Inkster	72	69	65	206	$33,750
Beth Daniel	66	68	72	206	20,812
(Inkster defeated Daniel on first hole of playoff.)					
Rosie Jones	74	66	70	210	11,109
Betsy King	70	69	71	210	11,109
Debbie Massey	69	69	72	210	11,109
Martha Nause	67	70	73	210	11,109
Sally Quinlan	71	69	71	211	6,637
Cathy Marino	72	73	67	212	5,569
Sandra Palmer	69	70	73	212	5,568
Sherri Turner	74	69	70	213	4,313
Kim Shipman	72	70	71	213	4,313
Colleen Walker	68	73	72	213	4,313
Mindy Moore	74	69	71	214	3,601
Kristi Albers	70	72	72	214	3,600
Jane Geddes	72	75	68	215	3,010

	SCORES			TOTAL	MONEY
Kathy Guadagnino	74	70	71	215	3,010
Judy Dickinson	73	71	71	215	3,010
Chris Johnson	71	73	71	215	3,010
Karin Mundinger	74	73	70	217	2,478
Marta Figueras-Dotti	69	76	72	217	2,478
Connie Chillemi	73	70	74	217	2,478
Kathy Postlewait	70	73	74	217	2,478
Lynn Adams	69	74	74	217	2,478
Sarah LeVeque	75	72	71	218	1,981
Kathryn Young	72	74	72	218	1,981
Ok-Hee Ku	73	72	73	218	1,981
Danielle Ammaccapane	72	73	73	218	1,981
Amy Benz	72	73	73	218	1,981
Donna White	71	74	73	218	1,980
Janet Anderson	73	70	75	218	1,980

Nestle World Championship

Stouffer PineIsle Resort, Buford, Georgia
Par 36-36 — 72; 6,107 yards

August 25-28
purse, $265,000

	SCORES				TOTAL	MONEY
Rosie Jones	70	69	66	74	279	$81,500
Liselotte Neumann	70	73	71	66	280	43,000
Patty Sheehan	70	73	68	70	281	21,167
Sherri Turner	71	70	70	70	281	21,167
Nancy Lopez	67	72	71	71	281	21,166
Ayako Okamoto	67	71	73	73	284	10,500
Amy Alcott	68	74	75	68	285	7,625
Colleen Walker	71	73	70	71	285	7,625
Judy Dickinson	71	79	66	70	286	5,067
Jan Stephenson	69	73	74	70	286	5,067
Sally Little	72	69	72	73	286	5,066
Kathy Postlewait	72	72	71	72	287	4,000
Betsy King	71	76	69	72	288	3,750
Juli Inkster	78	73	69	69	289	3,500
Marie-Laure de Lorenzi-Taya	75	73	68	75	291	3,125
Laura Davies	74	71	69	77	291	3,125

Ocean State Open

Alpine Country Club, Cranston, Rhode Island
Par 36-36 — 72; 6,210 yards

August 26-28
purse, $150,000

	SCORES			TOTAL	MONEY
Patty Jordan	73	68	70	211	$22,500
Mitzi Edge	72	72	69	213	7,988
Lynn Adams	74	69	70	213	7,988
Margaret Ward	72	70	71	213	7,988
Jill Briles	70	71	72	213	7,987
Sandra Palmer	71	69	73	213	7,987
Joan Pitcock	75	63	75	213	7,987
Susie Redman	71	71	72	214	3,525
Kathryn Young	69	73	72	214	3,525

	SCORES			TOTAL	MONEY
Martha Nause	73	67	74	214	3,525
Vicki Fergon	77	70	68	215	2,427
Jerilyn Britz	69	75	71	215	2,427
Penny Hammel	72	71	72	215	2,427
Sally Quinlan	69	73	73	215	2,426
Carolyn Hill	71	70	74	215	2,426
Cindy Mackey	70	70	75	215	2,426
Kathy Whitworth	75	74	67	216	1,889
Robin Walton	78	69	69	216	1,889
Missie Berteotti	73	72	71	216	1,889
Stephanie Farwig	78	70	69	217	1,541
Debbie Massey	74	74	69	217	1,541
Dottie Mochrie	73	72	72	217	1,541
Nancy White	73	71	73	217	1,541
Laura Hurlbut	72	71	74	217	1,541
Joan Joyce	71	72	74	217	1,540
Kristi Albers	72	70	75	217	1,540
Kathy Ahern	75	73	70	218	1,163
Nina Foust	72	76	70	218	1,163
Beth Daniel	73	73	72	218	1,162
Lori West	73	73	72	218	1,162
Karin Mundinger	76	69	73	218	1,162
Carol French	73	72	73	218	1,162
Nancy Ledbetter	71	73	74	218	1,162
Pam Allen	75	68	75	218	1,162
Sherri Steinhauer	72	71	75	218	1,162

Rail Charity Classic

Rail Golf Club, Springfield, Illinois
Par 36-36 — 72; 6,403 yards

September 3-5
purse, $250,000

	SCORES			TOTAL	MONEY
Betsy King	68	68	71	207	$37,500
Margaret Ward	70	68	71	209	23,125
Donna White	66	75	70	211	15,000
Sandra Palmer	69	70	72	211	15,000
Dale Eggeling	71	74	69	214	7,825
Cathy Marino	70	73	71	214	7,825
Vicki Fergon	68	74	72	214	7,825
Danielle Ammaccapane	71	69	74	214	7,825
Nancy Brown	68	70	76	214	7,825
Sandra Haynie	71	72	72	215	5,001
Alice Miller	70	70	75	215	5,000
Lenore Rittenhouse	75	71	70	216	3,772
Myra Blackwelder	72	71	73	216	3,772
Ayako Okamoto	68	75	73	216	3,772
Muffin Spencer-Devlin	75	67	74	216	3,772
Missie Berteotti	68	74	74	216	3,772
Susan Sanders	69	69	78	216	3,771
Cindy Figg-Currier	70	75	72	217	2,876
Joan Pitcock	70	74	73	217	2,876
Elaine Crosby	70	73	74	217	2,876
Janet Coles	70	70	77	217	2,876
Adele Lukken	67	72	78	217	2,875
Missie McGeorge	71	77	70	218	2,202
Terry-Jo Myers	73	74	71	218	2,202

	SCORES			TOTAL	MONEY
Deborah McHaffie	72	75	71	218	2,202
Sherrin Smyers	76	70	72	218	2,201
Penny Hammel	68	78	72	218	2,201
Alice Ritzman	73	72	73	218	2,201
Janet Anderson	71	73	74	218	2,201
Sue Ertl	70	74	74	218	2,201
Marta Figueras-Dotti	67	72	79	218	2,201

Cellular One-Ping Championship

Riverside Golf and Country Club, Portland, Oregon
Par 36-36 — 72; 6,253 yards

September 9-11
purse, $250,000

	SCORES			TOTAL	MONEY
Betsy King	71	70	72	213	$37,500
Colleen Walker	68	77	69	214	23,125
Susan Sanders	68	76	71	215	15,000
Myra Blackwelder	72	71	72	215	15,000
Jody Rosenthal	70	77	69	216	8,917
Sherri Turner	73	72	71	216	8,917
Penny Hammel	70	72	74	216	8,916
Cindy Rarick	76	70	71	217	5,875
Deborah McHaffie	73	72	72	217	5,875
Beth Daniel	71	72	74	217	5,875
Donna White	73	74	71	218	4,422
Jane Geddes	75	72	71	218	4,422
Sandra Haynie	71	71	76	218	4,421
Loretta Alderete	75	72	72	219	3,630
Ok-Hee Ku	72	74	73	219	3,630
Melissa Whitmire	70	73	76	219	3,630
Marta Figueras-Dotti	77	73	70	220	2,943
Kathryn Young	72	77	71	220	2,943
Sherri Steinhauer	72	76	72	220	2,942
Amy Benz	72	75	73	220	2,942
Deb Richard	73	71	76	220	2,942
Tammie Green	72	72	76	220	2,942
Sue Ertl	71	76	74	221	2,433
Danielle Ammaccapane	72	75	74	221	2,433
Nancy Brown	71	75	75	221	2,433
Anne Kelly	76	74	72	222	2,129
Mitzi Edge	73	77	72	222	2,129
Missie McGeorge	74	74	74	222	2,129
Juli Inkster	75	73	74	222	2,129
Mary Beth Zimmerman	71	74	77	222	2,129

Safeco Classic

Meridian Valley Country Club, Seattle, Washington
Par 36-36 — 72; 6,222 yards

September 15-18
purse, $225,000

	SCORES				TOTAL	MONEY
Juli Inkster	76	70	65	67	278	$33,750
Ok-Hee Ku	71	70	71	69	281	20,812
Jan Stephenson	71	72	67	72	282	15,187

	SCORES				TOTAL	MONEY
Sherri Turner	73	75	67	68	283	11,812
Danielle Ammaccapane	73	70	68	73	284	9,562
JoAnne Carner	70	71	70	74	285	7,256
Beth Daniel	71	69	71	74	285	7,256
Jane Geddes	74	73	72	67	286	5,288
Nancy Lopez	72	75	70	69	286	5,287
Rosie Jones	72	71	74	69	286	5,287
Connie Chillemi	76	73	69	69	287	4,107
Susie Redman	69	70	74	74	287	4,107
Carolyn Hill	74	73	72	69	288	3,488
Kathy Postlewait	72	76	69	71	288	3,488
Shirley Furlong	75	67	74	72	288	3,488
Cathy Morse	73	75	72	69	289	2,814
Penny Hammel	72	70	77	70	289	2,813
Cathy Johnston	69	76	73	71	289	2,813
Jody Rosenthal	73	73	71	72	289	2,813
Patty Sheehan	71	69	77	72	289	2,813
Meg Mallon	72	71	76	71	290	2,476
Allison Finney	71	71	71	78	291	2,363
Deedee Lasker	76	72	73	71	292	2,223
Sherrin Smyers	71	74	74	73	292	2,222
Lenore Rittenhouse	72	77	73	71	293	2,015
Janet Coles	73	73	76	71	293	2,015
Kim Williams	73	73	73	74	293	2,014
Nancy Brown	74	73	70	76	293	2,014
Colleen Walker	77	72	74	71	294	1,631
Nina Foust	75	73	75	71	294	1,631
Cathy Reynolds	76	69	78	71	294	1,631
Muffin Spencer-Devlin	74	73	75	72	294	1,631
Sandra Haynie	75	71	76	72	294	1,630
Jo Ann Washam	73	73	75	73	294	1,630
Amy Alcott	72	74	74	74	294	1,630
Kathryn Young	69	76	73	76	294	1,630

Santa Barbara Open

Santa Barbara, California

September 22-25
purse, $300,000

Sandpiper Golf Course
Par 36-36 — 72; 6,311 yards

La Purisima Golf Course
Par 36-36 — 72; 6,120 yards

	SCORES			TOTAL	MONEY
Rosie Jones	70	70	72	212	$45,000
Missie McGeorge	68	72	75	215	27,750
Myra Blackwelder	72	72	73	217	18,000
Kathy Postlewait	71	73	73	217	18,000
Sherri Turner	66	76	76	218	12,750
Carolyn Hill	71	76	72	219	7,701
Colleen Walker	74	72	73	219	7,701
Shirley Furlong	71	74	74	219	7,701
Ayako Okamoto	71	74	74	219	7,701
Sandra Palmer	71	73	75	219	7,701
Cathy Morse	70	73	76	219	7,700

	SCORES			TOTAL	MONEY
Amy Benz	79	68	73	220	4,530
Cindy Rarick	72	75	73	220	4,530
Penny Hammel	72	74	74	220	4,530
Juli Inkster	70	74	76	220	4,530
Betsy King	68	76	76	220	4,530
Lynn Connelly	72	71	77	220	4,530
Vicki Fergon	74	77	70	221	3,316
Tammie Green	74	75	72	221	3,316
Marci Bozarth	77	71	73	221	3,316
Lauren Howe	75	73	73	221	3,316
Martha Nause	75	73	73	221	3,316
Jan Stephenson	73	73	75	221	3,315
Alice Ritzman	74	71	76	221	3,315
Sally Little	72	75	75	222	2,645
Deb Richard	72	75	75	222	2,645
Allison Finney	75	71	76	222	2,645
Kathryn Young	72	74	76	222	2,645
Karin Mundinger	72	73	77	222	2,645
Danielle Ammaccapane	72	79	72	223	2,062
Bonnie Lauer	74	76	73	223	2,062
Meg Mallon	72	78	73	223	2,062
Jane Geddes	75	74	74	223	2,062
Janet Coles	76	72	75	223	2,062
Loretta Alderete	71	76	76	223	2,062
Kris Monaghan	74	73	76	223	2,061
Lenore Rittenhouse	72	75	76	223	2,061
Dawn Coe	70	76	77	223	2,061

Konica San Jose Classic

Almaden Golf and Country Club, San Jose, California
Par 36-36 — 72; 6,370 yards

September 30-October 2
purse, $300,000

	SCORES			TOTAL	MONEY
Kathy Guadagnino	69	71	67	207	$45,000
Cathy Marino	70	70	68	208	27,750
Rosie Jones	73	69	68	210	18,000
Missie McGeorge	69	69	72	210	18,000
Beth Daniel	73	70	68	211	12,750
Missie Berteotti	68	71	73	212	10,500
Kathryn Young	69	75	69	213	7,500
Lynn Adams	71	71	71	213	7,500
Kathy Postlewait	69	73	71	213	7,500
Juli Inkster	69	69	75	213	7,500
JoAnne Carner	71	74	69	214	4,852
Patti Rizzo	72	73	69	214	4,852
Kris Monaghan	72	71	71	214	4,852
Betsy King	73	69	72	214	4,852
Myra Blackwelder	71	69	74	214	4,852
Jan Stephenson	71	69	74	214	4,852
Amy Alcott	69	75	71	215	3,702
Colleen Walker	70	73	72	215	3,702
Robin Hood	71	70	74	215	3,702
Nancy Lopez	69	72	74	215	3,702
Mitzi Edge	73	72	71	216	3,066
Silvia Bertolaccini	73	71	72	216	3,066
Deb Richard	75	69	72	216	3,066

	SCORES			TOTAL	MONEY
Kristi Albers	76	68	72	216	3,066
Sherrin Smyers	74	69	73	216	3,066
Elaine Crosby	73	73	71	217	2,407
Kathy Whitworth	73	73	71	217	2,407
Jane Geddes	74	71	72	217	2,407
Cindy Rarick	72	73	72	217	2,407
Susan Sanders	70	75	72	217	2,407
Donna White	72	72	73	217	2,407
Janet Coles	74	69	74	217	2,407
Lori Garbacz	74	69	74	217	2,407
Judy Dickinson	67	73	77	217	2,407

Mazda Japan Classic

Musashigaoka Golf Club, Saitama, Japan

November 4-6

Par 36-36 — 72; 6,398 yards

purse, $450,000

	SCORES			TOTAL	MONEY
Patty Sheehan	72	67	67	206	$67,500
Liselotte Neumann	70	66	70	206	41,625
(Sheehan defeated Neumann on third hole of playoff.)					
Jody Rosenthal	70	73	67	210	27,000
Yuko Moriguchi	67	72	71	210	27,000
Robin Walton	69	74	68	211	16,050
Ayako Okamoto	73	68	70	211	16,050
Sally Little	70	70	71	211	16,050
Mitsuko Hamada	72	74	67	213	11,138
Tammie Green	71	74	68	213	11,137
Betsy King	75	70	69	214	8,081
Martha Nause	74	71	69	214	8,081
Amy Benz	72	69	73	214	8,081
Jan Stephenson	71	70	73	214	8,080
Tatsuko Ohsako	68	73	73	214	8,080
Debbie Massey	74	71	70	215	6,332
Colleen Walker	72	69	74	215	6,332
Dottie Mochrie	72	72	72	216	5,432
Myra Blackwelder	71	73	72	216	5,432
Laura Davies	69	75	72	216	5,432
Cindy Rarick	71	72	73	216	5,432
Vicki Fergon	72	67	77	216	5,432
Hiromi Kobayashi	75	72	70	217	4,420
Deb Richard	73	74	70	217	4,420
Rosie Jones	75	71	71	217	4,419
Ok-Hee Ku	75	69	73	217	4,419
Hiroko Inoue	73	70	74	217	4,419
Marta Figueras-Dotti	75	73	70	218	3,597
Erika Nakajima	72	75	71	218	3,597
Fukumi Tani	73	73	72	218	3,597
Miki Oda	73	72	73	218	3,597
Sherri Turner	71	72	75	218	3,596
Beth Daniel	71	71	76	218	3,596
Kathy Postlewait	74	67	77	218	3,596